Lydia White
2006

L2 Acquisition and Creole Genesis

# Language Acquisition & Language Disorders

Volumes in this series provide a forum for research contributing to theories of language acquisition (first and second, child and adult), language learnability, language attrition and language disorders.

Volume 42

L2 Acquisition and Creole Genesis: Dialogues
Edited by Claire Lefebvre, Lydia White and Christine Jourdan

# L2 Acquisition and Creole Genesis

Dialogues

*Edited by*

## Claire Lefebvre
University of Quebec, Montreal

## Lydia White
McGill University

## Christine Jourdan
Concordia University

John Benjamins Publishing Company

Amsterdam/Philadelphia

™ The paper used in this publication meets the minimum requirements
of American National Standard for Information Sciences – Permanence
of Paper for Printed Library Materials, ANSI z39.48-1984.

Library of Congress Cataloging-in-Publication Data

L2 acquisition and creole genesis : dialogues / edited by Claire Lefebvre, Lydia
White and Christine Jourdan.
        p.   cm. (Language Acquisition & Language Disorders, ISSN
0925–0123 ; v. 42)
        Includes bibliographical references and indexes.
        1. Second language acquisition. 2. Creole dialects. 3. Language in
contact. 4. Bilingualism.

    P118.2.L15  2006
401/.93--dc22                                               2006047804
ISBN 90 272 5302 1 (Hb; alk. paper)

John Benjamins Publishing Co. · P.O. Box 36224 · 1020 ME Amsterdam · The Netherlands
John Benjamins North America · P.O. Box 27519 · Philadelphia PA 19118-0519 · USA

# CONTENTS

## PART III
### PROCESSES: DEVELOPING GRAMMARS (RESTRUCTURING AND REANALYSIS)

## PART IV
### PROCESSES: FINAL STATE (FOSSILIZATION)

# PREFACE

The purpose of this volume is to contribute to rebuilding the dialogue between L2 acquisitionists and creolists. It focuses on shared processes that are at work in both L2 acquisition and creole genesis, and on the similarities and differences between these two situations.

The results reported on in this volume are based on a research project (2002–2005, funded by the Social Sciences and Humanities Research Council of Canada) entitled "Cognitive and Social Processes in the Formation and Acquisition of New Language Varieties" (Claire Lefebvre, Christine Jourdan and Lydia White). The objective of the project was to establish a multidisciplinary research network that would bring together researchers on pidgin, creole and mixed languages and second language acquisition (from the perspective of linguistics, anthropology, sociology and psychology, as well as related fields), whose research explicitly or implicitly takes account of such processes. We created an interactive website to connect the members of the network and to allow the exchange of ideas and data. With members of the network, we held a workshop at the Université du Québec à Montréal (August 27 to 29, 2004), entitled *Montreal Dialogues: Processes in L2 Acquisition and in Creole Genesis*. The chapters of this book constitute a selection of the papers presented at that workshop.

We would like to thank SSHRCC for financing these research activities. We are grateful to the students who contributed in one way or other to the realization of this project: Anne-Sophie Bally, Virginie Loranger, Annie Loyer and Isabelle Therrien. Our heartfelt thanks go out to all of the participants in the workshop and contributors to the book for their insightful contributions, discussions and dialogues. Gratitude is also due to Heather Goad, Stephen Matthews and Virginia Yip for their most helpful contributions in reviewing the papers for this volume. Finally, thanks to Zofia Laubitz for copy-editing the manuscripts, to Andrée Bélanger for formatting them, and to Claude Dionne and Lucie Kearns for preparing the indexes.

# INTRODUCTION

Claire Lefebvre
*Université du Québec à Montréal*

Lydia White
*McGill University*

Christine Jourdan
*Concordia University*

## 1. *Why This Volume?*

The purpose of this volume is to contribute to re-establishing a dialogue between researchers on second language (L2) acquisition and creolists. In the 1970s, there was a fruitful dialogue between these two disciplines (see Siegel, this volume). The dialogue ceased for a couple of decades, but now there is renewed interest in constructive exchanges between the two fields (see, for example, the papers in Kouwenberg & Patrick 2003). The present volume contributes to bringing the two fields together by focusing on processes that are at work in both L2 acquisition and creole genesis, such as transfer, relexification, restructuring, reanalysis and fossilization.

Pidgins and creoles develop in multilingual communities as a means of giving speakers who do not have a common language lingua franca. While features from the source languages are typically identifiable, pidgins/creoles and their source languages are not mutually intelligible. Pidgins and creoles have long been considered as distinct entities (Hymes 1971). However, there are some pidgins (still used only as a second language) that have expanded in the same way as the languages known as creoles (e.g., Hancock 1980: 64; Mufwene 1990: 2; Mühlhäusler 1980, 1986). For such reasons, scholars have started referring to pidgins and creoles as PCs, suggesting that they belong to a single category. This reflects the fact that they cannot be distinguished on the basis of the processes that play a role in their formation (Lefebvre 1998; Woolford 1983). In this book, therefore, we do not distinguish between them.

L2 acquisition (or SLA) refers to the sequential acquisition of another language by children or adults, after a first language (L1) has been acquired. The term L2 acquisition is not, in fact, restricted to the acquisition of a second language but is generally used to cover other cases of non-native acquisition (L3, L4, Ln), as well as what is sometimes referred to as foreign language learning. The language of L2 learners is often referred to as interlanguage (following Selinker 1972), and the grammars of individuals in the process of learning an L2 are known as interlanguage grammars, the proposal being that

L2 learners construct mental representations for the L2 input, which differ in various ways from those of native speakers of the L2 but which are nevertheless systematic and rule-governed. Bilinguals are speakers who have acquired and use more than one language; one language may be dominant or the two may be balanced (see Butler & Hakuta 2004). Bilingualism may be the outcome of L2 acquisition or of the simultaneous acquisition of two L1s (see Müller, this volume[1]).

The papers in this volume address multiple and interconnected themes; between them, they cover the lexical, morphological, phonological, semantic and syntactic properties of interlanguage grammars and creole grammars. We have grouped the papers thematically, recognizing that our classification is a somewhat arbitrary one. The volume opens with an overview by Jeff Siegel on the relationship between SLA research and PC research. The first group of papers addresses issues related to current language contact at either a societal or an individual level (Smith; Terrill and Dunn; Bruhn de Garavito and Atoche; Liceras et al.; Müller). The next selection of papers focuses on processes that characterize the various stages of L2 acquisition and creole genesis: relexification and transfer from the L1 and their role in the initial state (Sprouse; Schwartz; Kouwenberg; Aboh; Ionin); reanalysis and restructuring and their effects on development and elaboration (Sánchez; Brousseau and Nikiema; Steele and Brousseau); fossilization and its effects on the end state (Cornips and Hulk; Montrul; Lardiere). In this introduction, we will discuss these themes in the context of creole genesis and L2 acquisition.

## 2. *Language Contact*

Cultural contacts generally give rise to language contact between groups and individuals who may or may not share an understanding of social and cultural life and of the role and place of language in culture. Situations of language contact and multilingualism are by no means exceptional (Romaine 2001). Indeed, throughout history, cultural groups have needed to engage and communicate with people speaking different languages. Whether we are talking of commercial links between groups (the fur trade between North American Indians and Europeans), the forced displacement of populations (African slavery in the Caribbean), the settlement of lands and continents (from the Mongol invasions to the "discovery" of America by Europeans), or migration (Mexican immigrants to the USA), cultural contacts have almost always had linguistic outcomes. These have been varied, ranging from heightened linguistic differences to signal ethnic differences (as in Amazonia or Melanesia), to language death (as in Tasmania) or the birth of contact languages such as koinés (Siegel 1995), as well as pidgins and creole languages.

---

[1] From now on, we will not use the designation *this volume* when referring to authors whose papers appear herein.

The studies in this volume refer to situations where speakers must find linguistic solutions to cultural contacts. Broadly construed, these solutions include code-switching (Liceras et al.), bilingualism (Cornips and Hulk; Montrul; Sánchez), transfer (Aboh; Müller; Sprouse; Schwartz; Terrill and Dunn), development of creoles (Brousseau and Nikiema; Steele and Brousseau; Kouwenberg; Smith), and variability or optionality (Bruhn de Garavito and Atoche; Ionin; Lardiere).

Clearly, there are different types of linguistic contacts. Linguistic contacts may be fleeting or intense, sporadic or continued, intended or unintended. They may lead to the development of new linguistic communities. They may involve egalitarian exchanges that foster options for speakers or they may take place within unequal power relationships such that hegemony, coercion and exploitation impinge on the status of the languages at hand, on their speakers, on language choice and on language change. This issue is particularly relevant to Smith's observations concerning the speed of creolization: is the birth of a creole linked to the unequal relationship existing on plantations between workers and master? Did the slaves have any intention of learning the language of their "employers"? If so, what would their motivation be? Did they have enough access to the L2 to be able to learn it? And finally, how slow or quick a process was creolization? Some of these questions resonate with Kouwenberg's argument about the respective importance of L1 and L2 acquisition strategies in the process of creole genesis: were the workers trying to learn an L2 or were they transforming an L1 in situ? According to Kouwenberg, while the L2 may have been the early target of language learning, an incipient pidgin rapidly took over as the target.

Scholars interested in contact-induced language change have sought to understand factors involved in the transmission of language between generations, or to other groups. Transmission without cultural breaks (Thomason & Kaufman 1988) seems to encourage language maintenance, with light or heavy restructuring depending on the nature of the contact. It may also lead to bilingualism (Sánchez), active code-switching (Liceras et al.) and shift (Bruhn de Garavito and Atoche). Linguistic transmission involving cultural breaks, for example, in cases of migrants or their descendents (Cornips and Hulk; Montrul) and with early plantation settings in the Caribbean (Smith; Kouwenberg) are likely to foster loss or changes to the language of origin in the former case and the development of contact languages in the latter. Terrill and Dunn hypothesize that contact, in this case without cultural break, will lead to semantic transference between the L1 and L2. Working in two separate language communities that speak different Papuan languages plus the local pidgin called Pijin, they show that spatial descriptions used by speakers of either Papuan language transfer into the local version of Pijin. These results echo research by Jourdan (2000) on kinship terminology in Solomons Pijin:

semantic transference makes it possible for L1 terms that are culturally relevant to L2 to be transferred into L2. Terrill and Dunn's findings suggest that semantic transference is widespread; nevertheless, preferred and less preferred strategies exist that affect the fit between L1 and L2.

This raises the question of variability within the same linguistic community. Is the speech of speakers with the same L1 influenced in the same way by contact with the same L2? This question is potentially important to our understanding of how pidgin and creoles develop. Bruhn de Garavito and Atoche look at contact Spanish spoken in Peru by monolinguals who live in close proximity to Quechua without actually acquiring that language. Nevertheless, their Spanish syntax, particularly clitics, appears to be affected by Quechua (see also Sánchez). Unlike Spanish speakers who are not in a contact situation, and like L2 learners of Spanish, these speakers demonstrate considerable variability in their use of clitics—variability which is subject to grammatical principles. In other words, contact does not produce haphazard changes in the grammar, but is highly constrained.

Other cases of constrained language contact are discussed by Liceras et al., who compare language mixing in bilinguals and in L2 learners, suggesting that bilingual code-switching is subject to different constraints from L2 code-switching. In particular, they examine how gender features are dealt with in mixes involving languages that differ over the realization of gender (e.g., English versus Spanish). In their view, the way feature mismatches (such as ±gender) are handled in code-switching may explain the loss of gender in creoles.

Müller's study of the use of complementizers by bilingual L1 acquirers (German-Italian and German-French) also shows that one language may influence the other in a constrained fashion: during the period when children's German grammar shows problems with German verb placement, the complementizer they use in German takes on properties of Romance complementizers. Müller suggests that there are interesting parallels with the development of prepositional complementizers in creole languages; in particular, she argues that in both child L1 bilingualism and creoles, cross-linguistic influence is only possible when there is a certain amount of overlap between the two languages, such that the input from one language is amenable to an analysis based on the grammar of the other.

The papers that we have grouped together under Language Contact are all concerned with the effects of one language on another or one grammar on another. While contact between populations or groups belongs in the social domain, the basis of language contact is in the individual's head (Weinreich 1953). This is the position that we adopt as we turn to the discussion of the cognitive processes involved in L2 acquisition and creole genesis.

## 3. *Processes*

We have chosen to group the various processes round three major stages in L2 acquisition and in creole genesis: the initial state (involving relexification and transfer), development and elaboration (involving restructuring and reanalysis) and the steady state (with particular reference to fossilization).

### 3.1 *Relexification and Transfer in the Initial State*

In this section, we consider in more detail some processes that are particularly relevant to accounting for cross-linguistic influence, namely relexification and transfer. Transfer has been identified as a process essential to creole formation and to L2 acquisition. The notion of transfer, which goes back at least to Weinreich (1953: 1), refers to the use of mother tongue features by speakers who are acquiring a second language. The presence of substratum features in creole lexicons is widely considered to be the result of transfer (Andersen 1980, 1983; Mufwene 1990, 1993; Naro 1978; Siegel 1995; etc.). Over the past 20 years, this concept has been refined and developed both by L2 researchers and by scholars interested in the genesis of creole languages.

In recent years, the Full Transfer/Full Access (FTFA) model has dominated generative-oriented approaches to L2 acquisition (e.g., Schwartz & Sprouse 1994, 1996; see also White 1989). According to the FTFA, at the outset of L2 acquisition, the L1 grammar transfers in its entirety (but excluding the phonetic matrices of lexical items), thus constituting the L2 initial state. This is what is meant by *full transfer*. Subsequently, the initial grammar will undergo restructuring, constrained by Universal Grammar (hence, *full access* to Universal Grammar).

In parallel fashion, the relexification model has dominated generatively oriented approaches to creole genesis (e.g., Lefebvre 1998; Lumsden 1999). Relexification is a particular type of transfer (Naro 1978: 337). It is a cognitive process that essentially consists in assigning to a lexical entry of language $L_1$ a new label drawn from language $L_2$. The resulting lexical entry has the semantic and syntactic properties of the original lexical entry in $L_1$, and a phonological representation derived from a form in $L_2$. In other words, the process of relexification reduces to relabeling. The process of relabeling is semantically driven, in the sense that the semantics of the two associated lexical entries must overlap at least partially (Muysken 1981: 62). Relabeling is thus constrained by what is available in $L_2$ to relabel a lexical entry from $L_1$ (Lefebvre & Lumsden 1994).

It seems, then, that there are strong parallels between full transfer, as conceived of in the FTFA model, and relexification, as conceived of in the relexification account of creole genesis. In this vein, Sprouse maintains that, despite superficial differences, there are significant similarities between the two. Given the current emphasis on the lexicon as the source of all morphosyntactic variation (e.g., Chomsky 1995), Sprouse suggests that:

> The only way for the "abstract properties" of the L1 to transfer and comprise the initial state of L2 acquisition is via retention of the L1 lexicon (minus phonetic labels). That is, Full Transfer's "abstract properties" appear to correspond in Minimalist terms to Relexification's lexical "features" (minus phonetic features).

In both fields (SLA and creole studies), there have been claims that functional categories are not subject to transfer (e.g., Vainikka & Young-Scholten 1994) or relexification (Muysken 1988). In the context of FTFA, Schwartz claims that all syntactic categories, including functional categories, undergo transfer. Drawing on a variety of evidence from different L2 experiments, Schwartz shows that CP does indeed transfer completely from the L1 to the L2, contrary to what has often been claimed. Similarly, Lefebvre (1998, 2006) shows that functional categories, including the complementizer system, may undergo relexification/relabeling.

Kouwenberg adopts a different position, maintaining that transfer in L2 acquisition is not the same as transfer in creoles, because transfer is a lasting phenomenon in creoles but not in L2 acquisition, where it is confined to the early stages and ceases to be relevant thereafter, in her view. In fact, there is now considerable evidence that shows lasting effects of transfer in L2 acquisition. FTFA does not claim that there will be a point after which transfer is irrelevant. Quite the reverse—L1 properties constitute the interlanguage representation initially and some L1 properties may remain permanently in the interlanguage representation. Nevertheless, it does indeed appear to be the case that transfer is more persistent in creoles. As Sprouse suggests (see below), this may relate to differences in the availability of L2 input in the two contexts.

Transfer has been identified as likely to have persistent effects on various interfaces (syntax-pragmatics, syntax-discourse, syntax-morphology, etc.) (Gürel 2002; Sorace 2003; Valenzuela 2006). Aboh makes the same case for creole genesis, proposing that language transfer in creoles is attributable to problems at the semantics-syntax interface, in particular that semantic properties are more liable to undergo persistent transfer than syntactic ones. Thus, while determiners in Surinamese creoles (e.g., Sranan and Saramaccan) reproduce the semantics of the Gbe languages, they show English word order. (See also Montrul—discussed in the next section—for evidence of interface problems in the L1 grammar of bilinguals.)

The group of papers on transfer concludes with Ionin's contribution, which raises the question of what happens in L2 acquisition when transfer cannot be implicated, because of the absence of some category in the L1 (in this case, the absence of articles in Korean and Russian) that is present in the L2 (English). The claim is that, initially at least, L2 learners will fluctuate between analyzing

English articles in terms of a universal specificity distinction (defined as ± *speaker intent to refer*) and in terms of a universal definiteness distinction. Ionin goes on to show that a number of creoles overtly encode specificity in their article systems, and suggests that this may be attributable to properties of the substrate languages. In such cases, then, relexification can be demonstrated to hold in creoles but transfer appears not to be implicated in L2 (because there is nothing to transfer).[2] (The effect is nevertheless similar, namely the overt realization of a specificity feature in the grammar, temporarily for the L2 learners, permanently in the creole.)

Both relexification theory and FTFA posit transfer, such that the L1 effectively *is* the interlanguage grammar or *is* the creole grammar. In the early stages of interlanguage and creole genesis, the mechanisms at work are similar, if not identical. As Sprouse points out: "the early L2 learner and the early creole cocreator are cognitively and epistemologically indistinguishable." A number of factors may explain subsequent differences between interlanguage grammars and PCs. Sprouse suggests that the differences are environmental: L2 learners are more likely than creole speakers to encounter sufficient L2 input to motivate grammar restructuring. However, this is not inevitably the case, as the paper by Cornips and Hulk points out; it shows that bilingual children of immigrants to the Netherlands never acquire certain aspects of Dutch gender. In addition, the social environment and the development of a creole-speaking community (Kouwenberg; Smith) may explain differences between interlanguage and PCs. Whereas interlanguage is the product of an individual grammar, creoles are, in some sense, the collective output of different interlanguages, themselves based on similar or different L1s.

*3.2 Restructuring and Reanalysis during Development*
Relexification and transfer are particularly relevant to the initial state of L2 acquisition and to the incipient creole. The papers in this section look at issues beyond the initial stages, examining parallels between developing interlanguage grammars and developing creoles. In other words, they examine processes that are involved in grammar change, either in individual interlanguage grammars or in developing creole grammars. In this context, two related processes are particularly relevant, namely restructuring and reanalysis. Although these terms are often used interchangeably, at least in SLA, differences of emphasis are involved. Restructuring implies change to the grammar itself, reanalysis concerns the kind of analysis imposed on the data (a new way of analyzing the data). Restructuring implies reanalysis; reanalysis can lead to restructuring. This is true of both historical change and language acquisition (Lightfoot 1999).

---

[2] See White (1996) versus Schwartz (1999) for a debate on whether there can ever truly be cases where there is nothing to transfer.

According to FTFA, grammar development involves (progressive) restructuring of the interlanguage grammar away from the L1 (and constrained by UG). In particular, data incompatible with—or not amenable to—an analysis in terms of the L1 grammar force the grammar to be restructured to accommodate them. As Sprouse suggests, L2 learners are more likely than PC acquirers to encounter such data. Restructuring may involve parameter resetting, from the L1 to the L2 setting or to some other setting (White 1989, 2003) or, as Lardiere (in press) has recently suggested, feature reassembly, whereby abstract morphosyntactic or semantic features that are represented in the L1 have to be remapped onto L2 lexical items. (This might seem to involve a particular case of relexification but, as Lardiere points out, L2 learners typically go beyond relexification.)

Sánchez's proposal is relevant to the issue of remapping or reassembly of features. She argues for functional convergence between the two grammars of bilingual speakers and suggests that morphological elaboration (in creoles) is a similar phenomenon. In each case, abstract functional features are dissociated from their morphological counterparts in one language and relinked to morphemes not previously associated with them. For example, Quechua has an evidentiality feature for first-hand information, which is associated with past tense distinctions in that language. Quechua-Spanish bilinguals associate this evidentiality feature with the pluperfect in Spanish, an association that does not exist in monolingual Spanish. Thus, compared to the monolingual Spanish grammar, the bilingual Spanish grammar has undergone restructuring at the featural level.

According to Brousseau and Nikiema, transfer and UG are both implicated in creole development. Their shows that the phonological system of Haitian Creole (HC) reflects properties of its substrate, Gbe, as well as its superstrate, French. The syllable structure of Haitian is more complex than that of Gbe and less complex than that of French, suggesting that transfer of phonological parameter settings and UG-constrained restructuring have both been involved in the development of HC phonology, consistent with full transfer and full access.

Steele and Brousseau point to the strong parallels between phonological processes observed in Haitian Creole and in the L1 and L2 acquisition of French. These comprise several processes that involve potential misanalyses (some L1-based and some not), including misparsing of input, as well as substitutions of perceptually similar items from the L1 or substrate in place of L2 or superstrate segments. Misanalyses in L1 acquisition are clearly not due to transfer; furthermore, reanalysis eventually occurs (French is acquired); in L2 acquisition, on the other hand, reanalysis is not inevitable (L1-based analyses may be maintained). In HC, the original misanalysis became the appropriate analysis.

Restructuring and reanalysis are essential ingredients of language change, leading to new language varieties historically. While most of the papers in this volume do not address the issue of language change directly (but see Montrul), all report examples of contact-induced language change. It is possible to think of creoles in terms of extreme language change: all the interlanguages produced by PC creators coalesce to form a new language variety for a new community. Is the same true of interlanguages? Are there interlanguages common to L2 communities? Do the interlanguage grammars of immigrants in the Netherlands, or bilingual children in Germany, or Spanish speakers in contact with Quechua in Peru, or Russian spoken in California have similar effects on the Dutch, German, Quechua, English, etc., spoken by the rest of the community? This seems unlikely: the properties of interlanguage grammars, by and large, remain properties of individual grammars and do not spread to the community (but see Montrul, as well as Cornips and Hulk, for speculation about the transmission of interlanguage properties across generations).

### 3.3 Fossilization in the Final State
The remaining papers in this volume address the final outcome of L2 acquisition. When language acquisition is no longer taking place, and speakers are bilingual (to a greater or lesser extent), one of the bilingual's grammars (the L2) may show evidence of fossilization. Fossilization is a term used to describe the fact that many L2 speakers stabilize at some point in their grammatical development short (often considerably short) of native-like attainment, showing evidence of long-lasting non-native performance (Long 2003). But, in fact, it is not only the L2 grammar that may be affected: the L1 grammar may also show "incomplete" acquisition, such that it appears fossilized in comparison to the grammars of monolinguals.

Fossilization is often noted in the domain of inflectional morphology. It takes a variety of forms, including omission of morphology, variable use of morphology, or use of default forms. One example of morphological fossilization in L2 is provided by Cornips and Hulk, who investigate Dutch gender, comparing the bilingual children of immigrants to the Netherlands (with a variety of L1s) with bidialectal children who speak Dutch and a local dialect. The bilingual children show fossilization (they do not fully acquire all properties of Dutch gender), in contrast to the bidialectal children. The effect of fossilization in this case is simplification of the gender system and this simplification is maintained in subsequent generations. Cornips and Hulk suggest that this may, in part, be the result of insufficient access to L2 input.

Montrul points out that Spanish heritage speakers in the USA (whose L1 in early childhood was Spanish) may have insufficient access to the L1, due to the pervasiveness of English, resulting in "incomplete" acquisition of Spanish. In other words, fossilization is not restricted to L2 contexts; however, in this case, at least, the problem is not related to morphology. Montrul shows that heritage speakers fail to observe rather subtle pragmatic constraints which determine the use of overt and null subjects in Spanish, while at the same time showing considerable accuracy with morphological properties, such as verbal agreement. (See Serratrice, Sorace & Paoli 2004 for similar findings in the case of Italian-English bilingualism.) Once again, this appears to be maintained across generations. Subtle discourse or pragmatic properties are also vulnerable in cases of loss of L1 (attrition) in older speakers who are continuously exposed to an L2 and who have reduced contact with the L1 (Gürel 2002; Sorace 2003).

Fossilization (of the L2) or incomplete acquisition (of the L1) may be the result of insufficient access to input, as suggested by Cornips and Hulk and by Montrul. Such situations may be analogous to situations typical of creole development, where creole speakers have insufficient access to the superstrate language (see Sprouse). In the final paper, Lardiere examines a case of fossilization that has occurred despite unlimited access to L2 input, a situation that presumably differs from the kind of access to the superstrate that creole speakers would have had. Lardiere shows that the subject of her case study goes beyond relexification: there are many subtle properties of English that she does acquire and that cannot be attributed to either of her L1s. At the same time, there are limits on what she achieves, particularly as far as inflectional morphology is concerned.

If fossilization is found even in the context of ample access to the L2, this raises the question of what other factors may be determinants of fossilization. The causes of fossilization may be multiple: lack of sufficient exposure to the L2; lack of motivation; properties of the L1 that make it impossible for certain features of the L2 to be acquired. This latter point brings us back, once again, to transfer and relexification.

Even when interlanguage grammars have undergone restructuring, this does not mean that transfer is no longer implicated. Sometimes, the initially adopted L1 grammar will impose a particular analysis on the L2 data, for which there is no disconfirming evidence; in such cases, reanalysis becomes impossible and transfer will be persistent and permanent (Brown 2000; Schwartz & Sprouse 1996; White 1989: Ch. 6).[3] In other words, FTFA does not claim that the outcome of L2 acquisition will inevitably be L2-like or that full access will inevitably win over full transfer. Transfer is not just an initial strategy adopted by L2 learners (contra Kouwenberg); rather, it involves the adoption of the L1 grammar as the appropriate analysis unless and until there is evidence to the contrary. In the absence of such evidence, L1 effects will

---

[3] It is not clear that the fossilization reported by Lardiere is susceptible to such an analysis, however, since her subject fails to supply inflectional morphology for which there is ample evidence in the L2 input.

persist even in the L2 steady state; similarly, in the case of creoles, relexification will remain in evidence in the long term.

## 4. *Directions for Future Research*

A number of common issues have emerged from the papers in this volume. One concerns interfaces. These have been identified in recent years as a source of problems in L2 acquisition and in bilingualism, in some cases leading to persistent L1 effects in the interlanguage grammar, as well as L2 effects on the L1 (syntax/discourse/pragmatics, Serratrice et al. 2004; Sorace 2003; Valenzuela 2006; morphology/phonology, Goad & White 2004; morphology/ syntax, Lardiere 2000). In the present volume, Montrul's paper examines problems at the syntax/discourse interface in the case of bilingualism, while Aboh emphasizes the importance of the syntax/semantics interface in the case of creoles. Schwartz and Müller address the issue of transfer in the C-domain, another interface area. The question that naturally presents itself is why interfaces should be so vulnerable. Can all cases of persistent cross-linguistic influence, in creole genesis as well as L2 acquisition, be located at the interfaces between the various components of the grammar?

Another issue that surfaces in some of the papers here (e.g., Müller; Sánchez) and that invites further exploration concerns the question of equivalence or overlap between the L1 and the L2. How much overlap must there be to motivate and facilitate transfer? As already mentioned, the relexification hypothesis assumes that relabeling will only take place if there is at least partial overlap in the semantics of two lexical items. What properties of the L2 or superstrate input determine that an analysis based on the L1 or substrate will work? What properties of the L2 input force a reanalysis, leading to the abandoning of the L1-based analysis? What kind of data can act as a trigger for language change? What kind of data fail to do so?

An area that has received surprisingly little explicit treatment in the present volume is the role of linguistic universals, specifically, access to UG. Several papers have drawn parallels between L2 acquisition and creole genesis as far as UG involvement is concerned (Ionin; Nikiema and Brousseau). And, of course, the claim that interlanguage grammars are UG-constrained forms a major component of the FTFA model. There is clearly room for further exploration here of the contribution of linguistic universals in both situations.

In conclusion, we hope that the papers in this volume will contribute to an ongoing and fruitful dialogue between two fields that for too long have failed to connect with each other. Most of these papers have pointed to similarities between the processes at work in L2 acquisition and creole genesis. Even if, in the end, one were to conclude that the differences outweigh the similarities, the dialogue can only help to focus discussion on the major outstanding issues pertaining to each field.

*References*

Andersen, R. W. 1980. Creolization and the acquisition of a second language as a first language. In *Theoretical Orientations in Creole Studies,* A. Valdman and A. R. Highfield (eds.), 273–295. New York, NY: Academic Press.

Andersen, R. W. 1983. A language acquisition interpretation of pidginization and creolization. In *Pidginization and Creolization as Language Acquisition,* R. W. Andersen (ed.), 1–59. Rowley, MA: Newbury House.

Brown, C. 2000. The interrelation between speech perception and phonological acquisition from infant to adult. In *Second Language Acquisition and Linguistic Theory,* J. Archibald (ed.), 4–63. Oxford: Blackwell.

Butler, Y. and K. Hakuta. 2004. Bilingualism and second language acquisition. In *The Handbook of Bilingualism,* T. Bhatia and W. Ritchie (eds.), 114–144. Oxford: Blackwell.

Chomsky, N. 1995. *The Minimalist Program.* Cambridge, MA: The MIT Press.

Goad, H. and L. White. 2004. Ultimate attainment of L2 inflection: Effects of L1 prosodic structure. In *EUROSLA Yearbook, Vol. 4*, S. Foster-Cohen, M. Sharwood Smith, A. Sorace and M. Ota (eds.), 119–145. Amsterdam: John Benjamins.

Gürel, A. 2002. Linguistic Characteristics of Second Language Acquisition and First Language Attrition: Turkish Overt versus Null Pronouns. Ph.D. dissertation, McGill University.

Hancock, I. 1980. Lexical expansion in creole languages. In *Theoretical Orientations in Creole Studies,* A. Valdman and A. R. Highfield (eds.), 63–87. New York, NY: Academic Press.

Hymes, D. 1971. Introduction. In D. Hyme (ed.) *Pidginization and Creolization of Languages* [Proceedings of a conference held at the University of the West Indies, Mona, Jamaica, 1968], 65–91. Cambridge: Cambridge University Press.

Jourdan, C. 2000. My Nephew is my Aunt: Features and Transformation of Kindship Terminology in Solomon Islands Pidgin. In J.Siegel (ed.) *Processes of Language contact: studies from Australia and the South Pacific*, 99–121. Montreal: Fides.

Kouwenberg, S. and P. Patrick (eds.). 2003. *Reconsidering the Role of SLA in Pidginization and Creolization.* Special issue of *Studies in Second Language Acquisition* 25(2).

Lardiere, D. 2000. Mapping features to forms in second language acquisition. In *Second Language Acquisition and Linguistic Theory*, J. Archibald (ed.), 102–129. Oxford: Blackwell.

Lardiere, D. In press. Feature-assembly in second language acquisition. In *The Role of Features in Second Language Acquisition,* J. Liceras, H. Goodluck and H. Zobl (eds.). Mahwah, NJ: Lawrence Erlbaum.

Lefebvre, C. 1998. *Creole Genesis and the Acquisition of Grammar: The Case of Haitian Creole.* Cambridge: Cambridge University Press.

Lefebvre, C. 2006. The contribution of relexification, grammaticalization, reanalysis, and diffusion to contact-induced language change. Paper given at a special session on Contact-Induced Change, SPCL/LSA, Albuquerque, January 5–8.

Lefebvre, C. and J. S. Lumsden (eds.). 1994. *MIT Symposium on the Central Role of Relexification in Creole Genesis: The Case of Haitian Creole*. Research report prepared for SSHRCC on the project *La genèse du créole haïtien: un cas particulier d'investigation sur la forme de la grammaire universelle*. Université du Québec à Montréal, Montreal.

Lightfoot, D. 1999. *The Development of Language: Acquisition, Change and Evolution*. Oxford: Blackwell.

Long, M. 2003. Stabilization and fossilization in interlanguage development. In *Handbook of Second Language Acquisition,* C. Doughty and M. Long (eds.), 487–535. Oxford: Blackwell.

Lumsden, J.S. 1999. Language acquisition and creolization. In *Language Creation and Language Change,* M. DeGraff (ed.), 129–158. Cambridge, MA: The MIT Press.

Mufwene, S. 1990. Transfer and the substrate hypothesis in creolistics. *Studies in Second Language Acquisition* 12(1): 1–23.

Mufwene, S. 1993. Créole, créolisation, substrat, et autres notions apparentées: quelques réflexions sur *Des îles, des hommes, des langues. Langues créoles – cultures créoles* de Robert Chaudenson. *Études créoles* 16(2): 117–141.

Mühlhäusler, P. 1980. Structural expansion and the process of creolization. In *Theoretical Orientations in Creole Studies,* A. Valdman and A. R. Highfield (eds.), 19–56. New York, NY: Academic Press.

Mühlhäusler, P. 1986. *Pidgin and Creole Linguistics* [Language Society II]. Oxford: Basil Blackwell.

Muysken, P. C. 1981. Half-way between Quechua and Spanish: The case for relexification. In *Historicity and Variation in Creole Studies*, A. R. Highfield and A. Valdman (eds.), 52–79. Ann Arbor, MI: Karoma.

Muysken, P.C. 1988. Lexical restructuring in creole genesis, in Boretzky, Enninger and Stolz (eds.), pp. 193-210.

Naro, A. 1978. Study of the origins of pidginization. *Language* 54: 314–347.

Romaine, S. 2001. Multilingualism. In *The Handbook of Linguistics,* M. Aronoff and J. Rees-Miller (eds.), 512–532. Oxford: Blackwell.

Schwartz, B. D. 1999. Some specs on Specs in L2 acquisition. In *Specifiers: Minimalist Approaches,* D. Adger, S. Pintzuk, B. Plunkett and G. Tsoulas (eds.), 299–337. Oxford: Oxford University Press.

Schwartz, B. D. and R. A. Sprouse. 1994. Word order and nominative case in non-native language acquisition: A longitudinal study of (L1 Turkish) German interlanguage. In *Language Acquisition Studies in Generative Grammar: Papers in Honor of Kenneth Wexler from the 1991 GLOW Workshops*, T. Hoekstra and B. D. Schwartz (eds.), 317–368. Philadelphia: John Benjamins.

Schwartz, B.D. and Rex A. Sprouse. 1996. L2 cognitive states and the full transfer/full access model. *Second Language Research* 12: 40–72.

Selinker, L. 1972. Interlanguage. *International Review of Applied Linguistics* 10: 209–231.

Serratrice, L., A. Sorace and S. Paoli. 2004. Crosslinguistic influence at the syntax-pragmatics interface: Subjects and objects in English-Italian bilingual and monolingual acquisition. *Bilingualism: Language and Cognition* 7: 183–205.

Siegel, J. 1995. Koine formation and creole genesis. In *Creolization and Contact,* N. Smith and T. Veenstra (eds.), 175–198. Amsterdam: John Benjamins.

Sorace, A. 2003. Near-nativeness. In *Handbook of Second Language Acquisition,* C. Doughty and M. Long (eds.), 130–151. Oxford: Blackwell.

Thomason, S. G. and T. Kaufman. 1988. *Language Contact, Creolization, and Genetic Linguistics.* Berkeley, CA: University of California Press.

Vainikka, A. and M. Young-Scholten. 1994. Direct access to X'-theory: Evidence from Korean and Turkish adults learning German. In *Language Acquisition Studies in Generative Grammar: Papers in Honor of Kenneth Wexler from the 1991 GLOW Workshops*, T. Hoekstra and B. D. Schwartz (eds.), 265–316. Philadelphia: John Benjamins.

Valenzuela, E. 2006. L2 end state grammars and incomplete acquisition of the Spanish CLLD constructions. In *Inquiries in Linguistic Development: In Honor of Lydia White,* R. Slabakova, S. Montrul and P. Prévost (eds.), 283–304. Amsterdam: John Benjamins.

Weinreich, U. 1953. *Languages in Contact.* The Hague: Mouton.

White, L. 1989. *Universal Grammar and Second Language Acquisition.* Amsterdam: John Benjamins.

White, L. 1996. Clitics in L2 French. In *Generative Perspectives on Language Acquisition,* H. Clahsen (ed.), 335–367. Amsterdam: John Benjamins.

White, L. 2003. *Second Language Acquisition and Universal Grammar.* Cambridge: Cambridge University Press.

Woolford, E. 1983. Introduction: The social context of creolization. In *The Social context of Creolization*, E. Woolford and W. Washabaugh (eds.), 1–9. Ann Arbor, MI: Karoma Publishers.

# LINKS BETWEEN SLA AND CREOLE STUDIES:
## PAST AND PRESENT*

Jeff Siegel

*University of New England (Australia) and University of Hawai'i*

This chapter examines the links between adult second language acquisition (SLA) and the genesis of pidgin and creole languages, focusing on two SLA processes: simplification and transfer. Some historical background is presented concerning each process, followed by a discussion of recent developments in pidgin and creole studies that have built upon research in the field of SLA. The chapter concludes that the "simplification" found in restricted pidgins is most likely a consequence of earlier SLA, with various social-psychological factors possibly responsible for the lack of further convergence with the L2. On the other hand, much of the grammatical expansion found in extended pidgins and creoles is the result of functional transfer from the L1, which occurs with extended second language use.

The possible links between adult second language acquisition (SLA) and the characteristics of pidgin and creole languages have been debated for more than a hundred years. In this chapter, I review the issues concerning the role of two SLA processes—simplification and transfer—in the genesis of pidgin and creole (P/C) languages. For each process, I present some historical background, followed by a discussion of recent developments in P/C studies, especially those that have built upon research in the field of SLA.

## 1. *Simplification*

### 1.1 *Background*

Although linguists frequently make use of the term "simplification," they do not necessarily agree on its precise meaning. For example, some use the term to refer to a reduction in complexity (Hymes 1971) and others to a lack of development of complexity (Corder 1981). In P/C studies, it usually refers to comparative formal simplicity—that is, simplicity in the quantitative rather than psycholinguistic sense. In other words, one variety is considered simpler or less complex than another if it has fewer components and fewer rules, but it is not necessarily easier to process. Thus, comparing one variety to another (or comparing subsets of features of two varieties), simplification includes characteristics such as a smaller lexicon, a reduced phonemic inventory, fewer grammatical categories, less bound morphology and fewer exceptions to rules. Traditionally, pidgins and creoles have been compared to their lexifier (or superstrate) language, and according to this definition, nearly all creolists would

* This chapter is a revised and expanded version of "Pidgins/Creoles and Second Language Acquisition," to appear in the *Handbook of Pidgins and Creoles* edited by J. V. Singler and S. Kouwenberg.

agree that P/Cs are characterized by simplification in at least some aspects of phonology, morphosyntax or lexicon.[1] Consider these two sentences from Tok Pisin:

(1) a.  *Asde        mi   wok   long    haus.*
         yesterday  I    work  at      home
         ·'Yesterday I worked at home.'
    b.  *Yu    no    kam     long  haus  bilong  mi*[2].
         you   NEG   come    to    house POS     me
         'You don't come to my house.'

These sentences illustrate the following aspects of simplification (compared to the lexifier, English): lack of verbal morphology (no past tense marking), no auxiliaries, a single negative marker before the verb, just one form of the pronoun (*mi*), and reduced lexicon, for instance, *long* meaning both 'at' and 'to.'

In order to explain this kind of simplification in P/Cs, Adolpho Coelho first proposed in the 1880s what is now known as the "imperfect learning theory" (Siegel 1987: 19–20) or the "imperfect second language learning theory" (Muysken & Smith 1995: 10). According to this theory, these simplified features are the result of incomplete acquisition due to insufficient access to the target language (i.e., the lexifier). Similarities among various pidgins and creoles could then be explained by the universal properties of the simplification that occurs in the early stages of second language learning. The theory was in opposition to the view that simplification arises because of speakers of the lexifier using simplified versions of their own speech (or "foreigner talk") in talking to non-native speakers. The imperfect acquisition theory in P/C genesis was subscribed to by later linguists, such as Jesperson (1922) and Bloomfield (1933), and by early modern creolists, such as Hall (1966) and Samarin (1971).

While the field of P/C studies expanded rapidly in the late 1960s and early 1970s, the study of SLA was just starting to emerge as a separate subfield of linguistics. Thus, creolists such as Bickerton (1977) could comment that "the whole area of natural second language acquisition—a process that affects

---

[1] Of course, if P/Cs are compared to their substrate languages, simplification is not so clear-cut. For example, while the amount of inflectional morphology in Haitian Creole is less than in French, it is similar to that of the Gbe (West African) substrate languages. On the other hand, Haitian Creole has more derivational affixes than the Gbe languages (Lefebvre 1998, 2003).

[2] List of abbreviations used in linguistic examples:

POS    possession
NEG    negative
ANT    anterior
COMP   completive
ASP    aspect
EXT    extreme
TRAN   transitive
3SG    3$^{rd}$ person singular

countless millions of persons—remains a vast and grotesque lacuna in our knowledge of language" (p. 54). Nevertheless, he asserted that "pidginization is second-language learning with restricted input" (p. 49). Ferguson and DeBose (1977) also noted that there were "few studies of adult 'natural' acquisition" (p. 108), but they drew on the recent SLA research into the nature of learners' grammars—that is, transient internal representations of the structure of the target language called "approximative systems" (Nemser 1971) or "interlanguage" (Selinker 1972). Ferguson and DeBose called learners' actual productions of the target language—characterized by relative formal simplicity, a carryover of features from the first language, and great variability among learners—"broken language" (pp. 108–109). They also broadened the definition of pidginization, describing it as "a process that accepts normal language as input and produces a reduced, hybridized, and unstable variety of language as output" (p. 111), which included both broken language in SLA and foreigner talk.

It was during this period that some scholars in the nascent field of SLA looked to P/C studies for explanations of the processes involved in learning a second language. Schumann (1978a), for example, equated early SLA and pidginization in his book *The Pidginization Process: A Model for Second Language Acquisition*. The basis for this model was a longitudinal study of six native speakers of Spanish learning English outside the classroom setting. One of the learners, Alberto, remained in the early stages of development with regard to the linguistic features being studied. His English output resembled pidgins in terms of simplification, and specifically in particular features found in English-derived pidgins, such as the following (Schumann 1978a: 66):

1. negatives formed by *no* preceding the verb
2. absence of inversion in questions
3. no auxiliaries
4. unmarked possessives
5. absence of *-ed* past tense marking

Schumann's claim was not that Alberto spoke a pidgin, but that this simplification was evidence of pidginization. Schumann surmised "that pidginization may characterize all early second language acquisition in general and that under conditions of social and psychological distance it persists" (p. 110). He also suggested, following Kay and Sankoff (1974), that the pidginized form of speech found in early second language acquisition and pidgins may approximate the universal underlying structure of language.

Schumann's model was criticized by scholars in both P/C studies and SLA. Washabaugh and Eckman (1980: 455) noted, among other criticisms, that creolists do not agree that the definition of pidginization necessarily includes simplification, or that a definable process of pidginization even exists! Corder (1981: 148–149) took the point of view that pidginization is a linguistic process that results in the formation of a pidgin language, not a psycholinguistic process involving simplification of the superstrate, because people cannot simplify a language that they do not know.

In contrast to Corder, however, Andersen (1980, 1981, 1983a) distinguished between individual pidginization, a psycholinguistic process that results in individual second language varieties, and group (or social) pidginization, a sociolinguistic process results in a pidgin language with its own norms:

> Individual pidginization arises from the interaction between an individual language learner's brain and the linguistic input that the brain processes during SLA. Group pidginization results from communication among speakers who have undergone or are undergoing individual pidginization. (Andersen 1980: 274)

In a 1979 study (published as Andersen 1981), he made a detailed comparison of the speech of Alberto (Schumann 1978a) and the speech of speakers of Hawai'i Pidgin English (Bickerton & Odo 1976), and found features very similar to those listed above. On the basis of this study, Andersen (1980: 274) concluded, in agreement with Schumann and Bickerton, that "SLA and individual pidginization are really the same phenomenon viewed from different perspectives and often, although not always, occurring under different circumstances." He noted that researchers in SLA have focused mainly on "depidginization," defined as "the gradual acquisition of TL [target language] norms" (1980: 275), while researchers in P/C studies have focused on pidginization. He concluded, however, that they are studying basically the same pidginization-depidginization continuum. There was general agreement on this point at a symposium held in 1979 on the relationship between pidginization, creolization and language acquisition (Andersen 1983b). Soon afterwards, Valdman (1980: 297) noted: "The notion that the incipient IL [interlanguage] is the product of pidginization has gained wide acceptance."

Unlike previous scholars, Andersen also addressed the issue of the specific relationship between SLA and creolization, not just pidginization. He again made a distinction between two types of creolization. Social creolization refers to the process that results in a creole language, generally thought to occur when a pidgin or pre-pidgin (i.e., a continuum of second language varieties) becomes the mother tongue of a community of speakers. Individual creolization is defined as individual pidginization plus

> the creation of form-meaning relationships which serve the creator's (learner's) communicative and expressive needs, but which cannot be explained as having been "acquired" from the input. The forms themselves come from the input, but the meanings they convey are provided by the learner and are not those they have in the input. (Andersen 1983a: 9)

Andersen (1983a: 9–10) believed that both children and adults have the capacity to create these new form-meaning relationships, and by implication, that certain SLA processes may be involved:

> If the circumstances require further growth in the language and the input is inadequate for this growth (as in the settings where pidgin and creole languages develop), this growth must take place within the linguistic system created by the learner. The learners must utilize the limited linguistic resources available to them and complicate and expand their linguistic system. Both adults and children can do this ...

It was with regard to the expansion and complication in creolization that Andersen and Bickerton parted company. Bickerton believed (and still does) that only children have the innate capacity to create linguistic systems without adequate models—thus his well-known distinction in the full version of the quotation given earlier: "that pidginization is second-language learning with restricted input, and that creolization is first-language learning with restricted input" (1977: 49). Bickerton's view (1981, 1984a, 1988, 1999a, 1999b) is that creoles are created by children learning their first language and drawing upon their innate "bioprogram" in absence of any fully developed linguistic model. This abrupt creolization occurs "in the space of a single generation" (1999a: 49) among the first generation of locally born children of plantation slaves or indentured laborers. Thus, according to Bickerton, creole genesis is the result of child first language acquisition, not adult second language acquisition.

Bickerton's Language Bioprogram Hypothesis was highly controversial and is certainly not universally accepted. But because of its impact, the main thrust of research in P/C studies in the later 1980s and early 1990s shifted away from pidgin genesis to concentrate on creole genesis and what it could tell us about the nature of humans' inborn language capacity. The focus was on the "core features" of creoles that demonstrate expansion and complication rather than on other common creole features that demonstrate earlier simplification. Thus, as Arends, Muysken and Smith (1995: 320) observed: "Earlier ideas regarding possible parallels between creolization and pidginization on the one hand and natural second language on the other ... have not been followed up by many creolists."

## 1.2 *Recent developments*

Later in the 1990s, however, fewer creolists remained convinced by Bickerton's point of view. First of all, it could not explain the clear presence of features from substrate languages in many creoles. Second, new historical findings contradicted his scenario for the development of creoles, showing that many of them had developed gradually over several generations (Arends 1993; Singler 1990; and various chapters in Arends 1995). According to the "gradualist model" which emerged from these findings, the rate of nativization (i.e., becoming a native language) was slow and speakers of the emerging creole were mainly adults. This led to a renewed interest in the role of adult second language acquisition in creole genesis. For example, in a chapter in a volume he edited on creole languages and language acquisition, Wekker (1996: 146) views creolization as "a gradual process of imperfect second-language acquisition by successive cohorts of adult slaves, extending over generations."

Meanwhile, research in SLA has increased by leaps and bounds since the early 1980s, and today it is a much larger field than P/C studies. So while in the past the field of SLA looked toward P/C studies for data and insights, it would seem profitable now for P/C studies to look toward SLA. However, with the exception of scholars such as Mufwene (1990), DeGraff (1999), Clements (2001), Winford (2002), and others mentioned below, very few people writing about pidgins and creoles have delved into the recent SLA literature in any detail. The most detailed coverage is found in a recent book about language contact (Winford 2003) which includes a whole chapter on SLA and weaves recent SLA findings into explanations in later chapters about the genesis of pidgins and creoles.

Two areas of SLA research have led to findings that are directly relevant to issues surrounding simplification in P/C genesis (and also surrounding transfer —discussed below). First, detailed descriptions of the interlanguage (IL) of second language learners have provided more evidence that the same processes operating in SLA may be responsible for features of pidgins and creoles. Second, further investigations into the role of social-psychological factors in SLA help to explain why, if SLA was involved in their genesis, P/Cs did not continue along the developmental continuum to become more like their lexifiers, as in "normal" SLA. I will discuss each of these areas in turn.

1.2.1  *Descriptions of IL and P/C features.* The last decade has seen numerous detailed analyses of the ILs of learners of various European languages. These have led to many more studies along the lines of Andersen (1981), comparing ILs and P/Cs with the same language as the target or lexifier. First we will look at studies dealing with IL and specific non-English-lexified P/Cs. Then we will look at a study of IL features in general in comparison with typical features of restricted pidgins (i.e., pidgins that have not expanded grammatically).

Véronique (1994) describes many formal similarities between features found in the early interlanguages of first language (L1) Moroccan Arabic learners of French as a second language and what are considered "simplified" features of French-lexified creoles. These include the following (p. 133):

1. lack of formal distinction between word classes, especially between nouns and verbs
2. NP and VP morphology largely lacking (compared to French)
3. some nouns used without articles

4. verbs developing two forms: the bare stem and stem + /e/[3]
5. extended use of "presentationals" /jãna/ and /se/ 'there is'

He concludes (p.133): "The similarities between FBCs [French-based creoles] and ILs illustrate early attempts of naturalistic learners to understand and use TL [target language] input, to 'crack the code.'" Similarly, in an examination of the IL of West African L1 Ewe learners of French, Mather (2000) found some of the same and other features similar to those of French-lexified creoles, such as the lack of copulas, which he concludes were the result of the process of simplification in SLA.

Using data from several studies on Dutch SLA, Muysken (2001) compares learners' IL features with features of the now extinct Dutch-lexifier creole, Negerhollands. He reports many similarities in terms of formal simplicity, including rigid SVO word order, the absence of postpositions, preverbal negation, the absence of inflections on verbs and periphrastic possessives of the type *Mary her/his book.* Muysken concludes (p. 169): "A number of features of Negerhollands may well be explicable as deriving from the acquisition of Dutch as a second language."

Kotsinas (1996) illustrates numerous similarities between the features of the IL of Swedish immigrants where Swedish is the second language (L2), and those of Russenorsk, a pidgin which has closely related Norwegian as a lexifier—for example, extended use of the preposition *på.* A later work (Kotsinas 2001) shows similarities between the features of L2 versions of Swedish and those typical of pidgin languages.

A good indication of IL features in general came out of one of the largest studies ever done of naturalistic adult second language acquisition: the European Science Foundation (ESF) project that took place in the 1980s. This was a 30-month longitudinal study of 40 adult immigrants with various first languages: Arabic, Italian, Finnish, Spanish and Turkish. The target languages were Dutch, English, French, German and Swedish (Perdue 1993).[4] In an article about the results of the study, Klein and Perdue (1997) state that approximately one-third of the learners acquired only what they call "the Basic Variety," characterized by numerous simplified structural features.[5] These include the following features, which can be considered simplified because

---

[3] Note that this feature is found in only some French-lexified creoles, such as those of Réunion and Louisiana (Alleyne 2000: 129–130). It is also found in Mauritius, where it was a later rather than an early development (Baker & Corne 1982: 64–78).

[4] The core informants for the study were young adults ranging from 16 to 39 years of age, with an average age of 24.3. They were relatively recent immigrants, having been in the country from 1 to 19 months (average: 8.1 months). They had from 0 to 11 years of schooling in their L1 in their home country (average: 6.9 years) and from 0 to 600+ hours of instruction in the medium of the target language (L2) (average: 200+ hours) (Perdue 1993: 46).

[5] The other two-thirds of the learners also went through a stage characterized by the structural simplification of the Basic Variety, but later progressed from "a noun-based utterance organization" to "a finite-verb-based organization" (Klein & Perdue 1997: 309n).

they are reduced, regularized or more semantically transparent than the features of the target language:

1. no inflections
2. lexical items used in invariant form (multifunctionality)
3. invariant forms generally infinitive (verbs) or nominative (nouns) (but also some inflected forms)
4. lexical items noun-like and verb-like words with some adjectives and adverbs
5. most lexical items from the L2 but some from the L1 and other languages
6. minimal pronouns to refer to speaker, hearer and a third person
7. no anaphoric pronouns referring to inanimates
8. only a few quantifiers
9. a single word for negation
10. only a few prepositions
11. no overt complementizers
12. no expletive elements (e.g., *there is*)
13. use of temporal adverbs, rather than grammatical TMA markers, to indicate temporality, including: calendar type: Saturday, in the morning
    anaphoric: after, before
    deictic: yesterday, now
    frequency: always, often
    duration (usually nouns): two hours
14. specification of temporal relations: BEFORE, AFTER, SIMULTANEOUS, etc.
15. "boundary markers" to express the beginning or end of some situation, such as *work finish* 'after work is/was/will be over' (Klein & Perdue 1997: 321)

Significantly, the majority of these features are found in most restricted (i.e., unexpanded) pidgins including Pidgin Fijian and Pidgin Hindustani (Siegel 1987), Chinese Pidgin English (Baker 1987), Greenlandic Pidgin (van der Voort 1996), the Hiri Trading Languages (Eleman and Koriki) (Dutton 1997), Nauru Pidgin English (Siegel 1990), Ndyuka-Trio Pidgin (Huttar & Velantie 1997), Pidgin Delaware (Goddard 1997), Pidgin Hawaiian (Roberts 1995), Pidgin French of Vietnam (Reinecke 1971) and Russenorsk (Jahr 1996).

These similarities provide evidence that a large proportion of the "simplified" structural features of pidgins may be a consequence of SLA at an earlier stage of development. Some of these simplified features could also have been inherited by creoles in a later stage of development.

1.2.2 *Social-psychological factors and "imperfect" SLA*. If SLA was involved in the genesis of pidgins and creoles, we need to explain why acquisition did not progress further. In other words, why do P/C grammars remain so distinct from those of their lexifiers? Baker's view (1994, 1997, 2000) is that SLA is not relevant to P/C genesis. He believes that people of different ethnolinguistic backgrounds in contact situations are generally not interested in acquiring the language of the other groups but rather in constructing a new "medium for interethnic communication." However, a lot of evidence exists, such as that presented above, to support the involvement of SLA (see also Mufwene 2001; Siegel 2003), and the SLA literature itself contains a great deal of work on factors which lead to incomplete language acquisition.

Early social-psychological models of SLA, such as Schumann's (1978b) "acculturation model" considered social and psychological distance to be important factors. Other models used individual factors, such as motivation and social identity as well as socio-structural factors such as relative size, status and power of the L1 and L2 groups. (For overviews, see Ellis 1994; Siegel 2002.) However, more recent work has criticized these models for implying that learners are free to make choices about when they interact with L2 speakers or whether they are motivated to integrate with the L2 culture, and thus blaming the learner for lack of L2 attainment. Ethnographic studies in SLA–such as those by Norton Peirce (1995), Norton (2000) and McKay and Wong (1996)–take into account the socio-historical factors of power and domination which limit the choices available to learners, and also adopt the post-structuralist view that people have multiple and changing social identities, rather than the unitary static social identity of most social-psychological models.

Another recent perspective in the SLA literature considers that a variety which differs from that of an idealized native speaker does not necessarily represent its speakers' failure to attain L2 competence. As Rampton (1997: 294) observes: "People are not always concerned with improving their L2 interlanguage." An "imperfect" variety may be used to express a particular identity of the speaker, to show solidarity with a peer group or to indicate attitudes towards society in general. For example, stereotyped South Asian English is used by the adolescents in England studied by Rampton (1995) not because of any lack of proficiency in local varieties of English but for joking and ridiculing racist attitudes. As Firth and Wagner (1997: 292) observe, non-native-like structures may be "deployed resourcefully and strategically to accomplish social and interactional ends." Furthermore, the decision not to use native-like L2 forms or not to use the L2 at all may represent a form of resistance, which, alongside achievement and avoidance, is another kind of communication strategy (Rampton 1991: 239). It follows, then, that in many situations native-like proficiency is not the target of language learning.

Both these recent perspectives are relevant to P/C genesis in providing alternatives to the explanation positing a "lack of success" or "failure" in acquiring the lexifier that have been justifiably criticized by creolists such as Baker (1994). As Sebba (1997: 79) notes: "A more pragmatic view would be that pidgins represent *successful* second language learning from the point of view of their learners—who learn just enough to communicate what they want to communicate and no more." [italics in original] So rather than "imperfect SLA," a non-negative term such as "strategic" or "adaptive" SLA would be more appropriate.[6]

## 2. *Transfer*

### 2.1 Background

Like the role of simplification, the degree of influence of features of the substrate languages in pidgins and creoles has been debated since the earliest days of P/C studies. One of the first scholars to ascribe this influence to language learning was Hesseling in work that first appeared in 1933:

> [The African slaves] learn the surface structure of the European languages, although they make them suitable for their own manner of thinking. ... The masters hear their own words, however truncated or misshapen, while the slaves employ the foreign material in a way which is not in complete conflict with their inherited manner of expressing themselves. (Hesseling 1979: 69)

More recently, Alleyne (1971: 182) wrote along the same lines that "in attempting to speak English or French, Africans in Africa, as well as in the New World, interpreted English or French structural patterns in terms of native patterns."

Here I will focus on two types of substrate influence that appear to occur in pidgins and creoles. The first type is concerned with word order. An example is found in the pidginized English spoken by Japanese immigrants in Hawai'i, which uses Japanese OV word order:

(2)  *da pua  pipl    awl poteito  it.*                    (Bickerton 1981: 11)
     the poor people all   potato    eat
     'The poor people just eat potatoes.'

The influence of substrate word order can be seen most commonly in pre-pidgins or restricted pidgins, but it is occasionally found in creoles. For instance, Sranan, a creole spoken in Suriname, uses some postpositions, similar to its West African substrate languages, as with *ondro* 'under' in this example:

(3)  *a    buku  de   na    tafra   ondro.*              (McWhorter 1996: 485)
     the  book  is   LOC  table   under
     'The book is under the table.'

The second type of substrate influence is the use of forms from the lexifier with grammatical functions from the substrate languages. This is found in expanded pidgins or creoles, rather than in pre-pidgins or restricted pidgins. An

---

[6] Thanks to students in my seminar "Pidgins, Creoles and Other Language Contact Varieties" at the University of Hawai'i in 2003 for their help in coming up with these terms.

example is the subject-referencing pronoun in Melanesian Pidgin, as represented by Bislama.

(4) a. Bislama:   *Man  ya  i   stil-im   mane.*
                   man   DET 3SG steal-TR money
                   'This man stole the money.'

    b. Bislama:   *Ol  woman **oli**  kat-em   taro.*
                   PL   woman 3PL   cut-TR    taro
                   'The women cut the taro.'

The forms of the subject-referencing pronouns are derived from English morphemes (*he* and *all he*), but the function is typical of Eastern Oceanic substrate languages such as Arosi and Kwaio:

(5) a. Arosi:  *E    noni   a    ome-sia    i    ruma.*   (Lynch 1993: 143)
                ART  man   3SG see-TR.3SG  ART house
                'The man saw the house.'

    b. Kwaio: *Ta'a   geni   **la**   a'ari-a   go'u.*   (Keesing 1988: 220)
                people female 3PL   carry-TR  taro
                'The women carried taro.'

In the last three decades, some creolists have accounted for these kinds of substrate influence, and also to morphological expansion in creoles, by referring to another important process in SLA: language transfer. The term "transfer" refers to a form of cross-linguistic influence found in SLA that involves "carrying over of mother tongue patterns into the target language" (Sharwood Smith 1996: 71), or more accurately, into the interlanguage. In other words, learners use linguistic features of their L1—phonemes, grammatical rules, or meanings or functions of particular words—when speaking the L2. Such transfer can be either positive (when a feature in the L1 matches that of the L2) or negative (when corresponding features of the L1 and L2 do not match). Negative transfer, which I will concentrate on, is sometimes called "interference" and has been given other labels as well.

Here I focus on two types of transfer that correspond to the examples above: (i) syntactic or "word order" transfer, and (ii) what I call "functional transfer"—the use of L2 forms with L1 grammatical properties.

Bickerton was one of the first to refer to the role of transfer in P/C genesis. On the basis of his work in Hawai'i, Bickerton (1977: 54) saw pidginization as a process of "relexification"—where the substrate grammar is maintained but the L1 lexicon is gradually replaced by superstrate words, which are "rephonologized to accord with the substrate sound system and phonotactics." More superstrate lexicon is acquired later and for the most part "slotted into syntactic structures drawn from the substrate." Bickerton made a clear connection between this process and early SLA, saying that "second languages are naturally acquired via piecemeal relexification, productive calquing, and the utilization of mother tongue surface structure ... in the early stages at least" (pp. 54–55). The difference between pidginization and normal SLA lies in "the availability of target models and the amount of interaction with speakers of the target language" (p. 55).

While Bickerton said that relexification may be "complete down to grammatical items" (p. 54), the examples in Bickerton (1977) and in Bickerton and Odo (1976) mainly show the use of L1 phonology and word order in speaking the L2—what would be described as phonological and syntactic transfer in the SLA literature—for example, the use of Japanese SOV word order by Japanese speakers as seen in example (2) above and example (6) (Bickerton 1977: 53):

(6)    *as  kerosin  plænteishan  wan  mans   fo    gælan  giv.*
       us   kerosene  plantation   one   month  four  gallon  give
       'The plantation gave us four gallons of kerosene a month.'

Later, Bickerton (1984b: 152) referred explicitly to the process as learners "transferring rules of grammar from the grammar they already know to the grammar they are seeking to acquire."

In contrast to Bickerton, however, Naro (1978) claimed there was no substrate influence in Pidgin Portuguese, and therefore presumably no transfer in the pidginization process. Similarly, Manessy (1977) reported no substrate influence in African pidgins. Furthermore, in a work that had great influence on the field of P/C studies, Meisel (1983) argued that universal cognitive strategies of simplification, rather than transfer, are the most significant determinants of the features of interlanguage, and therefore transfer is not a significant factor in P/C genesis. This work reflected the prevailing attitudes in the field of SLA regarding the role of transfer in interlanguage development. Research in the 1970s (e.g., Dulay & Burt 1973) had shown that negative transfer accounted for only a small proportion of non-target forms in interlanguage, and that there were natural sequences of morphological and syntactic development that were unconnected with the L1. As a result of these findings and others, SLA research had ceased paying much attention to transfer and was concentrating instead on the role of universal processes of language acquisition.

With regard to creoles, Andersen (1983a: 31) believed that the substrate languages could be a possible source for the expansion and complication involved in creole genesis:

> In the absence of clear models in the input for a linguistic form needed to consistently convey a meaning the learner wants to communicate, the learner can (probably far below the level of consciousness) use a form (or forms) available in the input to convey the meaning and/or fulfill the function of an equivalent form in his native language ... with the distribution that form has in his native language.

Here Andersen was clearly talking about functional transfer. However, this possibility was discounted by Bickerton (1977, 1981, 1984a), who argued that the first generation of creole speakers did not know their ancestral languages and therefore only first language acquisition was involved in creole genesis. So from the late 1970s to the early 1990s, the combination of the earlier move away from research on transfer in the field of SLA and the dominance of Bickerton's paradigm meant that there was very little interest in the role of transfer in P/C genesis.

In contrast, during the 1980s and 1990s, the field of SLA once again became interested in research on language transfer, but with a new focus on identifying conditions that determine whether or not transfer occurs. These factors are called "constraints" (Ellis 1994: 315), though they are not absolute and may either promote or inhibit transfer. Two types of constraints were investigated. The first are situational constraints, such as the learner's degree of proficiency and the learning context (i.e., naturalistic vs. classroom); these affect whether or not transfer occurs in general (see Siegel 1999 for details). The second are linguistic constraints, such as markedness (discussed below); these affect whether or not particular linguistic features are transferred.

## 2.2 *Recent developments*

The first clear statement about the connection between the process of transfer in SLA and substrate influence in pidgins and creoles was made in 1990 by Mufwene (1990: 2):

> Transfers apply putatively in the speech of multilingual speakers and/or at the stage of SLA; substrate influence is observed in a language as a relatively crystallized system. Once transfers have been replicated by different speakers, repeated by most of them, and established in the contact situation's new linguistic system (even as variable features), they may be characterized genetically as substrate influence. The latter need not be associated synchronically with multilingual speakers and/or SLA.

In the late 1990s, Bickerton abandoned his claim that the first generation of Hawai'i Creole speakers did not know their ancestral languages, and left open the possibility of transfer—here described in terms of parameter settings:

> Most of the first creole generation simultaneously acquired one or more of their ancestral languages, so that, in principle, parameters could have been set according to those languages and the settings transferred to the nascent creole. (Bickerton 1999a: 55)

However, Bickerton asserts that such transfer did not actually occur. His argument is that the parameter settings of the contributing languages (Hawaiian, Japanese, Portuguese, etc.) are so radically different from one another that if transfer had occurred, one would have expected a Hawaiian-influenced creole, a Japanese-influenced creole, etc. But instead, he says, Hawai'i Creole is characterized by striking homogeneity.

In contrast, I suggest (Siegel 1997) that in a contact environment such as Hawai'i, one would find various L2 versions of the lexifier and these would include some features transferred from the speakers' L1s. These transferred features enter the pool of variants that are used by the community, and are therefore potential models for language acquisition. When a stable pidgin or creole emerges, leveling (or koineization) occurs. In this process, some of the variants are eliminated, while others are retained and incorporated into the grammar of the new contact language. This may occur gradually, as some features drop out from lack of use, or more rapidly, as children acquire some features but not others. The point is that some of the retained variants may be those that originally resulted from transfer.

Bickerton (1999a: 55) dismisses this view, saying that early examples of Hawai'i Creole were also homogeneous. However, Roberts (1998, 2000) demonstrates that the creole did not emerge in just one generation. The first generation of immigrant plantation laborers (G1) spoke a rudimentary English-lexified pre-pidgin or restricted pidgin. The first generation of locally born children of these immigrants (G2) were generally bilingual in their parents' language and a stabilizing and expanding pidgin, Hawai'i Pidgin English. It was most likely at this time that older children and adults of this generation transferred features from their parents' language into the expanding pidgin (Siegel 2000), and that there was variation in the pidgins spoken by the different ethnic groups. Many members of G2 shifted to this pidgin as their primary language, which they used to speak to their children. Thus, it was the second generation of locally born children (G3) who learned the expanded pidgin as their first language and were the original speakers of Hawai'i Creole. Leveling, and the emergence of a homogeneous creole, occurred with the second locally born generation, who were monolingual in the creole.[7]

One of the criticisms of the notion of substrate influence has been that no constraints or principles have been identified to explain why some substrate features are retained in various pidgins and creoles and others are not (e.g., Mufwene 1990: 6). In reaction to this criticism, and in line with the leveling model just described, I proposed that there must be both "availability constraints" that determine which substrate features actually reach the target pool of variants via transfer, and "reinforcement principles" that determine which of these transferred features are reinforced and therefore retained in the leveling process.

In order to identify specific availability constraints and reinforcement principles affecting pidgins and creoles, I examined the research on various constraints on transfer proposed in the SLA literature, and tested the validity of

---

[7] Jourdan (1985) and Smith (2002) report similar findings for Solomon Island Pijin and Tok Pisin.

these constraints using data from Melanesian Pidgin (MP) (Siegel 1999). The findings with regard to situational constraints are that the factors found to promote transfer in SLA are generally characteristic of the situations where pidgins such as MP emerge. These include a naturalistic and unfocused learning context, an immediate need to communicate, and the use of the L2 mainly with social equals.

With regard to linguistic constraints, which affect both transfer and retention, I examined 11 core morphosyntactic features of the Central Eastern Oceanic (CEO) languages that are the substrates for MP. Seven of these features are found in MP, while four are not. Then I identified various factors that researchers in SLA have postulated as influencing which linguistic features or aspects of particular features are more likely to be transferred by individuals in SLA. I related these to similar factors which researchers in P/C studies have proposed to explain which features are more likely to be "selected" or retained by the community in later stages. For the purpose of the study, six factors were isolated: markedness, perceptual salience, transparency, simplicity, frequency and congruence. These have to do with the linguistic properties of both the superstrate and substrate languages. Each of these factors was examined to see whether it could account for transfer and reinforcement of some of the CEO core features but not the others.

The most important factors appear to be perceptual salience and congruence. First, for a substrate feature to be transferred, it must have "somewhere to transfer to" (Andersen 1983c): there must be a morpheme (or string of morphemes) in the L2 that can be used or reanalyzed according to the rules of the L1 (here, the substrate). This L2 morpheme or string must be perceptually salient—a separate word, or words, or at least a stressed syllable—and it must have a function or meaning related to that of the corresponding L1 morpheme. Second, especially in situations where the emerging creole remains in contact with its lexifier, the substrate and superstrate morphemes should be morphosyntactically congruent, at least superficially. The absence of such a morpheme in the superstrate or the lack of structural congruence will constrain transfer, and thus the availability of the particular substrate feature. Another factor which may also play a part is transparency: transfer will be more likely if the L2 morpheme is invariant in form and has a single function.

For example, one core feature of the CEO languages is a preverbal marker that has a causative function or converts a stative or intransitive verb into a transitive one:

(7)  a.  Nguna:    *loaloa* 'dirty'      ***vaka**-loaloa* 'make dirty'
     b.  Kiribati: *kukurei* 'happy'    ***ka**-kukurei-a* 'make happy'

Another core feature is a preverbal reciprocal marker. Some examples are:

(8)   a.   Nguna:     *tawiri* 'marry'       ***pi***-*tawiri* 'get married (to each other)'
      b.   Kiribati:  *tangitangira* 'love' ***i***-*tangitangiria* 'love each other'

MP has a preverbal causative marker, *mekem*:

(9)   a.   Bislama:   *slip* 'sleep'          ***mekem*** *i slip* 'put to sleep'
      b.   Bislama:   *foldaon* 'fall'        ***mekem*** *i foldaon* 'cause to fall'

But it does not have a preverbal reciprocal marker.

The explanation is that with regard to the causative marker, the lexifier (English) has a preverbal string of morphemes that could be interpreted as a transitivizing causative marker: *make him* or *make'em*, as in *She'll make him happy* or *She'll make him go home*. Consequently, there was somewhere to transfer to, and so this substrate feature was available. But with regard to the reciprocal marker, *each other* occurs in English, but it occurs after the verb. There is no preverbal element congruent to the substrate feature that could be interpreted as marking reciprocity. Therefore, transfer could not occur, and so this substrate feature was not available in the developing pidgin.

At any rate, by the mid-1990s, more creolists were convinced that transfer plays an important role in P/C genesis. For example, Wekker (1996: 144) describes the process of creolization as "one of imperfect second-language acquisition, predominantly by adults, involving the usual language transfer from the learners' L1." Winford (2000: 216) describes the parallels between the formation of P/Cs and the processes of SLA, which include "L1 strategies," such as "L1 retention," the term he uses rather than transfer. (See also Migge 1998, 2000; Winford 2002, 2003.) Other scholars have also used different labels for basically the same processes. DeGraff (2001: 250) mentions the "retention and reanalysis of source-language structures in pidginization (and creolization)." In his work on Melanesian Pidgin, Keesing (1988) uses the term "calquing," implying an exact correspondence between rules in the substrate and in MP (which is not really the case).[8]

Writing about Haitian Creole, Lefebvre (e.g., 1986, 1996, 1997) and Lumsden (e.g., 1996) refer to the process of "relexification" to explain substrate influence. Relexification is described by Lefebvre (1998: 16) as "a mental process that builds new lexical entries by copying the lexical entries of an already established lexicon and replacing their phonological representations with representations derived from another language."[9] In recent work, these scholars have related relexification to L1 transfer. Lefebvre (1998: 34) makes it clear that "the type of data claimed to be associated with the notion of

---

[8] For example, the *fala* ending on adjectives in Solomons Pijin has no correspondence in the substrate languages.

[9] Lefebvre (2002) also regards reanalysis as a process available in the expansion of pidgins and creoles. She defines it as "a mental process whereby a particular form which signals one lexical entry becomes the signal of another lexical entry" (p. 255).

transfer in creole genesis corresponds to the result of the process of relexification ... That is, it is claimed that substratal features are transferred into the creole by means of relexification." Lumsden (1999a: 226) says that relexification "plays a significant role in second language acquisition in general" and uses the term "negative transfer error" to refer to an example of the process.

But is relexification the same as transfer? It seems to me that there is one important difference. According to my understanding of relexification, all the properties of L1 structures would be replicated in the L2 by the copying and relabeling of the L1 lexical entry (Lefebvre 1998: 16–17). But in transfer, morphemes with forms from the L2 or lexifier often have only some of the properties of the corresponding morphemes in the L1 or substrate. In other words, transfer is often partial. For example, the verbal suffixes in the CEO languages generally mark the person and number of the object as well as transitivity (see example 5a), but in MP, the suffixes, which supposedly result from transfer, mark only transitivity (example 4). (I will return to relexification later.)

Tense-modality-aspect (TMA) marking in expanded pidgins and creoles is one important grammatical area where functional transfer or relexification is argued to have played a role in development. For example, the Haitian Creole tense marker *te* (from French *été*) has the properties of the Fongbe anterior marker *kò,* as illustrated below (Lefebvre 1996: 282):

(10)  Haitian Creole:  *Mari   te    prepare pat.*
      Fongbe:          *Mari   kò    ɖà    wɔ.*
      Mary   ANT   prepare  dough
      'Mary had prepared dough.'

In my own work (Siegel 2000), I have referred specifically to transfer to account for the origins of some TMA markers in Hawai'i Creole—for example, the copula and progressive aspect marker *ste* (from English *stay*), which has the properties of *estar* from the Portuguese substrate, as in (11):

(11)  Hawai'i Creole:  *Ai   ste    wok.*
      Portuguese:      *Eu   estou a trabalhar.* (Hutchinson & Lloyd 1996: 72)
      I   PROG  work
      'I am working.'

In the discussion of simplification, we saw that some researchers in the field of SLA somewhat recklessly referred to the process of pidginization from P/C studies to explain findings in SLA. Now, the tables are turned and we find creolists, myself included, referring to the process of transfer from SLA to explain findings in P/C studies. But is this reference to transfer justified? In order to answer this question, we need to see whether the kinds of transfer evoked to account for substrate influence in pidgins and creoles actually occur in SLA. I will look first at word order transfer and then at functional transfer.

2.2.1  *Word order transfer in SLA*. In second language acquisition in general, there are many reported instances of word order transfer in the interlanguage of second language learners, for example:

(12)  L1 English, L2 French:   *\*Louise toujours mange du pain.*
      English:   'Louise always eats bread.'
      French:   *Louise mange toujours du pain.*

                        (Odlin 2003: 460)

(13)  L1 English, L2 German:   *Ich bin glücklich sein hier.*
      English:   'I am happy to be here.'
      German:   *Ich bin glücklich hier zu sein.*

                    (Krashen 1981/2002: 65)

But whether basic word order is transferred or not has been a controversial topic in the field of SLA. Rutherford (1983, 1986) and Zobl (1983, 1986) claimed that there is usually no transfer of basic word order. But Odlin (1990) presented 11 counterexamples, such as transfer of Japanese and Korean OV word order into English. And in the European Science Foundation (ESF) study mentioned above, there was evidence of transfer of word order in the earliest stages—for example, OV rather than VO order occurring in the IL of Punjabi learners of English and Turkish learners of Dutch (reported in Kellerman 1995: 137).

More recently, this topic has been revived in recent debates about the question of whether the principles of Universal Grammar (UG), especially parameters, are available to second language learners. Epstein, Flynn and Martohardjono (1996: 677) argue for what they call the "full access" hypothesis, which "asserts that UG in its entirety constrains L2 acquisition." This hypothesis plays down the role of transfer—in this context viewed as the use of prior linguistic knowledge in the construction of the L2 grammar.

However, other hypotheses or models accept continuing access to UG but still allow for the role of transfer, especially of parameter settings, such as the setting for the headedness parameter that determines basic word order. This would need to be transferable to account for the data presented by Odlin (1990), for example. One of these is the "Full Transfer/Full Access" hypothesis (Schwartz 1996, 1998; Schwartz & Sprouse 1996). According to this model, SLA in adults and children depends on three components—the L2 initial state, UG, and the target language (or L2) input. Significantly, the L2 initial state comprises the entirety of the L1 grammar, and therefore IL development is constrained by both the L1 grammar and UG. Thus, all the syntactic properties of the L1, including the setting for the headedness parameter, are initially transferred. To support this position, Schwartz (1998) presents an impressive array of examples of word order transfer, including OV order into English by Turkish learners and N-Adj order into German by Italian and Spanish learners. This model has also received a great deal of independent support in the recent literature (Bhatt & Hancin-Bhatt 1996; Camacho 1999; Slabakova 2000).

Referring to White (1991), Sharwood Smith (1996: 75) notes that UG is relevant to SLA but that "learners assume that L1 parameter settings will work for L2 unless *evidence turns up to disconfirm this assumption*" [italics in original]. According to Schwartz (1998: 147), the way that progress towards the L2 (or TL) takes place is that input from the L2 that cannot be accommodated to the L1 grammar causes the system to restructure. She observes: "In some cases, this revision may occur rapidly; in others, much more time may be needed."

For basic word order, the revision (or restructuring) occurs very rapidly. This explains the relative rarity of word order transfer reported in the earlier SLA literature, which led some scholars to claim that it does not occur (see above). This rapid adoption of L2 word order most probably happens because basic word order is quite a salient structural characteristic (Comrie 1997: 369; Odlin 1990: 110). In other words, learners normally have metalinguistic awareness of rules for the ordering of verb and object, unless there are a large number of rules involving structural detail (as in German and Dutch).

If we assume that transfer in SLA is relevant to P/C genesis, then this would explain why the word order of the substrate languages is not usually maintained in the resultant contact language if it differs from that of the lexifier (superstrate). Minimal exposure to the lexifier language would have caused rapid restructuring. But then the question is: Why would other features of L1 or substrate word order remain? The answer may be that other L2 features are not so accessible to consciousness. For example, Lightbown and Spada (2000) report that, because L1 English learners of French have no metalinguistic awareness of the rules they use for adverb placement, they do not notice how their English sentences differ from those of French. Thus, these learners use English patterns of adverb placement when speaking French. Lightbown and Spada conclude, therefore, that positive evidence is not always sufficient to lead to acquisition. Similarly, White (1991) argues that L2 learners, unlike L1 learners, need negative evidence to reset some parameters. In more general terms, Schwartz writes:

> [C]onvergence on the TL grammar is not guaranteed; this is because unlike L1 acquisition, the L2 starting point is not simply open or set to "defaults," and so the data needed to force L2 restructuring could be either nonexistent or obscure. (Schwartz 1998: 148)

If input from the lexifier language was restricted in P/C development, as most creolists believe, then these insights from SLA theory would explain the retention of substrate word order.[10] In the case of creoles, such as Sranan in Suriname (mentioned above), which have preserved aspects of basic word order from their substrate languages, we would have to assume that there was very little input from the lexifier. And this indeed was the case in Suriname: the lexifier, English, was the language of the colonial power only from 1651 to 1667, after which it was replaced by Dutch.

2.2.2  *Functional transfer in SLA.* In contrast to simplification and word order transfer, examples of functional transfer in the IL of second language learners are difficult to find. In the ESF study, for example, there was no evidence of the transfer of L1 properties onto L2 forms. Furthermore, in the studies of the IL of learners of French, Dutch and Swedish mentioned earlier, there is no evidence of any transfer of grammatical features of the kind found in pidgins or creoles with the same lexifier. Other creolists who have specifically looked at learners' L2 versions of the lexifier of a creole (Mather 2000; Véronique 1994) have found some similarities, but none that could be unambiguously attributed to functional transfer from the substrate.[11] And in the SLA literature in general, I am not aware of any examples that clearly show learners using L2 forms with the grammatical properties of the corresponding L1 morphemes.[12]

This includes TMA marking. We have seen that in the ESF study (Klein & Perdue 1997) learners used temporal adverbs, rather than grammatical TMA markers. Mather (2000: 258) refers to "the mystery" that, while TMA markers

---

[10] This point of view has been expressed in different terms by DeGraff (1996: 723).
[11] In a possible exception to this statement, Mather (2000) found the postposed determiner *la* modeled on the French postposed deictic *là* (as in French creoles) used in the interlanguage of Ewe-speaking learners of French. Significantly, postposed determiners are found in Ewe. However, while this may be an example of L1 influence, it may not be the result of transfer so much as substrate reinforcement of one stage of the normal developmental sequence in the acquisition of French by speakers of languages that have postnominal deictic markers (see Zobl 1982).
[12] Two possible exceptions are as follows. Pfaff (1992) shows that, in the interlanguage of Turkish children learning German, some independent lexical items come to be used as grammatical markers—for example, *mach* + Verb, as in the following example (p. 292):

Elefant    komm.   die    mach    hauen
[elephant  come    3SG    make    beat]
'(The) elephant comes. He is fighting.'

Pfaff first says that this provides "some, though rather slight evidence for a possible structural transfer" from Turkish (p. 292), but then concludes (p. 293) that "in periphrastic verbal constructions, used only by the Turkish bilinguals, there are striking parallels to Turkish structures (compound verb constructions), which does suggest that the L1 plays some role ...." Clements (2003) describes the study of a Mandarin-speaking learner of Spanish who used the adverb *ya* as a preverbal periphrastic perfective marker. Mandarin also has a perfective marker but it is a postverbal suffix. Examining the learner's TMA system as a whole, Clements concludes that, while transfer from Mandarin may be a factor, is the system can be better explained by reference to more universal hypotheses, such as the Primacy of Aspect (Andersen & Shirai 1996).

in French creoles appear to be similar to those of the substrate languages, "there is very little evidence of TMA markers in any French or other European interlanguage variety." In fact, Bardovi-Harlig (2000: 411) observes: "No significant L1 effect has been identified in the longitudinal studies of the acquisition of temporal expression." The lack of evidence of this kind of transfer in the interlanguage of L2 learners would seem to argue against transfer as an explanation of substrate influence in pidgins and creoles.

However, transfer is not associated just with L2 acquisition. Many scholars consider the overall field of SLA to be divided into two main areas of research: second language acquisition and second language use (e.g., Ellis 1994: 13; Gass 1998: 84). As we have seen, L2 acquisition, as opposed to L2 use, is concerned with the gradual attainment of linguistic competence in the L2—in other words, with the learning of the L2 grammar. L2 use, as opposed to L2 acquisition, looks at how learners make use of their existing knowledge of an L2, and other knowledge as well, when trying to communicate in the language. In fact, many researchers in SLA think of transfer primarily as a feature of L2 *use* rather than acquisition (Meisel 1983: 44). For example, Kellerman (1995: 130) notes that "what can be seen ... is not so much the role of the first language in second language development, but its role in second language use."

An important point here is that, while transfer in L2 acquisition involves the L2 as the target—that is, L1 structures are used or retained in an attempt to approximate the perceived norms of the L2—transfer in L2 use, on the other hand, is the result of speakers of an L2 falling back on their L1 knowledge when communicating in the L2. This occurs when their knowledge of the L2 is inadequate to express what they want to say. Sharwood Smith (1986: 15) says that cross-linguistic influence (i.e., transfer) typically occurs in two contexts: (1) "overload" situations or "moments of stress" when the existing L2 system cannot cope with immediate communicative demands, and (2) "through a desire to express messages of greater complexity than the developing control mechanisms can cope with." Therefore, transfer in L2 does not involve a target because the aim is not to approximate the norms of another language, but to compensate for a perceived shortage of the linguistic resources that are needed for successful communication in an existing language.

How speakers of an L2 compensate for inadequate L2 knowledge when they are under pressure to communicate in that language is studied under the heading of "communication strategies" (Poulisse 1996; Tarone 1981). The particular communication strategy that is relevant here is "transfer from the native language" (Tarone, Cohen & Dumas 1983: 5, 11). Blum-Kulka and Levenston (1983: 132) characterize the communication strategy of transfer as "attributing to a lexical item of the second language all the functions—referential and conceptual meaning, connotation, collocability, register restriction—of its assumed first-language equivalent." This, of course, is what I have been calling functional transfer.

But are there actual examples of this kind of transfer in studies of second language use? One is found in a study by Helms-Park (2003), which shows that causative serial verb constructions occur in the English of Vietnamese-speaking learners, but not in the English of Hindi-Urdu-speaking learners. Since Vietnamese has such serial verb constructions but Hindi-Urdu does not, their occurrence in the English spoken by Vietnamese speakers is attributed to language transfer. The author considers this transfer to be the result of a communication strategy, or

> a compensatory L1-based strategy used by learners to manage a situation in which they are compelled to produce TL constructions before adequate information about the grammatical behavior of the targeted verbs has been noted in the input ... (Helms-Park 2003: 230)

This is the result of the "communication stress" caused by "the elicitation of data through a tightly constrained test" (p. 230) in the study. (These findings are significant because similar serial verb constructions occur in creoles, such as Haitian Creole and Saramaccan, that have serializing substrate languages.)

Since studies that focus specifically on L2 language use are rare, however, most of the evidence for functional transfer in L2 use comes indirectly from features of indigenized varieties of English, which emerged from individuals' use of English as an L2. Evidence presented in an earlier article (Siegel 1997) is repeated here. First, in Singapore Colloquial English, *already* is used as a completive aspect marker, as in the following example (from Platt & Weber 1980: 66):

(14)  *I only went there once or twice already.*
     'I've been there only once or twice.'

This usage is believed to be influenced by the postverbal aspect marker *liáu* in the Hokkien substrate, as shown in this example (from Platt, Weber & Mian Lian 1984: 70):

(15)  *goá chiảh  pá    liáu*
     I     eat    full  COMP
     'I have finished eating.'

In Fiji English, the word *full* is used as a preverbal marker indicating an extreme or excess quality or action:

(16)  a. *The boy just full shouted.*
        'The boy shouted really loudly.'
     b. *The fella full sleeping over there.*
        'The guy's sound asleep over there.'

This closely parallels the Fijian use of *rui* as a preverbal marker with the same function, as in this example (from Schütz 1985: 272):

(17) *au   sā   rui   loma-ni        koya   vaka-levu.*
     I    ASP  EXT   care.for-TRAN   her    MANNER-big
     'I care for her very much.'

Another source of indirect evidence is substratum influence in language shift varieties, which are thought to be a consequence of second language use—e.g., South African Indian English (Mesthrie 1992) and Irish English (Winford 2003: 240–241). A well-known example is the recent past construction using *after* in Irish English (Harris 1984: 319).

(18) Irish English:     *She is after selling the boat.*
                        'She has (just) sold the boat.'
     Irish:             *Tá               sí    tréis    an    bád    a dhíol.*
                        be.NONPAST   she   after    the   boat   selling

With regard to pidgin and creole origins, the lack of evidence of functional transfer in restricted pidgins may be because they are the result of L2 acquisition where the lexifier is the target. However, evidence of functional transfer is found in expanded pidgins because they are the result of compensatory strategies of L2 use, where the L2 is the pidgin itself, not the lexifier (as illustrated above for Hawai'i). Evidence of functional transfer (substrate influence) is found in creoles as the result of transferred features having been acquired by children.

As Andersen (1983a: 30) observed more than 20 years ago, expansion and complication occur when the use of a pidginized variety is extended (for example, as a language of wider communication) and when there is immediate pressure to communicate without acquired competence. While a pre-pidgin or a restricted pidgin with little or no grammatical morphology may be adequate for speakers to use for intermittent basic communication, when they start to use it more frequently for wider purposes, they may sense that it lacks some necessary linguistic resources, especially compared to their first languages. The greatest extension of use, of course, is when speakers shift to the pidgin as their primary language, which they then pass on to their children. This is when functional transfer occurs. Thus, the reason grammatical elaboration and complication occur with the extension of use in expanded pidgins is that there is pressure to communicate more frequently and explicitly about wider topics, but the means to do so efficiently are not available in the pidgin.

## 3. *Summary and discussion*
In summary, we have seen that word order transfer can occur in the earliest stage of development as part of L2 acquisition, but it is generally short-lived unless, for example, there is extremely limited contact with the target

language. This would account for the substrate word order that we do find in pre-pidgins and restricted pidgins, and for the rarity of substrate influence on basic word order in expanded pidgins and creoles. We have also seen that functional transfer (the use of L2 forms with L1 grammatical properties) is not normally found in L2 acquisition, but it may occur as a strategy of expansion in L2 use. This would account for the evidence of substrate influence in grammatical marking in expanded pidgins and subsequent creoles, but not in pre-pidgins and restricted pidgins. It appears, then, that I was wrong in my earlier work (Siegel 1999) when I said that substrate influence in pidgins and creoles is the result of transfer that occurred in an earlier stage of development. It now seems that word order influences come from an early stage of L2 acquisition, but the use of forms from the lexifier with grammatical properties from the substrate comes from a later stage of L2 use. If this is correct, the relexification hypothesis may also need modifying.

We have seen earlier that the process of relexification is considered to be a particular type of transfer—closest to what I have been calling functional transfer. Lefebvre (1998: 10) maintains that creole genesis is a function of second language acquisition and states that "the process of relexification is used by speakers of the substratum languages as the main tool for acquiring a second language, the superstratum language." Thus, the hypothesis assumes that relexification is a process that occurs in "ordinary cases" of targeted second language acquisition (Lefebvre 1998: 34). Evidence is presented (pp. 34–35) from the work of Lumsden (later published in Lumsden 1999b); it concerns French reflexive verbs, where English-speaking learners of French leave out the reflexive pronouns in French whereas French-speaking learners of English incorrectly use reflexive pronouns with corresponding English verbs. While this could possibly be a result of relexification (as opposed to simplification or direct translation), it is not the kind of functional transfer that we have been focusing on: the kind involved in the origins of creole TMA markers, for example. And we have seen that that there is actually no clear evidence of what could be called relexification as "a tool for acquiring a second language." It may be, however, that a process similar to relexification can be used as a compensatory strategy in second language use.

## 4. *Conclusion*

This chapter has shown that important links exist between the fields of SLA and P/C studies, and that established areas of research in SLA—especially regarding simplification and word order transfer—can throw some light on the genesis of pidgin and creole languages. The new research into second language use may provide further insights, especially in the study of expansion strategies, such as transfer, and social-psychological factors, such as identity issues and resistance. But more work is needed in these areas—in both SLA and P/C studies.

## References

Alleyne, M.C. 1971. Acculturation and the cultural matrix of creolization. In *Pidginization and Creolization of Languages,* Dell Hymes (Ed.), 169–186. Cambridge: Cambridge University Press.

Alleyne, M.C. 2000. Opposite processes in "creolization". In *Degrees of Restructuring in Creole Languages,* Ingrid Neumann-Holzschuh and Edgar W. Schneider (Eds.), 125–133. Amsterdam/Philadelphia: John Benjamins.

Andersen, R.W. 1980. Creolization as the acquisition of a second language as a first language. In *Theoretical Orientations in Creole Studies,* Albert Valdman and Arnold Highfield (Eds.), 273–295. New York: Academic Press.

Andersen, R.W. 1981. Two perspectives on pidginization as second language acquisition. In *New Dimensions in Second Language Acquisition Research,* Roger W. Andersen (Ed.), 165–195. Rowley, MA: Newbury House.

Andersen, R.W. 1983a. Introduction: A language acquisition interpretation of pidginization and creolization. In *Pidginization and Creolization as Language Acquisition,* Roger W. Andersen (Ed.), 1–56. Rowley, MA: Newbury House.

Andersen, R.W. (Ed.), 1983b. *Pidginization and Creolization as Language Acquisition.* Rowley, MA: Newbury House.

Andersen, R.W. 1983c. Transfer to somewhere. In *Language Transfer in Language Learning,* Susan M. Gass and Larry Selinker (Eds.), 177–201. Rowley, MA: Newbury House.

Andersen, R.W. and Y. Shirai. 1996. The primacy of aspect in first and second language acquisition: The pidgin-creole connection. In *Handbook of Second Language Acquisition,* William C. Ritchie and Tej K. Bhatia (Eds.), 527–570. San Diego, CA: Academic Press.

Arends, J. 1993. Towards a gradualist model of creolization. In *The Atlantic Meets the Pacific: A Global View of Pidginization and Creolization,* Francis Byrne and John Holm (Eds.), 371–380. Amsterdam: John Benjamins.

Arends, J. (Ed.). 1995. *The early stages of creolization.* Amsterdam/Philadelphia: John Benjamins.

Arends, J., P. Muysken and N. Smith. 1995. Conclusions. In *Pidgins and Creoles: An Introduction,* Jacques Arends, Pieter Muysken and Norval Smith (Eds.), 319–330. Amsterdam/Philadelphia: John Benjamins.

Baker, P. 1987. The historical developments in Chinese pidgin English and the nature of the relationships between the various pidgin Englishes of the Pacific region. *Journal of Pidgin and Creole Languages* 2: 163–207.

Baker, P. 1994. Creativity in creole genesis. In *Creolization and Language Change,* Dany Adone and Ingo Plag (Eds.), 65–84. Tübingen: Max Niemeyer.

Baker, P. 1997. Directionality in pidginization and creolization. In *The Structure and Status of Pidgins and Creoles,* Arthur K. Spears and Donald Winford (Eds.), 91–109. Amsterdam/Philadelphia: John Benjamins.

Baker, P. 2000. Theories of creolization and the degree and nature of restructuring. In *Degrees of Restructuring in Creole Languages,* Ingrid Neumann-Holzschuh and Edgar W. Schneider (Eds.), 41–63. Amsterdam/Philadelphia: John Benjamins.

Baker, P. and C. Corne. 1982. *Isle de France Creole: Affinities and Origins.* Ann Arbor, MI: Karoma.

Bardovi-Harlig, K. 2000. *Tense and Aspect in Second Language Acquisition: Form, Meaning, and Use.* Oxford: Blackwell.

Bhatt, R.M. and B. Hancin-Bhatt. 1996. Transfer in L2 grammars. *Behavioral and Brain Sciences* 19: 715–716.

Bickerton, D. 1977. Pidginization and creolization: Acquisition and language universals. In *Pidgin and Creole Linguistics,* Albert Valdman (Ed.), 49–69. Bloomington, IN: Indiana University Press.

Bickerton, D. 1981. *Roots of Language.* Ann Arbor, MI: Karoma.

Bickerton, D. 1984a. The Language Bioprogram Hypothesis. *Behavioral and Brain Sciences* 7: 173–221.

Bickerton, D. 1984b. The Language Bioprogram Hypothesis and second language acquisition. In *Language Universals and Second Language Acquisition,* William E. Rutherford (Ed.), 141–161. Amsterdam/Philadelphia: John Benjamins.

Bickerton, D. 1988. Creole languages and the bioprogram. In *Linguistics: The Cambridge Survey. Volume II: Linguistic Theory: Extensions and Implications,* Frederick J. Newmeyer (Ed.), 268–284. Cambridge: Cambridge University Press.

Bickerton, D. 1999a. How to acquire language without positive evidence: What acquisitionists can learn from creoles. In *Language Creation and Language Change: Creolization, Diachrony, and Development,* Michel DeGraff (Ed.), 49–74. Cambridge, MA: The MIT Press.

Bickerton, D. 1999a. Creole languages, the Language Bioprogram Hypothesis, and language acquisition. In *Handbook of Child Language Acquisition,* William C. Ritchie and Tej K. Bhatia (Eds.), 195–220. San Diego, CA: Academic Press.

Bickerton, D. and C. Odo. 1976. *Change and variation in Hawaiian English, Vol. 1: General Phonology and Pidgin Syntax.* Honolulu, HI: Social Sciences and Linguistics Institute, University of Hawaii.

Bloomfield, L. 1933. *Language.* New York: Holt, Rinehart and Winston.

Blum-Kulka, S. and E.A. Levenston. 1983. Universals of lexical simplification. In *Strategies in Interlanguage Communication,* Claus Færch and Gabriele Kasper (Eds.), 119–139. London/New York: Longman.

Camacho, J. 1999. From SOV to SVO: The grammar of interlanguage word order. *Second Language Research* 15: 115–132.

Clements, J.C. 2001. The TMA system in interlanguage and pidgins. Paper presented at the conference of the Society for Pidgin and Creole Linguistics, Coimbra, Portugal, June.

Clements, J.C. 2003. The tense-aspect system in pidgins and naturalistically learned L2. *Studies in Second Language Acquisition* 25(2): 245–281.

Comrie, B. 1997. On the origin of the basic variety. *Second Language Research* 13: 367–373.

Corder, S.P. 1981. Formal simplicity and functional simplification in second language acquisition. In *New Dimensions in Second Language Research,* Roger W. Andersen (Ed.), 146–152. Rowley, MA: Newbury House.

DeGraff, M. 1996. UG and acquisition in pidginization and creolization. *Behavioral and Brain Sciences* 19: 723–724.

DeGraff, M. 1999. Creolization, language change, and language acquisition: An epilogue. In *Language Creation and Language Change: Creolization, Diachrony, and Development,* Michel DeGraff (Ed.), 473–543. Cambridge, MA/London: The MIT Press.

DeGraff, M. 2001. On the origins of creoles: A Cartesian critique of neo-Darwinian linguistics. *Linguistic Typology* 5: 213–310.

Dulay, H. and M. Burt. 1973. Should we teach children syntax? *Language Learning* 23: 245–258.

Dutton, T. 1997. Hiri Motu. In *Contact Languages: A Wider Perspective,* Sarah G. Thomason (Ed.), 9–41. Amsterdam/Philadelphia: John Benjamins.

Ellis, R. 1994. *The Study of Second Language Acquisition.* Oxford: Oxford University Press.

Epstein, S.D., S. Flynn and G. Martohardjono. 1996. Second language acquisition: Theoretical and experimental issues in contemporary research. *Behavioral and Brain Sciences* 19: 677–714.

Ferguson, C.A. and C.E. DeBose. 1977. Simplified registers, broken language and pidginization. In *Pidgin and Creole Languages,* Albert Valdman (Ed.), 99–125. Bloomington, IN: Indiana University Press.

Firth, A. and J. Wagner. 1997. On discourse, communication, and (some) fundamental concepts in SLA research. *The Modern Language Journal* 81: 285–300.

Gass, S. 1998. Apples and oranges: Or, why apples are not orange and don't need to be. A response to Firth and Wagner. *The Modern Language Journal* 82: 83–90.

Goddard, I. 1997. Pidgin Delaware. In *Contact Languages: A Wider Perspective,* Sarah G. Thomason (Ed.), 43–98. Amsterdam/Philadelphia: John Benjamins.

Hall, R.A., Jr. 1966. *Pidgin and Creole Languages.* Ithaca, NY: Cornell University Press.

Harris, J. 1984. Syntactic variation and dialect divergence. *Journal of Linguistics* 20: 303–327.

Helms-Park, R. 2003. Transfer in SLA and creoles: The implications of causative serial verbs in the interlanguage of Vietnamese ESL learners. *Studies in Second Language Acquisition* 25: 211–244.

Hesseling, D.C. 1979. On the Origin and Formation of Creoles: A Miscellany of Articles. Ann Arbor, MI: Karoma.

Hutchinson, A.P and J. Lloyd. 1996. *Portuguese: An Essential Grammar.* London/New York: Routledge.

Huttar, G.L. and F.J. Velantie. 1997. Ndjuka-Trio Pidgin. In *Contact Languages: A Wider Perspective,* Sarah G. Thomason (Ed.), 99–124. Amsterdam/Philadelphia: John Benjamins.

Hymes, D. 1971. Introduction [to Part III]. In *Pidginization and Creolization of Languages,* Dell Hymes (Ed.), 65–90. Cambridge: Cambridge University Press.

Jahr, E.H. 1996. On the status of Russenorsk. In *Languages in Contact in the Arctic: Northern Pidgins and Contact Languages,* Ernst Håkon Jahr and Ingvild Broch (Eds.), 107–122. Berlin: Mouton de Gruyter.

Jesperson, O. 1922. *Language: Its Nature, Development, and Origin.* London: Allen and Unwin.

Jourdan, C. 1985. Sapos Iumi Mitim Iumi: Urbanization and Creolization in Solomon Islands Pijin. Ph.D. dissertation, Australian National University, Canberra.

Kay, P. and G. Sankoff. 1974. A language universal approach to pidgins and creoles. In *Pidgins and Creoles: Current Trends and Prospects,* David DeCamp and Ian F. Hancock (Eds.), 61–72. Washington, DC: Georgetown University Press.

Keesing, R.M. 1988. *Melanesian Pidgin and the Oceanic Substrate.* Stanford, CA: Stanford University Press.

Kellerman, E. 1995. Crosslinguistic influence: Transfer to nowhere? *Annual Review of Applied Linguistics* 15: 125–150.

Klein, W. and C. Perdue. (1997. The basic variety (or: Couldn't natural languages be much simpler?). *Second Language Research* 13: 301–347.

Kotsinas, U.-B. 1996. Aspect marking and grammaticalization in Russenorsk compared with immigrant Swedish. In *Language Contact in the Arctic: Northern Pidgins and Contact Languages,* Ernst Håkon Jahr and Ingvild Broch (Eds.), 123–154. Berlin: Mouton de Gruyter.

Kotsinas, U.-B. 2001. Pidginization, creolization and creoloid in Stockholm, Sweden. In *Creolization and Contact,* Norval Smith and Tonjes Veenstra (Eds.), 125–155. Amsterdam/Philadelphia: Benjamins.

Krashen, S.D. 1981/2002. *Second Language Acquisition and Second Language Learning* (first internet edition). http://www.sdkrashen.com/SL_Acquisition_and_Learning.

Lefebvre, C. 1986. Relexification in creole genesis revisited: The case of Haitian creole. In *Substrata versus Universals in Creole Genesis,* Pieter Muysken and Norval Smith (Eds.), 279–300. Amsterdam: John Benjamins.

Lefebvre, C. 1996. The tense, mood and aspect system of Haitian Creole and the problem of transmission of grammar in creole genesis. *Journal of Pidgin and Creole Languages* 11: 231–311.

Lefebvre, C. 1997. Relexification in creole genesis: The case of demonstrative terms in Haitian Creole. *Journal of Pidgin and Creole Languages* 12: 181–201.

Lefebvre, C. 1998. *Creole Genesis and the Acquisition of Grammar: The Case of Haitian Creole.* Cambridge: Cambridge University Press.

Lefebvre, C. 2002. The field of pidgin and creole linguistics at the turn of the millennium: The problem of the genesis and development of PCs. In *Pidgin and Creole Linguistics in the Twenty-First Century,* Glenn Gilbert (Ed.), 247–285. New York: Peter Lang.

Lefebvre, C. 2003. The emergence of productive morphology in creole languages: The case of Haitian Creole. In *Yearbook of Morphology 2002,* Geert E. Booij and Jaap van Marle (Eds.), 35–80. Berlin: Mouton de Gruyter.

Lightbown, P.M. and N. Spada. 2000. Do they know what they're doing? L2 learners' awareness of L1 influence. *Language Awareness* 9: 198–217.

Lumsden, J.S. 1999a. The role of relexification in creole genesis. *Journal of Pidgin and Creole Languages* 14: 225–258.

Lumsden, J.S. 1999b. Language acquisition and creolization. In *Language Creation and Language Change: Creolization, Diachrony, and Development,* Michel DeGraff (Ed.), 129–158. Cambridge, MA/London: The MIT Press.

Lynch, J. 1993 *Pacific Languages: An Introduction.* Suva, Fiji: University of the South Pacific.

Manessy, G. 1977. Processes of pidginization in African languages. In *Pidgin and Creole Linguistics,* Albert Valdman (Ed.), 129–134. Bloomington, IN: Indiana University Press.

Mather, P.-A. 2000. Creole genesis: Evidence from West African L2 French. In *Languages in Contact,* Dicky G. Gilbers, John Nerbonne and Jos Schaeken (Eds.), 247–261. Amsterdam/Atlanta: Rodopi.

McKay, S.L. and S.-L. Cynthia Wong. 1996. Multiple discourses, multiple identities: Investment and agency in second-language learning among Chinese adolescent immigrant students. *Harvard Educational Review* 66: 577–608.

McWhorter, J.H. 1996. A deep breath and a second wind: The substrate hypothesis reassessed. *Anthropological Linguistics* 38: 461–494.

Meisel, J. 1983. Transfer as a second-language strategy. *Language and Communication* 3: 11–46.

Mesthrie, R. 1992. *English in Language Shift: The History, Structure and Sociolinguistics of South African Indian English.* Cambridge: Cambridge University Press.

Migge, B. 1998. Substrate influence in creole formation: The origin of *give*-type serial verb constructions in the Surinamese plantation creole. *Journal of Pidgin and Creole Languages* 13: 215–265.

Migge, B. 2000. The origin of the syntax and semantics of property items in the Surinamese plantation creole. In *Language Change and Language Contact in Pidgins and Creoles* John H. McWhorter (Ed.), 201–234. Amsterdam/Philadelphia: John Benjamins.

Mufwene, S.S. 1990. Transfer and the substrate hypothesis in creolistics. *Studies in Second Language Acquisition* 12: 1–23.

Mufwene, S.S. 2001. *The Ecology of Language Evolution.* Cambridge: Cambridge University Press.

Muysken, P. 2001. The origin of creole languages: The perspective of second language learning. In *Creolization and Contact,* Norval Smith and Tonjes Veenstra (Eds.), 157–173. Amsterdam/Philadelphia: John Benjamins.

Muysken, P. and N. Smith. 1995. The study of pidgin and creole languages. In *Pidgins and Creoles: An Introduction,* Jacques Arends, Pieter Muysken and Norval Smith (Eds.), 1–14. Amsterdam/Philadelphia: John Benjamins.

Naro, A.J. 1978. A study on the origins of pidginization. *Language* 54: 314–347.

Nemser, W. 1971. Approximative systems of foreign language learners. *International Review of Applied Linguistics in Language Learning* 9: 115–123.

Norton, B. 2000. *Identity and Language Learning: Gender, Ethnicity and Educational Change.* Harlow, UK: Pearson Education.

Norton Peirce, B. 1995. Social identity, investment, and language learning. *TESOL Quarterly* 29: 9–31.

Odlin, T. 1990. Word-order transfer, metalinguistic awareness and constraints on foreign language learning. In *Second Language Acquisition—Foreign Language Learning,* Bill Van Patten and James F. Lee (Eds.), 95–117. Clevedon, UK: Multilingual Matters.

Odlin, T. 2003. Cross-linguistic influence. In *The Handbook of Second Language Acquisition,* Catherine J. Doughty and Michael H. Long (Eds.), 436–486. Malden, MA/Oxford: Blackwell.

Perdue, C. (Ed.), 1993. *Adult Language Acquisition: Cross-Linguistic Perspectives,* Vol. I: Field Methods. Cambridge: Cambridge University Press.

Pfaff, C.W. 1992. The issue of grammaticalization in early German second language acquisition. *Studies in Second Language Acquisition* 14: 273–296.

Platt, J. and H. Weber. 1980. *English in Singapore and Malaysia: Status, Features, Functions.* Kuala Lumpur: Oxford University Press.

Platt, J., H. Weber and H. Mian Lian. 1984. *The New Englishes.* London: Routledge & Kegan Paul.

Poulisse, N. 1996. Strategies. In *Investigating Second Language Acquisition,* Peter Jordens and Josine Lalleman (Eds.), 135–163. Berlin: Mouton de Gruyter.

Rampton, B. 1995. *Crossing: Language and Ethnicity among Adolescents.* London: Longman.

Rampton, B. 1997. A sociolinguistic perspective on L2 communication strategies. In *Communication Strategies: Psycholinguistic and Sociolinguistic Perspectives,* Gabriele Kasper and Eric Kellerman (Eds.), 279–303. London/New York: Longman.

Rampton, M.B.H. 1991. Second language learners in a stratified multilingual setting. *Applied Linguistics* 12: 229–248.

Reinecke, J.E. 1971. Pidgin French in Vietnam. In *Pidginization and Creolization of Language,* Dell Hymes (Ed.), 47–56. Cambridge: Cambridge University Press.

Roberts, J.M. 1995. A structural sketch of Pidgin Hawaiian. *Amsterdam Creole Studies* 14: 97–126.

Roberts, S.J. 1998. The role of diffusion in the genesis of Hawaiian creole. *Language* 74: 1–39.

Roberts, S.J. 2000. Nativization and genesis of Hawaiian creole. In *Language Change and Language Contact in Pidgins and Creoles,* John H. McWhorter (Ed.), 257–300. Amsterdam/Philadelphia: John Benjamins.

Rutherford, W.E. 1983. Language typology and language transfer. In *Language Transfer in Language Learning,* Susan M. Gass and Larry Selinker (Eds.), 358–370. Rowley, MA: Newbury House.

Rutherford, W.E. 1986. Grammatical theory and L2 acquisition: A brief overview. *Second Language Studies* 2: 1–15.

Samarin, W.J. 1971. Salient and substantive pidginization. In *Pidginization and Creolization of Languages,* Dell Hymes (Ed.), 117–140. Cambridge: Cambridge University Press.

Schumann, J.H. 1978a. *The Pidginization Process: A Model for Second Language Acquisition.* Rowley, MA: Newbury House.

Schumann, J.H. 1978b. The acculturation model for second language acquisition. In *Second Language Acquisition and Foreign Language Teaching,* R. Gingras (Ed.), 27–50. Arlington, VA: Center for Applied Linguistics.

Schütz, A.J. 1985. *The Fijian Language.* Honolulu, HI: University of Hawai'i Press.

Schwartz, B.D. 1996. Now for some facts, with a focus on development and an explicit role for L1. *Behavioral and Brain Sciences* 19: 739–740.

Schwartz, B.D. 1998. The second language instinct. *Lingua* 106: 133–160.

Schwartz, B.D. and R.A. Sprouse. 1996. L2 cognitive states and the full transfer/full access model. *Second Language Research* 12: 40–72.

Sebba, M. 1997. *Contact Languages: Pidgins and Creoles.* New York: St Martin's Press.

Selinker, L. 1972. Interlanguage. *International Review of Applied Linguistics* 10: 209–232.

Sharwood Smith, M. 1986. The competence/control model, crosslinguistic influence and the creation of new grammars. In *Crosslinguistic Influence in Second Language Acquisition,* Michael Sharwood Smith and Eric Kellerman (Eds.), 10–20. Oxford: Pergamon Press.

Sharwood Smith, M. 1996. Crosslinguistic influence with special reference to the acquisition of grammar. In *Investigating Second Language Acquisition,* Peter Jordens and Josine Lalleman (Eds.), 71–83. Berlin: Mouton de Gruyter.

Siegel, J. 1987. *Language Contact in a Plantation Environment: A Sociolinguistic History of Fiji.* Cambridge: Cambridge University Press.

Siegel, J. 1990. Pidgin English in Nauru. *Journal of Pidgin and Creole Languages* 5: 157–186.

Siegel, J. 1997. Mixing, levelling and pidgin/creole development. In *The Structure and Status of Pidgins and Creoles,* Arthur K. Spears and Donald Winford (Eds.), 111–149. Amsterdam: John Benjamins.

Siegel, J. 1999. Transfer constraints and substrate influence in Melanesian pidgin. *Journal of Pidgin and Creole Languages* 14: 1–44.

Siegel, J. 2000. Substrate influence in Hawai'i Creole English. *Language in Society* 29: 197–236.

Siegel, J. 2002. Social context. In *Handbook of Second Language Acquisition,* C. Doughty and M. H. Long (Eds.), 178–223. Oxford: Blackwell.

Siegel, J. 2003. Substrate influence in creoles and the role of transfer in second language acquisition. *Studies in Second Language Acquisition* 25(2): 185–209.

Singler, J.V. 1990. On the use of sociohistorical criteria in the comparison of creoles. *Linguistics* 28: 645–659.

Slabakova, R. 2000. L1 transfer revisited: The L2 acquisition of telicity marking in English by Spanish and Bulgarian native speakers. *Linguistics* 38: 739–770.

Smith, G.P. 2002. *Growing Up with Tok Pisin: Contact, Creolization, and Change in Papua New Guinea's National Language.* London: Battlebridge.

Tarone, Elaine. 1981. Some thoughts on the notion of communication strategy. *TESOL Quarterly* 15: 285–295.

Tarone, E., A.D. Cohen and G. Dumas. 1983. A closer look at some interlanguage terminology: A framework for communication strategies. In *Strategies in Interlanguage Communication,* Claus Færch and Gabriele Kasper (Eds.), 4–14. London/New York: Longman.

Valdman, A. 1980. Creolization and second language acquisition. In *Theoretical Orientations in Creole Studies,* Albert Valdman and Arnold Highfield (Eds.), 297–311. New York: Academic Press.

van der Voort, H. 1996. Eskimo pidgin in West Greenland. In *Language Contact in the Arctic: Northern Pidgins and Contact Languages,* Ernst Håkon Jahr and Ingvild Broch (Eds.), 157–258. Berlin: Mouton de Gruyter.

Véronique, D. 1994. Naturalistic adult acquisition of French as L2 and French-based creole genesis compared: Insights into creolization and language change. In *Creolization and Language Change,* Dany Adone and Ingo Plag (Eds.), 117–137. Tübingen: Max Niemeyer.

Washabaugh, W. and F. Eckman. 1980. Review of *The pidginization process: A model for second language acquisition* by John Schumann. *Language* 56: 453–456.

Wekker, H. 1996. Creolization and the acquisition of English as a second language. In *Creole Languages and Language Acquisition,* Herman Wekker (Ed.), 139–149. Berlin: Mouton de Gruyter.

White, L. 1991. *Universal Grammar and Second Language Acquisition.* Amsterdam: John Benjamins.

Winford, D. 2000. "Intermediate" creoles and degrees of change in creole formation: The case of Bajan. In *Degrees of Restructuring in Creole Languages,* Ingrid Neumann-Holzschuh and Edgar W. Schneider (Eds.), 215–274. Amsterdam/Philadelphia: John Benjamins.

Winford, D. 2002. Creoles in the context of contact linguistics. In *Pidgins and Creoles in the Twenty-First Century,* Glenn Gilbert (Ed.), 287–354. New York: Peter Lang.

Winford, D. 2003. *An Introduction to Contact Linguistics.* Oxford: Blackwell.

Zobl, H. 1982. A direction for contrastive analysis: The comparative study of developmental sequences. *TESOL Quarterly* 16: 169–183.

Zobl, H. 1983. L1 acquisition, age of L2 acquisition and the learning of word order. In *Language Transfer in Language Learning,* Susan M. Gass and Larry Selinker (Eds.), 205–221. Rowley, MA: Newbury House.

Zobl, H. 1986. Word order typology, lexical government, and the prediction of multiple, graded effects in L2 word order. *Language Learning* 36: 159–183.

# PART I

## CONTACT

# VERY RAPID CREOLIZATION IN THE FRAMEWORK OF THE RESTRICTED MOTIVATION HYPOTHESIS

Norval Smith
*University of Amsterdam/ACLC*

In this article, I will introduce a hypothesis of creolization which I will refer to as the *Restricted Motivation Hypothesis*. I oppose the idea that a significant majority of slaves is required in a plantation colony as a precondition for the development of a creole. I oppose the idea that a majority of Europeans present in the early stages of such a colony would result in the early slaves automatically learning the colonial language. I also oppose the premise that such slaves would wish to learn such a colonial language. And I will claim that in most small colonies a new colony-wide slave ethnicity developed very rapidly. Parallel to this rapid development of a slave ethnicity, a medium for interethnic communication developed as a communication medium among the slaves. This rapidly crystallized into a medium for ethnic communication for the slave population. Evidence for this will be drawn from two sources: firstly, from pidgin-like L2-acquisition; and secondly from the crowded timetable of events associated with the development of the creole languages in the South American country of Surinam.

## 1. *Introduction*

In this short article, I will introduce a hypothesis of creolization, which I will refer to as the *Restricted Motivation Hypothesis*. I will also criticize various assumptions that I believe have held back our understanding of why the new languages that creole languages are develop in the way they do. Much of what I have to say is not new by any means. However, conceivably the combination of hypotheses and argumentation presented in this brief article is, to some extent, novel.

Here, I will be primarily concerned with the question of why creole languages developed in the originally English colony of Surinam.

## 2. *Assumptions*

The following assumptions, which seem to be particularly widespread, whether implicitly or explicitly, seem to me to get in the way of a proper understanding of creolization, apart from lacking any justification:

(a) the idea that a certain *proportion* of slaves was required in a plantation colony before creolization could take place (cf. Bickerton 1984).
(b) the assumption that in the earlier phases of plantation colonies, when there was certainly a proportionately large number of indentured laborers present on plantations, at least in the English colonies, this would automatically result in the slaves learning the colonial language, by reason of the easy access made possible by the large European population (e.g., Singler 1996: 223).

(c) the assumption that slaves would wish *en masse* to learn the languages of
    their oppressors. This assumption follows on from (b): if there is access to
    it, then slaves will learn English.
(d) the assumption that that plantations are social microcosms, that is, that the
    social relations entered into by slaves were mainly restricted to their own
    plantation. In other words, the assumption that slave society was dominated
    by vertical social relationships rather than horizontal ones. This assumption
    has been solidly refuted by Arends (2001: 299–303), but is still
    encountered.

First of all, however, it will be necessary to reflect on the speed of the
creolization process itself, something on which there has been intermittent
debate over the last two decades.

## 2.1 *Speed of creolization*

The debate about the speed of creolization has been conducted between those
creolists who believe in gradual creolization (e.g., Arends 1993) and those who
believe in one-generation creolization (e.g., Bickerton 1981, 1984). I will try
and liven this debate up by attempting to make a case for a third variant: *Very
Rapid Creolization*. By this, I mean creolization that would essentially be
completed within the space of a few years. In this, I wish to situate myself at or
below the bottom end of Thomason's *Abrupt genesis scenarios* (Thomason
2001: 177).

The debate became relevant when Bickerton developed his *Language
Bioprogram Hypothesis* (1984). This hypothesis crucially made reference to
children as creole formers, who filled in the gaps, based on their knowledge of
universals, in whatever pidgin they encountered in use by adults, and which
they set about trying to acquire as if it was a real language. In other words, the
children created the creole within a generation.

The criticism generated by Bickerton's work eventually led to much opposition among a group of creolists who came, or had come, to see creolization as
a gradual process extending over several generations. A further tendency grew
up among some gradualist-inclined creolists of regarding creoles as mere
dialects of whatever colonial language was involved, and therefore not as
creoles at all in the normal understanding of the term. This was presumably not
unconnected to the general and severe difficulty for gradualists of defining
when a creole had actually finished the creolization process, and had therefore
become a full language. It thus also got round the knotty problem of having
several generations of slaves who did not have a "full" language, while creolization was not yet completed.

I am assuming here that creoles are new *languages*. I refuse to see Sranan,
for example, as a dialect of English, and so far no one has explained in what

sense of the term *dialect* it might be considered to be entitled to that description.

With the question of the speed of creolization in the back of our minds, I will now address the four assumptions I want to discuss.

## 2.2 *Proportion of creolizers required*

Bickerton's ideas about children as creole formers sparked off a debate about the number of slave children present on plantations during the formative years of a creole, and whether these were (ever) sufficient to create a creole language. Most of the ammunition in this debate was fired off by gradualists. Arends (1993), for example, used the figures supplied by Postma (1990) on the Atlantic slave trade, which are particularly valuable for Surinam, to suggest that there were too few children present on plantations to have a role in creolization.

But the most important aspect of the whole debate was this: no independent argumentation was ever forthcoming from either proponents or opponents of the Bickerton's Language Bioprogram Hypothesis concerning just how many children would be required, or just how few might be sufficient, to create a creole language.

Similarly, such measures as were developed to help determine whether a creole would develop in a specific colony or not based on the numbers of imported slaves—whatever their ages—remained completely hypothetical. We can think of Bickerton's (1984) *pidginization index* as an example of this.

Both approaches involved theoretical assumptions plucked out of thin air. In addition, their application was usually crude. Account was only taken of global aspects, such as the population make-up of a whole plantation colony. Little or no account was taken of factors like local variations in the proportions of slaves to Europeans, or the presence of garrisons of European soldiers in important towns, and other such distorting factors.

## 2.3 *The question of access to the superstrate language*

Later on in the creolist debate, the realization dawned on creolists, as they paid more attention to historical facts, that the initial postcolonization periods in Caribbean plantation colonies were not characterized by slave majorities at all, but by European ones. The length of time it took for a colonist majority to be replaced by a slave majority varied considerably, but the early colonies always started out with a majority of *superstrate* speakers.

The slaves, most creolists thought, would therefore have had sufficient *access* to the colonial languages in the early phase of most colonies to have learned them in the normal fashion (Singler 1996: 223). Only when slave imports gathered momentum, and the African-European balance had swung around to a large majority of slaves, and in particular African-born slaves, would new slaves have insufficient access to the colonial languages to learn them under normal language-learning conditions. We have already seen that there is no actual measure that would tell us when such a point had been reached.

Still the problem remained of what constituted a sufficient proportion of slaves to cause a creole to develop. The idea was that, when new slaves started arriving in larger numbers than would allow normal second-language learning to take place, then a creole would start to develop, because of the lack of access that these slaves would have to the colonial language, however access was defined. The question of why the newer slaves would not just learn the colonial language from the older slaves remains something of a mystery. The newer, and more numerous, slaves may not have had sufficient access to white speakers of the colonial language—previous generations of slaves were, after all, supposed to have learned the colonial language in times of better access.

One might argue, and this has of course been argued, that during what has been termed the *expansion phase* of a colony, new slaves were being imported at a sufficiently high speed to nullify their opportunities for learning the colonial language. Still, if there had been a significant body of slaves speaking the colonial language, one would have thought that their status advantage over "salt-water" slaves would still have carried the day. What this makes clear is that one cannot simply do calculations based on black-white population proportions. Just demonstrating that at a particular moment in time there were more slaves than Europeans in a colony is no indication of what languages they spoke.

Having an "opportunity" to learn a colonial language is no guarantee, of course, that large numbers of slaves actually did so, and even less that it would become their first language. We know, of course, that the end result was similar in most plantation colonies of any size. This, then, raises the question of whether learning the colonial language was an *aim* at all, or at least using it as a community language. We will examine this question in the next section.

## 2.4 *Why would slaves want to learn the superstrate language? The question of motivation*[1]

This point has been made previously (Baker, 1990: 109; Schumann, 1978: 373), but has not been given sufficient prominence. So Thomason (2001: 180) says, "… in most cases there is probably no serious effort to learn the lexifier language as a whole." I disagree with the "in most cases" here, because in the creole case, it is clear that if there had been a serious intent to learn the language, then—given the sufficient access they are claimed to have had—our early slaves would have gone and done so. And Lefebvre (e.g., 2001) talks about the lexifier language as forming the (initial) target in the creolization process.

---

[1] I am indebted to Pieter Muysken for sowing the seeds of my concerns with motivation.

Starting from the obvious fact that Africans have the same second-language-learning abilities as anyone else, then the assumption has usually been made that the first slaves would automatically have learned the colonial language, and that this was a reason to postpone the period of creole development until later in the history of the plantation colony. I would like to replace *would* with *could* here. There is no question that under other circumstances, say, voluntary small-scale migration, this would have happened. However, these were not normal circumstances—these people had been violently enslaved. Some slaves would no doubt have seen the main chance and taken the opportunity of learning the colonial language, but this would perforce have involved a small number, or the exercise would have been pointless—you do not stand out by virtue of your abilities in the language of the colonizers if a large number of your fellows do the same. Moreover, it is doubtful whether the majority of slaves would have wished to do this anyway. What could possibly have been their motive to do so? On a polyglot plantation, where two, or three or four languages would have been spoken by the slaves themselves, say, a group of Fon-speakers, some Kikongo-speakers, a couple of Twi-speakers, and maybe a Nago (Yoruba-speaker), what would have been the motivation to learn, say, colonial English as well, rather than adopting alternative strategies to communicate with each other?

Why should mere access to a language cause someone to learn it? And here we have additional constraints in some situations, like that of the Dutch planters in Surinam whose slaves were expressly forbidden to speak Dutch. A total lack of access to a language will make it impossible to acquire, but it has been assumed too easily that the mere opportunity to learn a language would result in a whole (slave) community acquiring it. Once again, we can ask why many slaves should wish to learn the language of the enemy enslavers. What is the advantage to the community as a whole of such a move? It would only guarantee easier access to the community by the colonial power. The dangers of this are revealed by the following quote, dating from 1667:

> They are there a mixture of several nations, which are always clashing with one another, so that no conspiracy can be hatching, but it is presently detected by some party amongst themselves disaffected to the plot, because their enemies have a share in it. (Warren 1667)

We have to assume in any case that different African groups ("Of the negroes or slaves ... Who are most brought of *Guinea* in *Africa* to those parts"; Warren 1667) maintained their ethnic languages for several generations. Clearly, this quotation suggests that the different groups had some common means of communication. It does not tell us whether they communicated in an English-based pidgin, creole, or even some form of English itself. To attempt a more precise interpretation would certainly be egregious.

However, the initial period of undoubted greater access to the colonial language will, as we will see, prove to be a important datum. Creolization represents *some* kind of second language learning, however vestigial. But as DeGraff (e.g., 2003: 394) points out, it would be a highly racist and obviously ridiculous assumption to imagine that Africans were not capable of ordinary second language learning. So we have a conundrum that has only one obvious answer: that the African slaves just did not particularly want to learn French, Dutch or Portuguese or, in the case of Surinam, English.

Jourdain (to appear) takes things further than the mere lack of motivation to learn the enslaver's language. Talking about the plantation environment she suggests pidgins/creoles could function as a vehicle of empowerment, of resistance, of subversion.

"By virtue of having a new language at their disposal that was in continuity with their ancestral languages and making use of significant elements of the superstrate, PC [pidgin/creole, NS] makers set themselves on a course of linguistic independence that changed their relationships to the world and shaped their own identity.

### 2.5 *Plantations as social microcosms*

As for the fourth assumption, it is simply untenable. Rather than being a series of vertical microcosmic societies joined at the tops, it is more correct, at least for the later periods we know more about, to regard plantation colonies as being basically two superimposed horizontal societies, with vertical hierarchical downward links on each plantation linking the two planes. And why should we not extrapolate this model back to the earlier days of the colonies?

The plantations were prison camps, but without fences, and there was a great deal of socializing among plantations after the day's work was done. Slaves were kept on their plantations during working hours by the extreme sanctions that were applied in the case of marronnage (flight from slavery). After hours, though, there was absenteeism, partner-visiting, general wandering about, and so on (Arends 2001; Muyrers 1993). Why should these same things not have happened in the earlier days when there were fewer slaves, and therefore the slave population was easier to keep under control—and there was less need to do so anyway?

Arends (2001) divides the types of activities of slaves involving external (i.e. extra-plantation) contacts into four types: work, trade, leisure, and resistance. It would go too far to examine these in detail, but a brief mention of several more important factors is relevant.

Slaves were employed in the transport of goods and persons, etc., by boat to and from Paramaribo. Plantation slaves were also involved in this riverine traffic. As the boats employed were fairly small there was quite a lot of this traffic. Another labour-intensive work environment was the so-called *commando* service, a compulsory work levy on plantation owners to supply for various public works tasks such as digging ditches, and building defence works. Plantation-owners moved their slaves around as well. Often one owner would own more than one plantation, or lend slaves out. Also Arends mentions that the plantation provision-grounds were often located at some distance behind the plantation (all plantations fronted a river). Slaves were also sent out hunting and fishing, to supplement their and their owner's diet.

Trading took place on the plantations themselves. This involved trade with Indians, Whites, and even Maroons.

Among the leisure activities mentioned by Arends are visits by freed former slaves from Paramaribo. Some plantations apparently had special buildings where such former slaves could stay when visiting, which suggests that was a not infrequent occurrence.

Slaves from different plantations formed concubinage relationships. Herlein (1718: 97) mentions the existence of these.

Festivities involving slaves from more than one plantation are already mentioned in 1765. Examples of these would be the annual distributions of foods and goods around the New Year, dance parties, and musical performances by special societies. Price & Price (1980: 166) reproduce a painting of such a dance party from 1707.

African religious activities also took place both inside and outside the plantation, sometimes at sanctuaries shared by more than one plantation. Up till about the mid-eighteenth century no mission activities were allowed amongst slaves, leaving the field to the syncretic Winti religion, formed by a combination of Gbe, Kikongo, Twi and Amerindian panthea.

Under this heading Arends mentions the visits of Maroons to plantations, and the temporary residence of plantation slaves in Maroon communities (*petit marronnage*).

In this context, the *Code Noir de Colbert* (1685) has to be taken into account (Da Silva 1999). This was a set of rules applicable to slaves in French colonies, which were extremely restrictive, among other things, as regards the freedom of movement of slaves. The question is to what extent such legal frameworks were applied in practice. No doubt this varied from place to place.

It is clear that there *was* an overall *slave community* in the large majority of plantation colonies. And definable communities develop linguistic means to mark themselves off from other communities occupying the same *space*, whether they occupy discrete or intertwined spaces. And in the case of plantation societies these linguistic means are precisely creoles.

## 2.6 *Access again*

The question of access is important, however. It cannot be denied that there was access to the colonial language at the start of most plantation colonies, and that this access became more and more restricted later on, when the plantations became larger, and the European population on the plantations became reduced, for the simple reason that the superstrate language did *not* spread to any extent through the slave community—and that was because an alternative means of communication arose in competition to prevent this. So there is no reason, or at least evidence, for the assumption that creole formation was delayed until some hypothetical (im)balance of population had been achieved.

Thus, instead of regarding the moment of creation of creole languages as being delayed until African-born slaves became a significant majority of the population, I am going to turn things on their head and suggest that it was precisely in the period when slaves had *reasonable access* to the colonial language that creoles were formed.

Later in the history of some colonies, the numbers of slaves vs. Europeans were so disproportionate that it is indeed difficult to imagine there being sufficient access to learn anything much of the colonial language at all, especially if we get rid of the hypothetical previous generations of colonial-language-speaking slaves. Note that in Surinam, there were hardly any models of English available *at all* just one generation following colonization, due to the departure of most of the English(-speakers). Therefore, we do need a period of initial access so that some things could have been learned, but only those aspects of the colonial language that were called upon in the construction of a new language to fulfill the communicative needs of the new slave community.

Jourdain (to appear) makes the point that:

"work and work-related activities ... provided the only social context where regular, repeated, and sometimes prolonged communication could take place between workers and plantation overseers and owners ...."

and:

"Work was the common space, the common denominator that opened the door for exchange, cultural and linguistic, in other words for pidginicity to appear."

Such work-related contact between blacks and whites would be much more intense in the early days of small plantations with a more evenly-balanced workforce.

## 3. *A medium for interethnic communication? Yes, but not completely interethnic*

It is highly likely that Philip Baker (1990) was on the right lines with his idea that the first stage in the development of new means of communication was the development of a medium for interethnic communication (MIC), although I reject his suggestion that each plantation would have its own MIC, precisely because plantation colonies were not a combination of so many vertical mini-societies. Also, I do not consider that *all* the ethnic groups in a slave colony would have been involved in the formation of the MIC. Only the ethnic groups represented among the *slaves themselves* would have been. There was no motivation to develop a full range of communicative interactions with plantation owners and officials. Only a minimum of such interactions would be necessary.

What form would this early slave MIC take? I see no special role for children (*pace* Bickerton, and my own earlier stated opinions; Smith 1987). The proportions of children arriving in Surinam were variable, depending on what the slavers could pick up in West Africa. Basically, they took what was on offer. So, one shipment might have one child in six, while another might have twice that proportion.[2] I envisage the slave MIC as an average of the first/early interlanguage (IL) stages of the first learners—the combination of their IL1s, as it were (something similar to Lefebvre's dialect-leveling; Lefebvre 2001).

Some theories of L2 acquisition see early ILs as stripped-down forms of the L1 plus relexification—that is, with the replacement of L1 lexical items by their L2 "equivalents." In normal L2 learning, a series of ILs is produced, ideally ending up with a close approximation to L2. The importance of relexification for creolization has been most emphasized in the work of Lefebvre (e.g., 1998, 2004).

It is clear that the contributions of substrate and superstrate languages are not quite so neatly ordered as Lefebvre wishes, however. She says:

> ... while the forms of the lexical entries of a PC tend to be derived from the superstratum language, the syntactic and semantic properties of these lexical entries tend to follow the pattern of the substratum languages. (Lefebvre 2004: 11)

I myself believe that this probably *was* at least partly the case in the earliest phase of the development of the creoles, when they were not as yet anyone's native language. This is only to be expected as a result of the earliest interlanguage states of the various ethnic groups in the slave population at that time, assuming the correctness of theories of second-language learning involving interlanguages and relexification. We can see from the Surinam creoles, however, that the results are much more complex. Once again, these languages form a useful test bed, as the language that supplied the largest part of the basic vocabulary—English—was removed from the picture at a very early stage.

As far as phonology is concerned, it is clear that the input forms of such basic words were provided by English, as Lefebvre states. It is equally clear, however, that the (phonological) output forms were mediated by many of the same constraints, applied in the same order of importance, as in Fon (for instance, see Smith & Haabo, to appear). This is more obvious in Saramaccan

---

[2] For more detail on this point, see Smith (2001).

and Ndyuka than in Sranan, which was exposed to a long period of Dutch adstratal influence.

As far as syntax is concerned, we see that some features are clearly substratal, derived from the influence of Gbe languages, while others seem to come from English or French. For instance, take nominal structures where an adjective qualifies a noun. In Sranan, adjectives always precede nouns in NPs. This is opposite to the Gun/Fon noun-adjective order. In Haitian, we have noun-adjective as the normal word order, just like in Gun/Fon. But Haitian also has some prenominal adjectives. These are precisely the adjectives that correspond to the prenominal adjectives of French. In adjective positioning, then, Haitian follows the superstrate pattern.

If we turn to the syntax-pragmatics interface, we find a seeming mixture of substrate and superstrate influences. This is apparent from Aboh's work on the determiner system for instance (Aboh, this volume). Similarly, work by Essegbey (to appear) shows that verbal semantics can only be *partly* explained in terms of a Gbe substrate.

Smith (2001) asked why, when Lefebvre claims that the principal substrate language of Haitian is Fon, and this is clearly also the case for Saramaccan, there are such major grammatical differences between Haitian and Saramaccan.

For instance, let us consider the English inflectional system. The English inflections have disappeared completely from the present-day Surinam creoles. Our first records of these languages—dating from the beginning of the eighteenth century—show no trace of them either, some 40 years after the mid-1660s, when I claim they were formed.

English is an inflection-poor language, with fewer than ten regular inflectional suffixes.

(1) a.  Nominal inflections                     Example
        /-z/     [plural]                        bed**s**
    b.  Verbal inflections
        /-z/     [3rd person singular]           hate**s**
        /-ɪŋ/    [progressive]                   be hat**ing**
        /-d/     [perfective]                    hate**d**
        /-d/     [passive]                       be hate**d**
        /-d/     [perfect]                       have hate**d**
    c.  Adjectival inflections
        /-ər/    [comparative]                   nic**er**
        /-əst/   [superlative]                   nic**est**

I will ignore adjectival inflection in what follows.

One thing that is abundantly clear is that no post-head English inflectional suffix has survived as such in any of the Surinam creoles. Plurality is marked in definite noun phrases by prenominal *de(n)* as in (2). Similarly, verbal tense and aspectual features are marked by preverbal particles; the third-person singular clitic pronoun *a* could also be interpreted as such a particle.

(2)    *den pikin*              'the children'                    SRANAN

Verbal tenses and aspects are likewise marked in pre-head position, for example:

(3)    *tá sútu*        '… is shooting'        SARAMACCAN
       *e sutu*         '… is shooting'        SRANAN

In other words, English post-head inflections, which provide evidence for the movement of nominal and verbal material past the inflection, are replaced in the Surinam creoles by pre-head particles. I will not discuss this in more detail here. Note that in this respect, the Surinam creoles differ from both Haitian and the Gbe languages in general, which both make use of nominal suffixal inflections, and therefore involve leftward movement on the part of nominals. In general, English involves structures with a pre-head particle and a post-head inflection, in both nominal and verbal constructions. Bare structures—IPs or DPs—are actually atypical.

Considering the case of nominal inflections more closely, it is fairly obvious that it was not the lack of salience of plural inflections, nor any obvious phonological restrictions, that prevented the realization of plural /z/ with nouns. At least ten or so nouns actually appear in an etymologically plural form in the Surinam creoles:

(4)    | *English* | *Saramaccan* | *Ndyuka* | *Sranan* | *Gloss* |
|---|---|---|---|---|
| shoes | *súsu* | *susu* | *susu* | 'shoe' |
| clothes | *koósu* | *koosi* | *krosi* | 'cloth' |
| news | *njúnsu* | *nyunsu* | *nyunsu* | 'news' |
| yams | *njámisi* | *nyamisi* | *yamsi*[3] | 'yam' |
| paths | *pási* | *pasi* | *pasi* | 'path' |
| ears | *jési* | *yesi* | *yesi* | 'ear' |
| ants | *(h) ánsi* | — | — | 'ant' |
| ashes | — | *asisi* | *asisi* | 'ash(es)' |
| bricks | — | — | *briksi* | 'brick' |

Note that Sranan and Ndyuka both have the lexical item *nyun* with the meaning 'new,' but that this is not in a direct morphological relationship with *nyunsu*. However, it is clear that both singular and plural forms were available in the early period. Compare the following forms:

---

[3] Note that early Sranan had a similar NOCODA restriction to Ndyuka—final /n/ in fact indicates a nasalized vowel in Ndyuka.

(5)     *English*     *Ndyuka*     *Sranan*     *gloss*
          egg           igi          —          'egg'
          eggs          —           eksi        'egg'

Sranan and Ndyuka are closely related, Ndyuka having descended from an early eighteenth-century plantation dialect of Sranan. Note that all these forms are words for pairs of items or collectives in some sense. This indicates that it was *not* an inability to parse plural meanings out of plural forms that was at issue for the early creole formers: they ignored plural suffixes where the unmarked meaning was singular, and kept them for collective nouns, where the unmarked meaning was "plural." The real reason for the loss of a meaningful plural suffix was presumably the availability of more salient pre-head structures.

Take the following options, which presumably existed in the substandard English that would have been available to the early slaves:

(6)     the boat                        'the boat'
        that boat                       'that boat'
        the boats                       'the boats'
        them boats                      'those boats'

Not only has the plural inflection -*s* been lost, the unstressed clitic *the* has also disappeared. But the reason for its disappearance was presumably not so much its lack of stress as its lack of a feature expressing number as well as definiteness.

(7)     the boat       >        Ø
        that boat      >        *da boto*  >      *a boto*
        the boats      >        Ø
        them boats     >        *den boto*

So, we see that in this case we do not have relexification, but rather the adoption of aspects of English (i.e., superstrate) grammar, with the less salient and less feature-rich markers removed.

### 3.1 *MEC formation*
Two additional questions can be asked with respect to the initial early interlanguages of the first slave cohort:

(a) How did individual ILs become unified?
(b) What was the role of children in this process?

The first languages of the initial slave cohort were, of course, various African languages. The first children born in the colonies would certainly have had as their first languages at least the language spoken by their mothers, and conceivably others spoken in the slave community too.

The above-mentioned (see section 2.5) communal slave identity would very rapidly catalyze the creation of a means of ethnic communication (MEC) as an in-group language from the initial MIC. This can be assumed to be a uniformization of the early pidgin ILs of the slaves, along the lines suggested by Lefebvre (2001) and Siegel (1985).

The rapidity of the posited developments has to do with the social violence involved in plantation slavery. In conditions of social turbulence, language change—and development—occurs faster than otherwise. And there was an urgent need to form an MEC.

The Surinam creoles only display a sum total of about 700 roots derived from English. These give us a good idea of the size of the initial MIC. The MEC clearly—like any community language—required a larger vocabulary. Compound formation, reduplication, conversion, and the transfer of lexical items from Fon and Kikongo to the MEC would go a long way towards supplying this, as can clearly be seen from the modern lexica of the Surinam creoles, which make extensive use of all these possibilities.

Both children and adult slaves would be involved in creole formation as L2 learners. Any children involved at that time would arrive equipped with an African L1. And if we assume that the formation of the creole proceeded very rapidly, that is, within the space of a few years, we are relieved of the necessity to assign any special role to children. Note that children would never have had any problem learning the colonial language; children would not have problems learning any natural language, given proper access to it. This fact did not cause or help the colonial languages to take root among the slaves. The reason for this must be a motivational one. Once a basis of a common and usable pidginized form of the colonial language had been laid, such that a slave MIC and then MEC had been formed, there would be little motivation to develop things further in the direction of the colonial language.

We would get fossilization, as in the case of L1 Spanish-speaking Alberto —forever famous in the annals of a-language study (Schumann 1978, 1982). Once his English competence had reached the state in which it was sufficient for his limited social needs, he terminated the process of acquisition. This is called fossilization from the perspective of the second language, but in fact pidginization, as Schumann called it, is a better term from Alberto's point of view. All he needed was a pidgin, after all: his MIC.

An MEC would be the next step after the slave MIC, as I have just stated. The various slave MICs used by the different ethnic groups would differ, and uniformization (or dialect-leveling, as Lefebvre calls it) would swiftly follow.

Note that Alberto provides us with more than one object lesson. Firstly, as we have just seen, his pidginization provides us with an individual example of what I am claiming was a universal process among the first cohort of plantation slaves.

Secondly, he certainly had as much (potential) access to English as a slave on a plantation in early Surinam. This did not seem to cause him to acquire English, nor did it help those slaves, apparently.

Thirdly, he was not motivated to take his second-language learning beyond the bare minimum. His motivations were obviously different from those of slaves in early plantation colonies. The common factor was that there was not much in the way of motivation in either case.

And fourthly, he acquired his pidgin-like version of English rapidly. He did not have to spend a generation or two doing it. For the startled reader's information, a generation is a period of 25 to 30 years.

### 3.2 A final supporting argument from Surinam

In the case of Surinam, history provides with an additional useful tool in this context. There was a change of colonial language after only 16 years of settlement by the English. The creole languages that arose in Surinam were still largely English-lexifier creoles, however. And Schumann's eighteenth-century word lists are not full of Dutch lexical items by any means (Schumann 1778, 1783)—this, despite the fact that more than a hundred years of Dutch rule had elapsed since the Dutch takeover in 1667.

The question is, then, whether we can speak of a fully formed creole at the time of the English departure. In Smith (2002), I provide the following time-table of linguistically relevant events in Surinam. Similar arguments appear in Smith (2000) and McWhorter (1997). I have omitted some facts not directly relevant to my brief argumentation here.

(8) *Timetable of creole formation in Surinam*

| Date | Event |
|------|-------|
| 1651 | Settlement of Surinam by the English |
| ca. 1665 | *Sranan creolized from Caribbean Plantation Pidgin English* |
| 1665 | Jewish settlers arrive from Cayenne *with Portuguese Creole-speaking slaves* |
| 1667 | Treaty of Breda by which Surinam was surrendered to the Dutch |
| 1668–75 | More than 90% of the English leave with around 1,650 slaves |
| ca. 1680 | *Sranan partly relexified to Portuguese, resulting in Dju-Tongo ('Jew-language') on the Middle Suriname River plantations* |
| 1690 | Mass escape of slaves, who founded the Matjau clan of the Saramaccan tribe |

Before the English left Surinam, or otherwise by the early 1670s, all the English elements occurring in Sranan must have been present in whatever form of speech was a precursor to Sranan. This explains the date of around 1665 for the formation of Sranan. Arends (2002: 124) argues for a longer period of English influence, past the end of the seventeenth century, but there was undoubtedly a larger *Portuguese* Jewish presence at this time and, as the seventeenth century came to an end, more and more Dutch planters of course.

Price (1983) provides ample evidence for the creation of Saramaccan from 1690 onwards. The various groups that ended up forming the Saramaccan tribe had separate escape routes, and were often separated by large distances. But Saramaccan is a very homogeneous language, with little dialectal variation. This suggests that the Saramaccans must have spoken a partly Portuguese-relexified English creole prior to marronnage, say, by 1680.

The crowded nature of the above timetable is a serious problem for any type of gradualness in creole formation at all. And, as such, it reinforces the various positions I have adopted in respect of other factors.

## 4. *Conclusions*

To conclude this brief article, let me run through my points again.

*Speed*: I see no reason for assuming that the creolization proceeds slowly. The evidence for gradual creolization makes assumptions about creole languages that are not proven. My conclusion is that what we have is *Very Rapid Creolization*.

*Proportional demography*: No evidence has ever been provided bearing on how many children are required before Bickertonian creolization can take place, or what proportion of the slave population must be African-born before any creolization hypothesis can work out.

*Access*: I see no reason to believe that access to a colonial language would necessarily result in a slave community's learning it.

*Motivation*: Just as Alberto was not motivated to take his acquisition of English any further than was necessary for his social purposes, I see no reason to assume that the initial cohort of slaves in a plantation colony would acquire any more English than was sufficient to form an English interlanguage adequate to function as an MEC. So, I stand by the *Restricted Motivation Hypothesis*.

*Plantations*: Plantations were not socially microcosmic, but macrocosmic. A single *slave* ethnic group quickly arose.

*Access again*: It was in the initial phase of plantation colonies that there was sufficient access to colonial languages to allow the formation of interlanguages and MICs. The greater access to the colonial languages possible then was vital to the formation of creoles. They were formed *early*.

*The Surinam timetable*: The sequence of events involved in the formation of Sranan and then Saramaccan is completely incompatible with gradualism, and even with one-generational creolization.

In closing, I hope this brief article correctly conveys some of the excitement of the Montreal Dialogues workshop.

*References*

Arends, J. 1993. Towards a gradualist model of creolization. In *Atlantic meets Pacific*, F. Byrne and John Holm (eds.), 371–380. Amsterdam: John Benjamins Publishing Company.

Arends, J. 2001. Social stratifications and network relations in the formation of Sranan. In *Creolization and Contact,* N. Smith and T. Veenstra (eds.), 291–307. Amsterdam: John Benjamins Publishing Company.

Baker, P. 1990. Off target? *Journal of Pidgin and Creole Languages* 5: 107–119.

Bickerton, D. 1981. *Roots of Language.* Ann Arbor, MI: Karoma.

Bickerton, D. 1984. The Language Bioprogram Hypothesis. *The Behavioral and Brain Sciences* 7: 173–188.

Da Silva, U.-K. E. 1999. *Le code noir.* Porto-Novo: Grande Imprimerie du Bénin.

DeGraff, M. 2003. Against creole exceptionalism. *Language* 79: 391–410.

Essegbey, J. To appear. Verb semantics and argument structure. In *The Trans-Atlantic Sprachbund: Gbe and Surinam,* P. Muysken and N. Smith (eds.).

Herlein, J. 1718. *Beschrijvinge van de Volksplantinge Zuriname.* Leeuwarden: Injema.

Jourdain, C. To appear. The cultural in PC genesis. In *The handbook of pidgin and creole languages.* J. Singler and S. Kouwenberg (eds.). Oxford: Blackwell.

Lefebvre, C. 1998. *Creole Genesis and the Acquisition of Grammar: The Case of Haitian Creole.* Cambridge: Cambridge University Press.

Lefebvre, C. 2001. Relexification in creole genesis and its effects on the development of the creole. In *Creolization and Contact,* N. Smith and T. Veenstra (eds.), 9–42. Amsterdam: John Benjamins Publishing Company.

Lefebvre, C. 2004. *Issues in the Study of Pidgin and Creole Languages.* Amsterdam: John Benjamins Publishing Company.

McWhorter, J. 1997. *Towards a New Model of Creole Genesis.* New York: Peter Lang.

Muyrers, S. 1993. Het netwerk van de slaaf: Een onderzoek naar contacten van Surinaamse plantageslaven in de achtiende en negentiende eeuw. M.A. thesis, Erasmus University Rotterdam.

Postma, J. 1990. *The Dutch in the Atlantic Slave Trade, 1600–1815.* Cambridge: Cambridge University Press.

Price, R. 1983. *First time: The historical vision of an Afro-American people.* Baltimore: The Johns Hopkins University Press.

Price, R. and S. Price. 1980. *Afro-American arts of the Suriname rain forest.* Berkeley: University of California Press.

Schumann, C. 1778. Saramaccan Deutsches Wörter-Buch. MS., Moravian Brethren, Bambey, Surinam.

Schumann, C. 1783. Neger-Englisches Wörter-Buch. MS., Moravian Brethren, Paramaribo, Surinam.

Schumann, J. 1978. The relationship of pidginization, creolization and decreolization to second language acquisition. *Language Learning* 28(2): 367–379.

Schumann, J. 1982. Simplification, transfer, and relexification as aspects of pidginization and early second language acquisition, *Language Learning* 32(2): 337–366.

Siegel, J. 1985. Koines and koineization. *Language in Society* 14: 357–378.

Singler, J. 1996. Theories of creole genesis, sociohistorical considerations, and the evaluation of evidence: The case of Haitian Creole and the Relexification Hypothesis. *Journal of Pidgin and Creole Languages* 11.185-230.

Smith, N. 1987. The genesis of the creole languages of Surinam. D.Litt. dissertation, University of Amsterdam.

Smith, N. 2000. The linguistic effects of early marronnage. In *Proceedings of the 13th Biennial Conference of the Society for Caribbean Linguistics*, H. Devonish (ed.), 288–301. Mona, Jamaica: University of the West Indies.

Smith, N. 2001: Voodoo Chile: Differential substrate effects in Saramaccan and Haitian. In *Creolization and Contact,* N. Smith and T. Veenstra (eds.), 43–80. Amsterdam: John Benjamins Publishing Company.

Smith, N. 2002. The history of the Surinamese creoles II: Origin and differentiation. In *Language Atlas of Suriname,* J. Arends and E. Carlin (eds.), 131–151. Leiden: KITLV Press.

Smith, N. and V. Haabo. To appear. The Saramaccan implosives: Tools for linguistic archaeology? *Journal of Pidgin and Creole Languages*.

Thomason, S. G. 2001. *Language Contact*. Edinburgh: Edinburgh University Press.

Warren, George. 1667. *An Impartial Description of Surinam, upon the Continent of Guiana, in America. With a History of Several Strange Beasts, Birds, Fishes, Serpents, Insects, and Customs of that Colony*. London: W. Godbid.

# SEMANTIC TRANSFERENCE:
## TWO PRELIMINARY CASE STUDIES FROM THE SOLOMON ISLANDS

Angela Terrill
*Max Planck Institute for Psycholinguistics*
*Radboud University Nijmegen*

Michael Dunn
*Max Planck Institute for Psycholinguistics*
*Australian National University*

This study illustrates processes of semantic transference with two casestudies from the Solomon Islands. In each case study we investigate semantic transference in the structured semantic domain of spatial reference, from the local indigenous language to Solomon Island Pijin (SIP), the unofficial national language of the Solomon Islands. Semantic transference, the exchange of semantic structure apart from its morphological or lexical expression, has relevance to language contact and creole genesis, and is a relatively understudied area of language change. The individuals studied were members of two indigenous language communities: the Lavukal people of the Russell Islands (native speakers of Lavukaleve), and the Touo people of Rendova Island (native speakers of Touo), all of whom also speak SIP. Solomon Island Pijin is structurally close to Oceanic Austronesian languages. Selection of non-Austronesian 'Papuan' languages, not known to be related to each other or indeed to any other languages, as the matrix languages enabled intractable questions of historical relatedness versus contact-induced change to be avoided. The varieties of SIP spoken in the two language communities largely shared the same grammatical structures, but differed in their semantic structures. Results of the study showed that semantic structure was transferred from native language to second language only where suitable lexical and morphological means existed in the target language; in the case where there was no formal structural affordance semantic transfer did not take place.

## 1. *Introduction*[1]

This study sets out to investigate semantic transference: the ways in which speakers use semantic structures of their first language when speaking another—creole—language. An experimental investigation was carried out in a limited semantic domain—expressions of spatial configuration in small-scale

[1] This work was carried out in part while the authors were recipients of a grant from the European Science Foundation under its EUROCORES "Origin of Man, Language and Languages" scheme, via the Netherlands Organisation for Scientific Research (NWO), hosted by the Max Planck Institute for Psycholinguistics. The work was completed under an Australian Research Council grant hosted by the Australian National University and Max Planck Institute for Psycholinguistics (Dunn), and a grant from the Netherlands Organisation for Scientific Research (NWO), hosted by the Radboud University Nijmegen (Terrill). In addition, we would like to express our appreciation for the help given by members of the Touo and Lavukal communities who participated in the experiments reported on here. Finally, we are grateful to the participants in the Montreal Dialogues conference, to two anonymous reviewers, and to Andrej Malchukov for their comments on earlier versions of this paper.

space—to gather data to evaluate the hypothesis that semantic transference between a first language and a second language is the norm. The investigation involved an elicitation task run in two separate bilingual language communities in the Solomon Islands. In each community, people were first-language speakers of one of two unrelated Papuan isolates, Lavukaleve (Russell Islands) and Touo (Rendova Island), and were second-language speakers of the local varieties of Solomon Island Pijin (SIP), itself a variety of the creole language Melanesian Pidgin.

The results showed that the spatial descriptions employed by speakers using SIP parallel those of the speaker's first language. In both locations in the Solomon Islands, SIP has more or less the same grammatical structures. What differs in different areas is speakers' choice of expressions, or semantic structures—subtle elements that give flavor to their speech. It is these subtle semantic differences that are the target of the inquiry.

The study thus seeks to provide some evidence of a process of semantic transference in expressions of spatial configurations in small-scale space. It attempts to isolate in one semantic domain a microcosm of what could be a much wider picture of differential mother-tongue transference of semantic structures among different first-language speakers when speaking a second language.

## 2. *Background—semantic transference*

Within the broad field of language contact, there exists an extensive literature on substratum effects on phonology and the lexicon. There is less literature on substratum effects on syntax and discourse-pragmatics. Mithun's (1992) study on substratum effects of Central Pomo on English in larger discourse stretches is a fascinating exception. Still less work has been done on substratum effects on semantics (although see Aikhenvald (2005) for a brief discussion and review of the literature on the diffusion of semantic and pragmatic patterns). The present study focuses on this relatively under-researched area of substratum effects on structured semantic domains.

The study takes as its reference point Clyne's concept of "transference":

A "transfer" is an instance of transference, where the form, feature or construction has been taken over by the speaker from another language, whatever the motives or explanation for this. "Transference" is thus the process and a "transfer" the product. The terms have the advantage of covering lexical, semantic, phonetic/phonological, prosodic, tonemic, graphemic, morphological and syntactic transference, and any combinations of these. (Clyne, 2003: 76)

Semantic transference, then, is "the transference of meanings from words in one language to words in another with some morphemic or semantic correspondence" (Clyne, 2003: 77).

What is here called semantic transference has also been called calquing or loan translation, among other terms. We prefer the term "semantic transference" because it treats semantics as a separate, investigable unit of language structure; this accords well with our position of taking semantic structures as the unit of analysis.

Talmy (2000) makes a substantial contribution to the field of semantic transfer; the main aim of that paper is to provide a framework for semantic borrowing in language contact situations, by means of a detailed examination of the effect of Slavic semantic structures on Yiddish verb prefixes. Talmy uses the concept of "semantic space": "for any language, the patterns in which semantic domains are subdivided and in which the resulting concepts are represented among the surface morphemes" (p. 289); a broad concept that is also used in the present study, here referred to as "semantic structure" or "structured semantic domains." The paper sets up a framework of types of semantic borrowing, and in particular, types of accommodation. Many of the features of this framework are to be seen also in the data presented in our paper, and will be further discussed below; indeed, evidence of Talmy's "non-accommodation" will also be seen. The framework set up by Talmy proves most useful in thinking about processes of semantic transfer within a particular form class. However this paper approaches the problem from the other direction, by comparing semantic transfer within a particular semantic domain (and using a structured nonlinguistic elicitation task to make the problem of cross-linguistic comparability of semantic domains more tractable).

An interesting contribution to some aspects of this general topic is provided by Ross (2001a) who, in his discussion of semantico-syntactic borrowing, or "metatypy" as he calls it, argues that "reorganisation of the language's semantic patterns and 'ways of saying things'" is the first type of change to happen in a situation of contact-induced language change; only afterwards does syntactic restructuring occur (Ross, 2001a: 146). If this is correct, and semantic transference actually happens before any other type of borrowing, it would be extremely interesting and important to studies of language contact in general. Ross's work is based largely on contact-induced language change between Takia (Oceanic Austronesian) and Waskia (Papuan), which are geographically and culturally not so far from the Solomon Islands. The present study aims to further investigate the nature of semantic transference by describing a controlled case study in two regions in the Solomon Islands.

Siegel (1999), looking at the transfer of linguistic material from Central Eastern Oceanic substrate languages into Melanesian Pidgin, finds that "different constraining factors may limit which substrate features become available, determine which superstrate forms are used, and influence which transferred features are actually reinforced and incorporated into the language." Our paper aims to show that the process of semantic transference is constrained by morphological factors, and we extend Siegel's finding in two ways: firstly, we look at semantic transference, a type of transference not specifically addressed by Siegel; and secondly, the substrate languages are two of the handful of Papuan languages of the Solomon Islands, languages which have so far been almost completely neglected as sources for substrate influence in Melanesian Pidgin.

It is important to stress at the outset that the initial position of this study comes from the angle of language contact rather than creole genesis. The speakers whose data we cite in the study are not generating a creole; one is already being spoken in large towns of the Solomon Islands. Rather, our approach is that this is a situation of imperfect learning of a second language, although that second language happens to be a creole, or at least an extended pidgin. We believe that the fact that SIP is a creole is not in itself relevant here: we use SIP as the language of comparison because it is the only language spoken in both Papuan-speaking regions, and thus a direct comparison is possible.

Note that while we view this as a situation of language contact rather than creole genesis, the same mechanisms and processes should actually be involved, as Lumsden (1996), Lefebvre (1998) and others have made clear. And certainly the notion of transference, or transfer, has been used in both the second language acquisition and creole genesis literature.

So far, it has been assumed that semantic transference occurs in a context of substratum interference. In Thomason & Kaufman's (1988) view, borrowing takes place when native speakers of a recipient language import features from the source language into their native recipient language (Sankoff, 2002: 644). The converse is substratum interference: when foreign language speakers impose their own native language features on their use of their second language.

As Sankoff points out,

> local groups bilingual in externally imposed languages ... provide perhaps the most fertile ground for features of substratum origin to become established in the speech community as a whole. However, careful studies of such situations have often cautioned against jumping to conclusions about substratum influence, first, because sources other than substratum may be historically correct, and second, because descriptions of contact varieties may be descriptions of L2 speakers, not of stable bilingual or L1 speech. (Sankoff, 2002: 654)

Note that Sankoff is dealing with bilingualism, rather than the second language acquisition which occurs in the language situations to be described, but the caution remains relevant to the present study.

We are aware that by referring to a substrate in a creole as a source for linguistic features we are being thoroughly substratist—a position that not all scholars in the field would concur with. However as Rickford & McWhorter (1997: 250) point out, Melanesian Pidgin as a whole has long been considered a fertile ground for substrate factors: indeed, substratists "have received a big boost from the work of Keesing (1988) on the Oceanic substrate in Melanesian Pidgin English." And in fact, as Rickford & McWhorter later concede, most people recognize at least some substrate influence in creole formation.

## 3. *This study*

As a starting hypothesis, we took the position that semantic transference from the substrate language is pervasive in situations of language contact.

We investigated this hypothesis by carrying out an exploratory study of substrate effects on semantic transference in the spatial domain in three languages of the Solomon Islands: two unrelated Papuan languages, and the lingua franca of the Solomon Islands, Solomon Island Pijin.

The Solomon Islands have about 80 closely related Austronesian languages, and, spread among these, a handful of very divergent, and possibly unrelated Papuan languages (Todd, 1975; Ross, 2001b; Dunn, Reesink & Terrill, 2002; Lynch, Ross & Crowley, 2002). SIP is an extended pidgin (Muysken & Smith, 1995: 3; Lefebvre, 1998: 32), meaning that children of mixed marriages grow up using SIP as their native language, while others speak it as a second or later language. Perhaps because of this, SIP shows a lot of variation depending on the native language of each speaker (Jourdan & Maebiru, 2002).

This study was conducted in two separate locations, each one a Papuan-speaking environment. The Papuan languages in question are Lavukaleve (spoken in the Russell Islands, Central Province) and Touo (spoken on Rendova Island, Western Province). These two languages share almost no linguistic features, and any relationship between them must be of a very ancient and remote nature, if it exists at all (Dunn, Terrill, Reesink, Foley & Levinson, 2005).

The speakers in our study all had one of the two Papuan languages as their native language, some also spoke an Austronesian language, and all spoke SIP very well, usually having learned it at school, while some had also lived in town and used SIP as the language of daily communication.

The study compares the way in which speakers of the two Papuan languages use SIP. Data for the study come from fieldwork carried out *in situ* on Lavukaleve, SIP as spoken by Lavukaleve speakers, Touo, and SIP as spoken by Touo speakers. Accessible information on these varieties can be found in Terrill (2003) for Lavukaleve; Frahm (1998), Todd (1975), and Terrill & Dunn (2003) for Touo; and Keesing (1988) and Jourdan & Maebiru (2002) for SIP in general.

The languages chosen are well suited to the task: it is important to compare the unrelated or only very distantly related Papuan languages, rather than the closely related Austronesian languages, thus avoiding potentially complex and unresolvable issues to do with variable degrees of inheritance of semantic systems.

## 4. *The task*

The aim of the study is to compare the languages of interest in one controlled semantic domain. Semantic systems are subtle and often covert, and it can be difficult to identify and compare them between languages. The semantic domain of spatial reference was chosen as being a relatively confined and graspable domain. An elicitation task designed at the Max Planck Institute for Psycholinguistics, called "Man and Tree" (CARG, 1992), was used. This elicitation task looks at strategies for the spatial description of static location in small-scale space, and is thus ideal for eliciting otherwise natural conversation in a confined semantic domain, and enabling direct comparison from one language variety to another.

Man and Tree is not a single task but a family of related tasks; the data reported on in this paper are based on two: the Annie Senghas version (here called the "exhaustive" version), and Game 2 (here called the "distracter" version). The exhaustive version consists of two identical sets of sixteen color photographs, each one showing a static array of two objects: a small plastic man, and a small plastic tree (Figure 1). The set of photos includes the man and tree arranged in all sixteen possible spatial configurations with respect to each other, as well as having the man facing in all four possible directions. The distracter version contains a subset of the photos of the exhaustive version, plus some photos showing other objects aside from a man and a tree, for example, pigs and balls, intended as distracters. The photos from these two versions of the task overlap somewhat, and we have only used those photos which occur in both tasks.

Figure 1. *Two photos from the Man and Tree task*

The game is played by two people. One player (the director) is given one set of photos, from which she or he describes the scene shown in the photo, in such a way as to enable the other player (the matcher) to identify the correct photo from the second, identical, set. The matcher cannot see the photo that the director is describing. The matcher is free to ask questions. If the wrong picture is chosen, the matcher tries again until she or he gets the right picture. To solve the task, and enable the matcher to identify the correct photo, the director can give descriptions relating the elements inside the photos to spatial cues from the physical surroundings, outside the photos (i.e., picture-external cues); she or he may also use cues taken from within the photos themselves (i.e., picture-internal cues).

The rationale for using an elicitation task such as the one described above, as opposed to searching a corpus for naturally occurring examples, is that it is difficult or impossible to find enough instances of structured semantic relationships in a comparable domain without eliciting them. The spatial cues locating objects in small-scale space described in this study occur infrequently in the genres that comprise the standard linguistic corpus recorded in a fieldwork situation. The elicitation task has the advantage of controlling the environment of the task, making data across languages readily comparable, as well as vastly increasing the number of tokens of any given type of data. Finally, even though this is an artificial task, it generates plenty of natural problem-solving interaction between the two participants; such natural interactional data would be difficult to obtain otherwise.

## 5. *Results*

### 5.1 *Previous results from the task*
For this study, we coded only the picture-external spatial cues speakers used to relate spatial configurations in each photo. Languages differ greatly in the linguistic strategies they have available for their speakers to solve the Man and Tree task. There is an unlimited number of different types of picture-external cues potentially available to a speaker of a language to use: these can be based on the compass points (e.g., 'the man is facing north'), left and right (e.g., 'the tree is left of the man'), up and down (e.g., 'the man is up from the tree'), landmarks (e.g., 'the man is on the hill side of the tree'), ad hoc referents (e.g., 'the man is facing where the sun comes up'), social referents (e.g., 'the man is facing where Judy was sitting before') and so on. So, for example, to describe a given picture, a speaker of Dutch (Indo-European, northern Europe) might use an expression equivalent to 'the man is to the right of the tree, and he is looking at you,' whereas for the same picture a Tzeltal (Mayan) speaker might say 'the tree is on the uphill side, the man is downhill, he is looking towards the trail,' a Longgu (Austronesian, Solomon Islands) speaker might say 'the man is facing me towards the east, the tree is on the inland side,' while in Arrernte (Pama-Nyungan, Australia) the equivalent might be 'the man is facing us, on the east side, with the tree at his side' (Pederson, Danziger, Wilkins,

Levinson, Kita & Senft, 1998). Pederson et al. give a detailed explanation of the task and cross-linguistic results for a number of languages; see also Senft (2001) for an in-depth analysis of Kilivila (Oceanic, Austronesian) using this (among other) tasks. Note that while languages spoken in areas with similar geographical features may use those features similarly as spatial cues (and see Majid, Bowerman, Kita, Haun & Levinson (2004) who point out that there are some correlations between ecological situation and spatial frame of reference), it is by no means a hard-and-fast rule that they will do so; as we will see, even in languages spoken in geographically comparable Pacific island situations, very different spatial cues can be used.

While Pederson et al. (1998) were largely concerned with frames of reference, and indeed the Man and Tree task was conceived as a means of eliciting frames of reference, we do not discuss frames of reference in this paper. Rather, the study is confined to the types of spatial cues used in the spatial expressions elicited by the task, and no further abstractions are made.

The next sections of this paper discuss in turn the results of the Man and Tree task for the four language varieties to be considered: first Lavukaleve, then SIP as spoken by Lavukaleve speakers; then Touo, and the SIP spoken by Touo speakers. On the way, explicit comparisons between each variety will be made.

## 5.2 *Lavukaleve*

Lavukaleve Man and Tree data were collected in the Russell Islands by Angela Terrill in 2003. Ten sessions were carried out, four with the exhaustive variant of the task, and six with the distracter variant.

Lavukaleve is a Papuan language spoken by about 1,700 people in the Russell Islands, an island group in the Central Province of the Solomon Islands. Lavukal people mostly live on the smaller islands which cluster to the west and north of the two largest islands in the group. Most Lavukal speakers are subsistence farmers, practicing slash-and-burn agriculture and fishing, as well as participating to some extent in cash-cropping by running small family-based coconut plantations in order to sell the dried flesh, copra. Apart from two large Tikopian villages in the Russell Islands, and the one town on the island group, most people living in the Russells are Lavukal people, and grow up speaking Lavukaleve. Lavukaleve is beginning to give way to SIP in the town and in some areas of the east Russells but elsewhere it is the only language regularly heard.

Data were collected in the town, Yandina, and in one village of the west Russells, Mane Village. In order to solve the Man and Tree task, Lavukaleve speakers invariably first establish where the man is, with respect to a picture-external cue. This is always a compass point, landmark, geographical feature or speech-act participant. Lavukaleve speakers then establish where the tree is with respect to the man.

All speakers used cardinal directions as picture-external cues, but only to refer to where the man is facing. All informants but one used left and right, referring to the left and right of the man. In all cases, left and right were used in the context of 'the tree is to the man's left/right.' There were no examples in which left and right were used with respect to the speaker rather than the man in the scene. Even for those scenes where the tree is both to the man's left and to our left, it can be clearly seen in Lavukaleve that the speaker is referring to the man's left, in that the words for 'left' and 'right' require a possessor; a third-person singular possessor must be the man; otherwise, it would have to be a first- or second-person dual or plural possessor. Thus, morphology settles the potential question quite simply.

Not all speakers used external landmarks, but those who did used them both to describe where the man is facing and where the tree is with respect to the man.

Landmarks used included the sea, 'where the sun comes up,' inland, the bush, place names (Havun), and places, such as 'the office.'

Most speakers used the speaker/addressee as a reference point. This usually happened in the context of the man facing you/me/us, or showing his back to you/me/us. In a couple of instances, the tree was described as across from the man, or to the side of the man, which is of course only the case for the point of view of external viewers.

So, for example, a typical Lavukaleve response is the following:

(1) *Ali      na      vego me      e-hamail      fi      o-fem*
    man(m) sgmArt east SPEC.sgn 3sgnO-towards 3sgnFOC POSS-face(n)
    *o-lei.      O-mutu      me-hamail      aka*
    3sgS-exist 3sg POSS-back(n) 1pl.in-towards then
    *o-malege-n      fi      houla la      o-fale-re*
    3sg POSS-left-LOC 3sgnFOC tree(f) sgfArt 3sgS-stand-NF
    *o-lei.      Iire².*
    3sgS-exist yes
    'The man has his face towards the east. His back is towards us, and the tree is standing to his left.'

The orientation of the man is cued with respect to a compass point, and the tree is related to his back. The following example is similar. The man's

---

² Abbreviations: Art definite article; CCW counterclockwise; dir directional; f feminine gender; FOCus; in inclusive; INDEFinite; IRRealis; LOCative; m masculine gender; n neuter gender; n2 neuter-2 gender; NF nonfinite; O object; pl plural; POSSessive; PREDicative; PRESent; S subject; sg singular; SPECifier; STATive.

orientation is defined with respect to a landmark, the sea, and the position of the tree is related to the man's face:

(2) *Ali      na      tasi      e-hamail      kako-re,*
    man(m) sgmArt sea(n) 3sgnO-towards look.out-NF
    *o-femi-n            fi            houla la      o-lei.*
    3sgPOSS-face-LOC   3sgnFOC   tree(f) sgfArt 3sgS-exist
    'The man is looking out towards the sea, the tree is in his face.'

In summary,
- if speakers can say the tree is in the man's face/to his back, they do so;
- if speakers can say the man is facing north, they do so (i.e., north is always used if possible, whereas other compass points are less consistently used);
- if the man is facing another way, a variety of strategies are used across speakers (including east/where the sun goes up/bush, west/us/sea, south/Havun/inland, and others).

These kinds of expression accord well with how spatial reference works in Lavukaleve outside this controlled elicitation task. Further data from the Man and Tree task in Lavukaleve are given in Terrill and Burenhult (in press).

## 5.3 *SIP as spoken by Lavukals*

As was mentioned above, Lavukaleve is giving way to Solomon Island Pijin in some areas of the Russells, notably in the one town, Yandina, and in some villages and hamlets in the eastern part of the island group (Terrill, 2002). Children from the few mixed marriages in the Russells tend to grow up speaking SIP and Lavukaleve; otherwise, SIP is a language learned, and spoken, outside the Russells. Older men mostly learned SIP working on fishing boats or plantations; many older women do not speak the language, as they have never lived away from the Russells. Younger people mostly learn SIP at school if they leave their village for secondary schooling.

Man and Tree data for SIP as spoken by Lavukals consist of 14 sessions (seven of the exhaustive variant, and seven of the distracter variant), collected by Michael Dunn in the Russell Islands in 2003.

Based on the starting hypothesis, that semantic transference from the substrate language is pervasive in situations of language contact, the prediction is that Lavukaleve speakers should use the same spatial reference system in the task when they speak SIP as when they speak Lavukaleve. That is, the types of spatial cues used to refer to small-scale space within the Man and Tree task should be the same.

The hypothesis was confirmed by the data: in fact, exactly the same set of spatial cues was used: compass points, landmarks, geographical features and speech-act participants were used for picture-external reference. Picture-internal cues comprised body parts of the man in relation to the tree. The following are examples of the types of expressions used:

(3) *Wanfala man hem standap, hem fes    ist,    tri   hem lo    bihaen*
    INDEF    man 3sg stand    3sg   face east tree 3sg  LOC  at.back.of
    *lo    hem.*
    LOC  3sg
    'There's a man, he is standing facing east, the tree is behind him.'

(4) *Wanfala man hem i    standap, hem i    fes    lo    iumi, tri    hem*
    INDEF    man 3sg PRED stand    3sg PRED face LOC  2pl.in tree 3sg
    *lo    baksaed blo    hem*
    LOC  back    POSS   3sg
    'A man is standing, he is facing us, the tree is at his back.'

The differences between Lavukaleve and the SIP spoken by Lavukals occurred only in distribution of these cues: in Lavukaleve, landmarks were somewhat more commonly used than in SIP. Compass points were more used in Lavukaleve than SIP too (in SIP, only west and east were used, whereas in Lavukaleve all four points were used, albeit frequently incorrectly). Gesture was used frequently in SIP and not in Lavukaleve. These points are minor differences in distribution of what is in fact the same set of categories.

So far, the prediction holds: in SIP as spoken by Lavukals, spatial expressions in the task are identical to those used in Lavukaleve itself. Thus far, the two languages compared look rather similar, but it is difficult to establish a yardstick looking at only one area. The next part of the study moves to a second area to perform a further comparison. Looking at our second area, it immediately becomes obvious how similar Lavukaleve and Lavukaleve SIP are to each other; and how divergent they are from both Touo and Touo SIP.

## 5.4 *Touo*

Touo is a Papuan language, spoken by about 1,800 people on Rendova Island in the Western Province of the Solomon Islands. Rendova is a large volcanic island, and Touo people live on the southern half, with Oceanic-Austronesian Ughele people living on the northern half. Touo speakers are typically multilingual, many speaking Roviana, Marovo, Ughele and other Oceanic languages, as well as Solomon Island Pijin (Terrill & Dunn, 2003).

The Touo data consist of eight sessions, all of the exhaustive version of the Man and Tree task, collected on Rendova Island by Michael Dunn and Angela Terrill in 2001.

The basic strategy for solving the task is what we will call an island-based system. This system places all location in a plane consisting of four intersecting axes: inland, seaward, clockwise round the island, and counterclockwise round the island.

This basic type of system is not unknown: island-based systems have been reported before; for example, the nearby Austronesian languages Longgu (Hill, 1997) and Kokota (Palmer, 1999) (to name but two of many examples) have an east/west/inland/seaward system (the system works differently in each language); what is quite unusual in Touo is the clockwise/counterclockwise terms.

5.4.1  *Touo's clockwise/counterclockwise system of spatial reference.* Under Touo's clockwise/counterclockwise system of spatial reference, there are four terms for referring to direction and location in space. The system imagines a central point in the middle of Rendova. All movement or location from any point towards the middle to any point radiating outwards, is described as 'seaward.' Conversely, any movement or location from closer to the edge of the island to closer to the middle is described as inland. This axis is not problematic, and is shared by many island-based societies. However, the clockwise/counterclockwise dichotomy is interesting and unusual (although not unique—a similar system occurs for instance in at least three Austronesian languages; Makian Taba, Manam and Boumaa Fijian (François, 2004)). This system is used to describe motion or location along the island. It can easily be described in a right/left system: all movement or location rightwards along the island, if one is facing seaward, is clockwise. All movement or location leftwards along the island if one is facing seaward, is counterclockwise. Thus, one could circumnavigate the whole island and be going clockwise all the time, if one had the sea to one's left. (Of course, the Touo terms *avi* 'counterclockwise' and ruevu 'clockwise' do not actually refer to the motion of a clock.)

These four terms then, *fei* 'seaward,' *mugi* 'inland,' *avi* 'counterclockwise' and *ruevu* 'clockwise,' form a coherent system for describing spatial location and movement on an island. These terms are used instead of more familiar terms (to Westerners) such as 'left' and 'right' or 'up' and 'down'. For example, students sitting along a bench were asked to shift along 'seaward' to make more room. A group of children picking pomelos were calling to each other 'Clockwise! Clockwise!' to point out the location of more pomelos. An answer to the question 'Where did your sister go?' could be 'counterclockwise.' In short, the system is frequently used and fundamental to Touo.

Some examples from the Man and Tree task using this system:

(5) *Ngw   wrw-ngw        mugi        vaha fino-zo     avi-ri*
    3sgn2   tree/stick-3sgn2 there_inland side   person-sgm CCW-dir
    *rove-a.*
    look-REALIS
    'The tree is on the inland side, the man is looking counterclockwise.'

(6) *Fi-a*          *yenengw.*    *Wrw-ngw*
    start-REALIS now      tree/stick-3sgn2
    *mugi*          *vaha ia*     *zo*       *fino-zo*
    there_inland   side   already   3sgm     person-sgm
    *fei*          *zo*          *ya-enw.*        *Fei*        *zo*
    seaward    3sgm       stand-STAT.pln   seaward   3sgm
    *fino-zo*     *ya-enw*            *nodo-a.*
    person-sgm stand-STAT.pln      see-REALIS
    'Start now. The tree is on the inland side already and the man is seaward. He is standing looking seaward.'

The results obtained for the Touo Man and Tree task were all of this nature: the terms used to express this island-based system are pervasive and they are one of the most common things to be heard when Touo people are speaking, so it is not surprising that they were used during the Man and Tree task.

### 5.5 *SIP as spoken by Touo speakers*
Most Touo speakers speak Solomon Island Pijin, learning it not only while away from their home island, as is the case with Lavukals, but also in the large schools situated within villages in Touo-speaking communities. The only groups of people unlikely to speak SIP are very old women and very young children.

The Touo SIP data come from two sessions, one from 2002 and one from 2004, both with the exhaustive version of the task, collected by Michael Dunn on Rendova Island.

An interesting question is immediately raised when one tries to predict how a Touo speaker would make spatial reference in the Man and Tree task, when speaking SIP. In the Lavukaleve test case, spatial cues in Lavukaleve had good translation equivalents in SIP, and one could think of the Lavukals' SIP system as essentially a good fit with the Lavukaleve system. However, there is no good way to translate all of the Touo island-based terms into SIP, and they do not all have natural SIP equivalents. For inland, the SIP term *ap* can easily be used; this is widely found throughout Solomon Island Pijin, usually conflated with east or southeast. For seaward, the term *daon* can be used; again, this is common across SIP, and usually conflated with west/northwest. However for the clockwise/counterclockwise terms, there are no obvious words in SIP. We have heard clockwise referred to as *daon* and counterclockwise as *ap* or *ontop*; this represents a conflation of clockwise and seaward, versus counterclockwise and inland; thus, such a system makes only two distinctions instead of four. (That particular conflation is enabled in SIP as spoken by Touos, by another collapse, in Touo, of the verb *fara*, which means both 'come down' and 'come clockwise.') This is one possible solution to how to refer to space in SIP as spoken by Touos; but collapsing four terms into two may represent an unworkable compromise.

A second possibility is that speakers could use a different system entirely. Touo, like most languages, does have other ways of talking about space, for times when the island-based system is not appropriate. This happens, for example, when speakers are out at sea and thus away from the coordinates of an island, or when they are lost and do not know where the necessary coordinates are, or on a landmass which is not an island. In these contexts, the island-based system is not suitable, and various other strategies are used.

Thirdly, if the island-based strategy is deemed untranslatable, an entirely separate system might be used in the SIP spoken by Touos.

A fourth possibility is that there may just be a gap in SIP and speakers will not be able to complete the task. SIP is not a full language for these people, after all: it is an extended pidgin for most Touo speakers, rather than a fully-developed creole.

The results of the task show that speakers used entirely picture-internal cues. Consider examples (7) and (8):

(7) *Tri    an     man. Tri   ia     hem  i      long raetsaed blo   hem, man ia*
    tree   and    man  tree  FOC   3sg  PRED LOC  right       POSS  3sg  man FOC
    *hem  i     long leftsaed bat man ia /  baksaed blo   hem  lo*
    3sg  PRED LOC  left       but man FOC  back       POSS  3sg  LOC
    *desfala    tri.*
    this       tree
    'There's a tree and a man. The tree is on the right side, the man is on the left side, but the man has his back to the tree.'

(8) *Semfala  man  en     semfala tri   ia     bat destaem tri hem  lo      fran*
    same     man  and    same    tree  FOC   but this.time tree 3sg  LOC     front
    *nao  ia.   Bata boe  ia,   hem  i      lo     bihaen bat hem  i      baksaed*
    FOC  FOC   but  boy  FOC   3sg  PRED LOC  behind but 3sg  PRED back
    *kam       lo     tri     nomoa.*
    towards   LOC    tree    just
    'The same man and the same tree, but this time the tree is at the front. But the boy, he is at the back but his back is towards the tree.'

Speakers only used the following spatial cues: left and right, body parts of the man related to the tree, front/back (of the man, and of the picture itself) and the speaker/addressee as a ground object. They did not use the island-based system at all, in any form. Even when they could have used readily available SIP terms like *lo si* 'seaward' or *lo bus* 'inland,' they did not.

## 5.6 *More on Touo: Context-dependent systems*

Linguistic data are rarely as simple as they first seem, and our Touo sessions are no exception. As it happens, in one of the sessions some Touo speakers, speaking Touo, not SIP, did not use the island-based system. In this session, the director said things like this:

(9) *Zo        fino-zo       me        ngw*
   3sgm   person-sgm  um   3sgn2
   *wrw-ngw*            *gede        vaha        zo*
   tree/stick-3sgn2   left.side   side   3sgm
   *ya-e,        ngw        vaha       ngw        teo-ri        zo*
   stand-IRR   3sgn2   side   3sgn2   LOC-dir   3sgm
   *hiri-engw.*
   back-PRES
   'The man then the tree, the man is standing on the left side, he has his back to it [the tree].'

This was a problematic session in that the speakers had a great deal of trouble in describing and identifying pictures: there were long pauses during the director's description, longer response times and high error rates on the matcher's part, and a very great use of gesture. Halfway through this session, communication completely broke down, and the matcher used the island-based system to clarify the director's descriptions. From that point onward, the director switched entirely to the island-based system, and the session was completely very quickly and with no more errors.

We speculate that the reason these particular speakers first chose not to use the island-based system, but instead to use picture-internal cues, was our presence; they thought we would not understand the island-based system, and wanted to use the left and right terms, which they thought would be more readily understandable to us, even though they did not control them at all well. Touo's clockwise/counterclockwise system is sometimes pointed out by speakers as a shibboleth; they are well aware that other languages around them do not have such a thing, and are often at pains to describe it to us. The island-based system relies on shared knowledge of where the speaker and addressee are on the island and also of the lexical items used to express the system. Incidentally, it is not always immediately obvious where inland and seaward are; some villages are on small peninsulas, and the exact codification of directions is by culturally accepted practice. The system using picture-internal spatial cues, by contrast, requires no more information than what two speakers of any speech situation share: themselves and their own location, and the directly observable information contained in the spatial scene that the speakers are describing.

We suggest that this aberrant session represents accommodation: Touo speakers, like most people, accommodate to what they think their audience will understand. For Touo people, this means adapting their system of spatial reference to one which appears more transparent. Interestingly, when these two speakers abandoned the island-based system, they used exactly the same picture-internal spatial cues as Touo speakers used when speaking SIP.

So, to return to our predictions, Touo speakers do not collapse the four axes into two when speaking SIP, nor do they transport the Touo terms directly into their SIP; rather, they use a different system entirely: a system that is available in the language in other contexts (e.g., when the island-based system is not appropriate, or when the speaker thinks the audience might not understand). So this is indeed a case of semantic transference, but it turns out that semantic transference is not always a straightforward process.

## 6. *Conclusions: Is semantic transference the norm?*

In both the test cases presented above, semantic transference was the norm, as we predicted. The domain of spatial language has complex grammatical encoding which is, for the most part, opaque to speakers of the language. The semantics of linguistic spatial encoding serves to conventionalize the process of picking out relevant features of real spatial disposition. This process is highly non-iconic and arbitrary. Identification of figure and ground follows from psychological universals for dealing with salience, but the only communicatively efficient way to link these with a real spatial configuration requires one to rely on conventionalized patterns of encoding. Solomon Island Pijin is a nonstandardized language, spoken by many more second language speakers than first language speakers, and the linguistic conventions for spatial language are weakly established. The path of least resistance is to use the same conventions of spatial semantics in a second language as in the substrate, and so it is not particularly surprising to see (although it has rarely been clearly demonstrated) that this is a major strategy selected by speakers of Lavukaleve and Touo when speaking SIP.

We have seen that deviations from straightforward semantic transference occur in our data where Solomon Island Pijin does not have lexical or grammatical resources commensurate with the substrate structures; this finding is also discussed by Talmy (2000). We illustrate this with a model of semantic transfer of a functional domain into L2 which weighs semantic strategy against lexico-syntactic fit, as in Figure 2.

In this account, a straightforward translation of the substrate semantic structures onto the L2 semantic structure is only possible where the lexical or other formal expression of those semantic structures affords the process of transference.

| *L1* | more preferred | 3 | 1 |
|------|----------------|---|---|
| *semantic strategy* | less preferred | 4 | 2 |
| | | low | high |
| | | *lexical/morpho-* | |
| | | *syntactic fit L1 -> L2* | |

Figure 2. *Affordances: semantic vs. lexical/morphosyntactic*

The diagram shows two competing forces: there is a desire for a straightforward translation of the substrate semantic structures onto the L2 semantic structures, but the lexical or other formal expression of those semantic structures may or may not afford the process of transference. Box 1 includes cases, like the Lavukaleve one described above, in which the preferred semantic strategy can easily be expressed in the lexical or morphosyntactic devices available in the L2. The prediction is that Box 4 will not arise: these are cases in which a less preferred semantic strategy is used, and there is a low degree of fit between the L1 and L2 formal expressions of this less preferred strategy.

The interesting cases are Boxes 2 and 3. In these are expressed the tension between a good semantic fit from the substrate language into the target language, versus a good formal fit. Box 2 represents cases in which speakers choose the less preferred semantic strategy in favor of a good lexical or morphosyntactic fit. This is the Touo case outlined above, in which speakers used the dispreferred spatial system in favor of something that was easily expressible in SIP.

Box 3 is the opposite solution: that in which speakers prefer to retain their substrate semantic structures and force them into the formal structures of the target language; in other words, they change some forms in the target language. We think that Touo speakers refrained from doing this (i.e., they did not change any lexical or morphosyntactic structures in SIP) because there is a large buffer of other SIP speakers, who do not share this particular contact situation, and who do not have this problem of expression.

In cases where the L2 is not buffered by a community of other speakers, we hypothesize that lexical/morphosyntactic structure will give way to preferred semantic structures.

There are many examples of this in the literature: the cases of heavy semantico-syntactic borrowing discussed by Malcolm Ross for Takia (Oceanic Austronesian) and Waskia (Papuan) present just this kind of example (Ross, 1996; 2001a): both communities are involved in the language contact, and it is not buffered by a community of speakers not affected by the contact. The preceding argument is only speculative: to be any more certain, one would need more data from these two language situations, as well as further supporting data from other areas of the world. However if the hypothesis did prove to be true, it would provide an interesting and potentially useful way to think about semantic transference as it feeds into the wider picture of language contact, in terms of both second language acquisition and creole genesis.

*References*
Aikhenvald, AY. 2005. Grammars in contact: a cross-linguistic perspective. In: Research Centre for Linguistic Typology International Workshop 'Grammars in contact: A cross-linguistic perspective'. Melbourne.
CARG. 1992. Space Stimuli Kit 1.1. Cognitive Anthropology Research Group, Max Planck Institute for Psycholinguistics, Nijmegen, The Netherlands.
Clyne, M. 2003. Dynamics of language contact. Cambridge: Cambridge University Press.
Dunn, M., G. Reesink, and A. Terrill. 2002. The East Papuan languages: a preliminary typological appraisal. Oceanic Linguistics 41:28-62.
Dunn, M., A. Terrill, G. Reesink, R.A. Foley, and S.C.Levinson. 2005. Structural phylogenetics and the reconstruction of ancient language history. Science 309:2072-2075.
Frahm, R.M. 1998. Baniata serial verb constructions. In: The University of Auckland.
François, A. 2004. Reconstructing the geocentric system of proto-Oceanic. Oceanic Linguistics 43:1-31.
Hill, D. 1997. Finding your way in Longgu: geographical reference in a Solomon Islands language. In: Senft G, editor. Referring to space: Studies in Austronesian and Papuan languages. Oxford: Clarendon Press. p 101-126.
Jourdan, C., and E. Maebiru. 2002. Pijin: A trilingual cultural dictionary. Canberra: Pacific Linguistics 526.
Keesing, R.M. 1988. Melnesian Pidgin and the Oceanic substrate. Stanford: Stanford University Press.
Lefebvre, C. 1998. Creole genesis and the acquisition of grammar. Cambridge: Cambridge University Press.
Lumsden, J.S. 1996. On the acquisition of nominal structure in the genesis of Haitian Creole. In: Wekker H, editor. Creole languages and language acquisition. Berlin: Mouton de Gruyter. p 185-205.
Lynch, J., M. Ross, and T. Crowley. 2002. The Oceanic Languages. London: Curzon Press.
Majid, A., M. Bowerman, S. Kita, D.B.M. Haun, and S. Levinson. 2004. Can language restructure cognition? The case for space. Trends in Cognitive Science 8:108-.
Mithun, M. 1992. The substratum in grammar and discourse. In: Jahr EH, editor. Language contact: Theoretical and empirical studies. Berlin: Mouton de Gruyter. p 103-115.
Muysken, P., and N. Smith. 1995. The study of pidgin and creole languages. In: Arends J, Muysken P, Smith N, editors. Pidgins and creoles: an introduction. Amsterdam: John Benjamins. p 3-14.
Palmer, B. 1999. A grammar of the Kokota language, Santa Isabel, Solomon Islands. In: Department of Linguistics. Sydney: University of Sydney.
Pederson, E., E. Danziger, D. Wilkins, S. Levinson, S. Kita, and G. Senft. 1998. Semantic typology and spatial conceptualization. Language 74:557-589.

Rickford, J.R., and J. McWhorter. 1997. Language contact and language generation: Pidgins and creoles. In: Coulmas F, editor. The handbook of sociolinguistics. Oxford: Blackwell. p 238-256.

Ross, M. 1996. Contact-induced change and the comparative method: cases from Papua New Guinea. In: Durie M, Ross M, editors. The Comparative Method Reviewed. New York: Oxford University Press. p 180-217.

Ross, M. 2001a. Contact-induced change in Oceanic languages in north-west Melanesia. In: Aikhenvald A, Dixon RMW, editors. Areal diffusion and genetic inheritance: problems in comparative linguistics. Oxford: Oxford University Press. p 134-166.

Ross, M. 2001b. Is there an East Papuan phylum? Evidence from pronouns. In: Pawley A, Ross M, Tryon D, editors. The Boy from Bundaberg: Studies in Melanesian linguistics in honour of Tom Dutton. Canberra: Pacific Linguistics. p 301-321.

Sankoff, G. 2002. Linguistic outcomes of language contact. In: Chambers JK, Trudgill P, Schilling-Estes N, editors. The handbook of language variation and change. Massachusetts: Blackwell. p 638-668.

Senft, G. 2001. Frames of spatial reference in Kilivila. Studies in Language 25:521-555.

Siegel, J. 1999. Transfer components and substrate influence in Melanesian Pidgin. Journal of Pidgin and Creole Languages 14:1-44.

Talmy, L. 2000. Borrowing semantic space: diachronic hybridization. In: Towards a cognitive semantics Vol II. Cambridge, MA.: MIT Press. p 289-320.

Terrill, A. 2002. Why make books for people who don't read?: a perspective on documentation of an endangered language from Solomon Islands. International Journal of the Sociology of Language 155-156:205-219.

Terrill, A. 2003. A grammar of Lavukaleve. Berlin: Mouton de Gruyter.

Terrill, A., and N. Burenhult. in press. Orientation as a strategy of spatial reference. to appear in Studies in Language.

Terrill, A., and M. Dunn. 2003. Orthographic design in the Solomon Islands: the social, historical, and linguistic situation of Touo (Baniata). Written languages and literacy 6:177-192.

Thomason, S.G., and T. Kaufman. 1988. Language contact, creolization and genetic linguistics. Berkeley: University of California Press.

Todd, E. 1975. The Solomon Language Family. In: Wurm SA, editor. Papuan languages and the New Guinea linguistic scene. Canberra: Pacific Linguistics C-38. p 805-846.

# VARIABILITY IN CONTACT SPANISH:
## IMPLICATIONS FOR SECOND LANGUAGE ACQUISITION

Joyce Bruhn de Garavito and Cristina Atoche
*The University of Western Ontario*

It has been argued that lack of consistency in the production of different types of agreement morphology in adult second language (L2) acquisition is evidence for a deficit in the functional domain (see White 2003 for a review of the issues). In other words, there is an important difference between L1 and L2 acquisition, and as a result the L2 grammar will always differ in significant ways from the target language (Meisel 1997). This paper will show that the assumption that the production of agreement morphology in the L1 final state is not variable to any noticeable degree is not empirically supported. If variability is present in both first and second language production, it is not valid to argue that it is a sign of a deficit only in second language acquisition. On the other hand, we will show that the data studied here are constrained by the grammar, contra the position that grammars themselves are variable (Tarone 2002). We examine the production of 14 monolingual speakers of Spanish from the Andean region of Peru, where there is a long history of contact with Quechua. In particular, we focus on the clitic that, in these varieties of Spanish, is used to double direct and indirect objects. We find no significant difference between these speakers' output and standard varieties in dative clitic doubling of indirect objects. In contrast, there is significant variability in the production of accusative objects: no doubling, doubling with a dative clitic, doubling with correct gender agreement and doubling with incorrect gender agreement. This variation is found not only in the group results but also in the output of individual speakers. The results are reminiscent of the speech of second language learners and thus provide evidence against the Fundamental Difference Hypothesis (Bley-Vroman 1989, 1990).

## 1. *Introduction*

It has been argued that lack of consistency in the production of different types of agreement morphology in adult second language (L2) acquisition is evidence for a deficit in the functional domain (see White 2003 for a review of the issues). In other words, there is an important difference between L1 and L2 acquisition, and as a result the L2 grammar will always differ in significant ways from the target language (Meisel 1997). Variability is one of the symptoms of this difference (Bley-Vroman 1989). It is assumed that final state speakers do not exhibit variable performance in their first language.

This paper will show that there is no empirical support for the assumption that the production of agreement morphology is invariant in the L1 final state. If variability is present in both first and second language production it is not valid to argue that it is a sign of a deficit only in second language acquisition. On the other hand, we will show that the data studied here are constrained by the grammar, contra the position that grammars themselves are variable (Tarone 2002).

We will examine a phenomenon that appears to be widespread when Spanish comes into contact with other languages: variability in the expression of objects. Objects are frequently omitted in contexts in which this omission is illicit in the regional standard. When the object is present, it is often doubled by a clitic without the correct number and gender agreement. The treatment of objects in these contact varieties is usually taken as either a sign of convergence between Spanish and the contact language, and/or as a result of substratum influence.

The aims of this paper are twofold. The first is to report on the results of a field study carried out in Peru that focuses on the expression of objects in the speech of a group of speakers of Spanish. Although these speakers all claim to be monolingual in Spanish, they live in a region of heavy contact with Quechua. We will show that the results replicate in part many studies carried out mainly with bilingual speakers (Minaya & Luján 1982; Pozzi-Escot 1998; Sánchez 2004b). In the second place, we intend to demonstrate that some types of natural language, namely languages in contact situations, may provide evidence against a universal link between the production of morphology and syntax, and also against the claim that variability in the area of morphology constitutes support for an underlying deficit in second language acquisition. Thus, we highlight the significance of expanding the horizons of second language acquisition research in order to encompass not only first language development, for which there is a long tradition, but also adult bilingualism and monolingualism in areas of contact. The importance of this expansion has received some attention recently (see papers in this volume, also Bullock & Toribio 2004; Montrul 2004; Sánchez 2004a; Winford 2003), but the effects of this interest have yet to be felt in the field.

In the next section of this paper, we will look at the theoretical debate within generative linguistics regarding L2 acquisition and variability in the expression of morphology, followed by a description of objects and clitics in Spanish in Section 3. After a brief look at the literature on contact Spanish in Section 4, we will turn to the experiment and the analysis of the data. Finally, we discuss our conclusions.

## 2. *Variability in adult second language acquisition*

It is usually taken for granted that adult second language acquisition differs in certain ways from first language acquisition. According to Bley-Vroman (1989, 1990), for example, second language learners are characterized by their general lack of success in attaining the target language, variation in the level attained, and indeterminate intuitions, among other problems. The question that arises is whether these differences are due to a deficit at the level of representation, or whether perhaps they denote some other kind of problem.

There are two main positions that argue for a crucial difference between first and second language acquisition at the level of representation. On the one hand, it is claimed that second language learners no longer have access to Universal Grammar (UG), and consequently an adult L2 grammar will differ significantly from an L1 grammar, no matter how near-native the L2 speaker is (Bley-Vroman 1996, 1997; Clahsen & Muysken 1986; Meisel 1997). In contrast to this No-Access position, some researchers have argued that the difference between an L2 representation and an L1 mental grammar is not that drastic, but affects only certain areas of the grammar. Assuming that the difference between languages lies in the lexicon and, in particular, in the functional categories, features and feature values (Chomsky 1995), proponents of the Failed Functional Features Hypothesis (FFFH) (Hawkins 1998a, 1998b; Hawkins & Chan 1997; Hawkins & Franceschina 2004) argue that adult second language learners are not able to acquire functional categories or features that do not exist in their L1. Similarly, Tsimpli and Roussou (1991; see also Liceras & Díaz 1999) argue that L2 learners are constrained to the parameter values of their L1. Evidence for both of these positions comes mainly from the inconsistent production of morphology by adult L2 learners. Franceschina (2001) has argued that L2 researchers have to account for small differences in error rates between L2 and L1 speakers, for example in the case of gender agreement, because even small rates of errors are a symptom of an underlying deficit.

Counter to the above positions, some scholars have argued that L2 acquisition is not fundamentally different from L1 acquisition in that new functional categories, features and feature values are available. According to the Full Access Hypothesis (Prévost & White 2000; Schwartz & Sprouse 1996; White 1989, 2003), differences between L2 speakers and native speakers can be accounted for without assuming a deficit. Furthermore, a native-like representation is, in principle at least, possible.

One of the best documented cases of variability in the production of morphology is Patty, an L2 learner of English followed for over 10 years by Lardiere (1998a, 1998b, 2003). Patty was first recorded after she had lived in the United States for 10 years, and subsequently recorded several years later. She is therefore not a learner, but has reached an end-state grammar of the type often referred to as fossilized. Her production data differ in significant ways from those of a native speaker. On the one hand, Patty's production of verbal inflection is very low, while on the other, she performs in a way that is consistent with knowledge of the abstract features related to Tense and Agreement. Lardiere has argued that the fact that Patty's syntax is intact shows that the problems she has with morphology are not related to any deficit in the functional domain. In contrast to Lardiere's position, facts such as these are taken by those who defend the FFFH as evidence that the functional domain is in fact affected in second language acquisition. The assumption behind this, as pointed out by White, Valenzuela, Kozlowska-Macgregor and Leung (2004), is that errors in gender agreement or morphological variability in general are never found in first language acquisition. This is, of course, an empirical question that needs to be investigated. In this paper, we will show that this assumption is not warranted.

### 3. *Objects in Spanish*

Object clitics and clitic doubling have been the focus of extensive studies (among many others, see Harris 1995; Heap 2000, for morphological analyses; Uriagereka 1988, 1995, for the syntax of clitics; Suñer 1988; Bleam 1999, for object doubling). We will focus here on a description of clitics and clitic doubling in Spanish, touching briefly on possible analyses of the latter phenomenon.

Direct objects in the Spanish norm spoken in Peru and elsewhere are classified into two types: direct objects that refer to [+specific, +human][1] entities are marked by the pseudo-preposition *a* (often referred to as Personal *a*) (1), which is also used to indicate indirect objects; all other direct objects are unmarked (2). Objects of the verb *tener* 'to have' with a [+specific, +animate] object are never marked (3a), unless some sort of circumstantial information is added (3b).

(1)  *Veo   **a**   la   joven.*           [+animate, +specific]
     see-I   *a*   the  young woman
     'I see the young woman.'

(2) a.  *Veo   la       televisión.*         [−animate, +specific]
        see-I  the     television
        'I see the television.'

    b.  *Busco    una    secretaria.*        [+animate, −specific]
        search-I   a        secretary
        'I am looking for a secretary.'

(3) a.  *Tengo   un    hijo.*
        have-I    a     son
        'I have a son.'

    b.  *Tengo   a   un   hijo   en   el   hospital.*
        have-I   *a*   a    son    in   the  hospital
        'I have a son in hospital.'

---

[1] Although there is some variation in the case of animals, I will henceforth refer to this restriction as a restriction on animacy.

Differential object marking is important because, at least in some varieties of standard Spanish, it is related to the choice of clitic and the availability of clitic doubling.

Table 1 summarizes the Spanish third-person clitics as used "in Asturias, Aragón, Andalucía, the Canary Islands and America[2] (excepting parts of Ecuador, Paraguay and the Venezuelan Guyana" (Alarcos Llorach 1994: 203).[3]

| | Accusative | | | Dative |
|---|---|---|---|---|
| | masculine | feminine | neuter[4] | genderless |
| singular | lo | la | lo | le |
| plural | los | las | | les |

Table 1. *The clitic system of "standard" Spanish*

There is a great deal of dialect variation regarding Spanish clitics, and this often leads to variability in their production both between speakers and within the speech of the same speaker or writer, as shown in (4), in which the author first uses *le* to replace the direct object, and then uses *lo* for the same purpose in the second part of the sentence[5].

(4)  *Se    quedó    mirándo*le    *sin    atreverse    a*
     REFL  remained-he  regarding-DAT-CL  without  daring-REFL  to
     *despertar*lo.
     wake-ACC-CL
     'He remained looking at him without daring to wake him.'
     (Roa Bastos, Spanish author, cited in Alarcos Llorach 1994: 203).

There are in general four types of regional variations: the "standard," the distribution of which we see in Table 1; *leísmo*, the use of the dative for the masculine accusative; *laísmo*, the use of accusative gender markings on the dative feminine form; and *loísmo*, the use of the accusative for the dative in the masculine form. *Leísmo*, or the use of the dative *le* for the accusative *lo*, is generally, but not always (as example (4) shows), based on the type of object referred to. Masculine objects differentially marked, that is, accusative objects that are [+animate, +specific], trigger the use of the dative clitic *le*. The feminine may surface as *la* in these varieties. In summary, the choice of case

---

[2] "America" is far from being as homogeneous as this author suggests.
[3] Translated by Bruhn de Garavito.
[4] Neuter is used to replace sentences: *lo dijo*, 'he said it.' This will not be touched on in this paper.
[5] The following abbreviations are used throughout this paper: CL = clitic; DAT = dative; ACC = accusative; REFL = reflexive; DET = determiner; M = masculine; F = feminine; SG = singular; PL = plural.

and/or gender in clitics is subject to regional and, in some cases, personal variability.[6,7]

There is far less variation in the expression of datives in Spanish, although the omission of number agreement on the dative is common, subject to some syntactic restrictions (Bruhn de Garavito 2000). Dative clitic doubling of oblique DPs is very frequent (Bruhn de Garavito 2000; Cuervo 2003; Masullo 1992). Unlike accusative clitic doubling (see below), there is no restriction based on the specificity of the doubled NP (Suñer 1988).

Accusative clitic doubling of a pronoun is obligatory in most varieties of Spanish (5). Clitic doubling of an accusative full DP is less widespread, but it is common in the River Plate region, where the clitic preferred for doubling is the accusative *lo/la* (6), and in the North of Spain, where there is a preference for the dative *le* for both masculine and feminine objects (7) (Bleam 1999, 2001). It is also present in contact varieties of Spanish (Atoche 2001; Lastra 1992; Sánchez 2004b).

(5)  *Yo    *(lo)         vi       a él.*
     I     ACC-M-CL     saw-I    a  PRON-M-SG
     'I saw him.'

(6)  *La$_i$          vi       a Maria$_i$.*
     ACC-F-CL       saw-I    a  María
     'I saw María.'

(7)  *Le$_i$          vi       a Juan$_i$/María$_i$.*
     DAT-CL         saw-I    a  Juan/María
     'I saw Juan/María.'

According to the literature, accusative clitic doubling is only possible when the object carries the features [+specific, +animate], that is, the same class of objects that is differentially object marked. In particular, a doubled direct object cannot refer to a nonspecific element, as shown by the examples in (8) (from Suñer 1988: 396). It has been suggested that this is so because accusative clitics are inherently [+specific]. According to Bleam (1999), the referent must be referentially accessible. Uriagereka (1988, 1995) argues that the [+specific] interpretation of doubled DPs is due to the fact that accusative clitics in Spanish, unlike dative clitics, are definite determiners, occupying the D position. Contact varieties of Spanish also double [−animate] NPs (Atoche 2001; Godenzzi 1991; Sánchez 2004b) among others, but it is not clear whether specificity is involved.

---

[6] These are not recent phenomena; most can be traced back at least as far as the sixteenth century.
[7] There is also some variation in the expression of number, but it is not so great (Harris 1994).

(8) a.  *No oyeron      a   ningún  ladrón.  /  *No lo              oyeron*
        no heard-they  *a*  any      thief   /  *no  ACC-M-CL  heard-they
        *a   ningún  ladrón.*
        *a*  any      thief
        'They did not hear any thief.'

   b.  *La           oían      a Paca/  a la niña /  a la  gata.*
        ACC-F-CL  heard-they  *a* Paca /  *a* the child/  *a* the  cat.
        'They heard Paca / the girl / the cat.'

   c.  *\*La          compramos  esa  novela.* (possible in contact varieties)
        ACC-F-CL  bought-we    that novel-F
        'We bought that novel.'

In the *leísta* dialects of the north of Spain, in contrast to the River Plate Spanish illustrated above, only the dative clitic *le* can be used for doubling direct objects. Bleam (1999, 2001) shows that, in fact, this "dative" *le* doubling of accusative DPs is subject to the same specificity restrictions as accusative *lo/la* doubling, in contrast to dative doubling of an indirect object. As Bleam points out, this fact may lead us to conclude that there are two clitics *le* in the lexicon, one [+specific], that is available to double accusative DPs, and one not. If there is only one dative clitic, we must account for why it can double an accusative. This problem has not been resolved.

Before turning to the focus of the present study, the production of clitics in Andean Spanish, we will briefly review some of the literature on a few of the notable characteristics of contact Spanish.

## 4. *Contact Spanish*

With the exception of the studies of Spanish in contact with Quechua in the Andes, particularly in Peru (de Granda 1999; A. Escobar 1978; A. M. Escobar 2000; Godenzzi 1991; Klee 1990; Klee & Ocampo 1995; Minaya & Luján 1982; Sánchez 1999, 2004a, 2004b), and of Spanish in contact with English in the United States (Montrul 2004; Silva-Corvalán 1986, 1991, 1994), the work on Spanish in contact with other languages in the Americas is sporadic at best. Furthermore, with few exceptions, in most of the literature, examples are presented without information about the frequency of the phenomena. This field also seems to suffer from a lack of communication between scholars and, as a consequence, few seem to have realized the many commonalities these varieties of Spanish share. In most studies, it is either implied or stated that the cause of the change in Spanish is due to contact with the other language, although these contact languages may not belong to related language families. We will briefly mention some of the properties mentioned in the literature.

I. Spanish in contact with Mapudungun, an indigenous language spoken in Argentina and Chile by the Mapuche people (data from Acuña & Menegotto 1996a: 1996b). The informants were monolingual contact-Spanish-speaking adults.

(9) *Lack of gender and number agreement in the noun phrase.*
   a. (Norm: *un guante nuevo*)
      *Una          guante          nuevo.*
      DET-F-SG   glove-M-SG   new-M-SG
      'A new glove'
   b. (Norm: *es mala la gente ahora pues*)
      *Es malo        la          gente          ahora pues.*
      is  bad-M-SG DET-F-SG people-F-SG   now    *pues*
      'Well, the people are bad now.'

(10) *Lack of gender agreement between the referent and a clitic.*
    (Norm: ***la*** *hace pedazos*)
    *El   nene agarra la   foto          y      lo                    hace*
    the baby takes  the photo-F-SG and   ACC-M-SG-CL makes
    *pedazos.*
    pieces
    'The baby grabs the photo and tears it in pieces.'

(11) *Inconsistency in the production of reflexive clitics.*
    (Norm: *el otro* ***se*** *acuerda*)
    *Si  uno no  se     acuerda,   el   otro     acuerda.*
    if  one  no  REFL remembers, the other  ∅    remembers
    'If one doesn't remember, the other remembers.'

II. Spanish in contact with Otomí, a language spoken in Mexico (data from Lastra 1992). The participants were six adult bilingual Spanish/Otomí speakers.

(12) *Lack of gender and number agreement in the noun phrase.*
    (Norm: ***Estas niñas***)
    *Estos          niña*
    these-M-PL  girls-F-SG
    'These girls'

(13) *Inconsistency in the production of reflexive clitics.*
    a. (Norm: *Tú* ***te*** *peinas sola.*)
       Tú           peinas       sola.
       you    ∅    comb-2nd   alone.
       'You comb yourself alone.'

b.  (Norm: *De dónde va a salir …*)
    *De dónde se      va      a    salir      tanto      dinero?*
    from where  REFL  going  to  come out  so much  money
    'Where is so much money going to come from?'

(14)  *Lack of subject-verb agreement.*
      (Norm: *Ellos **compran***)
      Ellos           compra.
      They-3rd-PL     buy-3rd-SG
      'They buy'

(15)  *The doubling of objects by a clitic even when the object does not exhibit the properties of animacy and perhaps specificity. There is often a lack of gender agreement.*
      a.  (Norm: *¡Hasta colcha usamos!*)
          *¡Hasta  colcha            lo                   usamo!*
          Even    coverlet-F-SG  ACC-M-SG-CL   we use
          'We even use a coverlet.'
      b.  (Norm: *te **la** vas …*)
          *Hora ya      quítate                   tu      ropa            porque*
          now  already  take-off-you-REFL  your  clothing-F-SG  because
          *te        lo                    vas           a    ensuciar.*
          REFL  ACC-M-SG-CL   going-you   to  dirty
          'Now take off your clothes because you are going to get them dirty.'

III.  Spanish in contact with Nahuatl, a language spoken in Mexico (not related to Otomí) (data from Lastra 1992). The participants were five adult bilingual speakers and a group of Spanish-dominant children.

(16)  *Lack of gender and number agreement in the noun phrase.*
      (Norm: *tortillas aunque **martajaditas***)
      *tortillas           aunque     martajaditos.*
      tortillas-F-PL  although  mashed-M-PL
      'tortillas, but mashed'

(17)  *Lack of subject-verb agreement.*
      (Norm: *Las tortillas se le **quemaron***)
      *Las   tortillas        se     le         quemó.*
      the   tortillas-F-PL  REFL  DAT-CL  burned-3rd-SG
      'The tortillas got burned on him.'

(18)  *The doubling of objects by a clitic even when the object does not exhibit the properties of specificity and animacy. There is often a lack of gender agreement.*

    a.  (Norm: *Yo nunca he visto nada*)

        *Yo    nunca  lo                he     visto   nada.*
        I     never  ACC-M-SG-CL  have-I  seen   nothing
        'I have never seen anything.'

    b.  (Norm: *La tortilla más **quemada la** echa en medio de **las** demás.*)

        *La    tortilla        más   quemado        lo             echa*
        the  tortilla-F-SG  most  burned-M-SG  ACC-M-SG-CL  throw
        *en   medio  de   los           demás.*
        in   middle  of   DET-M-PL  rest
        'The most burned tortilla you throw (it) in with the others.'

IV.  Spanish in contact with Quechua, language spoken in Peru, Bolivia and Ecuador (data from several authors).

(19)  *Lack of gender and number agreement in the noun phrase.*
     (Norm: ***Nuestra** patria **peruana***)
     *Nuestro     patria      peruano*
     our-M-SG  land-F-SG  Peruvian-M-SG
     'Our Peruvian land'                       (Godenzzi 1991)

(20)  *Lack of subject-verb agreement.*
     (Norm: *que ellos **hablen** su quechua pues*)
     *Es  necesario  que   ellos        hable         su     quechua  pues*
     is  necessary  that   they-PL  speak-3rd-SG  their  Quechua  *pues*
     'It is necessary that they speak their Quechua, so.'  (A.M. Escobar 2000)

(21)  *The doubling of objects by a clitic even when the object does not exhibit the properties of specificity and animacy. There is often a lack of gender agreement.*
     (Norm: *mi mamá me compró dos truzas; me **las** compró*)
     *Mi  mamá  me       lo compró     dos   truzas.*
     my  mother  DAT-1$^{st}$  ACC-M-SG-CL  two  shorts-F-PL
     'My mother bought me two boxer shorts.'       (Pozzi-Escot 1998)

This paper will focus on the production of objects by Spanish speakers in Peru. At least since the 1970s, scholars have remarked that speakers of Andean Spanish, the product of contact between Spanish and Quechua, tend to exhibit a certain variability when expressing direct objects (Atoche 2001; A. M. Escobar 2000; Sánchez 2004a; 2004b). The most in-depth study of this phenomenon is by Sánchez (2004b). She studied three groups of children, two of which were relatively bilingual and one which was made up of speakers from a region of contact who did not speak Quechua. She compared the expression of direct objects in two tasks: a story-telling task, using the Frog picture books (Mayer 1969), and a picture identification task. Based on the fact that Quechua does not have clitics and objects can be left unexpressed, she expected to find a certain degree of object omissions among the bilingual children. In fact, the bilingual children did produce a significantly higher proportion of null pronouns than the monolingual children (6.7% and 5.2% for the bilingual children; 1.6% for the monolinguals). She also expected to find clitic doubling of a direct object DP. In this case, the numbers were quite similar across the three groups (18.5% and 25.4% for the bilinguals, 26.3% for the monolinguals). An analysis of the relation between antecedents and clitic-doubled objects led her to conclude that the clitic-doubled objects serve to recover topics in the course of the dialogue. Sánchez sees in these results evidence for both transfer and convergence between Quechua and Spanish.

Sánchez also found a great deal of variability in the gender of the clitic. In the case of masculine antecedents, there is in general no problem, but when the antecedent is feminine "the monolingual group has a similar distribution for *lo*, *la*, and *le*, as if the use were random, and the bilinguals, to the extent that they had clitics, used *le*" (Sánchez 2004b: 203). In a footnote, she wonders whether the monolinguals' results should be attributed to errors in performance. It is not clear why only the divergence from the norm by monolinguals should be attributed to performance, when all the participants completed the same performance-based task.

In the next section, we will examine the present study. As we will show, the results are very similar to those found by Sánchez (2004b), although the subjects are adult monolingual speakers of Spanish, not children.

## 5. *Description of the experiment*

Research was carried out in the town of Santa Rosa de Ocopa, which lies close to the city of Huancayo, in the department of Junín (Peru). The population is around 2,400 inhabitants.

The participants were 14 speakers of Spanish, whose ages ranged between 16 and 34 years. They had all finished or were about to finish high school in Spanish at the time of testing. Three had attended technical school as well. They all stated that they only spoke Spanish, with maybe a few words of Quechua. In fact, in most cases the parents did not speak Quechua either, but the grandparents did.

The tasks were very similar to those used in other studies of this type, using the picture book Frog stories (Mayer 1969). The speakers were asked to look at the picture book for about 10 minutes, and then to tell the story, using the pictures as a guide. Each participant told two of these stories, and in between the two stories they were asked to tell a legend or strange experience. The total interview lasted around an hour. It was recorded and transcribed.

Besides telling stories, the participants were asked to answer some questions based on pictures. Finally, they carried out an oral grammaticality judgment task, which we will not be reporting on here (see Atoche 2001 for the details).

Before turning to the results, we should explain that there were certain limitations on the story-telling task. The story revolves around a boy and some animals, including a dog, a turtle and two frogs. They all appear to live together and to be friends. The stories tell of their adventures. Most of the direct objects elicited refer to the child and his animals and, as a consequence, a higher proportion of [+specific] and [+animate] objects was produced, although there were enough objects of other types to make a meaningful comparison.

The second limitation on the task is that most of the characters in the story are masculine. The turtle, a minor character, is feminine in Spanish (*la tortuga*), although not all speakers used this word. The main characters were a boy and two frogs. Referring to the character of the frog, five of the participants used the word *rana*, which is feminine, but the remaining nine used the word *sapo* ('toad'), which is masculine; as a result, the opportunity for finding discrepancies in gender was somewhat reduced. We will see, however, that variability with gender was found.

In the next sections, we will examine the production of indirect objects, the use of direct object clitics replacing objects, clitic-doubled accusative objects, and objects that are not clitic-doubled.

## 6. *Results*

### 6.1 *Indirect objects*

Recall that the doubling of indirect object DPs is very common in all dialects of Spanish. The 14 participants produced a total of 143 indirect objects, of which 4 did not include a clitic. The breakdown of production of dative clitics is shown in Table 2.

| Clitics | | Clitic-doubled indirect object DPs | |
|---|---|---|---|
| +animate referent | −animate referent | +animate DP | −animate DP |
| 123 (88.5%) | 1 (0.7%) | 13 (9.4%) | 2 (1.4%) |

Table 2. *Production of indirect object clitics*

The third-person clitic used to express indirect objects was the standard *le*, as shown in example (22) for doubled DPs and (23) for non-doubling clitics. The only anomaly was lexical in nature.[8] In Spanish the verb 'to hit' and the

---

[8] There were two other problematic sentences. In one, the referent of the clitic was impossible to determine (i), and in the other, the speaker seems to have self-corrected (ii):
(i)   *Lo muerde la nariz al niño*. ("He bites the nose to the child.")

verb 'to stick' or 'glue' are the same, *pegar*. Spanish speakers generally express 'hit' with the dative, and 'glue' with the accusative.[9] Participant 9 produced the meaning 'to hit' with the accusative twice (24). Sentence (25) illustrates one of the sentences in which the indirect object DP is not doubled.

(22) a. *En eso   le            dijo    que  no  hiciera   bulla  al  perro.*
        in  that  DAT-SG-CL  told-he  that  no   make-he   noise  *a*   the dog
        'At that moment, he told the dog not to make noise." (Participant 4)

    b. *El  niño  le            pide      silencio  al   perro.*
        the  boy  DAT-SG-CL  asks-he  silence   *a*    the dog
        'The boy asks the dog for silence.'        (Participant 2)

(23) a. *... sale            una comadreja que  le da un       mordisco*
        ... comes-out-she a    weasel     that  DAT-SG-CL  gives-she
        *en   la    nariz.*
        a    bite   on the nose
        'A weasel comes out and gives him a bite on the nose.'(Participant 1)

    b. *... y   en castigo      le            dicen    que  ya    no*
        ... and as  punishment  DAT-SG-CL  tell-they  that  now   no
        *irán         con   ellas.*
        go-they     with  PRON-F-PL
        '... and as punishment they tell her that they will not go with them.'
        (Participant 12)

(24) *Entonces  el   sapo  lo            pega,  lo            pega.*
      then          the  toad  ACC-M-SG-CL  hits-he, ACC-M-SG-CL  hits-he
      'Then the toad hits him, hits him.'      (Participant 9)

(25) *Y    el    Paco dice        al   perro ...*
      and  the   Paco say-3rd-pres  *a*   the dog ...
      'And Paco says to the dog ...'      (Participant 11)

To summarize, the number of instances in which the production of indirect objects diverged from the norm was almost nil, and the clitic used was exclusively the dative *le*.

6.2 *Direct objects*
The speakers produced 583 direct objects including clitics, clitic-doubled DPs and non-doubled DPs, as shown in Table 3.[10]

---

(ii) *Y la tortuga lo avisó, le avisó y se enojó con ella.*
    ("The turtle advised him-ACC, advised him-DAT and got angry at her.")
[9] Animacy does not make a difference in interpretation in this case. 'To hit a table' would still be expressed with the dative *le*.
[10] Fewer than 10 null objects were found, and in most instances they appeared to the authors to be standard omissions, so null objects will not be considered in this paper.

| Clitics | Clitic-doubled DPs | DPs |
|---|---|---|
| 206 (35.5%) | 113 (19.38%) | 264 (45.28%) |

Table 3. *Distribution of overt direct objects.*

As mentioned before, it is important to consider animacy and specificity when examining the use of clitics, not only because these factors may affect the choice of clitic but also because they relate to the possibility of accusative object doubling (Bleam 1999; Suñer 1988). Table 4 shows the distribution of direct objects with respect to animacy.

| | Clitics | Clitic-doubled DPs | DPs |
|---|---|---|---|
| [+animate] | 191 (92.71%) | 107 (94.7%) | 115 (43.56%) |
| [−animate] | 15 (7.29%) | 6 (5.3%) | 149 (56.44%) |

Table 4. *Distribution of direct objects in terms of animacy*

Table 4 shows that, overwhelmingly, clitics were used to refer to animate objects, both when the clitic replaced the object (26) and when the clitic doubled the object (27). Non-doubled full DPs were used almost equally to refer to animate (28a) and inanimate objects (28b), and it is noticeable that inanimate objects were almost never doubled.

(26)   *Ven      que la ranita   no estaba en la  botella, pe- y     empiezan*
       see-they that the frog    no was    in the bottle,  pe,  and begin-they
       *a    buscarlo.*
       *a*   search-ACC-M-SG-CL
       'They see that the little frog was not in the bottle and they begin to
       search for him.'                                              (Participant 1)

(27) a. *El   niño lo              insulta    al  sapo     mayor.*
        the  boy  ACC-M-SG-CL insults-he *a*  the toad   older
        'The boy insults the older toad.'                            (Participant 3)

     b. *... porque le             había    empujado     a  la  otra ranita.*
        ... because DAT-SG-CL had-she pushed-PART *a*  the other frog
        '... because she had pushed the other little frog.'          (Participant 7)

(28) a. *Y   el  sapo mayor, como le          dije,  odia    al   sapito.*
        and the toad older,  as   DAT-CL told-I, hates-he *a*  the frog
        *más      chiquito*
        more     small
        'And the older frog, as I told you, hates the smaller frog.'
                                                                     (Participant 4)

     b. *Como  si  estuviese jalando un   palo.*
        as    if  were-it   pulling a    stick
        'As if it were pulling a stick.'                             (Participant 3)

Regarding specificity, 100% of objects that included a clitic referred to a specific object.[11] In fact, with one exception, all of the clitic-doubled DPs were marked with personal *a*. The most common source of indefinite [+animate] objects was the introduction of the story, which often began with the verb *tener* 'to have', which, as we have seen, generally does not trigger differential object marking. Table 5 shows the distribution of the non-doubled DPs with respect to specificity. Both specific and nonspecific objects appear without a clitic to a similar extent. Examples of non-doubled specific and nonspecific objects are given in (29).

| Specific | Nonspecific |
| --- | --- |
| 149 (56.44%) | 115 (43.56%) |

Table 5. *Distribution of non-doubled DPs regarding specificity*[12]

(29) a. *Van    a   cruzar  el   río   en   una  balsa.*
go-they  to  cross   the  river in   a    raft
'They are going to cross the river in a raft.'        (Participant 9)

   b. *El   niño tenía   unos  animales.*
the  boy  had     some  animals
'The boy had some animals.'                          (Participant 4)

To summarize, non-doubled DPs were produced equally often for animate and inanimate objects, and for specific and nonspecific ones. On the other hand, clitics and clitic-doubled objects referred almost exclusively to [+animate, +specific] objects. In spite of the limitations imposed by the structure of the story task that was used, it seems clear that clitics are associated with these features in the production of this group of speakers. However, the decision of when to double an object DP was subject to a great deal of variability. It was impossible to determine whether doubling obeyed pragmatic constraints, as suggested by Sánchez (2004b). Examples of intrasubject variability are shown in (30) and (31). Participant 7, in example (31a) fails to double the direct object, while in (32b), with the very same verb, the same participant doubles it with the dative clitic.

---

[11] There were three cases in which the clitic may have doubled a sentential object, but these were not included in the count because the interpretation was not clear.
[12] It is simple coincidence that the figures in Table 5 are identical to those in the last column of Table 4, which summarizes the distribution according to animacy. In total there were 82 non doubled DPs that were both [+animate] and [+specific].

(30)  Participant 1

    a.   ... *y*   *la*   *tortuga*  *llevaba*  *en*   *sus*  *espaldas* *a*  *la*  *ranita* *y* ...
        ... and the turtle    carried  on  her back    *a* the frog   and ...
        *a*   *las*  *dos*  *ranas.* (Not doubled)
        *a*   the  two  frogs.
        'And the turtle carried the frog ... the two frogs on her back.'

    b.   *Y*  *con*  *el*  *rencor* *la*   *rana logra*        *atacarla*
        and with the anger  the  frog  manages to   attack-ACC-F-SG-CL
        *a*  *la*   *pequeña*   *rana.* (Doubled)
        *a*   the  small       frog
        'And angrily, the frog manages to attack the small frog.'

    c.   ... *y*  *luego salen*    *al*  *campo*     *a*  *buscarle*
        ... and then  leave-they *a*   the countryside *a*  look-for-DAT-SG-CL
        *a*   *la*   *ranita.* (Doubled)
        *a*   the  frog
        '... and then they go out to the countryside to look for the little frog.'

    d.   ... *y*  *detrás de ese tronco hallan*    *al*  *sapo*   *con*  *su*  *pareja.*
        ... and behind of that trunk  find-they *a*   the toad with his friend
                                                 (Not doubled)
        '... and behind the trunk they find the toad with his friend.'

(31)  Participant 7

    a.   *Entonces, los dos preocupados salieron*  *a*  *buscar*  *a*  *la*  *ranita.*
        then,     the two worried      went-out *a*  look-for *a*  the frog
                                                   (Not doubled)
        'Then, worried, the two went out to look for the little frog.'

    b.   *Entonces el niñito con el perro seguían*   *y*    *seguían*
        then      the boy  with the dog  continued  and  continued
        *buscándole*          *a*  *la*  *ranita.* (Doubled)
        looking-DAT-SG-CL *a*  the  frog
        'Then the boy and the dog continued and continued looking for the frog.'

We also find a great deal of intersubject variability regarding the rate of doubling, as shown in Table 6.

| Subject # | Doubled DPs | Non-doubled DPs | 100% |
|-----------|-------------|-----------------|------|
| 1 | 10 (41.7%) | 14 (58.3%) | 24 |
| 2 | 9 (45%) | 11 (55%) | 20 |
| 3 | 9 (40.91%) | 13 (59.09%) | 22 |
| 4 | 11 (45.83%) | 13 (54.17%) | 24 |
| 5 | 11 (37.93%) | 18 (62.07%) | 29 |
| 6 | 1 (5.26%) | 18 (94.74%) | 19 |
| 7 | 17 (37.78%) | 28 (62.22%) | 45 |
| 8 | 10 (66.67%) | 5 (33.33%) | 15 |
| 9 | 12 (46.15%) | 14 (53.85%) | 26 |
| 10 | 1 (8.33%) | 11 (91.67%) | 12 |
| 11 | 13 (22.41%) | 45 (77.59%) | 58 |
| 12 | 2 (10%) | 18 (90%) | 20 |
| 13 | 4 (8.51%) | 43 (91.49%) | 47 |
| 14 | 3 (18.75%) | 13 (81.25%) | 16 |
| Totals | 113 | 264 | 377 |

Table 6. *Individual distribution of doubled and non-doubled DPs*

As Table 6 shows, although many of the speakers produced similar numbers of doubled and non-doubled objects, six participants (participants 6, 10, 11, 12, 13 and 14) show a strong preference for non-doubled DPs.

The variability in the use of object doubling was also present in the case of doubling of a pronoun, which is obligatory in standard Spanish. One of the tasks administered to the speakers involved a series of 12 questions relating to pictures, also based on the Frog stories. This produced a total of 167 sentences. The results are shown in Table 7.

| DPs | Clitics | Doubled DPs | Doubled pronouns | *Pronouns | Null objects | Total |
|-----|---------|-------------|------------------|-----------|--------------|-------|
| 60 | 35 | 12 | 23 | 23 | 14 | **167** |

Table 7. *Distribution of types of responses to questions*

The results include a number of null objects, which have been the subject of much research (Sánchez 2004b). We will not focus on this characteristic of Andean Spanish (see footnote 10). What is of interest to us here is the production of clitic-doubled strong pronouns and strong pronouns that were not doubled, the latter being unacceptable in the norm. Again, we find variability in the production of doubling, not only between subjects but also in the speech of the same subject, as the examples in (32) and (33) show.

(32) Participant 11
    a. *El sapo no mordió a ella.* (Ungrammatical according to the norm)
       the toad no bit    *a* PRON-3rd-SG
       'The toad did not bite her.'

    b. *Sí,  el  sapo lo*            *pateó  a  él.*
       yes, the toad  ACC-M-SG-CL  kicked  *a*  PRON-3rd-SG
       'Yes, the toad kicked him.'

(33)  Participant 7
    a. *Sí,  el  sapito lo*         *miró  a  él.*
       yes, the toad  ACC-M-SG-CL  looked-at  *a*  PRON-M-SG
       'Yes, the toad looked at him.'
    b. *Sí,  el  sapo pateó  a  él.* (Ungrammatical according to the norm)
       yes, the toad  kicked  *a*  PRON-M-SG
       'Yes, the toad kicked him.'

We will turn now to the problem of the choice of clitic. As we have mentioned, there is dialect variation in Spanish regarding the choice of *le* or *lo* for the masculine accusative, and we find both in this study. We will show that these participants also exhibited inconsistent gender agreement between the clitic and its referent.

In all, 319 clitics were produced. Table 8 shows their distribution according to the clitic used.

| | Masculine | | | Feminine | | | Totals |
|---|---|---|---|---|---|---|---|
| | *le* | *lo* | *\*la* | *\*le* | *\*lo* | *la* | |
| clitics | 36 | 114 | 6 | 16 | 8 | 26 | 206 |
| | (23.07%) | (73.08%) | (3.85%) | (32%) | (16%) | (52%) | |
| clitics + DPs | 30 | 51 | 0 | 19 | 8 | 5 | 113 |
| | (37.04%) | (62.96%) | 0% | (59.37%) | (25%) | (15.63%) | |
| Totals | 66 | 165 | 6 | 35 | 16 | 31 | 319 |

Table 8. *Distribution according to the clitic used*

As can be seen, the use of masculine clitics by the participants is generally grammatical according to the Spanish norm, that is, the clitic agrees with its referent, both in the clitic-doubled objects and in the case of clitics that replace the object DP. The exceptions were six instances of the feminine clitic used to refer to a masculine referent, and all of these were produced by one informant (Participant 6), and only when the clitic stood alone, not in the clitic-doubled constructions. There is a certain variation between the use of *le* and *lo*, although there is a preference for *lo*, particularly in the case of non-doubling clitics. Examples of masculine referents are given in (34).

(34) Participant 8

  a. ... *lo*                *buscaron, lo*              *buscaron,*
     ... ACC-M-SG-CL looked-for, ACC-M-SG-CL looked-for,
     *lo*                 *llamaron    y    no    estaba.*
     ACC-M-SG-CL called       and   no   was
     '... they looked for him, they looked for him, they called him and he
     wasn't there.'

  b. *Se    pasaron buscándole                    por los  bosques ...*
     REFL spent     looking-for-DAT-SG-CL by    the   woods
     'They spent their time looking for him in the woods.'

The production of clitics that refer to feminine objects is another story altogether. It is not the case that the speakers were not aware of the gender of the
noun itself, as the determiner always agreed with the noun. However, as we
see, the participants produced a masculine clitic, either *le* or *lo*, 48% of the
time when the clitic stood for a feminine referent, and a very surprising 84% of
the time in the case of clitic-doubled DPs. What is more surprising is that some
speakers varied the clitics used to refer to the very same referent. In examples
(35) and (36) below, the referent is always the feminine noun *ranita*, 'the little
frog.'

(35) Participant 1

  a. *La rana logra     atacarla            a   la   pequeña rana.*
     the frog manages attack-ACC-F-SG-CL *a* the little      frog-**F**
     'The frog manages to attack the little frog.'

  b. ... *de nuevo procedió empujándolo         a   la   ranita.*
     ... again       proceeded pushing-ACC-**M**-SG *a*  the  frog-**F**
     '... again she proceeded to push the little frog.'

  c. ... *lo                 dejan a  la   rana.*
     ... ACC-**M**-SG-CL leave *a* the  frog-**F**
     '... they leave the frog behind.'

  d. *Salen al   campo       a  buscarle          a   la   ranita.*
     leave *a*  the countryside *a* look-for-**DAT**-SG-CL *a*  the  frog-**F**
     'They leave for the countryside to look for the little frog.'

(36) Participant 7

  a. *La          empieza a   buscar.*
     ACC-**F**-SG-CL begins  *a*  look-for
     'He starts to look for her.'

  b. *Le            buscan  y   no  le             encuentran.*
     **DAT**-SG-CL look-for and  no  **DAT**-SG-CL find
     'They look for her and don't find her.'

    c.    *... y* ***lo***                *empiezan*    *a*    *buscar.*
           ... and ACC-**M**-SG-CL begin      to   look-for
           '... and they begin to look for him.'

    d.    *Se*       *fueron al campo*       *a*    *buscarla.*
           REFL   go *a*    the countryside *a*    look-for-ACC-**F**-SG-CL
           'They went off to the countryside to look for her.'

    e.    *Y*    *mientras tanto el perrito* ***le***            *buscaba debajo*    *de*
           and meantime      the dog    **DAT**-SG-CL look-for under    the
           *las rocas, debajo de las piedras* ***le***            *buscaba ...*
           rocks,    under    the   stones    **DAT**-SG-CL looked-for
           'And meantime the dog looked for her under the rocks, under the
           stones he looked for her.'

    f.    *... y* ***le***            *encuentran bien feliz*    *a la ranita.*
           ... and **DAT**-SG-CL find       well happy *a*   the little frog-**F**
           '... and they find the little frog very happy.'

    g.    ***Lo***                 *encontraron a la ranita.*
           ACC-**M**-SG-CL   found       *a*    the frog-**F**
           'They found the frog.'

The figures presented in Table 8 and the examples given in (35) and (36), besides many of the other examples used in this paper, show that the monolingual Spanish-speaking adults interviewed here exhibit a great deal of variability, particularly in the choice of gender on the clitic. In the next section, we will discuss these results.

## 7. *Discussion and conclusions*

In the literature, arguments for a general or particular deficit in the grammatical representation of adult L2 learners have often been based on the assumption that variability in the production of agreement morphology is never found in the speech of L1 speakers and therefore this kind of problem requires an explanation specific to L2 learners. This paper has shown that, in cases of language contact, this type of variability may actually be the norm rather than the exception. We focused on the production of monolingual speakers of Spanish who were raised in a Quechua-speaking environment, although they did not acquire this language. In particular, we looked at their production of clitics.

We have shown the presence of variability both between speakers and in the speech of individuals. We find variability in the frequency of doubling of DPs by a clitic, in the choice of clitic—dative or accusative—and in the expression of gender agreement between the clitic and its referent.[13] The degree

---

[13] We did not examine number agreement because there were not enough data, but in the two or three examples of clitic-doubled objects where the referent was plural, the clitic never agreed in number.

of variation is reminiscent of Patty, Lardiere's well-known subject (see Section 2). In particular, the third type of variation, lack of gender agreement, is generally associated with second language learners (Franceschina 2001; Hawkins 1998a, 1998b; Hawkins & Franceschina 2004).

Like second language learners, these speakers use the masculine form as the default, although, again as has been found for L2 speakers, one participant consistently used the feminine to refer to masculine objects. As with L2 speakers, the default is not used 100% of the time but alternates with the correct production of the clitic. Harris (1991) has proposed that the masculine is the default in Spanish, that is, items are unmarked for masculine gender in the mental lexicon. We may extend to clitics the proposals made by White et al. (2004) for determiner and adjective agreement. Appealing to distributed morphology (Halle & Marantz 1993), they propose that, assuming late insertion of lexical items in the syntax, when a feminine noun is inserted into a feminine DP, there is no clash in agreement between it and an unmarked (masculine) element such as a determiner or a clitic. However, if a masculine noun is inserted into a masculine DP, there would be a clash with any [+feminine] elements (see White, Valenzuela, Kozlowska-Macgregor and Leung 2004: 129).

We must mention, however, an important difference between these monolinguals and second language learners. We did not find any unexpected variation in the production of determiners, which almost always agreed with the noun.[14] What this tells us is a matter for future research.

Regarding the choice of clitic (accusative or dative), and clitic doubling of the object, we have shown that the data reported on here are not in free variation, but rather are constrained by principles of grammar. In all cases, clitic doubling (and the use of clitics in general) was applied to [+specific] objects, and very few examples of inanimate doubled objects were found, which is consistent with the features associated with object clitics in Spanish (Suñer 1989; Uriagereka 1995). The question of specificity in this dialect has not been addressed, as far as we know. The results regarding animacy are not consistent with the literature that has shown that Andean Spanish exhibits clitic doubling of inanimate objects (Atoche 2001; Sánchez 2004b).

The variability found in the doubling of pronouns was somewhat unexpected. Recall that doubling of pronouns in object position (*lo vi a él* 'I him-CL saw him-PRON') is obligatory in most standards of Spanish. However, for these speakers, doubling of a pronoun appears to be as optional as doubling of a DP. The representation of Spanish pronouns in this variety of Spanish must include strong features that are not present in the other grammars of Spanish.

---

[14] There were not enough adjectives in the data to permit any comparisons.

Either doubling or not doubling then becomes a possibility, perhaps based on pragmatic reasons.

We have presented our data to show there is no support for positing a fundamental difference between L2 grammars and L1 grammars based on variability in the production of morphology. It could be argued, however, that this is indeed the case, not because functional categories are unimpaired either in L2 acquisition or in contact varieties, but because all grammars are fundamentally variable (Tarone 2002). Our data do not support this position. We provided evidence that the production of clitics was constrained by the features associated with clitics in Spanish, and that, in the case of gender, divergence from the norm was not random, as would be expected if no grammatical principles were at work.

In conclusion, this paper shows that, if we want to understand language in general and second languages in particular, we should focus not only on the grammar of bilinguals, which has recently received some attention within the generative framework, but also of monolinguals, particularly of monolinguals whose language is the result of contact. We make many assumptions, including the assumption that variability is a symptom of an underlying deficit. We often also assume that divergence from the norm is due to the substratum language. However, as we have shown (Section 4), there is reason to believe that phenomena like those presented here are far more widespread than we have believed up to now, encompassing regions as far apart and diverse as Argentina, Chile, Mexico, Peru, and the Basque country, to name a few. It is true that in most cases grammatical gender does not exist in the contact language, but we wonder whether this is explanation enough. Bruhn de Garavito and White (2002) have shown that the production of gender by francophone learners, whose language exhibits gender, is similar to that of English speakers. Francophones may have an advantage in the initial stage of acquisition but Anglophones eventually catch up (White, Valenzuela, Kozlowska-Macgregor and Leung 2004). In language contact situations it may be that speakers have no interest in "catching up." Rather, certain possibilities latent in the structure of Spanish are exploited. Thus, Spanish is the guilty party, not Quechua.

## References

Acuña, M.L. and A.C. Menegotto. 1992. Dativo sin *a* y verbos pronominales sin *se*: rasgos dialectales del español de la zona mapuche. In *Lenguas Indígenas de Argentina 1492–1992*, E. H. Martín and A. Pérez Diez (eds.), 9-17. San Juan: Editorial Fundación Universidad Nacional de San Juan.

Acuña, M.L. and A.C. Menegotto. 1996. El contacto lingüístico español/mapuche en la Argentina. *Signo y Seña* 6: 235–274.

Alarcos Llorach, E. 1994. *Gramática de la Lengua Española*. Madrid: Espasa Calpe.

Atoche, C. 2001. Lenguas en contacto: el caso del español andino. M.A. thesis, University of Western Ontario.

Bleam, T.M. 1999. Leísta Spanish and the Syntax of Clitic Doubling. Ph.D. dissertation, University of Delaware.

Bleam, T.M. 2001. Properties of the double object construction in Spanish. In *A Romance Perspective in Language Knowledge and Use*, R. Núñez-Cedeño, L. López and R. Canero (eds.), 215–234. Amsterdam: John Benjamins.

Bley-Vroman, R. 1989. What is the logical problem of foreign language learning? In *Linguistic Perspectives on Second Language Acquisition*. S. Gass and J. Schachter (eds.), 41–68. Cambridge: Cambridge University Press.

Bley-Vroman, R. 1990. The logical problem of foreign language learning. *Linguistic Analysis* 20: 3–49.

Bley-Vroman, R. 1996. Conservative pattern accumulation in foreign language learning. Paper presented at EUROSLA 6, Nijmegen.

Bley-Vroman, R. 1997. Features and patterns of foreign language learning. Paper presented at SLRF, Michigan State University.

Bruhn de Garavito, J. 2000. The Syntax of Spanish Multifunctional Clitics and Near-Native Competence. Ph.D. dissertation, McGill University.

Bruhn de Garavito, J. and L. White. 2002. L2 acquisition of Spanish DPs: The status of grammatical features. In *The Acquisition of Spanish Morphosyntax: The L1/L2 Connection,* A. T. Pérez-Leroux and J. Liceras (eds.), 151–176. Dordrecht: Kluwer.

Bullock, B.E. and A.J. Toribio. 2004. Introduction: Convergence as an emergent property in bilingual speech. *Bilingualism: Language and Cognition* 7: 91–93.

Chomsky, N. 1995. *The Minimalist Program*. Cambridge, MA: MIT Press.

Clahsen, H. and P. Muysken. 1986. The availability of UG to adult and child learners: a study of the acquisition of German word order. *Second Language Research* 2: 93–119.

Cuervo, M.C. 2003. Datives at Large. Ph.D. dissertation, MIT.

de Granda, G. 1999. *Español y lenguas indoamericanas en Hispanoamérica. Estructuras, situaciones y transferencias*. Valladolid: Secretariado de Publicaciones e Intercambio Científico, Universidad de Valladolid.

Escobar, A. 1978. *Variaciones sociolingüísticas del castellano en el Perú*. Lima: Instituto de Estudios Peruanos.

Escobar, A.M. 2000. *Contacto social y lingüístico. El español en contacto con el quechua en el Perú*. Lima: Fondo Editorial de la Pontificia Universidad Católica del Perú.

Franceschina, F. 2001. Morphological or syntactic deficits in near-native speakers? An assessment of some current proposals. *Second Language Research* 17: 213–247.

Godenzzi, J.C. 1991. Discordancias gramaticales del español andino en Puno. *Lexis* XV: 107–118.

Halle, M. and A. Marantz. 1993. Distributed morphology and the pieces of inflection. In *The View from Building 20*, K. Hale and S. J. Keyser (eds.), 105–119. Cambridge, MA: MIT Press.

Harris, J.W. 1991. The exponence of gender in Spanish. *Linguistic Inquiry* 22: 27–62.

Harris, J.W. 1994. El traslado de pluralidad en los pronombres clíticos del español. Paper presented at Encuentro de lingüística en el noroeste, Mexico.

Harris, J.W. 1995. The morphology of Spanish clitics. In *Evolution and Revolution in Linguistic Theory*, H. Campos and P. Kempchinsky (eds.), 168–197. Washington, DC: Georgetown University Press.

Hawkins, R. 1998a. Explaining the difficulty of gender attribution for speakers of English. Paper presented at European Second Language Association, Paris.

Hawkins, R. 1998b. The inaccessibility of formal features of functional categories in second language acquisition. Paper presented at Pacific Second Language Research Forum, Tokyo.

Hawkins, R. and Y.-h.C. Chan. 1997. The partial availability of Universal Grammar in second language acquisition: The "failed functional features hypothesis". *Second Language Research* 13: 187–226.

Hawkins, R. and F. Franceschina. 2004. Explaining the acquisition and nonacquisition of determiner-noun gender concord in French and Spanish. In *The Acquisition of French in Different Contexts*, J. Paradis and P. Prévost (eds.), 175–205. Amsterdam: John Benjamins.

Heap, D. 2000. Morphological complexity and Spanish object clitic variation. In *Romance Syntax, Semantics and L2 Acquisition: Selected Papers from the XXXth Linguistic Symposium on Romance Languages, Gainesville, Florida, Feb. 2000*, C. R. Wiltshire and J. Camps (eds.), 55–67. Amsterdam: John Benjamins.

Klee, C. 1990. Spanish-Quechua language contact: The clitic pronoun system in Andean Spanish. *Word* 41: 35–46.

Klee, C.A. and A.M. Ocampo. 1995. The expression of past reference in Spanish narratives of Spanish-Quechua bilingual speakers. In *Spanish in Four Continents*, C. Silva-Corvalán (ed.), 52–70. Washington, DC: Georgetown University Press.

Lardiere, D. 1998a. Case and tense in the "fossilized" steady state. *Second Language Research* 14: 1–26.

Lardiere, D. 1998b. Dissociating syntax from morphology in a divergent end-state grammar. *Second Language Research* 14: 359–375.

Lardiere, D. 2003. Second language knowledge of [+/–past] vs. [+/–finite]. In *Proceedings of the 6th Generative Approaches to Second Language Acquisition Conference (GASLA 2002)*, J. M. Liceras, H. Zobl and H. Goodluck (eds.), 176–189. Somerville, MA: Cascadilla Press.

Lastra, Y. 1992. Is there an Indian Spanish? In *Contemporary Research in Romance Linguistics*, J. Amastae, G. Goodall, M. Montalbetti and M. Phinney (eds.), 123–133. Amsterdam, John Benjamins.

Liceras, J.M. and L. Díaz. 1999. Topic-drop versus pro-drop: Null subjects and pronominal subjects in the Spanish L2 of Chinese, English, French, German and Japanese speakers. *Second Language Research* 15: 1–77.

Masullo, P.J. 1992. Incorporation and Case Theory in Spanish. A Crosslinguistic Perspective. Ph.D. dissertation, University of Washington.

Mayer, M. 1969. *Frog: Where Are You?* New York: Pied Piper Books (Penguin).

Meisel, J. 1997. The acquisition of the syntax of negation in French and German: Contrasting first and second language acquisition. *Second Language Research* 13: 227–263.

Minaya, L. and M. Luján. 1982. Un patrón sintáctico híbrido en el habla de los niños bilingües en quechua y español. *Lexis* VI: 271–293.

Montrul, S. 2004. Subject and object expression in Spanish heritage speakers: A case of morpho-syntactic convergence. *Bilingualism: Language and Cognition* 7: 125–142.

Pozzi-Escot, I. 1998. *El multilingüismo en el Perú*. Cuzco: CBC – Centro de Estudios Regionales Andinos Bartolomé de las Casas.

Prévost, P. and L. White. 2000. Missing surface inflection or impairment in second language acquisition? Evidence from tense and agreement. *Second Language Research* 16: 103–133.

Sánchez, L. 1999. D⁰, Agr⁰ features and the direct object pronominal system of Andean Spanish. In *Advances in Hispanic Linguistics*, J. Gutiérrez-Rexach and F. Martínez-Gil (eds.), 530–545. Somerville, MA: Cascadilla Press.

Sánchez, L. 2004a. Functional convergence in the tense, evidentiality and aspectual systems of Quechua Spanish bilinguals. *Bilingualism: Language and Cognition* 7: 147–173.

Sánchez, L. 2004b. *Quechua-Spanish Bilingualism. Interference and Convergence in Functional Categories*. Amsterdam: John Benjamins.

Schwartz, B.D. and R. Sprouse. 1996. L2 cognitive states and the Full Transfer/Full Access model. *Second Language Research* 12: 40–72.

Silva-Corvalán, C. 1986. Bilingualism and language change: The extension of *estar* in Los Angeles Spanish. *Language* 62: 587–608.

Silva-Corvalán, C. 1991. Spanish language attrition in a contact situation with English. In *First Language Attrition*, H. W. Seliger and R. M. Vago (eds.), 151–171. Cambridge: Cambridge University Press.

Silva-Corvalán, C. 1994. *Language Contact and Change: Spanish in Los Angeles*. Oxford: Clarendon Press.

Suñer, M. 1988. The role of agreement in clitic doubled constructions. *Natural Language and Linguistic Theory* 6: 391–434.

Tarone, E. 2002. Frequency effects, noticing, and creativity. *Studies in Second Language Acquisition* 24: 287–296.

Tsimpli, I.-M. and A. Roussou. 1991. Parameter resetting in L2? *University College London Working Papers in Linguistics* 3: 149–169.

Uriagereka, J. 1988. On Government. Ph.D. dissertation, University of Connecticut.

Uriagereka, J. 1995. Aspects of the syntax of clitic placement in Western Romance. *Linguistic Inquiry* 26: 79–124.

White, L. 1989. *Universal Grammar and Second Language Acquisition*. Amsterdam: John Benjamins.

White, L. 2003. *Second Language Acquisition and Universal Grammar*. Cambridge: Cambridge University Press.

White, L., E. Valenzuela, M. Kozlowska-Macgregor and Y.-K. I. Leung. 2004. Gender agreement in nonnative Spanish: Evidence against failed features. *Applied Psycholinguistics* 25: 105–133.

Winford, D. 2003. *An Introduction to Contact Linguistics*. Oxford: Blackwell Publishing.

# L2 ACQUISITION AS A PROCESS OF CREOLIZATION:
## INSIGHTS FROM CHILD AND ADULT CODE-MIXING[*]

J. M. Liceras, C. Martínez, R. Pérez-Tattam and S. Perales
*University of Ottawa*

Raquel Fernández Fuertes
*Universidad de Valladolid*

Language contact which manifests itself as "code-mixing" constitutes a natural ground for investigating possible commonalities and differences between the L2 acquisition and pidginization/creolization processes. In this paper, we analyze spontaneous and experimental functional-lexical DP mixings in order to address the differences and similarities between the mental representation of language in the bilingual child, the bilingual adult and adult non-native language. Drawing a parallel with Pesetsky and Torrego's (2001) proposal concerning the relationship between nominative case (nominative case is a T feature on D) and agreement (phi) (agreement is a D feature on T), we assume that Gender is an N feature on D and Gender Agreement is a D feature on N. This dichotomy allows us to make a number of predictions as to how the native and non-native mental representation of these features determines the directionality of code-switching (which language contributes the functional or the lexical category). We will argue that the comparative priorities for the specification of uninterpretable features in a given pair of languages that are already present in the emergent bilingual grammar are transferred to the adult bilingual grammar but do not show up in the case of the non-native grammar. We attribute this to the fact that adult native speakers do not process and internalize formal abstract features from input in the same way as children do (Liceras 2003). Thus, in the spirit of Bickerton (1984, 1996, 1999), we will argue that adults do not "create" language and, in this respect, adult non-native systems and pidgins may share a number of properties, as initially proposed by Schumann (1978) or Andersen (1983) and recently discussed by DeGraff (1999) and Winford (2003), among others. However, in the case of the pidgin/creole continuum, the non-native system will eventually become a native-like system as it develops into a creole, although due to the special language contact situation, some formal features may only make it into the creole system in cases where contact between the creole and the lexifier persists through several generations.

---

[*] We would like to thank E. Álvarez, S. Muñiz, C. Senn and M. Sikorska for their help with the data collection, as well as the many students from the University of Valladolid and the University of Ottawa who kindly volunteered as subjects for the experimental part of the study. The general issues that we discuss here are related to the joint research program on language development and language contact housed at the Language Acquisition Labs of the University of Ottawa (Canada) and the University of Valladolid (Spain). Previous versions of this paper were presented at the Workshop on Contact Languages, Montreal Dialogues, Université du Québec à Montréal (UQAM), Montreal, August 27–29, 2004, and at the IV Congreso Internacional sobre la Adquisición de las Lenguas del Estado, Universidad de Salamanca, Salamanca, Spain, September 22–24, 2004. We would like to thank the audiences at these conferences for their feedback. We would also like to thank three anonymous reviewers for their useful comments and suggestions. This research was funded by the Spanish Ministry of Science and Technology, Dirección General de Investigación Científica and FEDER (DGICYT #BFF2002-00442), the Faculty of Arts of the University of Ottawa and the Social Sciences and Humanities Research Council of Canada (SSHRC #410-2004-2034).

1. *Introduction*

A large body of researchers shares the assumption that first language (L1) grammars and second language (L2) grammars are both constrained by Universal Grammar (UG), in the latter case via direct access to UG principles and/or via their implementation in the L1 (see Epstein, Flynn & Martohardjono 1996, and commentaries thereon). However, some argue that L1 and L2 acquisition differ with respect to the actual ways in which parameters are set (Liceras, Laguardia, Fernández, Fernández & Díaz 1998; Strozer 1994; Tsimpli & Roussou 1991) or in terms of how the features of functional categories are activated (Beck 1998; Eubank 1996; Hawkins & Chan 1997). For those researchers who do equate the L1 and L2 parameter-setting mechanisms and/or the activation of features (Bruhn de Garavito, forthcoming; Lardiere 1998; Schwartz & Sprouse 1996; Slabakova & Montrul, forthcoming; Sprouse 2004; White 2003, among many others),[1] accounting for the actual differences in the language development and ultimate attainment of L1 and L2 learners requires resorting to transitional L1 interference or to problems in the articulatory-perceptual or semantic-conceptual module. Thus, within the body of researchers who share a mentalist, UG-based view of the nature of the native and the non-native systems, whether differences are accounted for in terms of L1 influence, critical period or age factor effects affecting "narrow" syntax or interfaces, the fact is that not only are these differences acknowledged but also that second language acquisition (L2A) literature has systematically made L1 transfer and the activation of UG principles an intrinsic part of the L2A process. In some cases, metalinguistic abilities or processing mechanisms specific to adult L2 acquisition have been explicitly added as a third fundamental component of the L2A model (Adjémian & Liceras 1982; Liceras 1996, 1998; Sprouse 2004).

Within the field of L2A, there have also been proposals equating the early stages of interlanguage development with the pidginization process (Schumann 1978) and attributing the idiosyncratic linguistic nature of both systems to the specific cognitive and social constraints that characterize these language contact situations. Expanding and elaborating on this proposal, Andersen (1979, 1983) described all four processes (L1A, L2A, pidginization and creolization) as constituting either nativization or denativization, depending on whether growth was characterized as independent (moving away from the L1/L2 or the substratum/superstratum system) or dependent on the external norm (moving towards the L1/L2 or the substratum/superstratum system).

In the case of the creation of pidgin and creole languages, the mentalist, UG-based positions can be described in terms of whether the main role in the

---

[1] Lardiere (forthcoming) argues that the parameter-setting metaphor is too comprehensive to account for the problems that adult L2 learners face when determining how the various features are distributed across the functional categories of a given language, and she suggests that what learners have to figure out is how features are assembled.

process is attributed to language universals, the L1 (substratum language) or the L2 (superstratum or lexifier language), thereby echoing the L2A/L1A relationship debate. In the view of some authors (Bickerton & Givón 1976; DeGraff 2005; Kay & Sankoff 1974), the language universals that are responsible for the development of any natural language are also responsible for the pidginization and creolization process. However, according to Bickerton (1981, 1984), creoles are not only "unique" (they have morphosyntactic characteristics specific to creoles) but, unlike pidgins, they are the result of L1 acquisition (Bickerton 1984).[2] According to Lefebvre and Lumsden (1994), Lefebvre (1996) and Lumsden (1999), the L1 (substratum language) plays the major role in the projection of the pidgin/creole grammar, while the L2 or superstratum language (also known as the lexifier) contributes the lexical resources. Researchers such as Chaudenson (2001) argue that the origin of the creole grammar is not a pidgin but an L2 variety of the superstratum, which gradually diverges from this L2 target via a process of "basilectalization" (Mufwene 1996). There are also compromise positions (DeGraff 1999; Mufwene 1990) which, as in the case of the L2A literature, maintain that the L1, input from the L2, principles of UG and very complex social and/or psychological constraints shape the projection of the creole grammar (see also Cornips & Hulk, this volume).

Researchers who share the mentalist, UG-based view of L1A and L2A, as well as of pidgin and creole formation, agree that all four systems are constrained by UG principles. However, they differ on how to account for the differences and similarities between L1 and L2 acquisition, on the one hand, and the role of the L1 and L2 in the projection of the creole grammar, on the other. In line with Smith and Tsimpli (1995), Strozer (1994), Otero (1996), Liceras (1996) and Hawkins and Chan (1997) for adult L2 acquisition, and Bickerton (1996) for the formation of creole languages, we assume that some sort of critical period or age factor effect, which affects L2 learners' sensitivity to language input, compromises their activation of features in the target grammar (Liceras 2003). In the case of the DP component, for instance, we have argued (Liceras 2003) that while L1 learners of Romance languages produce monosyllabic placeholders that demonstrate how these learners go about encoding the Gender D feature and the Gender Agreement noun feature which has to be activated, L2 learners do not seem to follow a similar path.[3]

---

[2] The "unique" nature of creoles has been challenged by many researchers (i.e., commentary on Bickerton 1984; DeGraff 2005; Plag 1994) and it is difficult to accommodate within a mentalist, UG view of language. While admitting that creoles are UG-constrained, Bickerton (1999) argues that what makes creoles "unique" is their potential to be "pure" representations of the unmarked (default) options of the various parameters.

[3] The placeholders that have been isolated in child L2 data do not seem to have the same status as their apparent equivalents in child L1 data (Liceras 2003); at least, this seems to be the case of the *is* that appears, if not massively then rather systematically, in the L2 English of Spanish and Spanish/Basque children (Fleta 1999; García Mayo, Lázaro & Liceras 2005; Lázaro 2000).

Code-switching constitutes a natural ground for investigating possible commonalities and differences between the L2 acquisition and pidginization/ creolization processes because, in a highly idealized view, creole formation may be seen as a continuum going from a code-switching stage to an internalized diglossia stage along the lines proposed by Kroch (1994) for diachronic change processes, until it reaches the final full-fledged creole stage, where parameters (and feature activation) are set via L1 acquisition. Taking the Relexification Hypothesis (Lefebvre 1998; Lefebvre & Lumsden 1989; Lumsden 1999) as a point of departure, it would be plausible to assume an initial code-switching stage where, building on MacSwan's (2000) assumptions about the bilingual language faculty, the learner's grammar would contain two lexicons, a computational system and a phonological system. However, given the special circumstances of language contact in the pidgin-creole continuum, the two lexicons could initially result in an "unbalanced bilingual grammar" (as in Figure 1). In code-switching communities, access to the two systems is considered to be the basis for native-like competence in both languages. However, most of the literature on creole formation assumes that full access to the L2/lexifier does not exist. This leads us to propose that in the initial stage of pidgin formation, one of the lexicons—the superstrate/L2—might not contain functional categories. The issue is whether the language contact situation in which the pidgin is emerging leads to the spelling-out of functional categories at all and, if so, which L1 functional categories are spelled out.

| Lexicon 1 | Lexicon 2 |
|---|---|
| $LCs_1$ / $FCs_1$ | $LCs_2$ |
| *Computational component* | |
| $PF_1$ | $PF_2$ |

LC = lexical category; FC = functional category; PF = phonological form

Figure 1. *Code-switching (pidgin)*

This period would be followed by an internalized diglossia stage, in which the fact that functional categories from both languages are at work in the speaker's grammar would be reflected in the existence of competing grammars, as in Figure 2.

| Lexicon 1 | Lexicon 2 |
|---|---|
| $LCs_1$ / $FCs_1$.... $fc_1$ | $LCs_2$ / $fc_2$.... $FC_2$ |
| *Computational component* | |
| $PF_{(pidgin)}$ | |

Figure 2. *Diglossia (different stages of pidginization: towards creolization)*

In the initial diglossia stage, spelled-out L1 functional categories (if any) would predominate. However, more contact with the lexifier language could result in a subsequent diglossia stage with more reliance on L2 functional categories. Finally, the full-fledged creole would appear when L1 acquisition entered the picture and the child would project a single grammar "disregarding" the diglossic nature of the primary linguistic data and not necessarily relying on default forms (contra Bickerton 1999). In other words, the monolingual or bilingual acquirer of the L1 creole will regularize (or level out the variability of) the adult diglossic system.[4]

Within the specific type of "language contact" that manifests itself as code-switching, we investigate the characteristics of Determiner + Noun code-mixings produced and/or interpreted by child and adult English-Spanish bilinguals and non-native speakers of English and Spanish, and extrapolate our findings to the characteristics of DPs in the pidgin/creole continuum.

Our chapter is organized as follows: section 2 provides an account of how syntactic theory deals with functional-lexical mixings. In section 3 we follow Pesetsky and Torrego's (2001) "dual" feature-checking mechanism to analyze the status of the Gender features in D + Noun English-Spanish and Spanish-English lexical-functional mixings, paying special attention to the issue of the directionality of the code-switched items (i.e., whether Spanish or English contributes the functional category). In section 4, after discussing the code-switched DP data produced by English-Spanish bilingual children and adults, we present the research questions we attempted to answer in the experimental study described in section 5. In section 6, we provide a succinct overview of the DP in pidgin and creole languages, paying particular attention to creoles with Romance lexifiers, and discuss the implications of our findings with respect to the bilingual and the native and non-native code-mixing patterns for the theories of creole formation. The last section of this chapter is devoted to conclusions and suggestions for further research.

## 2. *Functional-lexical mixings and the theory of grammar*

Some researchers do not consider functional-lexical mixings such as those in (1), which are produced by early bilingual children, to be a grammatical option in adult bilingualism (Belazi, Rubin & Toribio 1994; Di Sciullo, Muysken & Singh 1986; Joshi 1985; Toribio 2001), even though they have been widely attested (Azuma 1993; Jake, Myers-Scotton & Gross 2002; Myers-Scotton 1997; Myers-Scotton & Jake 2001; Poplack 1980).

(1) a. UN rabbit         [Mario 3;5] (Fantini 1985)
   a (masc. sing.)
  b. OTRO book       [Manuela 1;9] (Deuchar CHILDES)[5]
   another (masc. sing.)
  c. UN sheep   [Leo 2;7] (Spradlin, Liceras & Fernández Fuertes 2003)
   a (masc. sing.)

---

[4] We will not try to account for the very complex scenarios that obtain in many language contact situations (i.e., the case of plantation creoles) since we simply want to depict a scenario where L1 (monolingual or bilingual) and L2 contact with a given language input are compared.
[5] MacWhinney, B. 2000. *The CHILDES project: tools for analyzing talk*. Third Edition. Mahwah, NJ: Lawrence Erlbaum Associates.

    d. DAS bateau                    [Ivar 2;00] (Köppe & Meisel 1995)
       the (neuter sing.)
    e. LE man                      [Michael] (Swain & Wesche 1975)
       the (masc. sing.)
    f. UNA bird                     (Lindholm & Padilla 1978)
       (fem. sing.)

In the case of child bilingualism, these types of mixings are rather pervasive (though not abundant). Köppe and Meisel (1995) argue that functional-lexical mixings are possible in child language only before the corresponding functional category is projected or, if we rephrase this in terms of features, before the features for the two language systems have been fully specified.

## 2.1 Code-mixing and feature matching

In order to account for the types of functional-lexical mixings shown in (1), we have to assume that the realization (instantiation) of the computational system accesses the lexicons of both languages. Therefore, the bilingual child will have to specify the array of features that give form to the functional categories in each language so that the operations MERGE, AGREE and MOVE converge. It follows that the choices and code-mixing patterns that the emergent bilingual systems display may provide us with information about the features that are activated and how this is accomplished, thus constituting a reflection of how language is represented in the mind of the bilingual child. In the case of the adult bilingual systems, the code-mixing choices and patterns should also respect the constraints imposed by the computational system in that MERGE, AGREE and MOVE should not violate any checking requirements.

It has been argued that a basic conflict in the requirements of the two grammars is responsible for ungrammaticality in adult code-switching (Belazi et al. 1994; Di Sciullo et al. 1986; Poplack 1980; Woolford 1983, 1984). Along these lines, MacSwan (2000) adopts Chomsky's (1995) stipulation that features cannot "mismatch" if the derivation is to converge, and accounts for the (un)grammaticality of the Spanish-Nahuatl code-mixing examples in (2) and (3) on the basis of a mismatch in the phi-features (person and gender) of the Spanish versus the Nahuatl pronominal systems (examples from MacSwan 2000: 49)[6].

---

[6]The U which appear on the trees besides some of the categories stands for 'unvalued'. The abreviations below the Nahuatl examples should be interpreted as follows:

1S = first person subject agreement (unspecified for number)
2S = second person subject agreement (unspecified for number)
3Os = third person singular object agreement
3S = third person subject agreement (unspecified for number)
FUT = future tense
NSF = noun suffix (sometimes called absolute)
PL = plural marking (on nouns or verbs)
SING= singular

(2) a.  *Yo *nikoas*              *tlakemetl*
        yo    ni-k-koa-s          tlake-me-tl
        I     1S-3Os-buy-FUT garment-PL-NSF
        'I will buy clothes.'
    b.  *Tú      *tikoas*              *tlakemetl*
        tú          ti-k-koa-s          tlake-me-tl
        you/SING 2S-3Os-buy-FUT garment-PL-NSF
        'You will buy clothes.'

(3) a.  Él *kikoas*              *tlakemetl*
        él    ø-ki-koa-s          tlak-eme-tl
        he  3S-3Os-buy-FUT   garment-PL-NSF
        'He will buy clothes.'
    b.  Ella *kikoas*              *tlakemetl*
        ella   ø-ki-koa-s          tlake-me-tl
        she   3S-3Os-buy-FUT garment-PL-NSF
        'She will buy clothes.'

Sentences (2a) and (2b) are ungrammatical because the D phi-features of the Spanish pronoun do not match the D phi-features borne by T in the first and second persons of the Nahuatl verb, as shown in (4a). In the case of (3a) and (3b), there is no mismatch because no D phi-features are borne by T on the third person of the Nahuatl verb, as in (4b).

(4) a.

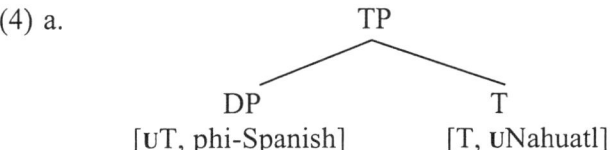

b.

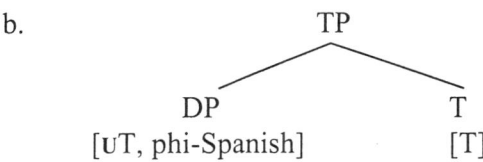

    This implies that not all instances of functional-lexical mixing are necessarily ungrammatical in the adult bilingual grammar and that we should be able to account for the functional-lexical mixings involving a determiner and a noun attested in the adult bilingual data in (5).

(5) a.  SE ***hombre*** *kikoas*                *se kalli*          (MacSwan 2000)
        se    hombre  0-ki-koa-s          se kalli
        a     man      3S-3Os-buy-FUT a   house
        'A man will buy a house.'

b. EL doorway                                             (Jake et al. 2002)
   EL research
   EL vacuum
   EL weekend
   UNA broom
   UNA pier
   TANTAS things
   TUS co-workers
c. AL (a + el) [to + the] mall                    (Arias & Lakshmanan 2003)
   UNA big ball

Franceschina (2001) also maintains that these types of mixings are produced
by Martin, an English near-native speaker of Spanish, and by his L1 Spanish-
speaking interlocutor when code-mixing with English. However, according to
Franceschina, while all of Martin's examples have a masculine determiner,
those produced by the native Spanish speaker contain masculine and feminine
determiners that abide by the so-called "analogical criterion" (Otheguy &
Lapidus 2005) in that the English noun is assigned the gender of the Spanish
lexical item that it displaces.

### 2.2 *The bilingual (English-Spanish) DP system*
The English DP and the Spanish DP share the feature Number but not the
feature Gender. We will assume, drawing a parallel with Pesetsky and
Torrego's (2001) proposal concerning the relationship between nominative
case (nominative case is a T feature on D) and agreement (phi) (agreement is a
D feature on T), that Gender is an N feature on D (thus, it is interpretable on N
and uninterpretable on D) and Gender Agreement (phi) is a D feature on N
(thus, it is interpretable on D and uninterpretable on N). This implies that
Gender and Gender Agreement must be valued and deleted in the case of the
Spanish DPs in (6a), but do not have to be valued in the case of the English
DPs in (6b).

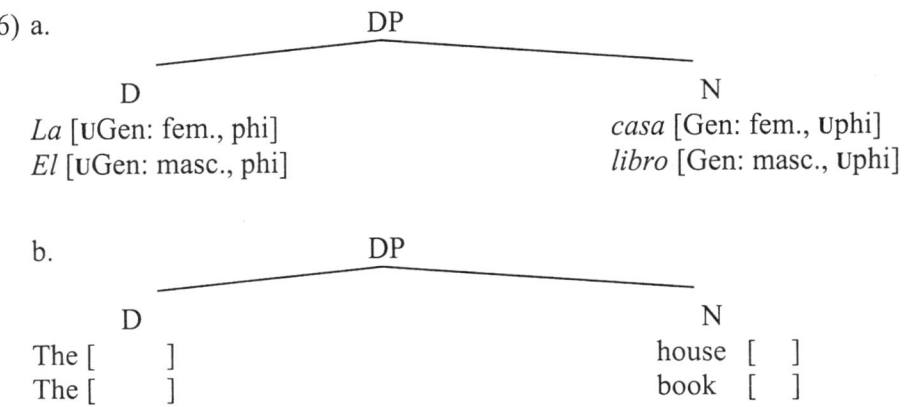

(6) a.                          DP

         D                                      N
   *La* [uGen: fem., phi]              *casa* [Gen: fem., uphi]
   *El* [uGen: masc., phi]             *libro* [Gen: masc., uphi]


    b.                          DP

         D                                      N
   The [     ]                          house  [    ]
   The [     ]                          book   [    ]

If we follow MacSwan's (2000) rationale that ungrammaticality occurs only when there is a feature mismatch, all the code-mixed DPs in (7) would be possible because, even though the Spanish determiner bears the uninterpretable N feature Gender and the interpretable Gender Agreement feature, the English N does not bear either of the two features, as shown in (8).

(7) a.  La house    /   La woman
    b.  La book     /   La man
    c.  El book     /   El man
    d.  El house    /   El woman

(8)                                DP
        _____
              D                                        N
        La [uGen: fem., phi]                      house [   ]
        El [uGen: masc., phi]                     book [   ]

However, if we assume that the D feature of the Spanish determiner requires the noun to bear a matching feature, none of the mixings in (7) would be possible, unless the English noun is assigned the D feature of the Spanish translation equivalent, in which case (7a) and (7c) would be grammatical in a Spanish-English (or English-Spanish) bilingual grammar.

Spanish grammarians (Harris 1991; Roca 1989) have proposed that the masculine determiner is the default form. If this is interpreted as implying that it can value a masculine or a feminine Gender Agreement phi-feature, (7d) would also be a grammatical option. In fact, based on the code-mixed DPs produced by Martin, the near-native speaker of Spanish and his native interlocutor, Franceschina (2001) argues that the masculine determiner may be the default form for non-native and near-native speakers but not for native speakers, since only the latter use both masculine and feminine Spanish determiners with English nouns.

With respect to the cases of code mixings where the determiner is provided by English, the prediction would also be that both of the examples in (9) would be possible because the English determiner does not bear any N Gender feature, as shown in (10).

(9) a.  *The casa*   / *The mujer*
    b.  *The libro*  / *The hombre*

(10)                               DP
        _____
              D                                        N
        *The* [    ]                          *casa* [Gen: fem., uphi]
        *The* [    ]                          *libro* [Gen: masc., uphi]

Alternatively, none would be possible if the presence of the corresponding Gender Agreement phi-feature on D is a requirement.

Thus, in terms of feature matching, it would appear that the theory allows any or none of the possible code-mixing alternatives (depending on whether the absence of a feature is considered to lead to convergence or not). What the child and adult code-mixing data tell us is that we may have to review the theory because there are some clear-cut tendencies that should be accounted for.

Within this system, provided we take the view that all these mixings are grammatical, can we predict any preference in terms of directionality? In a DP consisting of a Spanish D + English N such as the one in (8), the D Gender Agreement phi-feature is not borne by the noun, and the N itself does not have the intrinsic G feature that is borne by the Spanish determiner. On the other hand, in a DP consisting of an English D + Spanish N such as the one in (10), the N Gender feature is not borne by the English determiner, and this determiner does not have the intrinsic Gender agreement phi-feature which is borne by the Spanish noun. Thus, assuming that valuing and deleting are operations of the computational system that is also active in the code-mixing grammar (Chomsky 1998), the question is, which operation is more problematic: not valuing and deleting Gender Agreement (the D phi-feature which is uninterpretable in N) or not valuing and deleting Gender (the N feature which is uninterpretable in D)? In the former case, the English D mixings would be the preferred option, while the mixings where Spanish provides the D would be preferred if the latter obtains.

## 3. *D + N mixings in child and adult bilingual spontaneous data*

Table 1 provides a summary of the D + N mixings produced by English-Spanish and German-Italian children growing up with two languages. In the case of the English-Spanish data, the DPs with a Spanish D are more abundant than the DPs with an English D. We believe that this is so because the Spanish determiner projects the interpretable Gender Agreement feature, which is responsible for the Agreement operation, and it also carries the uninterpretable inherent Gender feature of the noun. In other words, it is the determiner (the functional category that projects) that imposes agreement on the DP. Thus, for a child who has to activate the Gender and Gender Agreement features, a D (the Spanish one) that has this potential is more salient than a D (the English one) that does not. In the case of the German and Italian DPs, determiners in both languages bear the Gender Agreement feature and the uninterpretable N feature Gender; they are equally important for the activation of these features by the bilingual children and, therefore, no clear preference for either D is observed.

|  | Spanish D | English D |
|---|---|---|
| Manuela (Deuchar & Quay, 2000) | 16 | 2 |
| Mario (Fantini 1985) | 43 | 0 |
| Simon and Leo (Fernández Fuertes, Liceras & Spradlin 2002–2005) | 27 | 5 |
| 5 children (Lindholm & Padilla 1978) | 18 | 3 |
|  | German D | Italian D |
| Lisa (Taeschner 1983) | 13 | 16 |
| Giulia (Taeschner 1983) | 17 | 17 |

Table 1. *Child bilingual D-N mixings: Spanish-English; French-English and Italian-German*

Thus, what these data suggest is that child bilinguals have to specify the features that adjust the computational component to two different types of input data, which leads them to prefer the items that are involved in Agreement operations. This happens because L1 children are extremely receptive to the cues provided by the input, and when a given feature must be activated, they do not shy away from it. Children's receptiveness to gender features is also obvious in the case of the "old" bilingual (Dutch-Heerlen dialect) children discussed in Cornips and Hulk (this volume), since they activate the neuter gender feature of standard Dutch faster than monolinguals and do not fossilize it like the "new" bilinguals (the children whose parents are new immigrants), who are exposed to their parents' adult L2 Dutch. These speakers "frequently delete the [Dutch] determiner and/or overgeneralize non-neuter gender."

In Liceras (2002), Spradlin et al. (2003) and Liceras and Fernández Fuertes (2005), we argued that child bilingual language dominance should not be defined in terms of the language that provides the functional category in a functional-lexical mixed utterance, as argued by Petersen (1988) and Lanza (1993), but in terms of the language whose functional category is made up of more uninterpretable features.[7] Thus, in the case of English and Spanish, mixings where Spanish provides the functional category (*la house*) should be favored over mixings where English does (*the casa*) because the Spanish DP bears Gender and Number features, while the English DP only has Number features. We have formulated this account of code-mixing priorities, the Grammatical Features Spell-Out Hypothesis (GFSH), as follows: in the process of activating the features of the two grammars, the bilingual child will make code-switching

---

[7] Language dominance has been defined in various ways, including relative proficiency (Grosjean 1982), the language that is developing more rapidly than the other (Wapole 2000), and/or relative vocabulary size in each of the two languages (Nicoladis & Secco 1998). Genesee, Nicoladis and Paradis (1995) propose four indices of relative dominance, including MLU and upper bound, multimorphemic utterances, and word types. Bernardini and Schlyter (2004) also used the MLU and upper bound as quantitative criteria to differentiate between Weaker and Stronger Languages, a distinction which is at the center of their "Ivy Hypothesis."

choices that favor the functional categories containing the largest array of uninterpretable features.[8]

In the case of the adult bilingual, the process of feature activation has already taken place (the DP is specified for the Gender and the Gender Agreement features that are valued and deleted upon projection), which implies that the English-Spanish bilinguals may apply the "analogical criterion" to the code-mixed pattern so that the Spanish D agrees with the Spanish N displaced by the English noun. In other words, it is possible that the valuing and deleting requirements were met by assigning inherent gender to the English noun. However, the recent production data that are available (DuBord 2004; Jake et al. 2002; Myers-Scotton & Jake 2001; Otheguy & Lapidus 2005) do not support this assumption.[9]

In terms of Gender, Jake et al. (2002) report that, of the 161 Spanish determiners that appeared with English nouns, 151 were marked for gender (the other 10 were possessives or appeared with proper nouns) and 78 (52%) out of the 151 matched the gender of the Spanish counterpart. Thus, the authors conclude, like Poplack, Pousada and Sankoff (1982), that neither phonology nor the translation equivalent predicts the gender of the determiner in a code-switched DP.

These adult bilinguals do not behave like the native Spanish speaker in Franceschina's (2001) study but rather like Martin, the near-native speaker, in that they seem to use masculine as a default: out of the 78 matching DPs, 64 (82%) are masculine, and out of the 73 non-matching DPs, 71 (almost 100%) are masculine as well.

In the data from the New York contact Spanish speakers reported in Otheguy and Lapidus (2005) masculine determiners are predominant with English nouns, regardless of whether the Spanish equivalent would be masculine or feminine. In fact, they report that their subjects are even reluctant to make English lexical insertions feminine when they end in /-a/.

The production of these bilinguals shows that, with English lexical insertions, they choose the masculine as the default option, in spite of the fact that their Spanish grammar has the Gender feature. In other words, it seems that they do not establish Gender Agreement with the "displaced" noun (the analogical criterion does not apply).

---

[8] Our hypothesis differs from Bernardini and Schlyter's (2004) "Ivy Hypothesis" in that the main tenet of their proposal is that in a code-switching utterance, the Stronger Language contributes the higher projection in the tree, which implies that at the DP level, the Stronger Language would always provide the determiner, while the Weaker Language would contribute the noun. However, Weak and Strong are not defined in terms of the array of formal features in a given functional category but in terms of the comparative structural development of the two languages in a given bilingual speaker.

[9] Zamora (1975) and Weinreich (1953) maintain that bilingual production adheres to the "analogical criterion."

## 4.· D+N mixings in adult experimental data

Based on the confirmation that the code-mixing patterns support the GFSH in that the Spanish D + English N DPs are the preferred option, we hypothesized: (i) that the representation of Gender and Gender Agreement in the Spanish DP would also lead native Spanish speakers with English as a second language to favor the Spanish D when presented with code-mixed DPs; and (ii) that the GFSH could be a diagnostic for native-like competence in the case of L2 learners of Spanish. In order to test these hypotheses, we formulated a series of research questions and carried out the experiment that is described below. The second aim of our study was to determine whether the experimental data would shed light on the mixed results reported with respect to the analogical criterion in the case of the bilinguals, and the different results reported for the Spanish native speaker and the near-native speaker in Franceschina's (2001) study.

### 4.1 Subjects

We tested 72 native speakers of Spanish studying English at a Spanish university and 61 native speakers of English and 74 native speakers of French studying Spanish at a Canadian university.

Subjects were assigned to four different levels (Table 2) determined by the CANTEST (Cloze test and reading comprehension) and the SGEL test (multiple choice test).

|        | L1 English | L1 French | L1 Spanish |
|--------|------------|-----------|------------|
| A      | N = 20     | N = 12    | N = 6      |
| B      | N = 15     | N = 24    | N = 23     |
| C      | N = 15     | N = 24    | N = 36     |
| D      | N = 11     | N = 14    | N = 7      |
| TOTAL  | N = 61     | N = 74    | N = 72     |

Lowest = A; highest = D

Table 2. Distribution of subjects according to proficiency levels in L2

Subjects were also given a general questionnaire to find out their parents' native language, their age, time spent in a Spanish- or English-speaking country, knowledge of other languages and languages spoken at home, at school and at work, if applicable.

### 4.2 Code-switching test

The main features of the code-switching test were as follows:
- Subjects rated each sentence on a scale of 1 to 5 (1 = sounds bad; 5 = sounds good).
- [+animate] nouns were not included.
- All entries included very frequent words.
- We avoided cognates and loan words that are used in English or Spanish (suéter, pueblo, Ciudad Juárez), as well as words that graphically could be

interpreted as belonging to either language (e.g., *pared* 'wall,' which could also be an English verb).

- None of the nouns started with a vowel.
- No words starting with "l" after *el* were included.
- We used different nouns in Spanish and English.
- Each sentence had between 7 and 10 words.
- Past and future tenses were avoided so that the sentences would be transparent for bilinguals at all levels.
- Common contractions were used.
- The gender of all the French nouns used in the experiment matched the gender of their Spanish equivalents.

4.3 *The test items were distributed as follows:*

- **32 Spanish determiner + English noun**: 16 with the article *el,* as in (11)—8 matching/8 non-matching—and 16 with the article *la,* as in (12).

(11) a. *Me resulta difícil dormir en el plane.*
      'I find it difficult to sleep on the plane.'
   b. *Voy a comprar flores para el church.*
      'I'm going to buy flowers for the church.'

(12) a. *Adriana se pasa las vacaciones en la beach.*
      'Adriana spends her vacation at the beach.'
   b. *Los pájaros están haciendo un nido en la tree.*
      'The birds are making a nest in the tree.'

- **32 English determiner + Spanish noun**: 16 masculine nouns, as in (13), and 16 feminine nouns, as in (14).

(13)    Peter's mother wants him to sweep the suelo. ('floor')

(14)    You have to be careful when driving in the nieve. ('snow')

- **18 distracters**, which consisted of intrasentential code-switchings at the pronominal subject/verb point: 9 begin in Spanish and finish in English, as in (15), and 9 begin in English and finish in Spanish, as in (16).

(15) a. *Ana sabe que nosotros eat dinner late.*
   b. 'Ana knows that we eat dinner late.'

(16) a. *Professor Martin says that you eres un buen estudiante.*
   b. 'Professor Martin says that you are a good student.'

- **18 fillers**, which consisted of sentences with possible and impossible deverbal compounds, 9 in Spanish and 9 in English, as in (17) and (18), respectively.

(17) a. *En esa estación de tren hay dos **botaslimpia***. [limpiabotas]
    b. 'In that train station there are two shoe-shine stands.'

(18)    That boxer looks like a real **breaker-bone**. [bone-breaker]

### 4.4 *Research questions*

Our research questions were the following:

(i)   Is there a preference for Spanish D in mixed DPs, as in the case of the production data from child and adult L1 bilingual English-Spanish speakers reported in the previous section?

(ii)  Do the L1 English speakers prefer the English D?

(iii) Do the L1 French speakers behave like the L1 Spanish speakers or like the L1 English speakers?

(iv) Is there evidence supporting the analogical criterion in that matching items (i.e., items in which the Spanish translation of the English N matches the gender feature of the Spanish D) are more acceptable than non-matching items?

(v)   Is there evidence for the claim that masculine is the default form?

### 4.5 *Results*

Figure 3 shows that all three groups gave higher ratings to mixed DPs with an English determiner (13 and 14) than to sentences containing mixed DPs with a Spanish determiner (11 and 12). The difference is significant in the case of all three groups.

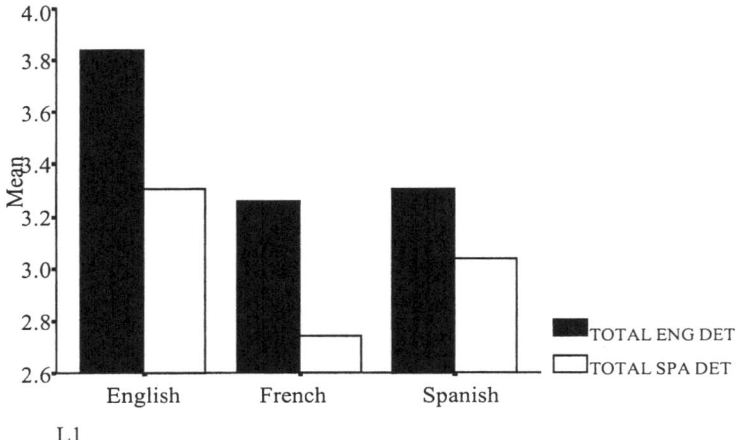

Figure 3. *English D versus Spanish D overall by L1*

When we compare the choice of English D (13 and 14) with the choice of Spanish D in the cases of gender-matching DPs (11a and 12a), the results are radically different for the L1 Spanish group, since this group shows a significant preference for the matching items (they abide by the analogical criterion).

However, the non-native Spanish groups continue to show a significant preference for the English determiner, as shown in Figure 4.

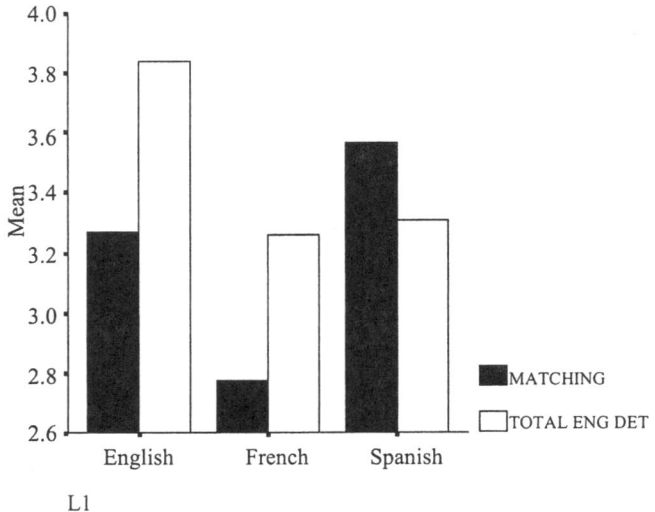

Figure 4. *English D versus Spanish matching D by L1*

In fact, as shown in Figure 5, the non-native Spanish speakers do not follow
the analogical criterion at all. This coincides with the pattern reported by
Franceschina in the case of Martin, the L1 English near-native speaker of
Spanish, who always produces Spanish masculine articles with English nouns.
It looks as though non-native speakers do not process the phi-feature of the
Spanish determiner, which results in their choice of the masculine as the
default form.

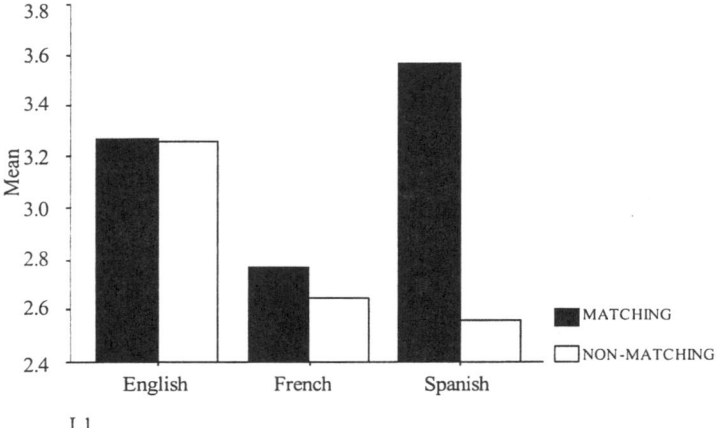

Figure 5. *Matching versus non-matching patterns by L1*

The Spanish speakers, on the other hand, show a strong preference for matching DPs (the ranking of the Spanish matching D in L1 Spanish versus L1 English is significant: DF1; f-value 27.398; p-value = .0001),[10] which we interpret as evidence that their computational system requires the English N to bear the interpretable Gender feature and the uninterpretable Gender Agreement feature of the "displaced" Spanish N, so that these features can be valued and deleted. Thus, their preferred choice is a DP as in (19), which has the same feature specification as the Spanish one in (6a) above.

(19)

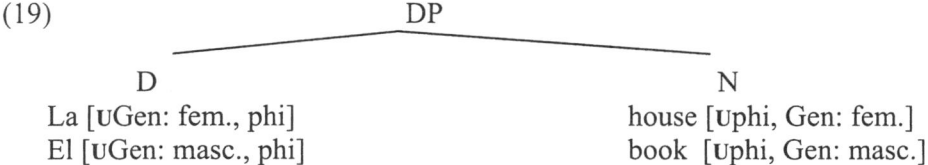

D
La [uGen: fem., phi]
El [uGen: masc., phi]

N
house [uphi, Gen: fem.]
book [uphi, Gen: masc.]

Figure 6 shows that the L1 Spanish subjects prefer both MM (masculine Spanish D, "masculine" English N) and FF (feminine Spanish D, "feminine" English N) significantly more than the L1 English speakers (p-value < .0001). The L1 Spanish speakers also disprefer the MF pattern significantly compared to the MM pattern (DF 1; f-value = 9.362; p =.0024). The L1 English subjects differ in that masculine is preferred over matching. In fact, they rate matching MM (mean = 3.023) and non-matching MF equally (mean = 3.022) and they prefer MM over FF and FM (p < .0001).

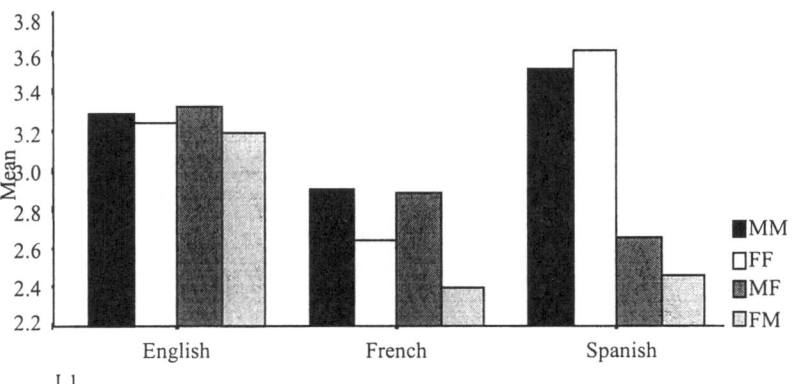

Figure 6. *Mixing pattern preferences by L1*

These results confirm that masculine is the preferred option for non-native speakers, which implies that they only deal with the unspecified phi-feature (the masculine as default—compare (8) above and (20) below).

---

[10] A paired t-test (DF 71; t-value = 4.010) indicates that the L1 Spanish groups significantly prefer Spanish matching D over English D (p-value = .0001).

(20)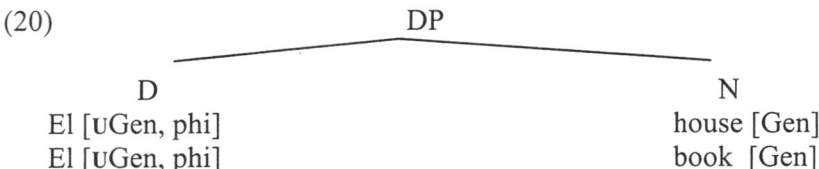
$$\text{DP}$$

| D | N |
|---|---|
| El [uGen, phi] | house [Gen] |
| El [uGen, phi] | book [Gen] |

With respect to whether competence in L2 makes a difference, Figure 7 shows that there is a negative correlation between proficiency and acceptance of code-switched DPs only in the case of the French subjects.

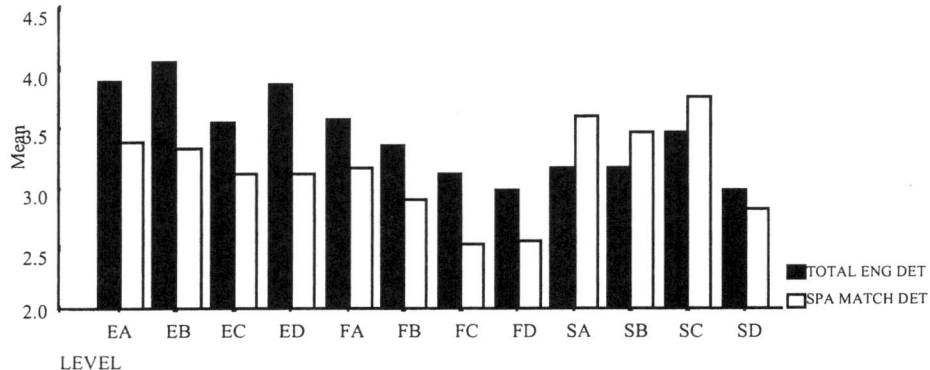

Figure 7. *English D versus Spanish matching D by L2 proficiency*

It also shows that greater proficiency in L2 Spanish does not lead to native-like judgments in terms of preference for the Spanish D in matching DPs versus the English D, a preference that the Spanish L1 group shows regardless of their proficiency in English. Paired t-tests indicate that the choice of Spanish matching D over English D is significant for all groups except the most advanced one (the group labeled SD in the chart). This seems to suggest some kind of "language attrition." However, we think it best to be cautious when dealing with these groupings because we do not think that the version of the CANTEST that we used allows us to discriminate proficiency levels in a refined way.

Based on the results described so far, the research questions that we formulated in the previous section can be answered as follows:[11]

---

[11] A reviewer points out that D/N is robustly attested in the production data analyzed by Bernardini and Schlyter (2004). However, they only provide five examples of mixed DPs: one is a combination of French D + Swedish N (*une bil* 'a car'), two are combinations of Swedish D + French N (*en bacca* 'a berry'/*en dame* 'a lady') and one is a combination of French N + Swedish D (*bouch-en* 'mouth-the'). According to these authors, whose Ivy Hypothesis predicts that the Stronger Language will contribute the higher category, the only exception would be the case of French D + Swedish N because Swedish was the children's Stronger Language. Since we are not given all the examples of mixed DPs, it is very difficult to compare these data with our own. Furthermore, the authors do not take into consideration the fact that there may

*(i) Is there a preference for Spanish D in mixed DPs, as in the case of the production data from child and adult L1 bilingual Spanish-English speakers?*

In contrast to the results of the child and adult bilingual production data, the L1 Spanish group does not show an overwhelming preference for the Spanish DP. In fact, overall, they prefer English D + Spanish N DPs. We would argue that this preference is due to the need to facilitate the interpretation of the code-switched DPs that they are presented with. Since it is the D that projects and triggers agreement, the English D is the one that creates fewest problems for the computational system: it does not have to trigger valuing and deleting the Gender features because it does not carry the uninterpretable Gender feature that is present in the Spanish D, nor does it have an intrinsic Gender Agreement feature. Because it is the D that projects, we assume that this judgment task favors the most neutral possible choice in terms of features: the one represented by the English D + Spanish N DP. However, in the case of the L1 Spanish speakers, this choice is overridden by the analogical criterion.

*(ii) Do the L1 English speakers prefer the English D?*

Just like the Spanish speakers, the English speakers also prefer the English D. For these speakers, this choice is also the least costly in terms of the demands that it imposes upon the computational system.

*(iii) Do the L1 French speakers behave like the L1 Spanish speakers or like the L1 English speakers?*

The French speakers in our experiment are closer to the English speakers in terms of choosing the English D. They differ from both the Spanish and English groups in that they are much more reluctant to accept mixed DPs. In terms of forcing agreement by choosing the matching DPs, it looks as if the phi-feature of the French D (and its computational value) is not "transferred" to their Spanish L2. This comes as no surprise to us because of the nature of this grammaticality judgment task: the fact that their L1 has the feature Gender brings these subjects closer to the Spanish subjects in terms of their sensitivity to the valuing and deleting Gender features. However, applying the analogical criterion (attributing the gender of the determiner to a displaced noun) would entail retrieving a lexical item in their L1, French, while the mixings that they are being asked to judge involve lexical items from their L2 and L3. In this respect, we should point out that, as stated above (section 4.2), all the Spanish

---

be a period in which these children produce monosyllabic placeholders, which implies that what are interpreted as instances of the Swedish determiner *en* may in fact be schwas. There is another issue that makes Swedish + Romance mixings different from English + Romance or German + Romance mixings: the existence of the postposed definite article in Swedish, as well as the special status of bound morphology in L1 acquisition (Liceras 2003).

translation equivalents of the English nouns bear the same inherent Gender feature as the French translation equivalents (i.e., *the house/la casa/la maison*). Nevertheless, these learners do not apply the "analogical criterion," which we attribute to the fact that being confronted with code-mixings in two non-native languages places greater cognitive demands on these subjects. This, we believe, explains why these subjects do not show a need to value the uninterpretable Gender feature of the Spanish determiner.

*(iv) Is there evidence supporting the analogical criterion in that matching items are more acceptable than non-matching items?*

Unlike the bilingual production data, which do not provide conclusive evidence regarding the analogical criterion, the L1 Spanish speakers in our experiment definitely abide by this criterion. In fact, this is by far the preferred option. We interpret these results as indirect evidence in favor of the GFSH in that the initial preference for the Spanish D by the child bilinguals—their need to activate the Gender features of the Spanish DP—is a reflection of how Gender features will be represented in the mind of the native speaker: the DP carries the inherent Gender Agreement and an interpretable Gender feature that the computational system requires to be valued and deleted, an operation that, in the case of the Spanish D + English N DP, is facilitated by the analogical criterion. This computational operation in relation to Gender is etched in the mind of the native speaker.

*(v) Is there evidence for the claim that masculine is the default form?*

This is the choice favored by the non-native speakers of Spanish (Figure 6 above), as was the case with Martin, the near-native speaker. We would like to argue that the different representation of Gender in the case of native and non-native speakers accounts for these choices. It is important to note that this choice is also mentioned as being the one preferred by some bilinguals, such as the ones in Otheguy and Lapidus's (2005) study.

## 5. *The creole DP and gender features*

In this section, we will briefly summarize the basic characteristics of the creole DP as far as Gender is concerned. We will also test the traditional generalizations of the creole DP system against a small corpus of data from different Atlantic creoles. As Holm (1988) noted, the elements that are present in the configuration of the creole DP—number, possession, definiteness or word order, to name a few—are so closely interrelated that none of them can be analyzed without reference to the others. Consequently, word order will be a key element in indicating natural gender, as we will see.

Since the seminal works of Bickerton (1984) and Holm (1988), two main assumptions have been made in the literature on creole DPs: on the one hand, the generalization that creoles labeled as "radical" or "basilectal" do not have any bound morphology at all; on the other hand, an assertion that creole languages lack Gender marking. In Table 3, we present a sample of the forms taken by determiners (definite articles and demonstratives) in different creoles:

|  | *the* man | *this* man | *these* men |
|---|---|---|---|
| Principe CP | omi *sé* | omi *faki* | *ine* omi *sé* |
| Haitian CF | nom *la* | nom *sa*-a | nom *sa*-yo |
| Papiamentu CS | *e* homber | e homber *aki* | e homber-*nan* aki |
| Saramaccan CE | *di* omi | di omi *aki* | *dee* omi aki |
| Sranan CE | *a* man | a man *disi* | *den* man disi |
| Jamaican CE | *di* man | *dis* man (*ya*) | *dem* man ya |

CE: Creole English; CF: Creole French; CP: Creole Portuguese; CS: Creole Spanish

(Adapted from Holm 1988: 191)

Table 3. *Determiners in various creole languages*

As Table 3 shows, creoles do not typically take over the definite articles of the lexifier language. Rather, they create them through a process of grammaticalization, usually taking the demonstratives of the lexifier as a point of departure.[12] However, in the so-called "decreolized" varieties of some Atlantic creoles, such as Jamaican CE, definite articles are borrowed from the lexifier language.[13] Furthermore, the uses of articles in Atlantic creoles do not necessarily parallel those of the lexifier languages. As noted by Bickerton (1981), creoles frequently have (i) a definite article to mark presupposed-specific NPs, (ii) an indefinite article for asserted-specific NPs, and (iii) a null article for nonspecific NPs.[14]

We generally do not find Gender distinctions in creoles, as was mentioned above and shown in (21), although biological gender is marked in these languages in certain cases, exemplified in (22) through (24):[15]

(21)  *un kasa ma bonito*                                          PALENQUERO
      'a prettier house'
      (cf. Spanish *una casa más bonita,* with *casa* 'house' feminine)

(22)  a.  *rei* ('king')                                            PAPIAMENTU
          (cf. Spanish *rey* 'king')
      b.  *reina* ('queen')
          (cf. Spanish *reina* 'queen')

---

[12] Note that this process of grammaticalization is very frequent in language change processes. For instance, and similarly to what we just saw for creoles, Romance languages created their determiner systems from certain elements of the Latin demonstrative paradigm.

[13] For the role of "decreolization" in the changes in the feature configuration in the creole DP, see section 6.

[14] For a discussion of these claims and partial counterevidence, see Holm (1988).

[15] Examples taken from Holm (1988).

(23)  a. *mucha homber* ('boy')                           PAPIAMENTU
         (cf. Spanish *muchacho* 'boy' and *hombre* 'man')
      b. *mucha muhe* ('girl')
         (cf. Spanish *mujer*, 'woman)

(24)  a. *gró* ('fat')                                     GUYANAIS
            (cf. French *gros* 'fat')
      b. *gros* ('pregnant')
         (cf. French *grosse* 'fat' feminine)

As shown above, Gender distinctions made by the use of inflections in the
European lexifier languages were not maintained in the creole nouns and
adjectives. As (21) shows, the Gender agreement of the Spanish DP *Una casa
más bonita* is not found in Palenquero *un_ kasa ma **bonito***. In some cases,
natural gender oppositions have been maintained in certain nouns, for instance
the Papiamentu *rei/reina* opposition in (22). Natural gender distinctions can
also be expressed through the juxtaposition of a noun indicating sex, as shown
in (23). According to Holm (1988), these cases appear to be calques on idioms
of the African substrate languages of these creoles. Finally, (24) shows that
even though most creole adjectives with European lexifiers have been built on
the lexifier's masculine form, certain feminine forms have been preserved,
sometimes with a distinction in meaning. Therefore, these data show that
grammatical Gender is generally not marked in creoles; in the specific cases
where they display some sort of natural gender marking, the mechanisms used
do not rely on inflectional morphology. However, Robert Papen (p.c.) notes
that in Indian Ocean Creoles, where (similarly to Atlantic creoles) Gender is
not generally marked, there are a number of (relatively productive) derivational
suffixes, such as *–ar* (derived from French *–ard*) and *–ris* (from French *–rice*)
that indicate natural Gender:

(25)  a. *ris-ar*                                          MAURITIAN CREOLE
         rich-natural masculine gender
         'rich man'
      b. *direkt-ris*                                       MAURITIAN CREOLE
         director-natural feminine gender
         'director (feminine)'

Therefore, we can conclude that so-called "radical" creole languages do not
have grammaticalized Gender. That is to say, they do not have Gender markers
such as free or bound morphemes, or any other grammatical means of marking
Gender on [–animate] entities.

   Unlike "radical" creoles, languages such as Reunion Creole French (RCF)
do encode a gender distinction in the DP. In fact, in the written and oral data
analyzed by Pierozak (2003) the articles *le* (*lo*)/*la* agree with masculine and

feminine nouns. This distinction also seems to be present in the demonstrative system. Note that some linguists argue that this creole is in the process of decreolization or that it is not a creole at all but a variety of French (Pierozak 2003 and references therein).

Also unlike "radical" creoles, but at the other end of the spectrum, was the so-called Lingua Franca, the trade language used by many communities around the Mediterranean from the beginning of the sixteenth century until the end of the nineteenth century, when it disappeared. There remains a written corpus of approximately 5,000 words (Arends 1998), which suggests that this language played a role in the formation of "classic" creoles (Arends 1999). The main lexical items in this language come from Italian and Spanish, although there also contributions from Arabic and Turkish. According to Muusse and Arends (2003), who analyze a corpus of three different sources consisting of approximately 1,500 words, this language constitutes an exception to prototypical "classic" creoles in that it has a rather rich inflectional morphology. For instance, besides the case and [+/−] definite markers on the DP system, which, interestingly, are not present in Italian or Spanish, it displays agreement between nouns and articles, demonstratives, possessives, numerals and adjectives. Specifically there is gender agreement between the noun and both the definite and indefinite articles (*il/oun café* 'the/a coffee,' *il/oun padré* 'the/a father,' *la/ouna parté* 'the/a part,' *la/ouna maré* 'the/a mother').

In the following sections we will explore the possible consequences of a specific language contact situation for the creole DP system. We will investigate how the GFSH could explain some of the facts related to this system—namely the differences in the DP system at different stages of the pidgin-creole continuum—and also the possible ways in which this system could be implemented via a continued language contact situation.

## 6. *Bilinguals, native speakers, non-native speakers and the pidgin-creole continuum*

In what follows, we discuss various issues and raise a number of questions, some of which we leave open for further research.

With respect to the functional category that is favored by English-Spanish bilinguals, the production data that we analyzed in Spradlin et al. (2003), Liceras and Fernández Fuertes (2005) and Liceras, Spradlin and Fernández (2005) show that L1 bilingual children prefer the Spanish D because they are in the process of specifying the uninterpretable features of the Spanish DP. In the early stages, their mixed DPs do not provide evidence that the masculine is the default form nor that they are following the analogical criterion. Some children, such as Mario (Fantini 1985), seem to avoid underspecification by choosing the default form, as in (20). This is also the choice that seems to be favored by many adult bilinguals, even though the feminine form emerges sometimes, as we saw in section 3. In fact, while the results of the recent production studies of adult bilinguals suggest a clear-cut preference for the masculine as default and a very minor role for the analogical criterion, native speakers of Spanish who happen to know English, such as the man in Franceschina's (2001) study, and the data from similar subjects cited by Zamora (1975) and Weinreich (1953), among others, display a clear preference for the analogical criterion. Again, the only data from a near-native Spanish speaker that we came across (Martin in Franceschina's 2001 study) suggest that, unlike the Spanish native speaker, the masculine as default defines this subject's code-switched DPs. This is also what our experimental data show overall: the Spanish speakers show a significant preference for the analogical criterion, while the non-native speakers show a preference for the English D + Spanish N DPs, with a secondary preference for the masculine as default.

Even though mixed DPs with English D have not previously been reported in adult bilingual speakers' output, the experimental data show that DPs with English or Spanish Ds can be rated in terms of their degree of grammaticality. However, for the L1 Spanish population, unless there is matching, the English D lacking Gender features seems to be the less problematic option. The presence of an underspecified phi-feature (the default option) is also less problematic than the presence of a specified phi-feature that does not trigger agreement. This is the reason why matching is the preferred option for the native speakers. The production data are not this clear-cut. Thus, we suggest that the GFSH accounts for how children activate features from a language contact situation and how features are represented in the minds of adult monolingual speakers but not adult bilinguals.

We will now speculate on the status of the GFSH in the case of permanent contact between two languages and language contact under special circumstances, such as the pidgin-creole situation. In other words, can the code-switching options be extrapolated to the pidgin-creole situation?

Let us assume, as we suggested above, that creole formation can be seen as a continuum which goes from a code-switching stage (Figure 3) to an internalized diglossia stage (Figure 4) and finally to the full-fledged creole stage, in which features are activated as in the case of child L1 acquisition. In the pidgin-creole continuum, the initial grammar is created by adult speakers. These non-native speakers seldom make use of the functional category that displays the largest array of formal features and certainly do not activate heavily grammaticalized features such as Gender and Gender Agreement. Although there are special cases such as that of Lingua Franca, which seemed to be the outcome of a language contact situation where all the various L1 languages had this specific feature, the limited input from the lexifier language, together with the adult's lack of sensitivity to the realization of abstract features in the input, will make the lexifier the source of the pidgin's content words but not of its functional categories in most cases of language contact.

Functional categories realized as free or bound morphemes could eventually be provided by the substratum, but such a choice would interfere with the much reduced chances of communication, since the native speakers of the lexifier language would not know the substratum language (or languages). Therefore, most pidgins do not display a DP system, which implies that the "unbalanced bilingual grammar" depicted in Figure 1, where the L1 provides the functional categories, is rarely realized, unless there are special circumstances as in the case of the Lingua Franca.

In the pidgin-creole continuum, further adult contact with the lexifier language may give rise to an L2-based grammar via relexification (i.e., the choice of the demonstrative as definite article), which is in fact a default representation of one of the languages in contact, namely the lexifier language, as is the case of the creoles presented in Table 3 above. This period may be followed by one where more balanced bilinguals go through an internalized diglossia stage in which functional categories from both languages are at work in the speaker's grammar so that we would have a situation of competing grammars, with a display of default forms.

Finally, the full-fledged creole comes into existence when the child (L1 acquisition) "regularizes" the creole system. If this child is confronted with a creole with a variable determiner system or with a system that contains feature agreement mismatches, he/she may make this system categorical and get rid of the mismatches.

The code-switching data that we have analyzed parallels the tension that any language contact situation reflects between production and judgments: in production, non-native speakers and bilingual speakers seem to favor the default options or the lexical realizations of functional categories that contain the smallest array of formal features (English D and masculine as default), while L1 children favor the most grammaticalized functional category. When it comes to judging mixed DPs, the L1 Spanish speakers favor the valuing and deleting of the Gender and Gender Agreement features via the analogical criterion. We do not have grammaticality judgment data from fluent bilingual speakers, but if the most advanced group of L2 English learners (the Spanish-speaking group from the Spanish university) is in fact different from the other groups because of its degree of bilingualism, we could conclude that bilinguals refrain from imposing the analogical criterion upon code-switched DPs. This leads us to speculate that highly grammaticalized features such as Gender and Gender Agreement may only enter a creole when there is already a determiner system in place and when second language learners with a dominant language that contains these features force the "analogical criterion" upon [−animate] nouns in the creole. It is at this point that L1 children learning the creole "analogical forms" coined by these second language speakers would assign an intrinsic Gender feature to the creole nouns—a feature that would have to be valued and deleted via its corresponding uninterpretable feature in the determiner. Thus, it looks as if complex processes of grammaticalization and "decreolization" have to be in place for highly grammaticalized features to enter the creole system.

## 7. *Conclusions*

We have proposed that code-switching data from children and adult bilinguals and from native and non-native speakers may shed light on the nature of the pidgin-creole continuum. Specifically, we have argued that the GFSH accounts for the code-switching options selected by L1 children and adult native speakers. We have also argued that the masculine as default option can be taken as a diagnostic for the role of bilingualism in creole formation, in that it is the bilingual speakers who incorporate an underspecified or unspecified option (via the analogical criterion) of the lexifier language into the creole system, thereby "decreolizing" it. Bilingualism seems to be behind the change from a demonstrative to a definite article in Jamaican Creole, while the creoles with a Romance lexifier always display the masculine (underspecified) form. If a creole is created via L1 acquisition and children are not in contact with a lexifier language that has Gender features, they have no reason to incorporate Gender features into that creole. However, if the creole speakers grow up in a bilingual situation (creole and lexifier), they would choose the lexifier language's determiner to activate the Gender feature. However, as they become adult bilinguals, they will keep the two systems separate and will make default choices in their potential mixed production. Furthermore, since Gender related to [–animacy] is a highly formal feature which, unlike elements such as the TMA (Tense/Mood/Aspect) markers or even Case, does not play any role in terms of semantic interpretation or theta-roles (agent, theme, benefactive), this feature may never make it into a creole system. We have speculated that, if it does, a complex contact situation where grammaticalization and "decreolization" processes such as the process triggered by the analogical criterion may have to be in place. This is precisely the contact situation that led to the implementation of the Gender feature in Reunion Creole French.

## *References*

Adjémian, C. and J. M. Liceras. 1982. Universal grammar, the intake component and L1: Accounting for adult acquisition of relative clauses. In *Universals of Second Language Acquisition,* F. Eckman, L. Bell and D. Nelson (eds.), 101–118. Rowley, MA: Newbury House.

Andersen, R. 1979. Expanding Schumann's pidginization hypothesis. *Language Learning* 29: 105–119.

Andersen, R. 1983. *Pidginization and Creolization as Language Acquisition.* Rowley, MA: Newbury House.

Arends, J. 1998. A bibliography of lingua franca. *Carrier Pidgin* 26(4–5): 33–35.

Arends, 1999. Lingua franca en de "Europese" creooltalen. *Gramma TTT* 7: 173–190.

Arias, R. and U. Lakshmanan. 2003. Code-switching in a Spanish-English bilingual child: A communication resource? Paper presented at the 4th International Symposium on Bilingualism (ISB4), Arizona State University.

Azuma, S. 1993. The frame-content hypothesis in speech production: Evidence from intrasentential code-switching. *Linguistics* 31: 1071–1093.

Beck, M-L. 1998. L2 acquisition and obligatory head movement. *Studies in Second Language Acquisition* 29: 311–348.

Belazi, H., E. Rubin and A. J. Toribio. 1994. Code-switching and X-bar theory: The functional head constraint. *Linguistic Inquiry* 25: 221–237.

Bernardini, P. and S. Schlyter. 2004. Growing syntactic structure and code-mixing in the weaker language: The Ivy Hypothesis. *Bilingualism: Language and Cognition* 7(1): 49–69.

Bickerton, D. 1981. *Roots of Language*. Ann Arbor, MI: Karoma.

Bickerton, D. 1984. The Language Bioprogram Hypothesis. *Behavioral and Brain Sciences* 7: 173–188.

Bickerton, D. 1996. A dim monocular view of Universal Grammar access. Commentary on S. Epstein, S. Flynn and G. Martohardjono. *Behavioral and Brain Sciences* 19: 716–717.

Bickerton, D. 1999. How to acquire language without positive evidence: What acquisitionists can learn from creoles. In *Language Creation and Language Change: Creolization, Diachrony and Development,* M. DeGraff (ed.), 49–74. Cambridge, MA: The MIT Press.

Bickerton, D. and T. Givón. 1976. Pidginization and syntactic change: From SXV and VSX to SVX. In *Papers from the Parasession on Diachronic Syntax,* S. B. Steever, C. A. Walker and S. Mufwene (eds.), 9–39. Chicago: Chicago Linguistic Society.

Bruhn de Garavito, J. Forthcoming. Acquisition of Spanish plural by French L1 speakers: The role of transfer. In *The Role of Formal Features in Second Language Acquisition,* J. M. Liceras, H. Zobl and H. Goodluck (eds.). Mahwah, NJ: Lawrence Erlbaum Associates, Inc.

Chaudenson, R. 2001. Créoles françaises et variétés de français. *L'information grammatical* 89: 32–37.

Chomsky, N. 1995. *The Minimalist Program*. Cambridge, MA: The MIT Press.

Chomsky, N. 1998. Minimalist inquiries: The framework. *MIT Occasional Papers in Linguistics* 15. (Reissued in 2000 in *Step by Step: Essays on Minimalist Syntax in Honor of Howard Lasnik,* R. Martin, D. Michaels and J. Uriagereka (eds.), 89–155. Cambridge, MA: The MIT Press.)

DeGraff, M. 1999. *Language Creation and Language Change: Creolization, Diachrony and Development*. Cambridge, MA: The MIT Press.

DeGraff, M. 2005. Morphology and word order in "creolization" and beyond. In *The Oxford Handbook of Comparative Syntax,* G. Cinque and R. Kayne (eds.), 293–372. New York: Oxford University Press.

Deuchar, M. and S. Quay. 2000. *Bilingual Acquisition: Theoretical Implications of a Case Study*. Oxford: Oxford University Press.

Di Sciullo, A. M., P. Muysken and R. Singh. 1986. Government and code-switching. *Journal of Linguistics* 22: 1–24.

DuBord, L. 2004. Gender assignment to English words in the Spanish of Southern Arizona. *Divergencias. Revista de estudios lingüísticos y literarios* 2(2): 27–39.

Epstein, S., S. Flynn and G. Martohardjono. 1996. Second language acquisition: Theoretical and experimental issues in contemporary research. *Behavioral and Brain Sciences* 19: 677–758.

Eubank, L. 1996. Negation in early German-English interlanguage: More valueless features in the L2 initial stage. *Second Language Research* 12: 73–106.

Fantini, A. E. 1985. *Language Acquisition of a Bilingual Child: A Sociolinguistic Perspective (to Age Ten)*. Clevedon, UK: Multilingual Matters.

Fernández Fuertes, R., J. M. Liceras and K. T. Spradlin. 2000–2005. Bilingualism (English/Spanish) as a First Language: A Case Study of Identical Twins. Research Project, University of Valladolid/University of Ottawa.

Fleta, M. T. 1999. La adquisición del inglés no nativo por niños: el desarrollo de la cláusula. Ph.D. dissertation, Instituto Universitario Ortega y Gasset, Universidad Complutense of Madrid.

Franceschina, F. 2001. Morphological or syntactic deficits in near-native speakers? An assessment of some current proposals. *Second Language Research* 17(3): 213–247.

García-Mayo, P., A. Lázaro Ibarrola and J. M. Liceras. 2005. Placeholders in the English interlanguage of bilingual (Basque/Spanish) children. *Language Learning* 55(3): 445–489.

Genesee, F., E. Nicoladis and J. Paradis. 1995. Language differentiation in early bilingual development. *Journal of Child Language* 22: 611–631.

Grosjean, F. 1982. *Life with Two Languages: An Introduction to Bilingualism*. Cambridge, MA: Harvard University Press.

Harris, J. 1991. The exponent of gender in Spanish. *Linguistic Inquiry* 22: 27–62.

Hawkins, R. and C. Chan. 1997. The partial availability of Universal Grammar in second language acquisition: The Failed Functional Features Hypothesis. *Second Language Research* 13: 187–226.

Holm, J. 1988. *Pidgins and Creoles, Vol. 1: Theory and Structure*. Cambridge: Cambridge University Press.

Jake, J. L., C. Myers-Scotton and S. Gross. 2002. Making a minimalist approach to codeswitching work: Adding the matrix language. *Bilingualism: Language and Cognition* 5(1): 69–91.

Joshi, A. 1985. Processing of sentences with intrasentential code-switching. In *Natural Language Parsing: Psychological, Computational and Theoretical Perspectives,* D. Dowty, L. Karttunen and A. Zwicky (eds.), 190–205. Cambridge: Cambridge University Press.

Kay, P. and G. Sankoff. 1974. A language-universals approach to pidgins and creoles. In *Pidgins and Creoles: Current Trends and Prospects*, D. DeCamp and E. F. Hancock (eds.), 61–72. Washington, DC: Georgetown University Press.

Köppe, R. and J. Meisel. 1995. Code-switching in bilingual first language acquisition. In *One Speaker, Two Languages,* L. Milroy and P. Muysken (eds.), 276–301. Cambridge: Cambridge University Press.

Kroch, A. 1994. Morphosyntactic variation. In *Papers from the 13th Regional Meeting of the Chicago Linguistic Society, Vol. 2: The Parasession on Variation and Linguistic Theory,* K. Beals (ed.), 180–201. Chicago: Chicago Linguistic Society.

Lanza, E. 1993. Language mixing and language dominance in bilingual first language acquisition. In *The Proceedings of the Twenty-Fourth Annual Child Language Research Forum,* E. V. Clark (ed.), 197–208. Stanford, CA: Center for the Study of Language and Information.

Lardiere, D. 1998. Case and tense in the "fossilized" steady-state. *Second Language Research* 14: 1–26.

Lardiere, D. Forthcoming. Feature-assembly in second language acquisition. In *The Role of Formal Features in L2 Acquisition,* J. M. Liceras, H. Zobl and H. Goodluck (eds.). Mahwah, NJ: Lawrence Erlbaum Associates, Inc.

Lázaro, A. 2000. El Programa Minimalista y el inglés/castellano-euskera de las ikastolas. M.A. thesis, University of Ottawa.

Lefebvre, C. 1996. The tense, mood and aspect system of Haitian Creole and the problem of transmission of grammar in creole genesis. *Journal of Pidgin and Creole Languages* 11(2): 231–311.

Lefebvre, C. 1998. *Creole Genesis and the Acquisition of Grammar: The Case of Haitian Creole.* Cambridge: Cambridge University Press.

Lefebvre, C. and J. Lumsden. 1989. Les langues créoles et la théorie linguistique. *Canadian Journal of Linguistics* 34: 319–337.

Lefebvre, C. and J. Lumsden. 1994. Relexification in creole genesis. In *The Central Role of Relexification in Creole Genesis: The Case of Haitian Creole,* C. Lefebvre and J. S. Lumsden (eds.) Research report prepared for SSHRCC on the project *La genèse du créole haïtien: un cas particulier d'investigation sur la forme de la grammaire universelle,* Université du Québec à Montréal.

Liceras, J. M. 1996. "To grow" and what "to grow": That is one question. Commentary on S. Epstein, S. Flynn and G. Martohardjono. *Behavioral and Brain Sciences* 19: 677–758.

Liceras, J. M. 1998. On the specific nature of non-native grammars: The whys, whens, wheres and ... hows. In *Issues in Second Language Acquisition and Learning, LynX: A Monographic Series in Linguistics and World Perception 6,* J. Fernández-González and J. de Santiago Guervós (eds.), 58–96. Valencia: Servei de Publicacions.

Liceras, J. M. 2002. Uninterpretable features in bilingual acquisition and the issue of language dominance. Paper presented at the European Research Conference on Theoretical and Experimental Linguistics. Corinth, Greece, June 1 – 6.

Liceras, J. M. 2003. Monosyllabic place holders in early child language and the L1/L2 "Fundamental Difference Hypothesis". In *Theory, Practice and Acquisition. Papers from the 6th Hispanic Linguistics Symposium and the 5th Conference on the Acquisition of Spanish and Portuguese,* P. Kempchinsky and C-L. Piñeros (eds.), 258–283. Somerville, MA: Cascadilla Press.

Liceras, J. M., B. Laguardia, Z. Fernández, R. Fernández and L. Díaz. 1998. Licensing and identification of null categories in Spanish non-native grammars. In *Theoretical Analyses on Romance Languages*, J. Lema and E. Treviño (eds.), 263–282. Amsterdam: John Benjamins.

Liceras, J. and R. Fernández Fuertes. 2005. Formal features in adult code-switching. *Cuadernos de Lingüística* XII: 139-154. Madrid: Instituto Universitario Ortega y Gasset.

Liceras, J. M., T. Spradlin and R. Fernández Fuertes (2005). Bilingual early functional-lexical mixing and the activation of formal features. *International Journal of Bilingualism* 9(2): 227–252.

Lindholm, K. J. and A. M. Padilla. 1978. Language mixing in bilingual children. *Journal of Child Language* 5: 327–335.

Lumsden, J. 1999. Language acquisition and creolization. In *Language Creation and Language Change: Creolization, Diachrony and Development*, M. DeGraff (ed.), 129–157. Cambridge, MA: The MIT Press.

MacSwan, J. 2000. The architecture of the bilingual language faculty: Evidence from intrasentential code-switching. *Bilingualism: Language and Cognition* 3(1): 37–54.

Mufwene, S. 1990. Transfer and the substrate hypothesis in creolistics. *Studies in Second Language Acquisition* 12: 1–23.

Mufwene, S. 1996. The development of American Englishes: Some questions from a creole genesis perspective. In *Varieties of English Around the World: Focus on the USA*, E. W. Schneider (ed.), 231–264. Amsterdam: John Benjamins.

Muusse, E. and J. Arends. 2003. La morphologie flexionnelle dans le syntagme nominal de la lingua franca. In *Grammaticalisation et réanalyse. Approches de la variation créole et française*, S. Kriegel (ed.), 325–334. Paris: CNRS Éditions.

Myers-Scotton, C. 1997. Code switching. In *The Handbook of Sociolinguistics*, F. Coulmas (ed.), 217–237. Oxford: Blackwell.

Myers-Scotton, C. and J. L. Jake. 2001. Explaining aspects of code-switching and their implications. In *One Mind, Two Languages: Bilingual Language Processing*, J. L. Nicol (ed.), 84–116. Malden, MA: Blackwell.

Nicoladis, E. and G. Secco. 1998. The role of translation equivalents in a bilingual family's code-switching. In *Proceedings of the 22nd Annual Boston University Conference on Language Development*, A. Greenhill, M. Hughes, H. Littlefield, and H. Walsh (eds.), 576–585. Somerville, MA: Cascadilla Press.

Otero, C. 1996. Language growth after puberty? Commentary on S. Epstein, S. Flynn and G. Martohardjono. *Behavioral and Brain Sciences* 19: 738–739.

Otheguy, N. and R. Lapidus. 2005. An adaptive approach to noun gender in New York contact Spanish. Ms., Graduate Center, City University of New York.

Pesetsky, D. and E. Torrego. 2001. T-to-C movement: Causes and consequences. In *Ken Hale: A Life in Language,* M. Kenstowicz (ed.), 355–426. Cambridge, MA: The MIT Press.

Petersen, J. 1988. Word-internal code-switching constraints in a bilingual child's grammar. *Linguistics* 26: 479–493.

Pierozak, I. 2003. Éléments de réflexion à partir du "genre" en créole réunionnais: grammaticalisation, variation et écriture. In *Grammaticalisation et réanalyse. Approches de la variation créole et française*, S. Kriegel (ed.), 303–323. Paris: CNRS Éditions.

Plag, I. 1994. Creolization and language change: A comparison. In *Creolization and Language Change*, D. Adone and I. Plag (eds.), 3–22. Tübingen: Max Niemeyer Verlag.

Poplack, S. 1980. "Sometimes I'll start a sentence in Spanish y termino en español": Toward a typology of code-switching. *Linguistics* 18: 581–618.

Poplack, S., A. Pousada and D. Sankoff. 1982. Competing influences on gender assignment: Variable process, stable outcome. *Lingua* 56: 139–166.

Roca, I. 1989. The organization of grammatical gender. *Transactions of the Philological Society* 87: 1–32.

Schumann, J. 1978. *The Pidginization Process: A Model for Second Language Acquisition*. Rowley, MA: Newbury House.

Schwartz, B. and R. Sprouse. 1996. L2 cognitive states and the full transfer/full access model. *Second Language Research* 12: 40–72.

Slabakova, R. and S. Montrul. Forthcoming. Aspectual shifts: Grammatical and pragmatic knowledge in L2 acquisition. In *The role of formal features in L2 acquisition*, J. M. Liceras, H. Zobl and H. Goodluck (eds.). Mahwah, NJ: Lawrence Erlbaum Associates, Inc.

Smith, N. and I.-M. Tsimpli. 1995. *The Mind of the Savant*. Oxford: Blackwell.

Spradlin, K. T., J. M. Liceras and R. Fernández Fuertes. 2003. Functional-lexical code-mixing patterns as evidence for language dominance in young bilingual children: A minimalist approach. In *Proceedings of the 2002 Generative Approaches to Second Language Acquisition (GASLA-6) Conference: L2 Links*, J. M. Liceras, H. Zobl and H. Goodluck (eds.), 298–307. Somerville, MA: Cascadilla Press.

Sprouse, R. 2004. The bankruptcy of the stimulus. Plenary talk presented at the Generative Approaches to Language Acquisition North America (GALANA 2004) conference, University of Hawai'i at Manoa, December 17–20.

Strozer, J. 1994. *Language Acquisition after Puberty*. Washington, DC: Georgetown University Press.

Swain, M. and M. Wesche. 1975. Linguistic interaction: Case study of a bilingual child. *Language Sciences* October: 17–22.

Taeschner, T. 1983. *The Sun Is Feminine*. Berlin: Springer-Verlag.

Toribio, A. J. 2001. On the emergence of bilingual code-switching competence. *Bilingualism: Language and Cognition* 4(3): 203–231.

Tsimpli, I. M. and A. Roussou. 1991. Parameter resetting in L2? *UCL Working Papers in Linguistics* 3: 149–169.

Wapole, C. 2000. The bilingual child: One system or two? In *The Proceedings of the Thirtieth Annual Child Language Research Forum*, E. V. Clark (ed.), 187–194. Stanford, CA: CSLI.

Weinreich, U. 1953. *Languages in Contact*. New York: Linguistic Circle of New York.

White, L. 2003. *Second Language Acquisition and Universal Grammar*. Cambridge: Cambridge University Press.

Woolford, E. 1983. Bilingual code switching and syntactic theory. *Linguistic Inquiry* 14: 520–536.

Woolford, E. 1984. Why creoles won't reveal properties of Universal Grammar. *The Behavioral and Brain Sciences* 7: 211–212.

Zamora, J. C. 1975. Morfología bilingüe: la asignación de género a los préstamos. *Bilingual Review* 2: 239–247.

# EMERGING COMPLEMENTIZERS:
## GERMAN IN CONTACT WITH FRENCH/ITALIAN
Natascha Müller
*Bergische Universität Wuppertal*

This study investigates the use of the prepositional complementizer für by two German-French and three German-Italian bilingual children aged 2 to 5 years old. The main observation to be explained is that children who exhibit problems with finite verb placement in German subordinate clauses make their way into the complementizer system by using für with the same syntactic derivation as pour/per. The Romance derivation of the prepositional complementizers pour/per is not only extended to German für, but to all German complementizers in child grammar. Kayne (1999) has argued that prepositional complementizers in French and Italian do not form a constituent with the infinitival IP they are associated with. Bilingual children extend this analysis to the prepositional complementizer für in German and, later in the developmental process, to all complementizers. Target-deviant finite verb placement in German subordinate clauses is the result of the Romance derivation for complementizers. The paper shows that the development of prepositional complementizers in early childhood bilingualism is intimately connected with the emergence of complementizers in creoles. What is striking about French-based creoles is that they have developed a prepositional complementizer pu (French: pour), just as the bilingual children have.

## 1. *Introduction: Cross-linguistic influence and language separation*

Research into bilingual first language acquisition has been guided by two main approaches (cf. Müller, Kupisch, Schmitz & Cantone 2006): either it was argued that bilingual children are not able to separate their two languages from an early stage since the two languages influence each other (e.g., Taeschner 1983) or it is claimed that bilingual children are able to separate their two languages early on and that there is no evidence of cross-linguistic influence (Genesee, 1989; Genesee, Nicoladis & Paradis 1995; Meisel 1989, 1994). In other words, language separation and cross-linguistic influence have been considered to be mutually exclusive. The main reason for the assumption of mutual exclusiveness is that most research has conceptualized separation and influence as involving whole language systems (or languages). Recently, some researchers have become interested in the possibility that only certain domains in simultaneous bilingualism are vulnerable to cross-linguistic influence while others are developed by the children without any sign of influence. This paper looks at the development of complementizers, with a focus on German, in particular the use of the preposition *für* to introduce clauses in child language.

Recent studies that have observed cross-linguistic influence have explained that influence in terms of language dominance (Bernardini Röst 2001; Döpke 1992; Gawlitzek-Maiwald & Tracy 1996; Hulk 1997; Schlyter 1993; Tracy

1995): the stronger or "more developed" language influences the weaker or "less developed" one. Most authors have defined language dominance on the basis of a comparison of MLU values in the bilingual child's two languages and/or language use (the number of utterances in the two languages used during a recording session). Others presuppose that the child's dominant language corresponds to the dominant language of the community. This paper will compare bilingual children with different degrees of language balance and will conclude that cross-linguistic influence cannot be explained on the basis of dominance. Hulk and Müller (2000) and Müller and Hulk (2000, 2001) argue that language-internal factors open up the possibility for cross-linguistic influence to occur. One prerequisite for such influence is that there must be a certain amount of overlap of the two languages: a construction in language A allows for more than one analysis (from the child's perspective) and language B provides positive evidence supporting one of those possible analyses (cf. Müller, Cantone, Kupisch & Schmitz 2002). Overlap of the two language systems is a necessary but not sufficient condition for cross-linguistic influence to occur. Müller et al. (2002) argue that the direction of the influence (which of the two languages is influenced) depends on the computational complexity of the grammatical analysis in the sense of Jakubowicz (2000): children prefer less complex analyses to more complex analyses. The present paper will help to eliminate the possibility that language dominance may account for cross-linguistic influence.

## 2.  *The research project*

The data to be presented are part of the "Frühkindliche Zweisprachigkeit: Italienisch/Deutsch und Französisch/Deutsch im Vergleich" (Bilingualism in Early Childhood: Comparing Italian/German and French/German)[1] research project. The bilingual children are presented in Table 1. All of the children have been raised bilingually (German-Italian/French) from birth in (northern) Germany. The parents decided to raise them according to the *"une personne, une langue"* (one parent, one language) strategy (Ronjat 1913). In most cases (Céline is the exception), the mother speaks the Romance language to the child and the father speaks German. The corpus consists of video recordings (every two weeks). Most of the recordings started at age 1;6. The languages were kept separate during the recordings: the German interviewer spoke German with the child, while the Romance interviewer interacted with the child in his or her particular Romance language. In this paper, the main focus will be on Alexander and Carlotta.

---

[1] The project was financed by the Deutsche Forschungsgemeinschaft from 1999 to 2005 and was directed by this author. The project is currently being conducted at Bergische Universität Wuppertal, again with a research grant from the Deutsche Forschungsgemeinschaft.

| Alexander | French/German | recordings started at 2;2,6 |
|-----------|---------------|------------------------------|
| Céline | French/German | recordings started at 2;0,9 |
| Carlotta | Italian/German | recordings started at 1;8,28 |
| Lukas | Italian/German | recordings started at 1;7,12 |
| Jan | Italian/German | recordings started at 2;0,11 |

Table 1. *Children under investigation*

## 2.1 *Language dominance*

In what follows, we will start with the German-French children Alexander and Céline. We will confine ourselves to the children's MLU values in order to determine their degree of language balance. More details are provided in Kupisch, Cantone, Schmitz and Müller (2005). Figure 1 shows that Alexander is a mildly French-dominant child: his French MLU is slightly higher at all points in his development than the values he reached in German. In contrast to Alexander, Céline has one clearly dominant language, namely German. Her French MLU values differ considerably from those in German, as can be seen in Figure 2. In some recordings, the difference between the two languages amounts to more than 1.

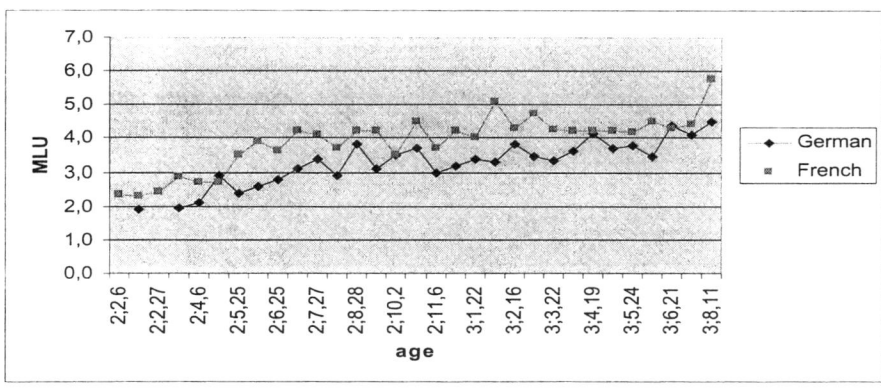

Figure 1. *MLU: Alexander (French-German)*

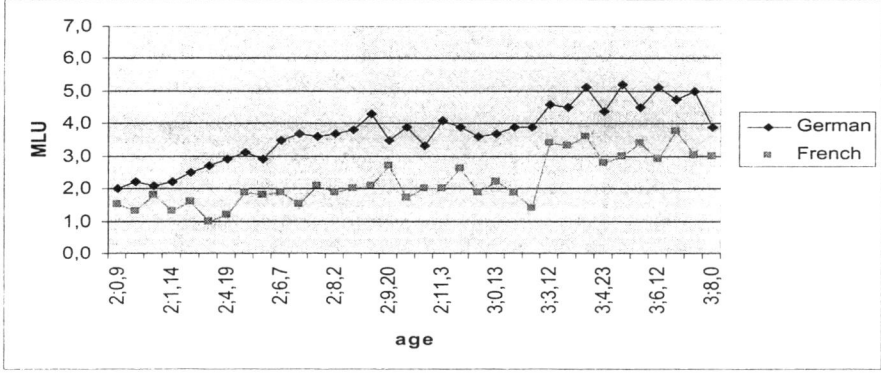

Figure 2. *MLU: Céline (French-German)*

Let us now turn to the German-Italian children (Loconte 2001). Figure 3 shows Carlotta's MLU in both languages; she can be regarded as a balanced bilingual child. Figure 4 presents the MLU values for Lukas. Until the age of approximately 3;3, he can be considered as the most balanced child in the project. After that age, he uses Italian less and less, most of his utterances in the Italian recordings being German or mixed utterances. Finally, Figure 5 presents Jan's MLU values. He is a non-balanced child like Céline, which is reflected in the considerable difference between his Italian and German MLUs until approximately age 3. His German is stronger than his Italian. However, unlike Céline, who uses not French but German with the French interviewer, Jan likes to speak Italian and mostly uses Italian during his Italian recording session.

To sum up, the children differ with respect to their degree of balance. We will return to language dominance and whether it relates to cross-linguistic influence below.

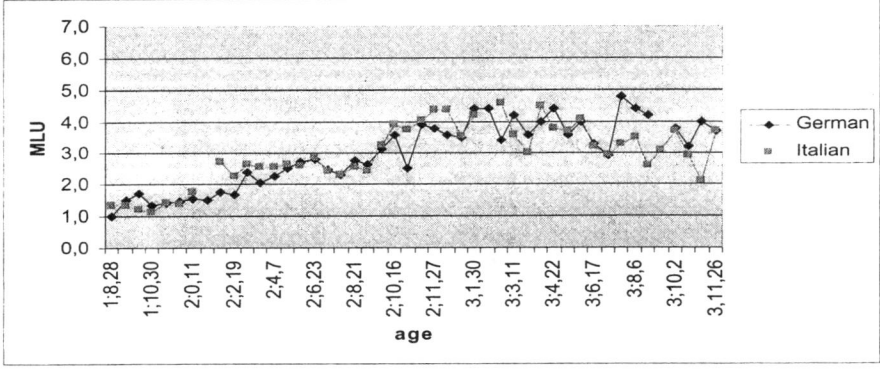

Figure 3. *MLU: Carlotta (Italian-German)*

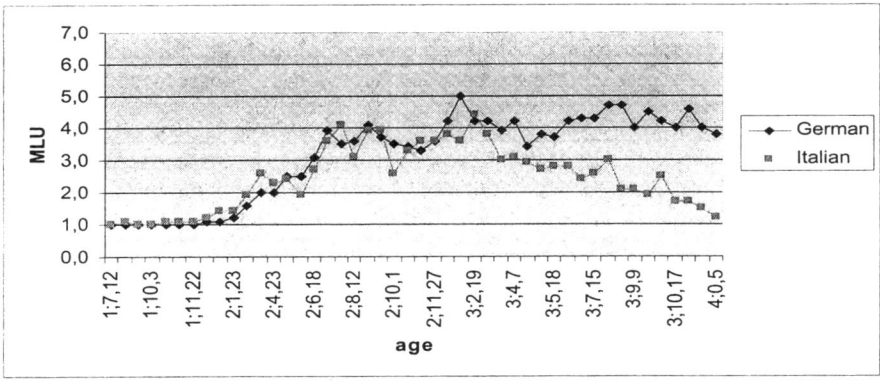

Figure 4. *MLU: Lukas (Italian-German)*

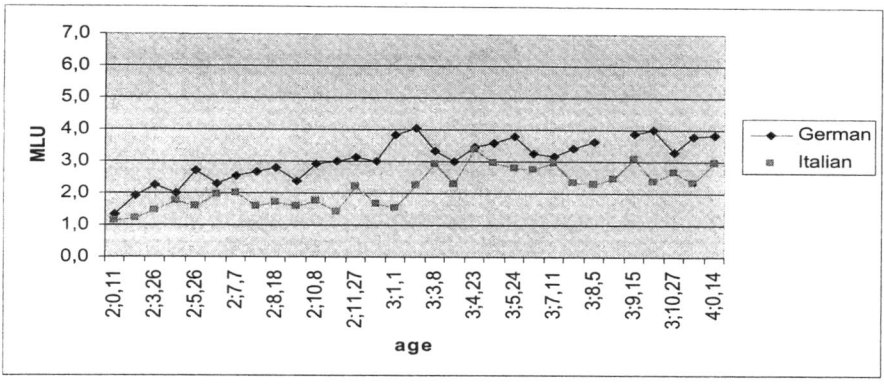

Figure 5. *MLU: Jan (Italian-German)*

## 3. *Cross-linguistic influence*

### 3.1 *The emergence of complementizers: German* **für** *and finite verb placement in subordinate clauses*

German and the two Romance languages, Italian and French, have a series of conjunctions that introduce subordinate clauses. Adult speakers of both German and the Romance languages use complementizers to introduce finite subordinate clauses, as well as a declarative and an interrogative complementizer (*dass/ob, que/si, che/se*).

(1) a. *Jean dit que ces étudiants ont compris le sujet.*
       'John says that these students understood the topic.'
    b. *Jean se demande si ces étudiants ont compris le sujet.*
       'John wonders whether these students understood the topic.'

These languages also contain a series of prepositions that introduce infinitival clauses, *pour/per* among them, as shown in (2).

(2)    *Jean est allé à la fête pour danser une valse.*
       'John went to the party to dance a waltz.'

As a first difference between the Romance languages and German, one notices that *für* does not figure among the prepositions that introduce infinitival clauses in standard German. Instead, the particle *zu* is used in German infinitival constructions. *Für*-infinitives are, however, in use in the Ruhr area.

(3)    *360 Eier   für  mitten   Auto   fahrn.*
       360  eggs   for  with-the car    drive
       '360 bucks for driving the car.'              (Gawlitzek-Maiwald 1997: 35)

The preposition *für* replaces *um* in *für*-infinitives; *um* is the most common preposition introducing infinitival clauses, as the infinitival particle *zu* is often not realized. *Für*-infinitives allow for the realization of the subject, which is otherwise impossible in infinitivals (Voyles 1983, cited in Gawlitzek-Maiwald 1997: 35).

(4) a.  *Menschen zu irren ist möglich.*
        People to err is possible
    b.  *Für Menschen zu irren ist möglich.*
        'For people to err is possible.'

The bilingual children investigated in the present study were raised in the northern regions of Germany; they did not have *für*-infinitives in their input. Notwithstanding, they do create these infinitives, as will be discussed in the following paragraphs.

A second difference between adult German and the Romance languages is that subordinate clauses, irrespective of whether they are finite or infinitival, are verb-final in German:[2]

(5) a.  *Hans sagt dass seine Studenten* [*den Stoff*]$_{Obj}$ [*verstanden*]$V_{lexical}$ [*haben*]$V_{finite}$
        John says that his students the topic understood have
    b.  *Hans ist auf die Party gegangen u m* [*einen Walser*]$_{Obj}$ *zu* [*tanzen*]$V_{infinitive}$.
        John has gone to the party for a waltz to dance

In the literature it is often assumed that German is an S-O-V-INFL language, where INFL is the category that hosts the finite verb. In other words, the position of the finite verb in subordinate clauses is the base position. In order to derive a V2 main clause, the finite verb has to move into the field above the subject, the left periphery which hosts the complementizer. The Romance languages are assumed to be S-INFL-V-O languages. In main (declarative) as well as in subordinate clauses, the finite verb follows the subject and is unrelated to the left periphery in the syntactic component of the grammar.

Müller (1993, 1994, 1998) observed a bilingual French-German child who had considerable problems in the domain of German subordinate clauses. The clause-final pattern, which is obligatory in subordinate clauses that are introduced by a conjunction or any other lexical element such as a *wh*-word, was acquired by this child at the age of 5. Müller (1993) also observed that the first element used to introduce infinitival and finite clauses is the preposition *für* in German and *pour* with infinitivals in French. Interestingly enough, the phonological shape of *für* is altered by this child, as can be seen in the examples below: *fü, fum, fo*. These phonological alternations with *für* are not possible in the adult language.

---

[2] Main clauses are verb-second in German: *[Dass seine Studenten den Stoff verstanden haben] [sagte]$_{Vfinite}$ Hans.*

(6) a. *[det] fü hm hin im     im     zoo* (=das) 2;7,17
      this for hm to  into-the into-the zoo
   b. *fum tiere   weg  nich [n]aufen* (=laufen) 2;7,17
      for animals away not  run
   c. *muß da  sei  rein  guck pour pour tie[j]e  nich nich weg[n]aufen*
      (=Tiere, weglaufen) 2;8,1
      must there there inside look for  for  animals not  not away-run
   d. *der will  fum  fum  besuch jemand  fum fum  krank* 2;9,5
      he  wants for  for  visit  someone for for  sick
   e. *fo  de fo  de  reiten  komm du* 2;9,18
      for it for it  (to) ride come  you
   f. *emm das das für  k[j]em[d]en* (=klemmen) 2;10,11
      emm this this for  (to) press
   g. *das  für  k[j]emmen deine   haare* (=klemmen) 2;10,11
      this for  (to) press your   hair

Müller argued that this first complementizer in German is a prepositional complementizer because at that time the child also used *pour* to introduce clauses in French. In contrast to German, French *pour*-clauses are always infinitival. The examples in (6) show a few finite clauses introduced by *für*. After the age of 2;10, that is, at the time when the child started to use adult-like complementizers, there are more examples of finite clauses introduced by *für*, some of which are shown in (7).

(7) a. *fü,  für  nich der  [n]öwe  beißt* (2;11,21)
      for for not the lion    bites
   b. *das  is  für der  rauch  geht hoch, in  das haus* (3;4,9)
      this is  for the  smoke  goes up,  in  the house
   c. *fum björn  hat das  abgerißt* (3;4,23)
      for björn  has it  off-torn
   d. *so  föm  föm  für die kinder,    kann das  abrissen* (3;4,23)
      like this for  for for the children can it    off-tear

Müller (1993) observed the use of the preposition *für* as the first lexical element to introduce subordinate clauses in German, together with problems in the acquisition of clause-final placement of finite verbs in subordinate clauses in one bilingual child, and suggested that these phenomena are connected. In what follows, it will be shown that both observations can be generalized to other bilingual French-German and also Italian-German children. In section 3.3., an explanation will be offered for the connection between finiteness, verb placement and the use of *für*.

We would like to start with the observation, already made by Müller (1998) on the basis of a review of the literature, that about half of all German bilingual children have problems with finite verb placement in German subordinate clauses, if their other first language is an S-INFL-V-O language, such as French, Italian or English. Interesting, two of the five children investigated have severe problems with finite verb placement in German subordinate clauses—Alexander in the French-German study, and Carlotta in the Italian-German study.

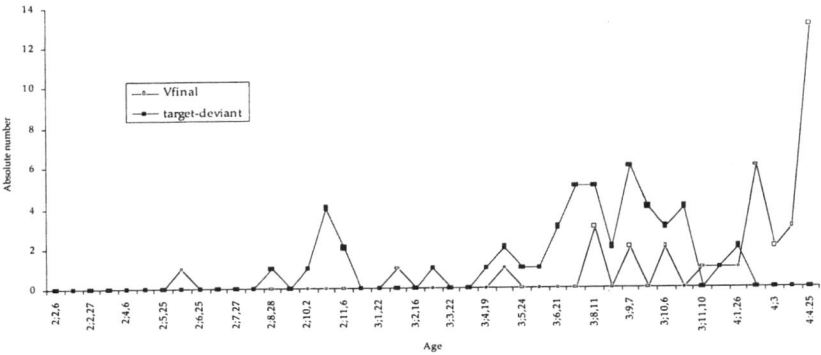

Figure 6. *German subordinate clauses: Alexander (French-German)*

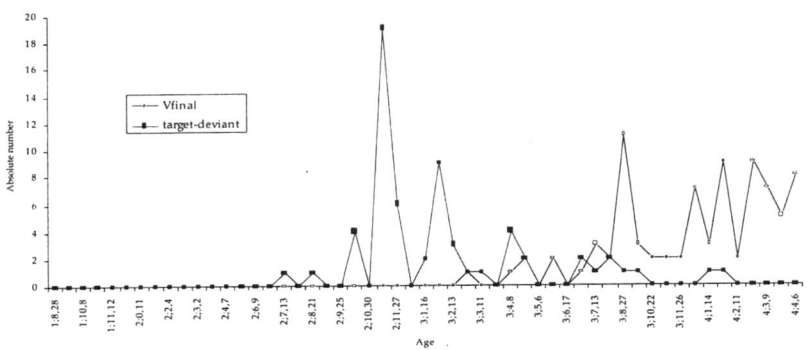

Figure 7. *German subordinate clauses: Carlotta (Italian-German)*

As can be seen in Figures 6 and 7, target-deviant verb placement ceases to appear in both children's speech only at the age of 4; in other words, German verb placement in subordinate clauses can be regarded as a late-acquired grammatical domain.

The other three children either have no problems at all, that is, the target-like placement of finite verbs (Vfinal) is acquired instantaneously and error-free (Jan), or their development shows marginal root word order in subordinate clauses (Lukas, Céline). This is shown in Figures 8, 9 and 10 for Jan, Lukas and Céline.

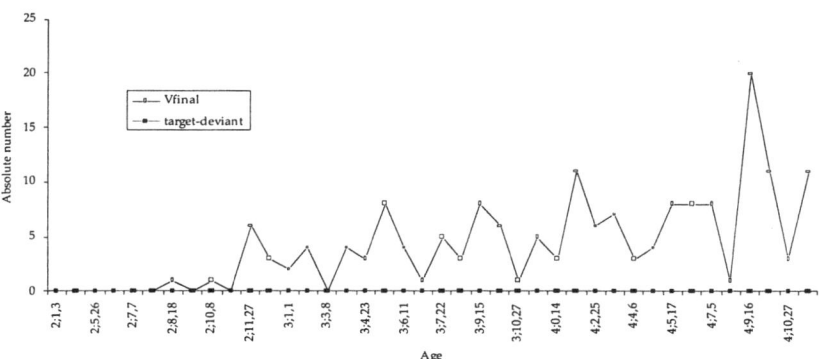

Figure 8. *German subordinate clauses: Jan (Italian-German)*

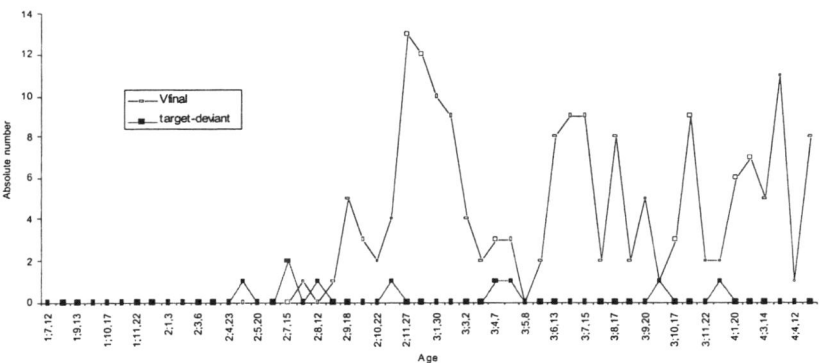

Figure 9. *German subordinate clauses: Lukas (Italian-German)*

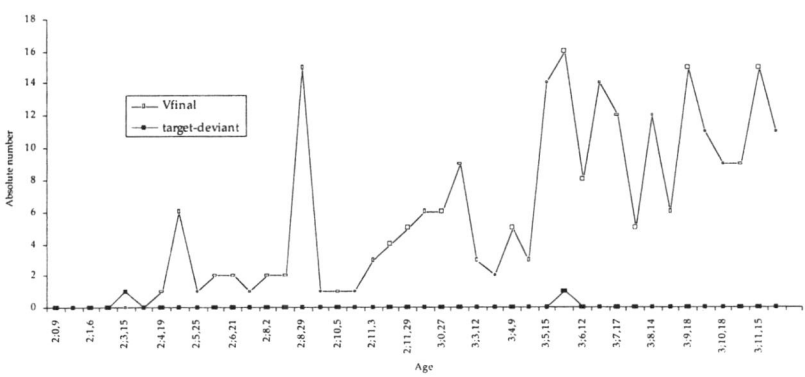

Figure 10. *German subordinate clauses: Céline (French-German)*

Furthermore, only the children who exhibit problems with finite verb placement also use *für* in German as one of the first elements introducing clauses,
with both finite and with infinitival clauses (cf. Gawlitzek-Maiwald 1997 on
the development of infinitival clauses in German by monolingual and bilingual
children).

(8) a. *für setzen* (Carlotta, 2;7,13)
        for (to) sit
    b. *für  es    macht* (Carlotta, 2;10,16)
        for  it    makes
    c. *für  gucken  und für  katzen* (Carlotta, 2;10,16)
        for  (to) look and for  cats
    d. *für  das   macht  musik* (Carlotta, 2;10,30)
        for  it    makes  musik
    e. *das  ist  doch      für  einkaufen* (Carlotta, 2;10,30)
        this is   however   for  (to go) shopping
    f. *für  rutschen* (Carlotta, 3;0,25)
        for  (to) slide
    g. *und  für  skiern* (Carlotta, 3;1,30)
        and  for  (to) ski
    h. *hier für  skiern* (Carlotta, 3;1,30)
        here for  (to) ski
    i. *für  der  machen* (Carlotta, 3;1,30)
        for  he   (to) make
    j. *für  machen   das* (Carlotta, 3;2,13)
        für  (to) make it
    k. *für  mein – mein kuchen   aufessen* (Carlotta, 3;3,11)
        for  my – my    cake      (to) all-eat

(9) a. *für   die   bahn   kann* (Alexander, 2;11,20)
        for   the   train  can
    b. *für   grattieren* (=kratzen, Alexander, 2;7,6)
        for   (to) scratch
    c. *noch so ein tier  für   die   kemmt* (=kommt) (Alexander, 3;2,2)
        another animal  for   it    comes
    d. *auch  für    das    kleben* (Alexander, 3;5,3)
        also  for    it     (to) glue
    e. *ja  für die – für die – die  haie    kann nich  die – äh – die  fischen*
        yes for the – for the – the sharks cannot     the – uh – the fish
        *essen* (Alexander, 3;5,3)
        eat

At the same time, the children use *für* as a preposition and alter its phonological shape to *fom, füm,* etc.

Since we are dealing with longitudinal data, absence of data should be
avoided as an argument for or against hypotheses concerning language development. However, it is the case that only the children who exhibit word order

problems also use *für* in order to introduce finite and infinitival clauses. This is probably not a mere coincidence.

### 3.2 *Why* für*? The emergence of prepositional complementizers*

Creolists such as Bakker (1987), Bickerton (1981), Byrne (1984) Koopman and Lefebvre (1981, 1982), Washabaugh (1975) and Woolford (1979) have observed that French-based creoles have developed *pu* (French: *pour*) in order to introduce clauses, and English-based creoles *fo, fi, fu, u* (English: *for*). The categorial status of this element has been the subject of a lively debate.

Koopman and Lefebvre (1981, 1982) argue in the case of Haitian creole that the possibility of introducing clauses was the first step in a reanalysis of the preposition *pu* as a complementizer. As a complementizer, *pu* always introduces finite clauses. Complementizers are included within S', whereas prepositions introduce or subcategorize an NP complement. The authors suggest several tests to determine whether *pu* is a preposition or a complementizer, one of which is pronominalization. As a complementizer, *pu* is substituted by the pronoun, for example, (10a) transforms into (10b), but not into (10c).

(10) a. *m   vle       pu    l   venir*
      *je   vouloir  pour  il  venir*
      I     want     for   he  come
   b. *m   vle       sa    a*
      *je   vouloir  cela  DET*
      I     want     that  DET
   c. *m   vle       pu  sa*
      I     want     for  that

Where does the prepositional complementizer come from? A study of interest is Siegel's (2000) analysis of *fo* in Hawai'i Creole English (HCE). *Fo* is a complementizer in HCE and can also introduce finite complements. Moreover, clauses introduced by *fo* contain overt subjects that are in the nominative case (Siegel 2000: 223).

(11) One keki been tell da udder one fo go buy ice cream for dey eat up on top
     da bus.
     'One kid told another one to buy ice cream for them$_{NOM}$ to eat on the bus.'

Influence from a substrate language (Portuguese) is one possibility to account for the emergence of *fo*. The Portuguese word *para* is functionally and syntactically similar to HCE *fo*. The syntactic similarities are the existence of overt (nominative-case-marked) subjects and the inflected infinitive of Portuguese *para*-clauses. Relexification could account for the similarities between Portuguese *para* and HCE *fo*. According to Lefebvre (1998: 16), "relexification is a mental process that builds new lexical entries by copying the lexical entries of an already established lexicon and replacing their phonological representations with representations derived from another language." However, there are also differences between *para*-clauses in Portuguese and *fo*-clauses in HCE which are unexpected under an analysis in terms of relexification but suggest the "extension of a pattern of grammaticalization that had already begun," according to Siegel (2000: 225 ff.). For one thing, Portuguese *para*-clauses are untensed, while HCE *fo*-clauses may be tensed.

The creole studies reveal parallels with the situation described in the bilingual children Alexander and Carlotta. These children use a preposition which exists in the German adult system—*für*—in order to introduce infinitival and finite clauses, a possibility that does not exist in the German adult system but, at least for infinitival clauses, does exist in French (*pour*) and in Italian (*per*). In the output of the child studied by Müller (1993), we also saw phonological variations like *fum* and *föm*, which are nonexistent in the child's input. Note that other prepositions in German are inflected for case, such as *an – am*, *in – im*, etc. The child extends this possibility to the prepositional complementizer *für*. Another parallel with the creole studies is that *für*-clauses in German can be finite while *pour-/per*-clauses in the Romance languages are infinitival. An explanation in terms of relexification for children's use of *für* is therefore not sufficient. Siegel (this volume) proposes for creole genesis that "there must be both 'availability constraints' that determine which substrate features actually reach the target pool of variants via transfer, and 'reinforcement principles' that determine which of the transferred features are reinforced and retained in the leveling process." Siegel presents perceptual salience and congruence as the most important factors. In the present case, the function and meaning of *für*—the prepositional complementizer—are related to *pour/per* in the Romance languages. Also, *für* and *pour/per* are morphosyntactically congruent, since they both introduce clauses. Semantically, *für* and *pour/per* express causality or finality. It is likely that the semantic value plays an important role here. *Weil* 'because' is one of the first target-like conjunctions to appear in child language. It is likely that causal (and temporal) relations are first expressed by children using a subordinate clause. *Pour, per* and *für* serve this function. On the other hand, prepositions like *de/di* lack semantic content altogether; they simply spell out functional features; this could be one reason why children opt for *für, pour, per* as their first complementizers.[3]

Müller and Hulk (2001) argued that one prerequisite for cross-linguistic influence to occur in bilingual children is that there must be a certain amount of overlap between the child's two languages: a construction in language A allows

---

[3] Within the framework of Distributed Morphology (cf. Halle & Marantz 1993), we might assume that some complementizers are merged as feature bundles and are inserted late in the derivational process, while others are merged as complete lexical items. Those complementizers that are mere functional elements spelling out functional features appear late in child language development. The "real" complementizers are the last connectors to be used by children. The privileged status of *für* in child language, as well as in creole genesis, may therefore have semantic reasons.

for more than one analysis (from the child's perspective) and language B contains positive evidence supporting one of those possible analyses. This condition is similar to Siegel's reinforcement principles in creole genesis, and is compatible with his view of the development of *fo* in HCE, for which extension of a pattern of grammaticalization that had already begun was plausible. In other words, in bilingual development as well as in creole genesis, the new pattern that emerges must be supported by positive evidence in that language; not only are the features that transfer restricted but so is their development in the recipient language. To enable us to discuss what kind of positive evidence the bilingual children need in order to use finite *für*-clauses in German, the syntactic derivation of prepositional complementizers in the Romance languages will be presented in the following section. The syntactic analysis will also shed light on the possible reason why those bilingual children who "find their way" into subordination via the *für*-route, that is, via a preposition, have problems with finite verb placement in German subordinate clauses.

3.3 *The syntax of French and Italian prepositional complementizers, extended to German*

In generative syntax and other frameworks, complementizers are assumed to form a constituent with the infinitival IP they are associated with. For instance, in the sentence *Il est important de chanter* 'It is important *de* sing-inf,' *de* is often analyzed as forming a constituent with *chanter*, since *de* requires an infinitival, and therefore is not compatible with a finite phrase: *\*Il est important de vous chantiez* 'It is important *de* you sing-subjunc' (Kayne 1999: 41). The same can be proposed for Italian *di,* which is compatible with an infinitival only, as its French counterpart. Kayne (1999) argued that the French and Italian prepositional complementizers enter the derivation above the VP, and not as sister to the IP they are associated with. The relation between complementizer and IP is expressed by movement of the (infinitival) IP to the specifier position of the complementizer. Subsequent movement of the complementizer to a head W, followed by phrasal movement to Spec,W accounts for the observed word order in these languages. The main hypothesis is that prepositional complementizers do not form a constituent with the infinitival IP they are associated with. For a sentence like *Gianni ha tentato di cantare* 'Gianni has tried *di* sing-inf,' the following derivational steps are necessary: the infinitival IP *cantare* is merged with the main verb *tentato*, not with *di*. *Di* is subsequently merged with *tentato cantare*, the result being *di tentato cantare*. *Di* then attracts the infinitival IP *cantare* to its Spec, resulting in *cantare$_i$ di tentato t$_i$*. *Di* further raises to an immediately higher head W, *di$_j$+W cantare$_i$ t$_j$ tentato t$_i$*. *Di+W* then attracts VP to its Spec: *[tentato t$_i$]$_k$ di$_j$+W cantare$_i$ t$_j$ t$_k$*.

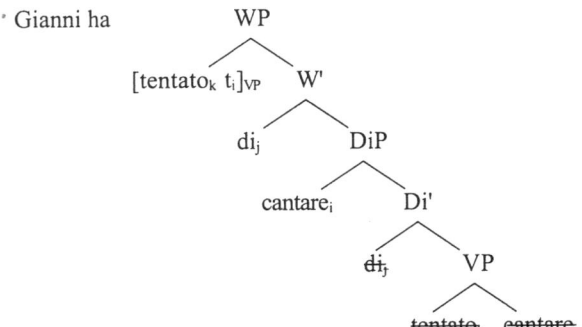

Figure 11. *Derivation of [...]* tentato di cantare

Kayne (1999) advances several arguments for his analysis. The first type of argument relates to the nominal character of French and Italian infinitives. French *de* and Italian *di* require an infinitival and are not compatible with a finite phrase (Kayne 1999: 40 ff.).

(12) a. *Il    est    important    de    chanter*
         It    is    important    *de*    sing-inf
      b. *\*Il est    important    de    vous chantez*
         It    is    important    *de*  you  sing-subjunc
      c. *Gianni  dice  di  aver      capito*
         Gianni  says  *di*  have-inf  understood
      d. *\*Gianni dice  di  (lui)  ha    capito*
         Gianni  says  *di*  (he)  has   understood

Both Romance languages use another complementizer for finite clauses, *que/che*. The same generalization extends to *pour* and *per* in the Romance languages. They are restricted to infinitival clauses. If a finite clause is expressed, French uses *pour que*, Italian *perchè*.

The second type of argument relates to the observation that, in French and Italian, infinitives, despite their nominal character, do not occupy DP positions. To sum up, French and Italian infinitives must be licensed in a special way; one way is to be preceded by *de/di*, or, extending Kayne's proposal, by *pour/per*. The new idea in Kayne's approach is that the prepositional complementizers do not form a constituent with the infinitival IP they are associated with. Consequently, the complementizer is not part of the argument of the (main) verb, but enters the derivation subsequent to the merger of the infinitival IP and the main verb.[4]

---

[4] Kayne's proposal allows us to analyze some puzzles in French and Italian as artifacts of the common assumption that *di/de* plus infinitive phrase is a constituent. One puzzle is that a subcategorized preposition can never be followed by *de/di* in French and Italian: *\*Contavo su di essere onesto* 'I-counted on *di* be-inf honest.' It is not the case that Italian disallows this sequence of two prepositions in general: *Contavo su di lui* 'I-counted on of him' (Kayne 1999:

Let us assume that Romance children have the correct analysis of infinitival clauses from the beginning. If Kayne's analysis is extended to *pour/per*, we would have the derivation in Figure 12 for the French child sentence *c'est pour dormir* 'it's for sleeping.'

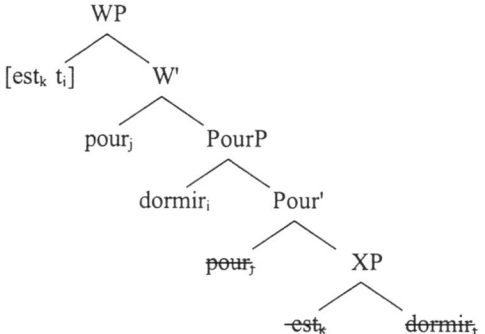

Figure 12. *Derivation of infinitival introduced by* pour

This structure would conform to the adult system. Bilingual French-German and Italian-German children may extend this kind of analysis to *für* in German. Thus, a child sentence like *das ist für einkaufen* 'it's for shopping' has the derivation in Figure 13:

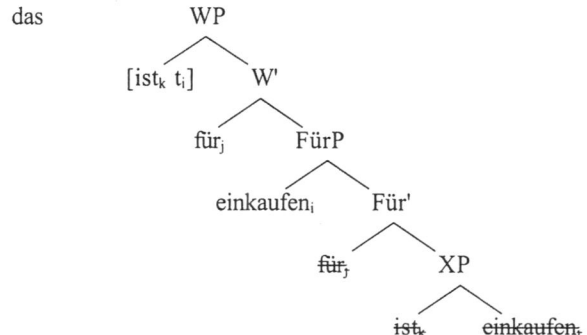

Figure 13. *Derivation of infinitival introduced by* für

---

53). Let us examine the ungrammatical sentence *Contavo su di essere onesto* under Kayne's proposal. Subcategorized prepositions will enter the derivation before the prepositional complementizer *di*, or only after the complex *contavo su essere onesto* has been formed: *di contavo su essere onesto*. *Di* then attracts the infinitival IP *essere onesto* to its Spec, resulting in *[essere onesto]ᵢ di contavo su tᵢ*. *Di* further raises to an immediately higher head W, *diⱼ+W [essere onesto]ᵢ tⱼ contavo su tᵢ*. *Di+W* then attracts VP to its Spec, *[contavo su tᵢ]ₖ diⱼ+W [essere onesto]ᵢ tⱼ tₖ*, giving rise to the surface sequence of elements. The ungrammaticality of the sequence follows naturally from the analysis, since the derivational step *[essere onesto]ᵢ di contavo su tᵢ.* represents an instance of preposition stranding, in which the argument of the preposition *su—essere onesto*—has been moved alone, without taking the preposition along with it. Italian has a general prohibition against preposition stranding, which Kayne exemplifies by the ungrammaticality of *Chi contavi su?* 'Who were-you-counting on?' (Kayne 1999: 52).

Kayne (1999) mentions the possibility that this kind of analysis extends to
the real complementizers *que/che* in the Romance languages. Let us assume that
this is indeed the case. We would then also assume that the bilingual children
extend the possibility they have encountered for *für* to the German
complementizers, that is, to finite clauses. As a consequence, they would merge
a finite clause with matrix word order with the matrix verb and subsequently
insert the complementizer *dass* (cf. Figure 14); thus, the absence of sentence-
final placement of the finite verb in these children's output is predicted. This
link between the first prepositional complementizer *für*, which is syntactically
analyzed like French *pour* and Italian *per*, and the persistent problems with
finite verb placement in German subordinate clauses, may make a key
contribution to the picture presented here, namely that children who have
problems with German subordinate clauses begin to grasp the complementizer
system by using *für* with the same syntactic derivation as *pour/per*. That the
syntactic derivation of the prepositional complementizer introducing infinitival
clauses is indeed extended to real complementizers is indicated by the
observation that the prepositional complementizers can also introduce finite
clauses in the children's grammar.

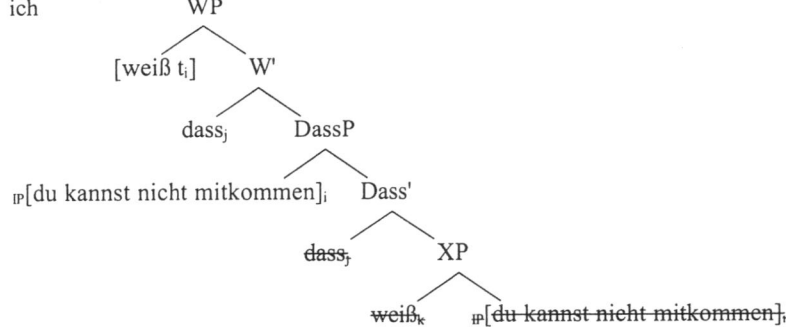

Figure 14. *Derivation of finite subordinate clause in German*
*with a Romance* pour/per-*analysis*

Interestingly, the bilingual children have positive evidence favoring the Romance analysis of complementizers in German. German subordinate clauses
that are not introduced by any lexical element do not show clause-final placement of the finite verb, but main clause word order instead, as shown in (13a)
in contrast to (13b).

(13) a. *ich   weiß   du   kannst   nicht   mitkommen*
      I     know  you  cannot   join    us
    b. *ich   weiß   dass du      nicht   mitkommen kannst*
      I     know  that  you     not     join us        can

Thus, for a sentence without a lexical complementizer, the *für*-derivation would yield the correct analysis. In other words, the Romance syntactic derivation does not transfer "blindly" into child German, but is supported by positive evidence.

Finally, one reviewer asked why the bilingual children do not extend *pour/per* to finite clauses in French and Italian as well. The extension would be expected, if—as we have assumed here—finite complements exhibit the same syntactic derivation as infinitivals (neither the complementizer introducing finite clauses in Romance nor prepositions introducing infinitivals are sisters to the constituent which they introduce in the syntactic derivation), but is unfortunately absent from the child corpora. The English children studied by Brown (1973), Adam and Eve, use *for* to introduce finite clauses as well, for example, *for Mummy help me reach* (Adam). The observation that *for* can introduce finite clauses even without language contact is important for the interpretation of the bilingual data, since it supports Siegel's and Hulk and Müller's view that, in the bilingual or creole case, positive evidence is a prerequisite for the observed development. The positive evidence in the monolingual case would constitute the possibility that finite subordinate clauses are compatible with an analysis à la Kayne for prepositional complementizers.

3.4 *Language dominance*

A final issue is the problem of individual variation. Why do only some bilingual children choose the *für*-path and exhibit word order problems in German subordinate clauses (i.e., Alexander and Carlotta but not Céline, Lukas and Jan)? In what follows, we would like to rule out the possibility that Alexander and Carlotta are extending the Romance analysis of prepositional complementizers to German because of language dominance or unbalanced bilingualism. We presented the two children's MLU values in section 2.1. In the case of Alexander, we could argue that since his German is weaker than his French, he will naturally try the Romance option for German. However, note that this argument does not generalize to Carlotta's case. She can be considered as a balanced bilingual; nevertheless, she opts for the Romance analysis. Finite verb placement is a vulnerable domain in bilingual first language acquisition, even among balanced bilingual children.

Results from a non-vulnerable grammatical domain, negation, reinforce the claim that dominance is not the crucial factor: these domains are non-vulnerable also in unbalanced bilingual children. We know from Meisel's (1997) work, that negation is not a vulnerable domain in monolingual and bilingual acquisition of French. This is also true of the French-German bilingual children of the present investigation. Céline's results are particularly revealing because her French is weak. Alexander's speech was studied for placement of the negator *pas* until the age of 2;6. Since Céline rarely spoke French with the French interviewer, her corpus was analyzed until the age of 4;0. Interestingly, Alexander produced 199 instances of *pas* with a verb until the age of 2;6. Céline produced 208 by the age of 4;0. Table 2 shows the results.

| Child | $V_{finite}$ + *pas* | *pas* + $V_{finite}$ | $V_{non\text{-}finite}$ + *pas* | *pas* + $V_{non\text{-}finite}$ |
|---|---|---|---|---|
| Alexander | | | | |
| verb types | 53 | — | 1 | 8 |
| verb tokens | 188 | — | 1 | 10 |
| Céline | | | | |
| verb types | 94 | 2 | — | 10 |
| verb tokens | 195 | 2 | — | 11 |

Table 2. *Position of* pas *in child speech*

Target-deviant placement (*pas* + $V_{finite}$, $V_{non\text{-}finite}$ + *pas*) amounts to only 0.5% of cases in Alexander's speech, and, more interestingly, 1% in Céline's. Thus, Céline's weak language, French, develops more slowly than her strong language, but is qualitatively similar to Alexander's French (cf. Cordes 2001 and Müller & Kupisch 2003 for the development of further grammatical domains in Céline's language). Language dominance is therefore not the explanation of the assumed analysis of *für*-clauses either. Further research is necessary in order to explain the individual aspects of cross-linguistic influence (cf. Müller et al., 2006 for further discussion).

## 4. *Conclusion*

A final issue that must be addressed is whether the cross-linguistic influence we have observed with *für* is related to language use or to underlying linguistic competence. Siegel (this volume) discusses the possibility of transfer in second language acquisition as a compensatory strategy, one that is involved in language use, not in language knowledge. Two observations seem to support this view of our data: (i) although it develops late, the bilingual children eventually learn the target-like word order in German subordinate clauses and do not continue to use *für* with finite clauses; (ii) subordinate clauses are one of the grammatical aspects of language that tend to be acquired late. Based on these observations, one might argue that pressure to communicate in the absence of the necessary competence is the reason for transfer as a compensatory strategy. Although this seems plausible at first sight, the developmental path of unlearning the incorrect word order in German subordinate clauses reveals that the competence system is involved in cross-linguistic influence: Müller (1993, 1998) shows that bilingual children unlearn target-deviant word order for each complementizer separately, a process that lasts as long as two years in some children. Another observation is that acceleration is one quantitative effect of cross-linguistic influence (Müller et al., 2006), which is quite a surprising result if one assumes that pressure is the cause of the influence.

In conclusion, this investigation has attempted to link two observations concerning child language, namely the use of a preposition as a complementizer and problems with finite verb placement in German. The conclusion drawn is that bilingual children make use of a syntactic derivation from language A to derive a similar syntactic phenomenon in language B. Positive evidence in language B is needed in order for cross-linguistic influence to occur. The case described has interesting parallels with the development of prepositional complementizers in creole languages and may contribute to our understanding of the importance of language contact in the development of languages.

*References*
Bakker, P. 1987. A Basque nautical pidgin: A missing link in the history of *fu*. *Journal of Pidgin and Creole Languages* 2(1): 1–30.
Bernardini Röst, P. 2001. Lo squilibrio nell'acquisizione di due lingue nell'infanzia: indagine longitudinale sullo sviluppo della sintassi nominale. Licentiate thesis, University of Lund.
Bickerton, D. 1981. *Roots of Language*. Ann Arbor, MI: Karoma.
Brown, R. 1973. *A First Language: The Early Stages*. Cambridge, MA: Harvard University Press.
Byrne, F. 1984. *Fi* and *fu*: Origins and functions in some Caribbean English-based creoles. *Lingua* 62: 92–120.
Cordes, J. 2001. Zum unausgewogenen doppelten Erstspracherwerb eines deutsch-französisch aufwachsenden Kindes: Eine empirische Untersuchung. M.A. thesis, University of Hamburg.
Döpke, S. 1992. *One Parent, One Language: An Interactional Approach*. Amsterdam/Philadelphia: Benjamins.
Gawlitzek-Maiwald, I. 1997. Der monolinguale und bilinguale Erwerb von Infinitivkonstruktionen. Ein Vergleich von Deutsch und Englisch. Tübingen: Niemeyer.
Gawlitzek-Maiwald, I. and R. Tracy. 1996. Bilingual bootstrapping. *Linguistics* 34: 901–926.
Genesee, F. 1989. Early bilingual development: one language or two? *Journal of Child Language* 16: 161–179.
Genesee, F., E. Nicoladis and J. Paradis. 1995. Language differentiation in early bilingual development. *Journal of Child Language* 22: 611–631.
Halle, M. and A. Marantz. 1993. Distributed morphology and the pieces of inflection. In *The View from Building 20*, K. Hale and S. Keyser (eds.), 111–176. Cambridge, MA: MIT Press.
Hulk, A. 1997. The acquisition of French object pronouns by a Dutch/French bilingual child. In *Language Acquisition: Knowledge, Representation and Processing. Proceedings of the GALA '97 Conference on Language Acquisition*, A. Sorace, C. Heycock and R. Shillcock (eds.), 521–526. Edinburgh: University of Edinburgh Press.
Hulk, A. and N. Müller. 2000. Crosslinguistic influence at the interface between syntax and pragmatics. *Bilingualism: Language and Cognition* 3(3): 227–244.
Jakubowicz, C. 2000. Functional Categories in (Ab)normal Language Acquisition. MS., CNRS, Paris.

Kayne, R. 1999. Prepositional complementizers as attractors. *Probus* 11: 39–73.

Koopman, H. and C. Lefebvre. 1981. Haitian creole *pu*. In *Generative Studies on Creole Languages*, P. Muysken (ed.), 201–221. Dordrecht: Foris.

Koopman, H. and C. Lefebvre. 1982. *Pu*: marqueur du mode, préposition et complémenteur. In *Syntaxe de l'Haïtien*, C. Lefebvre, H. Magloire-Holly and N. Piou (eds.), 64–91. Ann Arbor, MI: Karoma.

Kupisch, T., K. Cantone, K. Schmitz and N. Müller. 2005. Redefining language dominance in bilingual children. Submitted for publication.

Lefebvre, C. 1998. Creole Genesis and the Acquisition of Grammar: The Case of Haitian Creole. Cambridge: Cambridge University Press.

Loconte, A. 2001. Zur Sprachdominanz bei bilingual deutsch-italienischen Kindern. M.A. thesis, University of Hamburg.

Meisel, J. M. 1989. Early differentiation of languages in bilingual children. In *Bilingualism Across the Lifespan: Aspects of Acquisition, Maturity, and Loss*, K. Hyltenstam and L. Obler (eds.), 13–40. Cambridge: Cambridge University Press.

Meisel, J. M. (ed.). 1994. *Bilingual First Language Acquisition: German and French*. Amsterdam/Philadelphia: Benjamins.

Meisel, J. M. 1997. The acquisition of syntax of negation in French and German: Contrasting first and second language development. *Second Language Research* 13: 227–263.

Müller, N. 1993. Komplexe Sätze. Der Erwerb von COMP und von Wortstellungsmustern bei bilingualen Kindern (Französisch/Deutsch). Tübingen: Narr.

Müller, N. 1994. Parameters cannot be reset: Evidence from the development of COMP. In *Bilingual First Language Acquisition. French and German Grammatical Development*, J. M. Meisel (ed.), 235–269. Amsterdam/Philadelphia: Benjamins.

Müller, N. 1998. Transfer in bilingual first language acquisition. *Bilingualism: Language and Cognition* 1(3): 151–171.

Müller, N., K. Cantone, T. Kupisch and K. Schmitz. 2002. Zum Spracheneinfluss im bilingualen Erstspracherwerb: Italienisch-Deutsch. *Linguistische Berichte* 190: 157–206.

Müller, N. and A. Hulk. 2000. Crosslinguistic influence in bilingual children: Object omissions and root infinitives. In *Proceedings of the 24th Annual Boston University Conference on Language Development*, C. Howell, S. A. Fish and T. Keith-Lucas (eds.), 546–557. Somerville, MA: Cascadilla Press.

Müller, N. and A. Hulk. 2001. Crosslinguistic influence in bilingual language acquisition: Italian and French as recipient languages. *Bilingualism: Language and Cognition* 4(1): 1–21.

Müller, N. and T. Kupisch. 2003. Zum simultanen Erwerb des Deutschen und des Französischen bei (un)ausgeglichen bilingualen Kindern. *Vox Romanica* 62: 145–169.

Müller, N., T. Kupisch, K. Schmitz and K. Cantone. 2006. *Einführung in die Mehrsprachigkeitsforschung*. Tübingen: Narr.

Ronjat, J. 1913. *Le développement du langage observé chez un enfant bilingue*. Paris: Champion.

Schlyter, S. 1993. The weaker language in bilingual Swedish-French children. In *Progression and Regression in Language,* K. Hyltenstam and A. Viberg (eds.), 289–308. Cambridge: Cambridge University Press.

Siegel, J. 2000. Substrate influence in Hawai'i Creole English. *Language in Society* 29: 197–236.

Taeschner, T. 1983. *The Sun is Feminine: A Study of Language Acquisition in Bilingual Children.* Berlin: Springer.

Tracy, R. 1995. Child Languages in Contact: Bilingual Language Acquisition in Early Childhood. Post-doctoral thesis, University of Tübingen.

Voyles, J. 1983. *Ansätze zu einer deutschen Grammatik.* Göppingen: Kümmerle.

Washabaugh, W. 1975. On the development of complementizers in creolization. *Working Papers in Language Universals* 17: 109–140.

Woolford, E. 1979. The developing complementizer system of Tok Pisin: Syntactic change in process. In *The Genesis of Language*, K. C. Hill (ed.), 108–124. Ann Arbor, MI: Karoma.

# PART II

## PROCESSES: INITIAL STATE
## (TRANSFER AND RELEXIFICATION)

# FULL TRANSFER AND RELEXIFICATION:
## SECOND LANGUAGE ACQUISITION AND CREOLE GENESIS

Rex A. Sprouse
*Indiana University*

This paper identifies and examines a generally unnoticed convergence between a model of (adult) second language acquisition (Schwartz & Sprouse's 1994, 1996 Full Transfer/Full Access, FT/FA) and an influential model of creole genesis (Lefebvre's 1998 Relexification Hypothesis, RH), both framed within generative grammar. It is shown that both FT/FA and RH make virtually identical claims about the initial state of adult grammatical development in the general case. In other words, Schwartz and Sprouse's full transfer and Lefebvre's relexification are complementary conceptualizations of the same basic phenomenon. To the extent that one of these hypotheses finds empirical support, the other does as well. Subsequent to the initial state, "canonical" second language development and creole development exhibit striking differences. This paper argues that these differences arise not from divergent underlying mechanisms, but rather from the quality and quantity of "target language" input: in creole genesis, this input is extremely limited, and the "target language" serves primarily as the source for the relexification process alone. In more typical second language acquisition (particularly in tutored acquisition), the input is robust and persistent, and it is typically the case that morphosyntactic parameters are reset. This is because the resetting of morphosyntactic parameters results from failure-driven development, which is possible only if sufficient input is available. The paper will also comment on differences between two scholarly communities: second language acquisition scholars and creole scholars. It is suggested that the historicist emphasis of creole studies and the cognitive emphasis of second language studies obscure potentially valuable insights across the two subfields; scholars in each community are urged to become better acquainted with the controversies and findings of the other.

## 1. *Introduction*

The organizers of the *Montreal Dialogues: Processes in L2 Acquisition and Creole Genesis*, held at Université du Québec à Montréal in late August 2004, sought to bring together second language (L2) acquisition scholars and creolists to learn about each other's fields and see whether they might have useful insights to share.* In that spirit, the primary goal of this paper is to show that a particular model of L2 acquisition and a particular model of creole genesis have much in common. In fact, the differences between them are essentially straightforward functions of the different acquisitional settings each is designed to characterize. A weak version of the claim of this paper is thus that

---
* I wish to thank the organizers of the Montreal Dialogues for one of the most intellectually invigorating professional meetings I have ever had the pleasure of attending. I also thank Laurent Dekydtspotter, Claire Lefebvre, Kevin Rottet, Bonnie D. Schwartz, David Stringer, Lydia White, and audiences at the University of Utrecht and at the Indiana University Second Language Research Group for helpful comments and suggestions.

there is a generally unnoticed convergence between Schwartz and Sprouse's (1994, 1996) Full Transfer/Full Access model of L2 acquisition and Lefebvre's (1998) Relexification model of the genesis of (Haitian) creole. A stronger version of the claim is that Full Transfer can be restated in terms of Relexification and that Relexification is at the core of the second language instinct, accounting both for the L2 initial state and for the frequent failure of failure-driven (UG-constrained) revision ("learning") to effect convergence on the target language.

The paper is structured as follows: Section 2 lays out the basic claims of Full Transfer/Full Access and the Relexification Hypothesis and provides some contextualization for each. Section 3 discusses the basic similarity of the two hypotheses. Section 4 suggests that differences in formulation are primarily due to the anticipation of divergent outcomes in canonical interlanguage development vs. creole formation, which are due to external factors, and not to essential differences in the cognitive processes of early interlanguage learners and early creole creators. Section 5 offers brief treatments of four areas of interest for L2 researchers where Full Transfer as Relexification might shed some immediate light. Section 6 offers concluding remarks, including an observation on the different "cultures" of L2 acquisitionists and creolists.

## 2. *Summary of the Two Models*

### 2.1 *Full Transfer/Full Access (Schwartz & Sprouse 1994, 1996)*
Over the past decade, Schwartz and Sprouse's (1994, 1996) Full Transfer/Full Access model has attracted and sustained a substantial amount of attention within generative-oriented approaches to L2 acquisition. (See, for example, recent textbook treatments by Hawkins 2001 and White 2003a.) Full Transfer/Full Access claims that in L2 acquisition, all of the "abstract properties" of the L1 grammar are transferred and comprise the initial L2 state; further UG-constrained syntactic development arises from an inability to assign/license structures to target language (TL) input. This can be graphically represented as in (1).

(1)    Full Transfer/Full Access
       L1:   ... $G_{end}$

       L2:   $\bar{G}_0$, $G_1$, $G_2$, ...

Full Transfer/Full Access is far from the only model currently under investigation by L2 acquisitionists. Competing theories generally fall into four broad classes: (1) those that limit the role of the L1 grammar in some principled way; (2) those that accept Full Transfer, but place limits on subsequent development; (3) those that posit local impairments of either transfer or subsequent development; and (4) those that claim that interlanguage systems inhabit an epistemological space distinct from that inhabited by native grammars. Theories that limit the role of the L1 grammar may do so by denying transfer altogether (Epstein, Flynn & Martohardjono 1996); by limiting the domain of transfer to lexical categories (Vainikka & Young-Scholten's 1994, 1996a Minimal Trees); by allowing the transfer of functional categories, but not the associated feature values of their heads (Eubank's 1993/1994 Valueless Features); or by allowing transfer of some, but not all, functional categories (Bhatt & Hancin-Bhatt's 2002 Structural Minimality). One particularly influential model that places limits on subsequent development is Hawkins and Chan's (1997) Failed Functional Features, which claims that only those morphosyntactic features instantiated in the L1 are available for L2 development. Local impairment hypotheses include Beck's (1998) assertion that L2 learners cannot value the feature strength of I and Bley-Vroman and Joo's (2001) claim that L2 learners are unable to construct narrow-range rules for argument-structure realization alternations. Finally, hypotheses that there are essential differences between native and non-native grammars range from Bley-Vroman's (1990) rather moderate Fundamental Difference hypothesis, which claims that interlanguage grammars are merely "language-like," to Meisel's (1997) extreme claim that interlanguage systems employ linear sequencing strategies rather than hierarchical phrase structure representations.

Even focusing solely on the Full Transfer aspect of Full Transfer/Full Access, considerations of space would preclude a discussion of each of these alternatives. For our present purposes, we shall confine ourselves to stating that the strongest empirical evidence for Full Transfer is the demonstration of divergent developmental paths in the acquisition of a given TL as an L2 by speakers of typologically diverse L1s. For example, in acquiring German (SOV), Romance (SVO) speakers begin with SVO word order, but Turkish and Korean (SOV) speakers begin with SOV (Vainikka & Young-Scholten 1994, 1996b). Likewise, in acquiring German (Adj-N), Romance (N-Adj/Adj-N) speakers exhibit a persistent use of both N-Adj and Adj-N, but Turkish and Korean (N-Adj) speakers produce only Adj-N from the beginning (Parodi, Clahsen & Schwartz 1997). Similarly, in acquiring Spanish (dative case; clitics; clitic doubling), French (dative case; clitics; no clitic doubling) speakers acquire clitic-doubled dative experiencer subjects significantly sooner than otherwise matched English (no dative case; no pronominal clitics) speakers (Montrul 1998).

## 2.2 Relexification Hypothesis (Lefebvre 1998)
We turn now to the most linguistically sophisticated model of creole genesis currently available, Lefebvre's (1998) Relexification Hypothesis, which is demonstrated primarily on the basis of the origin of Haitian Creole. Lefebvre (Lefebvre 1998: 9) states the basic hypothesis as follows:

[T]he creators of a creole language, adult native speakers of the substratum languages, use the properties of their native lexicons, the parametric values and semantic interpretation rules of their native grammars in creating the creole. Creole lexical entries are mainly created by the process of relexification. Two other processes fed by the output of relexification, dialect levelling and reanalysis, also play a role in the development of the creole.

The relexification process can be represented graphically as in (2):

(2)   Lefebvre's (1998) Relexification Hypothesis

| $phon_i$ $sem_k$ $syn_l$ ... m | | [phonetic string]$_j$, perceived in semantico-pragmatic context | | $phon_{p(j)}$ $sem_k$ $syn_l$ ... m |
|---|---|---|---|---|
| L1 lexical entry | + | Lexifier language input | ⇒ | New lexical entry |

The lexical entries of a language consist of sets of phonetic, semantic, syntactic, and other features. The phonetic features may be thought of as the label for a given entry. A cocreator of a creole language seeks to relabel any given entry of his or her L1 lexicon with the appropriate label of the corresponding entry in the lexifier language. However, creole creators have no direct access to the lexical entries of the lexifier language. Rather, they have access only to their perception of phonetic strings perceived in semantico-pragmatic contexts. Furthermore, it is quite likely that for any given L1 lexical entry, there will be no entry in the lexifier language lexicon with the same precise set of semantic, syntactic, and other features, and it is likely that even the phonetic features perceived by the creators of a creole will not correspond perfectly to phonetic features available in the lexifier language. Thus, a new lexical entry for the creole consists of the creator's perception of a phonetic string of the lexifier language together with the set of nonphonetic features constituting an L1 lexical entry. Such a model is "substratalist" in the sense that the result of this process is a community of speakers with creole lexicons reflecting the structural properties of their L1s (which are then subject to further reanalysis and/or dialect leveling).

As with Full Transfer/Full Access, it would be inaccurate to suggest that the Relexification Hypothesis is the only approach currently under consideration. Competing theories include superstratalist approaches, which consider the creole to be essentially a variety of the Lexifier Language, and universalist approaches, which claim that creole grammars represent unmarked or default grammatical options. For example, the superstratalist Chaudenson (1993, 1996) views Haitian Creole as the result of an "approximation of an approximation" of French, whereas the universalist Bickerton (1981, 1984) sees creole grammars in general as largely reflecting default options of the human linguistic bioprogram.

Particularly strong empirical support for Lefebvre's Relexification Hypothesis comes from three-way comparisons of (one of) the L1(s) spoken by the creole creators, French, and Haitian Creole. For the sake of concreteness, Lefebvre's work relies heavily on Fongbe as representative of the range of languages spoken by the creators of Haitian Creole. Consider, for instance, the items in (3) to (5), from Lefebvre (1998: 250–251), comparing the expression of predicates of discomfort.

(3) a. *Vant     mwen ap   fè    m    mal.*              HAITIAN CREOLE
       stomach   me   IMP  do   me   hurt
       "I have a stomachache."

   b. *J' ai     mal au      ventre.*                      FRENCH
       I  have   pain in-the  stomach

   c. *Xɔ́mɛ      wíli   mi.*                                FONGBE
       stomach   hold   me

(4) a. *Tèt   mwen ap   fè   m     mal.*                 HAITIAN CREOLE
       head me      IMP  do  me    hurt
       "I have a headache."

   b. *J' ai     mal à   la    tête.*                      FRENCH
       I  have   pain in  the   head

   c. *Tà    ɖǔ   mi.*                                    FONGBE
       head  eat  me

(5) a. *Dan   ap    manje m.*                            HAITIAN CREOLE
       tooth IMP  eat    me
       "I have a toothache."

   b. *J'  ai    mal aux     dents.*                       FRENCH
       I   have  pain in-the  teeth

   c. *Àɖú   ɖɔ̀ ɖúɖu  mi    wɛ̀.*                          FONGBE
       tooth at eat     me    PART

In each case, the same pattern arises: the Haitian Creole example in (a) and the Fongbe example in (c) express discomfort by saying literally that the body part is hurting the experiencer, while the French example in (b), where literally the experiencer has pain in the body part, is the odd one out. It is important to understand that the power of Lefebvre's work lies in the *preponderance* of the evidence: Lefebvre considers definite determiners, plural markers, indefinite markers, case markers, tense-mood-aspect inflection, personal pronouns, possessives, pronominal clitics, expletives, reflexives, wh-words, complementizers, conjunctions, negation markers, question markers, raising verbs, existential verbs, meteorological predicates, inherent object verbs, ditransitives, etc. The overwhelming generalization is that Haitian Creole patterns structurally with Fongbe and is structurally unlike French.

## 3. *The Un(der)noticed Equivalence*

While Full Transfer and Relexification may seem superficially to be dissimilar, further reflection suggests that there is a significant similarity. In a theory of grammar in which all morphosyntactic variation (within and across languages) is encoded in the lexicon, such as Chomsky's (1995) Minimalist Program, the only way for the "abstract properties" of the L1 to transfer and comprise the initial state of L2 acquisition is via retention of the L1 lexicon (minus phonetic labels). That is, Full Transfer's "abstract properties" appear to correspond in Minimalist terms to Relexification's lexical "features" (minus phonetic features).

Perhaps two mutually neutralizing notes of caution are appropriate at this point. First, Schwartz and Sprouse (2000) warn against unmotivated reliance on the details of a particular syntactic theory in developing models of L2 acquisition. We may wish to pause before declaring that Full Transfer and Relexification are notional variants describing precisely the same process and ask whether we would be led to the same conclusion on the assumption of a syntactic theory that does not seek to encode all morphosyntactic variation in the lexicon (such as Chomsky's 1981 classic Government-Binding Theory). On the other hand, given its "abstract" interpretation of morphosyntactic features, the Minimalist Program may offer L2 researchers very little on which to "over-rely" in the first place:

> The properties of features and assembly form a large part of the subject matter of traditional and modern linguistics; I will put these topics aside here, including questions about organization of assembled features within a lexical item LI. Also left to the side is the question of whether LI is assembled in a single operation or at several stages of the derivation, as in Distributed Morphology (Halle & Marantz 1993). (Chomsky 1998: 13, n. 27, cited by Lardiere 2005: 189, n. 2)

(See Lardiere 2005 for a powerful critique of reliance on the mechanisms of the Minimalist Program in an attempt to account for target-deviant morphological competence in L2 acquisition.)

Here I would like to suggest that Full Transfer and Relexification, if not in fact notional variants, naturally extend to each other. All pieces of the non-phonetic information in a lexical item are presumably part of the "abstract properties" that Full Transfer claims are transferred. Likewise, assuming a theory of syntax that is less lexically oriented than Minimalism, several sorts of phenomena now conceptualized or conceptualizable as features of lexical items reemerge as modules or submodules of the grammar. To the extent that Relexification has correctly allowed one to capture the relevant historical developments in creole genesis, on the assumption that these properties were lexically encoded, it is natural under the less lexical syntactic theory to seek to extend Relexification to encompass more general "abstract properties."

Before moving on, it may be helpful to point out another difference in formulation that obscures an underlying similarity. In general, neither the early L2 learner nor the early creole cocreator can express very much with the new system. One might suppose that Full Transfer suggests that the early L2 learner is in possession of an enormously complex system of grammar, but just a handful of vocabulary items, while Relexification seems to posit an early creole cocreator with a small set of lexical items that have been relabeled, and also a very modest grammar. This is a misperception derived from a too literal interpretation of both hypotheses. Assuming Relexification, one could just as easily say that the early creole cocreator has a fully fledged lexicon with the same number of items as his or her L1 lexicon. The knowledge of all of the feature sets of a full lexicon is mentally represented; however, a feature set cannot be put to use for communication until it has been relabeled. There is no empirical basis for saying that only lexical items that have been relabeled can compose the lexicon of the new system. Both Full Transfer and Relexification (before the actual relabeling is accomplished) are the same thing: nothing has "happened" except (perhaps) for the mind's recognition that one is being exposed to a new kind of input that will allow one to begin to construct a new system.

## 4. *The Difference between Interlanguage and Creoles*

The real difference between canonical L2 acquisition and creole genesis lies not in distinct underlying mechanisms, but in the quality and quantity of input available for error-driving hypothesis revision ("learning"). In the case of canonical (especially tutored) L2 acquisition, the TL input is robust and persistent. Potentially, the presentation of at least some of the input is structured in order to enhance acquisition. The learner at state $G_0$ is confronted with TL input that $G_0$ cannot license. Morphosyntactic "parameters" can be revalued, yielding $G_1$. $G_1$ is confronted with TL input that it cannot license; revaluation yields $G_2$, etc.

The course of creole development is quite different. lexifier language input is rare or absent for many in the emerging creole speech community. Taking the first set of associations of lexical entries with new labels as $G_0$, $G_0$ based on one substrate language is confronted with input licensed by $G_0$ based on other substrate languages. This may encourage stabilization, or dialect leveling or reanalysis may ensue. Unless societal change brings emerging creole speakers into substantially more contact with Lexifier Language speakers, there is no motivation to revise $G_0$ (or $G_1, \ldots G_n$) to bring it more in line with Lexifier Language input.

In this view, the early L2 learner and the early creole cocreator are cognitively and epistemologically indistinguishable. Different outcomes associated with interlanguage development and creole genesis are functions exclusively of the environment.

## 5. *Thinking about L2 Acquisition in Terms of Relexification*

In this section, we briefly consider a range of well-known L2 acquisition phenomena, all of which receive an immediate account (or, at least, crucial elements of the outline of an account) on the assumption that relexification, in the sense of relabeling is a pervasive mechanism of the Second Language Instinct.

### 5.1 *Classic "Interference" in L2 Acquisition*

The anecdotal experience of virtually every classroom language teacher in the world is that a typical L2 learner's interlanguage production is chockablock with lexical items with phonetic features based on the target language and syntactico-semantic features transparently reflecting the L2 learner's L1 lexicon. Consider the following examples from the author's own experience as a 20-plus-year veteran of teaching German to English-speaking learners.

(6) a.  Maria hat die Frage geantwortet.                    ENGLISH-GERMAN
    b.  Maria hat auf die Frage geantwortet.                      GERMAN
    c.  Maria answered the question.                              ENGLISH

(7) a.  Haben wir ein Bier!                                 ENGLISH-GERMAN
    b.  Trinken wir ein Bier!                                     GERMAN
    c.  Let's have a beer!                                        ENGLISH

(8) a.  Brecht hat die Kommunistische Partei verbunden.     ENGLISH-GERMAN
    b.  Brecht ist der Kommunistischen Partei beigetreten.       GERMAN
    c.  Brecht joined the Communist Party.                       ENGLISH

(9) a.  Ich erwarte meinen Freund um 9 Uhr anzukommen.      ENGLISH-GERMAN
    b.  Ich erwarte, dass mein Freund um 9 Uhr ankommt.          GERMAN
    c.  I expect my friend to arrive at 9:00.                    ENGLISH

(10) a. Wann musst du verlassen?                            ENGLISH-GERMAN
     b. Wann musst du gehen?                                     GERMAN
     c. When do you have to leave?                               ENGLISH

The English-German examples have been altered only to make their morphophonology target-like. While the English verb *to answer* can take a direct object (6c), its German translation *antworten* requires that the question answered be mapped onto a PP with the P *auf* 'on' (6b). English-German learners routinely treat *antworten* as a simple transitive verb (6a). The English verb *to have* can be used not only for possession, but also for consumption (7c), while German generally uses a specific verb of consumption (such as *trinken* 'drink'), rather than the German *haben* in the latter context (7b). English-German learners routinely extend *haben* to contexts where consumption is the intended meaning (7a). The English verb *to join* can be used to mean that someone brings two or more objects together (German *verbinden*) or that someone becomes a member of a group (German *beitreten*). English-German learners frequently appear to have a single lexical entry with both meanings and the label *verbinden*. Thus, they use *verbinden* in contexts where German would require *beitreten* (8). Whereas the English verb *to expect* can be used in the accusativus-cum-infinitivo (or Exceptional Case Marking) construction (9c), with clausal complementation, its German translation *erwarten* permits only finite clauses (9b). Nevertheless, English-German L2 learners frequently use *erwarten* with the accusativus-cum-infinitivo construction (9a). Finally, the English verb *to leave* can be used either transitively (German *verlassen*) or intransitively (German *gehen*). English-German L2 learners frequently use *verlassen* in contexts where German would require *gehen* (10).

It is important to realize that some learners will revise their interlanguage lexical entries to make them more target-like. However, the prevalence of these "errors" in spontaneous learner speech receives an immediate account on the assumption of a version of Full Transfer that reaches down into the morpho-syntax of individual lexical items, precisely as the Relexification Hypothesis does.

## 5.2 *The Age-Dependent Decline in Ultimate Attainment in L2*
Johnson and Newport (1991) document empirically a longstanding intuition that the age of initial intense exposure to a new language is inversely propor-tionate to ultimate attainment in the morphosyntax of that new language, although it should be kept in mind that individual differences become particu-larly striking when the age of contact/arrival is 18 years or older. With an inter-pretation of Full Transfer as Relexification, the so-called "critical period" or "sensitive period" may be reconceptualized, at least in part, as a stabilization of the L1 lexicon. After the critical/sensitive period, it may become more difficult to relabel the L1 lexicon and the amount of TL input required to revalue—much less reassemble features in lexical items (Lardiere 2005)—may greatly increase.

## 5.3 *Bound vs. Free Inflection Asymmetries in L2 Acquisition*
L2 learners appear to have more difficulty mastering bound inflectional morphemes than free grammatical morphemes. Consider White's (2003b) results on accuracy of verb inflection on a picture description task completed by native English speakers and by high intermediate/low advanced French-English and Mandarin-English adult L2 learners, summarized in Table 1.

|                          | Copula/auxiliary | Past irregular | Past regular | 3rd sg. pres. -*s* |
|--------------------------|------------------|----------------|--------------|---------------------|
| native English (n = 19)  | 248/248 (100%)   | 88/88 (100%)   | 54/54 (100%) | 408/408 (100%)      |
| French-English (n = 19)  | 328/334 (98%)    | 106/127 (83.5%)| 24/48 (50%)  | 156/259 (60%)       |
| Mandarin-English (n = 24)| 342/370 (92.5%)  | 128/153 (83.5%)| 25/53 (47%)  | 110/340 (32.5%)     |

Table 1. *Results on picture description task (based on White's 2003b: 33, Table 2)*

Both learner groups perform quite well on free morphology (copulas and auxiliaries) and on irregular past tense verbs, which in English generally involve synchronically unpredictable ablaut and no past tense ending. For both learner groups, accuracy drops off significantly for regular past tense verbs, which involve an inflectional suffix; for Mandarin-English learners, accuracy drops even further on third person singular present tense -*s* (while it improves a bit for French-English learners).

White (2003b) accounts for these asymmetries by invoking Goad and White's (2003) Prosodic Transfer Hypothesis, making reference to the phonological structures licensed by English, French, and Mandarin. However, this asymmetry also receives an account within a Relexification model, where the lexical status of free and irregular inflection is encoded differently from regular bound inflection. Relexification is concerned primarily with relabeling lexical items as a whole, not with regular bound inflection. Thus, the presence of irregular past tense forms, copulas, and auxiliaries in the input will lead to the positing of new lexical items in the interlanguage lexicon. We may well expect these form-meaning pairings to be more easily acquired and accessed than the representations required for regular bound inflection, which does not operate at the word level.

### 5.4 *Locative Alternation: Challenges for Unlearning*
Consider finally the "ground" verbs in the much studied locative alternation. English has both alternating ground verbs, such as *load* (11), and non-alternating ground verbs, such as *fill* (12). In Korean, all ground verbs alternate, including *chaywuta* 'fill' (13).

(11)  a.  Mary loaded the truck with apples.
      b.  Mary loaded the apples onto a truck.

(12)  a.  James filled the glass with water.
      b.  *James filled the water into a glass.

(13)  a.  Minsu-ka      kulut-ul    mwul-lo     chaywuta.
          Minsu-nom     bowl-acc    water-obl   fill
      b.  Minsu-ka      mwul-ul     kulut-ey    chaywuta.
          Minsu-nom     water-acc   bowl-obl    fill        (=(10) in Joo 2000: 22)

Joo (2000) and Bley-Vroman and Joo (2001) argue that Korean-English L2 learners' difficulty in establishing narrow range verb classes such as those distinguishing the acceptability patterns in (11) vs. (12) suggests that adult L2 learners' development no longer has an important aspect of Universal Grammar to guide them. However, assuming that Korean-English L2 learners relabel the lexical entry *chaywuta* as *fill*, we expect learners initially to license both (12a) and (12b).

In fact, this perspective shifts the aspect of development calling for an explanation. To the extent that Korean-English L2 learners eventually come to reject (13b) (Dekydtspotter, Schwartz, Sprouse & Bullock 2005), we need to develop alternative accounts of L2 lexical reanalysis, since there is clearly nothing in the target language input that could trigger this reanalysis. This suggests that there may be aspects of interlanguage lexical development that the field has genuinely not begun to appreciate.

## 6. *Conclusion*

It is curious that the Full Transfer Hypothesis and the Relexification Hypothesis should have arisen in generative L2 acquisition research and in generative creole research, respectively, more or less simultaneously, and without influencing each other—in fact, the relevant literature in each field does not even mention the hypothesis from the other one. I would like to suggest that this is perhaps due in part to a general difference in the nature of the two fields.

L2 acquisition research tends to study groups of learners (or single learners longitudinally) with an eye towards making generalizations across non-native language acquirers. It is axiomatic that most of the systems studied are unstable, and there is relatively little "external" interest in any given learner's interlanguage. Investigating L2 developmental stages in terms of resetting of parameters in the sense of the classic Government-Binding Theory of Chomsky (1981) made immediate sense to the pioneers of generative approaches to L2 acquisition in the early and mid-1980s.

Creole research, on the other hand, has an inherently historical aspect. It is axiomatic (at least, to linguists) that creole languages are "real languages" and there is an inherent interest in describing their history and structure in detail. A striking amount of creole research is devoted to discussing the source of particular lexical items or constructions in particular creole languages, aspects of the mental grammar that do not generally lend themselves so readily to characterization in terms of the classic parameter setting theory of the 1980s.

My real conclusion is a personal note. The Montreal Dialogues placed creole research squarely in my field of vision as an L2 researcher in a way that had never been the case before. Subsequently, I have only gained a deeper appreciation for the potential for fertile cross-pollination across the two fields.

I hope that researchers centered in each of these fields will find it useful to consider insights from the other.

## References

Beck, L.-M. 1998. L2 acquisition and obligatory head movement: English-speaking learners of German and the local impairment hypothesis. *Studies in Second Language Acquisition* 20: 311–348.

Bhatt, R. M. and Barbara Hancin-Bhatt. 2002. Structural Minimality, CP and the initial state in second language acquisition. *Second Language Research* 18: 348–392.

Bickerton, D. 1981. *Roots of Language*. Ann Arbor, MI: Karoma Press.

Bickerton, D. 1984. The language bioprogram hypothesis. *Behavioral and Brain Sciences* 7: 173–221.

Bley-Vroman, R. 1990. The logical problem of foreign language learning. *Linguistic Analysis* 20: 3–49.

Bley-Vroman, R. and H.-R. Joo. 2001. The acquisition and interpretation of English locative constructions by native speakers of Korean. *Studies in Second Language Acquisition* 23: 207–219.

Chaudenson, R. 1993. De l'hypothèse aux exemples. Un cas de créolisation: Selon la formation des systèmes de démonstratifs créoles. *Études créoles* 16: 17–38.

Chaudenson, R. 1996. Démystification de la relexification. *Études créoles* 19: 93–109.

Chomsky, N. 1981. *Lectures on Government and Binding: The Pisa Lectures.* (Studies in Generative Grammar, 9.) Dordrecht: Foris.

Chomsky, N. 1995. *The Minimalist Program*. Cambridge, MA: The MIT Press.

Chomsky, N. 1998. Minimalist inquiries: The framework. *MIT Occasional Papers in Linguistics* 15, *MIT Working Papers in Linguistics*.

Dekydtspotter, L., B.D. Schwartz, R.A. Sprouse and G. Bullock. 2005. Locative verbs in Korean-English interlanguage and the universal grammar question: Disentangling lexical semantics, syntax and pragmatics. Manuscript, Indiana University and University of Hawai'i at Manoa.

Epstein, S., S. Flynn and G. Martohardjono. 1996. Second language acquisition: Theoretical and experimental issues in contemporary research. *Behavioral and Brain Sciences* 19: 677–714.

Eubank, L. 1993/1994. On the transfer of parametric values in L2 development. *Language Acquisition* 3: 183–208.

Goad, H. and L. White. 2003. (Non)native-like ultimate attainment: The influence of L1 prosodic structure on L2 morphology. Paper presented at the Boston University Conference on Language Development, Boston University.

Halle, M. and A. Marantz. 1993. Distributed morphology and the pieces of inflection. In *The View from Building 20*, Kenneth Hale and S. J. Keyser (eds.), 111–176. Cambridge, MA: The MIT Press.

Hawkins, R. 2001. *Second Language Syntax: A Generative Introduction*. Malden, MA: Blackwell.

Hawkins, R. and C.Y. Chan. 1997. The partial availability of Universal Grammar in second language acquisition: The "failed functional features hypothesis". *Second Language Research* 13: 187–226.

Johnson, J.S. and E.L. Newport. 1989. Critical period effects in second language learning: The influence of maturational state on the acquisition of English as a second language. *Cognitive Psychology* 21: 60–99.

Joo, H.-R. 2000. Acquisition of the Argument Structure of Locative Verbs: Korean EFL Learners. Unpublished M.A. thesis, University of Hawaiʲi at M_noa.

Lardiere, D. 2005. On morphological competence. In *Proceedings of the 7th Generative Approaches to Second Language Acquisition Conference (GASLA 2004)*, Laurent Dekydtspotter, Rex A. Sprouse and Audrey Liljestrand (eds.), 178–192. Somerville, MA: Cascadilla Press.

Lefebvre, C. 1998. *Creole Genesis and the Acquisition of Grammar: The Case of Haitian Creole*. New York: Cambridge University Press.

Meisel, J. 1997. The acquisition of the syntax of negation in French and German. *Second Language Research* 13: 227–263.

Montrul, S.A. 1998. The L2 acquisition of dative experiencer subjects. *Second Language Research* 14: 27–61.

Parodi, T., H. Clahsen and B.D. Schwartz. 1997. On the L2 acquisition of morphosyntax of German nominals. *Essex Working Papers in Linguistics* 15: 1–43.

Schwartz, B.D. and R.A. Sprouse. 1994. Word order and nominative case in non-native language acquisition: A longitudinal study of (L1 Turkish) German interlanguage. In *Language Acquisition Studies in Generative Grammar: Papers in Honor of Kenneth Wexler from the 1991 GLOW Workshops*, Teun Hoekstra and Bonnie D. Schwartz (eds.), 317–368. Philadelphia: John Benjamins.

Schwartz, B.D. and R.A. Sprouse. 1996. L2 cognitive states and the full transfer/full access model. *Second Language Research* 12: 40–72.

Schwartz, B.D. and R.A. Sprouse. 2000. When syntactic theories evolve: Consequences for L2 acquisition research. In *Second Language Acquisition and Linguistic Theory*, John Archibald (ed.), 156–186. Malden, MA: Blackwell.

Vainikka, A. and M. Young-Scholten. 1994. Direct access to X'-theory: Evidence from Korean and Turkish adults learning German. In *Language Acquisition Studies in Generative Grammar: Papers in Honor of Kenneth Wexler from the 1991 GLOW Workshops*, Teun Hoekstra and Bonnie D. Schwartz (eds.), 265–316. Philadelphia: John Benjamins.

Vainikka, A. and M. Young-Scholten. 1996a. Gradual development of L2 phrase structure. *Second Language Research* 12: 7–39.

Vainikka, A. and M. Young-Scholten. 1996b. The early stages in adult L2 syntax: Additional evidence from Romance speakers. *Second Language Research* 12: 140–176.

White, L. 2003a. *Second Language Acquisition and Universal Grammar*. Cambridge: Cambridge University Press.

White, L. 2003b. Some puzzling features of L2 features. Ms., McGill University.

# TRANSFER AS BOOTSTRAPPING[*]

Bonnie D. Schwartz
*University of Hawai'i*

This paper addresses the issue of the extent of L1 transfer in L2 acquisition, concentrating on the highest functional layer of the clause—abbreviated here to "the C-domain"—a syntactic domain little studied in L2 research. Evaluating a range of (very) early Interlanguage data (with a variety of source- and target-language pairings), I argue that the evidence is clear-cut, straightforwardly implicating—from the earliest points of L2 development—the (full) transfer of the L1-specified C-domain. I turn to broader theoretical implications in the conclusion, including a few observations on the relation of relexification to transfer vis à vis both L2 acquisition and creole genesis.

## 1. *Introduction*

Native language (L1) influence, or transfer, has long been an important construct in research on nonnative language (L2) acquisition. Most L2 researchers, regardless of theoretical persuasion, acknowledge a definite if not prominent role for the L1 in (adult) L2 acquisition. And within generative studies of L2 acquisition, in addition to the issue of the extent of Universal Grammar (UG) involvement, the other main issue has indeed been the extent of L1 transfer. These two components of L2 theorizing—UG involvement and L1 transfer—are independent. This is set out in (1):

(1) *Orthogonal relation between L1 transfer and UG involvement in (adult) L2 acquisition*

| L1 transfer | UG involvement (beyond the L1) | Examples |
|---|---|---|
| – | – | Clahsen & Muysken (1986); Meisel (1997) |
| – | + | Epstein, Flynn & Martohardjono (1996); Platzack (1996) |
| + | – | Bley-Vroman (1989); Clahsen & Muysken (1989); Hawkins & Chan (1997); Liceras (1997); Müller (1998); Schachter (1989); Tsimpli & Roussou (1991) |
| + | + | Bhatt & Hancin-Bhatt (2002); Eubank (1993/94); Hulk (1991); Schwartz & Sprouse (1994); Vainikka & Young-Scholten (1994); White (1989, 2003) |

---

[*] For a very informative, stimulating and congenial workshop, my sincere thanks to the Montreal Dialogues organizers—Claire Lefebvre, Christine Jourdan and Lydia White—and to all the other Montreal Dialoguers, especially Jeff Siegel and Rex A. Sprouse.

There are thus four logical combinations—and I hasten to point out that within each of these four, there are various theoretical shadings. The last row is the most relevant to the topic I was asked to address, given in (2):

(2) "Can all syntactic categories, including functional categories, undergo transfer/relexification? What are the implications with respect to parameter settings?"

The various positions in the last row in (1) are united by the overarching idea that L1 transfer and UG work in tandem but crucially differ on the hypothesized extent of L1 transfer.

In this paper, I will argue that the answer to the first question in (2) is "yes, all functional categories in the L1 grammar do transfer," illustrating some of the consequences of this with respect to parameter setting. To do so, I will focus on a domain of functional syntax that has received relatively little attention in the generative L2 literature: the C-domain—or the highest level of syntactic projection in the clause, sometimes referred to as the "left periphery" (Rizzi 1997).[1] This is the syntactic domain that is associated with the structure of several phenomena, such as questions (e.g., (3a)), verb second (e.g., (3b)) and embedded clauses (e.g., (3c)).

(3) **CP**   a. Question: [CP *Which papers* [C' *are* [IP you [VP working on]]]]?

**IP**   b. Verb second: [CP *Gestern* [C' *hat* [IP Johan [VP das Buch gelesen]]]]
                                                                      GERMAN
                  Yesterday   has      Johan     the   book   read
**VP**            'Yesterday Johan read the book.'

         c. Embedded:    No one knows [CP [C' *that* [IP we [VP waited so long]]]].

While evidence of transfer in the C-domain does not necessarily entail that all functional projections below it transfer as well, it nevertheless provides suggestive evidence for this position.

The paper is organized as follows. First I review the different positions that fall into that last row of the table in (1). All but one propose that transfer is restricted in some sense. I critically assess the empirical evidence underpinning these "partial transfer" views that leads their proponents to conclude that the properties of the L1 C-domain do not transfer, either in part or in full. I then present the results of several studies that demonstrate that the L1 C-domain does in fact transfer completely. The conclusion turns to broader theoretical implications of my take on the question in (2), including a few brief remarks on how I see the rela-

---

[1] Some of the first empirical L2 investigations into the early presence of CP are Kaplan (1993) for L2 Japanese and Lakshmanan (1993/94) and Lakshmanan and Selinker (1994) for L2 English. These are not discussed here because of the limited size of the databases. Another reason the Lakshmanan papers—as well as the work by Grondin and White (1996) and Haznedar (1997, 2003)—are not considered is because the participants in these studies were young L2 children.

tion of relexification to transfer as it pertains to both L2 acquisition and creole genesis.

## 2. *Background: [+transfer, +UG] (L2 initial state) proposals*

In the mid-1990s, the issue of L1 transfer was reconceptualized in terms of the initial state of L2 acquisition, that is, in terms of how much of the L1 grammar constitutes the starting point of L2 development (Hoekstra & Schwartz 1994; Schwartz & Eubank 1996). The motivation for doing so was twofold: first, to make explicit the extent (and timing) of transfer, and second, to "get a handle" (Schwartz 1997) on how the unfolding of L2 development actually proceeds, because how one conceives of the initial state inextricably determines the possible explanations for (UG-constrained) development (Schwartz & Eubank 1996; but cf. Hawkins 2001).

Four hypotheses concerning the L2 initial state are listed in (4), going from the least amount of transfer to the most. Note that these simultaneously correspond to the extent of syntactic structure claimed to characterize the L2 initial state, again going from least to most.

(4)  *Hypotheses on the L2 initial state (which assume further L2 development is UG-constrained)*

| Model | Extent of L1 transfer (→ initial L2 syntactic structure) |
|---|---|
| Minimal Trees (MT) (Vainikka & Young-Scholten) | lexical projections (e.g., VP, NP) and their headedness values, but not any functional projections (e.g., CP, IP, DP) |
| Structural Minimality (SM) (Bhatt & Hancin-Bhatt) | "all and only properties of [the] L1 associated with theIP-system (and below)" (B&H-B 2002: 366, (8)) |
| Valueless Features (VF) (Eubank) | lexical and functional projections, but not the "feature value strength" associated with specific functional heads (e.g., IP) |
| Full Transfer/Full Access (FT/FA) (Schwartz & Sprouse) | "the entirety of the L1 grammar (excluding the phonetic matrices of lexical/morphological items)" (S&S 1996: 41) |

### 2.1 *Minimal Trees (Vainikka and Young-Scholten)*

The Minimal Trees (MT) hypothesis of Vainikka and Young-Scholten (e.g., 1994, 1996) restricts transfer to lexical projections and their headedness values. As transfer of any and all functional projections is excluded under MT, the L2 initial state of the clause is thus only VP. With respect to there not being a CP, the evidence Vainikka and Young-Scholten offer comes from very early L2 German production data on the part of L1 speakers of Romance, Korean and Turkish, and consists of three types: (i) the *absence* of questions; (ii) the *absence* of (non-subject-initial) verb second (V2) sentences (see, e.g., (3b)); and (iii) the *absence* of embedded clauses, particularly the absence of lexical items associated with C, i.e., complementizers such as *dass* 'that' and *ob* 'if.'

(5) *Vainikka and Young-Scholten (e.g., 1994, 1996)*
   a. L1 = Italian, Portuguese, Spanish (SVO, [–V2]); Korean, Turkish (SOV, [–V2])
   b. Target Language = German (SOV, [+V2])
   c. natural and elicited production data

2.2 *Structural Minimality (Bhatt and Hancin-Bhatt)*
The second hypothesis, which Bhatt and Hancin-Bhatt (2002) dub Structural Minimality (SM), is perhaps less well known. It singles out the C-domain as the only one not subject to transfer. Specifically, according to SM, the syntactic structure of the L2 initial state consists of the L1 IP. The data Bhatt and Hancin-Bhatt offer in support come from their study that explicitly set out to test for CP in the early L2 English of Hindi speakers. They sought to assess the presence of CP via two tasks targeting distinct phenomena.

(6) *Bhatt and Hancin-Bhatt (2002)*
   a. L1 = Hindi (SOV, [–wh mvt]); Target Language = English (SVO, [+wh mvt])
   b. two tasks targeting the C-domain (and two studies, the preliminary study and the main study)
      i.   written question-production task
      ii.  adverbial-construal comprehension task
   c. 100+ participants, spanning four or five levels of English instruction, the first (testable) being elementary

In the written question-production task, participants were asked to supply the missing questions in short English dialogues. The ways to form questions in Hindi and English differ. First, Hindi is a *wh-in-situ* language: in constituent questions, such as (7a), neither the *wh*-phrase nor any auxiliary element (if there is one) moves to the C-level. Second, Hindi yes/no questions consist of a declarative clause preceded by a question particle (*kyaa* 'what'), as in (7b):

(7) a. *vah kal        hoTal meN kyaa khaa rahaa thaa*              HINDI
        he  yesterday hotel in   what eat   prog  was
        'What was he eating in the hotel yesterday?'
    b. *kyaa usne khanaa   khaayaa?*
        what  he    food     ate
        'Did he eat food?'                    (Bhatt & Hancin-Bhatt 2002: 354, (3), (4))

The L2 data, collected from more than 100 Hindi speakers across five levels of English instruction, essentially show the progression laid out in (8):

(8) *Hindi-English development of questions*
   a. *wh-in-situ* (in the preliminary study)
   b. *wh*-phrases in sentence-initial position
   c. Subject-Aux Inversion in yes/no questions
   d. target-like *wh*-questions

And the developmental pattern in (8) leads Bhatt and Hancin-Bhatt to argue that

> knowledge of English CP is initially not available ... [because if] the CP projection were present, then all *wh*-phrases should have moved to Spec-CP, with Aux simultaneously moving to Comp. (Bhatt & Hancin-Bhatt 2002: 363–364)

The second task concerned interclausal adverbial construal. In this task, participants were asked first to read a brief narrative in Hindi, in which, for example, Peter made a statement in a car about seeing a dog somewhere else, or Peter made a statement, let us say, in the kitchen about having seen a dog in the car. Presented with an English sentence of one of the types in (9), they were to judge whether that sentence was true or false in the context of the narrative.

(9)  a. **PP-Comp**: Peter said in the car that he saw a dog. *upstairs* PP-construal
    b. **Comp-PP**: Peter said that in the car he saw a dog. *downstairs*
                                                            PP-construal
    c. **no overt Comp**: Peter said in the car he saw a dog.    *ambiguous*
                  (adapted from Bhatt & Hancin-Bhatt 2002: 372 (13))

In (9a), the PP *in the car* precedes the complementizer *that* and so is construed with the (upstairs) "saying"-event, whereas in (9b) the PP follows the complementizer and so is construed with the (downstairs) "seeing"-event. As for (9c), there is no complementizer and so this sentence is ambiguous, i.e., the PP could be construed with the matrix clause or with the embedded clause.

The mean number of correct judgments on the 16 experimental items containing an overt complementizer (i.e., of type (9a) or type (9b)) is given in (10):

(10) *Mean number and percentage correct: Adverbial construal (overt complementizer conditions)\**

| Group | Mean (SD) | Percentage |
|---|---|---|
| Grade 7 (n = 25) | 7.8 (2.0) | 55.7% |
| Grade 9 (n = 25) | 8.4 (1.7) | 60.0% |
| Grade 11 (n = 23) | 11.9 (2.4) | 85.0% |
| Grade 13 (n = 28) | 13.1 (1.4) | 92.9% |

\* This reproduces the numbers as reported in Bhatt and Hancin-Bhatt, although the reported percentages appear to assume 14, not 16, as the denominator.

(adapted from Bhatt & Hancin-Bhatt 2002: 375, Table 8)

On the basis of these results, Bhatt and Hancin-Bhatt argue that learners in the first two levels do not show any covert [sic] evidence of the presence of the $C^0$/CP projection, as indicated by their close-to-chance performance. If the CP projection were available either via UG or via transfer from L1, then we would expect all our learners to perform uniformly across the grade levels, using this projection from relatively early on. (Bhatt & Hancin-Bhatt 2002: 375)

In sum, there are two types of evidence that Bhatt and Hancin-Bhatt use to argue that CP does not transfer from the L1: (i) *nontarget-like* questions; and (ii) *nontarget-like* interpretive consequences associated with the C-domain.

## 2.3 *Valueless Features (Eubank)*
The third position about the L2 initial state is Eubank's (e.g., 1993/94, 1996) Valueless Features (VF) hypothesis. This proposal was explicitly created in response to L2 data targeting the I-domain—specifically, White's (1990/91, 1991, 1992) well-known studies on French-English Interlanguage documenting the alternation between SAVO and *SVAO—but Valueless Features can in principle be extended to the C-domain.

(11) *French-English Interlanguage: Verb placement vis à vis adverbs*
  a. **SAVO**: Marie often takes the metro ($\sqrt{}$ in English)
  b. **SVAO**: Marie takes often the metro (*in English)
                                                    (White 1990/91, 1991, 1992)

The basic idea of VF is that although the full complement of lexical and functional projections in the L1 grammar transfers as the L2 initial state, the L1 (strength) values of features in functional categories do not. Rather, they are left unspecified (termed "inert"). That feature values are not specified as either [+] or [−] strong, according to Eubank, results in "optional movement." Note that this stipulation, made with respect to verb movement to the functional heads in the I-domain, should apply equally well to the functional heads in the C-domain. What this therefore predicts is that the L1-specified CP, i.e., a CP with L1 feature values, should not transfer.

## 2.4 *Full Transfer/Full Access (Schwartz and Sprouse)*
The last proposal on the L2 initial state is the one that Rex Sprouse and I have been advocating for about a decade (e.g., Schwartz & Sprouse 1994, 1996, 2000). The Full Transfer part of Full Transfer/Full Access (FT/FA) hypothesizes that the whole of the L1 grammar (excluding the phonetic matrices of lexical/morphological items) transfers and thus constitutes the L2 initial state. According to Full Transfer, then, the L2 initial state should include the structure and properties of the L1 C-domain.

## 3. *Reconsidering the no-transfer-of-CP evidence encountered so far*
Let us now consider how FT/FA responds to the empirical evidence presented so far in support of the idea that the L1 C-domain does not transfer in full. This evidence is recapped in (12) and (13):

(12) *MT: Evidence against CP transfer (Romance-/Korean-/Turkish-German production data)*
   a. ***absence*** of questions
   b. ***absence*** of (non-subject-initial) V2 sentences
   c. ***absence*** of embedded clauses, particularly lexical items associated with C, i.e., complementizers such as *dass* 'that' and *ob* 'if'

(Vainikka & Young-Scholten 1994, 1996)

(13) *SM: Evidence against CP transfer (Hindi-English production and comprehension data)*
   a. ***nontarget-like*** questions (NB: lowest L2ers had 73/130 [56.1%] *wh-in-situ* questions)
   b. ***nontarget-like*** interpretive consequences associated with the C-domain

(Bhatt & Hancin-Bhatt 2002)

One reason to question the type of evidence in (12a) and (12c) is the familiar adage "absence of evidence is not evidence of absence." This is to say, the fact that neither the spontaneous nor elicited L2 production data contained, for instance, questions or embedded clauses could well be an artifact of the discourse and/or the task, and not indicative, in principle, of lack of knowledge, i.e., lack of the C-domain. Another reason to question (12c) has to do with distinguishing between a syntactic category, e.g., C, and the lexical/morphological material associated with that category, e.g., *dass* 'that.' In short, the absence of lexical items associated with C does not entail that the syntactic category C itself is absent (Hyams 1994; Schwartz 1998). Lexical items, after all, do have to be learned.

This point about learning likewise extends, although in a somewhat different fashion, to the evidence of type (12b): absence of V2 utterances. Here parametric differences between the Target Language (TL), on the one hand, and the L1s, on the other, come into play. Given that none of the L1s—Italian, Korean, Portuguese, Spanish and Turkish—is a V2 language, then under Full Transfer one expects the early Interlanguages based on these L1s to lack V2. This, then, is a case where the parameter value of the L1, call it [−V2] for simplicity's sake, needs to be relinquished and reset to the German value, [+V2] (i.e., invoking Full Access). This, too, necessitates some kind of learning or "trigger," the specifics of which depend on the analysis of V2 (which I leave to the side here).

This same line of reasoning also undermines the type of evidence in (13a). Recall that questions in Hindi and English differ with respect to *wh*-fronting, again representing a parametric difference; call Hindi [−wh mvt] and English [+wh mvt]. Again, the prediction of Full Transfer in this case is that the earliest Interlanguage will be like Hindi, with *wh-in-situ* questions—which is indeed what was found: of the 130 attempted questions in the lowest (testable) level, 73 (56.1%) had the *wh-*

phrase *in situ*.[2] Since the L1 parameter value, [–], has to be reset to the TL value, [+], based on TL input (again, invoking Full Access), there is clearly no reason to expect target-like English questions straightaway.

But the problem with (13a) as well as (13b) is in fact more general, since the criterion used in both is *target-like performance*. The fallacy here, as noted by Dekydtspotter, Schwartz, Sprouse and Liljestrand (2005), is that knowledge of CP for these Hindi acquirers of English does not necessarily entail the *English-particular* parameter settings for main-clause questions, that is, the fronting of auxiliaries and *wh*-phrases to, respectively, C and Spec,CP. Subject-Aux Inversion (SAI) on its own in yes/no questions (cf. (8c)) could be taken as evidence of the C-domain, as could *wh*-fronting on its own, i.e., without the concomitant SAI, in constituent questions (cf. (8b)). The latter represents a possibility for main-clause questions in French: when *wh*-phrases move to Spec,CP, the verb can (14a) but need not (14b) raise to C.[3]

(14) a.  [$_{CP}$ Où      [$_{C'}$ vas-tu ]]?          (French: [$_I$V+I] complex in C)
             where         go  you
             'Where are you going?'

      b.  [$_{CP}$ Où      [$_{C'}$ [$_{IP}$ tu   vas]]]?      (French: [$_I$V+I] complex not in C)
             where                 you go
             'Where are you going?'                          (Rizzi & Roberts 1989)

Target-like performance, on its own, is again the criterion used in the adverbial-construal task, and so, again, (13b) is in principle subject to the criticism offered against (13a). Unfortunately, the way the data are presented in Bhatt and Hancin-Bhatt (2002) makes it impossible to determine if there is in fact *nontarget-like* evidence for the existence of CP. The participants' responses are categorized only as correct or incorrect; crucially missing in the latter is the further separation of "wrong-upstairs" interpretations from "wrong-downstairs" interpretations (see (9)). Unable to attempt a reanalysis of these data, Dekydtspotter et al. (2005) instead report on a very similar study by Garcia (1998), which also looked at upstairs (i.e., main clause) vs. downstairs (i.e., embedded clause) adverbial construal in very early L2 English.

### 3.1 *An early interpretive asymmetry implicating (the transfer of) CP: Garcia (1998)*

Garcia employed an oral picture-selection design, where participants listened twice to each of the recorded test items and were asked to choose one of three

---

[2] Whether these questions are evidence for the presence of CP depends on one's theory of question interpretation at LF, a matter I will not pursue here.
[3] SAI in French is possible only with pronominal subjects.

pictures for each item.[4] Pauses sandwiched both the PP adverbial and the comple-mentizer. So, a test item would have been heard as in (15):

(15) Charles told Anne *[PAUSE]* in the winter *[PAUSE]* that *[PAUSE]* he played tennis.

In all, there were 48 test items, comprising five sentence types, three of which were similar to those used in the Bhatt and Hancin-Bhatt study.[5]

(16) *Three types of sentences tested in Garcia's (1998) oral picture-selection task*
    a. **PP-Comp**: Charles told Anne in the winter that he played tennis.
       (k = 12: 9 *that*; 3 *if*)
    b. **Comp-PP**: Charles told Anne that in the winter he played tennis.
       (k = 12: 9 *that*; 3 *if*)
    c. **no overt Comp**: Charles told Anne in the winter he played tennis.
       (k = 12)

Garcia's study included 10 Arabic speakers and 8 Chinese speakers with quite rudimentary English proficiency; and 4 native English speakers served as controls.

(17) *Participants in Garcia (1998)*
    a. L1 Arabic     (n = 10, Cloze-score range of 15.8%–34.2%)
    b. L1 Chinese    (n = 8,   Cloze-score range of 15.8%–34.2%)
    c. Native speakers (n = 4)

The results of the three groups for PP-Comp and Comp-PP items are given in (18):

(18) *Mean percentage correct: Adverbial construal (overt complementizer conditions)*

| Group | PP-Comp (k = 12)[a] | Comp-PP (k = 12)[b] |
|---|---|---|
| Native English (n = 4) | 87.5% | 98.0% |
| L1 Arabic (n = 10) | 66.7% | 79.2% |
| L1 Chinese (n = 8) | 50.0% | 81.2% |

[a] e.g., Charles told Anne in the winter that he played tennis.
[b] e.g., Charles told Anne that in the winter he played tennis.

(based on Garcia 1998: x, Appendix 5)

The results in (18) show that all groups, on average, are more accurate on Comp-PP items (last column) than PP-Comp items (and this difference is statisti-cally significant for the L2ers). That is, when the PP precedes the complementi-zer, the Arabic L2ers incorrectly construe the PP with the embedded clause, on

---

[4] "I don't know" (with no clear relation depicted between the characters) was the third option, virtually never taken.
[5] The two other sentence types were PP-initial and PP-final:
   (i) a. **PP-initial**: In the winter Charles told Anne that he played tennis. (k = 6)
     b. **PP-final**: Charles told Anne that he played tennis in the winter. (k = 6)

average, 33.3% of the time, and the Chinese L2ers do this, on average, 50% of the time.

What's crucial here is the fact that the L2ers are differentiating between the two sentence types. Dekydtspotter et al. take this to suggest that, despite the *nontarget-like* performance, the L2ers' early Interlanguage does indeed project an embedded CP, for if there weren't one, there would be no reason for them to perform *asymmetrically* on PP-Comp vs. Comp-PP sentences.[6]

(19) *Reason to question the type of evidence in (13b) (Dekydtspotter et al. 2005)*
Evidence from Garcia (1998) of **asymmetric** (***nontarget-like***) interpretive consequences associated with the C-domain in very early Interlanguage (i.e., significantly more incorrect downstairs PP-construal on PP-Comp than incorrect upstairs PP-construal on Comp-PP).

### 3.2 *Summary*

So far, then, the L2 data that purportedly argue against the transfer of CP seem less than convincing. First, independent discourse-anchored reasons can explain why certain phenomena that implicate the C-domain do not occur in L2 production. Second, "absence of evidence" for the C-domain is not necessarily "evidence of absence" of the C-domain. Third, it is incorrect to equate the absence of lexical items that fill C with the absence of the category C itself. Fourth, a hypothesis that claims that L2ers initially adhere to their L1 parameter value which does *not* (overtly) implicate the C-domain can explain their early lack of TL phenomena whose parameter value *does* (overtly) implicate the C-domain. And fifth, it is misguided to adopt the criterion of target-like performance on phenomena implicating the C-domain, since (at least in some cases) nontarget-like performance can in fact provide evidence for its presence. In a nutshell, the L2 data considered thus far are unproblematic for the Full Transfer hypothesis.

### 4. *More (seemingly) problematic data for FT: Håkansson, Pienemann and Sayehli (2002)*

Interestingly, though, there are other L2 data that on the face of it directly contest Full Transfer in the C-domain. These data concern the L2 acquisition of a V2 language by speakers whose L1 is also V2. Clearly, under Full Transfer, the presence of V2 in the L1 should lead to speedy—indeed immediate—convergence on V2 in the TL, but this is not what was found.

The study is by Håkansson, Pienemann and Sayehli (2002), who look at the L2 acquisition of German by native Swedish speakers. Swedish is an SVO

---

[6] Dekydtspotter and Liljestrand (in press) have since found the same asymmetry in English-French Interlanguage, using locational PP adverbials (e.g., *dans la maison* 'in the house') in both a forced interpretation task and an online self-paced reading task, as have Bullock, Omaki, Schulz, Schwartz and Tremblay (to appear), using deictic temporal adverbials (e.g., *yesterday*), in Japanese-English Interlanguage as well as native English, in a tense-meaning (mis)match acceptability judgment task, although, interestingly, not in their online self-paced reading task.

language, unlike German, which is (in the relevant sense—see (3b)) SOV, but both are Germanic V2 languages.

An elicited-narration task was used to collect L2 German production data. A native German speaker interviewed the 20 L2 students who took part. These participants were evenly divided between first-year German (age 13) and second-year German (age 14).

(20) *Håkansson, Pienemann and Sayehli (2002)*
   a.  L1 = Swedish (SVO, [+V2]); Target Language = German (SOV, [+V2])
   b.  production data from an elicited-narration task
   c.  20 participants: 10 in first-year German (age 13); 10 in second-year German (age 14)

Håkansson et al. restrict the database to declarative main clauses that contain at least a subject and a verb (p. 256) and report only the incidence of V2 in utterances that have a sentence-initial adverbial. Although they provide the breakdown by individual participants, so striking are the results that no information is lost by grouping them by level, as in (21):

(21) *V2 in Swedish speakers' adverb-initial German*

| Group | Number of declarative main clauses with a subject and verb | Incidence of V2 out of all adverb-initial utterances |
|---|---|---|
| 1st-year German (n = 10) | 155 | **0/12 (0%)** |
| 2nd-year German (n = 10) | 303 | 10/37 (27.0%) |

\* Only four produce adverb-initial V2 at all, and only two do so consistently (2/2 and 6/8)

(adapted from Håkansson et al. 2002: 256–257, Tables 2 and 3)

In the first-year group, only 12 adverb-initial utterances are produced (representing six participants), and not a single one is V2 (they are instead "V3," i.e., \*AdvSV ...). The second-year group is only slightly more target-like: out of the 37 adverb-initial utterances (representing eight participants), only 27% are V2.

Meager though these data are, they still pose a challenge to advocates of Full Transfer. The good news is that the recent work of Ute Bohnacker superbly rises to this challenge.

## 5.  *Indisputable evidence for the transfer of CP*

### 5.1 *Bohnacker (2005, to appear)*

Bohnacker has carried out a series of studies on the acquisition of German by L1 Swedish speakers as well as one on the acquisition of Swedish by L1 German speakers (Bohnacker 2003, 2005, to appear). Although she confronts several generally accepted "myths" in the L2 acquisition literature, of interest to us is her research on the Swedish *ab initio* acquirers of German.

As Bohnacker rightly observes, there is a serious potential confound in the Håkansson et al. (2002) study, because all of their participants

> had had at least 3 years of English before their first exposure to German, and 4–6 years of English by the time their German was tested. Thus German was their third language, and syntactic properties of English (a non-V2 SVO language) may have transferred to their L3 German. (Bohnacker to appear: 4)

To determine whether English is the source of the V2 problem in the Håkansson et al. study, Bohnacker carefully compares German production data from two sets of Swedish speakers: for three of them, German is the first L2; and for the other three, English is the first L2 and German the second, i.e., their L3. Thus the latter group's language profile closely corresponds to the language profile of the participants in the Håkansson et al. study.

(22) *Bohnacker (2005, to appear)*
  a.  L1 = Swedish (SVO, [+V2]); Target Language = German (SOV, [+V2])
  b.  6 *ab initio* participants
      i.   3 who knew no other language  (i.e., German = L2)
      ii.  3 who knew English         (i.e., German = L3)
  c.  production data at two data points
      i.   after 4 months of exposure
          1.  15-minute monologues: German = L2 for 2; German = L3 for 2
          2.  2 hours alone with monolingual German: German = L2 for 1; German = L3 for 1
      ii.  after 9 months of exposure: 30-minute monologues from all 6 participants

Data were collected at two points, first after a mere four months of German classes and then after five months more. In both sessions, Bohnacker individually recorded the participants talking about what they did or would like to do in their spare time. At the first session, two participants—one who knew English and one who did not—were unable to carry out the task because their German was so minimal, and the four others each spoke for about 15 minutes. A few days later, Bohnacker recorded two of these same four participants—again, one who knew English and one who did not—during separate two-hour, one-on-one interactions with a monolingual speaker of German. Finally, during the second monologue session after nine months of German, data were collected from each of the six participants, since this time all were able to complete the task, speaking on average for about 30 minutes.

As might be expected, Bohnacker's data are much more extensive than those of Håkansson et al. And while Bohnacker provides very detailed quantitative and qualitative analyses of the data, the main finding remains crystal-clear in the collapsed data, given in (23):

(23) *Word order in the L2 vs. L3 German of L1 Swedish speakers*

| Exposure | SVX | V1 | V2[a] | "V3" | V2 instead of "V3"[b] |
|---|---|---|---|---|---|
| **4 MONTHS** | | | | | |
| German = L2 | 200/315 (63.5%) | 22/253 (8.7%) | 93/315 (29.5%) | **0** **(0%)** | 93/93 (100%) |
| German = L3 (English = L2) | 194/302 (64.2%) | 8/224 (3.6%) | 54/302 (17.9%) | **46/302** **(15.2%)** | 54/100 (54.0%) |
| **9 MONTHS** | | | | | |
| German = L2 | 357/518 (68.9%) | 2/206 (1.0%) | 158/518 (30.5%) | **1/24** **(0.8%)** | 158/159 (99.4%) |
| German = L3 (English = L2) | 304/439 (69.3%) | 0 (0%) | 304/439 (17.3%) | **59/439** **(13.4%)** | 304/363 (83.8%) |

[a] V2 = non-subject-initial V2
[b] This is the incidence of (non-subject-initial)V2 out of all opportunities for (non-subject-initial) V2.

(adapted from Bohnacker to appear: Table 3)

These data are robust and unequivocal: L1 Swedes who do know English allow both V2 and "V3" from the very beginning, whereas L1 Swedes who do not know English immediately converge on the V2 property of German (in all 93 instances, i.e., 100% of the time).[7] The obvious conclusion that Bohnacker comes to is that Swedish V2 transfers in the L2 group, and Swedish V2 and English "V3" both transfer in the L3 group. These findings are thus a strong confirmation that the initial state of nonnative language acquisition includes the transfer of the configuration(s) of CP.

Note that Bohnacker's results are important not only because they overturn the Håkansson et al. (2002) no-transfer conclusion, but also because no other study on the L2 development of German/Dutch verb placement—where crucially, the L1s were *not* V2—has found immediate convergence on V2 (e.g., Beck 1998; duPlessis, Solin, Travis & White 1987; Jagtman & Bongaerts 1994; Jansen, Lalleman & Muysken 1981; Jordens 1988; Meisel, Clahsen & Pienemann 1981; Schwartz & Sprouse 1994; Vainikka & Young-Scholten 1994). In other words, only when the L1 is V2 do we see immediate L2 convergence on the V2 property of the TL, in line with Full Transfer.

---

[7] Note that unlike the participants in the Håkansson et al. study (see (21)), Bohnacker's corresponding L3 participants are not limited to "V3" utterances when the first constituent is a non-subject. At both four and nine months, their overall V2 rate is around 17%; and if one calculates the rate of V2 out of only those that could be V2, i.e., out of all utterances that begin with a non-subject (last column), the V2 rate is 54% (54/100) at four months and 83.8% (304/363) at nine months.

So, in this first clear case of CP transfer, the L1 and the TL are both V2. Next we look at a study that tests for transfer at the CP level when the L1 is non-V2 but the TL is V2. And the final case of CP transfer we will consider is where the L1 is V2 but the TL is not.

(24) *L1-TL [±] V2 constellations for testing transfer at the C-domain*

| V2 in L1? | V2 in TL? | Study |
|-----------|-----------|-------|
| +<br>(Swedish) | +<br>(German) | Bohnacker (2005, to appear) |
| –<br>(English) | +<br>(German) | Grüter (2004) |
| +<br>(Dutch) | –<br>(French) | Hulk (1991) |

### 5.2 *Grüter (2004)*

Grüter (2004) in fact set out to test—specifically targeting CP—whether the full clause structure of English speakers transfers in their L2 acquisition of German. The data were collected by means of a very clever picture-interpretation task. It exploits certain properties of German morphosyntax (morphological syncretism, V2 and OV) that together can sometimes lead to *wh*-questions being ambiguous as either subject questions or object questions, as exemplified in (25):

(25) a.  *Was beisst die Katze?*
           what       bites    the  cat
           'What is biting the cat?'  ← [$_{CP}$ **Was$_i$** [$_{C'}$ beisst [$_{IP}$ t$_i$ [$_{VP}$ die Katze]]]]
           'What is the cat biting?'  ← [$_{CP}$ **Was$_i$** [$_{C'}$ beisst [$_{IP}$ die Katze [$_{VP}$ t$_i$]]]]?
      b.  *Was hat die Katze gebissen?*
           what       has the    cat  bitten
           'What has the cat bitten?'  ← [$_{CP}$ **Was$_i$** [$_{C'}$ hat [$_{IP}$ die Katze [$_{VP}$ t$_i$
                                                                                        gebissen]]]]?
           'What has bitten the cat?'  ← [$_{CP}$ **Was$_i$** [$_{C'}$ hat [$_{IP}$ t$_i$ [$_{VP}$ die Katze
                                                                                        gebissen]]]]?
                                                        (adapted from Grüter 2004: 7–8)

Note that in English the analogue of neither (25a) nor (25b) is ambiguous. With the simplex verb in the present tense, *What bites the cat?* can only be a subject question, and with the periphrastic present perfect, *What has the cat bitten?* can only be an object question. As such, Grüter hypothesized that if L2ers initially rely on their L1 grammar, then native English speakers will initially be prone to interpret, on the one hand, German present-tense questions like (25a) as only subject questions, but, on the other, German present-perfect questions like (25b) as only object questions. It was assumed that native Germans would be able to see the ambiguity and answer accordingly.

Seventeen English-speaking students of German and 15 native controls took part in the experiment. The L2ers were extremely low level, having had a mere 8 to 10 weeks of formal German instruction prior to the study. The participants were asked to circle the answer or answers to questions given in the context of pictures. In addition to distracter questions, there were 10 tokens of each of the types in (25a) and (25b), and each one could be truthfully answered in two ways: as A doing something to B or as B doing something C.

(26) *Grüter (2004)*
   a.  L1 = English (SVO, [–V2]); Target Language = German (SOV, [+V2])
   b.  picture-comprehension task (including 10 items like (25a) and 10 items like (25b))
   c.  participants: 17 complete beginners of German whose L1 is English; 15 native controls

The results, in percentages, are given in (27).

(27) *Interpretation of (ambiguous) German* wh-*questions*

| | Subject Q[a] | Object Q[b] | Both | Neither |
|---|---|---|---|---|
| **SIMPLE PRESENT (k = 10)** | | | | |
| Native German controls (n = 15) | 16.0% | 43.3% | **40.7%** | 0% |
| English-speaking L2ers of German (n = 17) | **71.2%** | 28.8% | 0% | 0% |
| **PRESENT PERFECT (k = 10)** | | | | |
| Native German controls (n = 15) | 7.3% | 47.3% | **45.3%** | 0% |
| English-speaking L2ers of German (n = 17) | 2.4% | **97.1%** | 0% | 0.6% |

[a] e.g., Was beisst die Katze? (interpreted as 'What is biting the cat?' and not 'What is the cat biting?')
[b] e.g., Was hat die Katze gebissen? (interpreted as 'What has the cat bitten?' and not 'What has bitten the cat?')

(adapted from Grüter 2004: 19, Figures 2 and 3)

The responses of the two groups diverge. While the natives mark both types of questions as ambiguous over 40% of the time (the "Both" column), the L2 participants never do so. The Germans are thus treating the two types of questions the same. By contrast, the L2ers treat the two types of questions as utterly different: simple-present wh-questions are interpreted as *subject* questions at a rate of 71.2%; present-perfect wh-questions are interpreted as *object* questions at a rate of 97.1%.

These L2 findings, then, straightforwardly align with the grammar of English *wh*-questions, and so constitute solid evidence of the L1 transfer of the C-domain.[8]

### 5.3 *Hulk (1991)*

The last study involving V2 that we will consider is that of Hulk (1991), which investigated the L2 acquisition of French by native Dutch speakers. Dutch is an SOV, [+V2] language and French is an SVO, [–V2] language.

Manipulating these two properties—[+V2] vs. [–V2] and [OV] vs. [VO]—Hulk devised a 40-item French acceptability judgment task that consisted of both possible and impossible word orders in both Dutch and French. A total of 131 Dutch students of French took part in the study, divided into four groups. Here we concentrate on the 26 beginners in first-level high-school French, since they had "just started learning French" (Hulk 1991: 21) and our interest is the initial L2 representation of CP. Specifically, we want to know whether these beginners initially adopt the [+V2] parameter value of Dutch in their L2 French.

(28) *Hulk (1991)*
    a.  L1 = Dutch (SOV, [+V2]); Target Language = French (SVO, [–V2])
    b.  40-item (written) acceptability judgment task
    c.  participants: 131 students of French, 26 of whom were beginners

And the answer is that indeed they do, as summarized in (29):

(29) *Acceptance of (non-subject-initial) French V2 vs. V3 by the beginning Dutch L2ers*

| Sentence pattern | Sentence type | Possible in Dutch? | Acceptance rate |
|---|---|---|---|
| Adv V S O | [+V2], [OV/VO] | yes | 92% |
| Adv Aux S O V | [+V2], [OV] | yes | 92% |
| Adv Aux S V O | [+V2], [VO] | no | 38% |
| Adv S V O | [–V2], [VO] | no | 38% |
| Adv S Aux V O | [–V2], [VO] | no | 19% |
| Adv S Aux O V | [–V2], [OV] | no | 30% |

(based on Hulk 1991: 24)

---

[8] Grüter frames the research question in terms of Full Transfer vs. Minimal Trees (see (4)), whose predictions
    converge in the case of the present tense: both accounts predict English-speaking learners of German at the initial state to interpret ambiguous constituent *wh*-questions as subject questions only. For questions in the perfect tense, however, predictions differ. While [FT] predicts an object question interpretation only, [MT] makes no principled predictions since the relevant string cannot be accommodated within the syntactic representations available to learners at this stage. If any bias can be expected, it would have to be based on non-syntactic strategies for interpretation .... (Grüter 2004: 11–12).

Comparing the first two rows to all others, we see that only when the word order is possible in Dutch, i.e., V2 plus OV, do these beginning L2ers robustly accept the French sentences—and in fact they do so at the very high rate of 92%. In short, just like the data from the two previous studies, Hulk's data argue that the L1 C-domain transfers in full.

## 6. *Conclusion: Transfer as bootstrapping*

Let me now return to the original question in (2), "Can all syntactic categories, including functional categories, undergo transfer/relexification?What are the implications with respect to parameter settings?" In response, this paper argued that the L1 properties of the highest functional layer of the clause, abbreviated here as CP, are initially adopted at the onset of L2 acquisition (which, if true, would suggest that the L1 properties of all lower functional layers are initially adopted as well). Interlanguage evidence that had been claimed to argue for the initial absence of CP or against the initial L1 instantiation of CP was found wanting, whereas the evidence reviewed here (in the work by Bohnacker, Grüter and Hulk) for the L1-specified CP in very early Interlanguage is, in my view, compelling. Along the way, I have also given hints where parameter resetting would be needed in this domain, that is to say, where the grammars of the L1 and Target Language diverge in the CP layer (e.g., [±wh mvt], [±V2]).

I have not, however, addressed the issue of relexification, that is, the relabeling of entries in a source language lexicon, including items that fill functional heads, with target language phonetic matrices. In the field of creole linguistics, for instance, Lefebvre (1998) has amassed an impressive array of evidence showing that the lexico-syntactic properties of Haitian Creole derive from the (superstratum French) relexification of (substratum) Fongbe. Indeed, she argues extensively for the idea that relexification applies to items associated with functional categories, such as determiners (D), tense-mood-aspect inflection (I) and complementizers (C), each with the expected syntactic consequences. Such creole findings are clearly compatible with (early) Interlanguage findings regarding the transfer of functional categories (as argued here for the C-domain, for example). Embracing Lefebvre's position that relexification is basic to creole genesis, Sprouse (this volume) claims, and I concur, that the role of relexification in L2 acquisition has been under-appreciated by the field. His contribution here is an attempt to show just how great the fundamental intellectual convergence is between Schwartz and Sprouse's conceptualization of Full Transfer in L2 acquisition and Lefebvre's Relexification Hypothesis in creole genesis, where the difference is merely one of emphasis: FT/FA has focused on abstract (morphosyntactic) properties of grammars; the Relexification Hypothesis has focused on lexical items and their grammatical consequences.

Yet I do not see transfer and relexification as co-extensive. I would argue that relexification is, rather, a subtype of the more general construct of transfer; while some relexification may well explain certain L2/creole syntactic phenomena, such as the realization of argument structure, other L2/creole syntactic phenomena that stem from L1 influence are not amenable to a relexification account, for instance, transfer of V2 (see section 5 above). V2 is a system-wide property, a property of the *grammar*, and even if (in the spirit of Borer 1984 and Chomsky 1995, among others) the locus of [+V2] is in the lexicon in the guise of some abstract feature, the latter has no phonetic matrix—and hence by definition cannot be relexified. Similarly with respect to the original question in (2): while functional *categories* (or the features from which they are constituted) can transfer, they cannot, strictly speaking, be *relexified*, since syntactic categories themselves have no phonetic matrix; only the items that overtly fill them do (and so they can be relexified).[9]

Finally, one might well ask *why* the L1 configuration of CP, or any of the L1 (including the lexicon) for that matter, should transfer. One possible answer, from the perspective of the mind as it embarks on L2 acquisition, is that the language-acquiring function makes use of what already works for language as it attempts to analyze TL input; and what already works for language is a particular instantiation of UG: the L1 grammar. So, from this mind's-eye view, the properties of the L1 grammar (and the L1 lexicon) are initially imposed onto TL input, and it is in this sense that L1 transfer bootstraps L2 acquisition, of which creole genesis—albeit thwarted due to deprivation of target language input—may be a particular instance.

### References

Beck, M.-L. 1998. L2 acquisition and obligatory head movement: English-speaking learners of German and the local impairment hypothesis. *Studies in Second Language Acquisition* 20: 311–348.

Bhatt, R. M. and B. Hancin-Bhatt. 2002. Structural Minimality, CP and the initial state in second language acquisition. *Second Language Research* 18: 348–392.

Bley-Vroman, R. 1989. What is the logical problem of foreign language learning? In *Linguistic Perspectives on Second Language Acquisition,* S. Gass and J. Schachter (eds.), 41–68. New York: Cambridge University Press.

Bohnacker, U. 2003. Residual word order problems in advanced adult L2 Swedish and German. In *Grammar in Focus: Festschrift for Christer Platzack, Vol. 2,* L.-O. Delsing, C. Falk, G. Josefsson and H. Sigurdsson (eds.), 37–45. Lund: Wallin and Dalholm.

Bohnacker, U. 2005. Nonnative acquisition of Verb Second: On the empirical underpinnings of universal L2 claims. In *The Function of Function Words and Functional Categories,* M. den Dikken and C. M. Tortora (eds.), 41–77. Philadelphia: John Benjamins.

---

[9] Likewise for (overt) [+wh mvt] languages: it is implausible that the *wh*-words are themselves inherently specified as [+mvt] (however technically implemented), given that *wh*-phrases do not always move overtly, as with multiple *wh*-questions, for instance, *When will Rex be thanked for what?*

Bohnacker, U. to appear. When Swedes begin to learn German: From V2 to V2. *Second Language Research.*

Borer, H. 1984. *Parametric Syntax.* Dordrecht: Foris.

Bullock, G., A. Omaki, B. Schulz, B. D. Schwartz and A. Tremblay. to appear. Where do L2ers attach interclausal adverbials? In *Proceedings of GALA 2005,* A. Belletti (ed.). Cambridge: Cambridge Scholars Press/CSP.

Chomsky, N. 1995. *The Minimalist Program.* Cambridge, MA: MIT Press.

Clahsen, H. and P. Muysken. 1986. The availability of Universal Grammar to adult and child learners—A study of the acquisition of German word order. *Second Language Research* 2: 93–119.

Clahsen, H. and P. Muysken. 1989. The UG paradox in L2 acquisition. *Second Language Research* 5: 1–29.

Dekydtspotter, L. and A. Liljestrand. in press. (Mis)interpretations of adverbials at the left-edge in early English-French as a reflex of the sentence processor. In *The Proceedings of the Inaugural Conference on Generative Approaches to Language Acquisition—North America, Honolulu, HI, UCONN Occasional Papers in Linguistics 4,* K. U. Deen, J. Nomura, B. Schulz and B. D. Schwartz (eds.).

Dekydtspotter, L., B. D. Schwartz, R. A. Sprouse and A. Liljestrand. 2005. Evidence for the C-domain in early Interlanguage. In *EuroSLA Yearbook,* S. H. Foster-Cohen, M. García Mayo and J. Cenoz (eds.), 7–34. Philadelphia: John Benjamins.

duPlessis, J., D. Solin, L. Travis and L. White. 1987. UG or not UG, that is the question: A reply to Clahsen and Muysken. *Second Language Research* 3: 56–75.

Epstein, S., S. Flynn and G. Martohardjono. 1996. Second language acquisition: Theoretical and experimental issues in contemporary research. *Behavioral and Brain Sciences* 19: 677–758.

Eubank, L. 1993/94. On the transfer of parametric values in L2 development. *Language Acquisition* 3: 183–208.

Eubank, L. 1996. Negation in early German-English interlanguage: More valueless features in the L2 initial state. *Second Language Research* 12: 73–106.

Garcia, B. 1998. The L2 Initial State: Minimal Trees or Full Transfer/Full Access? M.A. thesis, University of Durham.

Grondin, N. and L. White. 1996. Functional categories in child L2 acquisition of French. *Language Acquisition* 5: 1–34.

Grüter, T. 2004. Another take on the L2 initial state: Evidence from comprehension in German. *McGill Working Papers in Linguistics* 18: 1–24.

Håkansson, G., M. Pienemann and S. Sayehli. 2002. Transfer and typological proximity in the context of second language processing. *Second Language Research* 18: 250–273.

Hawkins, R. 2001. *Second Language Syntax.* Oxford: Blackwell.

Hawkins, R. and C. Chan. 1997. The partial availability of Universal Grammar in second language acquisition: The "failed functional features hypothesis". *Second Language Research* 13: 187–226.

Haznedar, B. 1997. Child Second Language Acquisition of English: A Longitudinal Case Study of a Turkish-Speaking Child. Ph.D. dissertation, University of Durham.

Haznedar, B. 2003. The status of functional categories in child second language acquisition: Evidence from the acquisition of CP. *Second Language Research* 19: 1–41.

Hoekstra, T. and B. D. Schwartz. 1994. Introduction: On the initial states of language acquisition. In *Language Acquisition Studies in Generative Grammar: Papers in Honor of Kenneth Wexler from the 1991 GLOW Workshops,* T. Hoekstra and B. D. Schwartz (eds.), 1–19. Philadelphia: John Benjamins.

Hulk, A. 1991. Parameter setting and the acquisition of word order in L2 French. *Second Language Research* 7: 1–34.

Hyams, N. 1994. V2, null arguments and COMP projections. In *Language Acquisition Studies in Generative Grammar: Papers in Honor of Kenneth Wexler from the 1991 GLOW Workshops,* T. Hoekstra and B. D. Schwartz (eds.), 21–55. Philadelphia: John Benjamins.

Jagtman, M. and T. Bongaerts. 1994. Verb placement in L2 Dutch. Paper presented at the America Association for Applied Linguistics (AAAL), Baltimore, 8 March (Ms. Delft University of Technology/University of Nijmegen).

Jansen, B., J. Lalleman and P. Muysken. 1981. The alternation hypothesis: Acquisition of Dutch word order by Turkish and Moroccan foreign workers. *Language Learning* 31: 315–36.

Jordens, P. 1988. The acquisition of word order in L2 Dutch and German. In *Language Development,* P. Jordens and J. Lalleman (eds.), 149–180. Dordrecht: Foris.

Kaplan, T. 1993. The Second Language Acquisition of Functional Categories: Complementizer Phrases in English and Japanese. Ph.D. dissertation, Cornell University.

Lakshmanan, U. 1993/94. "The boy for the cookie"—Some evidence for the nonviolation of the Case Filter in child second language acquisition. *Language Acquisition* 3: 55–91.

Lakshmanan, U. and L. Selinker. 1994. The status of CP and the tensed complementizer *that* in the developing L2 grammars of English. *Second Language Research* 10: 25–48.

Lefebvre, C. 1998. *Creole Genesis and the Acquisition of Grammar: The Case of Haitian Creole.* Cambridge: Cambridge University Press.

Liceras, J. 1997. The then and now of L2 growing pains. In *Views on the Acquisition and Use of a Second Language,* L. Díaz and C. Pérez (eds.), 65–85. Barcelona: Universitat Pompeu Fabra.

Meisel, J. M. 1997. The acquisition of the syntax of negation in French and German: Contrasting first and second language development. *Second Language Research* 13: 227–263.

Meisel, J. M., H. Clahsen and M. Pienemann. 1981. On determining developmental stages in natural second language acquisition. *Studies in Second Language Acquisition* 3: 109–135.

Müller, N. 1998. UG access without parameter setting: A longitudinal study of (L1 Italian) German as a second language. In *Morphology and its Interfaces in L2 Knowledge,* M.-L. Beck (ed.), 115–163. Philadelphia: John Benjamins.

Platzack, C. 1996. The initial hypothesis of syntax: A Minimalist perspective on language acquisition and attrition. In *Generative Perspectives on Language Acquisition,* H. Clahsen (ed.), 369–414. Philadelphia: John Benjamins.

Rizzi, L. 1997. The fine structure of the left periphery. In *Elements of Grammar: Handbook in Generative Syntax,* L. Haegeman (ed.), 281–337. Dordrecht: Kluwer.

Rizzi, L. and I. Roberts. 1989. Complex inversion in French. *Probus* 1: 1–30. (Reprinted 1996 in *Parameters and Functional Heads: Essays in Comparative Syntax,* A. Belletti and L. Rizzi (eds.), 91–116. Oxford: Oxford University Press.)

Schachter, J. 1989. Testing a proposed universal. In *Linguistic Perspectives on Second Language Acquisition,* S. Gass and J. Schachter (eds.), 73–88. Cambridge: Cambridge University Press.

Schwartz, B. D. 1997. On the basis of the Basic Variety .... *Second Language Research* 13: 386–402.

Schwartz, B. D. 1998. On two hypotheses of "Transfer" in L2A: Minimal trees and absolute L1 influence. In *The Generative Study of Second Language Acquisition,* S. Flynn, G. Martohardjono and W. O'Neil (eds.), 35–59. Mahwah, NJ: Lawrence Erlbaum.

Schwartz, B. D. and L. Eubank. 1996. What is the L2 initial state? Introduction. *Second Language Research* 12: 1–5.

Schwartz, B. D. and R. A. Sprouse. 1994. Word order and nominative case in non-native language acquisition: A longitudinal study of (L1 Turkish) German interlanguage. In *Language Acquisition Studies in Generative Grammar: Papers in Honor of Kenneth Wexler from the 1991 GLOW Workshops,* T. Hoekstra and B. D. Schwartz (eds.), 317–368. Philadelphia: John Benjamins.

Schwartz, B. D. and R. A. Sprouse. 1996. L2 cognitive states and the Full Transfer/Full Access model. *Second Language Research* 12: 40–72.

Schwartz, B. D. and R. A. Sprouse. 2000. When syntactic theories evolve: Consequences for L2 acquisition research. In *Second Language Acquisition and Linguistic Theory,* J. Archibald (ed.), 156–186. Malden, MA: Blackwell.

Sprouse, R. A. this volume. Full transfer and relexification: Second language acquisition and creole genesis.

Tsimpli, I.-M. and A. Roussou. 1991. Parameter-resetting in L2? *UCL Working Papers in Linguistics* 3: 149–169.

Vainikka, A. and M. Young-Scholten. 1994. Direct access to X'-theory: Evidence from Korean and Turkish adults learning German. In *Language Acquisition Studies in Generative Grammar: Papers in Honor of Kenneth Wexler from the 1991 GLOW Workshops,* T. Hoekstra and B. D. Schwartz (eds.), 256–316. Philadelphia: John Benjamins.

Vainikka, A. and M. Young-Scholten. 1996. Gradual development in L2 phrase structure. *Second Language Acquisition* 12: 7–39.

White, L. 1989. *Universal Grammar and Second Language Acquisition.* Philadelphia: John Benjamins.

White, L. 1990/91. The verb-movement parameter in second language acquisition. *Language Acquisition* 1: 337–360.

White, L. 1991. Adverb placement in second language acquisition: Some effects of positive and negative evidence in the classroom. *Second Language Research* 7: 133–161.

White, L. 1992. Long and short verb movement in second language acquisition. *Canadian Journal of Linguistics* 37: 273–286.

White, L. 2003. *Second Language Acquisition and Universal Grammar.* Cambridge: Cambridge University Press.

# L1 TRANSFER AND THE CUT-OFF POINT
## FOR L2 ACQUISITION PROCESSES IN CREOLE FORMATION

Silvia Kouwenberg
*University of the West Indies, Mona Campus*

Although L1 transfer can account for substrate-related properties of creole languages, I argue that this is largely unrelated to L2 acquisition. Paradoxically, the more evidence of L1 transfer we see in creole languages, the less reason we have for assuming that L2 acquisition has played a significant role in creole formation. This finding can be explained by the fact that in creolization, L1 transfer does not stop at target shift— that is, the point in time at which the superstrate ceases to be of direct relevance, and hence the point at which processes of L2 acquisition can be assumed to end. Moreover, L1 transfer in creole genesis may have the effect of assigning new grammatical functions to superstrate material, an effect not seen in L2 acquisition. Thus, L1 transfer in creolization and in L2 acquisition differ both in the quantity and quality of transfer. The upshot is that substrate-relatable properties in creole languages cannot be taken as an indication that L2 acquisition is a relevant process in creole formation.

## 1. *Introduction*

Evidence for the role of L2 acquisition in creole formation[1] has been sought in similarities between the morphosyntax of creole languages and their presumed substrate languages[2]—similarities which are thought to result from L1 transfer. It is fair to say, then, that the question of the role played by L1 transfer is central to the evaluation of the relation between L2 acquisition and creole formation.

In this paper, I will argue that L1 transfer can indeed be called upon to account for substrate-related properties of creole languages, but that, by and large, it is unlikely that this is related to L2 acquisition. In fact, paradoxically, the more evidence of L1 transfer we see, the less reason we have for assuming that L2 acquisition has played a significant role in creole formation. In short, L1 transfer in creole genesis is independent of L2 acquisition.

This position is implied in much recent creolist work. There appears to be consensus on the existence of a "cut-off point" in creole formation, after which the European lexifier ceases to be relevant as a resource in the emergence of

---

[1] I wish to thank Claire Lefebvre at UQAM for hosting me during the fall of 2004 and facilitating some of the work on which this paper is based. I also thank the University of the West Indies for the award of a Mona Campus Research Fellowship which allowed me the time for research on substrate-related issues. Finally, I would like to acknowledge the valuable discussions at the Montreal Dialogues workshop and the input from two anonymous reviewers of this paper.
[2] Despite the now well-known problems associated with the use of the terms "substrate" and "superstrate," no viable alternatives have emerged to date. I will use the terms here, but wish to note that they are not intended to convey an *a priori* commitment to the role of the languages so denoted in the process of creole emergence.

the contact variety which is to facilitate communication in the plantation context.[3] This cut-off point coincides with the time when the incipient contact language itself becomes a target language for newly arriving slaves (see Baker 1990: 109), the point of "target shift." On the assumption that L1 transfer constitutes an L2 acquisition strategy, this cut-off point should also signal the point at which L1 transfer ceases to be of relevance. But we will see below that L1-driven strategies not only continue to direct creole language formation beyond that point, but that L1 transfer increases in significance after the superstrate ceases to be relevant, that is, when it no longer constitutes a target of L2 acquisition. Thus, the persistent influence of L1 transfer beyond the point of target shift constitutes a striking contrast between L2 acquisition and creolization.

We will also see further that L2 acquisition and creole formation differ not only in the *amount* of substrate transfer which can be seen in individual cases, but also in the *quality* of this transfer. Thus, the reinterpretation of target-language material to take on grammatical functions is unheard of in L2 acquisition, but is attested in every creole language, and is frequently attributable to L1 transfer.

It is now recognized that L1 transfer is not uniform across creole languages, even where the same substrate language or languages seem to have been dominant. The question of the role of L1 transfer is, thus, linked to the question of cross-creole variation. In this chapter, I will consider the implications of cross-creole variation for our views of creole genesis. Of particular interest is the fact that variation in the extent to which L1 transfer can be recognized in individual creole languages cannot be effectively explained by calling on different processes of creole genesis. It appears that the sociohistorical factors which lead to target shift need to be taken into account.

## 2. *Cross-creole variation and uniformity*

In his 1986 paper entitled "The universalist and substrate hypotheses complement one another," Mufwene claims that "it is certainly safe to assume that creolists generally agree on the nature of the sociohistorical contexts which have produced these languages [i.e., pidgins and creoles], but they disagree essentially on the natures of the linguistic processes which resulted in them" (p. 129). At that time, creolist debates were premised on a rather undifferentiated view of plantation society and the institution of slavery. Moreover, creole grammars were broadly assumed to be comparable, and, by and large, creolists agreed on the features of grammar which were thought to be typical of creole

---

[3] I refer to the European lexifier or superstrate language here as a "resource," mindful of Baker's (1990) point that we have no reason to assume that African slaves aspired to fluency in the European lexifier. (See also Kouwenberg 1996b on superstrate and substrate as resource languages in creole genesis.) For argument's sake, I will adopt the usual terminology which designates the European lexifier as a "target" in the remainder of this paper.

languages. The debates of the 1980s—a boom period for creole studies—centered on different views of the nature of the linguistic processes which resulted in the formation of creole languages.

The past twenty years have seen a reversal of the position of the 1980s. It is now widely recognized that our earlier view of plantation society as a total institution, characterized by strict separation of classes of individuals and isolation of each plantation from the larger society, including other plantations, is not generally tenable: the structure of plantation societies and of the institution of slavery shows considerable variation related to time period, nature of crops, size of colony, nature of geographical terrain, and many other factors which are yet to be explored in detail (Arends 1995; Jourdan forthcoming; Mufwene 2001; Singler 1995). Moreover, better access to records pertaining to the slave trade has shown that earlier assumptions about the demographics of the slave trade, and therefore about the presence of different ethnolinguistic groups at different times, as well as the gender and age composition of the enslaved population in plantation societies, are not upheld (Arends forthcoming). All this means that the social conditions under which creole languages emerged must have been diverse. The idea that a "crisis of communication" obtained almost from the inception of these societies may be true only of particular plantation societies during particular historical periods, and it is doubtful that creole formation took place only in this context. This insight opens the door to serious research on the social and demographic contexts of creole genesis in individual cases, and in particular, on the linguistic implications of these contexts (e.g., Arends 2001 constitutes research of this kind).

The presumed uniformity of creole grammar has also come under fire. Detailed work on various aspects of the grammars of creole languages has shown that profound differences exist below the layer of superficial resemblances and that this holds true in all modules of grammar. With the exception of basic SVO word order, I cannot now think of a single creole "universal" that can still be claimed to hold across, for instance, the creole languages of the Caribbean. And as we unearth new facts about creole languages, we continue to find evidence for differences between them. A point made by Kusters and Muysken (2001: 183) comes to mind, namely that creole languages "were often assumed to be instantly known by observers in the colonial era and theoretical linguists in the post-colonial era, due to their European lexicon and simple root shapes," and that this "has stood in the way of serious description." With more serious descriptions of different aspects of creole grammars becoming available, we find ourselves challenged to explain variation, rather than uniformity.

When it comes to accounting for cross-creole variation, creolists have the choice of seeking its source in different creole formation processes, in changes after the initial establishment of a creole language according to some uniform standard, or in extralinguistic factors:

(i)   cross-creole variation results from differences in post-creole developments;
(ii)  cross-creole variation results from differences in the processes which give rise to creole languages;
(iii) cross-creole variation results from differences in the (sociohistorical) context of emergence.

The first-mentioned option is one which we can dismiss out of hand. Caribbean creole languages for which early data are available have not shown any dramatic divergences from their earliest known properties. Substantial early data exist for the Surinam creole languages[4] (e.g., Arends & Perl 1995) and for Negerhollands (Van Rossem & Van der Voort 1996), and Baker (1990: 109) points out that a Mauritian Creole text of 1749, just 28 years after the start of settlement, is consistent with later examples. Below, I will return to the question of whether post-creole developments can be called upon to account for cross-creole variation when considering decreolization; at this point, suffice it to say that, at best, decreolization can account for the selection of different forms, not for the existence of distinct properties of grammar.

I will first consider the idea that cross-creole variation results from differences in the processes by which creole languages are formed (section 3), before turning briefly to the issue of differences in the sociohistorical context (section 4). This is followed by a discussion of L1 transfer in creolization and its comparison to L2 acquisition (section 5).

## 3. *Differences in creole genesis processes*

The question of whether the creole genesis views of the 1980s are able to deal with cross-creole variation boils down to the question of how much these views rely on cross-creole uniformity. The clearest instance of this is Derek Bickerton's 1980s version of the Language Bioprogram Hypothesis (e.g., Bickerton 1984), which is able to take variation into account *only* where it is explainable as decreolization, in other words, as resulting from the incorporation of superstrate properties in a creole base. Although the past decade has seen increasing acceptance in the field of superstrate-oriented explanations, there is little evidence that substantial superstrate contributions to creole grammar are made *after* some supposed process of creole genesis.

As an example, I will briefly explore the puzzle of different tense systems in Caribbean creole languages: some languages use a relative tense system

---

[4] In fact, the date for the earliest known creole texts continues to be pushed back as we take advantage of previously unexplored sources, as shown by the fact that court proceedings of the first decade of the seventeenth century now constitute the earliest known recordings of Sranan (Van den Berg & Arends 2004).

while others use an absolute tense system. In the former, a distinction between stative and nonstative verbs is relevant to tense marking: out of context, a past tense interpretation results where nonstative verbs are used without overt tense marking, whereas stative verbs require overt tense marking. In creole languages which employ an absolute tense distinction, a stative-nonstative distinction is not relevant. Compare the Sranan and Papiamentu examples in (1) and (2).

(1) a. *Mi  waka*          b. *Mi ben waka*      c. *Mi e        waka*  SRANAN
       1s   walk             1s TENSE-walk          1s ASPECT walk
       'I walked, have walked'  'I had walked'      'I walk, am walking'
                                                (adapted from Voorhoeve 1957: 383)

(2) a. *Mi  *(ta)  kana*        b. *Mi  tabata  kana*           PAPIAMENTU
       1s   TENSE  walk            1s   TENSE   walk
       'I walk'/'I am walking'     'I was walking'
                                                (Kouwenberg & Lefebvre forthcoming)

The Sranan examples in (1) are typical of a relative tense system, where the bare use of the nonstative verb *waka* 'to walk' signals a past tense, as in (1a),[5] whereas its tense-marked use signals an anterior tense, as in (1b). Such a system exists also in, among others, Jamaican, Guyanese and Haitian. The Papiamentu examples in (2) are typical of an absolute tense system. Here, some form of tense-aspect marking is required to give nonstative *kana* its tense interpretation. Berbice Dutch similarly employs an absolute tense system.

Bickerton postulates relative tense as part of the creole prototype. Since the absolute tense system of languages such as Papiamentu and Berbice Dutch is clearly closer to the superstrate model, it would appear that this must have come about as a result of decreolization, replacing an earlier more prototypical relative tense system. There is, however, no evidence that such a system is introduced via a process of decreolization. Thus, an examination of the Guyanese and Jamaican creole continua—where mesolectal levels are assumed to have arisen via decreolization—shows that the relative tense system of the basilect is maintained throughout the mesolect; no switch from relative to absolute tense can be observed at that level, despite the choice of more superstrate-like forms (e.g., Winford 1990). Even Bahamian, which is thought to be quite close to its English lexifier, employs a tense system which is unlike that of English in this respect (McPhee 2003). In short, proximity to the lexifier

---

[5] One should note that *Mi waka* is not to be interpreted as a past imperfective. Voorhoeve's translation of *Mi waka* is a present perfect ('I have walked') rather than a simple past ('I walked'), presumably to avoid the confusion of a possible imperfective interpretation of English 'I walked.' This becomes clear when we consider his translation of *Mi ben e waka* [1s TENSE ASPECT walk] 'I walked, I was walking'—the presence of preverbal *e* marks this as imperfective.

is not a predictor for the type of tense system. It is much more likely that languages such as Papiamentu and Berbice Dutch employed absolute tense marking from their inception.

Bickerton's later modifications (e.g., Bickerton 1989) allowed for substrate contributions. This introduced another potential source of variation, this time from the other end, so to speak—but only via the adoption of substrate morphemes. Unfortunately, most substrate-related properties of creole languages do not come wholesale with substrate-derived morphemes. The discovery of a Gbe-derived focus morpheme *wɛ* in Saramaccan (Smith 1996) marks the exception. Take, for instance, the spatial postpositional nouns of Berbice Dutch (BD). Although the existence of this class of items seems to be modeled on the Ijo substrate, it is not associated with the incorporation of the relevant substrate morphemes. Thus, BD postpositions *ben* 'in(side),' *bofu* 'top, on,' *ondro* 'under(side),' *foro* 'front, in front of,' etc., derive from Dutch adverbs and prepositions. The sole Ijo-derived postposition, *anga*, a general postposition used in both locative and directional contexts corresponding to English *at* and *to,* acquired its postpositional use in BD; its Ijo etymon is a noun meaning 'place' which is not used postpositionally (Kouwenberg 1992). Nor is BD alone in having a class of postpositions: it shares this property with the Surinam creole languages, where the spatial nouns derive mostly from English prepositions.

What was considered the opposing view to Bickerton's in the 1980s—that associated with Mervyn Alleyne's work (e.g., Alleyne 1980)—is in fact only one of several substratist approaches, and is limited in scope to the Caribbean situation. With its reliance on some kind of "generalized West African grammar," Alleyne's approach is able to account for uniformity, not variation, among Caribbean creole grammars. Moreover, despite the lasting popularity of this approach among many substratist creolists, the presumed uniformity of the grammars of West African languages turns out to be as illusory as that of Caribbean creoles. In this regard, I would like to cite Africanist historian Richard Rathbone, who says:

> Few Africanists can read the Caribbean and American material without wincing when it adverts to the "African background." For the most part such allusions are generalised, often based on rather ancient scholarship and shy of both the complexity and the dynamism of the history of Africa (Rathbone 1988: 173)

Like the scholarship which Rathbone refers to, substratist research of the 1980s often resorted to generalizations over West African source languages, assuming rather than demonstrating typological uniformity to an extent which even allowed individual languages to represent the entire Niger Congo family. More recently, the recognition that Niger Congo is typologically diverse, and that typological uniformity is often a property of branches rather than the family, has changed the way in which substratist research is carried out.

The more successful recent substratist research projects have focused on specific cases of substrate transfer. For the Caribbean, this includes work on the relation between Berbice Dutch and its Ijo substrate (e.g., Kouwenberg 1992, 1996a, 1996b; Smith, Robertson & Williamson 1987), on the Surinam creoles and the Gbe substrate (e.g., Migge 1998; papers in Muysken & Smith In preparation), and on Haitian Creole and the Gbe substrate (e.g., Lefebvre 1998, 2001). Although research of this kind is sometimes able to identify substrate sources down to specific dialects, it can make no claims beyond the creole-specific findings. Where the West African source languages can be shown to differ (e.g., Ijo vs. Gbe vs. ...), this approach clearly has the potential to account for cross-creole variation. But where the substrate is presumed to be the same, whereas the creole languages which are thought to have emerged under its influence are not, other questions arise. Thus, Muysken (1994) and Smith (2001) point to the difference between Saramaccan and Haitian in substrate-relatable properties; for both, Gbe languages have been argued to constitute the dominant substrate. If, then, transfer of L1 properties accounts for substrate-relatable properties, why does one creole language display more evidence of such properties than others, and why does it seem that different properties are transferred in different languages? It seems inherently unlikely that the differences result from differences in the process of L1 transfer itself. This means that, instead, there must be factors—possibly both linguistic *and* extralinguistic—which "disturb" L1 transfer, resulting in a lack of correspondence between substrate and creole.

In conclusion, existing views of creole genesis are hard-put to deal with cross-creole variation. And yet it seems that an account of variation has to consider the inception of the creole languages, rather than any later developments. I will now turn briefly to differences in the sociohistorical context of creole genesis which may throw light on this issue, before considering L1 transfer effects in creolization, and its comparison with L2 acquisition.

## 4. *The sociohistorical context as a source of cross-creole variation*

The ratio of African slaves (substrate speakers) to whites (superstrate speakers) and in particular the rapidity of the change in this ratio, as measured by the number of years to numerical parity between blacks and whites and the number of years to the presence of a sizeable creole population (see discussion in Arends, forthcoming), has long been accepted as the most significant social/demographic factor in the timetable of creolization: a ratio that severely disadvantages individual substrate speakers in terms of their access to the superstrate favors early creolization. An extreme version of this is provided by the Surinam case, where superstrate speakers were removed altogether.

Singler (1988) has argued that homogeneity of substratal input—itself tied in with ethnolinguistic homogeneity in the substrate population—is an important determinant in substratal influence: the more homogeneous the substratal input, the greater the extent of substratal influence in the creole. This is probably due to the fact—as recognized in particular in Bickerton's work —that a heterogeneous substrate translates into heterogeneous L2 versions or "jargons." These versions constitute so many competing forms; in that situation, leveling is likely to obliterate the evidence for L1 transfer, as pointed out by Thomason and Kaufman (1988).

It appears, then, that early creolization, spurred by the demographic factors noted above and combined with ethnolinguistic homogeneity in the substrate population, provides the most favorable context for L1 transfer.

In considering the range of substrate properties which appear to have fed the developing grammars of creole languages, one is struck by the fact that L1 transfer seems to have obtained to vastly different extents in different creole languages, and has involved different properties in the different languages. Compare, for instance, the existence of a postposed clausal determiner in Haitian (e.g., Lefebvre & Massam 1988), modeled on the Gbe substrate, with the complete absence of any form with a comparable function in other creole languages, including the Surinam creoles. In contrast, the Surinam creoles display clear parallels with many Gbe properties in phonology, morphology and syntax where Haitian does not. Smith (2001: 75), comparing different substrate effects in Saramaccan and Haitian, submits that "[i]t is most unlikely that precisely the same conditions pertained in the formative years of the two creoles" and argues that different substrate effects are correlated with different timing of the point at which target shift takes place, that is, the point in time when the superstrate ceases to be relevant in the contact situation, and the contact variety itself becomes a target for language learning. With regard to the Surinam creoles, the early withdrawal of English meant an early target shift, possibly within less than two decades of initial colonization in 1651 (see Smith 1999); such early target shift did not obtain in Haiti. Although demographic data suggest that Gbe speakers were an early dominant presence in Surinam, their dominance was interrupted by Bantu speakers and was not reestablished until the 1690s—the formative period of Saramaccan maroon society. In view of the fact that some Gbe-related properties of Saramaccan are not found in other Surinam creoles (for instance, prenasalized stops, some Gbe-derived question words, w_-focus; see Smith 2001), it appears that Gbe-driven restructuring obtained both in the early period and again in the later period when maroon society was formed, therefore both before and after target shift. In other words, ethnolinguistic homogeneity also facilitates later transfer, in the developmental stage after target shift.

In sum, although the formative processes in creolization do not appear to differ from one creole to another, the evidence for their effects varies widely, as is seen when considering the effects of L1 transfer in creole formation. This suggests that the relative weighting of the different processes, including L1 transfer, differs from one creole to another. It has been pointed out that this is at least partially related to the timing of the target shift and the ethnolinguistic homogeneity/heterogeneity of the shifting population. This points to the relevance of nonlinguistic factors—those pertaining to the demographic and social context of communication in plantation and maroon societies.

## 5. *How creole formation differs from L2 acquisition*

Creolists pursuing substratist research have been happy to point to possible cases of transfer, but have stayed away from considering the technicalities of this process, content to use the term transfer without further qualification, as also noted by Winford (2005). Nevertheless, transfer is associated with processes of adult second language acquisition (SLA), and its application to creole language formation needs to be evaluated against the background of findings in SLA research. After all, there is no *a priori* reason to think that transfer is a different process in creole genesis than elsewhere. I will argue that, in fact, there is evidence that transfer *is* different in creole genesis. Before we proceed, it may be useful to point out that despite some similarities between learners' interlanguages and creole languages (see discussion in Siegel, this volume), untutored second language acquisition as documented in currently existing contexts—typically involving migrant workers—never results in creole formation, whether across communities or in individuals.[6] There is simply no documented interlanguage stage that resembles a creole language, that is, a variety which is morphosyntactically independent of the "target," underscoring the fact that creole formation is not simply the result of failed L2 acquisition.[7]

Current work suggests two ways in which creole formation differs from L2 acquisition:

(i) persistence of L1-related properties of grammar,

(ii) reinterpretation of superstrate material.

As an example of the first point, Helms-Park (2003) compares early interlanguage versions of English by speakers of Vietnamese, a serializing language, and Hindi-Urdu, which is non-serializing. Serial-type constructions occur in the early interlanguage of the former, but not of the latter. Its

[6] One comes across statements to the effect that interlanguage varieties show creolization tendencies, namely in their simplification of target systems. There are two problems with such statements. First, among creolists, the notion of simplification has long been problematized (e.g., Muysken 1988), and it is no longer considered useful in describing the relation between creole languages and their superstrates, or in designating the process of creolization itself (see Kouwenberg & Patrick 2003). Second, I know of no work which claims that targeted L2 acquisition, like creolization, results in a variety which is morphosyntactically independent of the target. Where restructuring occurs in L2 acquisition, it is in the direction of the target language, unlike restructuring in creolization, which is independent of the superstrate.
[7] But note that Field (2004) argues that it may be possible to identify the extent to which L2 acquisition applied in creole formation by comparing the properties of different stages in L2 acquisition with the properties of creole languages.

occurrence, she notes, is restricted to lower levels of lexical proficiency, suggesting that L1 transfer is used as a conversational strategy under communicative pressure at very early stages of proficiency in the L2. At more advanced levels of proficiency, serial-type constructions disappear—in contrast with their conservation in creole languages, especially those of the Caribbean. She concludes that the nature of the target language is the most influential factor in these developments, concurring with Baker (1990) and others that the target in creolization comprises non-native varieties. In this respect, creolization contrasts with the situation that obtains in SLA, where non-native varieties are not considered acquisition targets. Whatever the explanation, it supports the point that, in creole genesis, the L1 does not cease to be relevant after initial L2 acquisition.[8]

For the second issue, that of the reinterpretation of superstrate material, recall the example of spatial nouns in the Surinam creole languages and in Berbice Dutch (see section 3). These derive mostly from prepositions and adverbs in the European lexifiers, and even where they derive from nouns, the forms have been reinterpreted as having spatial reference. Thus, English *face* and *back* have cognate forms in Sranan, *fesi* and *baka,* respectively. In addition to their English source meanings, the Sranan forms have the relational meanings 'in front' and 'behind.' Thus, *na a oso fesi/baka* [LOC DET house face/back] 'in front of/behind the house' (Bruyn 1996; Muysken 1987: 96ff).

Even more compelling than the reinterpretation of the categorial status of lexical material is the evidence for *functional* reinterpretation. This results in forms being put to grammatical uses which they lack in the target or lexifier languages. Such cases abound in creoles. For example, Becker and Veenstra (2003) compare the treatment of verb inflection in French interlanguage varieties with its treatment in French-lexifier creoles. Considering the long-short verb alternation which exists in several French-lexifier creoles (e.g., Mauritian Creole short *manz* vs. long *manze* 'eat'), they argue that "only the formal properties of French inflectional morphology survived the processes involved in creolization, and there was a break in transmission with respect to the functions attached to the formal opposition" (p. 294). Thus, in Mauritian Creole, the choice of the long or short form depends on the selectional properties of the verb, and bears no relation to the tense/aspect values expressed by the French counterparts from which they are assumed to derive (cf. "short" *mange* vs. "long" *manger, mangé, mangeais*). In this case, the reinterpretation of the superstrate material has resulted in functional differentiation of the variation in verb forms. This reinterpretation of French inflections can be compared to their treatment in the database compiled through the European

---

[8] One anonymous reviewer points out that persistence of L1-related properties happens in cases of fossilization in SLA. While this is true, the point is that transfer continues as a *process* in creole formation at a stage where it no longer does in L2 acquisition.

Science Foundation (ESF) project, which represents a longitudinal study of untutored second language acquisition in the European context of migrant worker communities. Klein and Perdue (1997) distinguish three levels of L2 development: prebasic, basic, and postbasic, corresponding to different levels of morphosyntactic elaboration. The ESF corpus shows that in the L2 basic variety of French, verbs appear in different formal variants, but without functional differentiation at this level. Where L2 acquisition continues, the tense/aspect values associated with the standard French forms are acquired. Importantly, where L2 fails to continue, formal variation persists without functional value.

Thus, there is a clear contrast between the cases of failed L2 acquisition in the ESF corpus, where development halts altogether, and creole formation, where development is independent of L2 acquisition, and therefore does not stop at the point where L2 acquisition ceases. Becker and Veenstra argue that the reinterpretation of superstrate material seen in these cases is made possible by target shift. It is noteworthy that not all French-lexifier creoles have a short-long verb distinction (Haitian lacks it), and that its function is not the same in all languages where it appears. In other words, functional reinterpretation can take different routes in different cases.

Cases of functional reinterpretation frequently seem to parallel similar uses in substrate languages. Where the reinterpretation can be seen as substrate-driven, Siegel's term "functional transfer" is applicable, that is, the use of a form from the lexifier with a grammatical function from the substrate (Siegel, this volume). Becker and Veenstra do not address the question of whether the kind of reinterpretation which they identify is L1-driven, but we can turn to work on the Gbe sources of the grammars of Haitian and the Surinam creoles, among others, where reinterpretation resulting from L1 transfer is explored in detail. For instance, Bruyn (1995) discusses the Gbe-driven development of the proximate demonstrative *disi* (< *this*) into a relative clause introducer in Sranan. Another example is provided by Aboh (this volume), who, considering the determiner systems of Haitian, Sranan and Saramaccan, argues for transfer of the functions associated with the definite determiner of the Gbe substrate, whereas transfer of the syntactic pattern that results in the postnominal position of that determiner took place in Haitian only.

Based on an extensive survey of the literature, Siegel (this volume) points out that functional transfer is not normally found in interlanguage development. This is surprising in light of the popularity of the view that the interlanguage initial state in L2 acquisition consists of the L1 grammar, as in the "Full Transfer/Full Access" model. According to this model, restructuring of the initial state grammar is triggered by L2 data that the L1 grammar cannot accommodate. With this in mind, let us consider the dilemma of a learner who has assigned an L1-based grammatical function to a L2 form, say, a hypothetical Gbe speaker targeting English who assigns the function of relative clause introducer to demonstrative *this*. Such a learner would not be confronted with input data that show this to be wrong unless it was explicitly pointed out to her/him. In the best case, the learner would notice the absence of this usage in native speaker production and deduce that she/he hypothesized wrongly. The learner might also notice that the target language uses a different form for this function (in this case *that,* along with a number of relative pronouns), and modify her/his usage accordingly. But the point is that the input that would lead to the restructuring which ensures the weeding-out of L1-type functional uses of L2 forms would be *negative* evidence rather than positive evidence. In all, one would expect lots of functional transfer—the use of an L2 item with an L1 grammatical function—at least in early interlanguage. The fact that this is apparently not attested suggests either that Full Transfer does not take place, or that independent constraints are at work. Either way, interlanguages differ markedly from creole languages in this respect.

This point is further underscored by Muysken's (2000: 165–171) discussion of the relevance of the lexical-functional distinction in widely different contexts (language mixing, speech production, agrammatic speech, language development, foreigner talk, language change, creolization, lexical borrowing). His overview shows that the lexical-functional distinction is useful, but that different dimensions of the distinction appear to be involved in different domains. It seems that creole genesis is unique in its radical restructuring of the overall inventory of grammatical elements.

## 6. *Conclusion*

In conclusion, in both creolization and L2 acquisition the target language may cease to be a potential target of L2 acquisition. However, subsequent developments differ widely for the two situations: where L2 acquisition is incomplete, the result is a "frozen" variety characterized by low or intermediate levels of proficiency. In contrast, development does not stop at the point of target shift in creolization. Nor does L1 transfer stop at target shift in creolization, in contrast to L2 acquisition. Moreover, L1 transfer may have the effect of assigning new grammatical functions to superstrate or target language material (functional transfer), an effect not seen in L2 acquisition.

Thus, the view that L1 transfer is a function of the relevance of L2 acquisition in creolization turns out to be too restrictive: late L1 transfer is independent of L2 acquisition, and the more evidence we see of L1 transfer, the less likely it is that L2 acquisition had anything much to do with it. This is because, the more L2 acquisition takes place, the more the transferred properties are weeded out of the interlanguage variety, as the learner progresses towards higher levels of competence in the target.

This means that substrate-relatable properties in creole languages—evidence for L1 transfer—cannot automatically be taken as an indication that L2 acquisition is a relevant process in creole formation.

A final point pertains to the extent of L1 transfer in creolization. We have noted that its effects differ greatly across creole languages—a fact which we can only explain by considering extralinguistic factors such as the demographics and social conditions of early plantation societies. In contrast, although SLA studies have identified social factors as important determinants in successful acquisition, there is no evidence that L1 transfer is determined by anything other than the acquisitional stage reached by the individual learners.

## References

Alleyne, M. C. 1980. *Comparative Afro-American*. Ann Arbor, MI: Karoma.

Arends, J. 1995. Demographic factors in the formation of Sranan. In *The Early Stages of Creolization,* J. Arends (ed.), 233–285. Amsterdam: John Benjamins.

Arends, J. 2001. Social stratification and network relations in the formation of Sranan. In *Creolization and Contact,* N. Smith and T. Veenstra (eds.), 291–307. Amsterdam: John Benjamins.

Arends, J. Forthcoming. A demographic perspective on creole formation. In *Handbook of Pidgin and Creole Studies,* S. Kouwenberg and J. V. Singler (eds.). Oxford: Blackwell.

Arends, J. and M. Perl. 1995. Early Suriname Creole Texts. A Collection of Eighteenth Century Sranan and Saramaccan Documents. Frankfurt: Vervuert.

Baker, P. 1990. Off target? *Journal of Pidgin and Creole Languages* 5(1): 107–119.

Becker, A. and T. Veenstra. 2003. The survival of inflectional morphology in French-related creoles. In *Reconsidering the Role of Second Language Acquisition in Pidginization and Creolization,* S. Kouwenberg and P. Patrick (eds.). *Studies in Second Language Acquisition (special issue)* 25: 283–306.

Bickerton, D. 1984. The Language Bioprogram Hypothesis. *Brain and Behavioral Sciences* 7: 173–188.

Bickerton, D. 1989. The lexical learning hypothesis and the pidgin-creole cycle. In *Wheels within Wheels. Papers of the Duisburg Symposium on Pidgin and Creole Languages,* M. Pütz and R. Dirvin (eds.), 11–31. Frankfurt: Peter Lang.

Bruyn, A. 1995. *Grammaticalization in Creoles: The Development of Determiners and Relative Clauses in Sranan.* Amsterdam: IFOTT.

Bruyn, A. 1996. On identifying instances of grammaticalization in creole languages. In *Changing Meanings, Changing Functions. Papers Relating to Grammaticalization in Contact Languages,* P. Baker and A. Syea (eds.), 29–46. London: University of Westminster Press.

Field, F. 2004. Second language acquisition in creole genesis. In *Creoles, Contact, and Language Change,* G. Escure and A. Schwegler (eds.), 127–160. Amsterdam: John Benjamins.

Helms-Park, R. 2003. Transfer in second language acquisition and creoles: The implications of causative serial verbs in the interlanguage of Vietnamese ESL learners. In *Reconsidering the Role of Second Language Acquisition in Pidginization and Creolization,* S. Kouwenberg and P. Patrick (eds.). *Studies in Second Language Acquisition (special issue)* 25: 211–244.

Jourdan, C. Forthcoming. The cultural in pidgin genesis. In *Handbook of Pidgin and Creole Studies,* S. Kouwenberg and J. V. Singler (eds.). Oxford: Blackwell.

Klein, W. and C. Perdue. 1997. The basic variety. *Second Language Research* 13: 301–347.

Kouwenberg, S. 1992. From OV to VO. Linguistic negotiation in the development of Berbice Dutch Creole. *Lingua* 88: 263–299.

Kouwenberg, S. 1996a. Grammaticalization and word order in the history of Berbice Dutch Creole. In *Changing Meanings, Changing Functions. Papers Relating to Grammaticalization in Contact Languages,* P. Baker and A. Syea (eds.), 207–218. London: University of Westminster Press.

Kouwenberg, S. 1996b. Substrate or superstrate: What's in a name? *Journal of Pidgin and Creole Languages* 11(2): 371–375.

Kouwenberg, S. and C. Lefebvre. Forthcoming. A new analysis of the Papiamentu clause structure. *Probus: International Journal of Latin and Romance Linguistics.*

Kouwenberg, S. and P. Patrick. 2003. Introduction. In *Reconsidering the Role of Second Language Acquisition in Pidginization and Creolization,* S. Kouwenberg and P. Patrick (eds.). *Studies in Second Language Acquisition* (special issue) 25: 1–9.

Kusters, W. and P. Muysken. 2001. The complexities of arguing about complexity. *Linguistic Typology* 5: 182-185.

Lefebvre, C. 1998. *Creole Genesis and the Acquisition of Grammar. The Case of Haitian Creole.* Cambridge: Cambridge University Press.

Lefebvre, C. 2001. Relexification in creole genesis and its effects on the development of the creole. In *Creolization and Contact,* N. Smith and T. Veenstra (eds.), 9–42. Amsterdam: John Benjamins.

Lefebvre, C. and D. Massam. 1988. Haitian Creole syntax: A case for DET as head. *Journal of Pidgin and Creole Languages* 3: 213–243.

McPhee, H. 2003. The grammatical features of TMA auxiliaries in Bahamian Creole. In *Contact Englishes of the Eastern Caribbean,* M. Aceto and J. Williams (eds.), 29–49. Amsterdam: John Benjamins.

Migge, B. 1998. Substrate Influence in the Formation of the Surinamese Plantation Creole. A Consideration of the Sociohistorical Data and Linguistic Data from Ndyuka and Gbe. Ph.D. dissertation, Ohio State University.

Mufwene, S. 1986. The universalist and substrate hypotheses complement one another. In *Substrata versus Universals in Creole Genesis,* P. Muysken and N. Smith (eds.), 129–162. Amsterdam: John Benjamins.

Mufwene, S. 2001. *The Ecology of Language Evolution.* Cambridge: Cambridge University Press.

Muysken, P. 1987. Prepositions and postpositions in Saramaccan. In *Studies in Saramaccan Language Structure,* M. Alleyne (ed.), 89–101. Amsterdam/Kingston: University of Amsterdam/University of the West Indies.

Muysken, P. 1988. Are creoles a special type of language? In *Linguistics: The Cambridge Survey, Volume II. Linguistic Theory: Extensions and Implications,* F. Newmeyer (ed.), 285–301. Cambridge: Cambridge University Press.

Muysken, P. 1994. Saramaccan and Haitian: A comparison. *Journal of Pidgin and Creole Languages* 9(2): 305–314.

Muysken, P. 2000. *Bilingual Speech. A Typology of Code-Mixing.* Cambridge: Cambridge University Press.

Muysken, P. and N. Smith. (eds.). In preparation. *From Alada to Paramaribo 1651–1750: What Happened to the Language?*

Rathbone, R. 1988. Resistance to enslavement in West Africa. In *De la traite à l'esclavage: Actes du colloque international sur la traite des noirs,* Nantes, 1985. Vol. 1, V^e–XVIII^e siècles, Serge Daget (ed.), 173–184. Paris: Harmattan.

Singler, J. V. 1988. The homogeneity of the substrate as a factor in pidgin/creole genesis. *Language* 64: 27–51.

Singler, J. V. 1995. The demographics of creole genesis in the Caribbean: A comparison of Martinique and Haiti. In *The Early Stages of Creolization,* J. Arends (ed.), 203–232. Amsterdam: John Benjamins.

Smith, N. 1996. Focus-marking *w_* in Saramaccan. Grammaticalization or substrate? In *Changing Meanings, Changing Functions. Papers Relating to Grammaticalization in Creole Languages,* P. Baker and A. Syea (eds.), 113–128. London: University of Westminster Press.

Smith, N. 1999. The vowel system of 18th-century St. Kitts Creole: Evidence for the history of the English creoles? In *St. Kitts and the Atlantic Creoles: The Texts of Samuel Augustus Mathews in Perspective,* P. Baker and A. Bruyn (eds.), 145–172. London: University of Westminster Press.

Smith, N. 2001. Voodoo Chile. Differential substrate effects in Saramaccan and Haitian. In *Creolization and Contact,* N. Smith and T. Veenstra (eds.), 43–80. Amsterdam: John Benjamins.

Smith, N., I. Robertson and K. Williamson. 1987. The Ijo element in Berbice Dutch. *Language in Society* 16: 49–90.

Thomason, S. G. and T. Kaufman. 1988. *Language Contact, Creolization, and Genetic Linguistics.* Berkeley, CA: University of California Press.

Van den Berg, M. and J. Arends. 2004. Court records as a source of authentic early Sranan. In *Creoles, Contact, and Language Change,* G. Escure and A. Schwegler (eds.), 21–34. Amsterdam: John Benjamins.

Van Rossem, C. and H. Van der Voort. 1996. *Die Creol Taal. 250 Years of Negerhollands Texts.* Amsterdam: Amsterdam University Press.

Voorhoeve, J. 1957. The verbal system of Sranan. *Lingua* 6: 374–396.

Winford, D. 1990. Copula variability, accountability, and the concept of "polylectal" grammars. *Journal of Pidgin and Creole Languages* 5: 223–252.

Winford, D. 2005. Contact-induced changes. Classification and processes. *Diachronica* 22: 373–427.

# THE ROLE OF THE SYNTAX-SEMANTICS INTERFACE
# IN LANGUAGE TRANSFER[*]

### Enoch Oladé Aboh
*University of Amsterdam*

It has been long observed that the determiner phrase in creole languages exhibits morphosyntactic variations that cannot be directly attributed to superstrate transfer, substrate transfer or independent UG development in any obvious way. This paper suggests that such variation results from the competition and selection process that arises in language contact situations. In such contexts, syntactic and semantic features from different languages compete to form the emerging grammar. The facts discussed indicate that this process affects functional categories differently depending on their semantic and licensing conditions (i.e., their syntax). Under the assumption that discourse-related features (e.g., definiteness, specificity) are visible at the syntax-discourse/semantics interface, it is argued that such competition may result in situations where the emerging language displays syntactic and semantic properties that combine those of their substrate and lexifier languages. For instance, it is shown that even though the Gbe languages act as a trigger for the emergence of specificity in the Surinamese creoles and in Haitian, only the latter adopted Gbe syntax to any extent, while English seems to have provided the syntax of the determiner in the former languages. The discussion further shows that language transfer, as described here, is subject to the vulnerability of interfaces in general, and more specifically to that of the syntax-semantics interface. By approaching the issue of creolization from the perspective of the nature of interfaces, this paper contributes to the ongoing debate on the role of interfaces in second language acquisition. A direct consequence of this view is that certain facts (e.g., loss of inflection) that are traditionally considered from the point of view of learnability might actually derive from the properties of interfaces.

## 1. *Introduction*

The major motivation for this paper is the fact that the determiner systems of creole languages exhibit morphosyntactic variations that cannot be directly attributed to superstrate transfer, substrate transfer or independent Universal Grammar (UG) development in any obvious way. For instance, the determiner systems of Haitian, Sranan, and Saramaccan display word order sequences that diverge from those found either in the superstrate languages (i.e., French and English) or in the substrate languages (e.g., Gungbe), or in both language types and cannot therefore be accounted for in terms of superstrate or substrate transfer.[1] Similarly, a UG-based account (e.g., Bickerton 1981) faces the

---

[*] Aspects of this paper were presented at the International Joint Conference of the SCL-SPCL-ACBLPE on Caribbean and Creole Languages, and at the Montreal Dialogues in August 2004. I would like to thank the participants in these events for their comments and suggestions. I am also grateful to Umberto Ansaldo, Norval Smith, Claire Lefebvre, Anne-Sophie Bally, and Lydia White, whose suggestions and criticisms helped improve this version significantly.

[1] Gungbe is a Gbe language (a subgroup of Kwa). According to Capo's (1991) classification, it belongs to the Fon cluster. While the Gbe languages often show strong (and sometime

problem of the wide range of variation these languages and other creoles display with regard to their determiner phrases.[2]

In this paper, I suggest that one way to approach such variation would be to propose that, in a situation of language contact, functional categories are affected differently depending on their semantic and licensing conditions (i.e., their syntax). Under the assumption that features such as definiteness, specificity, and number are visible at the syntax-discourse/semantics interface, I claim that language transfer results from a competition among features that may lead to a split between syntax and semantics. In other words, I propose that the emerging language may retain a feature (Fx) from a competing language (Lx) and adopt its function (i.e., discourse semantics) and morphosyntax (i.e., formal licensing properties). This situation is represented in (1a). On the other hand, the emerging language may select a feature (Fx) on the basis of its function in a competing language (Lx), while leaving its syntax unfixed, as represented in (1b). I informally refer to the former situation as pattern transmission and to the latter as feature transmission. In this case, I conclude that the emerging language may develop a syntax of its own under pressure from other competing languages (e.g., the superstrate) and/or based on the principles of UG.

(1) a. $F_x$ [Function = $L_x$;     Syntax = $L_x$] → Pattern transmission
    b. $F_x$ [Function = $L_x$      Syntax = …] → Feature transmission

The description in (1) indicates that pattern transmission includes retention of a feature, its function and its syntax, while feature transmission involves the selection of a feature and its function. Within the framework of Principles and Parameters, or Minimalism, such a split between syntax and semantics appears reasonable if we assume that a feature (F) is associated with a unique semantic/pragmatic representation cross-linguistically, while its syntax is subject to parametric variation. This would mean that the same feature may be valued differently in natural languages, even though its semantics remains the same. For instance, specificity is encoded by a demonstrative in French and English, while, in Gungbe, it requires fronting of the noun phrase to the left of a designated specificity marker within the determiner phrase (Aboh 2004a, 2004b). I further argue that, in a situation of language contact, these different patterns (e.g., Gbe versus Germanic/Romance) may compete for the same function at the syntax-semantics interface, leading to a particular combination in the emerging language.

---

predictable) similarities, it is worth keeping in mind that they may also show striking syntactic and/or semantic variations in certain domains (e.g., negation, tense, aspect; see Aboh 2004a; Essegbey 1999, for discussion). In this paper, I use Gungbe as a representative for the Gbe cluster where these languages show similar behavior. When necessary, the differences between languages are mentioned.
[2] See Aboh (2004c) for discussion.

The paper is structured as follows. Section 2 presents the general properties of the DP in Haitian, Sranan and Saramaccan, and contrasts them with corresponding data from French, English and Gungbe. The choice of these languages is interesting because they are considered to have the same substrate languages (i.e., Gbe; Arends 1989; Lefebvre 1998; Smith 1987) but different lexifier languages (i.e., English/Portuguese for Sranan/Saramaccan, and French for Haitian).[3] However, the discussion shows that the difference in lexifiers cannot explain the variation among these creoles. Instead, it will be shown in section 3 that the creoles often display syntactic and semantic properties that combine those of their substrate and lexifier languages. For instance, I will argue that even though the Gbe languages acted as a trigger for the emergence of the feature specificity in these creoles, only Haitian Creole adopted Gbe syntax to any degree, while English seems to have provided the basis for the syntax of the determiner in Sranan and Saramaccan. In addition, the discussion of the Haitian data suggests that pattern transmission does not entail a perfect replica of the source system in the emerging language. In this respect, I argue that language transfer results from the vulnerability of interfaces in general, and more specifically, that of the semantic-syntax interface. This view clearly differs from previous theories of creole genesis (e.g., Relexification) in which the substrate languages are thought to systematically provide syntactico-semantic features, while the superstrate languages mainly contribute to the lexico-phonetic forms, and from alternative theories of genesis such as the language bioprogram or superstrate influence. Instead, the proposed analysis presupposes that, in a situation of language contact, any competing language may affect any module of the grammar of the emerging language (see Mufwene 2001, 2002 for discussion). Section 4 concludes the paper.

## 2.  *Comparing the creoles to their source languages*

In this section, I discuss the general properties of noun phrases in the creoles as opposed to their lexifiers (e.g., French, English) and substrate languages (e.g., Gungbe). Of particular interest to us are the properties of the determiners related to features such as definiteness and specificity.

By specificity, I refer to discourse-anaphoric noun phrases that link back to referents that are pre-established in the discourse, or known or familiar to the participants (Pesetsky 1987).[4] On the other hand, definiteness refers to a pre-identified set of referents that is not necessarily discourse-linked. These informal definitions imply that specificity requires a smaller set of referents than definiteness. For the sake of discussion, I tentatively propose that specificity

---

[3] This paper does not discuss the influence of Portuguese on Saramaccan syntax; I hope to return to this issue in future work.

[4] This definition is compatible with Prince's (1981) notion of *assumed familiarity* for topics, and suggests that topic and specificity interact (Aboh 2004b).

identifies a subset of the set of contextually given or assumed elements for which a comment holds, by excluding the complementary subset for which this comment does not hold. This would mean that specificity expresses exhaustive identification, unlike definiteness, which only selects a contextually identified set.[5]

Specificity and definiteness combine in some languages (e.g., Gungbe), leading to the following characterization:

(i) A specific definite noun phrase is strongly D(iscourse)-linked and represents a unique referent assumed to be known to both speaker and hearer, and which the speaker intends to refer to.

(ii) A specific indefinite noun phrase need not be D-linked. It represents an existing referent that the hearer may not know about, but which the speaker has in mind and intends to refer to.

The description of specific definites in (i) is compatible with the notion of *assertion of existence,* as discussed in the literature (Bickerton 1981), while specific indefinites, described in (ii), recall Ionin's (this volume) notion of speaker *intent to refer.* In the Gbe languages, these two notions are properties of two different determiners, which exclude each other and which I assume to be expressions of the nominal left periphery (Aboh 2004a, 2004b). In these languages, noun phrases are never ambiguous with respect to specificity because they are marked. On the other hand, nonspecific noun phrases, whether definite, indefinite or generic, take no marking even though they may be modified by adjectives, demonstrative, numerals or relatives. I refer to such noun phrases as "bare noun phrases."[6] Building on this, I propose that specificity and definiteness are syntactic features anchored in distinct heads within the nominal left periphery (Aboh 2004a, 2004b; Szabolcsi 1994).

The following sections describe how the creoles (Haitian, Sranan/ Saramaccan) and their source languages encode definiteness, specificity, and number, as well as the types of determiners used to express these notions. In so doing, I pay particular attention to the contexts where such determiners can occur and word order variations inside the noun phrase that they may bring about. I also consider the position of the noun with regard to other nominal modifiers such as relative clauses, adjectives, demonstratives, and genitives. I will start with Haitian Creole, Gungbe and French.

---

[5] This characterization is inspired by Kiss's (1998) account of exhaustive or identificational focus.
[6] I am therefore assuming, contra Enç (1991), that definite noun phrases are not necessarily specific. In fact, the Gbe languages provide numerous examples of definite noun phrases that derive their definiteness from the context or from the modifiers that they are associated with (e.g., relative clause, demonstrative, genitive).

## 2.1 *Haitian Creole versus Gungbe and French*

Studies of the properties and distribution of the determiners in these languages suggest that determiner phrases (DPs) show strong parallels in Haitian and Gungbe, as opposed to French.[7] For instance, Haitian and Gungbe lack pure indefinite or definite articles, whether singular or plural. Indeed, these languages include a postnominal specificity marker, which occurs with the noun phrase if and only if it refers to some entity that is pre-established in discourse and/or is assumed by the speaker to be familiar to the addressee (i.e., specific definite). In addition, these languages have a separate postnominal number marker to express number. The number marker also expresses definiteness (Aboh 2002, 2004a, 2004b; Lefebvre 1998). The following examples illustrate these properties.

The Haitian and Gungbe examples in (2a–b) involve the specificity determiners, and the noun phrases are interpreted as referring to shared/known information only. This restriction does not apply to French, where the determiner is ambiguous (2c).[8]

(2)   a.   *Pè-a*                                                HAITIAN
           Priest-Det[9]
           'The *aforementioned* priest'                   (from Sylvain 1976: 55)
           *'The priest (e.g., that we know of)'
      b.   *Mɔ̀pè        lɔ́*                                     GUNGBE
           Priest        Det
           'The *aforementioned* priest'
           *'The priest (e.g., that we know of)'
      c.   *Le prêtre*                                          FRENCH
           'The priest (e.g., that we know of)'
           'The *aforementioned* priest'

The sentences in (3) indicate that the specificity determiner need not occur with definite or generic nouns in Haitian and Gungbe. As a result, these languages use bare noun phrases in a wide range of contexts. French, on the other hand, does not allow bare nouns as indicated by the ungrammatical sentence (3c). As one can see from the grammatical French example (3d), sequences that are most comparable to Haitian and Gungbe bare nouns necessarily involve conjoined plural nouns (Roodenburg 2004). Such a constraint does not hold on Gungbe and Haitian bare noun phrases.

---

[7] See also Brousseau and Lumsden (1992), Bruyn (1995a), DeGraff (1992, 1995, 2000), Déprez (2001) and Lefebvre (1998), for a discussion of creoles; Aboh (2004a, 2004b) and Lefebvre and Brousseau (2002) for studies of Gbe languages; and Bernstein (1997, 2001a, 2001b) and Giusti (1996, 1997) for the analysis of Romance and Germanic languages.
[8] Translations of and emphasis in the Haitian examples are mine.
[9] Det: Determiner; Dem: Demonstrative; Fut: Future; Hab: Habitual, Loc: Locative; Neg: Negative; Num: Number; pl: Plural; Poss: Possessive; Pst: Past; Rel: Relative; Sg: Singular

(3)  a.  *Wosiyòl     manje kowosòl*                            HAITIAN
         nightingale eat    soursop
         'Nightingales eat soursop.'                        (from DeGraff 1992: 105)
     b.  *Àlúé        nɔ̀         ɖù     gbàdó*                       GUNGBE
         magpie     Hab        eat    corn
         'Magpie(s) habitually eat(s) corn.'
     c.  *\*Pie mange maïs*                                        FRENCH
     d.  *Parlementaires et politiques de tous bords ont approuvé les mesures*
         *d'aide à l'emploi du gouvernement.*
         'Parliamentarians and politicians of all stripes approved the
         government's employment assistance measures.'

When they co-occur, determiners and pronominal possessors cluster in postnominal position in Haitian and Gungbe (4). Note in passing the absence of
number inflection and gender specification in these languages.

(4)  a.  *Krab    mwen     sa      a      yo*                      HAITIAN
                                                          (from Lefebvre 1998: 78)
     b.  *Àgásá cè        éhè     lɔ́     lɛ́*                           GUNGBE
         crab   1sg-Poss Dem    Det    Num
         'These crabs of mine'
     c.  N > Poss > Dem > Det > Num

It is worth noting, though, that, unlike Haitian, Gungbe does have a distinct
class of weak possessive pronouns, which, with the exception of first-person
singular (*cè* 'my') and second-person singular (*tòwè* 'your') derive from a
combination of weak personal pronouns plus the genitive marker *tɔ̀n* as in *mì-
tɔ̀n* (1pl + Poss = 'our'); *mì-tɔ̀n* (2pl + Poss = 'your'); *yé-tɔ̀n* (3pl + Poss =
'their') (Aboh 2002, 2004a).[10] However, given that Haitian does not have
possessive marker of any sort and only expresses possession by [Possessee]-
[Possessor] juxtaposition, it is arguable that, in sequences such as *krab mwen*
in (4a), the possessive marker is null. As Lefebvre (1998) argues, this means
that the word order and the form of the pronoun are parallel in Haitian and
Gungbe, the only difference being that Haitian lacks an overt possessive
marker.

In French, however, determiners and modifiers occur prenominally and
bear gender and number inflection (5a–c; 5a'–c'). Furthermore, demonstratives, possessive pronouns and definite determiners are mutually exclusive
(5d).

---

[10] This set of weak pronouns must be distinguished from the set of strong pronouns, which
uniformly includes the combination of a strong pronoun and the genitive marker: *nyè-tɔ̀n* 'my,'
*jè-tɔ̀n* 'your,' *úɔ̀-tɔ̀n* 'his/her,' *mìlé-tɔ̀n* 'our,' *mìlé-tɔ̀n* 'your,' *yélé-tɔ̀n* 'their'; see Aboh
(2004a) for discussion.

(5)  a.  *Le(s)*    *crabe(s)*              a'. *La table*              FRENCH
         'the crab(s)'                         'the table'
     b.  *Ce(s)*    *crabe(s)*              b'. *Cette table*
         'this/these crab(s)'                  'this table'
     c.  *Mon/mes crabe/s*                  c'. *Ma table*
         'my crab(s)'                           'my table'
         **Le(s) ce(s) mes crabes*
         'the/this/these my crab(s)'

Finally, Haitian and Gungbe display bare nouns that function as head nouns in relative clauses.

(6)  a.  [*Moun*]  *ki*   *pa*   *travay  p     ap     touché*        HAITIAN
         people    Rel   Neg   work    Neg   Fut    get-paid
         'Those who don't work won't get paid.'          (from DeGraff, p.c.)
     b.  [*Mè*]  *ɖê   má    wà àzɔ́n   má    ná    yí*      *kwé*     GUNGBE
         One     Rel   Neg   do work   Neg   Fut   receive   money
         'Anyone who doesn't work will not get money.'

When these nouns co-occur with the specificity marker, the head noun precedes the relative clause, which in turn precedes the specificity marker, as follows: head noun > [relative clause] > specificity marker and/or number marker.[11]

(7)  a.  [*Fam    ki    vini    wè-u*]   *la*             HAITIAN
         woman   Rel   come    see-2pl   Det
         'The *aforementioned* woman who came to visit you'
                                               (from Sylvain 1976: 69)
     b.  [*Fam    ki    rete*]   *yo*                     HAITIAN
         woman   Rel   arrest   3pl/Num
         'The women who arrested them'
         or 'The women who were arrested'       (from Sylvain 1976: 62)
     c.  [*Náwè   ɖê    wá    kpɔ́n    mì*]   *lɔ́   lé*     GUNGBE
         woman   Rel   come   see     2pl    Det   Num
         'The *aforementioned* women who came to visit you'

French, on the other hand, lacks bare nouns in relative clauses, whence the ungrammatical example (8a), which contrasts with the grammatical example (8b). As sequenced in (8c), the French definite determiner must precede the relative head noun, which in turn precedes the relative clause.

---

[11] What matters here is the position of the relative clause vis-à-vis the head noun and the determiners. The interested reader is referred to Koopman (1982a, 1982b), DeGraff (1992), Lefebvre (1998) and Aboh (2002, 2005) for the analysis of relative clauses in Haitian and Gungbe, respectively.

(8)  a.  *Homme   que j'ai    vu                                    FRENCH
          man            that I.have  seen
     b.  L'homme   que  j'ai    vu
          Det.man   that  I.have  seen
          'The man that I saw'
     c.  Determiner > noun > [relative clause]

It appears from this description that Haitian and Gungbe pattern alike in a way
that is different from French. While these similarities point to a close structural
relationship between Haitian and Gungbe, they should not obscure the fact that
Haitian Creole and French do share a number of properties, some of which
distinguish them from Gungbe (and related languages). For example, Haitian
exhibits prenominal and postnominal adjectives, like French. Gungbe,
however, has postnominal adjectives only.

     Similarly, our earlier discussion suggested that French lacks a proper speci-
ficity marker, and one might conclude from this that this language does not
encode specificity syntactically. Such a conclusion might be wrong since
French makes use of demonstrative articles (e.g., *ce, cette*), in combination
with the postnominal deictic locative *là*, to encode specificity, as shown in
(9a). The ungrammatical example (9b) shows that the postnominal deictic
element cannot occur in postnominal position by itself, unlike in Gungbe and
Haitian.

(9)  a.  *Cette* guitare-*là* me plaît beaucoup                      FRENCH
          that guitar there me pleases very much
          'I like that guitar (there) very much.'
     b.  *Guitare-*là* me plait beaucoup
          guitar-there me pleases very much

Yet, the deictic locative *là* is the source of the Haitian specificity marker *la*,
suggesting that the existence of the construction in (9a) in French might have
reinforced the emergence of the Gbe pattern in Haitian (see Lefebvre 1998 and
references cited therein). I will not elaborate on the possible reinforcing role of
French here, however, and the interested reader is referred to Mufwene (2001),
Siegel (2004), and Ansaldo (2005) for some ideas. Instead, I propose that part
of the nominal structure in Haitian has its source in the Gbe languages.

     Anticipating the discussion in section 3, the analysis proposed in this paper
follows Szabolcsi (1987) and much related work in assuming parallels between
the noun phrase and the sentence. It is argued that the noun phrase includes
three layers, starting with the core predicate layer where the (lexical) noun
head merges and introduces its arguments (e.g., in possessive constructions).
This layer further extends to a functional layer that consists of distinct functional projections responsible for agreement features, whose specifiers host

noun modifiers such as numerals and adjectives. In the approach of Cinque (1994, 1999), this would mean that nominal modifiers are to the noun phrase what adverbs are to the verb phrase. Keeping the parallel between the clause and the noun phrase, I refer to this layer as the nominal inflectional domain, whose head, the nominal counterpart of clausal I, encodes deixis and may host definite articles (Szabolcsi 1994).

The nominal inflectional domain is projected under a nominal left periphery headed by D, which Szabolcsi shows to have properties of a subordinator and therefore to parallel the clausal left periphery C. Under Rizzi's (1997) split-C hypothesis, the clausal periphery involves discrete functional projections responsible for force (i.e., clause-typing), topic, focus, and finiteness. Adopting this view, Aboh (2002, 2004a, 2004b, 2005) shows, on the basis of the Gbe languages, that the nominal left periphery can be split just like the clausal left periphery. It is therefore argued that the Gungbe specificity and number markers are the overt realizations of the two borderlines of the nominal left periphery. *Lɔ́* encodes DP as the highest projection that links the noun phrase to the discourse, while *lé* expresses NumP that links the nominal left periphery to the lower predicate. The core of this paper concerns transfer within the nominal left periphery. I will return to the details of the analysis in section 3.

With this description in mind, let us take a step back and consider the parallels we have observed between Haitian and Gungbe. What we seem to find here is that the Haitian specificity determiner *la* and the number marker *yo* express the nominal periphery similarly to their Gungbe counterparts *lɔ́* and *lé* (Aboh 2004a, 2004b). In terms of the analysis proposed here, such a parallel is regarded as an instance of pattern transmission (see section 3.2 for discussion).

The data further suggest that Haitian Creole shows a split in its noun phrase: the left periphery has a structure from the Gbe languages while the nominal inflectional structure derives from French syntax. For instance, French and Haitian have both prenominal and postnominal adjectives, which I assume, following Cinque (1994, 1999) and much related work, realize the nominal inflectional domain. I claim that such a hybrid system involving a left periphery that has been influenced by Gbe and an inflectional domain that has been influenced by French can be accounted for straightforwardly only if one adopts a modular approach to creolization, like the one developed here. Further empirical evidence comes from Sranan and Saramaccan.

*2.2 Sranan (and Saramaccan) versus Gungbe and English*
The facts described for Haitian, Gungbe, and French are replicated in Sranan, Saramaccan, and English with the difference that the Surinamese creoles use specificity determiners in the Haitian and Gungbe way, even though English syntax is evident. Data concerning the Surinamese creoles are mainly drawn from Sranan, but the conclusion reached here also applies to Saramaccan.

The Sranan sentences in (10) indicate that these creoles freely use indefinite, definite, and generic bare noun phrases, as Haitian and Gungbe do but English does not. Observe from the following examples that the bare noun *bana* 'banana' is interpreted as generic (10a) or definite, as in the second instance of *bana* in (10b). However, the sequence *a bana* in (10b) is read as specific.

(10) a. *Kofi, go na wowoyo go bai **bana** tya kon gi   mi* SRANAN
         Kofi go Loc market  go buy  banana carry come give 1sg
         'Kofi, go to the market to buy me banana(s).'

    b. *Na  a  bana    di  Ppa    tya  kon,  dati a    nyan.*
       Cop Det banana Rel father carry come  that 3sg  eat
       *A   bere   hati,   a    nyan  **bana***
       3sg stomach hurt   3sg  eat   banana
       'THE *aforementioned* BANANA that father brought is what he ate. His stomach is aching because he ate the banana.'

As the sentences in (11) show, the corresponding English examples involving bare nouns are ungrammatical.

(11) a  *John went to the market to buy **banana**
    b.  ***Banana** that Daddy bought yesterday

Like Haitian and Gungbe, Sranan has a singular specificity marker that is realized as *(n)a*. Note from sentences (10b) and (12a–b) that the presence of this element to the left of the noun triggers the specific reading. In example (12a), the first instance of *bana* is interpreted as specific (i.e., 'the aforementioned banana') as opposed to *bana* in (12b), which is understood as (in)definite.

(12) a. *Kofi, teki **a** **bana** tya  gi   mi.*           SRANAN
         Kofi take Det banana carry give 1sg
         'Kofi, give me the *aforementioned* banana [e.g., the one I brought yesterday].'

    b. *Kofi, teki **bana** tya  gi   mi.*
       Kofi take banana carry give 1sg
       'Kofi, give me a (or the) banana.'

Again, English does not make such a specific versus nonspecific distinction between bare nouns and nouns that occur with the determiner.

(13) a. I like trains very much.                        [Generic]
    b. Every day, I take the train to Amsterdam.    [Definite, nonspecific]

In addition, specificity may be encoded in English by various elements including (in)definite articles, demonstratives, and quantifiers.

While Sranan parallels Haitian and Gungbe with regard to encoding specificity, it differs from them because it lacks a distinct number marker. Hence, the plural counterpart of example (12a) involves the plural specificity marker, as in (14).

(14) *Kofi,   teki   **den**   **bana**   tya   gi   mi.*       SRANAN
     Kofi   take   Det   banana   carry   give   1sg
     'Kofi, give me the *aforementioned* bananas [e.g., the ones I brought yesterday].'

These variations point to a possible structural difference between the DP in Sranan, on one hand, and in Haitian and Gungbe, on the other. That this might be the correct description is further suggested by the fact that the specificity determiner precedes the noun in Sranan, but follows it in Gungbe and Haitian. This pattern is replicated in relative clauses, where the specificity determiner precedes the relativized noun, which in turn precedes the relative clause in Sranan (10b), while the relative clause is sandwiched between the head noun and the determiners in Gungbe and Haitian (6–7). I will argue that such syntactic properties emerged in Sranan under the pressure of English.

## 2.3 Summary

It appears from the above description that Haitian and Sranan use determiners (and number markers) in a way parallel to Gungbe and other Gbe languages. These languages mainly distinguish between specific and nonspecific referents. French and English, on the other hand, mainly differentiate between definite and indefinite noun phrases. Table 1 recapitulates the possible featural combinations and expressions of determiners in all five languages considered.

| D-features | Gungbe | Sranan | Haitian | English | French |
|---|---|---|---|---|---|
| [+spec +def, +plur] | ló, lé | den | la yo | the | Les, ces...ci |
| [+spec, +def, –plur] | ló | na | la | the | le, la |
| [+spec, –def, +plur] | dé, lé | Ø (wan tu) | — | some, certain | certains |
| [+spec, –def, –plur] | dé | wan | yon | a, some, certain | certain |
| [–spec, +def, +plur] | lé | den(?), Ø | yo | the | les |
| [–spec, +def, –plur] | Ø [definite] | Ø [definite] | Ø [definite] | the | le, la |
| [–spec, –def, +plur] | Ø [generic] | Ø [generic] | Ø [generic] | Ø, any [generic] | des |
| [–spec, –def, –plur] | Ø [indef] | Ø [indef] | Ø [indef] | a, some | un |

Table 1. *Feature combinations and determiner expression*
*in creoles and their donor languages*

With regard to the distribution of the determiners and the noun phrase, however, it appears that the creoles do not always show syntactic patterns that exactly coincide with those of the languages from which the function was retained. For instance, Haitian has postnominal determiners like Gungbe and prenominal adjectives like French, while Sranan has prenominal determiners and noun modifiers like English. This would mean that Haitian combines properties of the Gbe languages and French in both semantics and syntax, while Sranan seems to have mapped semantic features from Gbe onto syntactic patterns from English. These combinations are illustrated in Table 2.

| Determiners | Creoles | | | Lexifier | | Substrate |
|---|---|---|---|---|---|---|
| | HC | SC | SR | Fr | En | Gu |
| Bare NP generic, (in)definite | + | + | + | – | – | + |
| Specificity determiner (singular) | + | + | + | + | – | + |
| Specificity determiner (plural) | – | + | + | – | – | – |
| Specificity determiner (singular/plural) | – | + | + | + | + | – |
| (In)definite singular/plural articles also used for encoding specificity | – | – | – | + | + | – |
| Separate number marker (encoding definiteness) | + | – | – | – | – | + |
| Free use of bare (in)definite/generic NPs | + | + | + | – | – | + |
| Specificity determiner (singular/plural) before N | – | + | + | – | – | – |
| N before specificity determiner (singular/plural) | + | – | – | + | – | + |
| N before number marker | + | – | – | – | – | + |
| N before specificity marker preceding number marker | ? | – | – | – | – | + |
| Relative clause before specificity determiner singular | + | – | – | + | – | + |
| Relative clause before number marker | + | – | – | – | – | + |
| Relative clause before specificity determiner preceding number marker | ? | – | – | – | – | + |
| Specificity determiner (singular/plural) before relative clause | – | + | + | + | + | – |
| Adjective before N | + | + | + | + | + | – |
| N before adjective | + | + | ? | + | – | + |

HC: Haitian Creole; SC: Saramaccan; SR: Sranan; Fr: French; En: English; Gu: Gungbe

Table 2. *Function and distribution of determiners in creoles and their donor languages*

I conclude from the data presented in Tables 1 and 2 that syntactic and semantic patterns are not always uniformly transmitted from a single donor language (e.g., superstrate or substrate) to the emerging languages. Instead, I propose that, in a situation of language contact where various languages enter a competition that may lead to the emergence of a new language, the latter combines different syntactic and semantic properties selected from the competitor languages in a nontrivial way. More specifically, I propose that the new language emerges from the combination of syntactic and semantic features from

the competing languages. This means in principle that the core syntactic properties of the new language and those of its donors will not match perfectly. I
further argue that certain semantic and syntactic feature combinations (call the
process selection) could be favored by interface conditions (e.g., whether
certain interfaces are more sensitive to language transfer). I will now discuss
the possible role of the syntax-semantics interface in language contact on the
basis of the described facts in Haitian, Sranan, Gungbe, French, and English.

### 3. *On the vulnerability of interfaces*
In order to account for the similarities and variations between the creoles and
their donor languages, I propose that the way the determiner system (henceforth D-system) is affected in a situation of language contact depends on
whether the relevant features, their function, *and* their morphosyntax are
retained from a competing language or whether just the feature and its function
are retained, leaving it up to the emerging language to develop the relevant
licensing mechanisms, under pressure from other competing languages or on
the basis of UG principles. This line of thinking suggests that UG universally
determines linguistic features, their semantics and their related parameters.
These features, however, need appropriate triggers to emerge in a language. I
claim that competing languages provide the emerging language with such
triggers.

In this study, I propose that Haitian and Sranan show signs of substrate
transfer because the function and interpretation of the Haitian and Sranan
determiners (i.e., the specificity markers) are adapted from the Gbe languages,
as a result of D-feature transmission. Yet Haitian and Sranan D-elements
require different formal licensing conditions. It appears that Haitian patterns
like Gbe (and partly like French), while Sranan behaves like English and
unlike Gbe.[12] On the assumption that D-features (and their related parameters)
are properties of UG (Abney 1987), I conclude that the Gbe languages constituted the relevant triggers for fixing the parameters of the target D-features in
Haitian, while English played a similar role in the case of Sranan. Such a view
presupposes that UG acts as the ultimate filter for the relevant combinatory
possibilities, and only those that are UG-compatible can converge. For instance, cross-categorial combinations, say, between V and D, are filtered out
by UG. Similarly, if one adopts Cinque's (1999) fixed universal functional hierarchy, then free recombination of the features and morphosyntax of different
functional projections will be excluded by UG as being non-converging. Under
this restrictive view, no emerging language would be able to develop an
aspectual system where the specifier and the head of an aspect phrase are

---

[12] In terms of this approach, it is conceivable that Portuguese may have also played a role in
the development of prenominal left peripheral markers in Saramaccan, but I will not discuss
this possibility here.

simultaneously or optionally filled by the corresponding adverb and marker from both the lexifier and the substrate.

The proposed analysis for language transfer therefore implies an interaction between two levels: (i) the retention of syntactic features (i.e., the syntactic and semantic features that enter into competition as potential properties of the emerging language); and (ii) the formal requirement that UG sets for these features to be properly licensed.

### 3.1 Feature selection and the syntax-discourse interface

One question that arises at this stage of the discussion is what features can be retained and why. In other words, which features are contact-sensitive and why may such features be retained/selected in a situation of language contact?

Given our current limited knowledge of intralinguistic and extralinguistic factors that interact in a situation of language contact, there seems to be no obvious answer to the question of why a feature ($F_1$) should be selected over another feature ($F_2$).[13] These complications aside, it seems reasonable to assume that the features that are most likely to be selected are the ones that are associated with discourse/semantics and therefore relate to interfaces. Put differently, only discourse-interpretable features enter into competition and may be selected in the emerging language.[14] This would mean that certain domains of the Faculty of Language (e.g., the syntax-discourse interface) may be more sensitive to language contact phenomena than others.

This, in turn, leads us to conclude that certain aspects of core syntax (e.g., order of merging, structure of predicate) might be immune (or less sensitive) to language transfer. For example, under Kayne's (1994) antisymmetry and Sportiche's (1988) VP-internal subject hypothesis, the rigid SVO or head-complement pattern found across creoles appears to be a consequence of the merging order imposed by UG. Heads merge first with their complement, and the set formed in that way merges with the specifier. Similarly, if we adopt Cinque's (1999) universal hierarchy of the clause structure, then the mood-tense-mood-aspect-verb sequence found in creoles as well as other non-creole languages reduces to a simple expression of UG.[15] The only difference between creoles and superficially different languages resides in whether a language expresses the head position or the specifier position of a particular functional

---

[13] Other properties as frequency and saliency, as well as social factors such as prestige and markedness, could play a role in favoring one particular feature over another one, but very little is known about the role of such factors in language contact and language change in general.

[14] I further assume that feature competition is subject to a principle of economy that guarantees that two identical features cannot be selected in the emerging language. Accordingly, economy dictates that a creole cannot have two specificity markers, one derived from the substrate and one from the superstrate, to fulfill exactly the same syntactic and discourse functions.

[15] See Aboh (2006) for a discussion of mood sequences in Saramaccan and certain other English-based creoles.

projection within the clause structure. In the view advocated here, competing languages provide the trigger to set such parameters in the emerging language.

Assuming that UG acts as such a filter in language genesis, we may be able to approach the question of inflection in a completely different way. It is often argued in the literature that inflectional morphology (e.g., verbal inflection and noun inflection) is typically lost in language contact situations, mainly due to imperfect second language acquisition. Extended to creoles, this would mean that they lack inflectional morphology due to imperfect second language acquisition, itself conditioned by restricted access to the target language. While this may look like a reasonable account, it does force one to construct a special scenario that requires imperfect second language acquisition by a whole population—a rather complicated matter. For instance, how can we ensure that a significant (or determining) number of slave learners will fail to acquire the relevant inflectional paradigm regardless of their socio-economic position in the community? How can we account for such a failure in a principled way? And how can we accommodate both the absence of verbal inflection and the presence of derivational morphology in the nominal domain in such a framework? More specifically, how can we account for the fact that, even though Haitian lacks verbal endings (e.g., affixes) of the French type, the language does have nominal endings of the type –(s)yon in words such as *dekoupasyon* 'dividing a wall,' *vivasyon* 'conviviality,' as well as other nominal affixes as discussed by DeGraff (2002)? There seems to be no way of formulating such a difference in terms of a failure of second language acquisition.

In the analysis developed here, however, domains of grammar show different sensitivity to language transfer, depending on whether or not they relate to the syntax-semantics interface. Accordingly, the loss of inflection in language contact situation would follow in a straightforward manner if we assume that inflectional morphology (and agreement in general) is a by-product of core syntactic configurations (e.g., specifier-head vs. complement-head relations). As such, inflectional morphology is a property of core syntax. It does not play a crucial role at the syntax-discourse/semantics interface, and will therefore not be selected in language transfer. In other words, I suggest that inflection is a weak competitor that is hardly visible to language creators. This would mean that the loss of inflection in a language contact situation should by and large be dissociated from issues related to second language acquisition proper. The proposed analysis therefore distinguishes between inflectional morphology and derivational morphology in a principled way because the latter, but not the former, often has semantic content.

### 3.2 C and D as vulnerable interfaces

Following this line of thinking, I assume that interfaces (e.g., discourse-sensitive domains) are generally vulnerable and more permeable to language transfer. Platzack (2001), for instance, argues that the complementizer system (i.e., the interface between sentence and discourse) is a vulnerable domain for language transfer. Related proposals have been made concerning transfer between the bilingual child's grammars in L1 acquisition (e.g., Müller & Hulk 2000), transfer from the L1 in L2 acquisition (Valenzuela 2005), and L1 attrition under the influence of the L2 (Sorace 2000). Under such a general view of the properties of interfaces in language contact situations, it seems reasonable to hypothesize that the domains where new languages (e.g., creoles) display variations are those domains that relate to interfaces. This idea appears compatible with the fact that, even though creoles generally have SVO order and display a rigid hierarchy with regard to the ordering of tense, mood, and aspect markers, they display a wide range of variation as to the position of the determiner with respect to the noun. This is shown in Tables 3 and 4, which summarize the distribution of the determiner within the noun phrase in French-based creoles (Table 3), and across creoles with different lexifiers (Table 4).

| Creoles | Singular | | Plural | |
|---|---|---|---|---|
| Seychelles | sa N | Dem > N | sa ban N | Dem > Pl > N |
| Mauritian | sa N la | Dem > N > Def | sa ban N la | Dem > Pl > N > Def |
| Antillean | N sa (l)a | N > Dem > Def | se N sa (l)a | Pl > N > Dem > Def |
|  | N ta (l)a |  | se N ta (l)a |  |
| Guadaloupean | N la sa | N > Def > Dem | se N la sa | Pl > N > Def > Dem |
| New Louisiana | (la) N sa la | (Def) > N > Dem > (Def) | le N sa la | (Def/Pl) > N > Dem > (Def) |
| Old Louisiana | N la | N > Def | N (sila) ye | N > sila > Pl |
| Guyanese | sa N la | Dem > N > Def | sa N y(e-l)a | Dem > N > Pl > Def |
| Haitian | N sa a | N > Dem > Def | N sa yo | N > Dem > Pl |

Table 3. *Distribution of definite, demonstrative and plural markers across French-based creoles (adapted from Déprez 2001: 52)*

| Creoles | Ordering of Dem, N, Adj, Num |
|---|---|
| Bahamian | Dem-Num-Adj-N |
| Kriyol, Tok Pisin, Seychelles, Mauritian, Capeverdian | Dem-Num-N-Adj |
| Bislama, Berbice Dutch, Sranan | Num-Adj-N-Dem |
| Fa d'Ambu, Nubi | N-Adj-Num-Dem |
| Haitian, Papiamentu, Tayo, St. Lucian, Angolar, Louisiana | Num-N-Adj-Dem |
| Sango | Adj-N-Num-Dem |
| Lingala | N-Adj-Dem-Num |

Table 4. *Relative ordering of demonstrative, noun, adjective, and numeral in different creoles (adapted from Haddican 2002)*

The variation among creoles with the same lexifier (Table 3) and across creoles with different lexifiers (Table 4) suggests that such sequencing cannot simply derive from the different types of lexifiers, but rather must stem from a more general process such as the properties of the interfaces.

In this regard, the idea that interfaces are vulnerable to language transfer offers a new way of looking at such variation. Under such a view, the variation in Tables 3 and 4 is expected if we assume that the clause structure and the nominal structure include specific syntactic articulations that represent the point of interaction (i.e., the interface) between syntax and semantics. As Rizzi (1997) shows, the complementizer system represents such an articulation in the clause. It encodes two types of information: ForceP, which relates the clause to the discourse and expresses clause type, and FinP, which links the complementizer system to the proposition and indicates finiteness/modality (15). Topic and focus projections occur between ForceP and FinP (see Aboh 2006, in press for a discussion of the clausal periphery in Gungbe and Saramaccan).

(15)  **Discourse**........    [ForceP ...[TopP...[FocP....[FinP.........**Proposition**....]]]]

As was briefly discussed in section 2.1., this paper assumes, following Szabolcsi (1994), Aboh (2002, 2004a, 2004b) and much related work, that the determiner system represents a corresponding articulation within the noun phrase. DP is the highest projection that links the nominal sequence to the discourse. It is the nominal equivalent of ForceP. NumP, on the other hand, links the nominal left periphery to the nominal predicate. It is the nominal equivalent of FinP.

(16)  **Discourse**.............[DP ...[TopP......[FocP.......[NumP.....**Nominal predicate**....]]]]

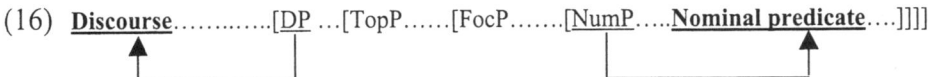

For the purposes of this paper, I shall ignore topic and focus projections within the DP. (See Giusti 1996 and Aboh 2004b for further discussion.)

*3.3 Transfers at the interfaces: Haitian and Sranan*
In terms of the proposed analysis, the determiner system, which I analyze in representation (16) as the interface between the nominal structure and the discourse, represents a potentially vulnerable domain. In what follows, I will suggest that the variation observed in Sranan and Haitian (as well as in the other creoles presented in Tables 3 and 4) can be understood as a reflection of such vulnerability. I start with Haitian, Gungbe, and French.

3.3.1  *Haitian and Gungbe versus French.* Starting from representation (16), I suggest that Haitian and Gungbe manifest the structure shown in (17), where the number markers *lé/yo* and the specificity markers *lɔ́/la* merge in Num and D respectively (Aboh 2002, 2004a, 2004b, 2005; Brousseau & Lumsden 1992; Ritter 1995).

(17)  [DP [D[±specific] *lɔ́/la* [NumP [Num[±plur, ±def] *lé/yo* ]]]]          HAITIAN, GUNGBE

Following previous analyses of Gungbe noun phrases, I further propose that Gungbe and Haitian D-elements surface postnominally because number and specificity are checked in these languages by overt movement of the nominal predicate to [spec NumP] and [spec DP], as shown in (18). Observe that this fronting rule is compulsory in Gungbe and Haitian, but not in French, where specificity and number may be checked by demonstratives, such as *ce*, *cet, cette, ces*.

(18)

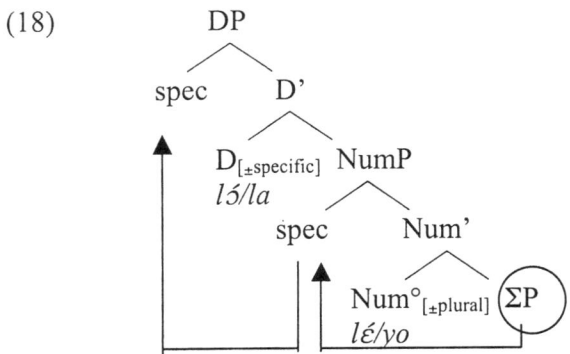

The same analysis carries over to the relative clause.[16] According to Kayne (1994), the relative clause involves a complementation structure similar to that in (19), where the determiner and the relative complementizer first merge in D and C, and the relativized noun raises to [spec CP].

(19)  [DP [D the [CP manᵢ [C° that [IP Mary will invite tᵢ...]]]]]

Recall from examples (6) and (7), repeated as (20) and (21) for convenience, that Haitian and Gungbe relative clauses differ from French relative clauses because they display the following general properties.

1.  The use of bare noun relatives.

(20) a.  [*Moun*]  ki    pa     travay p    ap     touché          HAITIAN
         people   Rel   Neg   work    Neg  Fut   get-paid
         'Those who don't work won't get paid.'          (from DeGraff, p.c.)

     b.  [*Mὲ*] ɖê    má    wà    àzɔ́n   má    ná    yí      kwε      GUNGBE
         One Rel   Neg   do    work   Neg  Fut  receive  money
         'Anyone who doesn't work will not get money.'

---

[16] The fact that the Gungbe and Haitian definite specificity markers display the same syntactic properties is supported by the fact that they can also function as clausal determiners (Aboh 2002, 2004a, 2005; DeGraff 2000; Lefebvre 1998).

2. The relative clause follows the noun, but precedes the specificity marker and/or the number marker.

(21) a. [*Fam    ki    vini    wè-u*]    *la*                    HAITIAN
        woman  Rel  come  see-2pl   Det
        'The *aforementioned* woman who came to visit you'
                                          (from Sylvain 1976: 69)

    b. [*Fam    ki    rete*]  *yo*                              HAITIAN
        woman  Rel  arrest  3pl/Num
        'The women who arrested them'
        or 'the women who were arrested'        (from Sylvain 1976: 62)

    c. [*Náwè   ɖê   wá    kpɔ́n mì*]  *lɔ́   lé*                GUNGBE
        woman  Rel  come  see  2pl   Det  Num
        'The *aforementioned* women who came to visit you'

Given that relative clauses may precede the specificity marker and a number marker in these languages, I propose to refine the representation in (16) as in (22) (Aboh 2002, 2005).[17]

(22) [$_{DP}$ [$_{D°}$ *lɔ́/la* [$_{NumP}$ [$_{Num°}$ *lé/yo* [$_{CP}$ [$_{C°}$ ɖ_/ki [$_{IP}$......]]]]]]]]

Since specificity and number licensing require fronting in Gungbe and Haitian, I conclude that the relative clause precedes the determiner in these languages because the relative CP-clause must raise to [spec NumP] and [spec DP], as represented in (23a) and (23b), respectively. Representation (23c) indicates that French does not allow such a fronting rule in its relative clauses (Aboh 2002, 2005; Zribi-Hertz 2002).

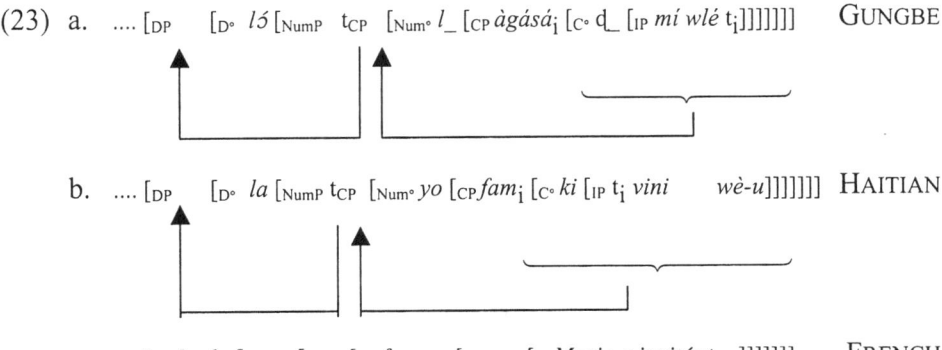

(23) a. .... [$_{DP}$   [$_{D°}$ *lɔ́* [$_{NumP}$ t$_{CP}$ [$_{Num°}$ *l_* [$_{CP}$ *àgásá*$_i$ [$_{C°}$ ɖ_ [$_{IP}$ *mí wlé* t$_i$]]]]]]]]   GUNGBE

    b. .... [$_{DP}$   [$_{D°}$ *la* [$_{NumP}$ t$_{CP}$ [$_{Num°}$ *yo* [$_{CP}$*fam*$_i$ [$_{C°}$ *ki* [$_{IP}$ t$_i$ *vini    wè-u*]]]]]]]]   HAITIAN

    c. ... [$_{DP}$ [$_{D}$ *la* [$_{NumP}$ [$_{Num°}$ [$_{CP}$*femme*$_i$ [$_{C°}$ *que* [$_{IP}$ *Marie a invitée* t$_i$...]]]]]]]]   FRENCH

Under the proposed analysis, the parallels between Haitian and Gungbe determiner phrases can be regarded as an instance of pattern transmission

---

[17] In this paper, I agree with Koopman (1982a, 1982b), DeGraff (1992), and Takahashi and Gracanin Yuksek (to appear) that *ki* is a complementizer, but see Lefebvre (1998) for alternative approaches.

because both languages share similar properties with regard to the function and syntax of the nominal left peripheral elements, such as the specificity markers *lɔ́/la* and the number markers *lé/yo*.

At this stage of the discussion, it is worth noting that pattern transmission, as described here, does not entail a perfect replica of the source system in the emerging language. That is, pattern transmission need not mean that the source language (whether the substrate or the superstrate) and the creole have to be isomorphic. Note, for instance, that even though the Gbe determiner encoding the feature specific definite can be equated with that of Haitian, as far as their syntax is concerned, the same does not hold true of the Gbe determiner that expresses specific indefinite. Indeed, all Gbe languages involve a distinct determiner that realizes specific indefinite, follows the noun phrase, and excludes the specific definite determiner, as illustrated in (24a–c). Examples (24d–e) indicate that the Gbe specificity determiners can co-occur with the number marker.

(24) a. *Súrù   kù     mótò   lɔ́    wá*                    Gungbe
        Suru   drive  car    Det   come
        'Suru drove the *aforementioned* car back [i.e., he came with that car]'
     b. *Súrù   kù     mótò   ɖé    wá*
        Suru   drive  car    Det   come
        'Suru drove *some* car back [i.e., he came with a certain car]'
     c. *\*Súrù   kù     mótò   lɔ́    ɖé    wá*
        Suru   drive  car    Det   Det   come
     d. *Súrù   kù     mótò   lɔ́    lé    wá*
        Suru   drive  car    Det   Num   come
        'Suru drove the *aforementioned* cars back [i.e., he came with those cars]'
     e. *Súrù   kù     mótò   ɖé    lé    wá*
        Suru   drive  car    Det   Num   come
        'Suru drove *some* cars back [i.e., he came with certain specific cars]'

Interestingly enough, Haitian lacks a distinct specific indefinite determiner. Instead, the language resorts to the (specific) indefinite determiner *yon*, which is also used as numeral one, corresponding to French *un*. This determiner occurs in prenominal position like numerals and adjectives. Haitian and French are similar in this regard.

(25) a. *Bouki  se    **yon**  bon   doktè*              (from DeGraff 1995: 242)
     b. *Bouki  est   **un**   bon   docteur*
        Bouki  Cop   Det    good  doctor
        'Bouki is a good doctor.'

For the time being, it is not clear to me what factors (either external or internal to language) blocked the development of a Haitian postnominal specific indefinite determiner modeled on the Gbe pattern. Given my previous assumption that transfer-sensitive features are those features that operate at the (syntax-semantics) interface, I conjecture that the Gbe specific indefinite determiner was disfavored because it was less visible (at the discourse-syntax interface) than the specific definite. This idea is compatible with the observation made previously that specific definite referents are strongly discourse-anaphoric and must be established in previous discourse (*assertion of existence*; Bickerton 1981). No such constraint, however, holds of specific indefinite noun phrases, which are not necessarily discourse-anaphoric, but only represent a referent that the speaker intends to refer to (i.e., *intent to refer*, Ionin, this volume).

The following French examples illustrate this asymmetry. The sequence *cette guitare* 'that guitar' in (26a) is definite specific because it represents information that is bound by a discourse antecedent known to both the speaker and the addressee (i.e., old/known information). In example (26b), however, the sequence *une certaine guitare* 'a certain guitar' is specific indefinite. It does not necessitate a discourse-antecedent and need not be known to the addressee, even though it is interpreted as specific.

(26) a. *J'ai acheté* cette guitare *qu'on a vue dans le magasin ce matin.* FRENCH
I have buy that guitar that 3sg has seen in the shop this morning
'I bought the guitar that we saw in the shop this morning.'

   b. *J'ai    vue* une certaine guitare *ce matin,    je ne me    rappelle*
I have seen a    certain guitar    this morning, I not 1sg-acc remember
*plus    la marque mais elle    ressemble beaucoup à la tienne.*
anymore the brand but it    resembles very.much to Det yours
'I saw a guitar this morning, I can't remember what brand but it really looked like yours.'

Compare these sentences to their Gungbe counterparts. Note from the translation that in Gungbe (even more than in French) the use of the specific definite determiner *ló* requires that both the speaker and the addressee know about the referent. No such requirement holds of the specific indefinite marker *ɖé*, however.

(27) a. *Ùn xɔ    gíntá ɖ_ mí    mɔ̀ tò    cɔ́fù    mɛ̀ égbè àfɔ́nú    ló* GUNGBE
1sg buy    guitar that 1pl see at    shop    in    today morning Det
'I bought that guitar that we saw in the shop this morning.'

b. Ùn mɔ̀ **gíntá** *ɖé* égbè   àfɔ́nú,   má    sɔ́    flín
1sg see guitar Det today  morning 1sg-Neg again  remember
*mákù   étɔ̀n    àmɔ́n é   ɖì      **gíntá** tòwè    lɔ́ kákà*
brand  3sg-Poss but    3sg  resemble guitar 2sg-Poss Det a lot
'I saw a *certain* guitar this morning, I can't remember what brand but
it really looked like that guitar of yours.'

The idea that specific indefinite referents are less visible than specific definites
at the discourse-syntax interface (26–27), and are therefore disfavored in the
competition and selection process, appears compatible with findings in second
language acquisition studies. Ionin (this volume), for instance, shows that
errors of article misuse (i.e., overuse of *the*) mainly arise with specific indefinites. On the other hand, learners seem to use *the* appropriately for assumed or
pre-established referents (i.e., specific definite in our terms). I interpret this
asymmetry as a result of the weakness of specific indefinite versus the strength
(or prominence) of specific definite at the syntax-discourse/semantics
interface.

Recall also from our previous discussion of specific definite marking in
Haitian that the French use of the postnominal deictic locative *là* to encode
specificity may have reinforced the Gbe pattern (see section 2.1). With regard
to specific indefinites, however, French does not seem to provide any congruent paradigm that could have reinforced the Gbe pattern. This would add to
the weak discourse properties of specific indefinites in disfavoring the emergence of distinct specific indefinite determiner in Haitian modeled on that in
Gbe. This state of affairs further points to the potential role of typological
(di)similarities among the competing languages in boosting or disfavoring the
emergence of a pattern in the creole. More study is needed before we achieve a
better understanding of these phenomena.

At this stage of the discussion, however, it appears that the facts presented
here support the idea that domains of transfer in a language contact situation
involve those points (or articulations) that interact with the interfaces. This
paper focuses on instances concerning the syntax-discourse/semantic interface,
but it is reasonable to think that other interfaces (e.g., syntax-phonology/
morphology) are relevant as well, as has already been demonstrated for second
language acquisition (e.g., Goad, White & Steele 2003; Lardiere 2000); and I
hope to return to this in future work.[18]

The next section discusses the properties of the determiner phrase in
Sranan and compares them to those of the determiner phrase in English and
Gungbe. It is argued that Sranan retains only the function of the specificity
feature as it appears in the Gbe languages. The syntax of this feature is,
however, modeled on English syntax.

---

[18] See also DeGraff (2000) for a discussion of creoles.

3.3.2 *Sranan and English versus Gungbe.* I propose that the Sranan noun phrase involves the internal structure shown in (28). However, unlike in Haitian and in Gungbe where D and Num are realized individually and force movement of the complement noun phrase to [spec NumP] and [spec DP], as illustrated in (18), the Sranan determiner merges under Num but raises to D to encode an otherwise empty head. In other words, the determiner binds two positions (i.e., D and Num) in these languages.

(28)

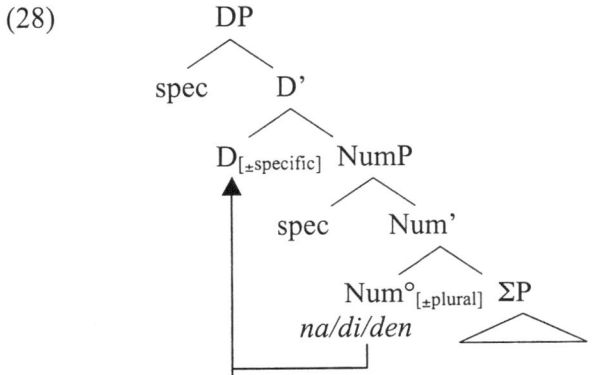

Representation (28) accounts for the fact that Sranan involves one determiner form, *na,* that expresses the feature combination [+specific, –plural], and one, *den,* that encodes the feature combination [+specific, +plural]. This is clearly different from Haitian and Gungbe, where the expression of specificity and number is dissociated (17). In this respect, Sranan appears similar to Germanic and Romance languages, which conflate definiteness and number in a single morphological form (e.g., *le/la, un/une* versus *les, des* in French, and *the/a*[singular] versus *the/∅*[plural] in English). The link between Sranan and the Germanic (and Romance) languages further translates into Num-to-D movement within the noun phrase, even though the semantics of the determiner originates in the Gbe languages (28).

Recall that Sranan clusters with Haitian and the Gbe-type languages in discriminating between specific and nonspecific referents only. For instance, these languages have bare nouns that are interpreted as (in)definite or generic depending on the context, while noun phrases that are associated with a specificity marker are necessarily discourse-anaphoric. In terms of the syntax-discourse interface, this property (i.e., the split between specificity and definiteness) clearly sets these creoles and the Gbe-type languages apart from Romance and Germanic languages, where the two notions often derive from a single determiner overtly realized in the noun phrase. We therefore face a situation where Sranan displays a hybrid noun phrase system with the function (or semantics) of the determiner developing from Gbe languages and the syntax resulting from English (and possibly Portuguese, in the case of Saramaccan).

However, Sranan and Haitian are parallel (and unlike Gbe) with regard to the expression of the specific indefinite marker. We conclude in section 3.3 that Haitian lacks a specific indefinite marker due to the weakness of such markers at the syntax-discourse interface. The same holds of Sranan: the language does not have a specific indefinite marker. Instead, some speakers use the combination *wan-tu* ('one-two') with the meaning of 'some/certain,' as in *Kofi nyan wan tu bana* 'Kofi ate some bananas.' These Sranan facts support the analysis in terms of the vulnerability of interfaces. Indeed, because the specific indefinite marker is weak in discourse, it fails to reach the interface and could not be selected in Haitian or in Sranan.

With this in mind, I conclude that the functional similarities between Sranan and Gungbe with regard to the specific definite are accounted for in terms of a substrate-induced feature, where the Gbe languages provided the relevant trigger for the feature [specificity] to emerge in the creole. The formal licensing of this feature, however, deviates from the Gbe pattern (or syntax), as a consequence of the influence of English. The latter can be measured through several properties that are common to English and Sranan noun phrases, but absent from the Gbe languages.

1. Modifier-noun order
Both English and Sranan display prenominal modifiers. In Gbe (e.g., Gungbe), however, all modifiers must occur postnominally. Example (29) shows this contrast.

(29) a. *Den  bigi  bana*                                              Sranan
        Det  big   banana
        'The/those big bananas'
     b. *The big banana(s)*
     c. *Àkwékwè  dàxó  lé*
        banana    big   Det
        'The big bananas'

2. Word order in possessive
Sranan and English display superficially similar possessive constructions that differ from those found in Gbe. For instance, example (30) indicates that Sranan and English have possessee-preposition-possessor as well as possessor-genitive-possessee sequences. In the latter case, Sranan differs from English in exhibiting a morphologically null Genitive marker only. Finally, Sranan and English have pronominal possessors in prenominal position. Compare the following Sranan examples to their English translations.

(30) a. *a    oso   fu  a    datra*                                    Sranan
        Det  house  of  Det  doctor
        'The house of the doctor'          (from Bruyn 1995a: 266, 267, 269)

b.  *a   datra   oso*
'The doctor's house'

c.  *Den oso*
'Their houses'

In Gungbe, on the contrary, possessive constructions manifest the orders possessor-genitive-possessee and possessee-possessor-genitive. While sequence (31a) might look similar to the English and Sranan cases in (30b), it is worth remembering that in the Gbe languages the determiner is postnominal. In addition, the sequence in (30b) is unavailable in English and Sranan. Taken together, these facts could be interpreted as evidence that the two language-types (e.g., Gungbe versus English) do not use the same pattern in possessive constructions and Sranan appears to have selected the English pattern (Aboh 2002, 2004a).

(31)  a.  *Dàwè   lɔ́   sín   xwé   lɔ́*                                GUNGBE
          man     Det   Poss  house  Det
          'The man's house [i.e., the aforementioned house of the
          aforementioned man]'

     b.  *Òxwé   dàwè   lɔ́   tɔ̀n   lɔ́*
         House   man    Det  Poss  Det
         'The man's house [i.e., the aforementioned house of the
         aforementioned man]'

3.  Demonstrative reinforcer constructions

Another difference between Gbe languages versus Sranan and English is that the latter display a typical construction in Germanic/Romance languages that has been referred to as the demonstrative reinforcer construction in the literature (Bernstein 2001a, 2001b). Some examples in Germanic and Romance are given under (32).

(32)  a.  *Ce livre-**ci***                                           FRENCH
          this book here

     b.  *El  libro interesante     **este***                        SPANISH
         the book interesting      this
         'This interesting book here'

     c.  That book **there**                                         ENGLISH

Similar constructions are found in Sranan, where the demonstrative element, which normally occurs prenominally as in (33a), surfaces postnominally to encode emphasis, as in (33b).

(33) a  *A   kisi   wan   pikin,   dan   **dati**   mofo   ben   langa   leki*
       3sg get   Det   child,   then   that   mouth   Pst   long   like
       *turtur   kayman*
       turtle   caiman
       'She got a child, then that mouth (of her) was long like that of a
       turtle-caiman.'                    (from Bruyn 1995b: 112, footnote 35)
    b.  *Den   pikin   **disi/dyà***
       Det   child   this/here
       'These children'                          (Bruyn 1995a: 265)

We can therefore conclude that Sranan behaves like Germanic/Romance
languages in making use of both pre- and postnominal positions for nominal
modification (as does Saramaccan). Such word order alternations inside the
noun phrase are simply unavailable in the Gbe languages, where the head noun
always precedes other nominal modifiers, in the rigid order noun-adjective-
numeral-demonstrative, and any word order alteration leads to ungrammaticality (see Aboh 2004a, 2004b for discussion).

4.  Determiner-noun-[relative] order
Finally, I have mentioned previously that Sranan and English display relative
clauses where the determiner precedes the head noun, which in turn precedes
the relative clause, as illustrated in (34a). The Gungbe example in (34b) indicates that in these languages the relative clause must appear between the noun
phrase and the determiner. Put differently, the relative clause appears to share
the same space as nominal modifiers in Gbe, while this is not the case in
Sranan and English (see Bruyn 1995b for discussion of relative clauses in
Sranan).

(34) a.  *Den uma   di   mi   si   na   a   wowoyo*                     SRANAN
      Det woman   Rel   1sg   see   Loc   Det   market
      'Those women that I saw at the market'
    b.  *Náwè   [ɖ_   ùn   mɔ̀n   tò   àxìmὲ]   lɔ́*                     GUNGBE
      woman   that   1sg   see   at   market   Det
      'That *aforementioned* woman that I saw at the market'

I conclude from these facts that, even though the Sranan noun phrase is
sensitive to the specific versus nonspecific distinction, like Gungbe and
Haitian, the syntax of the noun phrase in Sranan differs from that of Gungbe or
Haitian noun phrases. Sranan appears to have inherited English syntax, which
is why noun phrases in both languages share a significant number of syntactic
properties.

Assuming this description, the question arises of how to account for such
asymmetry between two creole types that are supposed to have the same
substrate languages (i.e., Gbe). It seems clear to me that the answer to this

question cannot be simply the difference in lexifiers (i.e., French versus English). Indeed, even though these two languages show significant morpho-syntactic differences, they share a number of properties when it comes to the determiner phrase. Both languages have prenominal determiners that encode (in)definiteness. They include prenominal modifiers (e.g., adjective, numeral, demonstrative) and have headed relatives where the determiner precedes the head noun, which precedes the relative clause. Finally, both English and French have demonstrative reinforcer constructions.

All these converging features in French and English emerged in Sranan and Saramaccan, but not in Haitian. Instead, what we seem to find is that the creoles that arose from the contact between French, English and the Gbe languages developed various syntactic patterns that do not perfectly replicate either the Germanic/Romance or the Gbe situation. For instance, Haitian has postnominal specificity and number markers but prenominal modifiers (e.g., adjectives). Similarly, Sranan and Saramaccan have specificity markers of the Gbe type, but these occur prenominally together with nominal modifiers.

In order to account for this asymmetry, it is conceivable that the prominent use of the specificity marker for discourse-anaphoric (i.e., specific) referents only in Gbe must have favored the emergence of this feature in these creoles. That is, I assume that discourse prominence and frequency conspired to make the feature [specific, definite] active at the syntax-discourse interface and so it was selected in the emerging language. Such a situation must have been made possible by the fact that English determiner is ambiguous with regard to definiteness and specificity and appears to be a weak competitor (see Ionin, this volume, for studies of second language acquisition).

With regard to syntax, however, English determiner syntax seems to have won the competition. Observe, for instance, that unlike Haitian and Gungbe, the licensing of the feature specificity does not require fronting of the noun phrase complement in Sranan or Saramaccan. Instead, the Surinamese creoles resort to a null operator in [spec DP] that checks the specificity feature under D, as in (35a). According to Campbell (1996), such a null operator exists in English noun phrases, where it binds an empty category in the nominal inflectional domain, as shown in (35b).[19]

---

[19] Even though the data discussed here support this scenario, it is still not clear to me what factors determine the selection of some licensing conditions (e.g., first merge of an operator versus movement of a goal to some designated specifier position) over others. I hope to return to this in future work.

(35)    a.                        b.

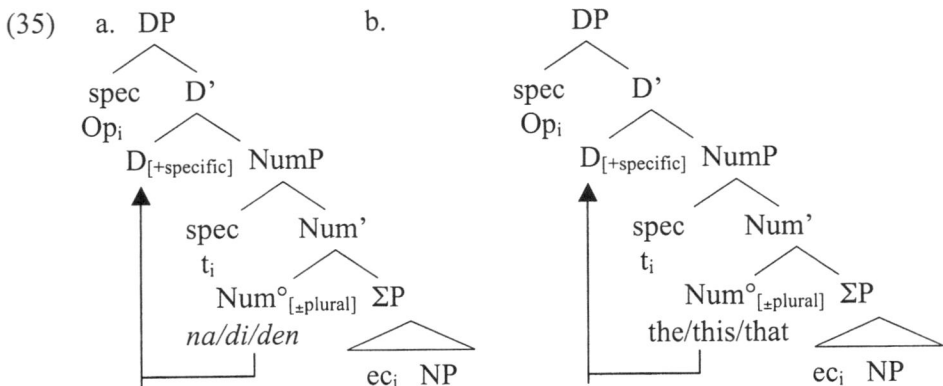

In this analysis, we also expect these creoles to differ from Haitian and Gungbe with regard to the syntax of relative clauses. Indeed, the following sentences indicate that, just like English determiners, the Sranan (and Saramaccan) specificity markers precede the head noun, which precedes the relative clause.

(36) a. *Den uma      di    mi   si  na   a    wowoyo*          SRANAN
        Det  woman   Rel  1sg  see Loc  Det  market
        'Those women that I saw at the market'
     b. *Di    womi   di    mi   go   kai   a    kon*            SARAMACCAN
        Det  man    Rel  1sg  go   call  3sg  come
        'The man that I went out to call came'
     c. The man that Mary will invite                           ENGLISH

In terms of the analysis proposed for relative clauses in (35a), Sranan and Saramaccan are like French and English and unlike Gungbe and Haitian. Indeed, the Surinamese creoles involve a null operator in [spec DP] to license specificity. The presence of this null operator in [spec DP] in Germanic/ Romance-type languages blocks fronting of the noun phrase complement or relative clause to [spec NumP] and [spec DP], unlike in Haitian and Gungbe. Sranan, Saramaccan and English relative clauses can therefore be derived as in (37).

(37) a. [DP [D° *Den* [NumP [Num° t_den [CP *uma* [C° *di* [IP *mi si* t_uma *na a wowoyo*]]]]]]]  SRANAN
     b. [DP [D° *Di* [NumP [Num° t_di [CP *womi* [C° *di* [IP *mi go kai* t_womi *a kon*]]]]]]]  SARAMACCAN
     c. [DP [D The [NumP [Num° [CP man [C° that [IP Mary will invite t_man...]]]]]]  ENGLISH

It is obvious from these representations that all these languages are characterized by Germanic/Romance determiner syntax.

## 4. *Concluding remarks*

This paper suggests that Sranan, Saramaccan, Haitian, and Gungbe specificity markers differ in syntax even though they are parallel with regard to function.

The major distinguishing factor is that Gungbe-type languages require NP-fronting to license specificity while the English-type languages (and to some extent the French-type languages) resort to a (null) operator (Aboh 2004a). This difference suggests the following parametric variation:

(38) Specificity licensing requires:
    a. NP-fronting to [spec DP] (via [spec NumP]) (Gungbe, Haitian),
    b. Null operator merging in [spec DP] (English, French, Sranan/Saramaccan),
    c. Other operator (e.g., demonstrative) plus partial raising (French).

Haitian Creole adopts (38a), while Sranan and Saramaccan make use of (38b). Given that these languages have emerged as a consequence of language contact, I argue that the Gbe languages triggered the selection of (38a) in Haitian, while English (and possibly Portuguese) provided the basis for Sranan and Saramaccan to select (38b). Haitian does not seem to have constructions of the type *ce* NP-*ci/là*. Accordingly, I suggest that the French pattern in (38c) did not fully contribute to fixing the parameters of the Haitian D-system even though the use of the locative deictic *là* might have reinforced the Gbe pattern. Finally, I conclude that the apparent mismatch between the so-called source languages and the emerging creole results from the vulnerability of interfaces, which allows combinations of semantic and syntactic features from different sources, provided that the selected combination is UG-compatible.

## References

Abney, P.S. 1987. The English Noun Phrase in Its Sentential Aspect. Ph.D. dissertation, MIT.

Aboh, E.O. 2002. La morphosyntaxe de la péripherie gauche nominale. In *Recherches linguistiques de Vincennes 31: La syntaxe de la definitude 2002,* Anne Zribi-Hertz and Anne Daladier (eds.), 9–26. Paris: PUV.

Aboh, E.O. 2004a. *The Morphosyntax of Complement-Head Sequences. Clause Structure and Word Order Patterns in Kwa.* Oxford/New York: Oxford University Press.

Aboh, E.O. 2004b. Topic and focus within D. *Linguistics in The Netherlands* 21: 1–12.

Aboh, E.O. 2004c Toward a modular theory of creole genesis. Paper presented at the International Joint Conference of the SCL-SPCL-ACBLPE on Caribbean and Creole Languages, August 11–15, 2004.

Aboh, E.O. 2005. Deriving relative and factive constructions in Kwa. In *Contributions to the Thirtieth Incontro di Grammatica Generativa,* W. Schweikert and N. Munaro (eds.), 265–285. Venice: Cafoscarina.

Aboh, E.O. 2006. Complementation in Saramaccan and Gungbe: The case of C-type modal particles. *Natural Language and Linguistic Theory* 24(1): 1–55.

Aboh, E.O. In press. La genèse de la périphérie gauche du saramaka: un cas d'influence du substrat. In *Grammaires créoles et grammaire comparative,* A. Zribi-Hertz (ed.). Paris: L'Harmattan.

Ansaldo, U. 2005. Typological convergence and admixture in Sri Lanka Malay. The case of Kirinda Java. Ms., University of Amsterdam.

Arends, J. 1989. Syntactic developments in Sranan. Ph.D. dissertation, University of Nijmegen.

Bernstein, J. 1997. Demonstratives and reinforcers in Romance and Germanic languages. *Lingua* 102: 87–113.

Bernstein, J. 2001a. Focusing the "right" way in Romance determiner phrases. *Probus* 13(1): 1–29.

Bernstein, J. 2001b. The DP hypothesis: Identifying clausal properties in the nominal domain. In *The Handbook of Contemporary Syntactic Theory,* M. Baltin and C. Collins (eds.), 536–561. Oxford: Blackwell.

Bickerton, D. 1981. *Roots of Language.* Ann Arbor, MI: Karoma.

Brousseau, A.-M. and J.S. Lumsden. 1992. Nominal structure in Fongbe. *The Journal of West African Languages* 22: 5–25.

Bruyn, A. 1995a. Noun phrases. In *Pidgins and Creoles: An Introduction,* Jacques Arends, Pieter Muysken, and Norval Smith (eds.), 259–270. Amsterdam: John Benjamins.

Bruyn, A. 1995b. *Grammaticalization in Creoles: The Development of Determiners and Relative Clauses in Sranan.* Studies in Language and Language Use 21. Amsterdam: IFOTT.

Campbell, R. 1996. Specificity operators in SpecDP. *Studia Linguistica* 2: 161–188.

Capo, H.B.C. 1991. *A Comparative Phonology of Gbe.* Publications in African Languages and Linguistics. Berlin/New York: Foris.

Cinque, G. 1994. On the evidence for partial N-movement in the Romance DP. In *Paths towards Universal Grammar,* Guglielmo Cinque, Jan Koster, Jean-Yves Pollock, Luigi Rizzi, and Raffaella Zanuttini (eds.), 85–110. Washington, DC: Georgetown University Press.

Cinque, G. 1999. *Adverbs and Functional Heads, A Cross-Linguistic Perspective.* New York: Oxford University Press.

DeGraff, M. 1992. Creole Grammars and Acquisition of Syntax: The Case of Haitian Creole. Ph.D. dissertation, University of Pennsylvania.

DeGraff, M. 1995. On certain differences between Haitian and French predicative constructions. In *Contemporary Research in Romance Linguistics,* J. Amastae, G. Goodall, M. Montalbetti and M. Phinney (eds.), 237–256. Amsterdam: John Benjamins.

DeGraff, M. 2000. The morphology-syntax interface in "creolization" and beyond. Ms., MIT.

DeGraff, M. 2002. Relexification: A reevaluation. *Anthropological Linguistics* 44: 321–414.

Déprez, V. 2001. Determiner architecture and phrasal movement in French lexifier creoles. In *Romance Languages and Linguistic Theory 2001,* J. Quer, J. Schroten, M. Scorretti, P. Sleeman and E. Verheugd (eds.), 49–74. Amsterdam: John Benjamins.

Enç, M. 1991. The semantics of specificity. *Linguistic Inquiry* 22: 1–26.

Essegbey, J. 1999. *Inherent Complement Verbs Revisited: Towards an Understanding of Argument Structure in Ewe.* Wageningen, The Netherlands: Ponsen and Looijen bv.

Giusti, G. 1996. Is there a FocusP and a TopicP in the noun phrase structure? *University of Venice Working Papers in Linguistics* 6: 105–128.

Giusti, G. 1997. The categorial status of determiners. In *The New Comparative Syntax,* Liliane Haegeman (ed.), 95–123. London: Longman Linguistics Library.

Goad, H., L. White and J. Steele. 2003. Missing inflection in L2 acquisition: Defective syntax or L1-constrained prosodic representations? *Canadian Journal of Linguistics* 48: 243–263.

Haddican, B. 2002 Aspects of DP word order across creoles. Ms., New York University.

Kayne, R.S. 1994. *The Antisymmetry of Syntax*. Cambridge, MA: The MIT Press.

Kiss, K.É. 1998. Identificational focus versus information focus. *Language* 74: 245–273.

Koopman, H. 1982a. Les constructions relatives. In *Syntaxe de l'Haïtien,* C. Lefebvre, H. Magloire-Holly, and N. Piou (eds.), 167–203. Ann Arbor, MI: Karoma.

Koopman, H. 1982b. Les questions. In *Syntaxe de l'Haïtien,* C. Lefebvre, H. Magloire-Holly, and N. Piou (eds.), 204–241. Ann Arbor, MI: Karoma.

Lardiere, D. (2000). Mapping features to forms in second language acquisition. In *Second Language Acquisition and Linguistic Theory,* J. Archibald (ed.), 102–129. Oxford: Blackwell.

Lefebvre, C. 1998. *Creole Genesis and the Acquisition of Grammar. The Case of Haitian Creole.* Cambridge: Cambridge University Press.

Lefebvre, C. and A.-M. Brousseau. 2002. *A Grammar of Fongbe.* Berlin: Mouton de Gruyter.

Mufwene, S.S. 2001. *The Ecology of Language Evolution.* Cambridge: Cambridge University Press.

Mufwene, S.S. 2002 Competition and selection in language evolution. *Selection* 3: 45–56.

Müller, N. and A. Hulk. 2000. Bilingual first language acquisition at the interface between syntax and pragmatics. *Bilingualism: Language and Cognition* 3: 227–244.

Pesetsky, D. 1987. Wh-in-situ: Movement and unselective binding. In *The Representation of (In)definiteness,* Eric Reuland and Alice ter Meulen, (eds.), 98–129. Cambridge, MA: The MIT Press.

Platzack, C. 2001. The vulnerable C-domain. *Brain and Language* 77: 364–377.

Prince, F.E. 1981. Toward a taxonomy of given-new information. In *Radical Pragmatics,* P. Cole (ed.), 223–255. New York: Academic Press.

Ritter, E. 1995. On the syntactic category of pronouns and agreement. *Natural Language and Linguistic Theory* 13: 405–443.

Rizzi, L. 1997. The fine structure of the left periphery. In *Elements of Grammar,* Liliane Haegeman, (ed.), 281–337. Dordrecht: Kluwer.

Roodenburg, J. 2004. *Pour une approche scalaire de la déficience nominale: la position du français dans une théorie des "noms nus".* LOT Ph.D. series 99. Utrecht: LOT.

Siegel, J. 2004. Morphological elaboration. *Journal of Pidgin and Creole Languages* 19: 333–362.

Smith, N. 1987. The Genesis of the Creole Languages of Surinam. Ph.D. dissertation, University of Amsterdam.

Sorace, A. 2000. Differential effects of attrition in the L1 syntax of near-native L2 speakers. In *Proceedings of the 24th Annual Boston University Conference on Language Development,* C. Howell, S. Fish and T. Keith-Lucas (eds.), 719–725. Somerville, MA: Cascadilla Press.

Sportiche, D. 1988. A theory of floating quantifiers and its corollaries for constituent structure. *Linguistic Inquiry* 19: 425–449.

Sylvain, S. 1976. *Le créole haïtien. Morphologie et syntaxe.* Geneva: Slatkine Reprints.

Szabolcsi, A. 1987. Functional categories in the noun phrase. In *Approaches to Hungarian,* István Kenesei (ed.), 167–189. Szeged: JATE.

Szabolcsi, A. 1994. The noun phrase. In *Syntax and Semantics 27: The Syntactic Structure of Hungarian,* Ferenc Kiefer and Katalin E. Kiss (eds.), 179–274. New York: Academic Press.

Takahashi, S. and M. Gracanin Yuksek. To appear. The Syntax of Ki in Haitian Creole. In *MIT Working Papers on Endangered and Less Familiar Languages*, ed. by Michael Kenstowicz. Cambridge, MA: MITWPL.

Valenzuela, E. 2005. L2 Ultimate Attainment and the Syntax-Discourse Interface: The Acquisition of Topic Constructions in Non-Native Spanish and English. Ph.D. dissertation, McGill University.

Zribi-Hertz, A. 2002. The DP hypothesis and the syntax of identification. *Recherches linguistiques de Vincennes* 31: 127–142.

# A COMPARISON OF ARTICLE SEMANTICS IN L2 ACQUISITION AND CREOLE LANGUAGES *

Tania Ionin
*University of Southern California*

This paper compares the article systems in L2 English and in some creole languages, examining the roles of the semantic features *definiteness* and *specificity* in both. The L2-English data come from the studies of Ionin (2003b) and Ionin, Ko and Wexler (2003, 2004), which examine the acquisition of English articles by adult speakers of Russian and Korean, languages that lack article systems. It is shown that these L2 learners' errors of article misuse are not random, but are traceable to an association of *the* with the feature *specificity*. Different definitions of specificity are examined, and it is shown that the traditional view of specificity as *existence* (Bickerton 1981; Huebner 1983) cannot account for the L2-English data; a more restricted definition of specificity is proposed, which involves *speaker intent to refer* (cf. Fodor & Sag 1982) and *noteworthiness*. It is argued that the use of articles to mark specificity as speaker intent to refer is an option available to L2 learners through access to semantic universals. The question then is whether this option is also available in creole languages. The literature on the article systems of several creole languages (Hawaiian Creole English: Bickerton 1981; Givón 1981, 2001; Guyanese Creole English: Bickerton 1981; and Berbice Dutch Creole: Kouwenberg, to appear) is examined in an attempt to answer this question.

## 1. *Introduction*

Cross-linguistically, articles encode a number of semantic distinctions, including *definiteness* and *specificity*. For instance, the English articles *the* and *a* encode the *definiteness* distinction, while the Samoan articles *le* and *se* encode the specificity distinction (Mosel & Hovdhaugen 1992). These distinctions have been argued to play a role both in second language (L2) acquisition (Ionin 2003a; Thomas 1989), and in creole languages (Bickerton 1981; Givón 2001). The goal of this paper is to explore the nature of these semantic distinctions, and to draw parallels between L2 acquisition and creole languages. The specific goals of this paper are as follows:

i) To provide a precise semantics for *specificity*, arguing for specificity as *speaker intent to refer* (cf. Fodor & Sag 1982) rather than as *assertion of existence*.

ii) To present empirical evidence that *specificity as speaker intent to refer* plays a role in the acquisition of English by adult second language learners.

---

* I am grateful to the audience of the Montreal Dialogues workshop for helpful comments and suggestions, and especially to Silvia Kouwenberg for sharing with me her paper on bare NPs in Berbice Dutch. Thanks to two anonymous reviewers for very helpful comments and suggestions. All remaining errors are my own.

iii) To examine whether *specificity as speaker intent to refer* also plays a role in the article systems of (at least some) creole languages.

The data on L2 acquisition discussed here come from elicitation studies with adult L1-Russian and L1-Korean learners of English (Ionin 2003b; Ionin, Ko & Wexler 2003, 2004). The creole data come from Hawaiian Creole English and Guyanese Creole English (Bickerton 1981), as well as from Berbice Dutch Creole (Kouwenberg, to appear).

It is well known that L2-English learners make errors using English articles. Such errors are generally found to be more prevalent for L2 learners whose native language (L1) lacks articles, such as Korean and Japanese, than for L2 learners whose L1 has articles, such as Spanish (Thomas 1989). For the purposes of this paper, we focus on the former case: L2-English learners who do not have articles in their L1, and are unlikely to be influenced by L1 transfer. Such L2-English learners tend to exhibit both *article omission* and *article misuse*; in particular, they overuse *the* with indefinites (cf. Huebner 1983; Ionin et al. 2004; Master 1987; Parrish 1987; Thomas 1989). Some examples of *the* overuse from L2-English written production data (from Ionin et al. 2004) are given in (1); the referent of the highlighted phrase in each example has not been previously mentioned, and so use of *the* is infelicitous.

(1) *Written production data from adult L2-English learners:*
    a. *L1-Russian L2-English learner:*
       When I was living in Ulan-Ude yet unmarried my friends presented me **the small seamese kitten**.
    b. *L1-Korean L2-English learner:*
       The most valuable object that I have received is **the ball** and the signature of **the famous baseball player** is signed on it.

The hypothesis developed in Ionin (2003a) and Ionin et al. (2004) is that such errors of L2-English article misuse are not random, but are due to an association of *the* with specificity rather than definiteness. We argue that L2-English learners have access to the semantic distinctions of definiteness and specificity, but do not know, at least initially, that *the* marks definiteness rather than specificity.

After reviewing our proposal concerning articles in L2 acquisition, we will consider articles in some creole languages, specifically Bickerton's (1981) classification of creole articles on the basis of definiteness and specificity. We will tentatively suggest that articles in (at least some) creole languages may encode the same (or similar) distinction as articles in L2 English, although more work remains to be done, and will discuss the implications of such similarities.

This paper is organized as follows. In section 2, we briefly discuss the semantic concepts of definiteness and specificity. Section 3 summarizes our studies on article use in L2 English, showing that *specificity as speaker intent to refer* plays an important role. In section 4, we consider available data on article semantics in three creole languages, and draw comparisons with the L2 acquisition data. Section 5 concludes the paper, and discusses some open questions.

## 2. *Semantic universals*

This paper is concerned with two semantic universals: *definiteness* and *specificity*. We adopt a standard presuppositional view of definiteness. We also adopt a particular view of specificity as speaker intent to refer. This view is based on Fodor and Sag (1982), and developed in Ionin (2003a). The informal definitions of these concepts are provided in (2) (see Ionin 2003a for formal definitions).

(2) *Definiteness and specificity: informal definitions*
   If a Determiner Phrase (DP) of the form [D NP] is …
   a. [+definite], then the speaker assumes that the hearer shares the speaker's presupposition of the existence of a unique individual in the set denoted by the NP
   b. [+specific], then the speaker *intends to refer* to a unique individual in the set denoted by the NP, and considers this individual to possess some noteworthy property

### 2.1 *Definiteness in English*

English articles encode the definiteness distinction: *the* is definite, and *a* is indefinite. This is illustrated in (3).

(3) a. I saw **a cat**. **The cat** was drinking milk.
   b. **The winner of the race** received a prize.

In (3a), on the first mention of a cat, there is no presupposition that a unique cat exists in the domain of the discourse, so *a* is used. On the second mention, the presupposition of a unique salient cat has been established in the previous discourse, so *the* is used. Previous discourse is not the only way of establishing uniqueness: in (3b), is it established through our world knowledge of a race having just one winner. For more discussion of definiteness in English, including different formal analyses of definiteness, and the relationship between definites and indefinites, see Heim (1991).

### 2.2 *Specificity in English*

In the view of specificity established in (2a), specificity necessarily involves speaker intent to refer to a particular individual. There have, in fact, been many other views of specificity in both the theoretical and the acquisition literature. Much L2 literature (Huebner 1983; Master 1987; Robertson 2000; Thomas 1989; Young 1996) has used a view of specificity that goes back to Bickerton's

(1981) term *specific reference*. While Bickerton did not provide a precise definition of *specific reference*, many L2 researchers (notably Thomas 1989) have treated this term as meaning something like assertion of existence. (This is our term, not one used by previous L2 literature; see also Schaeffer and Matthewson (2005) for a corresponding view of L1 acquisition.)

With specificity defined as assertion of existence, a [+specific] DP denotes an individual asserted to exist in the actual world. On the other hand, in our view of specificity as speaker intent to refer (which goes back to Fodor & Sag 1982), a [+specific] DP denotes an individual that the speaker intends to refer to. This difference is illustrated in (4).

(4)  Specificity as speaker intent to refer ≠ assertion of existence:
  a.  ✓*assertion of existence*, ✓*speaker intent to refer*
      Janet bought **a beautiful cat** in the pet store: I played with it all day yesterday.
  b.  ✓*assertion of existence*, \**speaker intent to refer*
      Janet fed **a cat** *(≈some cat or other)* yesterday, but I have no idea what cat it was.
  c.  \**assertion of existence*, \**speaker intent to refer*
      Janet would like to buy **a cat**—any cat will do.

In (4a), the speaker intends to refer to a particular cat, and also asserts that cat's existence.[1] In (4b), the speaker asserts the existence of a particular cat (the one that Janet fed) but denies all knowledge of it, which makes intent to refer quite unlikely. In (4c), no particular cat is asserted to exist, and there is no speaker intent to refer. Note that speaker intent to refer without assertion of existence is impossible: the speaker cannot intend to refer (in the actual world) to an individual that the speaker does not assert to exist in the actual world. Thus, speaker intent to refer entails assertion of existence, but not vice versa. The relationship between these two concepts is discussed in more detail in Ionin (2003a). In the following sections, it will be shown that specificity as speaker intent to refer, rather than assertion of existence, is tied to article errors in L2 English. Throughout this paper, whenever we use the term *specificity* or *specific*, we will be assuming the view of specificity as speaker intent to refer, as in (2b).

The examples in (4) show that English *a* indefinites, such as *a cat*, may be used in either a [+specific] context (4a) or a [−specific] context (4b–c); that is, *a* indefinites are compatible with the conditions on specificity given in (2b),

---

[1] Strictly speaking, we can never be 100% certain of what the speaker intends to refer to—however, the description of the cat in (4a), and the fact that the speaker is personally acquainted with this cat, make speaker intent more likely than in (4b), where the speaker claims to have no knowledge of the cat. The only way we can be certain that speaker intent is in fact present is if an overt marker of specificity is used, such as referential *this*—more on this below.

but are also compatible with nonspecificity. In spoken/colloquial English, there are also indefinites which are obligatorily [+specific]: indefinites headed by referential *this* (Lyons 1999; Maclaran 1982; Prince 1981). This is illustrated in (5) and (6) below.

(5) a. Peter intends to marry **a/this merchant banker**—even though he doesn't get on at all with her.

    b. Peter intends to marry **a/??this merchant banker**—though he hasn't met one yet.                     (Lyons 1999: 176)

(6) a. John has **a/this weird purple telephone**.

    b. John has **a/#this telephone**, so you can reach me there.

                                     (Maclaran 1982: 88)

In (5a), the speaker intends to refer to a particular merchant banker, so use of *this* is fine; in (5b), no particular merchant banker is under discussion, and use of *this* is infelicitous. Similarly, in (6a), but not in (6b), the speaker intends to refer to a particular telephone—which has the noteworthy property "it is weird and purple."[2]

There are two things to note about the use of referential *this*. First, unlike the regular, demonstrative use of *this*, referential *this* is clearly indefinite: use of *the* in (5) and (6) would be infelicitous. Second, use of referential *this* requires speaker intent to refer, not just assertion of existence: in (6b), for instance, a particular telephone is asserted to exist, yet use of referential *this* is infelicitous because there is no speaker intent to refer. As Maclaran (1982: 90) states, referential indefinite *this* "draws attention to the fact that the speaker has a particular referent in mind, about which further information may be given."

The above discussion concerns specificity with indefinites only. However, definites may also be used in [+specific] contexts: in fact, previously mentioned definites, as in (7), are obligatorily [+specific].

(7) Louise saw a cat. **The cat** was drinking milk.

The speaker in (7) necessarily intends to refer to a particular cat: the one that Louise saw, that is, the one whose uniqueness has been established by previous discourse. In this paper, we will confine our discussion to previous-mention definites, which must be [+specific].[3]

---

[2] The proposal that specificity includes speaker intent to refer is based on Fodor and Sag's (1982) proposal regarding referential indefinites. The view that specificity also involves *a noteworthy property* is developed more fully in Ionin (2003a), where it is shown that use of indefinite *this* in English requires that the speaker say something *noteworthy* about the referent.

[3] It is not necessarily true that all definites are [+specific]. Definites such as those in (i) (which correspond to Donnellan's (1966) attributive (non-referential) definites) do not involve speaker intent to refer and are therefore [-specific] in the view of specificity discussed here.

(i) a. The reporter would like to interview **the winner of this race**-whoever that happens to be.

   b. **The murderer of Smith** (whoever that is) must be insane.

## 2.3 *Definiteness and specificity cross-linguistically*

Definiteness receives morphological expression in many languages (e.g., in Germanic and Romance languages). The morphological expression of specificity is less well studied, but there do appear to be a number of examples, besides referential *this*. These include the Samoan article *le* (Lyons 1999; Mosel & Hovdhaugen 1992), the Modern Hebrew postnominal marker *xad* (Borer 2005; Givón 2001) and the Sissala postnominal marker *n_* (Blass 1990).

Hebrew and Sissala, like spoken English, use separate lexical items to mark definiteness (*the* in English, *ha* in Hebrew) and specificity (referential *this* in English, *xad* in Hebrew). Samoan, on the other hand, apparently has no definiteness marker: it uses one article (*le*) to mark specificity, and a different article (*se*) in the absence of specificity. Thus, Samoan, like standard English, has two articles: standard English (with no referential *this*) has *the* and *a*, marking only the definiteness distinction, while Samoan has *le* and *se*, marking only the specificity distinction. Note that a language with only two articles cannot mark both the definiteness and specificity distinctions: if one article is [+definite] and the other is [+specific], a third article (or the absence of an article/a zero article) is needed, which is neither [+definite] nor [+specific].[4]

Thus, we conclude that a language with two articles may encode *either* the definiteness distinction *or* the specificity one, as represented pictorially in Table 1.[5]

| DP type | Distinction by definiteness (e.g., standard English) | Distinction by specificity (e.g., Samoan) |
|---|---|---|
| Previous-mention definites | *the* | *le* |
| Specific indefinites | *a* | |
| Nonspecific indefinites | | *se* |

Table 1. *Possible options for languages with two articles*

On the other hand, if a language has three articles (or two articles plus a zero article option for singular NPs), it encodes both definiteness and specificity, as summarized in Table 2.

See Ionin (2003a) for a discussion of [-specific] definites, and of the relationship between definiteness and specificity. In Ionin et al. (2004), we provide empirical evidence that L2-English learners distinguish between [+specific] and [-specific] definites in their article choice, overusing *a* only with the latter. For reasons of space, the present paper addresses the specificity distinction with indefinites only. The only definites considered here are previous-mention definites, which are obligatorily [+specific].

[4] For the purposes of this paper, we consider a "zero article" option (with singular NPs) to be on par with overt articles. What matters for us is whether a language marks a two-way distinction (definite vs. indefinite; specific vs. non-specific) or a three-way distinction (definite vs. specific vs. neither). We abstract away from the issue of whether bare NPs have a zero article or no article at all.

[5] This table considers only previous-mention definites, which are obligatorily [+specific]. See Ionin et al. (2004) for a revised classification, which includes [-specific] definites.

| DP type | Three-way distinction by definiteness and specificity | |
|---|---|---|
| | e.g., colloquial English | e.g., Modern Hebrew |
| Previous-mention definites | *the* | *ha* |
| Specific indefinites | referential indefinite *this* | *xad* |
| Nonspecific indefinites | *a* | *ø* |

Table 2. *Possible options for languages with three articles*

## 3. *Semantic universals in L2 acquisition*

Having briefly examined definiteness and specificity cross-linguistically, we now turn to the question of how L2-English learners, in particular those who speak article-less L1s, come to acquire the specifications of English articles. Learners of standard English are acquiring a language with two articles: *the* and *a*. How do they know that these articles encode the definiteness distinction rather than the specificity distinction?

The hypothesis put forth in Ionin (2003a) is that (i) L2 learners have access to the semantic universals of definiteness and specificity; and (ii) in the absence of L1 transfer, L2 learners do not (initially) know which semantic distinction is encoded by *the* and *a*. As a result, L2 learners fluctuate between the two possibilities (see Ionin 2003a for evidence of similar fluctuations in other domains of L2 grammar).

### 3.1 *Predictions about article use and misuse in L2 English*

The above hypothesis makes explicit predictions for L2-English article use among learners whose native languages lack articles.[6] On the hypothesis that these learners have access to the features of definiteness and specificity, they should appropriately use *the* for previous-mention definites and *a* for nonspecific indefinites, but should use *the* and *a* interchangeably when the definiteness and specificity settings are in conflict: with specific indefinites. This is shown in Table 3.

| DP type | Distinction by definiteness (e.g., standard English) | Distinction by specificity (e.g., Samoan) | L2 English: fluctuation |
|---|---|---|---|
| Previous-mention definites | *the* | *le* | *the* |
| Specific indefinites | *a* | | *the* / *a* |
| Nonspecific indefinites | | *se* | *a* |

Table 3. *Predictions for L2-English article use (singular contexts)*[7]

---

[6] An interesting question for further study is how L1 transfer and universal semantic distinctions interact in the case of L2 learners whose L1 does have articles (e.g., L1-Spanish L2-English learners). This is not examined here.

[7] The predictions for plural contexts are similar, except that instead of *a*, plural indefinite contexts require article omission or the use of determiners such as *some, several*, etc. In Ionin et al. (2003), we show that similar patterns of results obtain in singular and plural indefinite contexts.

There are two important points to note. First, Table 3 shows that article use is expected to be non-random: errors of article misuse will be confined to the category of [+specific] indefinites. Second, in our view of specificity, overuse of *the* is predicted to occur only when speaker intent to refer is present; assertion of existence alone should not lead to *the* overuse (contra previous L2 literature, e.g., Thomas 1989). This is shown in Table 4.

| DP type | Definiteness | Specificity (intent to refer) | Assertion of existence | Target | Predictions for L2 English |
|---|---|---|---|---|---|
| previous-mention definites | + | + | + | *the* | correct *the* use |
| **specific indefinites** | − | + | + | *a* | ***the* overuse** |
| nonspecific indefinites | − | − | + | *a* | correct *a* use |
| | − | − | − | *a* | correct *a* use |

Table 4. *Predictions for L2-English article choice: breakdown by semantic property*

### 3.2 *Methodology*
The predictions in Tables 3 and 4 were tested in a series of three studies with adult L1-Russian and/or L1-Korean learners of English. Both Russian and Korean lack articles, so L1 transfer effects are not expected.[8] In all three studies, learners took a written elicitation test targeting articles as well as the Michigan L2 proficiency test (plus some other tests not relevant here, such as naturalistic production). Since all of these studies have been reported elsewhere, we summarize them only briefly here. The participant information is summarized in Table 5.

The main tests were written elicitation (see the corresponding papers, and Ionin 2003a for details). Each test consisted of a series of dialogues, and each dialogue contained a target sentence with a missing article. The L2 learners had to fill in the appropriate article, on the basis of the context. The learners were given a choice of *a, the,* or a dash -- (article omission). The tests contained indefinite and definite contexts. All test items were piloted with native English speakers, who performed as expected.

| Study | Source | Number of L1-Russian participants | Number of L1-Korean participants |
|---|---|---|---|
| Study 1 | Ionin (2003b) | 27 (1 beginner, 10 intermediate, 16 advanced) | — |
| Study 2 | Ionin, Ko & Wexler (2003) | 37 (15 intermediate, 22 advanced) | 37 (12 intermediate, 25 advanced) |
| Study 3 | Ionin, Ko & Wexler (2004) | 26 (11 intermediate, 16 advanced) | 39 (6 intermediate, 33 advanced) |

Table 5. *Summary of participants*

---

[8] Russian and Korean also do not obligatorily encode definiteness or specificity outside of the article system; see Ionin (2003a: Ch. 3) for further discussion.

We report results for only a subset of the items here: those most relevant to the predictions in Tables 3 and 4. The relevant categories and context types are in Table 6, with examples in (8).[9]

| Category | Number of context types per given category | | |
|---|---|---|---|
| | Study 1 | Study 2 | Study 3 |
| previous-mention definites | 2 | 1 | 1 |
| [+specific] indefinites: speaker intent to refer | 3 | 2 | 2 |
| [-specific] indefinites with assertion of existence | 1 | 2 | 2 |
| [-specific] indefinites with no assertion of existence | 2 | 1 | 1 |

Table 6. *Relevant categories and context types (four test items per context type)*

(8) a. *previous-mention definite (Study 2)*

Richard:   I visited my friend Kelly yesterday. Kelly really likes animals—she has two cats and one dog. Kelly was busy last night—she was studying for an exam. So I helped her out with her animals.

Maryanne: What did you do?

Richard:   I took **the** dog for a walk.

  b. *[+specific] indefinite, speaker intent to refer (Study 3)*
**Phone conversation**

Jeweler:   Hello, this is Robertson's Jewelry. What can I do for you, ma'am? Are you looking for some new jewelry?

Client:   Not quite—I heard that you also buy back people's old jewelry.

Jeweler:   That is correct.

Client:   In that case, I would like to sell you **a** beautiful silver necklace. It is very valuable—it has been in my family for 100 years!

  c. *[-specific] indefinite, with assertion of existence (Study 2)*
**At a university**

Professor Clark: I'm looking for Professor Anne Peterson.

Secretary:       I'm afraid she is out right now.

Professor Clark: Do you know if she is meeting somebody?

Secretary:       I am not sure. This afternoon, she met with **a** student—but I don't know which one.

---

[9] The different numbers of contexts in the various cells in Table 6 stem from the fact that additional factors, such as presence vs. absence of intensional operators and RC modification, were varied in the tests. Special categories of indefinites tested in the studies (such as plurals) are not included above. Also not included are definites in contexts other than previous-mention, which were tested in Ionin et al. (2004). The data are grouped differently here than in the three papers cited above, since these papers were not expressly concerned with comparing speaker intent to refer to assertion of existence. See these papers for detailed results for all context types.

d. *[-specific] indefinite, no assertion of existence (Study 3)*
   **In a school**
   Student:  I am new in this school. This is my first day.
   Teacher:  Welcome! Are you going to be at the school party tonight?
   Student:  Yes. I'd like to get to know my classmates. I am planning
             to find **a** new good friend! I don't like being all alone.

## 3.3 *Results*

Article omission was an extremely rare response: the main responses were *the* and *a*. We therefore report here the mean percentage of *the* use by category. The remaining percentage points out of a hundred mostly involve use of *a*, plus some article omission. The results are reported in Figures 1 and 2 for L1-Russian and L1-Korean speakers, respectively.

The L1-Korean speakers were more accurate (exhibited less *the* overuse with indefinites) than L1-Russian speakers.[10] However, the patterns of *the* (mis)use were very similar across the two groups.

**Figure 1: Percentage of *the* use: L1-Russian speakers**

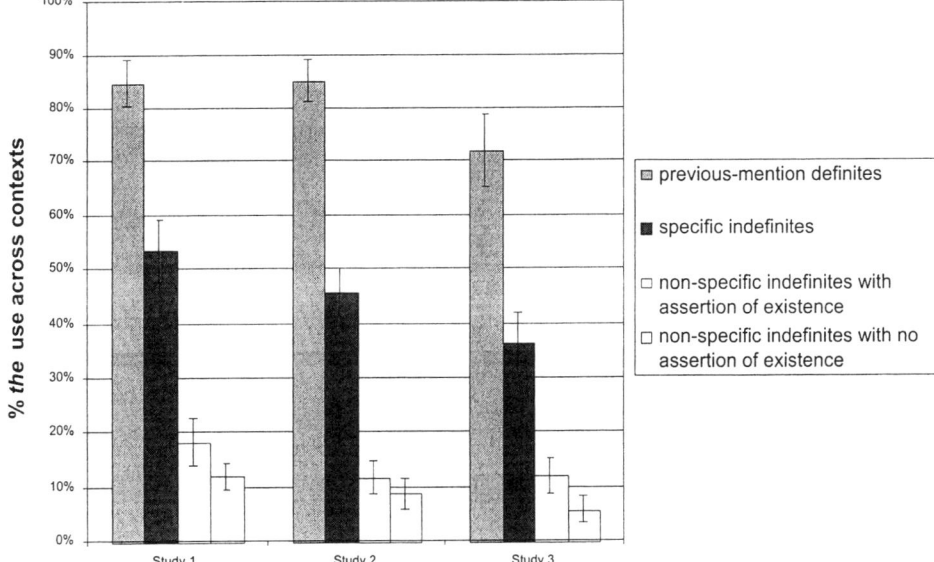

---

[10] In Study 3, the L1-Korean speakers had significantly higher L2 proficiency than the L1-Russian speakers; in Study 2, the two groups had similar proficiency levels, but the L1-Korean speakers were younger and had received more intensive exposure to English than the L1-Russian speakers.

Figure 2: %'the' use: L1-Korean speakers

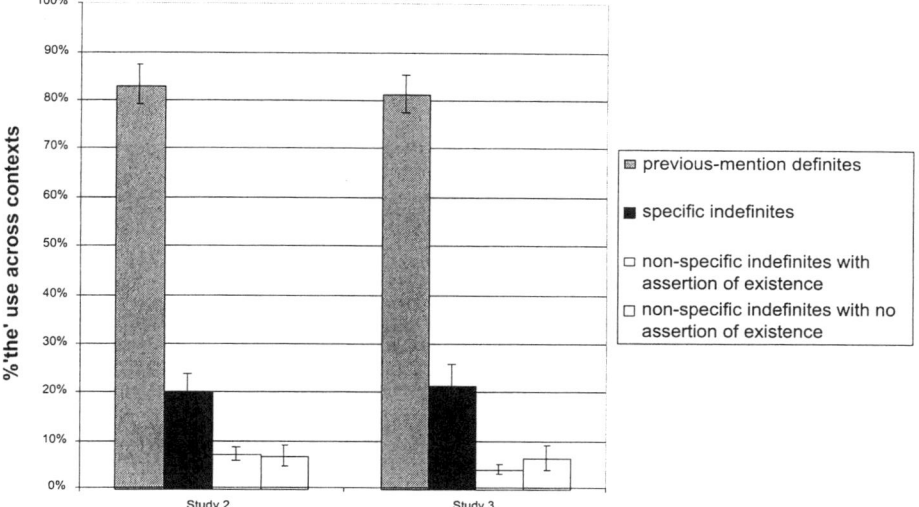

## 3.4 *Summary*

The main findings of our studies are summarized in Table 7. We see that, first of all, L2-English article choice is not random: the learners exhibit fairly accurate performance in definite and [-specific] indefinite contexts, compared to *the* overuse in [+specific] indefinite contexts. Thus, the learners show sensitivity to the semantic concepts of definiteness and specificity. Second, we see that L2-English article choice is affected by specificity as speaker intent to refer, not by assertion of existence: there is very low *the* overuse with [-specific] indefinites, regardless of the presence or absence of assertion of existence.

| | Definiteness | Specificity (intent to refer) | Assertion of existence | Target | Results for L2 English |
|---|---|---|---|---|---|
| previous-mention definites | + | + | + | *the* | correct *the* use |
| **specific indefinites** | – | + | + | *a* | ***the* overuse** |
| nonspecific indefinites | – | – | + | *a* | little *the* overuse |
| | – | – | – | *a* | little *the* overuse |

Table 7. *Summary of L2-English article choice in singular contexts*

On the basis of these findings, we conclude that L2 learners have linguistic knowledge which is not accounted for by L1 transfer (since their L1s lack articles) or L2 input (since English *the* does not encode specificity); rather, this knowledge stems from access to the semantic universal of *specificity*.

## 4. *Semantic universals in creole*

We now move on to a discussion of definiteness and specificity in creoles. If creole genesis is a special case of second language acquisition, then we would expect creole speakers, like L2 learners, to access the universal semantic feature *specificity as speaker intent to refer*. The proposal that creoles encode universal semantic distinctions goes back to the work of Bickerton (1981), who argued for the universal features of *specific reference* and *assumed known to hearer*. The latter corresponds quite closely to the term *definiteness,* as defined in (2a), while the former is related to our view of specificity, presented in (2b) (more on this below).

Bickerton's analysis was based largely on data from Hawaiian Creole English and Guyanese Creole English. In his analysis, these languages have a definite article (*da* or *di*), a specific indefinite article (*wan*), and a zero article used with nonspecific indefinites (as well as generics). Bickerton (1981: 23), discussing Hawaiian Creole, stated that

> The definite article *da* is used for all and only specific-reference NPs that can be assumed known to the listener ... The indefinite article *wan* is used for all and only specific-reference NPs that can be assumed unknown to the listener ... All other NPs have no article and no marker of plurality. This category includes generic NPs, NPs within the scope of negation—i.e., clearly nonspecific NPs—and cases where, while a specific referent may exist, the exact identity of that referent is either unknown to the speaker or irrelevant to the point at issue.

As a starting point, we can hypothesize that Hawaiian English Creole and Guyanese English Creole have a three-way article distinction, along the lines of spoken English and Modern Hebrew. This is summarized in Table 8 below. This table also includes Berbice Dutch Creole, another language with a three-way distinction; the nature of specificity marking in Berbice Dutch will be discussed in Section 4.1.3, based on Kouwenberg (to appear).

| DP type | Guyanese Creole | Hawaiian Creole | Berbice Dutch Creole |
|---|---|---|---|
| Previous-mention definites | *di* | *da* | *di* |
| Specific indefinites | *wan* | *wan* | *en* |
| Nonspecific indefinites | ø | ø | ø |

Table 8. Three-way distinction by definiteness and specificity in creole

As noted earlier, much L2 literature has adopted Bickerton's distinction, treating the term *specific reference* to essentially mean assertion of existence. In the previous section, we argued that L2-English data can be better explained if specificity is treated as speaker intent to refer. We now ask whether the same is true for creole languages: whether the distinction between *wan/en* and the zero article in these creoles is in fact related to specificity as speaker intent to refer rather than assertion of existence.

### 4.1 *The data*

In this section, we will examine the article systems of three creole languages: Guyanese Creole English, Hawaiian Creole English, and Berbice Dutch Creole.

4.1.1 *Guyanese Creole English.* The available data from Guyanese Creole English are limited but suggestive, as shown in (9).

(9) a. *Jan bai **di buk**.*
"John bought the book."
b. *Jan bai **wan buk**.*
"John bought a (particular) book."
c. *Jan bai **buk**.*
"John bought some book or other/books."    (Bickerton 1981:56)

While *di* in (9a) appears to be a straightforward counterpart to the English *the*, the distinction between (9b) and (9c) is less obvious. The relevant contrast between *wan* and the zero article does not appear to be assertion of existence: in both (9b) and (9c), at least one book is asserted to exist. Specificity as speaker intent to refer is a more likely candidate, since in (9b), the speaker appears to be drawing attention to a particular book, which is not the case in (9c). However, this information comes only from the glosses, and it is not possible to reach a definitive conclusion without more information about the felicity conditions on the use of *wan*.

4.1.2 *Hawaiian Creole English.* More data are available on the article system of Hawaiian Creole English (HCE). Considering definites first, we see that *da* in HCE is translated as *the* into English (10).

(10) *da* with definites
*I see **da book**.*
"I saw the book."    (Givón 1981:297)

We turn next to the use of *wan* with indefinites. As shown in (11), whenever *wan* is used, the speaker is clearly asserting the existence of a particular book.[11] The question is whether assertion of existence is enough, or whether speaker intent to refer is also present.

(11) *wan* with indefinites: √assertion of existence; ?speaker intent to refer
a. *hi get **wan bleak buik**. daet buk no du eni gud.*
"He has a black book. That book doesn't do any good."
(Bickerton 1981:23)
b. *I see **wan book**.*
"I saw a (specific) book."    (Givón 1981:297)

---

[11] Note that, in the examples (11) through (13), Bickerton and Givón use different transcription systems (more phonemic vs. closer to standard written English).

    c.   *i want rid **wan-buk**.*
        "He wanted to read a book." (>a specific book)    (Givón 2001:451)
    d.   Speaker 1:   *Hu stei upsteaz?*
                        "Who lives upstairs?"
        Speaker 2:   ***Wan wahine**, shi wrk ap in da nrs ples.*
                        "A woman, she works up in the nursing home."
                                                  (Bickerton 1977: 227)

In order to address this question, we have to consider the use of bare NPs: is the contrast between *wan* and bare NPs that of assertion of existence or of speaker intent to refer? We consider this by examining the bare indefinite NPs in (12).

(12)  bare NPs: √assertion of existence; ?no speaker intent to refer
     a. ***kaenejan waif**, ae, get.*
       "He has a Canadian wife."                 (Bickerton 1981:23)
     b. *He see **movie**.*
       "He saw a/some movie."                   (Givón 1981:297)

In (12), we see that a bare NP is possible when the existence of a particular wife or movie is asserted. This suggests that the contrast between bare NPs and *wan*-NPs is not that of assertion of existence. Rather, it would appear that use of a bare NP indicates lack of speaker intent to refer: the exact identity of the wife or book is irrelevant; this is emphasized in (12b) by the use of *some movie* in the gloss (as in "some movie—I have no idea which").

Finally, we note that bare NPs are used when both assertion of existence and speaker intent to refer are absent, as shown in (13). This is consistent with the picture so far: when no particular job or book is asserted to exist, the speaker is not intending to refer to a particular job or book, so the specificity marker *wan* is not expected.

(13)  bare NPs: no assertion of existence, no speaker intent to refer
     a. *bat nobadi gon get **jab**.*
       "But nobody will get a job."             (Bickerton 1981:24)
     b. *I no see **book**.*
       "I didn't see a/any book."               (Givón 1981:297)
     c. *i want rid **buk**.*
       "He wanted to read a book." (>no specific book)    (Givón 2001:451)

4.1.3 *Berbice Dutch Creole.* Finally, we note that English-based creoles are not the only ones that exhibit specificity marking. A detailed examination of article semantics in creole is found in Kouwenberg (to appear), which examines the distribution of articles and bare NPs in Berbice Dutch (BD) Creole in light of Bickerton's classification. In BD, NPs may appear with the definite article *di*, the indefinite article *en*, or no article. Kouwenberg's data suggest that the semantic distinction between *en* and bare NPs is not that of assertion of existence. We discuss below whether *en* can be considered a marker of specificity as speaker intent to refer on a par with English indefinite *this*. The uses of *di*, *en* and bare NPs in BD are exemplified in (14).[12]

(14) *andaka      iši   wa    habu  boki ...   iši  bi   iši  ma kopu kui₁  an*
    other_day  1p   PAST have  money ... 1p  say  1p   IRR buy  **cow**  and
    *iši   kopu-tɛ_   **en kui₂**    mɛtɛ      o.*
    1p    buy-PF    **IND cow**    with      3s
    *ɛkɛ  pama bifi  iši  mu    kopu  di      kui₃   in   kes*
    1s    tell  say  1p   must  buy   **DEF**    **cow**   in   case
    *aši   titi   ɛkɛ   doto-tɛ    o      habu   kui₄   fi   paši    o,*
    if    time  1s    die-PF     3s     have   **cow**   for  care    3s
    *bikas       o      kan   furkopu  di      kui₅.*
    because     3s     can   sell     **DEF**    **cow**
    "The other day we had some money (...) We said we would buy **a cow₁** and we bought **a cow₂** with it. I told (him) that we should buy **the cow₃**, just in case, when I die he will have **a cow₄** to secure him (financially), because he can sell **the cow₅**."        (=(2) in Kouwenberg, to appear)

On the first use of *kui*, the bare NP is nonspecific: there is no particular cow under discussion. The second use of *kui* corresponds to a specific indefinite reading (a particular cow is under discussion for the first time), so *en kui* is used. The third use of *kui* refers back to the previously mentioned cow, so *di kui* is used, with a definite determiner. The fourth use of *kui* is once again nonspecific, talking about a hypothetical state of events, while the fifth use is definite, a case of "donkey" anaphora referring back to the hypothetical cow. Given the above discussion, we now ask whether the distinction between bare *kui* and *en kui* corresponds to assertion of existence, speaker intent to refer, or yet another distinction.

Kouwenberg shows that a bare NP may be used even when existence of a specific referent is asserted, as in (15), where the bare NP *tau* is used even though a particular snake is asserted to exist (*di tau* is used upon the second mention). In our terminology, this suggests that the distinction between bare NPs and *en* indefinites is not that of assertion of existence.

(15) ***tau***      *biti-tɛ    o    ben    ši      fišpen.  **di   tau***     *biti-tɛ*
    **snake**    bite-PF   3s   inside 3s.poss fish pen. **DEF snake**   bite-PF
    *ši       fingri   an   o       doto-tɛ.*
    3s.poss  finger   and  3s      die-PF
    "**A snake** bit him inside his fish pen. **The snake** bit his finger and he died."

        (=(6) in Kouwenberg, to appear)

---

[12] Kouwenberg's examples below use the following abbreviations in the glosses (from Kouwenberg, to appear, footnote 8): DEF = definite article, HAB = habitual aspect, IND = indefinite article, IRR = irrealis mood, PF = perfective aspect. Pronouns are distinguished as s = singular, p = plural, poss = possessive.

However, we cannot automatically conclude that the distinction corresponds to speaker intent to refer. As Kouwenberg shows, the distribution of bare NPs in BD is in fact quite complex: for instance, bare NPs may be used in certain cases when the NP has a unique referent (where the uniqueness may be either absolute or established pragmatically in the immediate context), as shown in (16).[13]

(16) **sono** das    mja    lombo fi    ɛkɛ
     **sun**  HAB   make   bad    for   1s
     "**The sun** makes (it) hard for me [to work in the field]"
                                        (=(33) in Kouwenberg, to appear)

Kouwenberg links the availability of bare NPs in both indefinite and definite contexts to *non-identifiability*: in (15), for instance, use of a bare NP "suggests that this snake is not identified. In this manner, the speaker chooses to make the reference of *tau* existential ('some snake') rather than specific ('a snake')" (Kouwenberg, to appear: 14). Kouwenberg suggests that identifiability is also an issue for bare definites, but for a different reason: in the case of bare definites, "the identity of a noun's referent is not at issue, this time because it is given, either by the cultural context or the pragmatic context" (Kouwenberg, to appear: 16). Thus, Kouwenberg links the use of overt determiners (*en* as well as *di*) vs. bare NPs to the speaker's ability to identify the referent of the NP (see Lyons 1999, for more discussion of identifiability).

It may be possible to link the notion of *identifiability* to speaker intent to refer: arguably, a speaker intends to refer only to those individuals whose identity is known and important to the speaker. However, it is less clear whether the same link can be made for definites. Non-creole languages which have a marker of specificity as speaker intent to refer (e.g., colloquial English with indefinite *this* or modern Hebrew with *xad*) nevertheless require a definite article for definites with uniquely identifiable referents, such as *the sun*. Such definites also tend to appear with a definite article in L2 English: in our last study (Ionin et al. 2004), we used uniquely referring definites such as *the sun* as fillers, and found fairly accurate use of *the* for this category (but we did find overuse of *a* with definite DPs that lacked speaker intent to refer, such as those exemplified in footnote 3). Thus, more research into the link between speaker intent to refer and identifiability is needed.

### 4.2 Substrate influence

To sum up, there is some evidence that Hawaiian Creole English, Guyanese Creole English and Berbice Dutch Creole encode specificity as well as definiteness. Furthermore, the data suggest that the type of specificity encoded by

---

[13] Kouwenberg also discusses use of bare NPs vs. articles with mass and plural NPs, predicative NPs, and generic NPs, and furthermore makes a distinction between null determiners and truly bare NPs. These issues are beyond the immediate scope of the present paper.

*wan* does not correspond to assertion of existence; rather, there is suggestive evidence that *wan* encodes speaker intent to refer (and/or a similar concept such as identifiability).

Bickerton argued that specificity is a universal feature that is not traceable to the influence of the substrate or superstrate languages: according to Bickerton, specificity was not encoded in either English or pidgin, and "it is not a feature of any of the languages which were in contact there [in Hawaii]" (Bickerton 1977: 245). However, more recent work, in particular on HCE, has disagreed with this assertion. While a detailed examination of article semantics in the substrate languages of different creoles lies beyond the scope of this paper, we briefly summarize some relevant data for HCE, as discussed in Siegel (2000).

Siegel traces the use of *wan* as a marker of specificity with indefinites in HCE to substrate language influence. First, there is evidence that *one* was used as an indefinite article in Chinese Pidgin English, as shown in (17); second, Chinese speakers of Pidgin Hawaiian in the nineteenth century used *akahi* 'one' as an indefinite article as well (18); and finally, Hawaiian Pidgin English in the twentieth century also sometimes showed the use of *wan* as an indefinite article (19). According to Siegel (2000), all of these instances of the numeral 'one' are used to mark specific entities known by the speaker but not by the listener.

(17)  *Chinese Pidgin English*
      *He was welly much flight* **one Chinaman** *killee him if he no give back pipe!*
      ["He was very frightened a Chinaman would kill him if he didn't give back the pipe!"]
                                      (Grant 1888: 64, quoted in Roberts 1991:71)

(18)  *Pidgin Hawaiian*
      *Wau manao* **akahi pihi nui** *iaia paani kela wai.*
      1sg. think    indef fish big  3sg. play  def  water
      "I thought that a big fish was playing in the water."   (Roberts 1995:116)

(19)  *Hawaiian Pidgin English*
      *bambai mi waif hapai—bambai* **wan lil boi** *kam ...*
      later  me wife pregnant later  a    little boy come
      ["Later my wife got pregnant—later a little boy came ..."]
                                      (Roberts 1998:16–17)

Siegel (2000) suggests that this use of 'one' stems from Cantonese, which influenced Chinese Pidgin English, which in turn may have influenced pidgin and creole use in Hawaii. In Cantonese, *yat* 'one' is used to mark specific indefinites, in particular those preceding the main verb, as shown in (20).

Siegel also cites evidence (from Matthews & Pacioni 1997) that classifiers in Cantonese act as markers of specificity, at least for NPs preceding the verb, and suggests that the specificity distinction could have been transferred from Cantonese (and other southern Chinese languages) into HCE.

(20) *Cantonese*
    *Yáuh* **(yat)** **ga** **che** *jó-jyuh*      *go*     *cheut-háu.*
    have (one) cl   car   block-cont cl   exit-mouth
    "There's a car blocking the exit."         (Matthews & Yip 1994:89)

Thus, there is evidence that the presence of specificity marking in HCE is a result of substrate language influence.

### 4.3 *Summary: specificity in creole*

This paper started with the question of whether the same semantic distinctions are encoded in L2 acquisition and in creole languages. The available data from Hawaiian Creole English, Guyanese Creole English, and Berbice Dutch Creole provide a partial answer to this question. These languages do indeed appear to possess markers of specificity (*wan/en*), which are all derived from the numeral *one* (such a derivation is not uncommon—the Hebrew *xad* is also derived from the numeral for 'one,' *exad*). The semantic property marked by *wan/en* does not appear to be that of assertion of existence, since bare NPs may also be used to assert existence. Rather, the data and discussion in Bickerton (1981), Givón (2001) and Kouwenberg (to appear) suggest that the use of *wan/en* is tied to the referent of the indefinite's being important for the discourse and/or identifiable by the speaker. More investigation is needed, however, into whether identifiability (as encoded in creole) and speaker intent to refer (as encoded in L2 English) refer to the same semantic concept, or to two different (albeit similar) ones. More investigation into identifiability with definites is also necessary.

Furthermore, the presence of specificity marking in HCE (and possibly other creoles as well) may stem from corresponding marking in substrate languages. This suggests that while L2 acquisition and creole formation both make use of the semantic feature *specificity*, they may do so for different reasons: non-L1-related access to universally available features on the one hand, substrate influence on the other.

### 5. *Conclusion and open questions*

In this paper, we have argued that the semantic universals of definiteness and specificity are attested cross-linguistically, and available to L2-English learners. We have shown that specificity cross-linguistically and in L2 acquisition is tied to *speaker intent to refer* rather than to *assertion of existence*. We then posed the question of whether specificity as speaker intent to refer also receives morphological expression in creole languages. The evidence is suggestive: specificity does affect article semantics in at least some creole languages, and is clearly not tied to assertion of existence. The question is open as to whether the types of specificity encoded in L2 English and in creole are exactly the same or only somewhat similar; in order to answer this question, we would need to apply the same tests to both sets of data. Looking at data from more creole languages would also be beneficial.

Another important question is whether the role of specificity in L2 acquisition and in creole languages has the same source. In the case of L2 acquisition, we have argued that the role of specificity is not traceable to L1 transfer: speakers of two article-less and typologically different L1s (Russian and Korean) are sensitive to the semantics of specificity. We have proposed that learners have access to universal semantic features underlying articles cross-linguistically even if there are no articles in their L1. However, we cannot make a similar claim about creoles without further investigation into article semantics in the substrate languages. Data from HCE (Siegel 2000) suggest that, at least in this language, specificity marking is due to substrate influence. A further difference between creoles and L2 acquisition is that, while English- and Dutch-based creoles use forms of the numeral *one* to mark specificity, the L2-English learners discussed in this paper use the definite article *the* for this purpose. An interesting question is whether there are any creole languages that use the definite article of the superstrate language to mark specificity, and moreover, that do not do so as a result of substrate influence. Such a hypothetical creole language would provide the closest parallel to the L2 acquisition data discussed in this paper.

Finally, a comparison of article semantics in L2 acquisition and creole languages can look beyond specificity to other semantic features. Our more recent studies (Ko, Ionin & Wexler 2005; Perovic, Ko, Ionin & Wexler 2005) suggest that L2-English articles encode not only specificity but also partitivity (in the sense of *set membership*, cf. Enç 1991). An interesting question is whether this semantic distinction also plays a role in creole formation.

To conclude, there seems to be a fruitful research program in comparing article semantics in L2 acquisition and creole genesis. If creole genesis and L2 acquisition are similar types of processes, then we would expect either that (i) the same set of universal semantic distinctions is encoded in creole and in L2 learners' interlanguages, regardless of the L1/substrate languages; or (ii) article semantics in both creole genesis and L2 acquisition are traceable to L1 transfer. On the other hand, if these two processes treat article semantics differently (e.g., the role of specificity in L2 acquisition is *not* due to L1 transfer, as we have argued, while article semantics in creole *is* determined by the substrate languages), this would provide evidence that creole genesis is not a special type of L2 acquisition.

*References*

Bickerton, D. 1977. *Change and Variation in Hawaiian English, II: Creole Syntax*. Honolulu: Social Sciences and Linguistics Institute, University of Hawaii.

Bickerton, D. 1981. *Roots of Language*. Ann Arbor: Karoma.

Blass, R. 1990. *Relevance Relations in Discourse. A Study with Special Reference to Sissala*. Cambridge: Cambridge University Press.

Borer, H. 2005. *Structuring Sense, Volume I: In Name Only*. Oxford: Oxford University Press.

Donnellan, K. 1966. Reference and definite descriptions. *The Philosophical Review* 75: 281-304.

Enç, M. 1991. The semantics of specificity. *Linguistic Inquiry* 22: 1-25.

Fodor, J. and I. Sag. 1982. Referential and quantificational indefinites. *Linguistics and Philosophy* 5: 355-398.

Givón, T. 1981. On the development of the numeral 'one' as an indefinite marker. *Folia Linguistica Historica* 2(1): 35-53.

Givón, T. 2001. *Syntax: Volume 1*. Amsterdam: John Benjamins.

Grant, M.F. 1888. *Scenes in Hawaii; or, Life in the Sandwich Islands*. Toronto: Hart.

Heim, I. 1991. Articles and definiteness. Published in German as "Artikel und Definitheit," in *Semantics: An International Handbook of Contemporary Research*, A. v. Stechow & D. Wunderlich (eds.), 487-535. Berlin: de Gruyter.

Huebner, T. 1983. *A Longitudinal Analysis of the Acquisition of English*. Ann Arbor: Karoma.

Ionin, T. 2003a. Article Semantics in Second Language Acquisition. Ph.D. dissertation, MIT. Distributed by *MIT Working Papers in Linguistics*.

Ionin, T. 2003b. The interpretation of *the*: A new look at articles in L2-English. In *Proceedings of the 27$^{th}$ Boston University Conference on Language Development*, B. Beachley, A. Brown, and F. Conlin (eds.), 346-357. Somerville, MA: Cascadilla Press.

Ionin, T., H. Ko, and K. Wexler. 2003. Specificity as a grammatical notion: Evidence from L2-English article use. In *Proceedings of WCCFL 22*, G. Garding and M. Tsujimura (eds.), 245-258. Somerville, MA: Cascadilla Press.

Ionin, T., H. Ko, and K. Wexler. 2004. Article semantics in L2-acquisition: the role of specificity. *Language Acquisition,* 12, 3-69.

Ko, H., T. Ionin and K. Wexler. 2005. Adult L2-learners lack *the* Maximality Presupposition, too! To appear in *Proceedings of the 1$^{st}$ GALANA Conference*.

Kouwenberg, S. To appear. Bare nouns in Berbice Dutch Creole. To appear in *Bare Nouns in Creole Languages*, M. Baptista & J. Guéron (eds.). Amsterdam: John Benjamins.

Lyons, C. 1999. *Definiteness*. Cambridge: Cambridge University Press.

Maclaran, R. 1982. The Semantics and Pragmatics of the English Demonstratives. Ph.D. dissertation, Cornell University.

Master, P. 1987. A Cross-Linguistic Interlanguage Analysis of the Acquisition of the English Article System. Ph.D. dissertation, UCLA.

Matthews, S. and P. Pacioni. 1997. Specificity and genericity in Cantonese and Mandarin. In *The Referential Properties of Chinese Noun Phrases*, L. Xu (ed.), 45-59. Paris: Centre de Recherches Linguistiques sur l'Asie Orientale.

Matthews, S. and V. Yip. 1994. *Cantonese: A Comprehensive Grammar*. London: Routledge.

Mosel, U. and E. Hovdhaugen. 1992. *Samoan Reference Grammar*. Oslo: Scandinavian University Press.

Parrish, B. 1987. A new look at methodologies in the study of article acquisition for learners of ESL. *Language Learning* 37: 361-383.

Perovic, A., H. Ko, T. Ionin and K. Wexler. 2005. L2-acquisition of the English indefinite article by speakers of Serbo-Croatian. MS, MIT/Stony Brook University/USC.

Prince, E. 1981. On the inferencing of indefinite-*this* NPs. In *Elements of Discourse Understanding,* A. K. Joshi, B. L. Webber, and I. A. Sag (eds.), 231-250. Cambridge: Cambridge University Press.

Roberts, J.M. 1991. Language in Hawai'i in the nineteenth century and its relation to Hawaiian Pidgin English. MS, Hamilton Library, University of Hawai'i.

Roberts, J.M. 1995. A structural sketch of Pidgin Hawaiian. *Amsterdam Creole Studies* 12: 97-126.

Roberts, J.M. 1998. The role of diffusion in the genesis of Hawaiian creole. *Language* 74: 1-39.

Robertson, D. 2000. Variability in the use of the English article system by Chinese learners of English. *Second Language Research* 16: 135-172.

Schaeffer, J. and L. Matthewson. 2005. Grammar and pragmatics in the acquisition of article systems. *Natural Language and Linguistic Theory* 23: 53-101.

Siegel, J. 2000. Substrate influence in Hawai'i Creole English. *Language in Society* 29: 197-236.

Thomas, M. 1989. The acquisition of English articles by first- and second-language learners. *Applied Psycholinguistics* 10: 335-355.

Young, R. 1996. Form-function relations in articles in English interlanguage. In *Second Language Acquisition and Linguistic Variation,* R. Bayley and D. R. Preston (eds.), 135-175. Amsterdam: John Benjamins.

# PART III

## PROCESSES: DEVELOPING GRAMMARS
## (RESTRUCTURING AND REANALYSIS)

# BILINGUAL GRAMMARS AND CREOLES:
## SIMILARITIES BETWEEN FUNCTIONAL CONVERGENCE
## AND MORPHOLOGICAL ELABORATION*

Liliana Sánchez
*Rutgers University*

The paper examines the similarities between functional convergence in bilingual grammars (Sánchez 2003, 2004) and morphological elaboration in creole grammars (Siegel 2004). On the basis of an analysis of convergence in evidentiality and progressivity in Quechua-Spanish bilinguals and of the emergence of progressive markers in Hawaiian Creole English, the paper proposes that both processes take place irrespective of marked differences in the morphological configuration of the languages involved in the contact situation, and are favored by frequent activation of the two languages (Bao 2005; Sánchez 2004). Furthermore, such processes take place (and can be best observed) under specific discourse conditions that require the morphological expression of interpretable features in the L1 or the substratum languages. They are reminiscent of processes of feature reassembly in second languages (Lardiere 2005) and of systemic transfer constrained by the superstratum morphology in creoles (Bao 2005).

## 1. *Introduction*

In this paper, I examine the similarities between functional convergence in bilingual grammars (Sánchez 2003, 2004) and morphological elaboration in creole grammars (Siegel 2004). I propose that some examples of morphological elaboration in creole grammars presented in Siegel (2004) are similar to cases of functional convergence in bilinguals discussed in Sánchez (2003, 2004). Their common characteristic is that they involve the mapping of functional features from one language onto morphological units not previously associated with those features in another language. The purpose of this comparison is to engage in a dialogue between studies of bilingualism and studies of creole formation that may shed light on how similar psycholinguistic processes generate new linguistic forms in situations of language contact.

Following views originally proposed by Muysken (1981), Lefebvre (1998), Lardiere (1998), Myers-Scotton (2002), Prévost and White (2000) and White (2003), I argue that it is possible for bilinguals to dissociate abstract functional features from the overt morphological units to which they are linked in the input and to generate new feature-morpheme associations.[1] This process of

---

* I would like to thank the audience at the Montreal Dialogues Workshop (August 2004) and three anonymous reviewers for their comments. All errors are mine.
[1] In the case of "fossilized" L2 learners, the syntax can provide evidence that the mental representation includes abstract features present in the input that have no corresponding overt morphological unit in the production of the L2 speaker (Lardiere 1998; Prévost & White 2000; White 2003).

dissociation and relinking of features to morphological units might take place in the mind of second language (L2) learners in cases of transfer (Schwartz & Sprouse 1996) or reassembling of L1 features in the L2 (Lardiere 2005); among speakers of a pidgin or creole (Bao 2005; Lefebvre 1998) or a mixed language (Muysken 1981), as part of a general process of relexification; and among bilingual individuals who regularly activate two languages as cases in which subsets of functional features from two languages converge and generate a common set of features for both (Sánchez 2003, 2004).

In order to focus the discussion of how this process of dissociation works in bilinguals, I present evidence of functional convergence in the Tense/Mood/Aspect (TMA) systems of Quechua-Spanish bilingual grammars, using data from previous studies (Escobar 1994; Klee & Ocampo 1995; Sánchez 2003, 2004, forthcoming); this work underscores the relevance of pragmatic factors in favoring the use of morphological forms in bilingual Spanish that differ in extension and grammatical meaning from those found in non-contact varieties of Spanish and whose semantic import is very close to that of functional morphological units in Quechua. In the absence of appropriate morphology in the superstratum language (due to nonexistent forms or to incomplete acquisition of such forms), the bilingual grammar maps a functional feature in the substratum language onto an already existing morphological form in the superstratum language, resulting in convergent representations in the two languages.

I propose to extend the analysis of convergent feature specifications in TMA systems in bilinguals to some cases of the emergence of morphological forms in the TMA systems of creole speakers. These new morphemes have meanings that correspond more closely to those of a substrate or contact language than to those of the lexifier (Siegel 2004). Siegel proposes that these are cases of transfer of language use patterns in which features of one language are transferred to the morphological elements of the other due to the speakers' incomplete mastery of the linguistic resources in the L2. The proposal presented here extends Siegel's hypothesis by emphasizing the role that discourse conditions play in favoring convergence in bilingual TMA systems, as well as morphological elaboration in creole TMA systems. I propose that, as is the case among bilinguals living in language contact situations, speakers of pidgin languages are under pressure to maximize resources in the expression of discourse-oriented conditions. However, this maximization does not automatically imply the suppression of the abstract representation of features from their L1. These might be expressed using lexical units from the lexifier. Among creole speakers, who live in a language contact situation and speak "nativized" versions of the pidgin, the pragmatic conditions under which these lexical items are used in the pidgin provide the context for new associations between interpretable functional features from a substratum language and morpheme units from the lexifier. I hypothesize that in such cases the functional content of substrate languages serves as a prominent source for grammatical specifications that are mapped onto the morphological units from the lexifier.

## 2. *Functional convergence, morphological elaboration and the dissociation between features and morphemes*

In this section, I will present the definitions of two similar psycholinguistic processes that take place in the mind of bilingual speakers: functional convergence, a process whereby equivalent functional categories in the two languages spoken by a bilingual individual converge in their feature specifications (Sánchez 2003, 2004); and morphological elaboration, defined by Siegel (2004) as a process of language transfer that takes place in the minds of second language acquirers in the context of creole formation. I will propose that these two processes are similar in that what underlies them is the availability of abstract functional features that can be dissociated from their morphological counterparts in at least one of the languages spoken by a bilingual individual. Before I present the proposal in detail, I will discuss each of the definitions and the linguistic contexts in which they apply.

Convergence between bilingual grammars has been analyzed from many different perspectives (recent approaches include Backus 2004; Muysken 2001; Myers-Scotton 2002; Ross 2005). In this paper, I adopt an approach to convergence that is grounded on the view that human languages are basically characterized by a distinction between lexical and functional categories (Chomsky 1995). While lexical categories are relatively consistent across languages (Baker 2003), functional categories are the locus of cross-linguistic variation. Recently, a move to locate the grammatical properties of languages in functional features rather than functional categories has taken place (Chomsky 1995, 1999). This move has resulted in a consensus that abstract functional features, conceived of as minimal units that embody grammatical properties of language, are responsible for [all] cross-linguistic variation.

When convergence takes place in bilingual grammars, shared syntactic properties of the two languages follow from a common selection of functional features. Sánchez (2003, 2004) proposes that functional convergence is the "specification of a common set of features shared by equivalent functional categories in the two languages spoken by a bilingual individual"(Sánchez 2003: 15). This common specification is favored when the languages have partially similar matrices of features associated with the same functional category, and frequent activation of both matrices triggers convergence in features (Sánchez 2004). An example of such a case of convergence is provided by the common specification for evidentiality[2] among Quechua-

---

[2] A reviewer points out that Aikhenvald (2004) has proposed that evidentiality is prone to areal diffusion in Amazonian languages because it must be obligatorily marked in the morphological component. In this paper, I propose that diffusion is due to the fact that evidentiality is part of

Spanish bilinguals, who use imperfective forms in Spanish in the same contexts in which they use reportative past forms in Quechua to indicate that the information conveyed by a sentence is not first-hand information witnessed by the speaker. This is illustrated in the following examples from Sánchez (2004) and will be discussed in further detail in section 3:

(1)  *Paq  # pichikucha-ta  tarikuru-sqa*       *qilluchata.*
     bir  # birdy-ACC      find-PAST REPORT  yellow-ACC[3]
     '(She) found a yellow bird (second-hand information)'

(2)  *Le **había encontrado** un    pajarito # amarillo.*
     CL  **had    found**     a     birdy    # yellow
     '(S/he) had found a yellow bird (second-hand information)'

Morphological elaboration is also a psycholinguistic process that takes place in the case of a speaker living in a language contact situation. Siegel defines it as the "development and increased use of grammatical morphemes for expressing various meanings in a language, rather than relying on context or lexical items"(Siegel 2004: 335). An example of morphological elaboration is provided by the emergence of the progressive marker *stay* in Hawai'i Creole, even though Hawaiian Pidgin used the adverbial form *all time* and, at least in example (3), verb reduplication to mark progressivity. The following examples, originally from Roberts (1998, 2000), illustrate the changes from the pidgin to the creole expression of progressivity:

(3)  All time baby cry, cry play piano (Phases III–IV)      (Roberts 1998: 23)

(4)  He stay playing (Phase V)                            (Roberts 1998: 23)

Siegel notes that these two examples correspond to different phases or periods in the progression from Hawaiian pidgin to the actual elaboration of the Hawaiian Creole (Roberts 1998). In the earlier stages, represented by (3), reduplication and adverbs are linked to non-punctual aspect, while in the later stages, represented by (4), the independent head *stay* emerges as a marker of non-punctual aspect or progressivity.

Siegel views morphological elaboration as the transfer of second language use, in particular in those cases in which a lexical unit in one of the languages is used in a manner similar to that of another morphological unit in the other. In example (4) above, the English lexifier verb *stay* acquires a progressive meaning in the creole that it does not have in the superstratum language and that was conveyed through the use of a lexical adverb and reduplication in the

---

the inventory of functional features that require morphological expression in many Amazonian languages.
[3]  The following abbreviations are used in this article: ACC (accusative), PAST REPORT (reportative past tense), EVID REPORT (reportative evidential), PAST ATTEST (attested past tense).

pidgin. Siegel's main proposal is that morphological elaboration can be under-stood as a process of language transfer from the L1 into the L2 when "the linguistic forms needed to efficiently convey the required meaning are absent because the L2 at this stage is a restricted pidgin or pre-pidgin." (Siegel 2004: 353). The lexical entry *stay* is a better candidate to become a progressive morpheme than the actual *–ing* morpheme in the lexifier because the L2 available to the speaker is a restricted pidgin.

I would like to point out that some of the languages present in the contact situation that gave rise to Hawaiian Creole had a non-punctual feature. In fact, one could argue that the abstract progressivity feature is not absent in example (3) since the adverbial form and the reduplication of the verb appear to convey it. What is absent in this example is an overt morphological unit (bound or an independent) that is associated with the functional feature and that does not bear *lexical* content.[4]

The proposal presented here points out that functional convergence and morphological elaboration are two processes that can be better understood in light of the possible dissociation between functional features and their morphological counterparts in the minds of some bilingual individuals. This is particularly relevant in language contact situations such as those in which creole languages emerge, since input is provided by native speakers of several languages and by L2 acquirers of those languages. I would like to propose that what makes both the process of functional convergence in bilinguals and the process of morphological elaboration in creole languages possible is the abstract nature of the functional features in question. In the case of Tense/Mood/Aspect systems, these abstract features can be dissociated from their morphological counterparts in one of the languages spoken by a bilingual individual, as shown by research on second language acquisition by Lardiere (1998, 2003, 2005), Prévost and White (2000) and White (2003), and may be relinked to overt morphemes in the other languages or may simply have no phonetic representation. Lardiere's (1998, 2005) work in particular illustrates the dissociation between knowledge of morphology and knowledge of the values of functional features. Lardiere (1998) analyzes the speech of a native speaker of Chinese whose L2 English shows fossilization in verb agreement even after she had spent at least 10 years in the US, as evidenced by very low percentages of use of verbal morphology in obligatory contexts, especially in thematic verbs in non-past third-person forms. Despite this lack of overt morphology, her L2 speech shows evidence of syntactic knowledge in her production of obligatory overt subjects and negative sentences without verb-raising, a syntactic property triggered by weak features associated with verb

---

[4] It is important to note that Siegel (2004) distinguishes the process of morphological elaboration from the results of this process, which he terms "expanded morphology."

agreement morphology in English. Some of the examples presented by Lardiere show clearly that this speaker has preverbal adverbs and auxiliary verbs with negation:

(5)    He don't prepare it though.

(6)    My mom also speak Mandarin.

(7)    I eventually also get into the Chinese school.            (Lardiere 1998: 368)

Thus, Lardiere concludes that this subject "knows that the English feature value for syntactic verb raising is weak despite the fact that her agreement inflection rate is severely deficient" (Lardiere 1998: 369).

This process of dissociation between abstract features and overt morphological counterparts is at the basis of phenomena such as functional convergence and morphological elaboration in cases in which a functional value from a substratum language appears to be linked to a superstratum lexical morpheme in a creole language. Dissociation enables the relinking of functional features to morphemes not previously associated with them.[5] In more recent work, Lardiere (2005) refers to the process of relinking of features to their PF/morphological counterparts as a reassembly or a remapping of features that takes place at the level of morphology. I will adopt a very similar perspective to Lardiere's with respect to the remapping of abstract functional features onto PF/morphological forms, and I will advance a possible solution to the issue that she raises concerning the conditioning factors that guide the L2 acquirer in this remapping by focusing on the role that discourse conditions play in favoring feature relinking or remapping in bilinguals.

I would also like to point out that Siegel notes that he did not find in the literature on L2 acquisition examples of "L2 forms being used as grammatical morphemes with properties of corresponding L1 grammatical morphemes" (Siegel 2004: 349). He mentions that a closer observation of evidence of cross-linguistic interference in bilinguals could help us to better understand the processes involved in morphological elaboration. In this paper, I will undertake this task by examining cases of convergence in evidentiality and progressivity in bilinguals and the emergence of progressive markers and markers of completive aspect in two creoles discussed by Siegel (1998).

---

[5] I do not rule out the role played by grammaticalization in the evolution of certain forms. I assume that, as shown by Romaine (1999), it is possible that pidgin/creole languages such as Tok Pisin show gradual emergence of functional units that can be considered local developments. In situations of language contact, gradual processes of grammaticalization may also be favored by bilingualism (Heine & Kuteva 2003) and therefore it is very difficult to determine to what extent a process of grammaticalization corresponds to the relinking of a functional feature present in a substratum language or in one of the languages in the contact situation.

3.  *Functional convergence and morphological elaboration in TMA systems*
TMA systems are subject to cross-linguistic interference and functional convergence in bilinguals because they are the locus of micro-parametric variation in the values assigned to each of the categories involved: tense, mood and aspect. TMA systems are also the locus of variation from analytic to synthetic parameterization, that is, from one-to-one correspondences between features and morphemes (as in the notion of Feature-Scattering proposed by Giorgi & Pianesi 1997) to many-to-one correspondences in cases in which the feature values for these three categories are encoded in a single morpheme. As Siegel notes, it is probably not the case that the emergence of new morphemes in one of the lects of a creole continuum can be directly attributed to the shift from analyticity to syntheticity, nor is it true that functional convergence is blocked in bilinguals in cases in which one language favors the analytic parameter while the other favors the synthetic one (Muysken 2001). A more likely scenario is that cases of functional convergence and some cases of morphological elaboration in TMA systems correspond to situations in which functional features from the substratum language are associated to morpheme units (free or bound) from the superstratum or lexifier language.

In the particular case of the evolution from pidgins to creoles, morphological elaboration restores the association between abstract functional features and affixes or independent functional heads that had gone through an intermediate stage of association with a lexical unit in the earlier versions of the pidgin. Note that these abstract functional features are not necessarily absent from the pidgin since they might be linked to lexical items such as adverbs or they may correspond to phonologically null forms, as in the cases discussed by Lardiere (1998).

Creole speakers, like bilinguals, are sensitive to those conditions and, to the extent that they have access to input from both the substratum language and the lexifier, they can restore the association between functional features and morphemes (free or bound but more or less deprived of lexical content) under the appropriate discourse conditions. Thus, the types of elements on which dissociation and relinking might operate are: abstract functional features, lexical items, free functional morphemes and bound functional morphemes. Abstract functional features present in the substratum language(s) or L1s might have been preserved in a bilingual individual's mental representation in the L1 and the pidgin, in the latter through association with a lexical item in the lexifier such as an adverb or through reduplication. This is possible because the abstract feature is dissociated from its corresponding unit in the L1, as its phonetically overt expression. If the output of this particular speaker, along with that of other speakers of the pidgin with similar characteristics, is a salient part of the input, speakers of the nativized creole will have access to input in which the feature is available, although associated with a lexical item. In their representation, a new association is created so that, either gradually or abruptly, the functional feature becomes associated with a new grammatical unit that is bleached of its semantic content.

The features most likely to be imported from the substratum language into the creole would be features whose morphological expression is favored by discourse conditions that apply even in the pidgin. In the next section, I provide examples of how discourse conditions favor the expression or association of TMA functional features with morphemes in bilingual grammars and creoles.

## 4. *Convergence in bilingual grammars*

### 4.1 *Evidentiality*
One salient case of convergence in TMA functional features involves evidentiality values in bilingual varieties of Spanish spoken by Quechua speakers, as discussed in the first section. In Quechua, past tense suffixes and other discourse-level affixes convey evidentiality in terms of first-hand versus hearsay information (Cerrón-Palomino 1989; Cusihuamán 2001; Muysken 1995). In Spanish, on the other hand, past tense distinctions are conveyed by the use of suffixes and auxiliary verbs and are strongly associated with aspectual distinctions between perfectivity and imperfectivity (Acero 1990) and between background and foreground information in narrative forms (Bardovi-Harlig 1998). The Spanish of some Quechua-Spanish bilingual individuals shows consistent use of pluperfect forms throughout narrations in order to express the hearsay nature of the information conveyed (Sánchez 2004: 157):

(8) *Había*  *una*  *viejita*       *dice.*
    was    an    old woman   say
    '(There) was an old woman, (they) say.'

(9) *Había*  *sembrado*    *maíz.*
    had    sowed       corn
    '(S/he) had sowed corn.'

(10) *Le* *había* *encontrado* *un* *pajarito*  # *amarillo.*
     CL  **had**   **found**      a    birdy     # yellow
     '(S/he) had found a yellow bird.'

These correspond to the use of the reportative past morpheme -*sqa* in the corresponding narrative in Quechua (Sánchez 2004: 155):[6]

---

[6] The Quechua reportative past suffix –*sqa* has an attested past form counterpart –*rqa* that is used in discourse to convey first-hand information as in:
(i)  Llank'a-rqa-ni
     work- PAST ATTEST-1S
     '(I) worked.' (Cusihuamán 2001: 159)

(11)  *<Uk-si>*        [/] *uk-si*              *payacha ka-sqa*              y
      <once-REPORT> [/] once-EVID REPORT  old        be-PAST REPORT *and*
      #*sarata  tarpu-sqa.*
      #corn    SOW-PAST REPORT
      'Once there was an old woman *and* (they say she) was sowing corn'

(12)  *Paq*    # *pichikucha-ta  tarikuru-sqa*        *qilluchata.*
      bir     # birdy-ACC      find-PAST REPORT  yellow-ACC
      '(She) found a yellow bird.'

In order to test the hypothesis that the reportative value of the evidentiality feature has become part of the set of features associated with the pluperfect tense periphrastic verbal form, Sánchez (2004) conducted a study on the use of past tense forms in narration among Quechua-Spanish sequential bilingual children (ages 9 to 13). A story-retelling task was used to prompt the children to activate both languages and to convey hearsay information. The children were asked to listen to the story in (13). Then they were asked to retell the story first in Quechua and then in Spanish.

(13)  *Un día una viejita estaba sembrando maíz y se* **encontró** *un pajarito amarillo.*

> El pajarito estaba enfermo y no podía volar. La viejita lo *llevó* a su casa, lo *abrigó* y le *dio* un remedio. Al otro día el pajarito estaba sano. Entonces la viejita le *dio* de comer trigo, pan y agua. La viejita le *puso* de nombre Pío Pío y todos los días el pajarito canta para la viejita.

> 'One day, an old lady was sowing corn and (she) found a little yellow bird. The bird was sick and could not fly. The old lady took it to her house, warmed it and gave it medicine. The next day the bird was healthy. Then the old lady fed it wheat, bread and water. The old lady named it Pio Pio and the little bird sings every day for the old lady.' (Sánchez 2004: 154)

The input story has imperfective and perfective past tense forms (in italics) and contains no Spanish pluperfect forms. The story was retold by the children in Quechua and Spanish. Some of the bilingual children used Spanish pluperfect forms almost exclusively, as shown in the following narrative:

(14)  *Había una viejita dice.* **Había sembrado** *maíz. Ella sembraba maíz. Le* **había encontrado** *un pajarito # amarillo. Y le* **había llevado** *a su casa. Y le* **había hecho** *comer trigo # agua # pan.*
      '(There) was an old woman, (they) say. (S/he) had sowed corn. She sowed corn. (She) found a yellow bird for him/her. And (she) took him home. And (she) made him eat wheat, water and bread.'

(Sánchez 2004: 157–158)

In narratives such as (14), evidentiality features that are strongly associated with past tense distinctions in Quechua become part of the representation of the pluperfect in bilingual Spanish. Many of the children who used the Spanish pluperfect in Quechua also used the reportative form in their Quechua narrations (Sánchez 2004). Convergence in the use of the evidentiality value for first-hand information is favored by the discourse conditions imposed by a story retelling task that requires the expression of the reportative value of the past tense in Quechua.[7] Note that convergence in this case takes place independently of the different morphological forms used in each language (an auxiliary verb and a suffix in Spanish, and a suffix in Quechua).

Evidence of such convergence has been independently found in other studies conducted among adult and child Quechua-Spanish bilinguals. In a study on the use of past tense forms among Quechua-Spanish adult bilinguals in Calca (Cuzco), Peru, Klee and Ocampo (1995) found that some speakers used pluperfect past forms to express evidentiality. Although Klee and Ocampo focus on simple past imperfect forms, I would like to draw attention to the uses of pluperfect in the narrative:

(15) *¿Cuando* estaba *en estado del negrito? Un loco **había venido** y Caretas estaba así al cantito nomás, y ... "¡quiero esto!" le **había dicho**, entonces "¿donde está plata?" le **había dicho**.*
    'When she was expecting the negrito? A crazy man came [had come] and Caretas was there next to her, and ... "I want this!" he said [had said] to her, then "where is the money?" she said [had said] to him.'

(Klee & Ocampo 1995: 89)

The use of a pluperfect form in this narrative does not correspond to usage in non-contact varieties of Spanish. Non-contact varieties make use of the preterit form in these cases.

The narrative fragment in (15) is a hearsay narrative in which the speaker recounts the experiences of a third person. The hearsay quality of the information provided by the pluperfect corresponds to that conveyed by the reportative past form in Quechua shown in examples (11) and (12) above. In other varieties of Spanish, the expression of evidentiality is not grammaticalized as a distinction between past tense forms and therefore the contrasts between past tense forms focus on the punctual/discrete nature of the events or the distinction between events belonging to the background or foreground of the narrative (Acero 1990; Bardovi-Harlig 1998).

In a similar study on past tense uses in narratives by adult Quechua-Spanish bilinguals, Escobar (1994) also found evidence of evidentiality features associated with tense morphemes. This led her to propose that adult native speakers of Quechua who speak Spanish as a second language "have

---

[7] For an alternative pragmatic explanation of evidentiality features in Quechua, see Faller (2002).

grammaticalized a system of epistemic marking that seems to resemble the one found in Quechua" (Escobar 1997: 21). The data she analyzes show evidence of the use of pluperfect past forms to convey a reported meaning:

(16)  *no sé / porque no sé/ desde [que] mi [me he] nacido **dice** que cuando estuve chiquita / no sé / dice que me **había pateado** el gallo y de ahí no más me froté / entonces mi mamá me **había echado** el limón en los dos lados / ... con eso rojo así **había vuelto** mi ojo / ...*
'I don't know / because I don't know / since I was born it is said that when I was a child / I don't know / it is said that the rooster *had kicked* me [in the eyes] and then I rubbed [my eyes] / then my mother *had put* lemon in the two sides [of my face, in my eyes] / ...with that my eye *had turned* red / ...'

(Escobar 1997: 26–27)

Escobar notes that, in this example, the speaker uses the pluperfect to refer to events told to her, but she uses other past tense forms to refer to actions that she performed herself. Escobar points out that such reportative uses of the pluperfect appear in the data that she analyzes in co-occurrence with some form of the verb *decir* 'to say,' which reinforces the hearsay nature of the information provided by the speaker. She also notes that the speaker infers that the lemon must have damaged her sight.

The data presented and analyzed so far show that in the Spanish TMA system of some Quechua-Spanish bilingual children and adults, there is convergence of evidentiality and tense features under discourse conditions (such as the story retelling task) that require the expression of reportative features.

## 4.2 *Progressivity*

Progressive features are also part of TMA systems and are subject to cross-linguistic interference in Quechua-Spanish bilinguals. In Quechua, they may appear associated with a volitional and/or imminent feature. Sánchez (forthcoming) found evidence of modal progressive expressions used to convey the meaning of an imminent event among Lamas Kechwa-Spanish bilingual children living in a language contact situation. Lamas Kechwa, like many other Quechua dialects, has a wide range of suffixes that modify the meaning of the verb root, adding an aspectual value. According to Coombs, Coombs and Weber (1976), the desiderative suffix *–naya* indicates desire on the part of the subject of the verb to take the action expressed by the verb. Cerrón-Palomino (1994) notes that it also expresses the imminent nature of the verbal action:

(17)  *Miku-naya-ni*
eat-desiderative-1p
'(I) want to/am about to eat.'

This modal marker can be used with the progressive suffix –*yka*, considered by Cerrón-Palomino (1994) to be an imperfective aspectual suffix that expresses an action that lasts in time:

(18) *Kawa-yka-n*
     see-progressive-3p
     '(S/he) is seeing.'

While Quechua expresses progressivity through affixation, Spanish uses the auxiliary verb *estar* 'to be' followed by a gerund form such as *mirando* 'looking':

(19) *Est-á        mir-ando*
     be-3s.pres   look-gerund
     '(S/he) is looking.'

Spanish also has an independent modal verb *querer* 'to want' that expresses volition:

(20) *Quier-o        mir-ar*
     want-1s.pres   see-inf
     '(I) want (to) see.'

In the Spanish narratives of Lamas Kechwa-Spanish bilingual children the modal verb *querer* 'to want' is combined with the progressive expression, as in:

(21) *Est-á        quer-iendo       mir-ar*
     be-3s.pres   want-gerund   (to) see-inf
     '(S/he) is about to/wants to see.'

This combination of the auxiliary verb, gerund and infinitival forms to convey progressive aspect and modality does not occur frequently in most monolingual varieties of Spanish. If it does occur in a non-contact variety, it does not convey the idea of imminent action. Sánchez (forthcoming) found that in narratives elicited using a picture-based story-telling task, out of a total of thirty Lamas Kechwa-Spanish bilingual children (ages 9 to 13), ten used the modal progressive expression in both languages. Interestingly, none of the children in a comparison group of monolingual Spanish-speaking children used modal progressive forms. Moreover, just a few of the pictures elicited the majority of tokens of modal progressive forms. These were the pictures the children interpreted as portraying an imminent action. The following examples from two participants in the study illustrate such uses in bilingual Spanish and Lamas Kechwa:

### 4.2.1 *Participant L16 (Spanish)*

(22) *Y    el    perro*le  ***(e)stá queriendo morder***  *a    ese sapo.*
and  the  dog    is wanting  to bite   the  toad
'And the dog wants to/is about to bite the toad.'

### 4.2.2 *Participant L16 (Lamas Kechwa)*

(23) *Achku  miku-**naya-yka**-n*
dog    eat-des-prog-3
'The dog wants to/is about to bite.'

### 4.2.3 *Participant L25 (Spanish)*

(24) *Y    (a) su  sapo le  **está queriendo morder**  su  perro*
and  his   toad CL  is wanting  to bite   his  dog
'And his dog wants to/is about to bite his toad.'

### 4.2.4 *Participant L25 (Lamas Kechwa)*

(25) *Chay  achku  miku-**naya-yka**-n*
that   dog    eat-des-prog-3
'That dog wants to/is about to eat.'

These examples illustrate how functional convergence among bilinguals is favored by discourse conditions that require the expression of what the speaker perceives as an imminent action. In this particular case, the imminent and progressive features associated with suffixes in Lamas Kechwa converge with the modal progressive periphrasis in Spanish. This reassociation of features takes place irrespective of the different morphological patterns that characterize each of the languages. These examples also illustrate how functional convergence affects the grouping of features and their association with overt morphological forms under specific discourse conditions.

To sum up, convergence of reportative and imminent/progressive features in Quechua-Spanish bilinguals shows that TMA systems are sensitive to new associations between abstract functional features from one language and overt PF/morphological forms from another language. It also shows how these processes are favored by the selection of functional features whose insertion in a numeration is context-sensitive, as is the case with evidentiality or modal progressivity. In languages such as Quechua, the mapping of these abstract features onto PF/morphological forms is required under very specific discourse conditions. In the last section, I will consider how the obligatory nature of that mapping might also be involved in the evolution of TMA systems in creoles.

## 5. *Re-examining morphological elaboration from the perspective of dissociation and reassociation of functional features*

One of the examples identified by Siegel as a case of morphological elaboration is the emergence of the progressive marker *stay* (cf. pages 6 and 7) in the TMA system of Hawaiian Creole English (HCE) (Roberts 1998). According to Roberts (1998), the progressive marker *stay* emerged gradually in HCE and was not found in the earlier versions of the creole nor did it exist in the pidgin preceding the creole. Consequently, its presence in HCE cannot be attributed to the diffusion of substratum features. Roberts points out that this progressive marker is a local and gradual development in HCE and she provides examples from nineteenth-century fragments of speech from Japanese, Chinese, Hawaiian and Portuguese speakers that illustrate a lack of functional markers of past tense, future modality and aspect. It is interesting to note that, although morphological markings are absent from these fragments, there are other interesting characteristics that may illustrate how contact with other languages might have been a source of functional features that were not necessarily associated with bound morphemes or independent heads in the pidgin. In her report, Roberts includes a nineteenth-century English lexifier text attributed to a Portuguese immigrant from Kaua'i. She notes the use of reduplication and of the adverb *all time* to convey some form of non-punctual aspect:

(26)  Marie, he good woman, but talk, talk all time make me mad then
      *pilikia*[8]again.

Roberts (1998: 16)

Portuguese is a language that marks progressivity, so it is natural to hypothesize that abstract progressive features were part of this speaker's mental representation. In fact, Portuguese has forms similar to that found in HCE:

(27)  *Ele   fica   nadando*
      he    stays  swimming
      'He is still swimming.'

In the Portuguese speaker's use of the pidgin, progressive features associated with forms such as (27) could have been linked to verbal reduplication and to the adverbial expression *all time*. No evidence of such forms is found in the nineteenth-century pidgin fragments of speech by Japanese, Chinese or Hawaiian immigrants cited by Roberts (1998), but (27) raises the possibility that the abstract features associated with progressive forms in Portuguese were still part of the input heard by creole speakers.

---

[8] 'Trouble.' In italics in the original.

If this were the case, although the overt morphology was not necessarily inherited from the substratum language, creole speakers had some indication that the abstract feature of progressivity was linked to reduplication and adverbial forms. Some speakers with access to input in Portuguese might use a lexical item from the superstratum language similar to the Portuguese item. Therefore, the pidgin input that bilingual individuals heard did not in, fact, lack overt morphological expressions conveying this feature, although these were not instantiated in an independent functional head or a morpheme. As Roberts states, it was only in the later stages of the development of the creole (what she calls Phase V) in the early 1920s that the independent functional head *stay* emerged as a marker of progressivity, as shown in the following examples, which Roberts culled from different written sources:

(28) He stay playing (1921) [attributed to schoolchildren]

(29) He stay live Kaimuki (1948) [locally born Japanese student]

(30) He stay swimming (1937) [6-year-old Portuguese boy, Honolulu, O'ahu]

(Roberts 1998: 23)

It would be very difficult to demonstrate that a process of functional convergence took place in the bilingual grammars of Portuguese and pidgin speakers that affected the evolution of the creole, but the comparison with what happens with present-day bilingual children and adults could serve as a starting point in hypothesizing that similar processes might have taken place in the development of creole languages such as HCE.

Another example that Siegel presents as a case of morphological elaboration is the emergence of completive aspect in Singapore Colloquial English, which seems to have followed a pattern similar to the emergence of the progressive marker in HCE. Siegel cites an example from Platt and Weber (1980: 66):

(31) I only went there once or twice already.
     'I've been there only once or twice.'

Siegel points out that this example appears to be influenced by the use of the postverbal aspect marker *liau* in the Hokkien substrate, and he cites the following example from Platt and Weber (1984: 70):

(32) *Goá chiảh pá liáu*
     I    eat   full COMP
     'I have finished eating.'

In this case, the abstract feature of completive aspect would have been relinked in the bilingual representation to the adverb *already*. Bao (2005) provides a comprehensive analysis of the aspectual system of Singapore

English. He proposes that the entire aspectual subsystem of Chinese, of which progressivity is only one feature, has been transferred from the substratum language to Singapore English, a process that he dubs *system transfer*. This process complies with the *lexifier filter*, a restriction that stipulates that the morphosyntactic expression of substratum features must conform to the (surface) structural requirements of the lexifier language. What is crucially important to our proposal, as Bao points out, is that Singapore English speakers have constant access to input in both languages, a characteristic also found in the Quechua-Spanish contact situation. The cases of morphological elaboration analyzed by Siegel and Bao's *system transfer* analysis greatly resemble the process of *functional convergence* in bilingual speakers: in both cases, a feature associated with a functional morpheme in one of the languages spoken by a bilingual individual becomes relinked to a lexical item that had not previously been associated with that feature in the lexifier.

## 6. *Conclusion*
I have proposed that functional convergence in bilinguals (Sánchez 2003, 2004) and morphological elaboration in creoles (Siegel 2004) are two psycho-linguistic processes that require the dissociation of abstract functional features from their morphological counterparts in a substratum (Bao 2005) or first language (Lardiere 1998) and a subsequent relinking of the same abstract feature to a morphological element in a superstratum, L2 or contact language. This relinking has also been proposed as part of a feature reassembly process in the L2 representation (Lardiere 2005). In creole languages, it is constrained by the superstratum morphology (Bao 2005). As evidenced by convergence in the TMA systems of Quechua-Spanish bilinguals, this process takes place irrespective of strong differences in the morphological configurations of the languages involved in the contact situation, and it is favored by frequent activation of both languages (Bao 2005; Sánchez 2004). I have also argued that these processes take place (and can be best observed) under specific discourse conditions that require the morphological expression of interpretable features in the L1 or the substratum languages.

## *References*
Acero, J. 1990. Las ideas de Reichenbach acerca del tiempo verbal. In *Tiempo y aspecto en español*, Ignacio Bosque (ed.), 45–75. Madrid: Cátedra.
Aikhenvald, A. 2004. *Evidentiality*. Oxford: Oxford University Press.
Backus, A. 2004. Convergence as a mechanism of language change. *Bilingualism: Language and Cognition* 7(2): 179–181.
Baker, M. 2003. *Lexical Categories*. Cambridge: Cambridge University Press.
Bao, Z. 2005. The aspectual system of Singapore English and the systemic substrate explanation. *Journal of Linguistics* 41: 237–267.
Bardovi-Harlig, K. 1998. Narrative structure and lexical aspect. *Studies on Second Language Acquisition* 20(4): 471–508.

Cerrón-Palomino, R. 1989. *Lingüística Quechua*. Cuzco, Peru: Centro Bartolomé de las Casas.

Chomsky, N. 1995. *The Minimalist Program*. Cambridge, MA: The MIT Press.

Chomsky, N. 1999. Derivation by phase. *MIT Occasional Papers in Linguistics 18*.

Coombs, D., H. Coombs and R. Weber. 1976. *Gramática Quechua San Martín*. Lima, Peru: Instituto de Estudios Peruanos.

Cusihuamán, A. 2001. *Gramática Quechua Cuzco-Collao*. Cuzco, Peru: Centro Bartolomé de las Casas.

Escobar, A. M. 1994. Evidential uses in the Spanish of Quechua speakers in Peru. *Southwest Journal of Linguistics* 13(1–2): 21–43.

Escobar, A. M. 1997. Contrastive and innovative uses of the present perfect and the preterite in Spanish in contact with Quechua. *Hispania* 80(4): 859–879.

Faller, M. 2002. Semantics and Pragmatics of Evidentials in Cuzco Quechua. Ph.D. dissertation, Stanford University.

Giorgi, A. and F. Pianesi. 1997. *Tense and Aspect*. Oxford: Oxford University Press.

Heine, B. and T. Kuteva. 2003. On contact induced grammaticalization. *Studies in Language* 27(3): 529–572.

Klee, C. and A. Ocampo. 1995. The expression of past reference in Spanish narratives of Spanish-Quechua bilingual speakers. In *Spanish in Four Continents: Studies in Language Contact and Bilingualism*, Carmen Silva-Corvalán (ed.), 52–70. Washington, DC: Georgetown University Press.

Lardiere, D. 1998. Dissociating syntax from morphology in a divergent L2 end-state grammar. *Second Language Research* 14(4): 359–375.

Lardiere, D. 2003. Second language knowledge of [±past] vs. [±finite]. In *Proceedings of the 6th Generative Approaches to Second Language Acquisition Conference (GASLA 2002): L2 Links,* J. Liceras, H. Goodluck and H. Zobl (eds.), 176–189. Somerville, MA: Cascadilla Press.

Lardiere, D. 2005. On morphological competence. In *Proceedings of the 7th Generative Approaches to Second Language Acquisition Conference (GASLA 2004)*, Laurent Dekydtspotter, Rex A. Sprouse and Audrey Liljestrand (eds.), 178–192. Somerville, MA: Cascadilla Press.

Lefebvre, C. 1998. Creole Genesis and the Acquisition of Grammar: The Case of Haitian Creole. Cambridge: Cambridge University Press.

Muysken, P. 1981. Halfway between Quechua and Spanish: The case for relexification. In *Historicity and Variation in Creole Studies,* Arthur Highfield and Albert Valdman (eds.), 52–79. Ann Arbor, MI: Karoma.

Muysken, P. 1995. Focus in Quechua. In *Discourse Configurational Languages*, Katalin Kiss (ed.), 375–393. Oxford: Oxford University Press.

Muysken, P. 2001. *Bilingual Speech*. Cambridge: Cambridge University Press.

Myers-Scotton, Carol. 2002. *Contact Linguistics*. Oxford: Oxford University Press.

Prévost, P. and L. White. 2000. Missing surface inflection or impairment in second language acquisition. *Second Language Research* 16(2): 103–133.

Platt, J. and H. Weber. 1980. *English in Singapore and Malaysia: Status, Features, Functions*. Kuala Lumpur: Oxford University Press.

Roberts, S. 1998. The role of diffusion in the genesis of Hawaiian Creole. *Language* 74(2): 1–39.

Roberts, S. 2000. Nativization and the Genesis of Hawaiian Creole. In *Language Change and Language Conctact In Pidgins and Creoles*. McWhorter, John (ed.) Amsterdam: John Benjamins. 257-300.

Romaine, S. 1999. The grammaticalization of the proximative in Tok Pisin. *Language* 75(2): 322–346.

Ross, G. 2005. Partial creolization, restructuring and convergence in Bay Islands Englishes. *English World-Wide* 26(1): 43–76.

Sánchez, L. 2003. Quechua-Spanish Bilingualism. Interference and Convergence in Functional Categories. Amsterdam: John Benjamins.

Sánchez, L. 2004. Functional convergence in the tense, evidentiality and aspectual systems of Quechua-Spanish bilinguals. *Bilingualism: Language and Cognition* 7(2): 147–162.

Sánchez, L. Forthcoming. "Kechwa-Spanish bilingual grammars: testing hypotheses on functional interference and convergence" accepted for publication in *International Journal of Bilingual Education and Bilingualism*.

Schwartz, B. and R. Sprouse. 1996. L2 cognitive states and the full transfer/full access model. *Second Language Research* 12: 40–72.

Siegel, J. 1998. Substrate reinforcement and dialectal differences in Melanesian Pidgin. *Journal of Sociolinguistics*. 2(3): 347-373

Siegel, J. 2004. Morphological elaboration. *Journal of Pidgin and Creole Languages* 19(2): 333–362.

White, L. 2003. Fossilization at the steady state: Persistent problems with inflectional morphology. *Bilingualism: Language and Cognition* 6(2): 129–141.

# FROM GBE TO HAITIAN:
## THE MULTI-STAGE EVOLUTION OF SYLLABLE STRUCTURE[*]

Anne-Marie Brousseau and Emmanuel Nikiema
*University of Toronto*

In this paper, we examine the syllable properties of Haitian from the perspective of the elements of grammar that are responsible for the underlying representation of consonant sequences. We compare some aspects of the syllabic structure of Haitian to that of its contributing languages (French and Gbe) to determine how the properties of Haitian syllables can be traced to the properties of French and Gbe, given the processes involved in its genesis. We show that, while branching onsets are attested in Haitian, not all Obstruent-Liquid sequences can be analyzed as such. Some consonant sequences contain an intervening empty nuclear position. We propose a scenario for the genesis of Haitian syllable structure showing that the superficial similarities between Haitian and French were made possible by the existence of certain features of Gbe phonological grammar, namely the possibility of having empty nuclei in initial and medial syllables. This scenario adopts a multi-stage approach to the development of Haitian syllable structure, based on the distinction between second language use and second language acquisition.

## 1. *Introduction*

In this paper, we examine the syllable properties of Haitian by analyzing the elements of grammar responsible for the underlying representation of consonant sequences. We compare certain aspects of the syllabic structure of Haitian to that of its main contributing languages (French and Gbe) to determine how the properties of Haitian syllables can be traced to the properties of these languages, given the processes involved in the genesis of Haitian. We show that, while branching onsets are attested in Haitian, not all Obstruent-Liquid sequences should be analyzed as such. Some consonant sequences contain an intervening empty nuclear position. We propose a scenario for the genesis of Haitian syllable structure in which the superficial similarities between Haitian and French were made possible by the existence of certain features of Gbe phonological grammar, namely the possibility of having empty nuclei in initial and medial syllables.

The basic assumption behind our scenario is that the emergence of a creole is a particular case of second language acquisition (e.g., Anderson 1983). This is in line with Valdman (1983), who defines creolization as the "crystallization and subsequent elaboration of an autonomous interlanguage system" (p. 214).

---

[*] We would like to thank the participants in the Montreal Dialogues workshop and especially our discussant, Heather Goad, for their valuable comments.

If a creole equates to an interlanguage in a contact situation, we need to determine what mechanisms set the grammar of the creole/interlanguage apart from both the substrate/first language and the superstrate/second language. These mechanisms may involve general properties determined by Universal Grammar and transfer from the substrate (from a creolistic standpoint) or transfer from L1 (from a second language acquisition standpoint). In fact, there is an ongoing debate in both fields as to whether a sensible scenario of creole/ interlanguage development can be explained mostly, or even entirely, by either transfer or universals. We will adopt an intermediate view, which combines both concepts (cf. Alber & Plag 2001; Uffmann 2003, for a similar view of the phonology of creoles). From the standpoint of second language acquisition, we will adopt the "Full Transfer/Full Access Mode Hypothesis" (see section 5.1). From a creolistic point of view, we will adopt Anderson's (1983) "Transfer to Somewhere Principle" and we will follow Mufwene (1991), extending the morphosyntactic strategies he proposes to phonological strategies:

> A grammatical form will occur consistently and to a significant extent in the interlan-guage as a result of transfer if and only if (1) natural acquisition principles are consis-tent with the L1 structure or (2) there already exists within the L2 input the potential for (mis-)generalization from the input to produce the same form or structure. (Anderson 1983: 182).

> [Pidgins and creoles] seem to inherit their morphosyntactic strategies from some of the languages of the contact situation, a formative strategy predicted by USLAH [Universals of Second Language Acquisition Hypothesis]. In this, case "universals" may be interpreted as the regulatory principles that determine which grammatical features of the lexifier or of some other languages of the contact situation will be selected by a [pidgin or a creole]. (Mufwene 1991:137)

The paper is organized as follows. In the first three sections, we present in turn the syllable structures of the languages under comparison: Haitian (section 2), French (section 3), and Gbe languages (section 4), particularly Fongbe and Gengbe.[1] The presentation highlights the general features of the syllable struc-tures and focuses on justifying the representations that underlie consonant sequences of the type Obstruent-Liquid (O-L). In section 5, we discuss the similarities and differences between Haitian and its contributing languages and we propose a scenario of the emergence of the mixed properties of Haitian. We conclude briefly in section 6.

---

[1] Fongbe and Gengbe (also known as Mina) are two of the five main varieties that constitute the Gbe dialect cluster. The other three are Vhegbe (also known as Ewe), Ajagbe and Phla-Phera. Fongbe is the substrate language that played the most prominent role in the genesis of Haitian (see Lefebvre 1998 and the references therein).

## 2. *The syllabic structure of Haitian*

The syllable inventory of Haitian (cf. Anestin 1987; Cadely 1988, 1994; Valdman 1978) includes much more than the universal CV syllable. There are also V syllables (empty onsets), CCV syllables (branching onsets) and (C)VC strings, some of which may reasonably be analyzed as codas. All consonants (except [ɲ]) in Haitian are attested in prevocalic position, and with the exception of the rhotic [ɣ], any consonant is allowed in postvocalic position. Sequences of consonants are found both word-initially and word-medially, some of which are tautosyllabic and others heterosyllabic (i.e., consisting of either coda-onset clusters or onset-empty nucleus-onset sequences).

(1) Haitian consonant phonotactics[2]

| | Initial | | | | | | | Medial | | | | | | |
|---|---|---|---|---|---|---|---|---|---|---|---|---|---|---|
| | w | j | l | ɣ | m | n | X | w | j | l | ɣ | m | n | X |
| p | + | + | + | + | − | − | | + | + | + | + | + | − | s, t |
| b | + | + | + | + | − | − | | + | + | + | + | − | 1 | s |
| t | + | + | − | + | − | − | | + | + | + | + | + | + | s |
| d | + | + | 1 | + | 1 | − | | + | + | 3 | + | + | + | s |
| k | + | 2 | + | + | − | 1 | s/1 | + | + | + | + | + | + | s, t |
| g | + | − | + | + | − | − | | + | + | + | + | + | − | z |
| ʧ | 2 | − | − | − | − | − | | − | − | − | − | − | − | |
| ʤ | − | − | − | − | − | − | | − | − | − | − | − | − | |
| f | + | + | + | + | − | − | | + | + | + | + | + | 1 | |
| v | + | + | + | + | − | − | | + | + | + | + | + | + | |
| s | + | + | − | − | − | − | t/1 | + | + | + | + | + | − | |
| z | + | 1 | − | − | − | − | | + | + | 1 | − | + | 2 | |
| ʃ | + | + | − | − | − | − | | + | − | − | + | + | − | |
| ʒ | + | − | − | − | − | − | | + | + | − | + | + | 1 | |
| m | + | + | − | − | − | − | | + | + | − | + | + | + | |
| n | + | + | − | − | − | − | | + | + | − | 2 | + | − | |
| ɲ | | | | | | | | + | − | − | − | − | − | |
| l | + | + | − | − | − | − | | + | + | − | 1 | + | − | |
| ɣ | + | − | − | − | − | − | | − | + | − | − | − | − | |
| w | − | − | − | − | − | − | | − | − | − | − | − | − | |
| j | − | − | − | − | − | − | | − | − | − | − | − | − | |

Phonotactic constraints restrict the possible sequences of consonants. As shown in (1), sequences in initial position consist of any consonant followed

---

[2] The table in (1) was devised by examining all of the words in three dictionaries of Haitian: Bentolila (1976), Valdman (1981), and Ebenezer Mission (no date). The coding is as follows: (i) X stands for other consonants that occur marginally as the second consonant of a cluster (e.g., /ks/, /st/ in initial position); (ii) [ɲ] is never allowed in word-initial position, which explains the systematic gaps in the left-hand side of the table; (iii) where only one or two occurrences of the given cluster are found in the dictionaries consulted, this is indicated with a numeral.

by a glide, an obstruent followed by a liquid, or [f]/[v] followed by a liquid. However, a significantly larger set of combinations is found in word-medial position, which suggests that many consonant sequences in this position are heterosyllabic.

Focusing on the positions occupied by consonants in syllable structures, we now examine the various structures accommodating sequences of consonants (especially Obstruent-Liquid) and single consonants in word-final position.

### 2.1 Consonant sequences in initial and medial positions

Obstruent-Liquid sequences that are best analyzed as branching onsets are attested in Haitian. These sequences present the unmarked sonority profile that is typically found in onsets cross-linguistically (i.e., non-coronal obstruent followed by liquid), as shown in (2). However, we claim that not all O-L sequences in Haitian should be analyzed as tautosyllabic. O-L sequences such as those in (3a), as well as O-N and O-O sequences in (3b), may not constitute branching onsets.

(2)  a.  Initial O-L sequences

| flè | [flɛ] | 'flower' | grès | [gγɛs] | 'grease' |
| glas | [glas] | 'ice' | tris | [tγis] | 'sad' |
| ble | [ble] | 'blue' | krikèt | [kγikɛt] | 'cricket (insect)' |

     b.  Medial O-L sequences

| tranble | [tγãnble] | 'to shake' | agreyab | [agγejab] | 'agreeable' |
| eklèsi | [eklɛsi] | 'clearing (weather)' | ekri | [ekγi] | 'to write' |
| aplodi | [aplodi] | 'to cheer' | apre | [apγe] | 'after' |

(3) Non-typical consonant sequences

     a.  C-L sequences           b.  Other C-C sequences

| patisri | [patisγi] | 'pastry' | fabnak | [fabnak] | 'plastic shoe' |
| galri | [galγi] | 'gallery' | kondiktè | [kɔ̃diktɛ] | 'driver' |
| bouchri | [buʃγi] | 'butcher shop' | pwopte | [pwɔpte] | 'cleanliness' |
| vazlin | [vazlin] | 'petroleum jelly' | dejne | [deʒne] | 'breakfast' |
| matlo | [matlo] | 'sailor' | gadkòt | [gadkɔt] | 'body guard' |
| tannri | [tãnγi] | 'tannery' | kadna | [kadna] | 'padlock' |

While it is uncontroversial that the O-L sequences in (2) constitute branching onsets, another analysis is needed for the consonant sequences in (3) for the following two reasons. First, they never occur in word-initial position in Haitian, as the table in (1) shows, which is unexpected if they constitute branching onsets. Second, most of them do not correspond to typical branching onsets in that they do not exhibit the phonotactic restrictions typical of tautosyllabic consonants. For example, we find sequences of two obstruents (e.g., [kɔ̃diktɛ], [gadkɔt]), coronals before [l] (e.g., [vazlin], [matlo]), and sequences of two sonorants (e.g., [galγi], [tãnγi]).

The sequences in (3) could alternatively be analyzed as coda-onset sequences, thus explaining the absence of such sequences in word-initial position and the apparent violations of the phonotactic constraints that characterize branching onsets. While this alternative may account for forms such as *kondiktè, pwopte* and *gadkòt*, it leads in all other cases to a violation of the Sonority Sequencing Principle (Clements 1990; Selkirk 1982), which states that the consonant in onset position cannot have a higher degree of sonority than the consonant in the preceding coda.[3]

In order to avoid the sonority violation, we suggest, following Bhatt and Nikiema (in press) that the consonant sequences in (3) are separated by an empty nucleus. Forms such as *galri* and *bouchri* are thus trisyllabic: /galØɣi/ and /buʃØɣi/. In other words, the consonants in the sequence are not adjacent, but rather syllabify in two successive onset positions, as shown in (4).

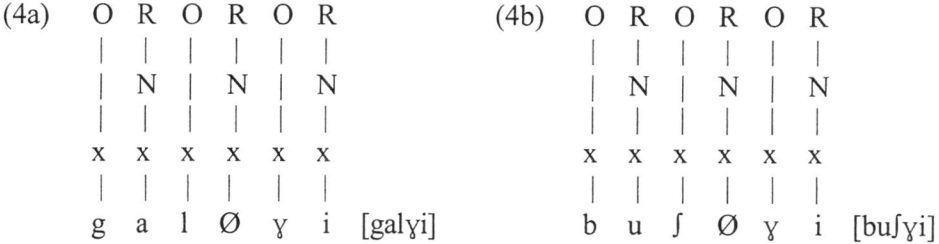

The presence of the intervening empty nucleus accounts for the absence of co-occurrence restrictions between the consonants in (3). It also accounts for the restricted distribution of these sequences, which are never found word-initially (or word-finally).

In sum, the sequences of consonants that are allowed word-initially are syllabified as branching onsets in both initial and medial positions while the atypical sequences that are found only word-medially occupy the onsets of two successive syllables, the first of which contains an empty nucleus. We do not analyze most word-internal sequences in (3b) as involving coda consonants for two reasons. First, they do not exhibit the asymmetry that characterizes coda-onset sequences. For example, if [tk] in [lɛtkaye] 'buttermilk' is assigned to a coda-onset structure, then the reverse sequence [kt] in [ɔktɔb] 'October' cannot have the same syllabic structure. Second, given that the coda is a structurally weak position, consonants appearing in coda position typically constitute a well-defined class of segments. For instance, Italian and Japanese allow only sonorants as single consonants in coda position (Itô 1988). In

---

[3] Other alternatives could be considered for the O-L sequences in (3a), namely that the liquid forms a complex consonant with the preceding obstruent or that the liquid forms a light diphthong with the following vowel. These alternate representations are ruled out for the same reasons as the equivalent representations in Gbe languages, as we will see in section 3.1.

Haitian, however, almost all consonants may appear as the first member of a word-internal consonant sequence. This lack of restriction suggests that such sequences contain an intervening empty nucleus.

### 2.2 Single consonants in word-final position

Haitian word-final consonants have traditionally been analyzed as codas (Anestin 1987; Cadely 1988, 1994). However, Nikiema (1999) and Bhatt and Nikiema (in press) argue that these word-final consonants are better analyzed as onsets of empty-headed syllables. As such, we analyze lexical items with a single word-final consonant, such as *rapid* 'fast', *legal* 'legal' or *piblik* 'public', as containing a final empty nucleus as in (5) below.

(5)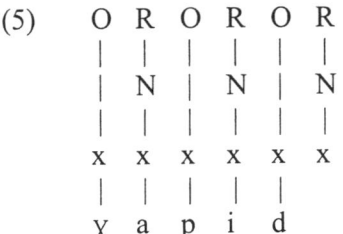

Almost all consonants of Haitian may appear in word-final position. This provides a first argument for syllabifying these consonants as onsets rather than codas. Proposals based on similar observations are found in the literature (Charette 1991; Goad & Brannen 2003; Kaye 1990; Piggott 1991, 1999) to account for various properties of word-final consonants in many genetically unrelated languages. A second argument stems from the way word-final consonants determine the allomorphic variation of the definite determiner. Paradoxically, the initial floating consonant of the definite determiner is realized after a consonant (*chat la* [ʃatla] 'the cat') but not after a vowel (*papa a* [papaa] 'the father'), as illustrated below.

(6) a.  **[la]** (oral consonant and oral vowel)
/ʃat + la/          [ʃatla]              'the cat'
/bagaj + la/        [bagajla]            'the thing'

b.  **[lã]** (oral consonant and obligatory nasal vowel)
/bãk + la/          [bãklã]              'the bank'
/plãt + la/         [plãtlã]             'the plant'

c.  **[na]** or **[nã]** (nasal consonant followed by an oral or nasal vowel)
/madam + la/        [madamna] or [madãmnã]   'the lady'
/wasin + la/        [wasinna] or [wasinnã]   'the root'

d.  **[nã]** (nasal consonant and nasal vowel)
/vyann + la/        [vjãnnã]             'the meat'
/ʒanm + la/         [ʒãmnã]              'the leg'

e.  [a] ('consonant deletion' followed by oral vowel)
    /papa + la/          [papaa]                 'the father'
    /bujwa + la/         [bujwaa]                'the kettle'

f.  [ã] ('consonant deletion' followed by nasal vowel)
    /laʒã + la/          [laʒãã]                 'the money'
    /dã + la/            [dãã]                   'the tooth'

To sum up, words that end in a consonant (cf. 6a–d) combine with the consonant-initial allomorph to create a sequence of two consonants, while words that end in a vowel (cf. 6e–f), combine with the vowel-initial allomorph to create a sequence of two vowels. This pattern is the exact opposite of that observed in languages such as French, where underlying consonants are usually retained before an empty onset (e.g., *grand étang* [gRãtetã] 'big pond') and dropped before a full onset (e.g., *grand lac* [gRãlak] 'big lake') in order to maintain a well-formed onset-rhyme structure (see Charette 1991).

The question thus arises as to why Haitian would create a sequence of two consonants when an empty onset allomorph is available and conversely create a sequence of two vowels when a consonant-initial allomorph is available. We can offer a natural explanation to this seemingly unnatural process if we adopt the hypothesis that the phonological representation of the determiner *la* includes a floating consonant, that is, a consonant that is not linked to the syllable structure.

(7) The floating consonant of the determiner /la/ (Cadely 1994; Nikiema 1999)

The floating consonant hypothesis is motivated by the fact that the patterns exhibited by the allomorphs of the determiner /la/ can be reduced to an l/Ø alternation that is typical of floating consonants.

Recall that, in forms such as [ʃat] 'cat,' the stem-final consonant is in the onset of a syllable with an empty nucleus while the determiner [la] includes an empty onset. The concatenation of these two forms results in a sequence of two adjacent empty positions (8a), which violates the conditions of proper government (see Nikiema 1999 for details). The floating [l] is forced to anchor to the onset position to rescue the structure, as shown in (8b).

(8) a.                                  b.

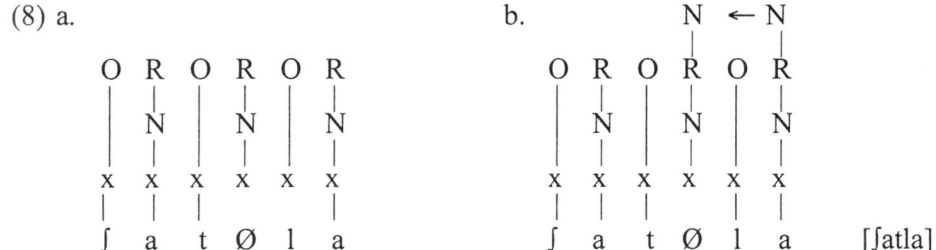

                                                                          [ʃatla]

According to the Empty Category Principle, or ECP (Kaye, Lowenstamm & Vergnaud 1990), empty positions in a phonological structure need to be properly governed. Because government is strictly local, this analysis predicts that only one of the two empty positions can be properly governed. Therefore, one of the two empty positions will necessarily violate the ECP, hence ruling out the entire form. In other words, if the final nucleus properly governs the empty onset in (8a) above, the final empty nucleus of the lexical item will not be governed. The floating consonant is anchored in exactly this context to avoid an ECP violation (8b). The floating consonant links to the empty onset (its sole available position) and leaves the government relation to occur between the two nuclei at the projection level. The non-final empty nucleus of [ʃat] is now properly governed by the vowel of [la]. Since the two consonants are linked to two onsets (rather than a coda and an onset), the consonant sequences do not have to obey the Sonority Sequencing Principle, as is the case with the sequences in (3a).

Let us examine now the derivation of [papaa] 'the father' provided in (9).

(9)

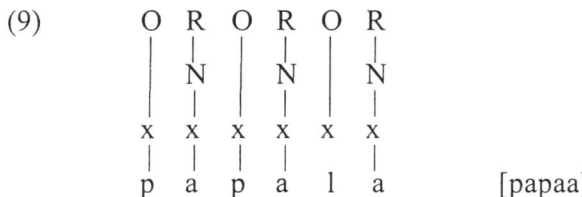

                              [papaa]

In this form, the determiner follows a vowel-final stem. Surprisingly, the floating consonant does not surface and a hiatus is created. This happens because the empty position containing the floating consonant is properly governed by the final vowel. Since nothing forces it to do so, the floating [l] does not anchor to the onset position and the form [papaa] results.

In [papaa], since the proper government between the empty onset and the following nucleus is linearly adjacent, it holds at the segmental level (the vowel governs the empty position in the onset). In [ʃatla], however, the government relation is between the two nuclei at the projection level.

To summarize, the underlying representation of the determiner /la/ consists of a bipositional syllable with an empty onset position. In forms such as [papaa], the empty onset position is properly governed by the following vowel. In forms such as [ʃatla], suffixation of /la/ creates a sequence of two empty positions that are subject to the ECP. The floating consonant is anchored in this context to avoid an ECP violation, producing the surface form [ʃatla] rather than *[ʃata].

The arguments provided so far seem to completely rule out the existence of codas in Haitian. As we have seen, forms such as *rapid*, *legal* or *chat* are best analyzed as containing a final consonant in the onset of an empty-headed syllable. However, another account may be needed for forms that exhibit medial CCC and CC sequences, such as those in (10).

(10)  a.  CCC medial sequences                          b.  CC medial sequences
         [ɛsklav]         'slave'                            [lɛtkaje]      'buttermilk'
         [elɛktɣik]       'electric'                         [saʒfam]       'midwife'
         [ẽskɣipsjɔ̃]      'inscription'                      [ɔktɔb]        'October'

The CCC sequences in (10a) constitute the best argument for the existence of a coda position in Haitian. As we have seen above, empty nuclei need to be properly governed (ECP) and phonological government is strictly local. Hence, these CCC sequences cannot be analyzed as three onsets [CØCØC], nor can they be analyzed as [CØCC] where the last two consonants constitute a branching onset. In the former case, the first empty nucleus would not be properly governed because of the locality condition imposed on governing relations (i.e., it is not adjacent to any possible governor). In the latter case, the empty nucleus is not licensed because the following branching onset, being the domain of a government relationship, is a barrier to proper government. Therefore, the CCC sequence must constitute a coda followed by a branching onset.

As for the CC sequences in (10b), there is no principled way to determine whether they are syllabified as two onsets or a coda-onset sequence. On the one hand, the sequences can be analyzed as coda-onset since they do not violate the Sonority Sequencing Principle (in contrast to those in (3a) already discussed). On the other hand, they can be analyzed as [CØC] since Haitian allows empty nuclei and an empty nucleus would be properly governed in this case. One possible distinguishing criterion is whether or not the sequences exhibit asymmetry in distribution. For example, the presence in Haitian of [ks] as in *aksidan* 'accident' and its reverse sequence [sk] as in *diskou* 'speech' suggests that both sequences cannot be analyzed as coda-onset sequences. If [sk] is a coda-onset sequence, then [ks] has to be analyzed as containing an empty nucleus. Such reverse sequences are attested in Haitian, such as those observed in *lètkaye/oktòb* and *metsin* 'medicine'/*istwa* 'story'. Because of the special status of [s] in syllabification patterns observed cross-linguistically, the unmarked hypothesis would be to propose that s-C sequences are coda-onset sequences, and that the reverse C-s sequences contain an empty nucleus. In fact, the presence of codas is expected in Haitian since the syllable structure includes branching onsets. According to the syllable markedness theory proposed in Kaye and Lowenstamm (1981) and Cairns & Feinstein (1982), the presence of branching onsets in a language entails the presence of branching rhymes. In sum, we have clear cases of codas in (10a) and possible cases of codas in (10b), although not for each form.

There are many Haitian words containing Ct sequences as in *oktòb* and *septanb* 'September', but very few with the reverse sequence tC as in *lètkaye* and *lotbò* 'across'. Given this segmental asymmetry, we need two different representations for these sequences, namely a coda-onset sequence or an alternative with two onsets separated by an empty nucleus. The former option is less marked than the latter because the latter requires additional principles of the grammar such as the ECP (Kaye, Lowenstamm & Vergnaud 1990) to account for the distribution of empty-headed syllables. The challenge is thus to determine which sequence should be assigned to which structure.

If one considers *lètkaye* as involving a coda-onset structure, then the low frequency of [tk] sequences in Haitian words would not correlate with the unmarked status of a coda-onset structure. Such a proposal would lead to a paradox in which more frequent sequences ([kt], [pt]) are assigned to the marked structure, whereas less frequent ones are assigned to the unmarked structure. Furthermore, unlike the common sequences [kt] and [pt], sequences such as [tk] and [tb] (in *lètkaye* and *lotbò*) are derived either from schwa deletion in the corresponding French etymon or from juxtaposition of two words (*lèt* + *kaye* and *lòt* + *bò* respectively). If, on the other hand, *oktòb* is assigned to a coda-onset structure, the consonant with a place feature (labial or dorsal) is in the weak (coda) position, whereas the placeless consonant (coronal) is in the onset. This is an unexpected situation, since in normal circumstances one expects the reverse (i.e., the placeless consonant to appear in the weak position). Note, however, that it is precisely in this context that the two consonants need to agree in voicing; they have both a [−voice] specification as exemplified in forms such as *elektrik* 'electric' and *adopte* 'to adopt', in contrast with forms such as *lotbò*. One may interpret this voicing requirement as a way to rescue the structure.

Incidentally, forms such as those in (10a) provide another argument supporting the existence of branching onsets in Haitian. If, on the contrary, CCC sequences as in *esklav* were to be analyzed as $/C_1C_2\emptyset C_3/$ sequences, the first consonant would be in a coda, while the second and third consonants would be in onsets with an intervening empty nucleus. This configuration would lead to a violation of Government-Licensing (Charette 1991) because: (i) the coda ($C_1$) needs to be governed by the following onset ($C_2$); (ii) the onset ($C_2$) needs to be licensed by a vowel in the nucleus of the same syllable in order to govern the preceding coda; (iii) since the nucleus is empty, the onset is not licensed and cannot govern the coda. This is precisely the reason why schwa does not delete in French forms such as *gouvernement* 'government', *garderie* 'daycare' and *chasteté* 'chastity.' In Haitian, forms such as those in (10a) would be the only case where Government-Licensing is violated if we were to reject the existence of branching onsets. We therefore reiterate that branching onsets are part of Haitian syllabic properties.

Overall, the syllable structures of Haitian are combinations of onsets (simple or branching) and rhymes (simple or branching), with each being able to dominate an empty position. Empty onsets are straightforwardly found in V-initial syllables. The presence of word-internal empty nuclei accounts for the fact that consonants that appear to be adjacent as in *kozri* 'talk' or *dejne* 'breakfast' are actually in the onsets of two adjacent syllables and therefore do not violate the Sonority Sequencing Principle. Moreover, the presence of empty nuclei accounts for the paradoxical distribution of the definite determiner in Haitian, which creates sequences of consonants or vowels.

## 3. *The syllabic structure of French*

In this section, we offer a cursory presentation of French syllable structure. Because of the abundant literature on French phonology and due to space limitations, we voluntarily limit our discussion of French syllables to aspects relevant to our comparison with Haitian and Gbe (for detailed accounts, see Dell 1985; Encrevé 1988; Schane 1968; Tranel 1981). With the notable exception of Lowenstamm (1996), all researchers agree that French allows branching rhymes (coda consonants) and branching onsets, that is, sequences of syllable-initial tautosyllabic consonants (Charette 1991; Dell 1985; Encrevé 1988; Kaye & Lowenstamm 1984). The consonants within typical branching onsets are combined in accordance with cross-linguistic phonotactic constraints or, in the terminology of Clements and Keyser (1983: 31), Syllable Structure Conditions. For example, a well-formed branching onset in French consists of a [–sonorant] consonant followed by another consonant specified as [+sonorant, –nasal]. Hence, a typical branching onset consists of any Obstruent-Liquid sequence except Coronal-Coronal and Coronal Fricative-Sonorant. These sequences define what Dell (1995: 7) calls obligatory clusters in French.

(11)  Typical branching onsets: obligatory clusters
      /pl, pr, bl, br, fl, fr, vl, vr, tr, dr, kl, kr, gl, gr/

We know that the above clusters do not exhaust all possible combinations of consonants observed in word-initial position in French (see Dell 1995: 11). In particular, sC sequences are exhibited in forms such as *spécial* 'special' and *stade* 'stadium' (cf. 12a). While sC sequences are common in the language, other sequences observed word-initially (cf. 12b) are rare, many of them occurring only in loanwords. We will not discuss these here because of their low frequency and their atypical sonority profile (i.e., many exhibit the same two consonants as in (12b) but in reverse order).

(12)  Other word-initial sequences
   a.  /sp, st, sk, sl, sm, sn, sv, sf, spl, spr, str, skl, skr/
   b.  /pn, ps, pf, pt, kn, km, kv, ks, kt, tl, tm, ts, tʃ, gn, gz, zl, zv, zb, zgr, mn, ft/

Note that Dell (1995) does not include Consonant-Glide (CG) sequences (e.g., [pje] 'foot,' [bwa] 'wood') among French clusters. In fact, there is no compelling argument to syllabify these sequences as branching onsets. Given the limits of this paper, we will assume without further discussion that glides are syllabified in the nucleus, forming a light diphthong with the following vowel (Bullock 2002; Kaye & Lowenstamm 1984; Kelly 2004).

The examples below illustrate French forms with typical branching onset consonants.

(13)  Typical branching onsets
   a.  Initial O-L sequences

| | | | | | |
|---|---|---|---|---|---|
| *fleur* | [flœR] | 'flower' | *graisse* | [gRɛs] | 'grease' |
| *glace* | [glas] | 'ice' | *triste* | [tRist] | 'sad' |
| *plaie* | [plɛ] | 'wound | *crochet* | [kRoʃɛ] | 'hook' |

   b.  Medial O-L sequences

| | | | | | |
|---|---|---|---|---|---|
| *trembler* | [tRãble] | 'to shake' | *agréable* | [agRejabl] | 'agreeable' |
| *éclater* | [eklate] | 'to burst' | *après* | [apRɛ] | 'after' |
| *couplet* | [kuplɛ] | 'verse' | *souscrire* | [suskRiR] | 'to subscribe' |

For word-internal consonants, Dell notes that there are many medial clusters that are not attested word-initially. Therefore such sequences must be parsed as heterosyllabic. The following assumptions are made.

(14)  Parsing of consonants in French (Dell 1995: 14)
   a.  a prevocalic consonant is tautosyllabic with the following vowel;
   b.  in an obligatory cluster (cf. (11) above), the two consonants are        tautosyllabic;
   c.  a postvocalic consonant is tautosyllabic with the preceding vowel,        provided no conflict arises with (a) and (b) above.

The first assumption ensures that a form such as *cinéma* 'cinema' will be parsed as *ci.né.ma* instead of *cin.ém.a*, whereas the second requires that *abri* 'shelter' be parsed as *a.bri* and not *ab.ri*. Finally, the third assumption ensures that *estropié* 'crippled' will be parsed as *es.tro.pié*.

A crucial aspect of French phonology is the presence of a rule that obligatorily deletes schwa after a VC sequence belonging to the same word as in /proʃte/ (*projeter* 'to project') and /atlaʒ/ (*attelage* 'harness'). This rule is particularly important since the deleted schwa is never observed in creole forms, as we will see in section 5. Due to the existence of this schwa deletion rule,[4] Dell (1995: 8) claims that any VCCV sequence occurring at the phonetic level may derive from an underlying /VCCV/ or /VCØCV/, and determining the underlying representation is not a trivial matter. Fortunately, the syllabification of VCCV sequences is more transparent in French than in Haitian, because in addition to the parsing rules in (14), Dell (1995: 16) posits that in French, a coda contains at most one consonant.

The consequences of the above assumptions are: (i) that word-final clusters (e.g., *astre* [astR] 'star', *sarcle* [sarRkl] 'hoe (verb form)') are coda plus onset sequences, and (ii) that a rhyme may end in one consonant at most, forcing the analysis of medial CCC sequences (e.g., *obstacle* [ɔpstakl] 'obstacle', *astral* [astRal] 'astral') as containing an empty-headed syllable. The data in (16) below illustrate coda consonants in French. We contrast them with the ones in (15) in order to show that a surface VCCV sequence in French may be derived from either /VCCV/ or /VCØCV/.

(15) Consonants followed by schwa

| *pâtisserie* | [patisRi] | 'pastry' |
|---|---|---|
| *samedi* | [samdi] | 'Saturday |
| *vaseline* | [vazlin] | 'petroleum jelly' |
| *tannerie* | [tanRi] | 'tannery' |
| *cadenas* | [kadna] | 'padlock' |

(16) Coda consonants

| *soldat* | [sɔlda] | 'private (army)' |
|---|---|---|
| *partie* | [paRti] | 'part' |
| *somnoler* | [sɔmnɔle] | 'to doze off' |
| *souscrire* | [suskRiR] | 'to subscribe' |
| *surprise* | [syRpRiz] | 'surprise' |

The surface consonant sequences in (15) all derive from schwa deletion, whereas those in (16) are underlying clusters. Except for [samdi], the forms in (15) cannot be analyzed as including coda-onset sequences because they would violate the Sonority Sequencing Principle. Furthermore, as Dell (1995) notes, assuming the presence of a schwa is the only way to avoid exceptions in otherwise exception-less patterns. This is precisely the case for the form [samdi], for which the expected pronunciation would be *[sãdi] according to the pattern of vowel nasalization (Dell 1985; Schane 1968), unless a schwa were posited between the two consonants.

In conclusion, French allows for branching onsets and branching rhymes (coda consonants), as well as empty-headed syllables (onset followed by an empty nucleus) and empty onsets (V(C) syllables).

---

[4] In the theoretical framework we adopt here, schwa is the phonetic realization of an empty nucleus that cannot remain empty because of a violation of the ECP. Dell's schwa deletion rule may be reformulated as follows: an empty nucleus remains empty (not phonetically realized) after a VC sequence belonging to the same word provided that it is properly governed.

## 4. *The syllabic structure of Gbe languages*

It is well accepted that Kwa languages in general and Gbe lects in particular are maximally CV (Greenberg 1963; Welmers 1973). Syllables in these languages contain maximally one onset position and one nuclear position. This is what we will refer to as the CV hypothesis. The problem with the CV hypothesis for Gbe lects is that they all exhibit sequences of consonants in both word-initial and word-medial position. For example, consonant sequences consisting of an obstruent followed by a liquid are very common in Gbe lects, as one can see from the table of possible combinations in (17) below.[5]

(17)  Fongbe consonant phonotactics

| | **Initial** | | | | | | **Medial** | | | | | |
|---|---|---|---|---|---|---|---|---|---|---|---|---|
| | w | j | l | r | m | n | w | j | l | r | m | n |
| t | | ?/1 | (+) | + | − | − | [+] | − | (+) | + | − | − |
| d | | − | (+) | + | − | − | [+] | − | (+) | + | − | − |
| k | [+] | ?/1 | + | − | − | − | [+] | − | + | − | − | − |
| g | [+] | ?/1 | + | − | − | − | [+] | − | + | − | − | − |
| ʧ | | + | (+)/1 | + | − | − | [+] | + | (+) | + | − | − |
| ʤ | | − | (+) | + | − | − | [+] | − | (+) | + | − | − |
| kp | | − | + | − | − | − | [+] | + | + | − | − | − |
| gb | | − | + | − | − | − | | + | + | − | − | − |
| xw | | −/1 | + | − | − | − | | − | + | − | − | − |
| ɣw | | −/4 | + | − | − | − | | − | + | − | − | − |
| f | + | + | + | − | − | − | [+] | + | + | − | − | − |
| v | +/− | + | + | − | − | − | [+] | + | + | − | − | − |
| s | [+] | + | (+) | + | − | − | [+] | + | (+) | + | − | − |
| z | [+] | +/1 | (+) | + | − | − | [+] | − | − | − | − | − |
| x | | +/1 | + | − | − | − | | − | + | − | − | − |
| ɣ | | + | + | − | − | − | | − | + | − | − | − |
| b | | + | + | − | − | − | [+] | − | + | − | − | − |
| ɖ | | +/1 | − | − | − | − | [+] | − | − | − | − | − |
| m | [+] | + | + | − | − | − | | + | + | − | − | − |
| n | | − | − | − | − | − | | − | − | − | − | − |
| ɲ | | − | (+) | + | − | − | | — | (+) | + | − | − |
| l | [+] | + | − | − | − | − | [+] | + | − | − | − | − |
| w | | +/1 | + | − | − | − | | − | + | − | − | − |
| j | [+] | − | (+) | + | − | − | | − | (+) | + | − | − |

---

[5] The table in (17) groups the phonotactic constraints listed in Capo (1991) with those that we devised by examining all of the words in Segurola and Rassinoux's (2000) dictionary. The coding is as follows: (i) cases where results from Capo (1991) and Segurola and Rassinoux (2000) are not consistent are indicated as follows: signs on the left of the slash are those in Capo (1991) while numbers on the right of the slash indicate the number of occurrences found in Segurola and Rassinoux (2000) for the combination in question; (ii) ? indicates a marginally acceptable form according to Capo (1991); (iii) (+) signifies that [l] appears in allophonic variation with [r] following coronals; (iv) [+] indicates the [w] in question is derived from the initial [+round] vowel of a VV string. Note that in Gbe, [ɣ] is a fricative, the voiced equivalent of [x].

Note that most obstruents can combine with non-nasal sonorants (i.e., liquids and glides), the exceptions being the complex consonants (ʍ, ɣw, kp and gb), which combine only with liquids. Given that the consonant inventory of Gbe lects is larger than that of French, the set of possible O-L and O-G combinations is also larger. No other types of consonant sequences are allowed in Gbe lects besides O-L and O-G, an observation that will prove important in the discussion to follow.

There are three generalizations that are known to be true for all Gbe lects, and any adequate analysis of the syllable structure of these languages must account for them. For ease of future reference, we name them as follows:

Generalization 1: The only consonant sequences observed in Gbe lects consist of an obstruent followed by a non-nasal sonorant (liquid or glide).

Generalization2: Almost all consonants in Gbe (including labio-velars, palatals and sonorants) may be followed by a liquid, and most may be followed by a glide.

Generalization 3: No consonant is allowed in word- or syllable-final position.

The Fongbe data in (18) show that C-L sequences are very common and as one can see, almost any consonant of the language may be the first member within a sequence, including glides, nasal, complex and labialized consonants[6].

(18) a.  Cl

| | | |
|---|---|---|
| *klu* | [klu] | 'to scratch' |
| *kple* | [kple] | 'to gather' |
| *hwla* | [ɣwla] | 'to hide' |
| *vlɛ* | [vlɛ] | 'to imitate' |
| *bli* | [bli] | 'to roll' |
| *mla* | [mla] | 'to coil, to fold' |
| *wla* | [wla] | 'variety of yam' |

b.  Cl ~ Cr

| | | |
|---|---|---|
| *tli* | [tli/tri] | 'to be thick' |
| *tlan* | [tlã/trã] | 'excessively' |
| *dlo* | [dlo/dro] | 'not fully ripe' |
| *jlɛ* | [dʒlɛ/dʒrɛ] | 'quarrel' |
| *slan* | [sla_/sra_] | 'mockery' |
| *zlɔ̃* | [zlɔ̃/zrɔ̃] | 'to put down' |
| *slu* | [slu/sru] | 'to vomit' |

As is the case in other Gbe lects, the examples in (18b) show an allophonic variation between [r] and [l] when the preceding consonant is coronal (see Capo 1991 for details). As mentioned earlier, the problem raised by the above data is that the CLV forms seem to contradict the CV hypothesis. Welmers (1973: 26–27), Vogler (1976) and Bole-Richard (1983) claim that the CLV sequences observed in most Kwa, Gbe and Kru languages should be analyzed as disyllabic, that is, as CvLV where v represents a very short vowel which is typically not realized phonetically. Capo (1991: 127) makes the same hypothesis for many Gbe lects although he concludes that these sequences are tautosyllabic in his reconstruction of proto-Gbe.

---

[6] Because they are not relevant to the present discussion, tonal specifications have been omitted in all Gbe examples.

The challenge raised by the CLV sequences observed in Gbe languages is the need to reconcile their syllabification with the hypothesis that all Gbe lects are maximally CV. Theoretically, there are five possible ways of analyzing the CLV sequences observed in Fongbe.

### 4.1 Five possible representations for CLV sequences

If the CV hypothesis for Gbe lects is correct, we are left with only two general options in analyzing CCV canonical forms: (i) to treat the strings as monosyllabic and make the three elements fit into the two available temporal positions, or (ii) to posit that there is more than one syllable involved in such forms. The first option amounts to posit the presence of complex consonants (19c) or light diphthongs (19d). The second option suggests the presence of two syllables, the first consisting of a consonant followed by an empty nucleus (19e). If the CV hypothesis is not correct, however, we have two other options: the sonorant is part of a branching onset (19a) or it is part of a branching nucleus (19b). We will examine each of these possibilities in turn.

(19)   a.                  b.                  c.                  d.                  e.

### 4.1.1 The branching onset hypothesis (19a).

This representation assumes that the two consonants (the initial consonant and the liquid) belong to the same syllabic constituent, as is the case in languages where branching onsets are allowed. Typical branching onset languages are French, English, Spanish and Italian (Davis 1990; Dell 1995; Encrevé 1988, Harris 1983, 1994; Nespor & Vogel 1986; Selkirk 1982). In these languages, branching onsets exhibit co-occurrence restrictions such as the exclusion of nasals and glides as the first member of the sequence. In contrast, there is no motivated co-occurrence restriction in Gbe: word-initial sequences such as [wl], [nl], [zr] and [sr] are attested. Since such potential branching onsets are not attested in typical branching onset languages, they would be highly marked in Gbe lects.

We have also mentioned the presence of an allophonic variation between [r] and [l] depending on whether the preceding consonant is coronal or not. Such an allophonic variation of the sonorant based on the initial consonant is very atypical of branching onset languages. For instance, none of the Romance languages exhibit similar behavior.[7]

Another unusual aspect of this hypothesis is that according to Greenberg (1963), typical branching onset languages allow for word-final consonants. Similarly, according to the syllable markedness theory proposed in Kaye and Lowenstamm (1981) and Cairns & Feinstein (1982), the presence of branching onsets in a language entails the presence of branching rhymes. Given the absence of word and syllable-final consonants in Gbe languages, the implicational relation leads us to assume the absence of branching onsets as well. For all of these reasons, we reject the branching onset structure in (19a) as a possible representation of Gbe O-L sequences.

4.1.2 *The branching nucleus hypothesis (19b)*. The branching nucleus structure assumes that the liquid and the following vowel form a heavy diphthong. What is inconsistent with such a representation is that heavy diphthongs are generally composed of elements with decreasing sonority. In other words, the head of the branching nucleus should be the vowel and its complement, the following liquid. The representation in (19b) has the opposite order, making it a highly marked type of branching nucleus.

If such marked branching nuclei were to be attested in Gbe lects, one would expect less marked branching nuclei such as (tautosyllabic) long vowels to be found as well. Long vowels are not observed in Gbe lects, a gap that could not be accounted for if the grammar allowed for branching nuclei. Finally, the branching nucleus hypothesis would be unable to account for the allophonic variation between [r] and [l] when the first consonant is coronal. According to the Free Occurrence Principle (Kaye, 1985: 290), every possible onset in a language may normally combine with every possible nucleus to create a syllable. For all these reasons, we reject the branching nucleus structure for the analysis of CLV sequences.

4.1.3 *The complex consonant hypothesis (19c)*. This analysis assumes that the two consonants are not separate segments, but rather a complex consonant (i.e., a two-root node segment consisting of a [–continuant] [+continuant] sequence). The problem with this hypothesis is that languages with complex segments seldom exhibit the complete range of combinations of stop-liquid and fricative-liquid (Greenberg 1963; Maddieson 1984). In fact, none of the 217 languages examined in Maddieson (1984) contain a full range of complex segments and Gbe languages would be unusual in this respect.

---

[7] One could interpret the allophonic variation between [r] and [l] as an indication that O-L sequences are in fact branching onsets. The variation would result from the phonotactic constraint that disfavors [tl] onsets. However, since this variation is optional in many Gbe lects, we contend that it is a weak argument that does not hold up against the stronger arguments that rule out the branching onset hypothesis.

Furthermore, this hypothesis would force one to posit complex consonants of the type [ml] and [ɲl] which are unlikely to occur in any language. Another unusual aspect of this hypothesis is that when a nasal and oral consonant combine to make a complex consonant, they are generally homorganic. The Gbe data do not fit this generalization. Rather than the expected [mb] and [ŋg] homorganic sequences, we find unexpected sequences such as [ml] and [ɲl] in Gbe.

Finally, since true complex consonants such as [kp] and [gb] are attested in Fongbe, the presence of combinations such as [kpl] and [gbl] would force one to posit unlikely segments composed of three root nodes. For all of these reasons, we reject the complex segment hypothesis for the analysis of CLV sequences.

4.1.4 *The light diphthong hypothesis (19d)*. Light diphthongs are defined in Kaye (1985), Hyman (1985) and Schane (1987) as the linking of two vocalic segments to the same nuclear position. This hypothesis assumes that the liquid (a vocalic element) and the vowel are both linked to the same nuclear position. It would therefore account for the lack of co-occurrence restrictions in Gbe lects between the initial consonant and the rest of the sequence. However, it could not account for the allophonic variation of [l], which is realized as /r/ when the first consonant is coronal, since there is no principled co-occurrence restriction between an onset and a following nucleus (Free Occurrence Principle: Kaye 1985). We therefore reject this representation for the analysis of CLV sequences in Gbe lects.[8]

4.1.5 *The empty nucleus hypothesis (19e)*. A cursory examination led us to reject four of the structures proposed for the representation of CLV sequences, namely those associated with the branching onset hypothesis, the branching nucleus hypothesis, the complex consonant hypothesis and the light diphthong hypothesis. The only remaining hypothesis to examine is the disyllabic representation in (19e). Not only does this representation comply with all principles of syllabic structure, it is also consistent with other phonological properties of Gbe languages, including tonal and reduplicative patterns (not discussed here because of space limitations). In the next section, we present a distributional gap that can only be accounted for if CLV sequences are considered to be disyllabic.

4.2 *A distributional gap*
As is the case in Fongbe, CLV sequences are very common in all Gbe lects (Bole-Richard 1983; Capo 1991; Welmers 1973), in both word-initial (20) and

---

[8] More compelling arguments against a light diphthong structure based on tonal and reduplication patterns can be made, but due to space limitations, we are unable to explore these aspects in detail (see Nikiema 1995 for discussion).

word-medial (21) positions. Furthermore, it has been long observed that CVLV sequences are prohibited when the two vowels are identical.

(20) a. Cl

| | | | | b. Cl ~ Cr | | | |
|---|---|---|---|---|---|---|---|
| *klu* | [klu] | 'to scratch' | | *tli* | [tli/tri] | 'to be thick' |
| *kple* | [kple] | 'to gather' | | *tlan* | [tlã/trã] | 'excessively' |
| *hwla* | [ɣwla] | 'to hide' | | *dlo* | [dlo/dro] | 'not fully ripe' |
| *vlɛ* | [vlɛ] | 'to imitate' | | *jlɛ* | [ʤlɛ/dʒrɛ] | 'quarrel' |
| *bli* | [bli] | 'to roll' | | *slan* | [slã/srã] | 'mockery' |
| *mla* | [mla] | 'to coil, to fold' | | *zlɔ* | [zlɔ/zrɔ] | 'to put down' |
| *wla* | [wla] | 'variety of yam' | | *slu* | [slu/sru] | 'to vomit' |

(21) a. Cl

| | | |
|---|---|---|
| *aglo* | [aglo] | 'bag' |
| *kplakpla* | [kplakpla] | 'raffia mat' |
| *jaxwle* | [dʒaxwle] | 'scraping' |
| *lɛvla* | [lɛvla] | 'latch' |
| *kabli* | [kabli] | 'monkey' |
| *gbɛtɔhla* | [gbɛtɔɣla] | 'brute' |
| *lanwliɖu* | [lãwliɖu] | 'canine (tooth)' |

b. Cl ~ Cr

| | | |
|---|---|---|
| *tlatla* | [tlatla/tratra] | 'skate (fish)' |
| *clɛclɛ* | [tʃlɛtʃlɛ/tʃrɛʃrɛ] | 'flowing a lot' |
| *adla* | [adla/adra] | 'calamity' |
| *ajlo* | [adʒlo/adʒro] | 'great' |
| *jijlɛ* | [dʒidʒlɛ/dʒidʒrɛ] | 'example' |
| *sislɛ* | [sislɛ/sisrɛ] | 'treason' |
| *azli* | [azli/azri] | 'vodoun (spec.)' |

In contrast, CVLV sequences are allowed when the two vowels are different (cf. 22), whereas CVCV sequences are allowed with non-distinct vowels when the second consonant is not /l/ (cf. 23).

(22)
| *bɛli* | [bɛli] | 'to bow' |
|---|---|---|
| *gali* | [gali] | 'cassava' |
| *gbelan* | [gbelã] | 'game (meat)' |
| *honli* | [hɔ̃li] | 'doorway' |

(23)
| *baba* | [baba] | 'mud' |
|---|---|---|
| *baka* | [baka] | 'canary' |
| *dɔjɔ* | [dɔʤɔ] | 'trembling' |
| *duwu* | [duwu] | 'big (with reference to eyes)' |
| *futu* | [futu] | 'to shuffle' |
| *logo* | [logo] | 'hip' |

This distributional gap could not easily be explained if we were to adopt one of the hypotheses we have rejected (two types of branching structures, two types of complex segments). However, an explanation is readily available with the hypothesis we have adopted. Following Nikiema (1995), we suggest that CLV sequences result from the deletion of an intervening vowel under an identity constraint. In other words, forms such as [aglo] and [klu] are derived (at least, historically) from /agolo/ and /kulu/ respectively.

This analysis is supported by Bole-Richard's (1983) observation that a deleted (identical) vowel reappears in Gengbe traditional songs: a form such as [fuflu], for instance, is realized [fufulu]. This form not only suggests that there was a vowel between the two consonants, but also that the deleted vowel was identical to the following one. Bole-Richard also provides examples of loanwords such as those in (24), which show deletion of the first of two identical vowels with an intervening liquid.

(24)  Borrowed forms from Ewe (Bole-Richard 1983: 75)

| Ewe | Gen | |
|---|---|---|
| *abolo* | *ablo* | 'cornbread' |
| *agala* | *agla* | 'crab' |
| *xɔlɔ* | *ɛxlɔ* | 'friend' |

If the disyllabic hypothesis is correct, then all underlying representations of CLV sequences are in fact disyllabic sequences with identical vowels, as illustrated in (25).[9]

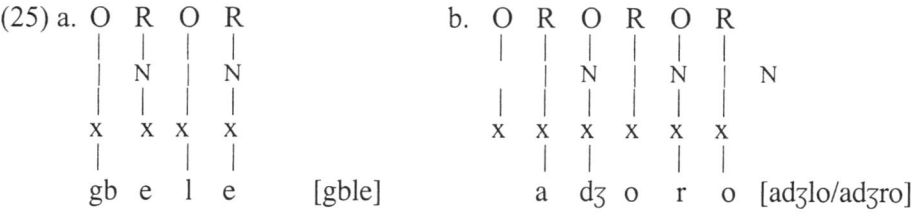

Two conditions must be met in order for CVLV sequences to reduce to CLV: (i) the two vowels must be identical, and (ii) the intervening consonant must be a liquid or a glide, an observation expressed in Capo (1991:92) in terms of a Morpheme Structure Condition. To recast this condition in phonological terms, we need to answer the following question: why does the vowel need to

---

[9] It is unclear whether the derivation still applies synchronically in the various Gbe lects or whether it applied only at some point in their history. The deletion of the first vowel in borrowed forms of Gengbe suggests the former while the reappearance of the identical vowels in traditional songs suggests the latter. For Fongbe, informants were divided as to the possibility of pronouncing the first of two identical vowels. When asked to pronounce a $CV_iLV_i$ word very slowly, some would not pronounce the first vowel at all, lengthening the first consonant instead. Others did pronounce the first vowel, while insisting that this pronunciation was reserved for very formal or literary speech.

be deleted in this particular context? In the next section, we show that the vowel deletion is a result of the application of the Obligatory Contour Principle (OCP).

4.3 *Deletion: a parametric option of the OCP*
Many variants of the OCP have been proposed in the literature, sometimes as a universal principle, sometimes as a language-specific constraint on representations (e.g., Kenstowicz & Kidda 1987; Lowenstamm & Prunet 1986; McCarthy 1981, 1986; Yip 1988). The OCP states that no identical elements (vowels, consonants, tones) may be adjacent at any given level of phonological representation. Yip (1988) suggests two ways of implementing the OCP: either through fusion (multiple linking) of the elements involved, as illustrated in (26a), or through deletion of one of them, as in (26b).

(26)  a. Double linking of segments

b. Segmental deletion

As shown in Nikiema (1995), the fact that liquids and glides are the only consonants allowing deletion under identity suggests, in the spirit of Paradis and Prunet (1991), that liquids and glides are transparent, unlike all other consonants, which are opaque. If liquids and glides are transparent in Gbe (i.e., placeless), then the vowels that immediately precede and follow them are adjacent. They are therefore subject to the OCP, whence the hypothesis that CLV sequences in Gbe emerge from the application of the deletion option of the OCP.

(27)  Deletion option of the OCP          /bala/ [bla] 'to tie'

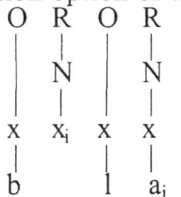

Given this analysis, we must still explain why it is always the first of the two identical vowels that deletes under the OCP application rather than the last. We claim that [bla] is a possible sequence, whereas [bal] is ruled out for reasons linked to the licensing conditions of empty nuclei. As a matter of fact, no consonant is allowed in word- or syllable-final position; we contend that

[bal] is ill-formed in Gbe because there is no vowel to the right to license the last empty position, since directionality of government is from right to left in this language.

The proposed disyllabic analysis accounts for the lack of co-occurrence restrictions between the first consonant and the following liquid, since they belong to different syllables. The analysis also provides a straightforward account for the allophonic variation between [r] and [l] based on the coronality of the first consonant. In terms of the Government Phonology approach to syllable structure, the allophonic variation is analyzed as an instance of government between two consonants in onset position.

To sum up, we have shown that, contrary to French, all CLV sequences in Gbe are disyllabic. In the next section, we will show by way of comparison, the syllabification of O-L sequences in Haitian, French, and Gbe lects.

## 5.  *The challenge raised by the syllabification of Haitian O-L sequences*
We have shown that there are two types of O-L sequences in Haitian:
1.  Tautosyllabic O-L sequences, which are observed in word-initial position, as well as in word-internal position. These consonants are linearly adjacent and analyzed as tautosyllabic, that is, they belong to the same onset constituent.
2.  Heterosyllabic O-L sequences, which, contrary to tautosyllabic ones, are not subject to co-occurrence restrictions. These O-L sequences are not linearly adjacent since they occur in two onset positions, separated by an intervening empty nuclear position.

We refer to the tautosyllabic O-L sequences as true clusters, and the heterosyllabic ones as false clusters. Our analysis explains why some O-L sequences are observed in word and syllable initial positions, whereas some others are limited to word-internal positions. The data in (28 and 29), repeated from (2 and 3), exemplify the distinction: the forms in (28) illustrate true O-L clusters while examples in (29) show false O-L and CL clusters.

(28) a.  Word-initial true clusters (branching onsets)

| *flè* | [flɛ] | 'flower' | *grès* | [gɣɛs] | 'grease' |
| *glas* | [glas] | 'ice' | *tris* | [tɣis] | 'sad' |
| *ble* | [ble] | 'blue' | *krikèt* | [kɣikɛt] | 'cricket (insect)' |

b.  Word-medial true clusters (branching onsets)

| *tranble* | [tɣãnble] | 'to shake' |
| *éklèsi* | [eklɛsi] | 'clearing (weather)' |
| *kuple* | [kuple] | 'verse' |
| *agreyab* | [agɣejab] | 'agreeable' |
| *maryaj* | [maɣjaʒ] | 'marriage' |

(29)   False clusters (empty nuclei)

a. *patisri*  [patisɣi]  'pastry'               b. *fabnak*   [fabnak]   'plastic shoe'
   *galri*    [galɣi]    'gallery'                 *kondiktè* [kɔ̃dikt̪]  'driver'
   *bouchri*  [buʃɣi]    'butcher shop'            *pwopte*   [pwɔpte]   'cleanliness'
   *vazlin*   [vazlin]   'petroleum jelly'         *dejne*    [deʒne]    'breakfast'
   *matlo*    [matlo]    'sailor'                  *gadkòt*   [gadkɔt]   'body guard'
   *tannri*   [tãnɣi]    'tannery'                 *kadna*    [kadna]    'padlock'

We have included other types of consonant sequences in (29) to provide a more complete picture of the scope of the phenomenon. It is important to note that all types of consonant sequences observed in Haitian are, without exception, also observed in French. More specifically, the syllabic properties of French presented in section 4 appear to be similar to those we have presented for Haitian so far. A comparison of the distribution and structure of O-L sequences in both French and Haitian reveals a convergence of constraints on syllabic structures at both the phonological and phonetic levels. This may be precisely the reason why the syllabic properties of Haitian have never been considered to be a challenge in phonological studies: most authors merely consider that the word-internal sequences in (29) are coda-onset sequences (e.g., Anestin 1987; Cadely 1988, 1994), analogous to their view of the French clusters as coda-onset sequences. We have demonstrated that these sequences cannot be analyzed as coda-onset sequences because of the Sonority Sequencing Principle (SSP), among other things. We have also shown that they must be analyzed as onset consonants separated by an intervening nuclear position.

We have to consider an important fact when comparing the syllabification of Haitian and French. Almost all of the French forms that are the source of the Haitian forms in (29) include an empty nucleus, intervening between the two consonants. More specifically, except for *fabnak* and *kondiktè*, all the Haitian forms in (29) correspond to cases in French where an empty nucleus is not phonetically realized. Hence, the similarity between the two languages exists at both the deep and surface levels of representation.

In contrast to the Haitian and French data, only O-L (and O-G) sequences are observed in Gbe lects: there are no other types of consonant sequences. We have analyzed all the O-L sequences in Gbe lects as disyllabic (onset consonants separated by an empty nucleus). We have seen that the set of O-L sequences (true and false clusters) observed in both Haitian and French is a subset of the O-L sequences attested in Gbe lects. In other words, the set of O-L sequences in Gbe is larger than that of French and Haitian. Since French and Gbe lects are considered to be the contact languages from which Haitian emerged, our question is the following: how can one determine whether the syllabification of O-L consonants in Haitian is similar to that of French or rather to that of Gbe lects? The relative contributions of first language and target language in cases of second language acquisition will provide the necessary elements to answer this question.

## 5.1 *Second language acquisition and the emergence of creole languages*

The phonological systems of Haitian appear to constitute a compromise between those of its contributing languages (cf. Brousseau 2003). The syllable structures of Haitian are less complex than those of French (e.g., codas only in medial position and a very limited number of CCC sequences in Haitian), but not to the point that they equate with the structural simplicity of those of Gbe (e.g., branching onsets and codas in Haitian). It is worth noting that this compromise can be observed in other areas of the phonology as well. While Haitian has the same vowel inventory as in Fongbe, it has a consonantal inventory that is very similar to French. The accentual system is also a kind of hybrid: it is a stress system (like French), realized at the level of the phonological word (like Fongbe). The hybrid character of Haitian is similar to what is typically found in interlanguages, in the more straightforward cases of second language acquisition, especially for phonology and prosody (cf. among others, Broselow 1983, for syllabic structures; Archibald 1998a, 1998b and Devonish 1989, for stress).[10]

The similarities are too striking to constitute a mere coincidence. Wode (1986) proposes that transfer occurs in all contact situations, since it is a major component of language-processing abilities. This implies that for any given pair of L1 and L2, the same transfer types will be found across age groups as well as across contact situations. Examining the way English consonants and vowels are realized in various contact situations (such as naturalistic L2 acquisition, tutored L2 acquisition, relearning of a language, and pidgins), Wode shows that the substitution patterns are the same in all situations. Therefore, transfer regularities may be explained by the only set of factors that is invariant enough to do so: the language background of the speaker. Different speakers who share a common language background use the same substitution patterns in different situations.

Theories that aim at explaining the development of an interlanguage in second language acquisition (SLA) may be subsumed under two well-known labels: the contrastive analysis (or Full Transfer Hypothesis) and the L2=L1 hypothesis (or Full Access Mode Hypothesis). The differences between the interlanguage and the target language are the consequence of transfer in the first hypothesis, and the consequence of universals involved in both L1 and L2 acquisition in the second hypothesis. Recent developments in SLA theory

---

[10] The issue of complexity needs a more careful evaluation because the overall complexity of a language may vary depending on its structural complexity (branching structures), its syntagmatic complexity (presence of empty positions), or the degree of markedness of its various components.

point to a reconciliation of these two opposing views. Most scholars would now agree on the following characterization of interlanguages. First, interlanguages are natural languages: they follow principles and constraints found in natural languages, and they reflect language universals. Second, the typological nature of both L1 and L2 determines the structural character of the interlanguage. Third, transfer is an integral part of second language learning and it is constrained by formal properties of L1 and L2. In other words, universals act as guiding principles in the process of developing an interlanguage, which also has recourse to the grammar of L1.

This reconciled view is best expressed by the Full Transfer/Full Access Mode Hypothesis (Schwartz & Spouse 1996; White 2000). According to this hypothesis, second language learners assume the grammar of L1 as a starting point (Full Transfer) and progressively restructure this initial grammar using principles and parameters of UG (Full Access). Learners maintain the parameter settings of L1 in the interlanguage unless they are exposed to evidence indicating the contrary: positive evidence in the target language triggers the resetting of the parameters in the interlanguage. In this view, an interlanguage is the "combination of (incorrect) L1 parameter settings, and the effect of Universal Grammar manifested in parameters that have been reset to the (correct) L2 value" (Archibald 1998a: 283). Since learners have full access to UG, the parallel developments between L1 and L2 are accounted for. UG guides both types of acquisition in a similar fashion. Yet at the same time, L1 and L2 acquisition show many differences in their respective development. The principles of UG do not allow language acquisition to develop as efficiently for adults as for children. This can be attributed to the fact that L1 involves parameter setting while L2 acquisition involves parameter *re*setting (cf. Flynn 1987; Flynn, Epstein & Martohardjono 1993; Youssef & Mazurkewich 1998).

Since the Full Transfer/Full Access Mode Hypothesis has proven very successful in accounting for phonological aspects of interlanguages (cf. Archibald 1998a, 1998b, Broselow & Finer 1991, Youssef & Mazurkewich 1998), we will assume that it is correct.

If Haitian (and creole languages in general) had emerged as an interlanguage, in which some properties are the consequence of transfers from the LI/substrate, we expect that the transfer constraints that affect the influence of L1 in the more straightforward cases of second language acquisition will help identify those features of the substrate that made their way into the creole and those that did not. In a detailed discussion of substrate influence and the role of transfers, Siegel (2003) proposes the following scenario:

> In attempting to speak a common L2, individuals transfer features from their L1 (the substrate languages) onto forms of the L2. This L2 may be some form of the superstrate language or a contact variety (a pidgin) lexified by the superstrate. These L2 forms with L1 properties join the pool of variants that are used in the contact

situation. When the community begins to shift from their L1 to the contact variety, leveling occurs: the elimination of some variants and the retention of others, which include some resulting from transfer. Thus, rather than features passing directly from the substrate languages into the creole, features are first transferred by individuals in using an L2 in the contact situation, and a subset of these features is later retained by the community when the creole emerges. (Siegel 2003: 187)

Siegel (2003: 200) identifies two main constraints, initially proposed by Anderson (1983),[11] that influence the availability of substrate features and/or their retention in the creole. They are both linked to the relative level of convergence between the two languages in contact. First, the Transfer to Somewhere Principle states that there must be an element (or string of elements) in L2 that can be used at the landing site of the transfer, and this element must be perceptually salient. Second, the Relexification Principle states that, when a structural pattern of L2 cannot be perceived, the strategy is to use the structure of L1 with lexical items from the second language. The Relexification Principle may be the only strategy available when the L2 input is not sufficient to promote transfer.

Siegel (2003: 198) also makes use of the distinction between transfer in L2 acquisition (gradually developing linguistic competence) and transfer in L2 use (handling the challenges of using and understanding L2). He concludes: "transfer in pidgin and creole genesis can occur in the earliest stage of development as part of L2 acquisition as well as in the latest stage of development as part of L2 use. With regard to pidgin and creole genesis, we would not expect evidence of transfer typical of early acquisition (e.g., basic word-order transfer) unless there was extremely limited contact with the lexifier."

Let us see how the various constraints on transfer may shed some light on the respective contributions of French and Gbe in the emergence of the syllable structure of Haitian.

### 5.2 A multi-stage scenario for the acquisition of Haitian consonant sequences

How can we determine whether the syllabification of O-L consonants in Haitian is similar to that of French or to that of Gbe lects? More generally, how can we evaluate the relative contributions of first language/substrate and target language/superstrate in the emergence of Haitian? We will consider some possible answers to these questions.

We have seen that the lexifier languages of Haitian have radically different syllabic structures: French has branching onsets and codas (although not in word-final position), whereas Gbe languages have none of these properties. There is, however, an overlap of both the types of segmental sequences and the syllabic properties (presence of empty nuclei) observed in the Haitian lexifier

---

[11] Anderson (1983) formulates the two principles in terms of morphemes, but we contend that the principles can apply similarly to structures or features of the grammar.

languages. As a result, it is not surprising that Haitian reflects aspects of the syllabic structures of both French and Gbe languages. Since, from a purely structural point of view, the syllabic properties of Gbe are a subset of those of French, its impact during the creation of Haitian is less obvious. This leads one to question how the Haitian syllabic structure was established.

Although, the creators of Haitian received minimal exposure to the French input (see Lefebvre 1998 and the references therein), let us assume that the input was sufficient to promote transfer from Gbe. For syllable structures, the elements that would be transferred are those that allow Obstruent-Liquid and Obstruent-Glide as the only possible consonant sequences. These elements are: (i) the possibility of having empty nuclei; and, probably,[12] (ii) the deletion option of the OCP that forces the deletion of the first of two identical vowels in CVLV sequences. These elements could be transferred only if there was a "somewhere" in French that could serve as a landing site for the transfer.

Since the bulk of the Haitian vocabulary comes from French, the "somewhere" should not be difficult to find: it corresponds to all words of French that need to be syllabified and that exhibit CLV (and CGV) sequences. The vast majority of these words are perceptually salient because a wide variety of nouns, verbs and adjectives of French (the most salient lexical items) include CLV and CGV sequences, and because the phonetic realization of a lexical item is among its most salient properties (in contrast to meaning, syntactic features, etc.). It is therefore reasonable to assume that the two elements (i.e., empty nuclei and the deletion option of the OCP) were transferred into Haitian, in accordance with the Transfer to Somewhere Principle. The conclusion may be the same if the input to which the creators of Haitian were exposed was not sufficient to promote transfer. In this case, they would resort to the Relexification Principle and they would use the structures of Gbe with lexical items of French, including empty nuclei and the deletion option of the OCP.

Because the consonant inventory of Gbe lects is significantly larger than that of French, and because there are no co-occurrence constraints on the heterosyllabic O-L sequences in Gbe, we would have expected the set of possible O-L sequences in Haitian to be larger than that in French. In fact, this is not the case because O-L sequences of Gbe such as [zl], [ml], or [wl] could not have made their way into Haitian unless French words exhibited such sequences as well. In this case, the absence of a larger set of O-L sequences than is found in French may be explained by the near-absence of Gbe words in Haitian. The gap is thus the consequence of an equivalent gap in the forms of French, not of the principles or parameters transferred from the L1 grammar.

---

[12] Recall that we cannot be sure whether the $CV_iLV_i$ structure underlying CLV sequences contained a first vowel or whether the structure was already CØLV at the time when Haitian was formed.

The transfer of the deletion option of the OCP poses a more serious problem. It does not explain why forms such as those in (29b), for example *kadna*, are possible. Since these forms involve sequences that are systematically banned in Gbe lects, we would expect them to be modified through vowel epenthesis or consonant deletion. Studies in loan phonology (Paradis & LaCharité 1997; Rose 2000) suggest that segmental epenthesis or deletion applies whenever the syllabic representation of loan words does not comply with the syllabic requirements of the source language. Gbe languages are no exception to this generalization when it comes to loans. For instance, the French forms [dɔktœR] and [pɔst] have been borrowed as [dotoo] and [pɔsu] respectively. In other words, the absence of vocalic epenthesis or consonant deletion in the Haitian words such as those in (29b)[13] is left unexplained, since Gbe lects do not allow such consonant sequences.

A multi-stage approach to the development of the Haitian syllable structure, based on the distinction between second language use and second language acquisition, may provide a solution to this problem. During the initial stage of second language acquisition, the CV properties of Gbe languages are the norm and O-L sequences are analyzed as heterosyllabic (with an intervening empty nucleus). Other consonant sequences are simplified by means of vowel epenthesis or consonant deletion. However, if Siegel (2003) is right, only a subset of the initially transferred features is later retained by the community. The simplified structures showing vocalic epenthesis or consonant deletion, like other transfers typical of early acquisition, are not likely to be retained.

At a later stage of language use, on the basis of positive evidence in the target language, subsequent generations of creole creators resort to Universal Grammar to reset the parameters of syllabic structures to the 'correct' L2 value (Archibald 1998a, 1998b), allowing for syllables that are closer to the French equivalents. In other words, subsequent generations of Haitian creators introduce a distinction between tautosyllabic O-L sequences and heterosyllabic O-L sequences, based on their use of the emerging creole. This leads exactly to the distinction we made between what we called true clusters (which exhibit co-occurrence restrictions) and false clusters (with an intervening empty nucleus).[14]

Based on the proposed scenario, one cannot strongly argue that the properties of Gbe lects played a pervasive role in the emergence of Haitian syllabic structure. However, one surprising aspect of Haitian may point to a contribution by Gbe lects. We observe that in all Haitian forms for which a schwa can

---

[13] There are only a few instances of consonant deletion in Haitian, typically with sC initial clusters of French (see Steele & Brousseau, this volume).

[14] The positive evidence in the target language that is needed for parametric resetting may imply, over time, a greater exposure to French or a lesser exposure to Gbe or both. Further research is needed in order to validate our scenario on the basis of migration and population data.

be posited in the corresponding French etymon, that schwa is generally absent, that is, the Haitian form does not show a phonetic realization for the empty nucleus, as illustrated in (30). Schwa is optional in the French etymons of these words, but absent in Haitian, which is precisely what we would expect if the empty nucleus option were transferred to Haitian from Gbe.

(30)  Marginally accepted realization of schwa

| Haitian | | French | | |
|---------|---------|--------|---------|---------|
| *anvlòp* | [ãvlɔp] | *enveloppe* | [ãv(ə)lɔp] | 'envelope' |
| *boulva* | [bulva] | *boulevard* | [bul(ə)vaʀ] | 'boulevard' |
| *salté* | [salte] | *saleté* | [sal(ə)te] | 'dirt, filth' |
| *samdi* | [samdi] | *samedi* | [sam(ə)di] | 'Saturday' |
| *soutni* | [sutni] | *soutenir* | [sut(ə)niʀ] | 'to support' |
| *kochma* | [koʃma] | *cauchemar* | [koʃ (ə)maʀ] | 'nightmare' |

In contrast, the etymons of the forms in (31) do not allow the empty nucleus to remain empty. Schwa is systematically realized in French to avoid sequences of three consonants. This obligatory realization of schwa known as the *Loi des trois consonnes* (law of three consonants) applies whenever a sequence of three consonants does not provide the configuration allowing an empty nucleus to be properly governed. The nucleus is thus realized as schwa in French and as [e] in Haitian, as exemplified below.

(31)  Mandatory realization of schwa

| Haitian | | French | | |
|---------|---------|--------|---------|---------|
| *vandredi* | [vãdɣedi] | *vendredi* | [vãdrədi] | 'Friday' |
| *mèkredi* | [mɛkɣedi] | *mercredi* | [mɛʀkʀədi] | 'Wednesday' |
| *senpleman* | [sẽplemã] | *simplement* | [sẽpləmã] | 'simply' |
| *gonfleman* | [gɔ̃flemã] | *gonflement* | [gɔ̃fləmã] | 'indigestion' |
| *direkteman* | [diɣɛktemã] | *directement* | [diʀɛktəmã] | 'directly' |

There is yet another context in Haitian where an empty nucleus needs to be realized, namely in the first syllable of a word, as illustrated below.

(32)  Schwa is maintained in the first syllable

| Haitian | | French | | |
|---------|---------|--------|---------|---------|
| *chemen/chimen* | [ʃemẽ/ʃimẽ] | *chemin* | [ʃ(ə)mẽ] | 'road' |
| *chemiz/chimiz* | [ʃemiz/ʃimiz] | *chemise* | [ʃ(ə)miz] | 'shirt' |
| *demen/denmen* | [demẽ/dẽmẽ] | *demain* | [d(ə)mẽ] | 'tomorrow' |
| *semèl* | [semɛl] | *semelle* | [s(ə)mɛl] | '(shoe) sole' |
| *vini* | [vini] | *venir* | [v(ə)niʀ] | 'to come' |

This observation raises the question as to why, contrary to French, an empty nucleus needs to be phonetically realized in the first syllable of Haitian forms. We suggest that this is precisely the place where Gbe lects may have played a role in the creation of Haitian. Since consonant sequences other than O-L are prohibited in Gbe lects, word-initial offending sequences were repaired by vocalic epenthesis, resulting in the presence of a phonetically realized vowel, in this case [i] or [e]. This Gbe constraint against consonant sequences other than O-L remained active in Haitian, forcing a simplification of the structure by means of the insertion of an epenthetic vowel,[15] but only in word-initial position. In subsequent stages, the constraint was turned off to allow consonant sequences other than O-L in word-internal position.

It is worth noting that we have found only four cases that are true exceptions to the generalization that the French schwa is maintained in the first syllable of Haitian words. Three of these cases are *dlo* 'water', *vlòp/vlope* 'envelope, to wrap' and *plo/plòt* '(wool)ball.' Interestingly enough, these three forms exhibit the type of consonant sequence that is allowed in Gbe languages, namely O-L sequences. The fourth case, *chwal/cheval* 'horse,' alternates between a schwa and a schwa-less form, the second of which exhibits the other type of consonant sequence that is allowed in Gbe languages: O-G sequences. The fact that these exceptional cases reflect precisely the constraints of Gbe languages is certainly not coincidental. Vowel epenthesis did not apply in these cases because they all conformed to the Gbe constraints on consonant sequences (e.g., neither *dilo* nor *delo* for *dlo*, neither *chewal* nor *chiwal* for *cheval*).

In summary, the similarity between Haitian and Gbe lects with respect to constraints on syllabic structure lies in the fact that empty nuclei are part of the underlying representations of both languages. However, vowel/zero alternations (vocalic epenthesis) are rare on the surface. Here is the proposed multi-stage scenario for the emergence of consonant sequences in Haitian.

1. All sequences other than O-L are prohibited, either because the severe constraints of Gbe lects have been transferred to the interlanguage (Transfer to Somewhere) or because the forms of French have been interpreted using the possible structures of L1 (Relexification).

2. Given that empty nuclei are available, other word-internal sequences of consonants are accepted in the interlanguage because the phonotactic constraints have been relaxed on the basis of positive evidence.

---

[15] Note that, in Haitian, [e] corresponds to three vowels of French: the phonetically realized schwa, [e] and [ø]. Furthermore, [i] is the epenthetic vowel used in Gbe to repair the ill-formed structures of loanwords. The forms in (32), where the vowel in the first syllable shows a variation (e.g., *chemen/chimen*), probably reflect the variation in the input. Depending on the context, words such as *chemin* in French are pronounced with or without the schwa. The Haitian form *chemin* would correspond to the French form with a pronounced schwa, on a par with the forms in (31) where schwa is reinterpreted as [e]. The Haitian form *chimin* would correspond to the French form with no pronounced schwa, the epenthetic [i] being used to phonetically realize the empty nucleus.

3. Word-final consonants are also accepted, that is, consonants in the onset of an empty-headed syllable, again because of the presence of empty nuclei and because the phonotactic constraints have been relaxed.
4. Possibly but not necessarily, word-initial O-L sequences which were originally heterosyllabic (Gbe) become tautosyllabic through second language usage of French. This would involve resetting the parameter on branching onsets from the Gbe value (no branching) to the French value (branching).
5. Possibly but not necessarily, a distinction between true and false clusters is introduced.

Within the multi-stage scenario, the transfer of the possibility of restricted empty nuclei accounts for the following properties of Haitian: (i) the presence of empty nuclei in medial sequences that cannot be analyzed as branching onsets or coda-onset; (ii) the absence of codas in word-final position, which may account, although not as straightforwardly, for (iii) the possibility of having codas in word-medial position. However, unless we assume a parameter resetting for which we have no clear evidence, it does not account for (iv) the presence of branching onsets.

The properties of (iii) and (iv) are theoretically linked. As we have seen, the presence of branching onsets in a language implies the presence of codas. In other words, if we could show that branching onsets are in fact heterosyllabic sequences of onsets with an intervening empty nucleus (a structure for which we have independent evidence), there would be no implicational need to posit the existence of codas in the language. Interestingly, we have noticed that the apparent cases of codas are not at all convincing. The clear cases (i.e., CCC sequences) are very rare in the language, while the more widespread cases could as well be analyzed as CØC sequences. In fact, the same situation holds with the apparent branching onsets. While nothing argues against analyzing them as complex onsets, there is not even an argument for such a structure. CC sequences in forms such as in [glas] or [tris] may very well constitute CØC sequences. The fact that the O-L sequences are limited by phonotactics word-initially but not word-medially would merely reflect the phonotactics of French, not those of Haitian.

Thus, the syllabic structure of Haitian would not include branching onsets or codas, making it much more similar to the structure of Gbe. With this revised analysis, the above scenario would become even simpler, involving only the first three steps. In a nutshell, the only modification that needs to apply to the structures transferred from Gbe is to relax the conditions that prevent an empty nucleus from appearing before any type of consonant. With these conditions relaxed, French would have provided a new set of consonant sequences to fill the neighboring positions of a more accommodating empty nucleus.

## 6. *Conclusion*

As in other areas of the phonology, the syllable structures of Haitian appear to be a compromise between those of its contributing languages. They are less complex than those of French but not to the point that they equate to the structural simplicity of Gbe syllabic structures. French allows for branching onsets and branching rhymes (coda consonants), while Gbe lects are maximally CV, allowing no branching constituents. Haitian seems to have negotiated a compromise in allowing for branching onsets and branching rhymes, two options that do not suffice, however, to accommodate the range of consonant sequences found in French forms.

Like both its contributing languages, Haitian allows for empty-headed syllables. However, the distribution of empty nuclei is not identical in the three languages. Whereas French has no further constraint on their distribution, Gbe restricts it to initial and medial positions. Haitian allows empty nuclei freely in any position (as French does) except the first syllable, where empty nuclei appear only when the following onset is filled by a liquid (or glide). This constraint is a relaxed version of the severe constraint of Gbe. It has no equivalent in French, which authorizes an empty nucleus in front of any consonant.

On the one hand, Haitian syllabic structure is similar to that of French in that both languages exhibit branching onsets, branching rimes and empty nuclei. On the other hand, Haitian is similar to Gbe in that it allows for O-L sequences that are separated by empty nuclei. Since both languages allow for O-L sequences in word-initial position, the presence of word and syllable-final consonants is the only feature that sets Haitian apart from Gbe languages. In other words, the syllabic structures of Haitian have substantially complexified when compared to those of Gbe. This complexification was made possible by the existence of certain features of the Gbe phonological grammar, namely the possibility of having empty nuclei in initial and medial syllables.

## *References*

Alber, B. and I. Plag. 2001. Epenthesis, deletion and the emergence of the optimal syllable in creole: The case of Sranan. *Lingua* 111: 811–840.

Anderson, R. (ed.). 1983. *Pidginization and Creolization as Language Acquisition*. Rowley, MA: Newbury House.

Anestin, A. 1987. Structure syllabique de l'haïtien et nasalisation. M.A. thesis, UQAM.

Archibald, J. 1998a. *Second Language Phonology*. Amsterdam: John Benjamins.

Archibald, J. 1998b. Metrical parameters and lexical dependency: Acquiring L2 stress. In *The Generative Study of Second Language Acquisition*, S. Flynn, G. Martohardjono and W. O'Neill (eds.), 280–301. Mahwah, NJ: Lawrence Erlbaum Associates.

Bentolila, A. (ed.). 1976. *Ti diksyonnè kreyol-franse: dictionnaire élémentaire créole haïtien-français*. Port-au-Prince: Éditions Caraïbes.

Bhatt, P. and E. Nikiema. In press. Empty positions in Haitian syllable structure. In *The Structure of Creole Words: Segmental, Syllabic and Morphological Aspects*, Parth Bhatt and Ingo Plag (eds.). Tübingen: Niemeyer.

Bole-Richard, R. 1983. *Systématique phonologique et grammaticale d'un parler éwé: le gen-mina du sud-togo et sud-bénin*. Paris: L'Harmattan.

Broselow, E. 1983. Nonobvious transfer: On predicting epenthesis error. In *Language Transfer in Language Learning*, S. M. Gass and L. Selinker (eds.), 269–281. Rowley, MA: Newbury House.

Broselow, E. and D. Finer. 1991. Parameter setting in second language phonology and syntax. *Second Language Research* 7: 35–39.

Brousseau, A.-M. 2003. The accentual system of Haitian Creole: The role of transfer and markedness values. In *The Phonology and Morphology of Creole Languages*, Ingo Plag (ed.), 3–23. Tübingen: Niemeyer.

Bullock, B. 2002. Constraining the vagaries of glide distribution in varieties of French. In *Romance Phonology and Variation*, Caroline Wiltshire and Joaquim Camps (eds.), 11–25. Philadelphia: John Benjamins Publishing Company.

Cadely, J.-R. 1988. Représentations syllabiques et distribution des diphtongues en créole haïtien. *Études créoles* 11: 9–40.

Cadely, J.-R. 1994. Aspects de la phonologie du créole haïtien. Ph.D. dissertation, UQAM.

Cairns, C. and M. Feinstein. 1982. Markedness and the theory of syllabus structure. *Linguistic Inquiry* 13: 193-225.

Capo, H. 1991. *A Comparative Phonology of Gbe*. Publications in African Languages and Linguistics 14. Dordrecht: Foris.

Charette, M. 1991. *Conditions on Phonological Government*. London: Cambridge University Press.

Clements, G.N. 1990. The role of the sonority cycle in core syllabification. In *Papers in Laboratory Phonology I: Between the Grammar and the Physics of Speech*, J. Kingston and M. Beckman (eds.), 283–333. Cambridge: Cambridge University Press.

Clements, G.N. and S.J. Keyser. 1983. *CV Phonology: A Generative Theory of the Syllable*. Cambridge, MA: MIT Press.

Davis, S. 1990. The onset as a constituent of the syllable: Evidence from Italian. In *Proceedings from the 26th Regional Meeting of the Chicago Linguistics Society*, 71–79.

Dell, F. 1985. *Les règles et les sons*. Second revised edition. Paris: Hermann.

Dell, F. 1995. Consonant clusters and phonological syllables in French. *Lingua* 95: 5–26.

Devonish, H. 1989. *Talking in Tones: A Study of Tone in Afro-European Languages*. London: Karia Press.

Ebenezer Mission. No date. *Kreyol to English Dictionary*. www.ebenezermission.com.

Encrevé, P. 1988. *La liaison avec et sans enchaînement: phonologie tridimentionelle et usages du français*. Paris: Seuil.

Flynn, S. 1987. *L2 Acquisition: Resetting the Parameters of Universal Grammar*. Dordrecht: Reidel.

Flynn, S, S.D. Epstein and G. Martohardjono. 1993. The full access hypothesis in SLA: Some evidence from the acquisition of functional categories. Paper presented at AILA, Amsterdam.

Goad, H. and K. Brannen. 2003. Phonetic evidence for phonological structure in syllabification. In *The Phonological Spectrum, Volume II: Suprasegmental Structure*. Jeroen van de Weijer, Vincent J. van Heuven and Harry van der Hulst (eds.), 3–30. Amsterdam: John Benjamins.

Greenberg, J. 1963. *The Languages of Africa*. Bloomington: Indiana Press.

Harris, J. 1983. *Syllable Structure and Stress in Spanish: A Non-Linear Analysis*. Linguistic Inquiry Monograph 8. Cambridge, MA: The MIT Press.

Harris, J. 1994. *English Sound Structure*. Oxford, UK/Cambridge, MA: Blackwell.

Hyman, L. 1973. Consonant types and tones. *Southern California Occasional Papers in Linguistics 1*. Los Angeles: University of Southern California.

Hyman, L. 1985. *A Theory of Phonological Weight*. Dordrecht: Foris.

Itô, J. 1988. Syllable thoery in prosodic phonology. New York: Garland Publishing.

Kaye, J. 1985. On the syllable structure of certain West African languages. In *African Linguistics, Essays in Memory of M. W. K. Semikenke*, D. Goyvaerts (ed.), 285–308. Studies in the Sciences of Language Series 6. Amsterdam: John Benjamins.

Kaye, J. 1990. Coda licensing. *Phonology* 7: 301–330.

Kaye, J. and J. Lowenstamm. 1981. Syllable structure and markedness theory. In *Theory of Markedness in Generative Grammar*, A. Belletti, L. Brandi and L. Rizzi (eds.), 287–316. Pisa: Scuola Normale Superiore di Pisa.

Kaye, J. and J. Lowenstamm. 1984. De la syllabicité. In *Formes sonores du langage: Structure des représentations en phonologie*, F. Dell, D. Hirst and J.-R. Vergnaud (eds.), 123–161. Paris: Hermann.

Kaye, J., J. Lowenstamm and J.-R. Vergnaud. 1990. Constituent structure and government in phonology. *Phonology* 7: 193–231.

Kelly, S. 2004. Theoretical implications of French nuclear diphthongisation. MOT workshop in phonology, University of Ottawa.

Kenstowicz M. and M. Kidda. 1987. The Obligatory Contour Principle and Tangale phonology. In *Current Approaches to African Linguistics 4*, D. Odden (ed.), 223–238. Dordrecht: Foris.

Lefebvre, C. 1998. *Creole Genesis and the Acquisition of Grammar: The Case of Haitian Creole*. Cambridge: Cambridge University Press.

Lowenstamm, J. 1996. CV as the only syllable type. In *Current Trends in Phonology: Models and Methods*, B. Laks and J. Durand (eds.), 419–441. Salford/Manchester: ESRI.

Lowenstamm, J. and J.-F. Prunet. 1986. Le tigrinya et le principe du contour obligatoire. *Revue québécoise de linguistique* 16: 181–208.

Maddieson, I. 1984. *Patterns of Sounds*. Cambridge: Cambridge University Press.

McCarthy, J. 1981. A prosodic theory of nonconcatenative morphology. *Linguistic Inquiry* 12: 373–418.

McCarthy, J. 1986. OCP effects: Gemination and antigemination. *Linguistic Inquiry* 17: 207–263.

Mufwene, S. 1991. Pidgins, creoles, typology and markedness. In *Development and Structure of Creole Languages*, F. Byrne and T. Huebner (eds.), 123–144. Amsterdam/ Philadelphia: John Benjamins.

Nespor, M. and I. Vogel. 1986. *Prosodic Phonology*. Dordrecht: Foris.

Nikiema, E. 1995. De la nécessité des positions vides dans les représentations syllabiques du gen. *Canadian Journal of Linguistics* 40: 319–349.

Nikiema, E. 1999. De la variation morphophonologique du déterminant /la/ dans les créoles haïtien et st-lucien. *Lingua* 107: 69–93.

Paradis, Carole and Darlene LaCharité. 1997. Preservation and minimality in loan adaptation. *Journal of Linguistics* 33: 379–430.

Paradis, C. and J.-F. Prunet. 1991. Asymmetry and visibility in consonant articulations. In *Phonetics and Phonology: The Special Status of Coronals*, C. Paradis and J.-F. Prunet (eds.), 1–28. New York: Academic Press.

Piggott, G.L. 1991. Empty onsets: Evidence for the skeleton in prosodic phonology. *McGill Working Papers in Linguistics* 7: 41–71.

Piggott, G.L. 1999. At the right edge of words. *The Linguistic Review* 16: 143–185.

Rose, Y. 2000. Headedness and Prosodic Licensing in the L1 Acquisition of Phonology. Ph.D. dissertation, McGill University.

Schane, S. 1968. *French Phonology and Morphology*. Cambridge, MA: MIT Press.

Schane, S. 1987. The resolution of hiatus. In *Papers from the 23rd Regional Meeting of the Chicago Linguistic Society. Part II: Parasessions on Autosegmental and Metrical Phonology*, Anna Bosch, Barbara Need and Eric Schiller (eds.), 279–290. Chicago: Chicago Linguistic Society.

Schwartz, B. and R. Spouse. 1996. L2 cognitive states and the full transfer/full access mode. *Second Language Research* 12: 40–72.

Segurola, B. and J. Rassinoux. 2000. *Dictionnaire fon-français*. Madrid: Société des Missions Africaines.

Selkirk, E. 1982. The syllable. In *The Structure of Phonological Representations* (Part 2), Harry van der Hulst and Norval Smith (eds.), 337–383. Dordrecht: Foris.

Siegel, J. 2003. Substrate influence in creoles and the role of transfer in second language acquisition. *Studies in Second Language Acquisition* 25: 185–209.

Tranel, B. 1981. *Concreteness in Generative Phonology: Evidence from French*. Berkeley, CA: University of California Press.

Uffmann, C. 2003. Markedness, faithfulness, and creolization: The retention of the unmarked. In *The Phonology and Morphology of Creole Languages*, Ingo Plag (ed.), 3–23. Tübingen: Niemeyer.

Valdman, A. 1978. *Le créole: statut et origine*. Paris: Klincksieck.

Valdman, A. 1981. *Haitian Creole-English-French Dictionary*. Bloomington, IN: Creole Institute.

Valdman, A. 1983. Creolization and second language acquisition. In *Pidginization and Creolization as Language Acquisition*, R. Anderson (ed.), 212–234. Rowley, MA: Newbury House.

Vogler, P. 1976. Description synchronique d'un parler kru: le vata. Ph.D. dissertation, Université René Descartes.

Welmers, W. 1973. *African Language Structures*. Berkeley/Los Angeles: University of California Press.

White, L. 2000. Second language acquisition: From initial to final state. In *Second Language Acquisition and Linguistic Theory*, J. Archibald (ed.), 130–155. Oxford: Blackwell.

Wode, H. 1986. Language transfer: A cognitive, functional and developmental view. In *Crosslinguistic Influence in Second Language Acquisition*, E. Kellerman and M. Sharwood Smith (eds.), 173–186, New York: Pergamon Institute of English.

Yip, M. 1988. The Obligatory Contour Principle and phonological rules: A loss of identity. *Linguistic Inquiry* 19: 65–100.

Youssef, A. and I. Mazurkewich. 1998. The acquisition of English metrical parameters and syllable structure by adult native speakers of Egyptian Arabic (Cairene dialect). In *The Generative Study of Second Language Acquisition*, S. Flynn, G. Martohardjono and W. O'Neill (eds.), 303–333. Mahwah, NJ: Lawrence Erlbaum Associates.

# PARALLELS IN PROCESS: COMPARING HAITIAN CREOLE AND FRENCH LEARNER PHONOLOGIES

Jeffrey Steele and Anne-Marie Brousseau
*University of Toronto*

In this paper, we focus on several aspects of Haitian Creole (HC) syllable structure and segmental adaptation that differ from its lexifier language, French. We seek to explain these differences as the result of non-native-like ultimate attainment of seventeenth-/eighteenth-century French by native speakers of Gbe. Specifically, we will demonstrate that such differences can be explained as the consequence of processes that are widely attested in L1 and L2 acquisition. For instance, the consonant-∅ alternations and initial syllable truncations of HC resemble forms attested in the production of L1 learners of French. Other HC forms mirror the outputs of L2 phonological processes; these include segmental equivalence classification, the transfer of allophonic rules, epenthesis in /sC/ clusters and the misperception of target forms. In summary, the differences in HC syllable structure vis-à-vis its substrate French and the patterns of segmental adaptation in question parallel forms observed in both child and adult learner French varieties.

## 1. *Introduction*

Many researchers have drawn parallels between creole and learner grammars, both those of adult learners (Andersen 1983; Muysken 2001; Valdman 1980, in general; Becker & Veenstra 2003; Mather 2000; Véronique 1994, for French in particular) and, to a lesser extent, those of children (Becker & Veenstra 2003; Corne 1999; DeGraff 1999; Roberts 2000). For example, creoles typically lack inflectional morphology or have inflectional systems that are significantly less complex than those of their lexifiers (Holm 1988; Lefebvre 1998; McWhorter 2001; Valdman 1978). Impoverished[1] verbal morphology also characterizes both first language (L1) (Brown 1973; Clark 2003) and second language (L2) grammars (Klein & Perdue 1997), at least at earlier stages of acquisition.

It is not only in the domain of morphosyntax that parallels are observed. In the present work, we will demonstrate that striking similarities also exist with respect to many phonetic and phonological properties of creole and learner grammars. Our comparison will be between Haitian Creole (HC) and French L1 and L2 learner varieties, with particular focus on their consonant systems and syllable structure. We assume that HC genesis can be understood in large part as the acquisition[2] of seventeenth-/eighteenth-century French by native

---

[1] The term "impoverished" is used here as it is common in the field of language acquisition. In the context of creoles, we prefer the terms "less complex" or "not as overspecified" (see McWhorter 2004 and Siegel 2004 for discussion).

[2] We assume that the processes that shape L1 and L2 acquisition are similar (e.g., White 2003 for syntax; Flege 1995 for phonetics and phonology). Consequently, we will draw parallels with processes attested in acquisition by children and adults.

speakers of Fongbe and other Gbe languages.[3] We will seek to explain a set of differences between this creole and its lexifier as the result of phonological and phonetic processes commonly observed in child French and interlanguage varieties. The processes in question include the misparsing of phonetic strings, segmental substitution due to both equivalence classification and transferred L1 allophonic rules, and syllable structure modification including truncation.

The remainder of this article is structured as follows. In section 2, we discuss those aspects of the Fongbe, French and HC consonant inventories and syllable structure relevant to the L1 and L2 phonetic and phonological processes in question. In sections 3 and 4, we discuss each of these processes in turn, demonstrating their effect in both HC and French learner varieties. We conclude briefly in section 5.

## 2.  Comparison of the consonant inventory and syllable structure of Fongbe, French and HC

The Fongbe consonant inventory includes 22 phonemes (see Appendix 1, Figure 2). Of particular interest to the present discussion is the velar [ɣ]. In section 4.1, we will argue that this L1 consonant served to adapt both seventeenth-/eighteenth-century French [ʁ] and [h] in HC. As for the combinatory possibilities of these segments, beyond the universal CV syllable that characterizes most West African languages (Greenberg 1963; Holm 1988; Welmers 1974), Fongbe allows for a limited set of syllable-initial clusters (see Appendix 1, Figure 1). Specifically, a cluster may consist of almost any consonant followed by a liquid (e.g., *tli* [t̪li/t̪ri] 'to be thick,' *klu* [klu] 'to scratch,' *slan* [sl̄ã/sr̄ã] 'mockery,' *mla* [ml̄a] 'to fold')[4] or a small subset of consonants followed by yod (e.g., *byo* [bjɔ] 'to ask,' *lya* [lja] 'to climb,' *myo* [mjɔ] 'fire'). A few /Cw/ initial clusters are also attested, but only in nominal forms. Following Capo (1991), we analyze these clusters as underlying CV sequences. Codas are prohibited.[5]

Modern French possesses 23 consonant phonemes including the voiced dorsal fricative [ʁ], the language's rhotic. Beyond this set, the seventeenth-

---

[3] Fongbe is one of the five main varieties that constitute the Gbe dialect cluster. The other four Gbe dialects are Vhegbe (also known as Ewe), Gengbe (or Mina), Ajagbe and Phla-Phera. Fongbe is the substrate language that played the most prominent role in the genesis of HC (Lefebvre 1998).

[4] The liquid /l/ is optionally realized as [r] following a coronal consonant. For simplicity's sake, tones are not indicated in the Fongbe examples.

[5] As concerns their phonological representation, glides can be analyzed as consonants (i.e., syllabified as onsets) or vowels (i.e., syllabified in the syllable nucleus). As discussed in Nikiema and Brousseau (this volume), the status of glides in the three languages under study is unclear. For this reason, we use the term "consonant+glide clusters" here to designate any linear sequence of a consonant followed by a glide. Similarly, the term "coda" is used descriptively to designate postvocalic, preconsonantal/prepausal consonants. The word-final HC consonants that we label as codas may be analyzed as rhymal consonants or as onsets followed by empty nuclei. See also Nikiema and Brousseau (this volume) for discussion.

/eighteenth-century varieties to which the originators of HC were exposed also possessed the laryngeal fricative [h] in words of Germanic origin (e.g., *haut* [ho] 'high,' *hacher* [haʃe] 'to chop'; Brousseau 2005), as well as two <r> variants (coronal [r] and dorsal [ʁ]). The set of French syllable-initial clusters is large, including obstruent+liquid (e.g., *clôture* [k̲l̲otyʁ] 'fence,' *entrée* [ãt̲ʁ̲e] 'entrance'),[6] obstruent+glide (*jouer* [ʒw̲e] 'play (inf.),' *méfiance* [m ef̲j̲ãs] 'mistrust') and, in initial clusters, stop+[s] (e.g., *psychique* [p̲s̲iʃik] 'psychic'), stop+nasal (e.g., *pneu* [p̲n̲ø] 'tire') and [s]+stop, nasal or liquid (e.g., *spécial* [s̲p̲esjal] 'special'; *snob* [s̲n̲ɔb] 'snob'; *slave* [s̲l̲av] 'Slavic'). Triconsonantal-initial clusters beginning with [s] are also possible (e.g., *strict* [s̲t̲ʁikt] 'strict,' *splendide* [s̲p̲l̲ãdid] 'splendid'). As concerns syllable-final consonants, French allows all obstruents and liquids. Moreover, nasals and clusters of up to three members are possible in word-final position (e.g., *pomme* [pɔm̲] 'apple'; *cercle* [sɛʁ̲k̲l̲] 'circle').

The HC consonant inventory closely ressembles that of its substrate Fongbe (see Appendices 1 and 2; Figures 2 and 4). The main differences are the absence of a labio-velar series and the retroflex [ɖ], and the presence of the alveo-palatal fricatives [ʃ,ʒ] (also present in its lexifier French). As concerns syllable structure (see Appendices 1 and 2, Figures 1 and 3), HC shows a greater degree of complexity than the Gbe languages. It allows coda consonants, as well as a more varied set of consonant clusters in medial position. Such clusters may consist of an obstruent+fricative (e.g., *absan* [aps̲ã] 'absent'), an obstruent+nasal (e.g., *atroupman* [atʏup̲m̲ã] 'crowd') or an [s]-nasal sequence (e.g., *dousman* [dus̲m̲ã] 'gently'). HC also allows triconsonantal clusters in medial position (e.g., *afèksyon* [afɛk̲s̲jɔ̃] 'fondness,' *electrik* [elɛk̲t̲ʏik] 'electric').

## 3. *Parallels in process: L1 acquisition*

Having outlined the relevant characteristics of the Fongbe, French and HC consonant inventories and syllable structure, we are now ready to examine six particular differences between HC and its lexifier French. For each of these differences, we will show that the phonological aspects of HC in question can be analyzed as resulting from processes observed in French learner varieties; we begin with parallels with L1 acquisition.

### 3.1 *Misparsing of target strings: liaison contexts*

In L1 acquisition, one of the first tasks faced by children is the parsing of the acoustic signal into its component units, including segments and words. In the case of the latter, cross-word syllabification may complicate the process, as it blurs boundaries between lexical items. One particular consequence of this for

---

[6] In French, the dorsal fricative [ʁ] patterns phonologically with [l] as a liquid.

child learners of French is the frequently observed misparsing of word boundaries in liaison contexts.

Liaison is a syllabification phenomenon in which a final consonant that is normally unrealized in preconsonantal or prepausal position is pronounced when followed by a vowel-initial morpheme or word syllabified within the same rythmic group (i.e., phonological phrase). The examples in (1) below illustrate liaison within the noun phrase, one of the most common obligatory contexts for its application. As shown in (1a), when the following noun begins with a consonant, the final consonant of the determiner or adjective is silent. In contrast, when followed by a vowel-initial word (1b), final [n], [z], and [t] are realized phonetically.

(1) French liaison
   a.  [_C]
       *un livre*       [œ̃.livʁ]        'a book'
       *des livres*     [de.livʁ]       'some books'
       *nos livres*     [no.livʁ]       'our books'
       *petit livre*    [pə.ti.livʁ]    'small book'
   b.  [_V]
       *un article*     [œ̃.naʁ.tikl]    'an article'
       *des articles*   [de.zaʁ.tikl]   'some articles'
       *nos articles*   [no.zaʁ.tikl]   'our articles'
       *petit article*  [pə.ti.taʁ.tikl] 'small article'

In parsing the strings in (1b), children typically begin by misanalyzing the liaison consonant as part of the root. The data in (2b) are representative of such misanalyses.

(2) Children's misparsing of liaison consonants (Côté 2005)
   a.  Adult form                      b.  Child learner forms
       *ours*    [uʁs]    'bear'            [uʁs], [nuʁs], [zuʁs], [tuʁs]

Inspection of the child learner forms in (2b) shows that, along with target-like vowel-initial realizations, children also produce [n]-, [z]- and [t]-initial variants. The misanalysis hypothesis is supported by the fact that the consonants attested in the child learner forms and those that appear in liaison contexts are identical.[7]

Alternations between consonant-initial HC lexical items and their corresponding French vowel-initial etymons (3) parallel the adult-child learner pairings in (2). Like the child learner forms in (2b), the HC forms in (3)

---

[7] Child forms such as [œ̃uʁs] (adult form *un ours* [œ̃nuʁs] 'a bear') further support the misanalysis hypothesis. Were the initial consonants of the forms in (2b) the result of a constraint requiring syllables to have onsets, one would not expect forms like [œ̃uʁs] to exist. Rather, children should simply reproduce the adult form containing the liaison consonant ([œ̃.nuʁs]).

contain a word-initial [n] or [z] absent in the French etymon.[8] Moreover, as is the case in L1 acquisition, both [n]- and [z]-initial variants of the same lexical item may coexist (e.g., French *homme* [ɔm]; HC *nonm* [nɔ̃m] and *zonm* [zɔ̃m]).

(3) Consonant-Ø HC-French alternations: liaison contexts

| | HC | | French etymon | | |
|---|---|---|---|---|---|
| a. | *nanm* | [nãm] | *âme* | [ɑm] | 'soul' |
| | *nechèl* | [neʃɛl] | *échelle* | [eʃɛl] | 'ladder' |
| | *nonm* | [nɔ̃m] | *homme* | [ɔm] | 'man' |
| b. | *zarenyen* | [zaɣɛ̃jɛ̃] | *araignée* | [aʁɛɲe] | 'spider' |
| | *zeb* | [zɛb] | *herbe* | [ɛʁb] | 'grass' |
| | *zwazo* | [zwazo] | *oiseau* | [wazo] | 'bird' |

The types of pairings given in (3) are frequent. We argue that the presence of initial [z] or [n] in the HC form is the consequence of Gbe-speaking learners' misanalysis of the liaison consonant as part of the noun in the early stages of the creole's formation. Note that the presence of this initial consonant is not likely driven by a constraint favoring consonant-initial words, as both the substrate and creole allow for vowel-initial lexical items (e.g., Fongbe *asu* [asu] 'husband'; HC *etid* [etid] 'study'). Such misanalyses parallel those observed in child French. Furthermore, they are not restricted to cases derived from the misanalysis of the final liaison consonant of preposed determiners. Indeed, the HC forms may also involve agglutinated determiners (4a)[9] and prepositions (4b).

(4) Consonant-Ø HC-French alternations: agglutinated determiners and prepositions

| | HC | | | French etymon | | |
|---|---|---|---|---|---|---|
| a. | Agglutinated determiners | | | | | |
| | *lajan* | [laʒã] | 'money' | *l'argent* | [laʁʒã] | '(the) money' |
| | *lafimen* | [lafimɛ̃] | 'smoke' | *la fumée* | [lafyme] | '(the) smoke' |
| b. | Agglutinated prepositions including partitives | | | | | |
| | *nannò* | [nãnnɔ] | 'North' | *dans le nord* | [dãl(ə)nɔʁ] | 'in the North' |
| | *dlo* | [dlo] | 'water' | *de l'eau* | [d(ə)lo] | 'some water' |
| | *danmou* | [dãmu] | 'love' | *d'amour* | [damuʁ] | '(of) love' |

---

[8] The lack of [t]-initial forms in HC is most likely related to its relatively low frequency as a liaison consonant. In the context of noun phrases, it occurs solely in the prenominal adjectives *petit* 'small,' *huit* 'eight,' and *second* 'second.' In contrast, [n] and [z] are highly frequent given their occurrence as the final consonants of the determiners *un* 'a (masc. sg.)' and *les* 'the (pl.).' That [n] and [z] occur most frequently as liaison consonants in prenominal determiners in French increases the likelihood of their being analyzed as part of the root by native speakers of languages with post-nominal determiners such as native speakers of Gbe.

[9] The French definite determiner agglutinated as part of the HC forms is not a separate morpheme in HC. Forms such as *lajan* and *lafimen* are bare nouns, which require an overt determiner in order to be interpreted as definite (e.g., *lajan an* 'the money,' *lafimen an* 'the smoke').

3.2 *Syllable truncation*

Children's earliest phonological outputs generally involve simplification vis-à-vis the target form. Such simplification not only involves the deletion of segments syllabified in marked syllable positions including codas; children may also delete entire syllables. Typical examples of truncation in early child French are given in (5a). In such cases, target items with three or more syllables are realized as disyllabic forms via deletion. In contrast, truncation is typically disfavored in French disyllabic targets (5b; e.g., Boysson-Bardies 1999: 167).[10] In the nontruncated forms, in spite of differences in segmental content, children's outputs resemble their targets in terms of syllable count. Many researchers have argued that the initial syllable deletion exemplified in (5a) serves to enforce a requirement that early words may maximally consist of a single disyllabic foot (e.g., Demuth 1995; Fee 1996).

(5) Truncation in early child French (Demuth & Johnson 2003)

|  | Adult form | | | Child form |
|---|---|---|---|---|
| a. | Tri- and quadrisyllabic targets | | | |
|  | *domino* | [dɔmino] | 'domino' | [ɔjɔ], [bojo] |
|  | *saucisson* | [sosisɔ̃] | 'sausage' | [tɔti] |
|  | *regardez* | [ʁəgaʁde] | 'look (imp.)' | [dade] |
|  | *parapluie* | [paʁaplɥi] | 'umbrella' | [api] |
| b. | Disyllabic targets | | | |
|  | *poupée* | [pupe] | 'doll' | [pepe] |
|  | *crayon* | [kʁɛjɔ̃] | 'pencil' | [ɔjɔ] |
|  | *café* | [kafe] | 'coffee' | [tata] |
|  | *couteau* | [kuto] | 'knife' | [toto] |

Similarly, the HC lexicon contains forms that are truncated vis-à-vis their French etymons. The examples in (6) are representative of the general pattern attested in the language. In all of these cases, the initial syllable of the French etymon fails to appear in the HC form. It is worth noting that, with the exception of a few forms (e.g., *oublier*), the initial syllable can potentially be analyzed as a separate morpheme. The vast majority of French lexical items that made their way into HC in a truncated form are verbs whose first syllable corresponds to a distinct morpheme in French: *a-*, *en-*, *é-*, *dé-* and *re-* are all prefixes that are or have historically been productive in the derivation of verbal forms. There is clear evidence that Gbe-speaking learners of French recognized the independent morphological status of the initial syllables in one case in particular: the prefix *dé-* was borrowed from French and is attested in HC to

---

[10] This is not to say that it is unattested. For example, Demuth and Johnson provide the example of target *merci* [mɛʁsi] 'thank you' realized as [si]/[ʃi] by their child learner.

this day (e.g., *mare* 'to tie,' *demare* 'to untie'; *grese* 'to get fat,' *degrese* 'to lose weight').[11]

(6) Initial syllable deletion: HC lexical items vis-à-vis French etymons

| HC | | French etymon | | |
|---|---|---|---|---|
| a. *tache* | [taʃe] | *attacher* | [ataʃe] | 'to tie' |
| *planni* | [plãni] | *aplanir* | [aplaniʁ] | 'to level' |
| *rive* | [ʁive] | *arriver* | [aʁive] | 'to arrive' |
| *limen* | [limẽ] | *allumer* | [alyme] | 'to light' |
| b. *janbe* | [ʒãbe] | *enjamber* | [ãʒãbe] | 'to straddle' |
| *tande* | [tãde] | *entendez* | [ãtãde] | 'to hear' |
| *voye* | [voje] | *envoyer* | [ãvwaje] | 'to send' |
| *vlope* | [vlope] | *envelopper* | [ãvlɔpe] | 'to wrap' |
| c. *chape* | [ʃape] | *échapper* | [eʃape] | 'to escape' |
| *grennen* | [gɣẽnẽ] | *égrener* | [egʁene] | 'to shell' |
| *klere* | [kleɣe] | *éclairer* | [eklɛʁe] | 'to brighten' |
| *bliye* | [blije] | *oublier* | [ublije] | 'to forget' |
| d. *boule* | [bule] | *débrouiller* | [deb‿uje] | 'to cope' |
| *chire* | [ʃiɣe] | *déchirer* | [deʃiʁe] | 'to shred' |
| *gade* | [gade] | *regarder* | [ʁəgaʁde] | 'to look at' |

As is the case in child French, HC truncation is most often attested in trisyllabic targets. However, also attested are truncations resulting in monosyllabic (e.g., French *attendre* [atãdʁ] > HC *tann* [tãn] 'to wait'; French *écume* [ekym] > HC *kim* [kim] 'foam') and trisyllabic forms (e.g., French *Américain* [ameʁikẽ] > HC *meriken* [meɣikẽ] 'American'; French *assaisonner* [asezɔne] > HC *sizonnen* [sizɔ̃nẽ] 'to season'). Moreover, nontruncated trisyllabic forms exist (e.g., *betize* [betize] 'to deceive,' *kreyati* [kɣejati] 'creature'). However, in the case of the latter, there is no evidence in French that could have led Gbe-speaking learners to analyze the initial syllables as independent morphemes. Regardless of the exact formal motivation,[12] it is nonetheless the case that the

---

[11] This is not to say that each of the French forms in (6) is a complex form containing a prefix or was a complex form at the time of the creation of HC. Rather, given the existence of such prefixes, the French forms in (6) may have been analyzed as containing a prefix by the originators of the creole.

[12] In Optimality-theoretic terms, this may be a case of the Emergence of the Unmarked (TETU; McCarthy & Prince 1994). TETU is a phenomenon in which Markedness constraints, including the constraint favoring disyllabic feet discussed here, are impeded from determining the shape of outputs (i.e., surface forms) due to higher-ranking Faithfulness constraints. In the case of the HC truncation discussed here, the higher-ranking Faithfulness constraint would be one that requires faithfulness to roots, one effect of which would be to block deletion in monomorphemic forms. The importance of satisfying root faithfulness over disyllabic feet would explain the absence of truncation with forms in which the initial syllable cannot be analyzed as a prefix. In contrast, if Gbe speakers posited a bimorphemic analysis for the forms in (6), the initial prefix of trisyllabic targets could be deleted. Deletion of the initial syllable would

forms in (6) show a clear preference for disyllabic outputs, in parallel to the early child French forms in (5a). Indeed, both sets of data are consistent with a process which creates prosodically simpler forms via the deletion of an initial syllable.

It is interesting to note that syllable structure modification motivated by foot constraints also occurs in L2 acquisition. Two studies that have proposed a role for foot structure in shaping L2 learner outputs are Broselow, Chen and Wang (1998) and Steele (2002), which examined Mandarin-speaking learners' acquisition of English word-final consonants and French onset clusters respectively. Analyzing data from Wang (1995), Broselow et al. (1998) argue that an epenthesis asymmetry existing between mono- and disyllabic targets is directly related to an L1-transferred Mandarin constraint favoring disyllabic feet; such a contraint parallels the one argued for here in child French and HC. As shown in Table 1 below, whereas the intermediate learners in question syllabified the final consonant of monosyllabic nonce forms such as *bim* via an epenthetic vowel ($V_e$) in 71.7% of cases, the final consonant of disyllabic targets such as *modit* were syllabified not via epenthesis but rather most often by deletion (62.5%). Broselow et al. point out correctly that both syllabification methods serve to ensure disyllabic feet. As such, foot structure shapes the intermediate Mandarin-speaking L2 learners' outputs.[13]

| Target | | | Epenthesis | | Deletion | |
|---|---|---|---|---|---|---|
| Shape | Example | n | Example | % | Example | % |
| CVC | *bim* | 60 | *bim*$V_e$ (CVCV) | **71.7** | *bi* (CV) | 8.3 |
| CVCVC | *modit* | 120 | *modit*$V_e$ (CVCVCV) | 17.5 | *modi* (CVCV) | **62.5** |

Table 1. *Foot binarity in Mandarin-English (Broselow et al. 1998)*

Steele (2002) reports a similar asymmetry for beginner Mandarin-speaking learners of French, this time with respect to complex onsets. The learners in the study were tested on their syllabification of stop+liquid clusters, including stop+/l/ initial forms. As shown in Table 2, the cluster of a target such as *plie* [pli] was syllabified via epenthesis (learner form [pəli]) in almost two-thirds (61%) of cases. In contrast, clusters in disyllabic targets having an identical segmental profile (e.g., *plateau* [plato]) were syllabified in a target-like manner, that is, without epenthesis, in almost the same percentage of cases (67%).

---

simultaneously fail to violate faithfulness to the root and satisfy the markedness constraint favoring disyllabic feet.

[13] Broselow et al. (1998) propose that this is a case of the Emergence of the Unmarked, as we have proposed for the HC truncations here (see Footnote 12).

| Target | | | Epenthesis $C_1VC_2$ | | Target-like | |
|---|---|---|---|---|---|---|
| Shape | Example | n | Example | % | Example | % |
| CCV | *plie* | 54 | [p_li] (CV$_e$CV) | **61.0** | [pli] (CCV) | 31.0 |
| CCVCV | *plateau* | 55 | [p_lato] (CV$_e$CVCV) | 25.0 | [plato] (CCVCV) | **67.0** |

Table 2. *Foot binarity in Mandarin-French (Steele 2002)*

Were epenthesis in targets such as *plie* driven solely by a phonotoactic constraint prohibiting onset clusters, one would expect similar rates of epenthesis with the initial clusters of forms such as *plateau*, which have an identical segmental profile. Rather, in the same spirit as Broselow et al., Steele argues that epenthesis in monosyllabic forms serves to create disyllabic outputs that satisfy the Mandarin-transferred constraint favoring disyllabic feet.

In summary, the HC truncations in (6) resemble truncations observed in child French. Moreover, under the assumption that the HC syllable deletions are driven at least in part by constraints requiring disyllabic feet, they parallel the epenthesis asymmetries found in Mandarin-speaking learners' outputs.

## 4. *Parallels in processes: L2 acquisition*
Parallels between HC and French L2 learner grammars involve not only changes in syllable count. In what follows, we will demonstrate that four other processes—namely segmental equivalence classification, the transfer of L1 allophonic rules, and two types of syllabification asymmetries—are observed in the interlanguage grammars of adult L2 learners, as well as in HC.

### 4.1 *Segmental equivalence classification*
When acquiring a second language, learners do not always produce new sounds or sounds closely resembling those of their L1 inventory accurately. Indeed, the substitution of target language phones with those deemed to be perceptually similar may occur (Flege 1987; Weinreich 1953). French [ʁ], a voiced dorsal fricative, is rare cross-linguistically and thus must typically be acquired by L2 learners of the language. Substitution of learners' L1 rhotic or some other post-coronal fricative is often observed. For example, in the experiment reported in Steele (2002), some of the beginner Mandarin-speaking learners realized target [ʁ] as the voiceless velar fricative [x] (7a) or the voiceless laryngeal fricative [h] (7b). Such subsitutions are motivated by L1 transfer: Mandarin has a velar but not a uvular series and all obstruents are voiceless. Moreover, [x] and [h] are allophones of the same phoneme (Duanmu 2000: 27).

(7) Mandarin-speaking learners' substitutions for French [ʁ] (Steele 2002)

| | Target form | | | L2 learner form |
|---|---|---|---|---|
| a. | *drapeau* | [dʁapo] | 'flag' | [dʲxapo] |
| | *martinet* | [maʁtinɛ] | 'swift (bird)' | [mʌxtinɛ] |
| b. | *brebis* | [bʁəbi] | 'lamb' | [bʲhɔbi] |
| | *corbillat* | [kɔʁbijɑ] | 'small crow' | [kɔhəbija] |

The adaptation of French *h-aspiré* words in HC shows a similar pattern of equivalence classification involving a post-coronal fricative. In modern French, there are numerous words containing an initial orthographic <h> (e.g., *habits* 'clothing,' *héros* 'hero,' *Hollandais* 'Dutchman,' *hôtel* 'hotel'). Modern French lacks a laryngeal fricative and all such words are phonetically realized as vowel-initial (i.e., [abi], [eʁo], [ɔlãdɛ], [otɛl]). The label "h-aspiré" refers to a subset of these words which pattern like consonant-initial words in blocking liaison (e.g., *un héros* [œ̃eʁo], *[œ̃neʁo]; *dez Hollandais* [deɔlãdɛ], *[dezɔlãdɛ]). "H-muet" words, in contrast, behave phonologically like any other vowel-initial word in triggering liaison (e.g., *un hôtel* [œ̃notɛl], *[œ̃otɛl]; *des habits* [dezabi], *[deabi]).

In words of Germanic origin, the initial <h> of h-aspiré items was historically realized in French, including in the seventeenth-/eighteenth-century varieties to which the Gbe-speaking originators of HC would have been exposed (Brousseau 2005). In contrast, h-muet words were never realized with an initial fricative. Such differences manifest themselves in the HC adaptation of French h-aspiré and h-muet etymons. In adapting the h-aspiré targets in (8), HC substituted the voiced velar fricative [ɣ].

(8) HC adaptation of French h-aspiré etymons

| HC | | French etymon | | |
|---|---|---|---|---|
| *rach* | [ɣaʃ] | *hache* | [haʃ] | 'axe' |
| *ranch* | [ɣãʃ] | *hanche* | [hãʃ] | 'hip' |
| *ranni* | [ɣãni] | *hennir* | [heniʁ] | 'to neigh' |
| *rayi* | [ɣaji] | *haïr* | [ha(j)iʁ] | 'to hate' |

In contrast, the adaptations of h-muet etymons are phonetically vowel-initial (e.g., French *habitude* [abityd] 'habit,' HC *abitid* [abitid]; French *heureuse* [øʁøz] 'happy,' HC *erèz* [eɣɛz]).

The adaptations in (8) parallel the Mandarin-speaking learners' forms in (7). The substrate (i.e., L1) Gbe lacks laryngeals. Accordingly, a Gbe-speaking learner of seventeenth-/eighteenth-century French would have had to acquire [h]. Like the native Mandarin speakers described in Steele (2002), the Gbe-speaking learners proceeded to adapt target [h] via equivalence classification, equating French [h] with [ɣ], an L1 segment that shares the manner and has the closest place of articulation to that of the target segment.

The equivalence classification hypothesis is further supported by the HC adaptation of targets involving [ʁ]. As illustrated by the examples in (9), here too a post-coronal fricative absent from the Gbe inventory is substituted with [ɣ].[14] The forms in (9) mirror the Mandarin-speaking learner forms in (7) even more directly. Both Mandarin and Gbe have a velar but not a uvular series. Accordingly, in an attempt to master target [ʁ], native speakers of both languages substitute the perceptually equivalent velar: [x] for Mandarin speakers and [ɣ] for speakers of Gbe.

(9) HC adaptation of French etymons involving [ʁ]

| HC | | French etymon | | |
|----|----|----|----|----|
| *rim* | [ɣim] | *rhume* | [ʁym] | 'cold (n.)' |
| *trete* | [tɣete] | *traiter* | [tʁete] | 'to treat' |
| *erèz* | [eɣɛz] | *heureuse* | [øʁøz] | 'happy' |
| *ipokrit* | [ipokɣit] | *hypocrite* | [ipokʁit] | 'hypocrite' |

The fact that this substitution also occurs after a coronal (e.g., *trete* [tɣete]), that is, in the only context where Gbe allows the coronal [r], confirms that the target [ʁ] is substituted by a sound that is perceptually equivalent, and not phonologically equivalent.

*4.2 Transfer of L1 allophonic rules*

Patterns of L1-influenced substitution are not driven by equivalence classification alone. L2 learners may acquire target-language sounds in a native-like manner yet apply allophonic rules transferred from the L1, resulting in non-target-like realizations in certain environments. For example, in many varieties of English, the lateral /l/ is velarized in coda (e.g., *lab* [læb], *ball* [bɑɫ], *[bɑl]). English-speaking learners of such varieties typically transfer this rule into their interlanguage French (e.g., target *il vole* [ilvɔl] 'he steals'; learner realization [iɫvɔɫ]). Transferred allophonic rules may be fossilized and hence exist even in the grammars of advanced learners.

Allophonic variation in the realization of HC /ɣ/ can also be understood as a case of the transfer and fossilization of an L1-based allophonic rule. As shown in (10b and c), in both singleton and complex onsets, HC /ɣ/ is realized as [w] in front of the rounded vowels [o], [ɔ] and [u]. In all other contexts, it is realized as [ɣ]. No such alternation exists in French, where [ʁ] can occur before any vowel.

---

[14] HC [ɣ] patterns as a sonorant rather than a fricative in such forms. As such, HC parallels Fongbe, for which it is necesssary to posit both a fricative and sonorant [ɣ]. A further parallel exists with French, where a post-coronal fricative ([ʁ]) patterns phonologically with sonorants.

(10)  Allophonic variation in HC /ɣ/

| | HC | | French etymon | | |
|---|---|---|---|---|---|
| a. | *ra* | [ɣa] | *rare* | [ʁaʁ] | 'rare' |
| | *chire* | [ʃiɣe] | *déchirer* | [deʃiʁe] | 'to shred' |
| | *pouri* | [puɣi] | *pourri* | [puʁi] | 'rotten' |
| | *debraye* | [debɣaje] | *débraillé* | [debʁaje] | 'sloppy' |
| | *chevrèt* | [ʃevɣɛt] | *crevette* | [kʁəvɛt]~[ʃəvʁɛt] | 'shrimp' |
| | *prete* | [pɣete] | *prêter* | [pʁete] | 'to lend' |
| b. | *nimero* | [nimewo] | *numéro* | [nymeʁo] | 'number' |
| | *paròl* | [pawɔl] | *parole* | [paʁɔl] | 'words' |
| | *ronfle* | [wɔ̃fle] | *ronfler* | [ʁɔ̃fle] | 'to snore' |
| | *roulo* | [wulo] | *rouleau* | [ʁulo] | 'roll' |
| | *tròp* | [twɔp] | *trop* | [tʁo] | 'too (much)' |
| | *gronde* | [gwɔ̃de] | *gronder* | [gʁɔ̃de] | 'to scold' |
| | *patron* | [patwɔ̃] | *patron* | [patʁɔ̃] | 'boss' |
| | *debrouye* | [debwuje] | *debrouiller* | [debʁuje] | 'to cope' |
| c. | *ro* | [wo] | *haut* | [ho] | 'high' |
| | *ront* | [wɔ̃t] | *honte* | [hɔ̃t] | 'shame' |
| | *rou* | [wu] | *houe* | [hu] | 'wake (water)' |

The identical allophonic variation occurs in some Gbe dialects. In these varieties, the sonorant [ɣ] is in complementary distribution with [w].[15] Its distribution is identical to that observed in HC: [w] occurs before back vowels, [ɣ] is found elsewhere. As such, the HC variation in the realization of /ɣ/ is a clear case of the transfer of an L1 allophonic rule.

### 4.3 *Asymmetries in the acquisition of initial clusters*

When acquiring a target language possessing a greater range of consonant clusters than those possible in the L1, L2 learners typically do not acquire all clusters with equal ease. In the case of onset clusters, previous research has demonstrated that clusters with an unmarked sonority profile are typically acquired first (Broselow & Finer 1991; Eckman & Iverson 1993).[16] Clusters with more marked sonority profiles, including obstruent+obstruent clusters and /s/+obstruent clusters, are generally acquired later.

The HC adaptation of three types of clusters that do not exist in Gbe also shows an asymmetrical pattern of treatment. Whereas stop+glide clusters

---

[15] This complementary distribution is found only in the Gbe dialects that have [ɣ] in their inventory. This includes Fongbe ([ɣ] = fricative and sonorant) and Phla-Phera ([ɣ] = fricative).

[16] Stop+liquid clusters (e.g., French *plateau* [plato] 'platter'), in which a low-sonority non-continuant is followed by a high-sonority continuant, are typically considered the unmarked case (Clements 1990).

present in French are also present in HC (11), initial stop+nasal and /sC/ clusters are not.[17]

(11)  Realization of French stop+glide clusters in HC

| HC | | French etymon | | |
|---|---|---|---|---|
| byè | [bjɛ] | bière | [bjɛʁ] | 'beer' |
| tyèd | [tjɛd] | tiède | [tjɛd] | 'lukewarm' |
| pwason | [pwasɔ̃] | poisson | [pwasɔ̃] | 'fish' |
| kwaf | [kwaf] | coiffe | [kwaf] | 'headdress' |

As shown in (12), French stop+nasal and stop+fricative clusters were adapted via deletion of the stop.

(12)  Realization of French stop+nasal/stop+fricative clusters in HC

| HC | | French etymon | | |
|---|---|---|---|---|
| nemoni | [nemoni] | pneumonie | [pnømɔni] | 'pneumonia' |
| sikyatri | [sikjatɣi] | psychiatrie | [psikiatʁi] | 'psychiatry' |

Initial /sC/ clusters, in contrast, are syllabified via epenthesis.[18]

(13)  Realization of French /sC/ clusters in HC

| HC | | French etymon | | |
|---|---|---|---|---|
| eskandal | [eskãdal] | scandale | [skãdal] | 'scandal' |
| eskolè | [eskolɛ] | scolaire | [skɔlɛʁ] | 'school (adj.)' |
| eskòpyon | [eskɔpjɔ̃] | scorpion | [skɔʁpjɔ̃] | 'scorpion' |
| estade | [estad] | stade | [stad] | 'stadium' |

In summary, the HC adaptation of French initial consonant clusters parallels asymmetries attested in L2 acquisition, where clusters of with an unmarked sonority profile are acquired first.

### 4.4 Asymmetries in the deletion of coda /l/ versus /r/

It is not only in the acquisition of clusters that asymmetries are attested to L2 acquisition. When acquiring new syllable positions including codas, L2 learners often do not acquire all contrasts within such positions in an all-or-none matter. Rather, a subset of the target-language contrasts is typically acquired first. For example, learners whose L1 lacks codas may master voiceless stops before their voiced counterparts (Eckman 1981; Flege & Davidian 1984).

A comparison of HC and French reveals a similar difference regarding the HC adaptation of coda /l/ and /ʁ/. As illustrated by the etymons in (14), French

---

[17] This asymmetry may also be due to the fact that a limited set of /Cj/ and /Cw/ clusters is present in Gbe. The acquisition of clusters such as /tj/ or /pw/ would have been facilitated by the convergence of two factors: their unmarked sonority profile and the presence of similar clusters in the substrate language.

[18] HC is unusual in this respect, as vowel prothesis is unusual in Atlantic creoles (Holm 1988: 110).

allows for both word-internal and word-final liquid codas. This contrasts starkly with Gbe, which prohibits codas of any type. Inspection of the HC adaptations shows a clear asymmetry between targets containing /l/ versus /r/ codas. In the case of the former, the HC and French forms are identical (14a).[19] In contrast, the HC variants of French targets containing rhotic codas (14b) all involve deletion of the [ʁ].

(14)  HC adaptation of French liquid codas

<table>
<tr><td></td><td colspan="2">HC</td><td colspan="2">French etymon</td><td></td></tr>
<tr><td>a.</td><td>pal</td><td>[pal]</td><td>pâle</td><td>[pɑl]</td><td>'pale'</td></tr>
<tr><td></td><td>kalm</td><td>[kalm]</td><td>calme</td><td>[kalm]</td><td>'respite'</td></tr>
<tr><td></td><td>elve</td><td>[elve]</td><td>elever</td><td>[elve]</td><td>'to raise'</td></tr>
<tr><td></td><td>salte</td><td>[salte]</td><td>saleté</td><td>[salte]</td><td>'dirtiness'</td></tr>
<tr><td>b.</td><td>pa</td><td>[pa]</td><td>part</td><td>[paʁ]</td><td>'share'</td></tr>
<tr><td></td><td>kat</td><td>[kat]</td><td>carte</td><td>[kaʁt]</td><td>'map'</td></tr>
<tr><td></td><td>mache</td><td>[maʃe]</td><td>marcher</td><td>[maʁʃe]</td><td>'to walk'</td></tr>
<tr><td></td><td>chabon</td><td>[ʃabõ]</td><td>charbon</td><td>[ʃaʁbõ]</td><td>'coal'</td></tr>
</table>

| Type | Target Example | n | Target-like | Syllabification Epenthesis | Deletion |
|---|---|---|---|---|---|
| ClV | plie /pli/ | 54 | **.31** | .61 | |
| CrV | pré /pʁe/ | 78 | **.18** | .43 | .27 |
| ClVCV | plateau /plato/ | 55 | **.67** | .25 | |
| CrVCV | préfet /pʁefɛ/ | 75 | **.20** | .36 | .33 |
| CVClV | chapelet /ʃaplɛ/ | 50 | **.66** | .28 | |
| CVCrV | cyprès /sipʁɛ/ | 47 | **.21** | .24 | .28 |
| CVClVCV | diplômé /diplome/ | 50 | **.90** | .08 | |
| CVCrVCV | soprano /sopʁano/ | 55 | **.11** | .13 | .60 |

Table 3. *Beginner Mandarin-speaking learners' syllabification of French stop+liquid onset clusters (Steele 2002)*

[19] Whereas forms with a singleton word-internal or -final /l/ coda are frequent in HC, forms with a final /lC/ coda are rare (e.g., [filt] 'filter,' [puls] 'pulse'). Furthermore, while one dictionary consulted provides [kalm] as the HC form for French *calme* [kalm] 'respite,' another provides the truncated form [kal].

Data from Steele's (2002) study of native Mandarin speakers' acquisition of syllable-initial stop+liquid clusters shows a similar asymmetry. As shown in Table 3, the beginner learners were more accurate with targets involving a lateral as the second member of the cluster for all stimuli shapes. For example, in the case of trisyllabic targets such as *diplômé* [diplome] 'graduate' and *soprano* [sopʁano] 'soprano,' the Mandarin-speaking learners were 90% accurate with the former targets versus a very low 11% with their rhotic counterparts. Of particular interest for the parallel being drawn here is that deletion is observed only with rhotics. This directly parallels the HC creole adaptation of French coda /r/.

As shown in (15), HC permits fricative codas including voiced [v] and [ʒ], which parallel French [ʁ] in manner and voicing. Consequently, deletion cannot result from a phonological constraint prohibiting syllable-final fricatives more generally.

(15)  HC fricative codas
| | | |
|---|---|---|
| *avni* | [aṿni] | 'avenue' |
| *diskite* | [diṣkite] | 'to discuss' |
| *achte* | [aʃte] | 'to buy' |
| *deranjman* | [deɣãʒmã] | 'pain' |

Ultimately, regardless of the motivation for coda [ʁ] deletion in HC, there exists a parallel asymmetry vis-à-vis the L2 data from Steele (2002). In both contexts, although a high degree of faithfulness to the target is witnessed with lateral targets, the realization of rhotic targets involves considerable deletion.

## 5.  *Summary and conclusion*

In this paper, we have examined six respects in which the phonology of HC differs from that of its lexifier French. These include initial C-∅ alternations and syllable truncations, segmental adaptation and substrate-based alternations not attested in the lexifier, and simplified syllable structure as concerns both word-initial consonant clusters and codas. For each of these differences, we have demonstrated parallel processes in the L1 and/or L2 acquistion of French. The processes in question have been of various sorts, including learners' misparsing of target forms, equivalence classification driven by perceived similarity between target and L1 phones, transferred allophonic rules, and prosodic constraints on both syllable and foot structure.

In contrast to previous research, which has tended to compare creoles, their substrates and lexifiers in terms of inventories and general sound patterns, we have chosen here to focus on specific phonetic and phonological processes using sets of lexical items. As has been demonstrated, such an approach reveals differences between the creole and its contributing languages that have previously gone unnoticed. For example, others have commented on creole syllable structure modification including onset cluster and coda simplification as a fairly unified phenomenon. However, the comparison made with learner grammars here reveals that their simplification is actually a multifaceted process driven by various constraints, including those on syllable and foot structure.

Our claim is not that creole formation can be reduced simply to non-native-like acquisition. Rather, the comparison between HC and its lexifier French that we have undertaken parallels that between L1/L2 learner varieties and target French. Such a comparison reveals strong similarities as concerns the processes involved in the formation of creole phonologies and those that shape learner grammars. One might argue that the processes investigated are isolated and that they played but a marginal role in shaping the HC phonological system. The present work is the first step in a larger project that will undertake a systematic comparison of HC, its contributing languages and French learner varieties. By applying the methodology adopted here to a broader range of segmental and prosodic phenomena, we hope to determine whether the patterns outlined are representative of a larger set of phonetic and phonological processes that shape creole sound systems.

*References*
Andersen, R. W. (ed.) 1983. *Pidginization and Creolization as Language Acquisition*. Rowley, MA: Newbury House.
Becker, A. and T. Veenstra. 2003. The survival of inflectional morphology in French-related creoles. *Studies in Second Language Acquisition* 25: 283–306.
Bentolila, A. (ed.) 1976. *Ti diksyonnè kreyol-franse: dictionnaire élémentaire créole haïtien-français*. Port-au Prince: Éditions Caraïbes.
Boysson-Bardies, de B. 1999. *Comment la parole vient aux enfants*. Paris: Éditions Odile Jacob.
Broselow, E., S.-I. Chen and C. Wang. 1998. The emergence of the unmarked in second language phonology. *Studies in Second Language Acquisition* 20(2): 261–280.
Broselow, E. and D. Finer. 1991. Parameter setting in second language phonology and syntax. *Second Language Research* 7(1): 35–59.
Brousseau, A.-M. 2005. The sociolect of 17th–18th century French settlers: Phonological clues from French creoles. In *Selected Papers from NWAVE 32, Penn Working Papers in Linguistics 10.2,* 45–60. Philadelphia, Penn Linguistics Club.
Brown, R. 1973. *A First Language: The Early Stages*. London: George Allen & Unwin.
Capo, H. B. C. 1991. *A Comparative Phonology of Gbe*. Dordrecht: Foris.
Clark, E. V. 2003. *First Language Acquisition*. Cambridge: Cambridge University Press.

Clements, G. N. 1990. The role of the sonority cycle in core syllabification. In *Papers in Laboratory Phonology I: Between the Grammar and Physics of Speech*, J. Kingston and M. E. Beckman (eds.), 283–333. New York: Cambridge University Press.

Corne, C. 1999. *From French to Creole: The Development of New Vernaculars in the French Colonial World*. London: University of Westminster.

Côté, M.-H. 2005. Le statut lexical des consonnes de liaison. *Langages* 158: 66–78.

DeGraff, M. 1999. Creolization, language change and language acquisition: An epilogue. In *Language Creation and Language Change: Creolization, Diachrony and Development*, M. DeGraff (ed.), 473–543. Cambridge, MA: MIT Press.

Demuth, K. 1995. Markedness and the development of prosodic structure. In *Proceedings of the North East Linguistic Society 25*, J. N. Beckman (ed.), 13–25. Amherst, MA: Graduate Linguistic Student Association.

Demuth, K. and M. Johnson. 2003. Truncation to subminimal words in Early French. *Canadian Journal of Linguistics* 48(3/4): 211–241.

Duanmu, S. 2000. *The Phonology of Standard Chinese*. Oxford: Oxford University Press.

Ebenezer Mission. No date. *Kreyol to English Dictionary*. www.ebenezermission.com.

Eckman, F. 1981. On the naturalness of interlanguage phonological rules. *Language Learning* 31: 195–216.

Eckman, F. and G. Iverson. 1993. Sonority and markedness among onset clusters in the interlanguage of ESL learners. *Second Language Research* 9: 234–252.

Fee, J. E. 1996. Syllable structure and minimal words. In *Proceedings of the International Conference on Phonological Acquisition*, B. Bernhardt, J. Gilbert and D. Ingram (eds.), 85–98. Somerville, MA: Cascadilla Press.

Flege, J. E. 1987. The production of "new" and "similar" phones in a foreign language: Evidence for the effect of equivalence classification. *Journal of Phonetics* 15: 47–65.

Flege, J. E. 1995. Second language speech learning: Theory, findings, and problems. In *Speech Perception and Linguistic Experience: Issues in Cross-Language Research*, W. Strange (ed.), 233–277. Timonium, MD: York Press.

Flege, J. E. and R. D. Davidian. 1984. Transfer and developmental processes in adult foreign language speech production. *Applied Psycholinguistics* 5(4): 323–347.

Greenberg, J. 1963. *The Languages of Africa*. Bloomington, IN: Indiana Press.

Holm, J. 1988. *Pidgins and Creoles*. Cambridge: Cambridge University Press.

Klein, W. and C. Perdue. 1997. The basic variety (or: Couldn't natural languages be much simpler?). *Second Language Research* 13(4): 301–347.

Lefebvre, C. 1998. *Creole Genesis and the Acquisition of Grammar: The Case of Haitian Creole*. Cambridge: Cambridge University Press.

Mather, P.-A. 2000. Cross-Linguistic Influence in Second Language Acquisition and in Creole Genesis. Ph.D. dissertation, University of Pittsburgh.

McCarthy, J. and A. Prince. 1994. The emergence of the unmarked: Optimality in prosodic morphology. In *Proceedings of the North East Linguistic Society 24*, M. González (ed.), 333–379. Amherst, MA: Graduate Linguistic Student Association.

McWhorter, J. 2001. The world's simplest grammars are creole grammars. *Linguistic Typology* 5: 125–156.

McWhorter, J. 2004. Saramaccan and Haitian as young grammars: The pitfalls of syntactocentrism in creole genesis research. *Journal of Pidgin and Creole Languages* 19(1): 77–139.

Muysken, P. 2001. The origin of creole languages: The perspective of second language learning. In *Creolization and Contact*, N. Smith and T. Veenstra (eds.), 157–173. Amsterdam/Philadelphia: John Benjamins.

Roberts, S. J. 2000. Nativization and genesis of Hawaiian Creole. In *Language Change and Language Contact in Pidgins and Creoles*, J. McWhorter (ed.), 257–300. Amsterdam: Benjamins.

Segurola, B. and J. Rassinoux. 2000. *Dictionnaire fon-français*. Madrid: Société des Missions Africaines.

Siegel, J. 2004. Morphological simplicity in pidgins and creoles. *Journal of Pidgin and Creole Languages* 19(1): 139–162.

Steele, J. 2002. Representation and Phonological Licensing in the Second Language Acquisition of Prosodic Structure. Ph.D. dissertation, McGill University.

Valdman, A. 1978. *Le créole: Structure, statut et origine*. Paris: Klincksieck.

Valdman, A. 1980. Creolization as second language acquisition. In *Theoretical Orientations in Creole Studies* A. Highfield (ed.), 297–311. New York: Academic Press.

Valdman, A. 1981. *Haitian Creole-English-French Dictionary*. Bloomington, IN: Creole Institute.

Véronique, D. 1994. Naturalistic adult acquisition of French as L2 and French-based creole genesis compared: Insights into creolization and language change. In *Creolization and Language Change*, D. Adone and I. Plag (eds.), 297–311. Tübingen: Max Niemeyer.

Wang, C. 1995. The Acquisition of English Word-Final Stops by Chinese Speakers. Ph.D. dissertation, State University of New York, Stony Brook.

Weinreich, U. 1953. *Languages in Contact: Findings and Problems*. The Hague: Mouton.

Welmers, W. 1974. *African Language Structures*. Berkeley/Los Angeles: University of California Press.

White, L. 2003. *Second Language Acquisition and Universal Grammar*. Cambridge: Cambridge University Press.

# FONGBE CONSONANTS BASED ON CAPO (1991) AND SEGUROLA AND RASSINOUX (2000)

| | Initial | | | | | | Medial | | | | | |
|-----|-----|-----|-----|-----|-----|-----|-----|-----|-----|-----|-----|-----|
| | w | j | l | r | m | n | w | j | l | r | m | n |
| t | | ?/1 | (+) | + | – | – | [+] | – | (+) | + | – | – |
| d | | – | (+) | + | – | – | [+] | – | (+) | + | – | – |
| k | [+] | ?/1 | + | – | – | – | [+] | – | + | – | – | – |
| g | [+] | ?/1 | + | – | – | – | [+] | – | + | – | – | – |
| tʃ | | + | (+)/1 | + | – | – | [+] | + | (+) | + | – | – |
| dʒ | | – | (+) | + | – | – | [+] | – | (+) | + | – | – |
| kp | | – | + | – | – | – | [+] | + | + | – | – | – |
| gb | | – | + | – | – | – | | + | + | – | – | – |
| xw | | –/1 | + | – | – | – | | – | + | – | – | – |
| ɣw | | –/4 | + | – | – | – | | – | + | – | – | – |
| f | | + | + | – | – | – | [+] | + | + | – | – | – |
| v | | +/0 | + | – | – | – | [+] | + | + | – | – | – |
| s | [+] | + | (+) | + | – | – | [+] | + | (+) | + | – | – |
| z | [+] | +/1 | (+) | + | – | – | [+] | – | – | – | – | – |
| x | | +/1 | + | – | – | – | | – | + | – | – | – |
| ɣ | | + | + | – | – | – | | – | + | – | – | – |
| b | | + | + | – | – | – | [+] | – | + | – | – | – |
| ɗ | | +/1 | – | – | – | – | [+] | – | – | – | – | – |
| m | [+] | + | + | – | – | – | | + | + | – | – | – |
| n | | – | – | – | – | – | | – | – | – | – | – |
| ɲ | | – | (+) | + | – | – | | – | (+) | + | – | – |
| l | [+] | + | – | – | – | – | [+] | + | – | – | – | – |
| w | | +/1 | + | – | – | – | | – | + | – | – | – |
| j | [+] | – | (+) | + | – | – | | – | (+) | + | – | – |

Figure 1. *Fongbe consonant phonotactics*[1]

---

[1] Coding: (i) cases where results from Capo (1991) and Segurola and Rassinoux (2000) are not consistent are indicated as follows: signs on the left of the slash are those in Capo (1991) while numbers on the right of the slash indicate the number of occurrences found in Segurola and Rassinoux (2000) for the combination in question; (ii) ? indicates a marginally acceptable form according to Capo (1991); (iii) (+) signifies that [l] appears in allophonic variation with [r] following coronals; (iv) [+] indicates that the [w] in question is derived from the initial [+round] vowel of a VV string.

| Bilabial | Labio-dental | Alveo-dental | Alveo-palatal | Palatal | Velar | Labio-velar |
|---|---|---|---|---|---|---|
| | | t,d | | | k,g | kp,gb |
| | f,v | s,z | | | x,ɣ | xw,ɣw |
| | | | tʃ,dʒ | | | |
| b [m]² | | ɖ [n] | | ɲ | | |
| | | l | | | | |
| w | | | | j [j̃] | | |

Figure 2. *Fongbe consonant inventory*

---

² Gbe [b] and [d] pattern with the language's sonorants with respect to tone. They are in complementary distribution with the nasals [m] and [n]: [b] and [d] appear before oral vowels, while the nasals appear elsewhere.

# HC CONSONANTS FOLLOWING BENTOLILA (1976), VALDMAN (1981) AND EBENEZER MISSION (NO DATE)

| | Initial | | | | | | | Medial | | | | | | |
|---|---|---|---|---|---|---|---|---|---|---|---|---|---|---|
| | w | j | l | ɣ | m | n | X | w | j | l | ɣ | m | n | X |
| p | + | + | + | + | − | − | | + | + | + | + | + | − | s, t |
| b | + | + | + | + | − | − | | + | + | + | + | − | 1 | s |
| t | + | + | − | + | − | − | | + | + | + | + | + | + | s |
| d | + | + | 1 | + | 1 | − | | + | + | 3 | + | + | + | s |
| k | + | 2 | + | + | − | 1 | 1-s | + | + | + | + | + | + | s, t |
| g | + | − | + | + | − | − | | + | + | + | + | + | − | z |
| tʃ | 2 | − | − | − | − | − | | − | − | − | − | − | − | |
| dʒ | − | − | − | − | − | − | | − | − | − | − | − | − | |
| f | + | + | + | + | − | − | | + | + | + | + | + | 1 | |
| v | + | + | + | + | − | − | | + | + | + | + | + | + | |
| s | + | + | − | − | − | − | 1-t | + | + | + | + | + | − | |
| z | + | 1 | − | − | − | − | | + | + | 1 | − | + | 2 | |
| ʃ | + | + | − | − | − | − | | + | − | − | + | + | − | |
| ʒ | + | − | − | − | − | − | | + | + | − | + | + | 1 | |
| m | + | + | − | − | − | − | | + | + | − | + | + | + | |
| n | + | + | − | − | − | − | | + | + | − | 2 | + | − | |
| ɲ | | | | | | | | + | − | − | − | − | − | |
| l | + | + | − | − | − | − | | + | + | − | 1 | + | − | |
| ɣ | + | − | − | − | − | − | | − | + | − | − | − | − | |
| w | − | − | − | − | − | − | | − | − | − | − | − | − | |
| j | − | − | − | − | − | − | | − | − | − | − | − | − | |

Figure 3. *HC consonant phonotactics*[1]

---

[1] Coding: (i) X stands for other consonants that occur marginally as the second consonant of a cluster; (ii) [ɲ] is never allowed in word-initial position, which explains the systematic gaps in the left-hand side of the table; (iii) where only one or two occurrences of the given cluster are found in the dictionaries consulted, this is indicated with a numeral.

| Bilabial | Labio-dental | Alveo-dental | Alveo-palatal | Palatal | Velar |
|---|---|---|---|---|---|
| p,b | | t,d | | | k,g |
| | f,v | s,z | ʃ,ʒ | | <ɣ>[2] |
| | | | tʃ,dʒ | | |
| m | | n | | ɲ | [ŋ] |
| | | l | w | | |
| w | | | | j [j̃] | <ɣ> |

Figure 4. *HC consonant inventory*

---

[2] See Footnote 14 for an explanation of the dual status of HC [ɣ].

# PART IV

## PROCESSES: FINAL STATE (FOSSILIZATION)

# EXTERNAL AND INTERNAL FACTORS IN BILINGUAL AND BIDIALECTAL LANGUAGE DEVELOPMENT:
## GRAMMATICAL GENDER OF THE DUTCH DEFINITE DETERMINER

Leonie Cornips
*Meertens Institute*

Aafke Hulk
*University of Amsterdam*

In the last few decades, many European countries have developed into bilingual societies. First, population shifts induced by large-scale technical and economic development have broadened the number and range of linguistic communities in contact in European cities. One of the outcomes is widespread bilingualism among the ethnic minority populations. The children born in these communities, even those who are raised bilingually from birth, are frequently exposed to language input from their parents, grandparents and siblings who have learned the language of the host country as adult L2 speakers in a non-instructed context. Second, bilingualism or bidialectalism has increased in geographical areas where local dialects are common, such that monolingual speakers of local dialects are now the exception. The aim of this paper is to examine the effects of language-internal and -external factors with respect to the acquisition of the grammatical gender of the Dutch definite determiner in both an ethnic minority and a standard-dialect community. The results of a sentence completion test in these two bilingual communities are very different. Compared to their monolingual peers, bilingual children in the ethnic minority communities show a non-target-like acquisition of the definite determiner *het* [neuter] ("fossilization" effect). This effect is creole-like in the sense that (i) it involves "simplification" of grammatical gender and (ii) it emerges rapidly in immigrants' speech and does not disappear in subsequent generations that are born in The Netherlands and acquire Dutch from birth onwards. In contrast, the bilingual/bidialectal children in the dialect community show an acceleration in the correct use of *het* [neuter] compared with their monolingual peers ("progressive" development). In this paper, we show that language-internal factors explain this effect. Finally, we consider the role of external factors, and show that it is not societal bilingualism per se that is relevant here. In other words, it is not the quantity of the Dutch input (which is the same for both types of bilingual communities) but the quality of the Dutch (parental) input that turns out to be the crucial factor.

## 1. *Introduction*

In many European countries, monolingualism is considered the norm. However, in the last few decades, countries such as the Netherlands have developed into bilingual societies. In this paper, we will focus on two types of bilingual communities, namely a "new" one and an "old" one. The "new" one is the result of population shifts, namely immigrants entering a new country, induced by large-scale technical and economic developments. These immigrants may shift to Dutch without completely taking over the grammatical system that exists in the grammar of native Dutch speakers (Thomason & Kaufman 1988). The "old" one refers to bilingual or bidialectal communities in geographical areas where nonstandard dialects are common. Nowadays, the phenomenon of bilingualism or bidialectalism has increased so much that monolingual speakers of nonstandard dialects have become the exception; that is, children often acquire a local dialect in addition to the standard language and are therefore raised bilingually, either from birth or from school age onwards.

In earlier work (Hulk & Cornips 2006) we found that bilingual children of the "new" bilingual type show a loss of grammatical gender in Dutch compared to their monolingual peers; that is to say, they "fossilize" with respect to the acquisition of the neuter definite determiner. The loss of grammatical gender is creole-like in the sense that it emerges rapidly in immigrants' speech and does not disappear in subsequent generations that are born in the Netherlands and acquire Dutch from birth onwards. Subsequently, the bilingual children have a potential role in contact effects as observed in creole and other languages. On the one hand, the loss of grammatical gender is well known in Dutch lexifier contact languages such as Negerhollands (Muysken 2001: 165), Berbice Dutch, Afrikaans (Donaldson 1993; Ponelis 2005), Curaçaos-Dutch (Joubert 2005), Surinamese-Dutch (Cornips 2005), and Indisch-Dutch (De Vries 2005). On the other, the loss of grammatical gender takes place in non ethnic minority communities in other countries too, such as the suburbs of Sweden where immigrants and their children learn Swedish as the target language (Kotsinas 2001: 150).

In comparison to the bilingual children of the new type, we will report new experimental results showing that bilingual children of the "old" type reveal an "accelerated" acquisition of the neuter gender of the Dutch definite determiner. In order to explain these striking differences in *societal* bilingual contexts, we will carefully disentangle various external and internal factors that play a role in language development. We will argue that the fossilization effect is due to (i) internal factors, and (ii) the quantity and the quality of Dutch in the (parental) input (Sorace 2005) the bilingual children are exposed to in their sociolinguistic context. We will suggest that the fossilization effect specifically arises in a multigenerational scenario in ethnic minority communities.

This paper is organized as follows. First, we will talk about the gender distinction in Dutch. Second, we will present our experimental results and linguistic factors involved in the (un)successful acquisition of grammatical gender by bilingual children of ethnic minority and bidialectal communities. Finally, we will discuss similarities and differences between the two types of bilingual communities.

## 2. *Gender distinction in standard Dutch determiners*

The acquisition of the gender of the Dutch definite determiner involves more than just lexicon and syntax. Definite determiners are obligatory under certain semantic and pragmatic conditions, which we will not discuss here. In the experiments considered (see sections 3.1 and 3.2), the conditions are such that the definite determiner is always obligatory. What interests us here is the morphology of this determiner. The definite determiner in standard Dutch is a prenominal morpheme. Unlike English, Dutch distinguishes between neuter and non-neuter nouns. This gender distinction is morphologically visible on the determiner if it has the features singular and definite: neuter nouns take *het* and non-neuter nouns take *de,* as illustrated in Table 1 and the examples in (1). In contrast, no gender distinction is reflected the indefinite article in Dutch, which is *een* for both neuter and non-neuter nouns.[1]

| Definite determiner | Singular | Plural | Indefinite | Diminutive |
|---|---|---|---|---|
| neuter noun *boek* 'book' | *het* | de | een | *het* boek*je* |
| non-neuter noun *tafel* 'table' | de | de | een | *het* tafel*tje* |

Table 1. *The morphology of the definite determiner in Dutch*

The only salient morphological cues on the noun are the diminutive suffix *–(t)je,* which always makes the noun neuter, as exemplified in (1a), and the plural suffixes *–en* or *–s,* which always require the determiner *de,* as illustrated in (1b) and Table 1 above:

(1) a. *het*            tafel*tje*       *het*            boek*je*
        the (NEUTER)  table + DIM  the (NEUTER)  book+DIM
   b. *de*     tafel*s*           *de*             boek*en*
        the      table +PLUR   the (PLUR)   book+PLUR

Linguistically speaking, (nominal) gender in Dutch can be analyzed as an [uninterpretable] feature, whose default value is [non-neuter]. The gender feature has to combine with the [+singular] number feature and the [interpretable] [+ definite] feature in order to morphologically realize the specific value [neuter] on the definite determiner.

From a developmental point of view, four stages can be distinguished in the *monolingual* acquisition of determiners in Dutch (cf. Bol & Kuiken 1988; De Houwer & Gillis 1998; Zonneveld 1992), as shown in Table 2. Crucially,

---

[1] Not only determiners, but also demonstrative determiners and personal and relative pronouns agree in gender with the accompanying noun in the singular. These elements are outside the scope of this paper, as are attributive adjectives, which also vary morphologically according to the gender of the noun, under certain conditions.

monolingual children do not acquire the target grammar before the age of six (Van de Velde 2004):

| |
|---|
| Stage 1:   only bare nouns |
| Stage 2:   schwa-element + noun which can be interpreted as the indefinite article |
|            *een* 'a(n)' (before the age of 2) |
| Stage 3a:   •   definite article *de* with both [non-neuter] and [neuter] nouns |
| Stage 3b:   •   first appearance of *het*, but massive *overgeneralization* of the non-neuter |
|            definite determiner *de* |
| Stage 4:   target grammar (not before the age of 6) |

Table 2. *Stages of determiner acquisition*

According to a dictionary-based estimate, roughly 75% of Dutch nouns are non-neuter (*de*-words) and only 25% are neuter (*het*-words). Van Berkum (1996) examined the relative distribution of *de*- and *het*-words in computerized databases and found that in running texts the estimate is roughly 2:1.

## 2.1 *Grammatical gender in the other languages of the bilingual children*

The bilingual children of ethnic minority communities are of Moroccan, Turkish, Ghanaian, Surinamese and French descent (see section 3.1). Consequently, the "other" languages of the children involved are Moroccan-Arabic, Berber, Turkish, Akan, Ewe, Sranan, and French. These languages widely vary in the way they express definiteness and grammatical gender. The determiner in standard Dutch is a prenominal morpheme and there is no apparent (structural) overlap with the determiner systems in the above-mentioned languages mentioned above. In addition, although French, Moroccan-Arabic and Berber have a gender distinction in their noun/determiner system, Turkish, Akan/Ewe and Sranan do not. We will discuss the issue of cross-linguistic influence in more detail later (section 3.1).

The language of the bidialectal children involved in our experiment is the local dialect of Heerlen. Heerlen is located in the province of Limburg in the southeastern part of the Netherlands; it is a town of about 90,000 inhabitants near the German and Belgian borders. The dialect of Heerlen is situated in the westernmost dialect-geographical transition zone of the Ripuarian dialects, a subbranch of the Franconian dialect group. From a linguistic point of view, it was heavily influenced by the German city of Cologne for centuries. In the speech repertoire in Heerlen, there is a structural or genetic relationship between standard Dutch and the local dialect. But the Heerlen dialect differs from standard Dutch in all linguistic aspects: lexical, phonological, morphological and syntactic (cf. Cornips 1994). In contrast to standard Dutch, the dialect of Heerlen makes a three-way distinction between masculine, feminine and neuter nouns that is morphologically visible on both the indefinite and definite determiner, as exemplified in Table 3.

| | DIALECT OF HEERLEN | | |
|---|---|---|---|
| | masculine | feminine neuter | |
| indefinite | *inne* | *ing* | *e* |
| definite | *d'r* | *de* | *'t* |

Table 3. *Definite and indefinite determiners in the local dialect of Heerlen*

As for language-internal factors that might play a role in the acquisition of Dutch grammatical gender, the determiner system of the Heerlen dialect shows a considerable structural and morphological gender overlap with the Dutch system, in contrast to the other languages of the ethnic minority children (see Table 1). Therefore, we expect cross-linguistic influence to be possible here since the input of the Heerlen dialect and standard Dutch may reinforce each other.

3. *The acquisition of grammatical gender, as reflected in the definite determiner, by bilingual subjects*

3.1 *Children from ethnic minority communities: the results of a sentence completion test*

In earlier work (Hulk & Cornips 2005) we replicated an experiment designed by Zuckerman (2001) to elicit production data reflecting the morphosyntax of inflected verbs. Later, in Hulk and Cornips (2006), we analyzed these data with respect to the production of the gender of the definite article. Zuckerman's experiment is a sentence completion test involving 40 picture pairs.[2] The experimenter presented first one picture with one conjunct and then a second picture with the second conjunct. Then, the experimenter presented the pictures again via a coordination structure in which the first conjunct was fully produced by the experimenter and the second conjunct was truncated. The children were asked to complete the sentence and to produce a finite verb and an object, hence a DP (see Hulk & Cornips 2006 for more details). In total, the children had to repeat 11 singular neuter nouns requiring *het* and 31 singular non-neuter nouns requiring *de*, as illustrated in (2):

(2) *Experimenter:*
Dit is de man die het brood snijdt en dit is de man die de tomaat
snijdt. Dus deze man snijdt het brood en deze man ...
"This is the man who cuts the bread and this is the man who cuts the
tomato. So, this man cuts the bread and this man ..."
*expected answer*: snijdt **de** tomaat "cuts the tomato"

The subjects were 20 children (14 bilingual and 6 monolingual controls), divided into three age groups: (i) 8 bilingual and 2 monolingual children between 3;0 and 3;10, (ii) 3 bilingual and 3 monolingual children between 4;11

---

[2] We added four test sentences to Zuckerman's (2001) original test.

and 5;2, and (iii) 3 bilinguals and 1 monolingual between 9;3 and 10;5. Thirteen bilinguals were born and raised in the Netherlands in ethnic minority communities, whereas the sociolinguistic setting of one French-Dutch bilingual child is more similar to the "one-parent, one-language" context (see section 4.1]). The youngest bilingual children are descendants of French, Ghanaian (Akan/Ewe) and Moroccan families (Moroccan-Arabic, Berber), the middle ones from Ghanaian and Suriname (-Russian) (Sranan) families, and the oldest ones from Moroccan and Turkish families. All the youngest and middle bilingual children attend three different (pre)schools in Amsterdam and the oldest ones attend a school in Utrecht. All schools are located in ethnic minority neighborhoods. The teachers or caregivers at preschool carefully selected these children to participate in the experiment on the basis of their proficiency in Dutch.

The cross-sectional character of the experiment with three age groups gives some insight into the development of the (correct) uses of the definite determiners *de* and *het*. If we interpret a statistically significant difference (Fisher Exact Test) between two age groups as indicating a developmental pattern (see Hulk & Cornips 2006), we can summarize the development as follows.

With respect to the correct use of *de*:
- In both monolingual and bilingual children, we see a clear development in the acquisition of its correct use*;*
- The bilingual children show a delay with respect to the monolingual children in this development, that is to say, there is still development going on between the middle and oldest age groups that is not visible in the monolingual distribution.

With respect to the correct use of *het*:
- In the data of the monolingual children, there is a clear development in the acquisition of its correct use;
- In the data of the bilingual children there is *no development* between the two age-agroups

With respect to overgeneralization of *de* where *het* is required:
- There is a clear trend to decreasing overgeneralization of *de* between the youngest and middle age groups of the monolingual children whereas this is not the case for the bilingual children.

These results can be interpreted as follows. First, the delay or quantitative difference in the bilingual children's correct use of *de* is not unexpected. In other studies of bilingual children in general and of these same children in particular (Hulk & Cornips 2006), a delay in comparison to the development of monolingual children is often found. Second, the monolingual children show a developmental pattern in which the overgeneralization of *de* decreases compared to the bilinguals. Moreover, unlike *de,* the development of the acquisition of the neuter determiner *het* is significantly different for monolingual and bilingual children. Thus, the bilingual children appear to be unable to acquire the correct use of *het*; they are somehow "fossilized" at a developmental stage in which they overgeneralize the non-neuter definite article *de*. The monolingual children also go through such a stage of overgeneralization (see the results of the youngest age group), but, unlike the bilingual children, the monolinguals pass through this stage. Crucially, it seems that the monolingual and bilingual children reveal a "qualitative difference" in their emerging grammars, in the sense that, for the older bilingual children but not for the monolingual ones, the acquisition of the target grammar/language is not successful. The non-target-like acquisition of neuter grammatical gender by bilingual children from ethnic minority communities seems to show a "creolization effect," or a simplification of the gender system. This is a striking and rather unexpected result since these children are exposed to Dutch input from birth onwards.

Hulk and Cornips (2006) identified language internal factors that might have played a role in this creolization effect, namely the fact that the gender of Dutch definite determiners has a default value, non-neuter, and a specific value, neuter. The default value is by far the most frequent in the input and is overgeneralized in the first stages of acquisition by monolingual children until at least age 6. The bilingual children from ethnic minority communities fossilize in this stage. Note that in the Swedish spoken by bilingual children and adults from ethnic minority communities, as well, grammatical gender is lost; that is, the n- and t-forms represent different genders and the most frequent form—*n*- as in *en boll* 'a ball'—often replaces the infrequent *t*-form as in *ett bord* 'a table' (Kotsinas 2001: 150). However, there is no evidence that a second potentially important factor, namely whether the "other" language instantiates a gender distinction in its noun/determiner system (French, Moroccan-Arabic, Berber) or not (Turkish, Akan/Ewe, Sranan) is relevant with respect to the fossilization of neuter gender; in other words, we found no evidence of cross-linguistic or substrate influence. Recall that there is no structural (morphological) overlap in the determiner systems in the languages under consideration. We will come back to possible language-external factors after discussing the (new) data from the bidialectal children.

### 3.2 Children from bidialectal communities: the results of a sentence completion test

3.2.1 *Introduction.* In this section, we will discuss the results of a sentence completion test concerning grammatical gender of the Dutch definite determiner by bidialectal children in Heerlen who were raised in both standard Dutch and the local dialect of Heerlen. Most speakers of a dialect, especially in the Netherlands, are bilingual in the sense that they can usually use a range of varieties along a continuum from the standard, as a supralocal variety, to a local (nonstandard/dialect) variety, depending on social and discourse context. There is, so to speak, no longer a clear-cut separation between the varieties; that is to say, speakers can change their way of speaking without a clear and abrupt point of transition between standard Dutch and the local dialect. However, the two varieties are clearly perceived as different by their speakers (Cornips in press).

Furthermore, Heerlen occupies an exceptional position with respect to other Dutch dialect areas: as early as 1920, it was already a bilingual community, that is, standard Dutch and the local dialect were spoken. Due to the expansion of the coalmining industry since 1900, Heerlen attracted numerous workers from elsewhere in the Netherlands and abroad. This immigration altered the linguistic setting in Heerlen, where formerly everyone had been a monolingual speaker of the local dialect. The native population of Heerlen became a minority within twenty years, and the emergence of Dutch spoken in the community led to (i) an increase in bidialectal speakers—dialect and Dutch—and (ii) a reduced use of the local dialect in public domains. Nowadays, Heerlen is still a bilingual community where no monolingual speakers of the local dialect exist any more but Dutch is always acquired in addition to the dialect.

3.2.2 *Subjects and methodology.* The experiment involved 30 children who were divided into two groups, one group of bilingual speakers (n = 13) who were exposed to both the local dialect of Heerlen (a Limburg dialect) and Dutch, and a group of monolingual children acquiring Dutch (L1, n = 17) as controls (see Table 8 in §4.2). Moreover, the children were distributed in four age groups: (i) between 2;0 and 3;0, (ii) between 3;0 and 4;0, (iii) between 4;0 and 5;0, and (iv) between 5;01 and 7;0. The children were selected from four different (pre)schools in Heerlen. Our experiment is a sentence completion test administering 30 standard Dutch test sentences similar to the one described in section 3.1 except that (i) the children were asked to produce an attributive adjective and (ii) the sentences were all administered in main clause conditions, as illustrated in (3).[3]

(3) *Experimenter:*
  a. Experimenter shows picture of a boy with a green flower
     Deze jongen tekent de groene bloem en   dit   meisje tekent ...
     this  boy    draws the green flower and this girl    draws

---

[3] It is important to point out that this type of completion test differs from the one discussed in section 3.1 since the children do not repeat a DP introduced by the experimenter. For this reason, the data from the "ethnic minority" children and dialect children and the monolinguals as controls cannot be compared directly since they are the result of two different experiments.

b. Experimenter shows picture of a girl with a yellow boat
*Child*:
... **de** *gele* <u>boot</u>
... the yellow boat

The sentences were divided into three conditions on the basis of noun gender in the dialect. To be more specific, ten sentences required the children to complete the sentence with a non-neuter definite determiner although the corresponding noun in the local dialect has [masculine] gender; ten other sentences also required the non-neuter definite determiner in Dutch although the corresponding noun in the local dialect has [feminine] gender; finally, ten more sentences required the [neuter] determiner, as does the corresponding noun in the local dialect. Examples are provided in (4).

(4) Standard test sentence                      Local dialect of Heerlen
    *required determiner in standard Dutch*      *local dialect*
    *de*  boot   'boat' [non-neuter]    *de*   boot   [feminine]
    *de*  man    'man' [non-neuter]     *d'r*  maan   [masculine]
    *het* mes    'knife' [neuter]       *'t*   mets   [neuter]

Table 4 presents the results for determiner production when the children had to complete the sentence with a DP which contained a non-neuter noun with the definite article *de*.

| | Monolingual Dutch | | | | Bilingual Dutch | | | |
|---|---|---|---|---|---|---|---|---|
| *Age* | Correct use of *de* | | Bare noun | | Correct use of *de* | | Bare noun | |
| 2;0–3;0 | n = 4 | | n = 4 | | — | | — | |
| | 5/9 | 95% | 77/99 | 78% | | | | |
| 3;01–4;0 | n = 7 | | n = 7 | | n = 3 | | n = 3 | |
| | 62/236 | 26% | 114/236 | 48% | 71/94 | 75% | 17/94 | 18% |
| 4;01–5;0 | n = 6 | | n = 6 | | n = 4 | | n = 4 | |
| | 107/190 | 56% | 56/190 | 29% | 94/133 | 71% | 23/133 | 17% |
| 5;01–7;0 | — | | — | | n = 6 | | n = 6 | |
| | | | | | 97/150 | 65% | 22/159 | 14% |

Table 4. *Correct use of* de *and bare noun production when non-neuter* de *is required*

The cross-sectional character of the experiment, with three age groups, allows us to say something about the development of the (correct) use of *de*. The significant results in Table 4 (Fisher Exact Test p < .01) show that the bilingual children (i) have already achieved a target grammar before the age of 3 regarding the low rate of use of bare nouns whereas the monolingual children are still in a developmental stage in all age groups, and (ii) have already acquired a target-like determiner *de* before the age of 3 whereas the monolingual children are still in a developmental stage.

Let us now consider the results regarding determiner production when the children had to complete the sentence with a DP which contains a neuter noun preceded by the definite article *het*.

| | Monolingual Dutch | | Bilingual Dutch | |
|---|---|---|---|---|
| *Age* | Correct use of *het* | Bare noun | Correct use of *het* | Bare noun |
| 2;0–3;0 | n = 4<br>2/36  6% | n = 4<br>27/36  75% | — | — |
| 3;01–4;0 | n = 7<br>6/91  6% | n = 7<br>52/91  57% | n = 3<br>2/38  5% | n = 3<br>6/38  16% |
| 4;01–5;0 | n = 6<br>8/89  10% | n = 6<br>30/89  34% | n = 4<br>19/64  30% | n = 4<br>16/64  25% |
| 5;01–7;0 | — | — | n = 6<br>43/75  57% | n = 6<br>10/75  13% |

Table 5. *Correct use of* het *and bare noun production when neuter* het *is required*

The significant differences (Fisher Exact Test p < .01) can be interpreted as follows. The monolingual children again show a developmental pattern in which they overcome the bare noun stage between 3;0 and 5;0 years of age whereas the bilingual children have already passed this stage by 3 years. Furthermore, the differences reveal a developmental pattern for the bilingual children with respect to the correct use of *het* whereas this is not the case for the monolingual children.

Finally, Table 6 reveals the overgeneralization of *de* in more detail, that is to say, between 4 and 5 years old the monolinguals show increased overgeneralization of *de* whereas the bilinguals show a decrease in this pattern. Thus, unlike the monolinguals, the bilinguals reveal a "progressive" reduction in the overgeneralization of *de*.

| Expected *neuter* **het** | | *Response non-neuter* **de** (completion) | |
|---|---|---|---|
| | | MONOLINGUALS | BILINGUALS |
| 2;0–3;0 | *de* | 2/36  6% | — |
| 3;01–4;0 | *de* | 10/91*  11% | 25/38**  66% |
| 4;01–5;0 | *de* | 40/89*  45% | 18/64**  28% |
| 5;01–7;0 | *de* | — | 11/75  15% |

*, **: significant (Fisher Exact Test, p < .01)

Table 6. *Overgeneralization of the non-neuter determiner* de *when completion involves a neuter noun with the definite article* het

### 3.3 Summary

In Dutch, the gender of the definite determiner has a default value, non-neuter, which is by far the most frequent in the input and which is overgeneralized in the first stages of acquisition by monolingual children. Similarly, the bilingual children from the ethnic minority communities adopt the un(der)specified, default value. As a result, they overgeneralize the definite determiner *de* and use it incorrectly with *het*-words too. These bilingual children do not acquire the specific value [neuter] in a target-like way and do not correctly produce the definite determiner *het*.

In contrast, the bidialectal children have already reached a target grammar between the ages of 2 and 3, whereas the monolingual children are still in a developmental stage where they have to acquire the determiner *de* in a target-like way. The monolingual children show that an increase in the correct use of *de* goes hand in hand with a decrease in the use of bare nouns. Strikingly, the monolingual children show a delay in comparison to their bidialectal peers. This result is completely opposite to what we found for the bilingual children in the ethnic minority communities.

With respect to the correct use of *het*, the monolingual children do not show a developmental pattern, that is, they use target-like *het* in only 10% of all cases when they are 5 years old, whereas the bidialectal children do show a development in the correct use of *het*. Further, the monolingual children show a developmental pattern in which they overcome the bare noun stage when the input is a neuter noun between 3;0 and 5;0 years old whereas the bilingual children have already passed this stage by 3 years old. Again, the monolingual children show a delay in comparison to their bidialectal peers, which is the opposite to what was found in the ethnic minority communities.

It is clear that with respect to the acquisition of grammatical gender in Dutch, the bilingual children from the ethnic minority communities (new type) differ substantially from the bilingual children of a bidialectal community (old type). The non-target-like effect in the new type is not due to cross-linguistic influence (substrate influence), that is to say, regardless of whether the "other" language has a gender distinction in its noun/determiner system (French, Moroccan-Arabic, Berber) or not (Turkish, Akan/Ewe, Sranan), it does not seem to make any difference. Probably, other internal factors are relevant in accounting for the creole-like effect. The determiner system in standard Dutch has no (structural) overlap with the other languages of the bilingual children from the ethnic minority communities involved. In contrast, if there is a structural, morphological overlap between the determiner systems of the two varieties, as is the case with the Heerlen dialect and standard Dutch, positive cross-linguistic influence occurs. In that situation, the dialect input and the Dutch input reinforce each other.

Let us now discuss the sociolinguistic context of the two types of bilingual communities in more detail and see what the role of this external factor may be.

## 4. *Similarities between new and old bilingual communities*

### 4.1 *Language choice in ethnic minority communities*
In addition to language-internal factors, we will argue that external factors are also relevant in order to explain the strikingly different findings concerning the

bilingual acquisition of grammatical gender in ethnic minority and bidialectal communities. It is important to examine the sociolinguistic context in which the languages of the individual bilingual child are acquired, since this is related to the quality and quantity of the Dutch input. The bilingual children who participated in our experiments—both the ethnic minority and the bidialectal children—differ considerably from those who have generally been examined in generative bilingual first language acquisition (henceforth: 2L1) research. In general, in 2L1 studies, the bilingual children (i) belong to middle-class families, (ii) have been raised bilingually from birth in an otherwise mono-lingual community, (iii) have been raised bilingually according to the well-known "one parent, one language" principle, and (iv) have parents who speak their respective varieties as native (L1) speakers.[4] Köppe and Meisel (1995: 283), for instance, describe a 2L1 child growing up in a middle-class family in Hamburg, Germany, where the mother speaks French to the child, and the father German, and the parents speak German to each other. In this family, a very rigid language separation is observed: the parents do not accept being spoken to in the other language. It is obvious that, with respect to linguistic behavior, these families function as small, isolated groups in which the lan-guage choice rules are not at all reflected in the surrounding community.

As we mentioned above, the bilingual children from ethnic minority communities, however, (i) belong to lower-class families, (ii) have been raised bilingually in a bilingual community, (iii) have one or both parents who are not native speakers of Dutch, and (iv) have been raised bilingually within a family in which language choice "rules" do not reflect a "one parent, one language" setting at all (see also section 3.1). Instead, according to Auer (1995: 115), in many if not in all "new" bilingual communities that have come into being in Europe as a consequence of work-related migration, language choice is often indecisive. In the classical view of the Language Bioprogram Hypothesis (cf. Bickerton 1981: 298), the first generation of locally born children plays a crucial role in the genesis of a creole, in developing "a vehicle for interethnic communication on the basis of a rudimentary pidgin when no other language would suffice for this purpose" (see Veenstra, in press, for an extensive discus-sion). However, in the sociolinguistic (migrant) settings in The Netherlands, or Europe in general, the conditions under which a creole may arise abruptly do not exist (Lefebvre 2004: 1–6). Migrants never settle in neighborhoods where no more than 20 percent of the inhabitants speak Dutch, with the remaining 80 percent speaking exclusively a variety of other languages (see Veenstra, in press). Moreover, the first generation of locally born children in this setting is bilingual; they acquire both their heritage language and Dutch. There is strong

---

[4] See, for example, De Houwer (1990), Gawlitzek-Maiwald and Tracy (1996), Hulk and Müller (2000), Meisel (1989), Müller and Hulk (2001) and Paradis and Genesee (1995).

evidence that, nowadays, Moroccan and Turkish families always speak Dutch at home. A recent extensive language survey (cf. Cornips & Jongenburger 1999; Jongenburger & Aarssen 2001) questioned Moroccan (N = 19) and Turkish (N = 15) households—family members living together in one house—in an ethnic minority community about their use of home languages (total households examined amounted to 275).[5] The reported behavior reveals that only in three Moroccan families is Dutch not spoken while all Turkish families use Dutch as a home language. Moreover, Table 7 reveals the patterns of language choice in the home domain of these families investigated. In particular, it shows that language-choice patterns vary in intergenerational communication practices (cf. Milroy & Wei 1995: 138). For the Moroccan and Turkish families, the heritage language is used more with mothers than with fathers and Dutch is used more between siblings. What is more, it appears that the exclusive use of Turkish, Berber and Arabic declines rapidly between older and younger siblings. This decline is most marked in the Berber-speaking families. By the same token, Dutch is also frequently used by the Moroccan families outside the home domain, namely to communicate with friends.

| Language | Mother | Father | Older brother/ sister | Younger brother/ sister | Friends |
|----------|--------|--------|----------------------|-------------------------|---------|
| Turkish | 88% | 72% | 85% | 14% | 44% |
| Dutch | 8% | 8% | 0% | 43% | 20% |
| Both | 4% | 20% | 15% | 43% | 36% |
| | | | | | |
| Berber | 84% | 74% | 17% | 0% | 28% |
| Dutch | 11% | 16% | 66% | 75% | 44% |
| Both | 5% | 11% | 17% | 25% | 28% |
| | | | | | |
| Arabic | 70% | 50% | 71% | 20% | 22% |
| Dutch | 30% | 38% | 14% | 60% | 33% |
| Both | 0% | 12% | 14% | 20% | 44% |

Table 7. *Language choice in the home domain of Turkish and Moroccan families in the Utrecht neighborhood Lombok/Transvaal (reported behavior; Jongenburger and Aarssen 2001)*

4.2 *Language choice in bidialectal communities*
The bidialectal subjects in our experiment (section 3.2) are in a sociolinguistic learning situation which is both different from and similar to the one ethnic minority children are in. It is different because the parents of the bidialectal children are not immigrants but are bilinguals themselves, speaking both the local dialect and standard Dutch as native speakers (cf. Cornips 1994). Furthermore, the duration and intensity of the contact situation between Dutch and the local dialect is long (about 100 years) and intensive. And dialect

---

[5] A school involved in our experiment (section 3.1) is located in this neighborhood.

speakers are not necessarily lower-class since the use of dialect in this type of community is not "socially stigmatized"; that is, it is used by speakers at all educational and occupational levels. However, one aspect of this type of community is similar to the ethnic minority communities: the bidialectal children have also been raised bilingually, not only in the family domain, but in a truly bilingual community. To be more specific, there is no "one parent, one language" setting but language choice patterns depend on particular interlocutors within the family domain, as illustrated in Table 8. For instance, Table 8 reveals for the 30 children participating in our experiment that grandparents always address their grandchildren in dialect.[6]

| number of children | n = 2 | n = 6 | n = 8 | n = 1 | n = 4 | n = 9 |
|---|---|---|---|---|---|---|
| *child speaks the local dialect* | no | no | no | no | **yes** | no |
| *mother speaks dialect in home* | no | yes | yes | yes | yes | no |
| *role relations in home domain*: | | | | | | |
| • mother: dialect to child | no | no | **yes** | **yes** | **yes** | no |
| • grandparents: dialect to grandchild | yes | yes | yes | — | yes | no |

Table 8. *Language choice patterns in the participating bidialectal families* (n = 30)

What is important is that in both types of bilingual community, that is, the new and old ones, (i) the family may be seen as an intermediate grouping between the individual and her community (Hazen 2002: 501), and (ii) the total exposure to the standard variety is reduced compared to that of monolingual speakers in standard-speaking communities.

## 5. *Differences between the two types of bilingual communities*
As for external factors, we have seen that the bilingual subjects of the "new" type are similar to the "old" ones in that they have been raised (i) bilingually in a bilingual community and (ii) within a family in which language choice "rules" do not reflect a "one parent, one language" setting. Moreover, the family may be seen as an intermediate grouping between the individual and the community. In addition, the total exposure to the standard variety of both types of bilingual children is reduced compared to that of monolingual standard-Dutch-speaking children. Consequently, it cannot be the case that the loss of grammatical gender by ethnic minority children and the progressive development by the dialect children is solely due to the "bilingual community" and/or "language choice" factor. Societal bilingualism per se cannot be the crucial factor in the loss of grammatical gender.

---

[6] We considered the children to be bilinguals when they are exposed to dialect input from birth onwards, namely (i) they are reported to speak the local dialect (n = 4), and/or (ii) their mother addresses them in the dialect (n = 9).

## 5.1 *Language contact situation*

Obviously, bilingual children of the new type differ from the bilinguals of the old type in (i) the duration and intensity of the contact between standard Dutch and their heritage languages, (ii) the fact that one or both of their parents do not speak Dutch as native speakers, and (iii) the fact that, in general, they belong to lower-class families. With respect to (i), the duration and intensity of the contact between standard Dutch and the local dialect of Heerlen is long (about 100 years) and intensive whereas this is not the case for the Moroccans and Turks. However, Turks and Moroccans differ from Surinamese families in this respect. The command of Dutch by the first-generation immigrant Surinamese is much higher as a consequence of the long period of contact with Dutch since colonial times. Furthermore, despite their frequently reported (oral) proficiency in Sranan, Surinamese households in which Sranan is spoken are generally oriented towards Dutch and none of the Surinamese subjects claim to speak Sranan better or to prefer to speak it rather than Dutch (Jongenburger & Aarssen 2001). It is also reported (Appel & Schoonen 2005) that children in Surinamese families often acquire Dutch as their first language, while Sranan—in most cases—is mainly used as a vernacular for in-group interaction.

It is plausible that these differences may account for the fact that the youngest bilingual children belonging to one "ethnic" group differ widely from each other in their correct use of the neuter definite article *het*, as shown in Table 9. The youngest Surinamese children perform much better than the Moroccan, French and Ghanaian children of the same age, with mean scores of 14% versus 2%, respectively. Moreover, one particular Surinamese child in the middle age group performs much better than the Ghanaian children of his age (38% versus 3%) and even uses *het* correctly as often as the oldest Moroccan and Turkish children. Finally, the Surinamese children show an increase in the correct use of *het* between the youngest and middle age groups (14% versus 38%).

| YOUNG | *Surinamese* | *French, Moroccan, Ghanaian* |
|---|---|---|
| | n = 3 | n = 5 |
| | 8/56 **14**% | 2/92 **2**% |
| MIDDLE | *Surinamese* | *Ghanaian* |
| | n = 1 | n = 2 |
| | 6/16 **38**% | 1/30 3% |
| OLD | | *Turk, Moroccan* |
| | | n = 3 |
| | | 13/41      32% |

Table 9. *Results of the Surinamese versus the other bilingual children with respect to the correct use of the neuter definite determiner*

5.2 *Adult L2 Dutch in the ethnic minority community*

As mentioned above, the parents and/or grandparents of the ethnic minority children did not acquire Dutch as L1 speakers but as adult L2 speakers in a non-instructed context. This is crucially different from the bidialectal parents and has important consequences for the quality of the input the ethnic minority children are exposed to. Furthermore, in contrast to bidialectal communities, ethnic minority communities consist of closed networks due to chain migration: the family or community may function quite autonomously within mainstream society. Consequently, people in neighborhoods with a high concentration of immigrants and their descendants tend to lack sufficient contact with native Dutch speakers in their neighborhood to acquire target-like Dutch. Thus, there is no routine of daily conversations with native monolingual speakers of Dutch (VROM 2005). This is similar to communities in which pidgins and creoles emerge, that is to say, where speakers of the substratum languages have very little access to the superstratum language (Lefebvre 2004: 8). These closed networks are a consequence of historical demographic patterns of immigration. According to Dabène and Moore (1995: 21), the early migrants encouraged family and village members to travel to the host county and join them in work. Newly arriving migrants often have friends and acquaintances in the closed group of people they already knew, directly or via other people, in their place of origin. Subsequently, specific migratory chains rapidly emerge, leading new arrivals to settle in specific city neighborhoods in the host country, and voluntary clustering and social encapsulation are strengthened. This explains the emergence of ethnic enclaves in cities with large migrant populations. This clustering, reinforced by the arrival of women and children, allows groups to function as a micro-society or an extended family. These migration patterns explain the over- or under-representations of specific ethnic groups in Dutch cities such as Amsterdam and Utrecht, for example, as shown in Table 10, which reveals that the relative proportions of Moroccans and Turks are roughly the same for both cities whereas Ghanaian and Surinamese immigrants are over-represented in Amsterdam. Moreover, it also shows that this represents a contact setting in which the immigrants form between 30% and 50% of the population.

| 2003 | *Utrecht* | | *Amsterdam* | |
|------|-----------|------|-------------|------|
| | 1st + 2nd generation | | 1st + 2nd generation | |
| Moroccan | 22,540 | 12% | 60,835 | 8% |
| Turk | 11,885 | 4% | 36,614 | 5% |
| Surinamese | 6,871 | 3% | 71,537 | 10% |
| Ghanaian | 222 | | 9,701 | 1% |
| % all non-indigenous | | 30% | | 47.2% |
| total all inhabitants | 270,244 | | 739,104 | |

© *Centraal Bureau voor de Statistiek, February 2005*

Table 10. *Over- or under-representation of non-indigenous groups in Utrecht and Amsterdam*

The mechanism of chain migration has significant repercussions on the restructuring of the various groups' social networks, and subsequently on their linguistic behaviors (Dabène & Moore 1995). In particular, the autonomization of migrant communities, and their recourse to a social structure based on models offered by the home culture, mean that members who do not have to maintain close links with the host society may develop only minimal skills in the majority language. This is especially true of newcomers, whereas their native-born children may differ from their parents and the community. In most immigrant communities, the children who most closely follow the language patterns of their parents are those belonging to families that immigrated more recently (Hazen 2002: 516). As the family becomes more integrated, the effects on older and younger siblings will differ. Whereas an older sibling may be more connected to the family when it has recently immigrated, a younger sibling a few years later may have more opportunity for peer group interaction. The effects on the children may also vary because of age and the relative prestige of the family's variety versus that of the community. To sum up, we can conclude that ethnic minority communities are still rather isolated within Dutch society and we would expect this to have effects on their acquisition of Dutch.

### 5.3 *Multigenerational scenario*
One consequence of the autonomization of migrant communities is that their children are not exposed every day to Dutch spoken by native monolingual speakers; instead, they are exposed to a variety of Dutch spoken by their older family/community members. The question then is, what is the quality and the quantity of the Dutch spoken in such communities? Let us therefore consider two generations in more detail from a linguistic perspective: the first immigrants (parents or grandparents) and their descendants.

*Generation 1: immigrants as adult second language acquirers*
Let us first focus on grammatical gender in the variety of Dutch spoken by immigrants. Immigrants entering the Netherlands learned Dutch as a second language in a non-instructed context. In a language shift scenario, neuter gender on the noun can be considered a marked feature; it is hard to produce (and perceive) for adult learners of Dutch. According to Muysken (1984) and Snow, Van Eeden and Muysken (1981), the Turkish and Moroccan immigrants entering the Netherlands frequently delete the determiner and/or overgeneralize non-neuter gender; in other words, they use *de* where *het* is required whereas the opposite never happens. (Consider also the results for the acquisition of German nouns found by the Heidelberger Forschungsprojekt "Pidgin-Deutsch," 1978: 14.) Snow et al. (1981: 90) analyzed foreigner talk conversations in two Amsterdam municipal offices. The existence of foreigner talk reveals that the immigrants are confronted with a reduced version of Dutch as

the superstrate language. Moreover, they are confronted with a version that is characterized by an absence of the functional category Determiner since it involves determiner deletion to a high degree (mean determiner deletion = 75%). The existence of foreigner talk is another indication that new immigrants have little access to the superstratum language (Lefebvre 2004: 13).

*Generation 2: locally born children as bilingual (first) language acquirers*
Around the end of the 1990s, a first generation of locally born immigrant children was examined on the basis of a corpus of spontaneous speech by Moroccan, Turkish and Surinamese youngsters who were born around 1980 (Bennis, Extra, Muysken & Nortier 2002). Within their community, they are exposed to the Dutch input of the first-generation immigrants. Sociolinguistic research reveals that these youngsters also overgeneralize the determiner *de* in their Dutch and hardly ever produce the determiner *het*, as illustrated by the following spontaneous speech examples (Cornips 2002):

(5) a.    zitten    we    in    *de*    laatste jaar
        are      we    in    the    final    year
        [*the* (NEUTER) *year*, Cengiz, Turkish ethnicity, Utrecht]
    b.   *de*    meest   serieuze   type
        the    most    serious   type
        [*the* (NEUTER) *type*, Abdelkhalek, Moroccan ethnicity, Berber, Utrecht]
    c.   de    man   met   *de*    boek
        the    man   with   the    book
        [*the* (NEUTER) *book*, Anouar, Moroccan ethnicity, Arabic, Utrecht]
    d.   Hij   had   *de*    juiste   merk aan
        he    wore   the    right   brand
        [*the* (NEUTER) *brand*, Ronald, Surinamese ethnicity, Rotterdam]

The children in our experiment were born around 2000. This generation of bilingual first language acquirers is overwhelmingly exposed to a Dutch variety in which overgeneralization of *de* takes place, as witness the adult L2 Dutch described above and the output of adolescents in their community, as illustrated in (5).

     Thus, the process of overgeneralization of *de* is transmitted (gradually) by two generations in a multilingual context, namely the immigrants and their native-born children. In this multigenerational scenario (see also Becker & Veenstra 2003), the immigrants and their descendants lack the access to monolingual standard Dutch that native Dutch children have. The insufficient quantity and quality of the input with respect to grammatical gender may explain why fossilization of grammatical gender happens so rapidly, as shown in Table 11.

| G1 (foreign-born immigrants): |
|---|
| L1 acquisition of heritage language(s) |
| **adult L2** acquisition of Dutch in a non-instructed context: |
| • deletion of determiners to a large extent (spontaneous speech) |
| • overgeneralization of *de* to a large extent (spontaneous speech) |
| sociolinguistic context (cf. Muysken 2001): |
| • the use of foreigner talk by target language speakers |
| • limited acquisition opportunities (close networks) |
| |
| G2 (native-born children) |
| L1 acquisition of heritage languages(s) (however, decline in case of youngest siblings?) |
| **child L2 / 2L1** acquisition of Dutch |
| • deletion of some determiners (spontaneous speech, Cornips 2002) |
| • overgeneralization of *de* to a large extent (spontaneous speech, experimental data) |
| sociolinguistic context: |
| • grammatical gender a marker/stereotype (Labov 2001) |
| • candidate for in-group speech, possibly serving as an ethnic marker |

Table 11. *Acquisition of Dutch in immigrant communities*

Very likely, the sociolinguistic context that favors the loss of grammatical gender is characterized by limited acquisition opportunities for the migrants due to their close networks or the autonomization of their ethnic communities and the use of foreigner talk by native speakers (Muysken 2001). With respect to the locally born bilingual children, an additional factor is whether the loss of grammatical gender is a candidate for in-group speech, possibly serving as an ethnic marker. If the latter is the case, we may conclude that, after all, these bilingual children successfully acquire Dutch—but a different variety.

In contrast, a generational scenario for the bidialectal community in Heerlen shows optimal acquisition conditions for both generations, as illustrated in Table 12.

| G1 (native-born) and G2 (native-born): |
|---|
| L1 or bilingual acquisition of standard Dutch |
| • standard Dutch use of determiners |
| sociolinguistic context: |
| • optimal acquisition conditions and access to L1 standard Dutch (open networks) |
| • stable bilingual community |

Table 12. *Acquisition of Dutch in bidialectal communities*

## 6. *Concluding remarks*

The aim of this paper was to examine the effects of language-internal and -external factors on the acquisition of the grammatical gender of the Dutch definite determiner. The results of a sentence completion test in two bilingual communities are very different. Bilingual children in an ethnic minority community, compared with their monolingual peers, reveal a delay in acquiring the definite determiner *de* [non-neuter] and a non-target-like acquisition of the definite determiner *het* [neuter]. In this case, their language development shows a "fossilization" effect. This effect is creole-like in the sense that (i) it involves "simplification" of grammatical gender, and (ii) it emerges rapidly in immigrants' speech and does not disappear in the speech of subsequent generations that are native-born and acquire Dutch from birth onwards. However, bilingual/bidialectal children in a –dialect-speaking community show an acceleration compared with their monolingual peers with respect to both *de* [non-neuter] and *het* [neuter]. Thus, taken together, compared with monolinguals, the bilinguals in an ethnic minority community reveal fossilization whereas bilinguals in a dialect community show "progressive" development.

In earlier work, we identified language internal-factors that might have played a role in the fossilization effect, such as the fact that the gender of Dutch definite determiner has a default value, non-neuter, which is by far the most frequently found in the input and which is overgeneralized in the first stages of acquisition by monolingual children. Second, we have discussed the possibility of cross-linguistic influence. The question of whether a gender distinction in the "other" language of the bilingual children facilitates the acquisition of grammatical gender in Dutch must be answered as follows. On the one hand, if there is no structural overlap between the determiner systems in the two languages, as is the case with the bilingual children from the ethnic minority communities, no cross-linguistic influence is expected. On the other hand, if there is a structural, morphological overlap between the determiner systems of the two varieties, as with the Heerlen dialect and standard Dutch, a positive cross-linguistic influence is predicted to occur. In such a case, the input of the dialect and the Dutch input will reinforce each other.

Finally, as for the external factors, we have shown that it is not societal bilingualism per se that is a relevant factor for fossilization. In other words, it is not the amount of Dutch input (which is the same for both types of bilingual communities) but the quality of the Dutch (parental) input that is relevant in explaining this effect. The quality of the parental input is standard-like in the bidialectal community, with optimal acquisition conditions and access to L1 standard Dutch due to open networks. However, it is not standard-like in the ethnic minority community. Another external factor favoring the rapid loss of grammatical gender as transmitted between two generations is the limited acquisition opportunities migrants have due to their close networks. As a result, the migrants (reinforced by the use of foreigner talk by native speakers) and their descendants tend not to have daily contact with native speakers of Dutch. With respect to the native-born bilingual children, a sociolinguistic context favoring the loss of grammatical gender is that this loss may be a candidate for in-group speech, possibly even serving as an ethnic marker. If this is the case, we may conclude that these bilingual children successfully acquire a different variety of Dutch.

*References*
Appel, R. and R. Schoonen. 2005. Street language: A multilingual youth register in the Netherlands. *Journal of Multilingual and Multicultural Development* 26(2): 85–117.
Auer, P. 1995. The pragmatics of code-switching: A sequential approach. In *One Speaker, Two Languages: Cross-Disciplinary Perspectives on Code-Switching,* L. Milroy and P. Muysken (eds.), 115–135. Cambridge: Cambridge University Press.
Becker, A. and T. Veenstra. 2003. The survival of inflectional morphology in French-related creoles. The role of SLA processes. *Studies in Second Language Acquisition* 25: 283–306.
Bennis, H., G. Extra, P. Muysken and J. Nortier. 2002. *Een buurt in beweging. Talen en culturen in het Utrechtse Lombok en Transvaal.* Amsterdam: Aksant.
Bickerton, D. 1981. *Roots of Language.* Ann Arbor, MI: Karoma Publishers.
Bol, G. W. and F. Kuiken. 1988. Grammaticale analyse van taalontwikkelingsstoornissen. Ph.D. dissertation, University of Amsterdam.
Cornips, L. 1994. Syntactische variatie in het Heerlens Algemeen Nederlands. Ph.D. dissertation, University of Amsterdam, IFFOT 7.
Cornips, L. & W. Jongenburger. 1999. Het TCULT-project. In: E. Huls en B. Weltens, *Artikelen van de Derde Sociolinguïstische Conferentie.* Delft: Eburon, 99-110.
Cornips, L. 2002. Etnisch Nederlands. In *Een buurt in beweging. Talen en culturen in het Utrechtse Lombok en Transvaal,* H. Bennis, G. Extra, P. Muysken and J. Nortier (eds.), 285–302. Amsterdam: Aksant.
Cornips, L. 2005. Het Surinaams-Nederlands in Nederland. In *Wereldnederlands. Oude en jonge variëteiten van het Nederlands,* N. van der Sijs (ed.), 131–147. The Hague: SDU.
Cornips, L. in press. Intermediate Syntactic Variants in a Dialect - Standard Speech Repertoire and Relative Acceptability. *Gradience in Grammar: Generative Perspectives.* G. Fanselow, C. Féry, M. Schlesewsky & R. Vogel (eds.). Oxford: Oxford University Press.
Dabène, Louise and Danièle Moore. 1995. Bilingual speech of migrant people. In *One Speaker, Two Languages: Cross-Disciplinary Perspectives on Code-Switching,* L. Milroy and P. Muysken (eds.), 17–44. Cambridge: Cambridge University Press.
De Houwer, A. 1990. *The Acquisition of Two Languages from Birth: A Case Study.* Cambridge: Cambridge University Press.
De Houwer, A. and S. Gillis. 1998. *The Acquisition of Dutch.* Amsterdam: John Benjamins.
De Vries, J. W. 2005. Indisch-Nederlands. In *Wereldnederlands. Oude en jonge variëteiten van het Nederlands,* N. van der Sijs (ed.), 59–77. The Hague: SDU.
Donaldson, Bruce. 1993. *A Grammar of Afrikaans.* Berlin: Mouton de Gruyter.
Gawlitzek-Maiwald, I. and R. Tracy. 1996. Bilingual bootstrapping. In *Two Languages. Studies in Bilingual First and Second Language Development,* special issue of *Linguistics,* N. Müller (ed.).

Hazen, Kirk. 2002. The family. In *The Handbook of Language Variation and Change,* J. K. Chambers, P. Trudgill and N. Schilling-Estes (eds.), 500–525. Malden, MA, and Oxford: Blackwell.

Heidelberger Forschungsprojekt Pidgin-Deutsch (HPD) 1978. The unguided learning of German by Spanish and Italian workers. *UNESCO Report SS-78/ Conf. 801/4.*

Hulk, A. C. J. and L. Cornips. 2005. Differences and similarities between L2 and (2)L1:DO-support in Child Dutch. In *Proceedings of the 7th Generative Approaches to Second Language Acquisition Conference (GASLA 2004),* L. Dekydtspotter, R. A. Sprouse and A. Liljestrand (eds.), 163–177. Somerville, MA: Cascadilla.

Hulk, A. C. J. and L. Cornips. 2006. Neuter gender and interface vulnerability in child L2/2L1 Dutch. In *Paths of Development in L1 and L2 Acquisition: In Honor of Bonnie D. Schwartz,* S. Unsworth, T. Parodi, A. Sorace and M. Young-Scholten (eds.), 107–134. Amsterdam: John Benjamins.

Hulk, A. C. J. and N. Müller. 2000. Bilingual first language acquisition at the interface between syntax and pragmatics. *Bilingualism: Language and Cognition* 3(3): 227–244.

Jongenburger, W. and J. Aarssen. 2001. Linguistic and cultural exchange and appropriation. A survey study in a multi-ethnic neighbourhood in the Netherlands. *Journal of Multilingual and Multicultural Development* 22(4): 293–308.

Joubert, S. M. 2005. Curaçaos-Nederlands. In *Wereldnederlands. Oude en jonge variëteiten van het Nederlands,* N. van der Sijs (ed.), 31–58. The Hague: SDU.

Köppe, R. and J. Meisel. 1995. Code-switching in bilingual first language acquisition. In *One Speaker, Two Languages: Cross-Disciplinary Perspectives on Code-Switching,* L. Milroy and P. Muysken (eds.), 267–301. Cambridge: Cambridge University Press.

Kotsinas, U. 2001. Pidginization, creolization and creoloids in Stockholm, Sweden. In *Creolization and Contact,* N. Smith and T. Veenstra (eds.), 125–156. Amsterdam: John Benjamins.

Labov, W. 2001. *Principles of Linguistic Change. Volume II: Social Factors.* Oxford: Blackwell.

Lefebvre, C. 2004. *Issues in the Study of Pidgin and Creole Languages.* Amsterdam/Philadelphia: John Benjamins.

Meisel, J. 1989. Early differentiation of language in bilingual children. In *Bilingualism across a Lifespan: Aspects of Acquisition, Maturity and Loss,* K. Hyltenstam and L. Obler (eds.), 13–40. Cambridge: Cambridge University Press.

Milroy, L. and Li Wei. 1995. A social network approach to code-switching: The example of a bilingual community in Britain. In *One Speaker, Two Languages: Cross-Disciplinary Perspectives on Code-Switching,* L. Milroy and P. Muysken (eds.), 136–157. Cambridge: Cambridge University Press.

Müller, N. and A. Hulk. 2001. Cross-linguistic influence in bilingual first language acquisition: Italian and French as recipient languages. *Bilingualism: Language and Cognition* 4(1): 1–21.

Muysken, P. 1984. Attitudes and experiences of discrimination: The Netherlandic of Moroccan foreign workers. In *Sociolinguistics in the Low Countries*, K. Deprez (ed.), 333–356. Amsterdam: John Benjamins.

Muysken, P. 2001. The origin of creole languages: The perspective of second language learning. In *Creolization and Contact,* N. Smith and T. Veenstra (eds.), 157–173. Amsterdam: John Benjamins.

Paradis, J. and F. Genesee. 1995. Language differentiation in early bilingual development. *Journal of Child Language* 22: 611–631.

Ponelis, F. 2005. Nederlands in Afrika: Het Afrikaans. In *Wereldnederlands. Oude en jonge variëteiten van het Nederlands,* N. van der Sijs (ed.), 15–30. The Hague: SDU.

Snow, C. E., R. Van Eeden and P. Muysken. 1981. The interactional origins of foreigner talk: Municipal employees and foreign workers. *International Journal of the Sociology of Language* 28: 81–92.

Sorace, A. 2005. Selective optionality in language development. In *Syntax and Variation. Reconciling the Biological with the Social,* L. Cornips and K. P. Corrigan (eds.), 55–80. Amsterdam/Philadelphia: John Benjamins.

Thomason, S. G. and T. Kaufman. 1988. *Language Contact, Creolization and Genetic Linguistics.* Berkeley, CA: University of California Press.

Van Berkum, J. J. A. 1996. *The Psycholinguistics of Grammatical Gender: Studies in Language Comprehension and Production.* Ph.D. dissertation, Max Planck Institute for Psycholinguistics.

Van Velde, M. 2004. "L'acquisition des déterminants en L1: une étude comparative entre le français et le néerlandais" *AILE*

Veenstra, Tonjes. in press. Pidgin/creole genesis: The impact of the Language Bioprogram Hypothesis. In *The Handbook of Pidgin and Creoles,* Silvia Kouwenberg and John V. Singler (eds.). Oxford: Blackwell.

VROM. 2005. Wonen in buurt met veel allochtonen belemmert integratie. Kenniscentrum Grote Steden (see http://www.kenniscentrumgrotesteden. nl/kcgs/dossiers/Sociaal/Integratie/algemeen/Wonen_in_buurt_met_veel_al lochtonen_belemmert_integratie_1923.html).

Zonneveld R. Van 1992. Het jonge hoofd - De Righthand Head Rule bij kinderen van 4 tot 7 jaar. *De Nieuwe Taalgids* 85 (1), 37-49.

Zuckerman, S. 2001. The Acquisition of "Optional" Movement. Ph.D. dissertation, Groningen University.

# INCOMPLETE ACQUISITION IN BILINGUALISM AS AN INSTANCE OF LANGUAGE CHANGE

Silvina Montrul
*University of Illinois at Urbana-Champaign*

Many simultaneous bilinguals exhibit the loss or incomplete acquisition of their heritage language under conditions of exposure to and use of the majority language (Montrul 2002; Polinsky 1997; Silva-Corvalán 1994, 2003; Toribio 2001). This study investigates argument expression in adult simultaneous bilinguals who are heritage speakers of Spanish and live in the USA. The results of an oral production task administered to 10 intermediate and 14 advanced bilingual speakers and 20 monolinguals showed that the intermediate-proficiency speakers produced more overt subjects than null subjects, more agreement errors, and more variability with the pragmatic distribution of overt and null subjects in Spanish, as compared to the other groups. With the erosion of pragmatic and semantic features, the grammars of the intermediate-proficiency Spanish heritage speakers appear to display morphosyntactic convergence with English. I will argue that, with reduced input in one of the languages, the grammars of these Spanish speakers exhibit relexification in reverse (from the L2 or superstratum to the L1 or substratum) and could also fall within the definition of dialect leveling, as described in Lefebvre (1998).

## 1. *Introduction*

Natural languages change over time. This can happen gradually over the course of several hundred years and successive generations, as in diachronic change. It can also happen much faster, as in the case of multilingual societies that bring languages into contact: for example, creole genesis, second language acquisition and other cases of bilingualism. According to DeGraff (1999), the development of linguistic systems that diverge from existing "target" systems defines successive stages of language change and language acquisition. "Both diachronic stages and learners' (intermediate) developmental stages are 'creole-like' insofar as they manifest properties (parameter values, as it were) that do not match those of earlier/older speakers" (p. 11). By "creole-like" DeGraff means "grammatical invention" in the sense of Rizzi (1999) or mismatches between the developing and target grammars, "the trying out of various UG options not adopted by the target system" (Rizzi 1999: 464). While many of the cognitive and linguistic processes involved in all of these language change situations are very similar, the outcome of change may differ depending on the speakers involved and the type, heterogeneity, and availability of the input (or primary linguistic evidence) that affects the development of the grammatical system. This chapter illustrates these outcomes through a comparison of subject expression in Spanish in early bilingualism and Spanish L2 acquisition.

Second language (L2) acquisition is a particular case of bilingualism. Second language learners are typically adults who start learning a second language (very often in a classroom setting) after puberty. Since the onset of bilingualism occurs quite late, L2 learners are late bilinguals. Because the acquisition of the L2 begins after the L1 has had a chance to develop completely, the L1 has a profound influence on the acquisition of the L2, especially at the earliest stages of acquisition. L1 transfer is a cognitive process that operates at all levels (lexicon, morphology, semantics, syntax) and plays a significant role in L2 acquisition, affecting both its development and the ultimate outcome (Schwartz Sprouse 1996; White 1989). The availability and type of input can be quite heterogeneous in the L2 acquisition situation: be abundant or not, and it may come from native speakers or not, depending on the situation. If L2 learners restructure or reanalyze their L1-based hypotheses concerning the L2 grammar through continuous access to L2 input, convergence with the target in certain grammatical domains is likely to occur. While success in many grammatical areas is possible and has been attested, the opposite outcome —fossilization—can occur even when L2 input is rich and abundant (see Lardiere, this volume), but for reasons not yet understood, the learner has failed to reanalyze or restructure the interlanguage system to match the target system. In L2 acquisition, reanalysis is contingent upon exposure to positive evidence. The outcome of L2 acquisition is typically incomplete, divergent, or even indeterminate, when compared with the target system (Sorace 1993).

If L2 acquisition is in some sense creole-like, what commonalities does it share with the process of creole genesis? Creole languages emerge in multilingual communities, when speakers of different L1s are brought together. As in L2 acquisition, the process of L1 transfer, which Lefebvre (1998) refers to as *substratum relexification*, plays a fundamental role in the creole creation process at earlier stages of development. According to Lefebvre (1998), in setting the parametric values of the new language, the creators of the creole use those parameters of their own grammars. In many ways, creole languages follow the semantic and syntactic patterns of the substratum languages. This is clearly like L1 transfer in L2 acquisition. Another process attested to both in creole genesis and in L2 acquisition is reanalysis, although the process operates in different ways. While reanalysis in L2 acquisition is fed by the input from the L2 (or superstrate) grammar (Meisel 2001; White 2004), in creole genesis it resembles the typical process attested in diachronic language change whereby lexical categories bleached of their semantic content become functional categories (i.e., grammaticalization). Finally, a process that takes place in creole genesis and that may also, in some sense, play a role in L2 acquisition is dialect leveling, which, according to Lefebvre, operates on the output of relexification. Through leveling, idiosyncratic features from the substrate language or languages may be eliminated in the creole. In L2 acquisition and bilingualism, leveling could account for why some complex or marked aspects of the L1 fail to transfer to the L2, even when the L2 has those features as well. Or L2 speakers of different L1s may level out differences in their L2 that are attributable to the influence of their respective L1s, which is parallel to the view of leveling prevalent in creole development.

In this chapter, I explore the consequences of these processes in a different but related situation of language contact and bilingualism. In particular, I ask what happens when bilingual speakers have abundant and continuous access to the superstrate, L2, or community language and varying access to input from the substrate (or L1). This is what happens to adult early bilinguals, particularly Spanish speakers living in the United States, who lose language skills in their heritage or family language under conditions of exposure to and use of the majority language (Lipski 1993, 1996; Montrul 2002; Polinsky 1997; Silva-Corvalán 1994; Toribio 2001; Valdés 2000). Unlike typical L2 learners, these are bilinguals for whom the onset of bilingualism occurred at birth or soon afterwards in early childhood. I call these cases of incomplete acquisition because in many respects the grammars of the family language (in this case Spanish) look like the grammars of intermediate and advanced L2 learners of Spanish (or late bilinguals) and not like the grammars of monolingual Spanish speakers. This may be the result of interrupted or incomplete acquisition of Spanish before English became dominant or of a change in language dominance at some point in the life span. Lipski (1993) refers to these speakers as transitional bilinguals and considers their behavior relevant to theories of creole formation. Lipski noted that these speakers exhibit patterns of morphological reduction in the areas of subject-verb agreement, gender and number agreement in nouns and subjunctive morphology, and errors with subject expression (backward anaphora), among many other features. Such morphological reduction is a feature of Romance-based creoles (Lipski 1996) when compared with the superstrate languages, and is also found among Latin Americans and Africans who use Spanish as a lingua franca.

A close study of this bilingual population is very relevant to the processes involved in L2 acquisition and creole genesis because, according to Meisel (2001), bilingual acquisition is indeed the most plausible source of grammatical reanalysis. In Meisel's view, reanalysis in diachronic change is an instance of transmission failure, and this is very likely to happen in cases of incomplete acquisition, or when one language is weaker than the other. The study will focus on the production of subject and object expression in second-generation Spanish-English bilinguals living in the US (also called heritage speakers, as in Valdés 2000), reported in Montrul (2004). To investigate whether transfer is a likely cause for the changes observed, the results will be compared to those of L2 learners of Spanish whose native language is English. I will show that, while early bilingual heritage speakers and L2 learners of Spanish are at different stages of language change at the morphosyntactic level, their grammars are similarly incomplete at the discourse-pragmatic level. Regardless of whether "non-target" indeterminacy at the discourse-pragmatic level is caused primarily by transfer from English or not, such erosion is in some ways akin to the process of dialect leveling that operates in creole genesis and other language contact situations.

## 2. *Spanish Subjects*

Spanish is a null subject language. Null subjects are possible because Spanish has rich verbal inflection (see Table 1), which allows person and number information about the subject to be recoverable, as in (1) and (2).

| Person/Number | | Pronouns | Agreement Paradigm | |
|---|---|---|---|---|
| 1st | sing. | yo | am-o | 'I love' |
| 2nd | sing. | tu | am-a-s | 'you love' |
| 3rd | sing. | el/ella/usted | am-a | 'he/she loves' |
| 1st | plural | nosostros | am-a-mos | 'we love' |
| 2nd | plural | vosotros | am-á-is | 'you love' |
| 3rd | plural | ellos/ellas/ustedes | am-a-m | 'they love' |

Table 1. *Spanish verb agreement paradigm*

(1) *Ellos/mis amigos llamaron a la puerta.*
they/my   friends   called-3rd-pl to the   door
'They/my friends knocked on the door.'

(2) *Ø Llamaron a la puerta.*
called-3rd-pl to the   door
'They knocked on the door.'

By contrast, English has impoverished agreement inflection (see translations in Table 1), and null subjects in English are typically not possible, except for imperative sentences. That is, the rich verbal inflection in Spanish allows pronominal and lexical subjects to be identified when they are omitted (under specific pragmatic conditions that I will review below). Thus, Spanish is a pro-drop language while English is a non-pro-drop language; these differences were subsumed under the Null Subject Parameter (Chomsky 1981; Jaeggli 1982; Rizzi 1982). Pro-drop languages allow postverbal subjects (VSO), do not have overt expletive pronouns (like English *it* as in *It is clear that)* and allow the *that*-trace effect, or the possibility of extracting a *wh*-element out of a subject position as in *Quién$_i$ dijiste que t$_i$ llamó?*, which is not possible in English (**Who did you say that called?*). A summary of the structures associated with the original formulation of the parameter is shown in Table 2. (For more recent accounts of these properties, see Alexiadou and Anagnostopoulou 1998 and Toribio 2000.)

| Setting | +pro-drop | −pro-drop |
|---|---|---|
| *Language* | Standard Spanish | English |
| *Properties* | rich verbal agreement inflection | poor verbal agreement inflection |
| | null and overt subjects | overt subjects |
| | null expletives | overt expletives |
| | preverbal and postverbal subjects | preverbal subjects |
| | *that*-t effect | *\*that*-t effect |

Table 2. *The Null Subject Parameter*

Even in cases of personal subjects, as in (1) and (2), the expression of overt/non-overt subjects is not entirely optional in Spanish, but depends on the discourse context. More specifically, the distribution of null and overt pronouns is regulated by discourse-pragmatic factors such as topic, focus, contrast, or known versus changed referent, as well as the lexical semantics of the verb. Overt pronouns can be focus (new information, contrast) or topic (old information). For example, when there is no switch in reference between a series of sentences in discourse, overt subjects are pragmatically infelicitous, as in (3). By contrast, null subjects are odd when a different referent is introduced (topic-shift), as in (4).

(3) *same referent*
*Pepe no vino hoy a trabajar. \*Pepe/?él/Ø estará enfermo.*
Pepe no came today to work Pepe/?he/Ø will be sick
'Pepe did not come to work today. He must be sick.'

(4) *different referent*
*Hoy no fui a trabajar. Pepe/él/\*Ø pensó que estaba enferma.*
today I no went to work Pepe/he/\*Ø thought that I was sick
'Today I did not go to work. Pepe/he thought I was sick.'

Overt subjects are strictly required when new information is introduced and a contrast is established in discourse. Sentences (5) and (6) illustrate this contrast. The answer to question (5) requires a focus. Focus must be expressed by an overt subject. In (6), the overt subject *él* is a topic if unstressed, but it can also be a contrastive focus if it is stressed. Unlike in (7), the pronoun in this case can corefer with the subject of the previous sentence because it emphasizes the subject.[1]

(5) *¿Quién vino*      *El/Mario/\*Ø vino.*                    *focus*
    'Who came?      He/Mario/\*Ø came.'

---

[1] For the interpretation and coreferentiality possibilities of overt or null subjects with referential (*Juan, María*) and variable expressions (*quien* 'who,' *nadie* 'nobody,' etc.) see Montalbetti (1984).

(6) *El    periodista<sub>i</sub> dijo que él<sub>i</sub>/ÉL<sub>i</sub>      no había escrito ese reporte.      topic*
    the journalist  said that he (himself)  not had   written that report
    'The journalist said that he had not written that report.'

In addition to their overt or non-overt expression, subjects in Spanish can appear in preverbal or postverbal position, depending both on the information structure of the clause and on the argument structure of verbs. Stylistically, in presentational contexts, subjects of unaccusative verbs show a marked tendency to appear in object position (postposed), as in (7), whereas subjects of unergative verbs, as in (8), prefer preverbal position (Contreras 1978; Suñer 1982).

(7) *María llegó ayer / Ayer llegó María.* [preferred]                      *unaccusative*
    Mary arrived yesterday. / *Yesterday arrived Mary.

(8) *María trabajó ayer.* [preferred] / *Ayer trabajó María.*            *unergative*
    Mary worked yesterday. / *Yesterday worked Mary.

In short, Spanish overt and null subjects in discourse are regulated by topic, focus, and topic-shift features (see Tsimpli, Sorace, Heycock, Filiaci & Bouba 2003 for Greek and Italian). While discourse-pragmatic context like new (focus) versus old (topic) information also plays a role in argument realization in English, this is accomplished via pronominalization, not omission.

### 3. *The Expression of Subjects in Bilingual Grammars*

Studies on a variety of languages that allow both overt and null subjects (Italian, Greek, Spanish, Russian) have reported that null subject expression is not completely lost in bilinguals exposed to a non-null-subject language like English, even though there might be an increase in the production of overt subjects. Bilinguals, however, seem to lose or display variability in the application of pragmatic constraints on overt subject distribution, such that they tend to produce redundant pronominal subjects when there is no change of referent (Lipski 1996; Silva-Corvalán 1994; Tsimpli et al. 2003). Moreover, in their experimental study on Greek and Italian, Tsimpli et al. (2003) found that, with respect to subject verb order, Italian-English bilinguals showed a marked preference for preverbal subjects regardless of the argument structure of verbs and specificity/definiteness of subjects. In a recent study (Montrul 2004), I investigated subject and object expression in bilinguals who are heritage speakers of Spanish (a minority language in the US). With respect to subjects, the research questions investigated were:

1. Is subject expression affected in the Spanish grammar of adult Spanish heritage speakers?
2. If so, to what extent is this structural domain affected by contact with English?

Based on the available theoretical and empirical findings, I hypothesized that, if language contact and subsequent reduction in Spanish as a minority language affects interface areas of competence more than purely syntactic domains, then Spanish heritage speakers should display robust knowledge of null subjects (regulated by morphosyntax) but variability in the pragmatic distribution of null vs. overt subjects (the syntax-pragmatics interface), as many other studies have documented.

The participants were 20 monolingually raised Spanish speakers from different Spanish-speaking countries (but, crucially, not from countries with Caribbean dialects) (mean age 32.76), and 24 adult Spanish-English speakers of Mexican-American background who were raised bilingually in the Unites States from an early age and who received their schooling in English (mean age 21.54). Spanish was spoken in these speakers' homes in early childhood and subsequent use of Spanish during the school years varied greatly from speaker to speaker, based on different family and sociolinguistic circumstances.

The monolinguals and the bilinguals took the vocabulary and Cloze sections of a standardized Spanish proficiency test (DELE). Table 3 shows the mean, range and standard deviations on the Spanish proficiency test. The difference between the mean scores of the monolinguals and the heritage speakers was significant according to a one-way ANOVA ($F(1,42) = 48.115, p < .0001$).

|  | Monolinguals (n = 20) | Heritage speakers (n = 24) |
|---|---|---|
| Mean | 48.95 | 39.95 |
| Range | 47–50 | 28–48 |
| SD | 1.14 | 6.24 |

Table 3. *Differences between monolinguals and bilingual Spanish heritage speakers in a proficiency test (maximum score of 50)*

In previous work (Montrul 2005), I have found that the most marked evidence of transfer, language loss, or grammatical variability in these bilinguals comes from those speakers with the lowest proficiency in the language. By contrast, those speakers who are advanced or as proficient as native speakers rarely show signs of linguistic change in their grammars. Accordingly, the Spanish heritage speakers were divided into two main groups: *intermediate* (n=10), those with proficiency scores ranging from 28/50 to 39/50 in the Spanish proficiency test, and *advanced* (n=14), those with proficiency scores of between 40/50 and 50/50. If transfer from or convergence with English is found in the Spanish of these speakers, it will most likely affect the lower-proficiency group.

Subject expression was evaluated by means of an oral retelling task, which is very appropriate for investigating the discourse pragmatic distribution of subjects. All participants were asked to tell the story of Little Red Riding Hood in Spanish. (These oral narratives were part of a larger study investigating tense and aspect.) Narratives were tape-recorded and transcribed. Two native speakers counted the number of conjugated verbs requiring subjects, and of overt and null subjects. Subjects were coded by type (lexical, pronominal or null) and by position in the clause (preverbal or postverbal). Overt and null subjects were further classified as correct (when the use of the null or overt subject followed the discourse rules), redundant (when overt subjects were repeated when they referred to the same person), or illicit (when null subjects were used instead of overt subjects in switch reference contexts). There was 92% agreement between the two coders. Percentages of production in each category were subject to statistical analysis.

Table 4 shows the percentage of production of null and overt subjects, as well as the percentage of pragmatically correct or illicit uses.

|  | Overt Subjects | | | Null Subjects | | |
|---|---|---|---|---|---|---|
|  | Total | Correct | Redundant | Total | Correct | Illicit |
| Monolinguals (n = 20) | 42.8 | 100 | 0 | 57.2 | > 99 | < 1 |
| Advanced HSs (n = 14) | 47.2 | 99.3 | 0.7 | 52.7 | 92 | 8 |
| Intermediate HSs (n =10) | 68.6 | 91.5 | 8.5 | 31.4 | 84.5 | 15.5 |

Table 4. *Percentage of null and overt subjects*

As can be seen from Table 4, both monolinguals and heritage speakers produced substantial percentages of null subjects, and this result clearly shows that the null subject option is part of the grammar of the bilingual heritage speakers. While there were no statistical differences in the production of null and overt subjects between the monolinguals and the advanced heritage speakers, both these groups were significantly different from the intermediate heritage speakers ($F(2,41) = 32.366, p < .0001$). According to a repeated measures ANOVA, there was a subject type (null, overt) by group (monolinguals, intermediate HS, advanced HS) interaction. While the monolinguals and advanced heritage speakers produced more null subjects (57.2% and 52.5%) than overt subjects (42.8% and 47.5%), it was only the intermediate heritage speakers who showed the opposite pattern, producing significantly more overt (68.8%) than null subjects (31.4%).

The heritage speakers were less accurate than the monolinguals, particularly with null subjects. However, as Table 4 shows, the greatest percentage of errors came from the intermediate heritage speakers, who produced 8.5% of redundant overt subjects when there was no change of referent and 15.5% of illicit null subjects when there was a change of referent. Note that the advanced heritage speakers produced 8% of these errors with null subjects. Examples (9) and (10) illustrate pragmatically illicit uses of null subjects in individual speakers' narratives, whereas examples (11) and (12) show redundant uses of overt pronominal subjects. (I use the symbol # to mean redundant, and ? for unclear referent.)

(9)   *Caperucita Roja salió a ir a la casa de su abuelita con una canasta de comida porque* pro *estaba,* pro *iba a visistarla porque* **\*pro** *estaba enferma.*
'Little Red Riding Hood went out to go to her grandmother's house with a basket of food because *pro* was, *pro* was going to visit her because *pro* was sick.'

(10)   *Entonces la Caperucita Roja encontró, pro fue a ver quién estaba en la cama, entonces* pro *encontró que era el lobo.* ?pro *estaba corriendo del lobo y entonces* pro *salió fuera, o* **\*pro** *se la comió,* **\*pro** *se comió a la abuelita y a la Caperucita.*
'So, the Little Red Riding Hood found, *pro* went to see who was in the bed, so *pro* found that was the wolf. *Pro* was running away from the wolf and then *pro* went out, or *pro* ate her up, *pro* ate up the grandmother and the Little Riding Hood.'

(11)   *Había una vez una niña chiquita que se llamaba Caperucita.* **Ella** *vivía con su mamá y* **#ella** *quería mucho a su abuelita. Y* **#ella** *le dijo a su mamá, mami quiero ir a visitar a mi abuelita. ... Y cuando llegó la Caperucita,* **#ella** *pensó que el lobo era su abuela. ... Y cuando se levantó el lobo,* **#él** *tenía piedras dentro y no pudo caminar.*
'Once upon a time there was a little girl whose name was Little Riding Hood. She lived with the mother and she loved her grandmother very much. And she told her mother, mommy I want to go visit my grandmother ... And when arrived the Little Riding Hood, she thought that the wolf was her grandmother ... And when the wolf got up, he had stones inside and could not walk.'

(12)   *Había una chica que vivía con su mamá y* **?ella** *va a visitar a su abuela. Y* **#ella** *trajo toda la comida para un regalo para la abuela. ... Cuando Caperucita llegó* **#ella** *estaba arreglando todos los flores que* **#ella** *recogía durante su camino* **#ella** *no notaba que el lobo estaba en la cama.*
'There was a girl who lived with her mother and she goes to visit her grandmother. And she brought all the food for a present for her grandmother ... When Little Riding Hood arrived, she was fixing all the flowers that she had gathered during her way, and she did not notice that the wolf was in the bed.'

The results in Table 4 and these examples are consistent with the hypothesis that while the null/overt subject distinction is not entirely lost, the pragmatic distribution of null and overt is substantially blurred in some of these bilinguals. Table 5 shows the results for position and types of overt subjects.

|                        | Preverbal Subjects |         |       | Postverbal Subjects |         |         |
|------------------------|--------------------|---------|-------|---------------------|---------|---------|
|                        | Total              | Lexical | Pron. | Total               | Unacc. V | Other V |
| Monolinguals (n = 20)  | 79.8               | 84.6    | 15.4  | 20.2                | 82.9    | 17.1    |
| Advanced HSs (n = 14)  | 68.2               | 74.3    | 25.7  | 31.8                | 89.5    | 10.5    |
| Intermediate HSs (n =10) | 75.7             | 69.8    | 30.2  | 24.3                | 95.5    | 4.5     |

Table 5. *Percentage of types of overt subjects*

Recall that, in Spanish, subjects can be in preverbal or postverbal position. All groups were very similar in their percentage of production of preverbal and postverbal subjects, and there were no significant differences among any of the groups. Bilinguals did not prefer preverbal subjects more than the native speakers ($F(2,41) = 3.153, p < .053$), nor did they fail to produce as many postverbal subjects as monolingual speakers ($F(2,41) = 3.045, p < .061$).

Within the category of overt preverbal subjects, subjects were further classified into lexical NPs vs. pronouns. No differences between the three groups were found for lexical or pronominal subjects either. However, since most of the redundant overt subjects produced were pronominal, the percentage of redundant pronominal subjects was 9% for the advanced heritage speakers and 50% for the intermediate heritage speakers. This difference between the two groups of heritage speakers was significant ($F(2,41) = 32.894, p < .0001$). As for postverbal subjects, all three groups produced the majority of postverbal subjects with unaccusative verbs (82.9%, 89.5% and 95.5%) as opposed to other verbs (12.1%, 10.5% and 4.5%), and the differences between the three groups were not significant here either.

In short, heritage speakers produced overt and null subjects and preverbal and postverbal subjects. Differences from monolinguals were apparent in the pragmatic, referential uses of overt and null subjects. The conclusion I reached was that, with the erosion of pragmatic and semantic features, the grammars of the intermediate-proficiency Spanish heritage speakers display a degree of morphosyntactic convergence with English in the expression of subject (and object) arguments. This is likely due to transfer from English. As Table 6 illustrates, Spanish subjects are more complex than English because there is an extra layer of features that interact with the pragmatic component. This layer (the shaded row in Table 6) is blurred or entirely eliminated in the output of some speakers.

| Language | Features | Consequences |
|---|---|---|
| Spanish | –interpretable | strong agreement |
|  | +interpretable | topic/focus |
| English | –interpretable | weak agreement |

Table 6. *Feature specification regulating the expression of Spanish and English subjects*

However, Silva-Corvalán (1994) argued that transfer from English is not the main cause underlying this phenomenon in Spanish in contact with English (specifically Mexican-Americans in Los Angeles). In her view, transfer from English is only "indirect" because it does not affect syntax directly but through semantic or pragmatic erosion. "In language contact situations, a number of changes affecting the secondary language have an internal motivation in that they are in progress in the model monolingual variety before intensive contact with the other language occurs" (Silva-Corvalán 1994: 214). Thus, it might be fruitful to consider whether the increase in overt subject production by Spanish-English bilinguals in the data shown is the result of an accelerated process of language change, similar to what is going on in the diachronic development of other pro-drop languages, such as Caribbean Spanish (Toribio 2000) or Brazilian Portuguese (Duarte 2000). Let us look at the case of Brazilian Portuguese, which is not in intense contact with English.

## 4. *Language Change in Progress*

In the last century, some pro-drop languages have been becoming progressively less pro-drop, as evidenced by the fact that there has been an increase in the production of overt subjects in places where null subjects are pragmatically licit. Two examples are Dominican Spanish (Toribio 2000) and Brazilian Portuguese (Duarte 2000). In these languages, the increase in overt subjects appears to be directly related to the weakening of the inflectional verbal paradigm (Duarte 2000; Roberts 1993; Toribio 2000; cf. Sprouse & Vance 1999 for a different view). The progressive erosion of agreement morphology with different persons in Brazilian Portuguese is shown in Table 7.

| Pers./No. | Pronouns | Paradigm 1 | Paradigm 2 | Paradigm 3 |
|---|---|---|---|---|
| 1st sing. | eu | am-o | am-o | am-o |
| 2nd sing. | tu | am-a-s | — | — |
|  | você | am-a | am-a | am-a |
| 3rd sing. | ele/ela | am-a | am-a | am-a |
| 1st plural | nós | am-a-mos | am-a-mos | — |
|  | a gente | — | am-a | am-a |
| 2nd plural | vós | am-a-is | — | — |
|  | vocês | am-a-m | am-a-m | am-a-m |
| 3rd plural | eles/elas | am-a-m | am-a-m | am-a-m |

Table 7. *Pronominal and inflectional paradigm in Brazilian Portuguese (Duarte 2000: 19)*

Table 7 shows three morphological paradigms that correspond to three periods in Duarte's analysis. The first period covers written and oral texts from 1845 to 1918. During this time, Brazilian Portuguese had six different agreement endings and 20%–25% overt subjects, which were only used for emphasis, focus, or switch reference, as in full pro-drop systems. During the second period (1937–1945), the agreement system lost the second-person singular (*am-a-s*) and plural (*am-ai-s*), and overt subjects increased to 46%–50%. The third period analyzed (1975–1992) only has a three-form distinction, having lost the first-person plural (*amamos* 'we love'). The incidence of overt pronouns in this period is 74%. Therefore, although the null subject option has not been entirely lost, it is used very infrequently (26%) compared with the frequency attested at the beginning of the century (75%–80%). What Duarte noticed is that the erosion of agreement endings is gradual and affects different persons. The most affected are second person (as in Caribbean Spanish dialects) and first person, while the least affected is the third person.

With the concomitant changes in the agreement paradigm, Brazilian Portuguese exhibits structures unattested in full pro-drop systems, such as left-dislocated subjects, as in (13), and the use of an overt expletive subject (*isso* 'that'), as in (14).[2]

(13)  *A    Clarinha_i   ela_i   cozinha    que    é    uma    maravilla.*
      the Clarinha      she     cooks      that   is   a      marvel
      'Clarinha, she can cook wonderfully.'

(14)  *Isso   era    em torno   de dez   pessoas.*
      that   was    around     of ten   people
      'It was around ten people.'

With this background on language change, I looked at the results presented Montrul (2004) to see whether there was any weakening of the verb agreement system in the Spanish-English bilinguals, whether there was differential use of overt/null subjects with first, second, and third persons, and whether bilinguals produced dislocated subjects and overt expletives. However, a caveat is in order. Although the oral production task used was appropriate to investigate the use of null and overt subjects in discourse, it was limited in other respects. While a few first- and second-person forms were attested, the task heavily favored the use of the third person (the least affected person in Duarte's data). Moreover, the task did not elicit any dislocated subject constructions or overt expletives. (See White 1989 for a discussion of the disadvantages of oral production tasks to investigate these aspects of the pro-drop parameter.)

---

[2] As a reviewer pointed out, this statement needs to be qualified. Left-dislocation is very productive in many Romance dialects (Poletto 2000) and also in Quebec French. However, these cases are usually analyzed as involving subject clitics, and it is not clear whether subject clitics are representative of "full pro-drop systems."

Table 8 shows the bilinguals heritage speakers' accuracy with verbal agreement. As can be seen, the control group and the advanced heritage speakers hardly produced any errors. More errors, although not many, were produced by the intermediate heritage speakers (12/471 = 2.54%).

|  | % correct | |
|---|---|---|
| Monolinguals (n = 20) | > 99 | (7/1019) |
| Advanced HSs (n = 14) | > 99 | (3/544) |
| Intermediate HSs (n =10) | 97.45 | (12/471) |

Table 8: *Percentage of correct person and number verbal agreement (raw error counts in parentheses)*

Tables 9 and 10 show the percentage of subject pronouns by person (Table 9) and the distribution of null vs. overt pronouns by person (Table 10). Table 9 shows that over 90% of pronouns were third person. Table 10 shows that the monolinguals produced 5% and 0% overt pronouns with the first and second person, while the bilinguals showed more variation: the advanced heritage speakers produced 0% overt pronouns with first person, and 50% overt pronouns with second person while the intermediate heritage speakers produced 100% overt pronouns with the first person and 0% with the second person. Even though the data are limited, it is still possible to see that the percentage of overt pronouns is much higher with the first and second persons than with the third person in the productions of heritage speakers.

|  | Total count | % 1st person | | % 2nd person | | % 3rd person | |
|---|---|---|---|---|---|---|---|
| Monolinguals (n = 20) | 613 | 3.26 | (20) | 5.5 | (34) | 91.19 | (559) |
| Advanced HSs (n = 14) | 313 | 1.60 | (5) | 2.56 | (8) | 95.85 | (300) |
| Intermediate HSs (n =10) | 250 | 1.6 | (4) | 3.20 | (8) | 95.20 | (238) |

Table 9. *Percentage of subject pronouns by person*

|  | 1st person | | 2nd person | | 3rd person | |
|---|---|---|---|---|---|---|
|  | *overt* | *null* | *overt* | *null* | *overt* | *null* |
| Monolinguals (n = 20) | 5% | 95% | 0% | 100% | 9.12 | 90.88 |
| Advanced HSs (n = 14) | 0% | 100% | **50%** | 50% | **15.33** | 84.67 |
| Intermediate HSs (n =10) | **100%** | 0% | 0% | 100% | **18.07** | 81.93 |

Table 10. *Percentage of overt and null subjects by person*

In conclusion, the patterns of null and overt subject expression in the bilingual heritage speakers are also compatible with the language change hypothesis, independently of the potential direct influence from English. Perhaps a better test case for the transfer hypothesis would be to compare the results of the bilinguals undergoing language loss with L2 learners of Spanish whose L1 is English.

## 5. *L2 Acquisition*

In this section, I ask whether the Spanish heritage speakers, who are early bilinguals, are like late bilinguals who are learning Spanish as their L2, since L2 acquisition constitutes language contact at the individual level as well. If L2 learners at intermediate and advanced stages of proficiency produce more overt subjects than the monolinguals, this is likely to be due to influence from English, their L1. If the pattern of performance is similar to that of the bilingual heritage speakers, then we can conclude that the pattern found in the heritage speakers is also due to transfer from English (the L2 or superstratum in this case).

The data comes from 32 comparable L2 learners of Spanish (see also Montrul & Rodríguez Louro, in press). These L2 learners were enrolled in intermediate and advanced Spanish classes at a research institution in the United States, and began learning Spanish at age 13 or later (mean 14.87). Their mean age at the time of testing was 20.55. The L2 learners took the same proficiency test and performed the same oral retelling task as the bilingual heritage speakers in the Montrul (2004) study. Based on their results on the proficiency test, the L2 learners were divided into intermediate (scores on the proficiency test ranging from 25/50 to 39/50) and advanced (scores ranging from 40/50 to 50/50). Figures 1 to 4 compare the results for the L2 learners and bilingual heritage speakers by proficiency level.

Figure 1 shows the results for percentage of correct agreement. The advanced L2 learners (L2) and the advanced heritage speakers (HS) had very comparable accuracy levels. The advanced L2 learners had the same error rate observed with the intermediate heritage speakers (around 97%). However, there were significant differences between the intermediate L2 learners and the intermediate heritage speakers, since the intermediate learners produced 12.55% agreement errors ($F(2, 26) = 5.678, p < .004$).

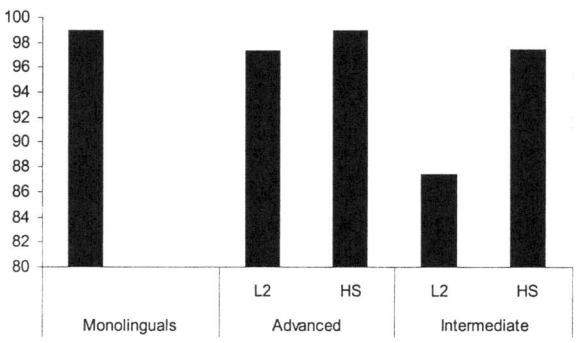

Figure 1. *Percentage correct subject-verb agreement*

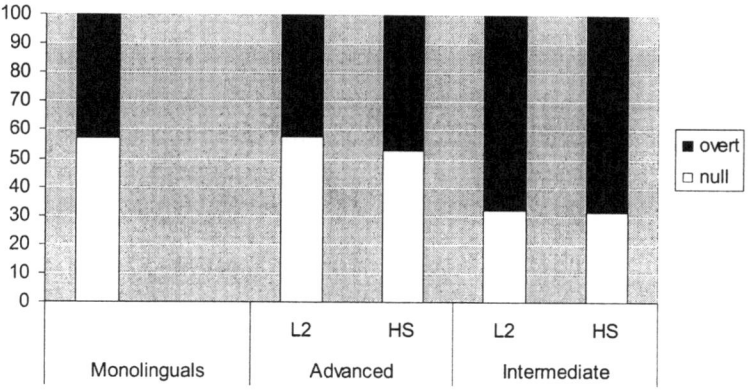

Figure 2. *Percentage of null and overt subjects by group*

Figure 2 displays the percentage totals of overt and null subjects. The advanced L2 learners and heritage speakers produced comparable percentages of null and overt subjects, which were no different from the percentages produced by the monolingual control group. The intermediate speakers were also very similar to each other, but different from the advanced groups and the monolinguals. There was a significant subject type by proficiency level interaction, since the intermediate speakers (L2 and bilinguals) produced significantly more overt (~ 68%) and fewer null subjects (~ 31%) than the advanced speakers.

Figure 3 displays the percentage production of preverbal and postverbal subjects.

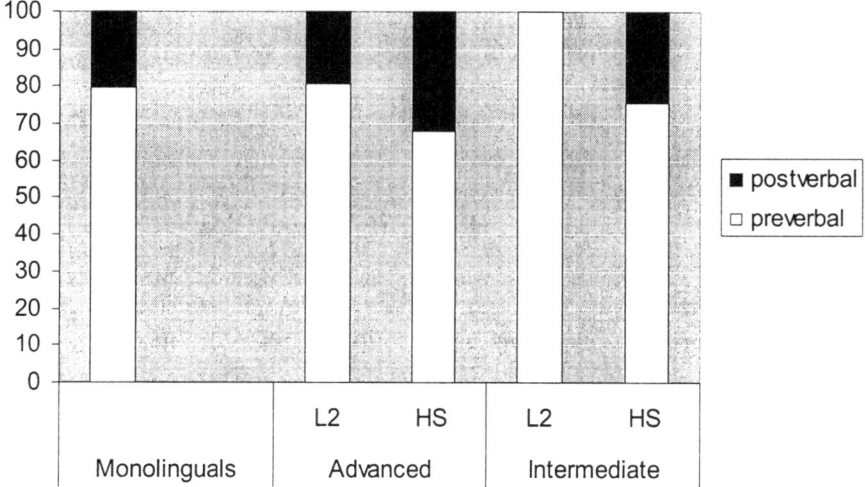

Figure 3. *Percentage preverbal and postverbal subjects*

As Figure 3 shows, the L2 learners produced more preverbal subjects than the heritage speakers ($F(3,53) = 5.543, p < .001$). While the intermediate heritage speakers produced 24.5% of postverbal subjects, the intermediate L2 learners produced none. Over 80% of the postverbal subjects produced by the monolinguals, the advanced L2 learners, and the heritage speakers occurred with unaccusative verbs. Thus, in terms of morphosyntactic properties of the Null Subject Parameter, the heritage speakers appear to have the parameter setting in place, while the intermediate L2 learners are in a state of language change, since their grammars are still in the process of resetting the parameter, judging by the number of errors with agreement they make, their overuse of overt subjects, and their exclusive preference for preverbal subjects.

Figure 4 shows accuracy with regard to the discourse-pragmatic distribution of null and overt subjects.

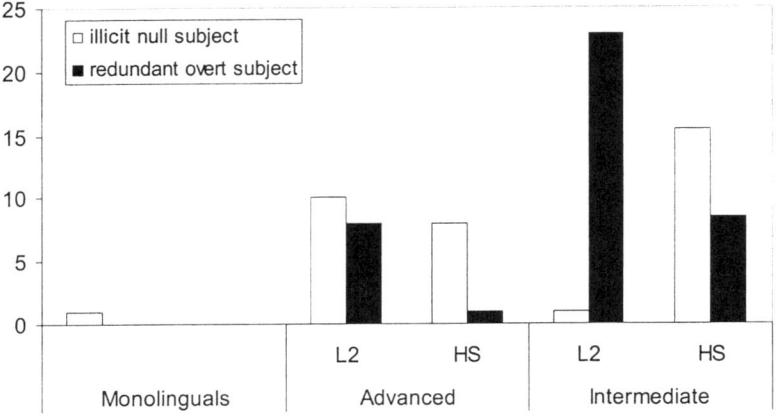

Figure 4. *Percentage of discourse-pragmatic errors with null and overt subjects*

In terms of pragmatic inaccuracy, there was a main effect for group ($F(3,53) = 7.986, p < .0001$), since both the heritage speakers and the L2 learners were less accurate than the monolinguals. When proficiency level was taken into account, there was a proficiency by type of error interaction. The intermediate L2 learners were more inaccurate than the intermediate and advanced heritage speakers with overt subjects (producing 22.9% of redundant subjects), while intermediate heritage speakers were more inaccurate than the other three groups when it came to null subjects (i.e., they produced 15.5% null subjects in switch reference contexts). Thus, while the heritage speakers have the morphosyntax of the Null Subject Parameter in place, like the L2 learners, they show a certain degree of uncertainty about the pragmatic distribution of null and overt subjects.

## 6. *Discussion and Conclusion*

As stated in the introduction, according to DeGraff (1999: 11), intermediate stages of L2 and bilingual acquisition are "creole-like" in many ways if the outcome does not match the target system. Like L1 acquirers, L2 acquirers and bilinguals try out parameter values that fall within the realm of UG options but are not sanctioned in the target language, or may be sanctioned in the target language but with a different domain of application. According to Meisel (2001), incomplete acquisition in bilingualism leads, perhaps inevitably, to language change after successive generations. I have illustrated these observations with the case of incomplete acquisition of Spanish by Spanish-English bilinguals living in the United States, where Spanish is a minority language. These bilinguals, especially those with lower proficiency in Spanish, have also been claimed to exhibit creole-like phenomena in their competence and production (Lipski 1993). I have also compared their grammars with cases of language change in progress and with stages of L2 acquisition.

The bilingual heritage speakers' results showed that the morphosyntactic aspects of the Null Subject Parameter were very intact, and there was no evidence of significant reduction of the verb agreement paradigm. However, there were other signs of "creole-like" effects like those reported by Lipski (1993). The heritage speakers with intermediate proficiency in the language produced more overt subjects than null subjects, and also made errors related to the discourse-pragmatic distribution of null and overt subjects: there were both redundant uses of overt subjects and overuse of null subjects in switch reference contexts (see Lafond, Hayes & Bhatt 2001 for similar results in an experimental study with L2 learners).

When it comes to the expression of subjects, Spanish and English differ in two important ways. First, English and Spanish have the opposite values for the Null Subject Parameter and, second, subject expression in Spanish has an added layer of complexity because the expression of subjects is regulated by discourse rules. While parameter values are not entirely unset, some aspects are affected, at least quantitatively. One possibility is that the erosion—or leveling as in creole genesis—of the complex pragmatic layer is caused by transfer from English, since as we will see, this is also common in L2 acquisition. Although this is very possible, there are other two pieces of evidence that conspire against transfer as the *only* cause in the process. One piece of evidence comes from an examination of language change in progress in Brazilian Portuguese, a language that is not in close contact with English. In the last century, Brazilian Portuguese has changed so that it is almost like a non-pro-drop language, with impoverished verb agreement morphology, more production of overt subjects, and the virtual elimination of discourse constraints on null/overt subject expression. Interestingly, the retention of null subjects is more pronounced with third-person forms than with first and second persons. Even though the data elicited from the bilingual narratives in my study were limited, the few instances of first and second persons found in the data from the heritage speakers were consistent with this trend in Brazilian Portuguese. The other piece of evidence that militates against the transfer hypothesis comes from a study of Spanish learners of Italian. Italian is a pro-drop language like Spanish. Bini (1993), who also used an oral production task, found that Spanish speakers also overused overt pronouns in Italian, most significantly with first and second person and less frequently with third person.

On the other hand, transfer from English in these contact Spanish grammars cannot be entirely ruled out, especially in the case of US-born and -raised bilinguals of Hispanic origin. Recall that Spanish dialects vary with respect to the incidence of overt subjects. In general, more overt subjects are produced in Caribbean dialects, and especially Dominican Spanish, than in dialects spoken in continental Latin America. In a recent study tracing the higher incidence of overt pronouns in speakers of Caribbean (Puerto Rican, Cuban and Dominican) and Continental (Mexican, Colombian and Ecuadorian) varieties of Spanish living in New York City and with different ages of arrival (recent arrivals born in Latin America vs. those born and raised in the US), Otheguy (2005) found that dialect leveling in the speech of recently arrived immigrants from these six countries (with speakers of Caribbean dialects behaving more like speakers of the continental dialects), while overt subject expression increased in *all* varieties due to the influence of English, especially in US-raised bilinguals (second generation). This study focused only on overt subjects and did not examine whether the overproduction of null subjects was also a feature of these grammars. Although the bilinguals who participated in my studies are of Mexican origin and are not residents of New York City, the overt pronoun data are very similar to Otheguy's and can be interpreted as indicating English influence as well.

That transfer from English plays a crucial role in the Spanish-English bilingual context is also evident when we consider the case of L2 acquisition by English speakers. The comparison between the heritage speakers and the L2 learners showed a clear dissociation between the morphosyntactic and discourse-pragmatic properties of the Null Subject Parameter according to proficiency level. The advanced L2 learners, who were very accurate with the morphosyntactic aspects of the Null Subject Parameter, showed comparable "inaccurate" performance with the overt/null distribution of subjects to that of the intermediate heritage speakers (around a 10% error rate).

The intermediate heritage speakers appeared to be in a more advanced stage of language change than the intermediate L2 learners, since the L2 learners were still in the process of resetting some aspects of the Null Subject Parameter. For example, of the L2 learners made more agreement errors, lacked postverbal subjects, and produced more than twice as many redundant overt subjects as the heritage speakers. Clearly, the intermediate L2 learners are in the process of reanalysis and parameter resetting toward the target. The intermediate heritage speakers, by contrast, had already set the morphosyntactic aspects of the parameter early in childhood, but they may have failed to develop the discourse-pragmatic properties of subject expression, probably as a result of intense contact with English early in childhood. There is evidence from simultaneous bilingualism in early childhood that bilingual children tend to simplify issues relating to the syntax-pragmatics interface. Paradis and Navarro (2003) compared the rates of overt/null subjects and their pragmatic distribution in a Spanish-English bilingual child exposed to Cuban Spanish (father) and non-native Spanish (mother). The bilingual child produced more overt subjects than matched monolingual controls and used overt subjects redundantly. Similar results are reported by Serratrice, Sorace and Paoli (2004) in early Italian-English bilingualism.

In conclusion, advanced bilingual and L2 grammars may be incomplete and "simplified" with respect to the target, as is also true of creoles. I have illustrated this phenomenon with the erosion, or leveling, of the discourse-pragmatics interface. Null subject expression is successfully acquired in L2 acquisition and is not entirely lost in cases of incomplete bilingual acquisition. Nevertheless, null subject distribution is affected in advanced bilingual and L2 grammars (La Fond et al. 2001; Lipski 1996, 1993; Silva-Corvalán 1994; Tsimpli et al. 2003), especially when the languages in contact (L1 and L2) have different parametric values. While I have not been able to confirm that the transfer of subject expression is unidirectional, as Sorace (2004) has argued, I agree with her that it might be the complexity of the syntax-pragmatics interface itself which causes these grammars to level off and remain incomplete and unspecified for pragmatic features. Finally, regardless of the particular forces behind the observed change (transfer and concomitant language change), these data point to the conclusion that bilingual and L2 grammars are systematic and undergo the same diachronic processes as other natural languages, including creole formation.

## References

Alexiadou, A. and E. Anagnostopoulou. 1998. Parameterizing Agr: Word order, V-movement and EPP checking. *Natural Language and Linguistic Theory* 16: 491–539.

Bini, M. 1993. La adquisición del Italiano: más allá de las propiedades sintácticas del parámetro pro-drop. In *La lingüística y el análisis de los sistemas no nativos,* J. Liceras (ed.), 126–139. Ottawa Hispanic Studies 12. Ottawa: Dovehouse.

Chomsky, N. 1981. *Lectures on Government and Binding.* Dordrecht: Foris.

Contreras, H. 1978. *El orden de las palabras en español.* Madrid: Cátedra.

398                                 SILVINA MONTRUL

DeGraff, M. 1999. Creolization, language change, and language acquisition: A prolegomenon. In *Language Creation and Language Change. Creolization, Diachrony, and Development*, M. DeGraff (ed.), 1–46. Cambridge, MA: The MIT Press.

Duarte, M. E. 2000. The loss of the "Avoid Pronoun Principle" in Brazilian Portuguese. In *Brazilian Portuguese and the Null Subject Parameter*, M. Kato and E. Negrão (eds.), 17–36. Madrid/Frankfurt: Verveut Iberoamericana.

Jaeggli, O. 1982. *Topics in Romance Syntax*. Dordrecht: Foris.

Lafond, L., R. Hayes and R. Bhatt. 2001. Constraint demotion and null subjects in Spanish L2 acquisition. In *Romance Syntax, Semantics and L2 Acquisition*, J. Camps and C. Wiltshire (eds.), 121–135. Amsterdam: John Benjamins.

Lefebvre, C. 1998. *Creole Genesis and the Acquisition of Grammar*. Cambridge: Cambridge University Press.

Lipski, J. 1993. Creoloid phenomena in the Spanish of transitional bilinguals. In *Spanish in the United States,* A. Roca and J. Lipski (eds.), 155–173. Berlin: Mouton de Gruyter.

Lipski, J. 1996. Patterns of pronominal evolution in Cuban-America bilinguals. In *Spanish in Contact,* A. Roca and J. Jensen (eds.), 159–186. Somerville, MA: Cascadilla Press.

Meisel, J. 2001. From bilingual language acquisition to theories of language change. Plenary talk, 3rd International Symposium on Bilingualism, Bristol, UK.

Montalbetti, M. 1984. After Binding. Ph.D. dissertation, MIT, Boston.

Montrul, S. 2002. Incomplete acquisition and attrition of Spanish tense/aspect distinctions in adult bilinguals. *Bilingualism: Language and Cognition* 5(1): 39–68.

Montrul, S. 2004. Subject and object expression in Spanish heritage speakers: A case of morpho-syntactic convergence. *Bilingualism: Language and Cognition* 7(2): 1–18. (Special issue on *Convergence,* edited by Jacqueline Toribio.)

Montrul, S. 2005. Second language acquisition and first language loss in adult early bilinguals: Exploring some differences and similarities. *Second Language Research* 21, 3.

Montrul, S. and C. Rodríguez Louro. in press. Beyond the syntax of the Null Subject Parameter: A look at the discourse-pragmatic distribution of null and overt subjects by L2 learners of Spanish. In *The Acquisition of Syntax in Romance Languages,* L. Escobar and V. Torrens (eds.). Amsterdam: John Benjamins.

Otheguy, R. 2005. Avances en el proyecto CUNY sobre el español en Nueva York: Variación, cambio e identidad en el uso variable del pronombre en seis comunidades hispanohablantes de la Gran Manzana. Paper presented at the 20th Conference on Spanish in the US, Chicago.

Paradis, J. and S. Navarro. 2003. Subject realization and crosslinguistic interference in the bilingual acquisition of Spanish and English: What is the role of the input? *Journal of Child Language* 30: 1–23.

Poletto, C. 2000. The Higher Functional Field. Evidence from Northern Italian Dialects. Oxford: Oxford University Press.

Polinsky, M. 1997. American Russian: Language loss meets language acquisition. *Proceedings of the Annual Workshop on Formal Approaches to Slavic Linguistics*, W. Brown et al. (eds.), 370–406. Ann Arbor, MI: Michigan Slavic Publications.

Rizzi, L. 1982. *Issues in Italian Syntax*. Dordrecht: Foris.

Rizzi, L. 1999. Broadening the empirical base of Universal Grammar models: A commentary. In *Language Creation and Language Change. Creolization, Diachrony, and Development*, M. DeGraff (ed.), 453–472. Cambridge, MA: The MIT Press.

Roberts, I. 1993. Verbs in Diachronic Syntax: A Comparative History of English and French. Dordrecht: Kluwer.

Schwartz, B. and R. Sprouse. 1996. L2 cognitive states and the full transfer/full access hypothesis. *Second Language Research* 12: 40–72.

Serratrice, L., A. Sorace and S. Paoli. 2004. Crosslinguistic influence at the syntax-pragmatics interface: Subjects and objects in English-Italian bilingual and monolingual acquisition. *Bilingualism: Language and Cognition* 7: 183–206.

Silva-Corvalán, C. 1994. *Language Contact and Change*. Oxford: Oxford University Press.

Silva-Corvalán, C. 2003. Linguistic consequences of reduced input in bilingual first language acquisition. In *Linguistic Theory and Language Development in Hispanic Languages*, S. Montrul and F. Ordóñez (eds.), 375–397. Sommerville, MA: Cascadilla Press.

Sorace, A. 1993. Incomplete vs. divergent representations of unaccusativity in native and non-native Italian grammars of Italian. *Second Language Research* 9: 22–47.

Sorace, A. 2004. Native language attrition and developmental instability at the syntax-discourse interface: data, interpretations and methods. *Bilingualism: Language and Cognition* 7: 143–145.

Sprouse, R. and B. Vance. 1999. An explanation for the decline of null pronouns in certain Germanic and Romance languages. In *Language Creation and Language Change. Creolization, Diachrony, and Development*, M. DeGraff (ed.), 257–284. Cambridge, MA: The MIT Press.

Suñer, M. 1982. *Syntax and Semantics of Presentational Sentences Types*. Washington, DC: Georgetown University Press.

Toribio, A. J. 2000. Setting parameter limits on dialectal variation in Spanish. *Lingua* 10: 315–341.

Toribio, A. 2001. On Spanish language decline. *Proceedings of the 25th Boston University Conference on Language Development*, pp. 768–779. Sommerville, MA: Cascadilla Press.

Tsimpli, I., A. Sorace, C. Heycock, F. Filiaci and B. Bouba. 2003. Subjects in L1 attrition: Evidence from Greek and Italian near-native speakers of English. In *Proceedings of the 27th Annual Boston University Conference on Language Development*, 787–797. Somerville, MA: Cascadilla Press.

Valdés, G. 2000. Spanish for Native Speakers: AATSP Professional Development Series Handbook for Teachers K-16 (Vol. 1). New York: Harcourt College Publishers.

White, L. 1989. Universal Grammar and Second Language Acquisition. Amsterdam: John Benjamins.

White, L. 2004. Reanalysis. Paper presented at the Montreal Dialogues between Creole Genesis and Second Language Acquisition, Université du Québec à Montréal.

# COMPARING CREOLE GENESIS WITH SLA
## IN UNLIMITED-ACCESS CONTEXTS:
### GOING BEYOND RELEXIFICATION

Donna Lardiere

*Georgetown University*

This paper considers the nature of ultimate attainment in adult second language acquisition in relation to the hypothesis put forward by Lefebvre (1998) regarding creole genesis: namely, that creole genesis is a particular case of second language acquisition within a context of limited access to the superstratum language. The less access learners have, the more "radical" and less target-like the resulting creole will be, as the substratum speakers relexify properties of their native lexicons, and retain the parametric values and semantic interpretation rules of their native grammars. Conversely, the more access learners have to the target language community, the more the creole is likely to resemble the superstratum language. In this paper, I discuss L2 ultimate attainment data from Patty, a native speaker of Mandarin and Hokkien Chinese who acquired English as an adult, and whose naturalistic acquisition in an unlimited-access context offers a potentially valuable case in testing the upper limits of this hypothesis. While the data appear to generally support the overall hypothesis that more exposure leads to more target-like acquisition, Patty's English idiolect has fossilized in some respects despite unlimited access; thus, we also need to tease apart the effects of degree of exposure from other factors such as maturation and possibly persistent effects of prior L1 knowledge.

## 1. *Introduction*

In this paper, I would like to reflect on the nature of ultimate attainment in adult second language acquisition in relation to the hypothesis put forward by Lefebvre (1998) regarding creole genesis: namely, that creole genesis is a particular case of second language acquisition (SLA) within a context of limited access to the superstratum language. The less access adult language learners have to the superstratum language, the more "radical" and less target-like the resulting creole will be, as the substratum speakers relexify or use the properties of their native lexicons, and retain the parametric values and semantic interpretation rules of their own native grammars (p. 9). Conversely, the more access the substratum speakers have to the target language community, the more the creole is likely to resemble the superstratum language (p. 2).

Given Lefebvre's hypothesis, I think it is possible to view the study of adult L2 ultimate attainment—particularly when it involves naturalistic acquisition in unlimited-access contexts—as potentially valuable in testing the upper limits of this hypothesis, and in teasing apart the effects of degree of exposure from other factors such as maturation and prior L1 knowledge. I will discuss the issue of ultimate attainment in relation to the case study I have been working on for the past several years, that of Patty, a native speaker of Mandarin and Hokkien Chinese who acquired English as an adult. While the data from Patty appear to generally support the overall hypothesis that more exposure will lead to more target-like acquisition, some interesting questions do arise.

First, since acquiring a more target-like representation of the L2 idiolect necessarily requires going beyond the relexification of native language features, functional categories, parametric settings and semantic interpretations, at what point along the continuum of degree of access to the L2 do the predictions of relexification become reversed? In other words, how much exposure is needed before we might predict that the learner will acquire the features, functional categories, parametric settings, etc., of the target language rather than simply relexifying the native language categories? While the data from Patty cannot answer this question exactly, it is clear that in many respects she does appear to have gone beyond relexification so that, for at least some areas of the grammar, it is indeed possible to do so eventually.

Second, although it is well beyond the scope of this paper to discuss the likely enormous impact of the psychological and sociolinguistic factors that distinguish the environmental circumstances in Patty's L2 acquisition case from those under which creolization typically occurs, these are nonetheless certain to play a significant role in ultimate attainment beyond the simple issue of "more or less access." As Lefebvre points out, creoles emerge in multilingual contexts where there is a need for a lingua franca and where the creators of this lingua franca generally have little access to the superstratum language. This scenario differs considerably from the environment in which Patty acquired English. Another distinguishing factor I will touch on briefly is the possible role of advanced literacy in the target language. At the very least, such literacy no doubt vastly increases the amount of exposure to the target language, especially exposure to complex sentences that may be helpful in working out some of the movement and extraction possibilities available in that language. As I will discuss, it may also play a role in the acquisition of derivational morphology.

Finally, as will become clear from the data, it seems unlikely that ultimate attainment in adult language acquisition can be reduced solely to a function of amount of access, although that is surely an important factor. Patty's English idiolect has clearly fossilized in some respects despite *unlimited* access; thus, we will also need to look for other factors to help account for the remaining areas of non-target-likeness. In this paper, I will consider the role of maturational constraints in particular, including recent research that is relevant to both creolization and adult SLA.

In the remainder of this paper, I briefly sketch some relevant points concerning Lefebvre's relexification proposal, followed by a brief introduction to Patty, my informant. Then I will compare the predictions of Lefebvre's relexification hypothesis and the results she observed in creolization with relevant data from Patty. I conclude with some findings concerning the role of maturational constraints in adult SLA. Throughout the paper, all references to Lefebvre's work are from Lefebvre (1998).

## 2. *Creole genesis and the relexification hypothesis*

Lefebvre observes that creole languages are mixed in the sense that some of their properties are derived from their substrate and some from their superstrate languages; however, she argues, the type of mix is not random. Rather, she claims, radical creoles are created primarily by the process of *relexification*, defined by Muysken (1981: 61) as "the process of vocabulary substitution in which the only information adopted from the target language in the lexical entry is the phonological representation" (Lefebvre 1998: 9). In other words, lexical items from the native (substrate) language(s) are "relabeled" using phonetic strings from the target language while nonetheless retaining their original semantic and syntactic properties—those of the native substrate languages.

Relexification is argued to be semantically driven, such that the learner perceives at least a partial overlap between the meaning of a target language phonetic string, as deduced from its context, and that of the lexical entry copied from the source language. Both major (lexical) and minor (functional) category items as well as derivational affixes are claimed to be relexified. For functional categories, however, the relexification process is argued to be "slightly more complex" than for lexical categories (p. 37), exhibiting the following characteristics (and testable predictions):

First, because of limited access, learners are hypothesized to be unable to identify the functional categories of the superstrate language. Thus, in setting the parametric values of the new language, the creators of a creole are predicted to use those of their native substratum language (p. 47).

Second, functional category lexical entries of the copied lexicon are claimed to be relabeled using major category lexical items (e.g., nouns, adjectives, verbs, adverbs and prepositions) from the target language. Since these categories are typically free morphemes, this accounts for why creoles tend to be isolating languages with little affixation, even when the source language is non-isolating (p. 49).

Third, because relexification is semantically driven, as mentioned above, only those functional categories from the source language that have some semantic content, such as determiners or demonstratives, will be relabeled with a phonetic form from the target language. Source language functional categories that have no semantic content, such as case markers or operators, may be abandoned, or else copied but assigned a phonologically null representation.

Finally, there is predicted to be a difference in word order for relabeled major lexical vs. minor functional category lexical items. Because learners identify phonetic strings of major category lexical items in the target language, they acquire the target language directionality properties of these items as well. Thus, the word order of major category lexical entries in the creole is predicted to follow that of major categories in the target language, such as the pre- or postnominal position of adjectives. However, because the substrate language properties of functional categories are retained in the creole, the order for functional category items should follow that of the substrate rather than target language, such as the pre- or postnominal position of determiners.

Readers familiar with the generative second language acquisition literature will notice a similarity between relexification and the notion of "full transfer," as proposed in the *full transfer/full access* (FT/FA) hypothesis of Schwartz and Sprouse (1994, 1996). Lefebvre makes the connection between relexification and transfer explicit, claiming that relexification applies in a situation which involves a particular case of SLA—that of creole genesis in limited-access contexts. More specifically, she argues that the notion of transfer is pertinent to both creole genesis and SLA, that it corresponds to the result of relexification in creole genesis, and that relexification also appears to play a role in SLA (p. 34).

It is important to note that *full transfer* is a theoretical construct hypothesized to hold true of learners at the initial state of SLA. The predictions of the relexification hypothesis are argued to hold for "radical" creoles— creoles that most resemble their substratum languages. It is not clear how to directly compare the notions of L2 *initial state* vs. *radical creole*. Perhaps the radical creole grammar "freezes" or fossilizes in the initial stages of the development of the language itself, due to its speakers' lack of access to the target language. By looking at an end-state grammar, we can observe the process of acquisition unfold under circumstances in which development is allowed to proceed naturally and fully. The predictions above thus provide a useful framework in which to examine whether learners are able to go beyond relexification if they are given greater access in an immersion second language context.

### 3. *SLA in an unlimited-access environment: the case of Patty*

Patty is a native speaker of Mandarin and Hokkien Chinese who was born into the Chinese expatriate community in Indonesia and then emigrated to mainland China as an adolescent, to Hong Kong two years later, and finally to the USA at age 22. Although she was exposed to some formal study of English during her high school years in Hong Kong, she acquired most of her English as an adult immigrant in the United States. Data collection was begun after she had already been living in the USA for about 10 years, and now includes samples of both spoken and written English extending over a period of more than 16 years. Over that entire time period, nearly all of Patty's daily interactions, not only within her community and workplace but also within her more intimate circles, that is, with her friends and at home with her husband and daughter, have been conducted almost exclusively in English.

It is impossible to estimate the millions of English sentences Patty has been exposed to since her arrival in the USA more than 25 years ago, including the written ones she has encountered throughout her entire undergraduate and graduate degree programs in accounting, as well as in the novels, magazines, newspapers, e-mail messages, work memos, IRS forms and instructions, recipes, and everything else she reads on a daily basis. But surely it overwhelmingly surpasses the six million or so sentences Birdsong (1999) estimates that children are exposed to over their first *five* years of life.

When I first began data collection, I was initially struck and frankly intrigued by how non-native-like her English appeared to be, even after 10 years of immersed living—working, studying and socializing—in the target language environment. Grammatical elements that tend to be omitted, especially from her spoken production data, include verbal inflections for regular past tense marking as in (1a), nonpast third-person singular agreement marking as in (1b), and past participle forms (1c); we also find the occasional overuse or omission of the present participle -*ing* form (1d–e), and the omission of copular and auxiliary *be* (1f–g), and for nouns, the occasional omission of regular plural (1h) and possessive clitic marking (1i).

(1) a.  I *call* Bill this morning and nobody *answer*
　　b.  because he *understand* better now
　　c.  yeah but we haven't *look* at it carefully
　　d.  my tears just can't *stopping* coming down
　　e.  I was *stay* by myself in the dormitory
　　f.  he ø around adult a lot
　　g.  she ø just hanging around
　　h.  I borrow a lot of *book* from her
　　i.  *Debbie* brother was very rich

Now, over two decades later, these generalizations still hold and do not seem to have changed; nonetheless, I have also in the meantime become aware of aspects of her L2 English idiolect that are strikingly target-like, and that moreover cannot necessarily be explained in terms of transfer or anything like a process of relexification from the L1. These acquired elements include knowledge of overall pronominal case-marking, and case-marking on subjects in particular as a function of clausal finiteness (2a), and various word-order-related phenomena such as the placement of verbs with respect to negation and adverbs (2b), robust relative clause formation, and *wh*-movement in general, including the appropriate stranding of prepositions (2c), and subject-aux inversion and *do*-support in questions (2d). Her use of possessive pronouns is native-like (2e) (except for the occasional confusing of gender in the third-person singular forms *his* and *her* in her spoken language only); and her use of determiners, while not completely native-like, is nonetheless surprisingly proficient (2f). Her use of overt rather than null subjects is overwhelmingly correct, and she correctly uses expletive subjects as shown in (2g–h).

(2) a.  maybe *they* don't want *us* to use it after office hour
    b.  his brother *never came* here
    c.  you don't know *who you should associate with*
    d.  *why do you* want me to go?
    e.  *our* hostess Julia and *her* family
    f.  say, um, he have *a* beer … when A. repeat *the* story to us *the* other day about *the* beer
    g.  *there's* political change in Indonesia
    h.  *it* is funny that you always late when the place you want to go is so close, isn't *it*?

In what follows, I would like to briefly outline and compare some of Lefebvre's predictions and findings regarding the relation of various parame-terized aspects of Haitian creole to both its sub- and super-stratum languages (Fongbe and French) to some corresponding data from Patty. Lefebvre found that for nearly every property she examined, the creole resembled the substrate grammar far more than that of the superstrate. My comparison will involve looking at a few of these grammatical properties as well, in a particular L2 idiolect, and likewise relating them to properties of the native grammar(s) (particularly Mandarin) or the target L2 (English), as well as to the predictions made by the relexification hypothesis.

The results strongly confirm Lefebvre's hypothesized role of degree of access to the target language in these domains, showing that when access increases, so does the resulting resemblance of the L2 idiolect to the target language. The areas I will look at are null and expletive subjects, verb raising, *wh*-movement and relativization, including preposition stranding, tense mark-ing, comparative and superlative affixation on adjectives and derivational affixation in general. Despite considerable evidence that much of what Patty knows about English has gone well beyond the relexification or relabeling of L1 lexical entries, the examples shown in (1) above nonetheless demonstrate that there are still apparent limits to what can be naturalistically acquired despite unlimited access to the target language. This residue of non-target-likeness must therefore be attributed to other factors.

### 3.1 *Null and expletive subjects*

Languages are thought to differ parametrically as to whether they allow null subjects or not. This is one property for which Haitian was argued by Lefebvre to differ from both of its source languages. Whereas both Fongbe and French are claimed to be null subject languages, Haitian is not.[1] In this case, the creators of Haitian apparently did reset the value of this hypothesized parameter to non-null subjects on the basis of exposure to strong subject pronouns in French, which are argued by Lefebvre to be major lexical category items (p. 148). The distinction between strong pronouns and weak syntactic pronominal clitics exists in both Fongbe and French; however, Haitian is thought to lack weak syntactic clitics. (This characteristic of Haitian seems surprising in light of the relexification hypothesis, and the reader is referred to Lefebvre (pp. 155–157) for a more extended discussion of possible analyses.)

As for the use of expletive subjects, Lefebvre observes that, whereas French has obligatory overt expletives, expletives in both Haitian and Fongbe may be optionally null; moreover, the possibility of overt vs. covert expletives in both Haitian and Fongbe is lexically determined by particular verbs. This is exactly what the relexification hypothesis would predict for Haitian Creole.

In Patty's case, Chinese is a null subject (or perhaps null topic) language, which does not make use of expletive subjects. English, on the other hand, requires overt subjects, including expletives. If this is a parameterized distinction, then Patty has clearly reset the parametric value to the target English value. She knows that overt subjects are required in English. Null subjects occur in only a tiny fraction (about 1.7%) of the more than 1,500 finite contexts examined that require overt subjects. This knowledge is, moreover, evident from the earliest recording, in which over 99% of her utterances requiring overt subjects had them, as shown in Table 1 below (from Lardiere, to appear).

| Recording | Overt | % | Null | % |
|---|---|---|---|---|
| 1 | 362 | 99.45 | | 2 00.55 |
| 2 | 788 | 97.89 | 17 | 02.11 |
| 3 | 329 | 97.92 | | 7 02.08 |
| TOTAL | 1,479 | 98.27 | 26 | 01.73 |

Table 1. *Patty's overt vs. null subjects in obligatory finite contexts (Recordings 1–3).*

Since there are no overt expletive subjects in Chinese and they have no semantic content in English, the relexification hypothesis would predict that these should not be available for relexification. However, Patty uses expletive subjects completely productively, a shown by the examples in (3) for expletive *it* and (4) for *there* in existential constructions:

(3) a. *it* was nice to hear from you finally
   b. *it* seems we have not really talk
   c. sorry *it* takes so long to reply
   d. *it* was especially helpful to me when my father went bankruptcy

---

[1] Both French and Fongbe are argued to be null subject languages on the assumption that their subject clitics should be analyzed as agreement markers (following Hulk 1986; Jaeggli 1984; Roberge 1990). The clitics are hypothesized to bind a small *pro* in subject position.

    e.  *it* was so fortunate that the police was there
    f.  to imagine how long *it* would take us to say hi to each daffodil

(4) a.  I think *there* was a breakdown in the agency
    b.  *there's* a poem that you have to memorize
    c.  *there* were some changes in my life recently
    d.  *there* are so many lessons to learn in your lifetime
    e.  I think *there* are differences between men and women
    f.  *there* is a signal to show you who are online

Thus, it appears that Patty has gone beyond relexification in acquiring obligatory overt subjects in English, including the purely formal properties of English expletive subjects.

### 3.2 *Pronominal case marking*

Under the relexification hypothesis, case markers have no semantic content and thus are predicted to be unable to be relexified or relabeled in the target language (Lefebvre, p. 101). This should be especially true in the case of a native Chinese speaker acquiring English, since Chinese has no overt case distinctions at all to begin with. In English, however, pronouns bear overt case distinctions, consisting of subject, object and possessive forms. In this section, I focus on subject, or nominative case, which is assigned only to subjects of finite clauses and thus entails knowledge of finiteness as well.

As reported in Lardiere (1998a), Patty has perfectly acquired the distribution of pronominal case marking in English. Her suppliance of nominative case marking on subjects in finite clauses is perfect, at 100%. Some examples are shown in (5):

(5) a.  *I* cried when *I* saw her videotape.
    b.  whether *they* have booked it or not
    c.  *she* started to cry last Tuesday when *I* said goodbye
    d.  *I* am sure *he* was getting in touch with you
    e.  *he* think that *they* are comparable
    f.  because *I* believe that *we* are soul mate

Moreover, if we compare her case marking on subjects in finite vs. nonfinite clauses, it is clear that it is actually the formal feature of finiteness rather than some functional property of "subjecthood" that determines the case marking. In nonfinite clauses and exceptional case marking contexts, she similarly chooses the correct *non*-nominative form of the pronoun 100% of the time. Some examples are shown in (6):

(6) a.  why do you want *me* to go?
    b.  that doesn't have anything to do with *me* leaving home
    c.  with the issue *my* getting pregnant

    d.  because China don't let *me* go there
    e.  maybe they don't want *us* to use it after office hour
    f.  so for *them* to learn English, you know …
    g.  not seeing *her* growing up
    h.  she wanted *us* to take her to Canada

In sum, it appears that Patty has certainly gone beyond relexification in terms of the accuracy of her pronominal case marking in the target language.

### 3.3 *Verb raising*

Languages have been claimed to vary parametrically according to whether or not they have verb raising, in which main verbs appear preposed before negative or adverbial elements, or invert with subjects in question formation (via I-to-C movement). It is thought by some to be tied to properties of verbal inflectional morphology, particularly more complex (or "strong") subject-verb agreement. Lefebvre shows that, in contrast to French, verb raising is not available in Fongbe, and that Haitian has retained the same non-raising value as Fongbe rather than resetting to the French value.

English is also a language in which there is little verbal agreement morphology and thematic verbs do not raise. As I have reported elsewhere (Lardiere 1998b, in press, to appear), Patty clearly does not allow verb raising in her own English L2 idiolect. However, since her L1 Chinese is also a non-raising language with no verbal agreement morphology, one might legitimately wonder whether Patty is not simply representing an L1 Chinese-like grammar in her L2 English idiolect, given that she not only rejects verb raising but also produces almost no third-person singular agreement inflection in her spoken English. There are a few reasons to doubt this, however.

For English, the kind of positive evidence that would inform learners that thematic verbs cannot raise is a bit different from that in Chinese, including the presence in English but not Chinese of *do*-support. There is also the possibility in English but not Chinese of raising finite forms of copular and auxiliary *be* over adverbs and NEG. It is clear in each of these cases that Patty's L2 English idiolect reflects the appropriate English rather than Chinese properties.

First, as shown in (7), it is clear that Patty has productively acquired *do*-support in English—a likely trigger or cue for setting the verb-raising parameter in English (to the non-raising value). *Do*-support is another purely formal construction with no semantic content, used to instantiate functional category features of number, person and tense (the last of which—tense—is itself often claimed not to exist in Chinese).

(7)  a.  we *do* not need to arrange any play date at all
     b.  I *did* not want to hurt your feeling
     c.  it *doesn't* stick anymore
     d.  *did* you watch Olympic?
     e.  *didn't* he know that it will get back to me?

Since the equivalent of *do*-support is not present in Chinese, there is no corresponding lexical entry from Patty's native language that could have been relabeled in her English idiolect; consequently, Patty's manifestation of *do*-support is the result of genuine acquisition, not relexification.

Next, Patty also knows that, unlike thematic lexical verbs, finite forms of *be* do in fact raise over adverbs and NEG in English, as shown in the examples in (8). Examples (8d–e) in particular contrast the position of *be* relative to adverbs with her production of the same adverbs occurring with thematic verbs. (Note also the correct use of agreement for the suppletive forms of *be*, another distinction that does not exist in Chinese but which Patty supplies highly consistently.)

(8) a.  my family *was not* rich
    b.  I *am not* going to miss you this time
    c.  *isn't* it generous gift?
    d.  although it *was never* obvious     (cf. his brother *never came* here)
    e.  because it *is always* there        (cf. I *always love* to be a dancer)

This distinction between verb placement with respect to *be* vs. lexical thematic verbs does not exist in Chinese where, on the other hand, NEG precedes the copula (*shi*) as well as thematic verbs:

(9) *Mandarin Chinese*                                  (Li & Thompson, 1981: 422)
    a.  *women* **bu** **zhidao**  *ta*    *zai*  *nar*
        we       not   know        s/he    at     where
        'We don't know where s/he is.'
    b.  *ta*    **bu** **shi**  *xiaozhang*
        s/he    not    be       school.chief
        'S/he is not the principal.'

In sum, it seems quite clear that Patty is not relying on a Chinese-type grammar but rather has acquired an English-like representation of the features governing verb raising in her L2 English idiolect.

### 3.4 *Wh-movement, relative clauses and preposition stranding*
Lefebvre demonstrates that Haitian *wh*-expressions correspond to the substrate Fongbe *wh*-expressions rather than superstrate French ones with respect to whether they are syntactic phrases as opposed to morphological simplexes (as in, for example, 'which person' vs. 'who' or 'which place' vs. 'where'). She therefore argues that *wh*-expressions are clearly relabeled lexical entries copied from Fongbe. She also notes that Haitian has *wh*-phrases exactly where Fongbe has them, and that their distribution in terms of their occurrence in questions but not relative clauses mirrors that of Fongbe rather than French. Furthermore, in both Haitian and Fongbe but not French, extraction out of the subject

position requires the use of a resumptive pronoun in the extraction site (pp. 179–180).

In comparing Chinese and English with respect to the syntactic vs. morphological shape of *wh*-expressions, these are quite similar across both languages with the exception of *weishenme* (lit. 'for what' = 'why'). It is clear, though, that Patty has acquired English *why*:

(10) a. *why* do you want me to go

    b. I asked myself *why* I never ever think of him

    c. *why* I was so cruel to him

    d. *why* so late, *why* don't you do it early

In English question formation, *yes-no* questions exhibit subject-aux inversion, and *wh*-questions require the fronting of the *wh*-expression to clause-initial position. Question formation in English also requires the use of *do*-support in case no other auxiliary is available for subject-aux inversion. In contrast, Chinese question formation looks very different. There is no subject-aux inversion or *wh*-movement; instead, question particles are used and the *wh*-expression remains *in situ*, as shown in (11) (examples from Li & Thompson, 1981):

(11) a. *ni    xihuan   nei-ben   shu    **ma**?*

      you   like      that-CL   book   Q

      'Do you like that book?'

    b. *women   jintian   wanshang    chi    **shenme**?*

      we       today    evening      eat    what

      'What are we having for supper tonight?'

    c. *ni    qu    **nar**?*

      you   go    where

      'Where are you going?'

The differences between English and Chinese question formation have been attributed to a parametric difference involving the strength or weakness of an interrogative [+wh] or [+Q] feature in C(omplementizer) position. In English, this feature is claimed to be strong, triggering movement of the *wh*-item into the CP to check the Q feature in C (Chomsky 1995; Freidin 1999). In Chinese, it is claimed to be weak (or absent), and thus the *wh*-expression remains in situ.

Turning now to Patty's data, she has clearly acquired the English feature values for question formation, including *wh*-movement, the use of *do*-support and subject-aux inversion, and the correct non-inversion of subject-aux in embedded questions, shown in (12):[2]

---

[2] As discussed in Lardiere (to appear), Patty's question formation in English still retains traces of earlier developmental stages as described by Pienemann et al. (1988). For example, she

(12) a.  did you visit your mom last weekend?
 b.  should I call you on the phone next time?
 c.  is it because of all the excitement?
 d.  are you relying on my answers to finish the book?
 e.  where's the cover, A.?
 f.  if I leave, who is going to do the job?
 g.  when are you coming back?
 h.  what are you doing for Thanksgiving?
 i.  I don't know how long we are going to wait
 j.  I don't know what they're doing with this system now

Let us now turn to relative clauses. In English, relative clauses can be introduced either by a *wh*-expression, or by the complementizer *that* or, in non-subject relatives, by a null operator, as shown in the examples in (13). Even in relative clauses with no *wh*-expression, as in (13b–c), it is assumed that a null operator has moved into clause-initial position. English also allows preposition-stranding, as shown in (13d).

(13) a.  the boy who I met
 b.  the boy that I met
 c.  the boy I met
 d.  the boy I gave a book to

Relative clauses in Chinese, on the other hand, precede the noun they modify, as opposed to English, in which they follow it, and the use of the relativizing particle *de* is required. In sharp contrast to English, preposition stranding is not allowed, and oblique relatives require the use of a resumptive pronoun, as shown in (14c) (examples from Li & Thompson, 1981):

(14) a. *qi    zixingche  de    ren*
   ride  bicycle    DE    person
   'people who ride bicycles'
 b. *wo   gei   ni    de    shu*
   I     give  you   DE    book
   'the book I gave you'

---

occasionally fails to invert the auxiliary and subject in *wh*-questions, even though the *wh*-expression has moved, as in (i), or conversely, incorrectly inverts the auxiliary in embedded questions, as in (ii):
(i)      why I was so cruel to him?
(ii)     I wonder what are they talking about
Nonetheless, it is clear from the data that she has achieved the final developmental stage on the Pienemann et al. scale, as shown by the examples in (10i–j). This final stage also includes the use of tag questions, which Patty has also acquired, as shown in (iii) below:
(iii)    it is funny that you always late when the place you want to go is so close, isn't it?

    c. *wo   song-gei  \*(ta)  yi-ben   xiaoshuo de   ren*
        I    give-to  3SG  one-CL  novel    DE  person
        'the person to whom I gave a novel'
        'the person I gave a novel to'

Aside from the issue of parameter-setting, for which the relexification hypothesis would predict that Patty should retain the values of her native Chinese, we also observe differences in functional category directionality for relative clauses in English and Chinese, for the complementizer *that* and relativizer *de,* respectively. In English, the CP headed by C follows the head noun, whereas in Chinese it precedes it. According to the relexification hypothesis, functional categories should follow the word order of the native rather than the target language. Thus, the data show that Patty has advanced beyond relexification, and instead appears to have acquired the relevant English settings for word order.

Turning again to the data, Patty always uses the correct, English-type word order, has obviously acquired the English complementizer *that* (again, a purely functional category with no semantic content), and has clearly acquired preposition stranding as well. Examples of subject, object and oblique relatives (including free relatives) are shown in (15) through (17), respectively. The examples in (17) in particular illustrate her robust use of preposition stranding.

(15)  a. my parents contributed in some way *that shaped me as who I am*
      b. and then they find this place *that will do the catering*
      c. they are the one *who clean your bathroom*
      d. a lot of teacher *who* # *who have a very good education*

(16)  a. there's a poem *that you have to memorize*
      b. the language *that you don't know*
      c. I got *what I wanted*
      d. the medicine *you mentioned*

(17)  a. he's the only person *I spoke to*
      b. I didn't understand *what he's talking about in the class*
      c. I have a couple # couple university *that I apply to*
      d. that is *what we are on earth for*

Patty's productive use of preposition stranding suggests that she is probably not simply base-generating the *wh*-expression in clause-initial position, as has been suggested by studies examining the so-called "null prep" phenomenon, in which learners tend to drop the required preposition rather than strand (or pied-pipe) it. Baker (2003) also takes preposition stranding as "particularly good evidence" of a syntactic derivation involving movement (p. 281). Thus, it appears that Patty has indeed acquired an English-like *wh*-operator and the feature values involved in triggering *wh*-movement.

### 3.5 *Tense marking*

Lefebvre observes that verbs in Haitian are always bare; there are none of the verbal inflectional affixes encoding distinctions for tense, mood, person and number that are required in French. In Fongbe, as in Haitian, however, verbs are bare, there are no subject-verb agreement markers, and no affixes for tense, mood or aspect; instead, these distinctions are indicated by markers occurring between the subject and the verb (pp. 111–112). In Haitian, these preverbal markers derive most of their semantic, syntactic and morphological properties from Fongbe, whereas their phonological form is derived from phonetic strings—mainly free morphemes such as prepositions or auxiliaries that occur in the same preverbal position—from French, as predicted by the relexification hypothesis.

Turning to consider Patty's case, I will focus on the categories of past tense vs. perfective aspect. Mandarin makes use of a perfective suffix -*le* which is used to indicate that an event is being viewed in its entirety or as a whole, that is, it is bounded temporally, spatially or conceptually (Li & Thompson 1981: 185). It is considered an aspect rather than a tense marker; Li and Thompson claim that Mandarin has no markers of tense (p. 184). If it is true that tense (or at least [+past]) does not exist as a functional category or feature in Chinese, then the relexification hypothesis would predict that past tense should be unacquirable in English.

Has Patty acquired past tense? In her spoken English, approximately one-third of verb forms in past contexts are past-tense-marked. In her written production, this percentage rises to about 78%. One might wonder, however, whether Patty's past tense marking truly indicates past tense as opposed to the functional category from her L1 with the highest degree of semantic overlap—perfective aspect. In other words, if relexification is semantically driven, then one possible candidate form for relabeling Chinese perfective aspect in English would be the regular past tense marker -*ed*, which, in addition to marking an event as occurring prior to the moment of speech, has also been argued to include the expression of perfective aspect for events (e.g., Ludlow 1999; see Lardiere 2003a, to appear, for further discussion). For example, a sentence like *John painted the kitchen* includes both the interpretation of the event of kitchen-painting as having occurred prior to the moment of speech *and* that the kitchen-painting was in fact completed in its entirety. Thus, there is at least partial semantic overlap for the forms -*le* and -*ed*.

From a syntactic and morphological standpoint, it is unlikely that Chinese perfective -*le* is being relexified with past tense marking in English: because -*le* follows the verb in Chinese, as does the English suffix -*ed*, the directionality condition for relexification is met; however, it appears that the English suffix -*ed*'s status as a functional category affix would preclude its being used to relabel perfective aspect in Patty's idiolect, assuming, as mentioned earlier, that functional category lexical entries of the copied lexicon are claimed to be relabeled using only major category lexical items from the target language. Lefebvre writes: "Relabelling of functional category lexical entries is thus constrained by what the superstratum language has to offer in terms of major category lexical items whose semantics and distribution are appropriate to provide a phonetic matrix for a copied functional category lexical entry" (p. 37). Another complication from a morphological standpoint is the highly frequent presence throughout the target language environment of *irregular* verb forms used in the same semantic and syntactic contexts as regular past tense verb forms in English. Since verbs in Chinese do not change their root form depending on aspectual or temporal interpretation, it is not clear what functional category or feature in Chinese is being relabeled with an irregular past form in English.

It seems then, that the sort of data that would indicate that Patty has gone beyond relexification and acquired past tense in English would include any of the following: consistent use of the regular past tense marker *-ed* in past tense contexts (although this is not the best indication for eventive predicates if there is a possibility that this morpheme is relexifying Chinese perfective *-le*, due to the degree of semantic overlap mentioned above), or use of English past tense marking (of any sort—regular or irregular) in appropriate English past tense contexts in which it would *not* be appropriate to use the Chinese aspectual marker *-le*. According to Li and Thompson, this would be for verbs expressing states that do not represent bounded events, verbs denoting ongoing actions, or verbs in negative sentences (since, according to Li and Thompson, the meaning "that some event does not take place or some state of affairs does not obtain is incompatible with the meaning of *-le*, which is to signal a bounded event" (p. 205)).

With respect to regular past tense marking, the data show that Patty does not use the regular past tense marker *-ed* consistently, although she uses it sometimes, with a huge difference between its use in her speech (about 6% suppliance in past tense contexts) vs. her writing (about 77% suppliance). The discrepancy between her spoken and written data suggests that (i) phonological factors are probably heavily implicated in the affix's relative absence from her spoken data, and (ii) that the suppliance rate in the written data is too high to dismiss as evidence that she has no representation at all of this functional category in English.

Looking at past tense marking overall, we should first note that Patty generally uses past tense marking where appropriate in English—about 94% of her use of past is appropriately supplied, and only about 2% is in temporally mismatched contexts (the other errors she makes are errors involving formally incorrect marking, as in doubly-marked clauses such as *they did went to school*, and instances of marking the main verb instead of the auxiliary for past, as in *we don't spoke that much English*). (See Lardiere (to appear) for a much more detailed discussion of Patty's past tense marking.[3])

What about the sorts of contexts in which the Chinese aspectual marker *-le* cannot be used? The first context is that of verbs expressing states that do not represent bounded events. There are many examples of such past-marked states in Patty's English data. A few examples are shown in (18):

(18)  a.  I *felt* terrific
      b.  I *thought* we have a special deal
      c.  J. always *treated* M. as a friend
      d.  it *was* so fortunate that the police was there
      e.  I *wanted* to have a house, a car, etc.
      f.  since my mom *was* a teacher

Second, ongoing actions would not be marked with *-le* in Chinese. In English, past tense marking of ongoing actions is most likely to be in the progressive, with past itself marked on the auxiliary (note the double-marking in example (19d)):

(19)  a.  D. and I *were* practicing the violin again
      b.  I *was* dating uh, um, a man that I met in a club
      c.  so we *were* living together for a year
      d.  I *was* still wrote to my friend
      e.  I *was* living with S.'s parents
      f.  while they *were* going to school

Finally, negative contexts are incompatible with aspectual *-le* marking in Chinese. There are many past negative contexts in the data; I have chosen examples in (20) below that are unlikely to be aspectually marked not only because of negation but also because they represent unbounded states.

(20)  a.  we *did* not expect it will be so fast
      b.  they *did* not know whether or not she will be back
      c.  we *were* unable to go over to the other end
      d.  I *did* not want to hurt your feeling
      e.  I *was* not bitter or anything

---

[3] A reviewer suggests that parallels regarding the lack of past-tense-marking consistency could be drawn with Ho and Platt's (1993) analysis of past tense marking for Singapore English, a contact language for which various Chinese dialects (including Hokkien) are known to be substrates. Ho and Platt provide a detailed verb-type analysis and conclude that aspectual factors such as telicity and phonological factors such as resultant consonant clustering could account for a considerable portion of the incidence of past tense marking in Singapore English. In fact, similar analyses have already been carried out for Patty's past tense marking (Lardiere 2003a, 2003b, to appear). In contrast to Ho and Platt's results for Singapore English, Patty's past tense marking showed no significant effect for telicity (in either spoken or written production); however, similar to Ho and Platt's findings, there was a striking avoidance of final consonant clusters in the spoken data.

In sum, Patty productively (although not consistently) uses past tense marking in English in contexts in which aspectual -*le* marking would not be allowed in Chinese. This suggests that she has acquired at least some knowledge of this functional category in English. and is not simply relabeling a Chinese one. But if she has acquired past tense, why is her usage not consistent? I will return to this issue below.

Another possibility for aspectual relexification, proposed by Bao (2005) for Singapore English, is that Chinese perfective *le* (Hokkien *u* and *liau*, Cantonese *tso*) is relabeled with the English lexical item *already*, as shown in the following examples (from Bao 2005: 239, citing Kwan-Terry 1989: 38):[4]

(21)  a.  I wash my hand *already*.
          'I have washed/washed my hand.'
      b.  Alice fell down in the hole *already*.
          'Alice has fallen/fell down in the hole.'

As a perfective aspectual marker, *already* does not require that an action must have taken place prior to the time of utterance, as shown by the following example (Bao 2005: 239):

(22)  After you wax the car *already*, I pay you.

Bao argues that the aspectual system of Singapore English is the entire grammatical subsystem of Chinese aspect, minus a few "missing" aspectual categories that are present in Chinese but could not be accommodated by the morphosyntax of the superstrate language (English), following Lefebvre's relexification hypothesis quite closely. Thus, other aspectual markers are also argued to be relexified in addition to perfective *le*: for example, experiential *guo* with English *ever*, as shown in (23); perfective negation *méi* with English *never* (24); emphatic completion of an event *yǒu* 'have' with English *got* (25) (all examples from Bao 2005):

(23) I *ever* see the movie.
     'I have seen the movie.'

(24) John *never* eat durian.
     'John didn't eat the durian.'

(25) I *got* wash my hand (already).
     'I did wash my hand.'

A search through all of Patty's spoken transcripts for the lexical items *already*, *ever*, *never*, and *got* suggests that she has not relexified her Chinese aspectual system with these English lexical items. All of these items are used appropriately in context and, to the extent that this can be determined, with the

---

[4] I thank a reviewer for pointing out this and related references to me.

expected English intended meaning. In Singapore English, *already* as a perfective marker is clause-final; in English (with its standard meaning) it can be either clause-final or preverbal. Patty produces *already* in both positions:

(26) a.  Well, I # I *already* know # knew [...] like, maybe I knew about hundred character...
   b.  I have to look at the book, I forgot *already*.

Since one of Bao's specific claims is that substrate influence is systemic—that is, the entire aspectual system transfers if it can be lexically accommodated in the lexifier language—we should also find evidence of examples such as those in (23–25) above. There are certainly none in all the data for examples like those in (23) with *ever* or (25) with *got* (Patty often uses *got* but it is appropriate and idiomatic, as in *and then the second year his father got a job*; *well, she got stuck on the first piece*). For *never*, which she also uses frequently, there is considerable semantic overlap with "perfective negation" in past time contexts anyway, so these are inconclusive (e.g., *his brother never came here?*), but Patty uses it appropriately in imperfective contexts as well (e.g., *although it was never obvious*), and in nonpast contexts it does not appear to have a perfective meaning (e.g., *because if I speak fast they can never catch ...*). In sum, Patty's L2 English idiolect appears to differ clearly from Singapore English in this respect.

### 3.6 *Other affixes: comparative and superlative forms*

Recall that Lefebvre suggests that the relexification process for functional features targets only free morphemes from the superstrate language that have direct counterparts in the substrate language in terms of their semantics and syntax, including their distribution and directionality. We can compare this prediction with Patty's case by looking at her production of comparative and superlative morphemes in English.

First, let us look briefly at how comparative and superlative constructions are formed in Patty's L1(s). (In this section, I include data from Hokkien as well since it is slightly different from Mandarin in a way that is possibly relevant for comparatives.) Chinese languages are isolating languages. Mandarin has a superlative free morpheme *zui* that is similar to the free morpheme *most* in English; there is no affixal form.

(27) *zhei-tiao weijin*  **zui**   *hao*                    (Li & Thompson 1981: 572)
   this-CL   scarf   *most*  good
   'This scarf is the best.'

The relexification prediction is that Patty should easily be able to relabel *zui* as *most* in English, and indeed she has:

(28) a. the *most* difficult for me is to write
    b. I have the *most* wonderful teacher there
    c. that is the *most* scary thing for me

It is not clear whether we should also expect suppletive forms such as *best* to be easily produced, since these would presumably have been relexified following the morphosyntactic properties of Chinese, which would use the syntactic phrase *zui hao* 'most good,' as in example (27) above. However, we do find several instances of *best* in the data (and no occurrences of *most good*):

(29) a. you are the *best*
    b. she play the *best* on that one
    c. it's the # her *best* one
    d. the table *best* sit for 12

However, we should not expect to find superlative *suffixes* as well, as shown below in (30), including the overextended (doubly marked) example in (30c):

(30) a. it's the *highest* point in my TOEFL
    b. but the *lowest* point is to hear
    c. I was the most *unhappiest* person on earth
    d. the *biggest* differences between A. and S. are ...

Thus, although it is possible that the semantics of superlative marking were contributed by the L1, it is unlikely that the concatenative rules for how they attach to their bases were, since superlative affixes do not exist in the native language(s). The situation is even more striking for the comparative forms. Here, it is not even clear that Mandarin has a true grammaticalized counterpart to English *more* (or *-er*), since it is usually omitted in true comparative contexts, as in (31) below, where the so-called comparative morpheme *bi* (similar to English *than*) serves to introduce the object of comparison and there is no formal equivalent of the English *-er* affix on *tall* (example from Li & Thompson, 1981: 564):

(31) *Ta bi     ni  gao*
    3SG COMPARE you tall
    'S/he is taller than you.'

However, Hokkien, Patty's other native language, does have such a grammaticalized equivalent which, although not affixal, behaves formally very much like the English free morpheme *more* (examples from Bodman 1987: 145).

(32) a. *cit-kieng lutiam pi       hit-kieng* **khaq** *hou*
      this-CL   hotel   COMPARE that-CL   *more*  good
      'This hotel is better than that one.'

   b. *hit pieng e       sua:      **khaq** kuai*
      over there ATTRIB mountain *more*   high
      'The mountains over there are higher.'

Again, we would expect Patty to have acquired the English morpheme *more*, and it is clear that she has:

(33) a.  then I'm *more* serious in dancing
     b.  women are *more* sensitive than men in many ways
     c.  A. is *more* impatient than me
     d.  I have to be *more* aggressive in my position

Similar to the suppletive superlative form, the suppletive comparative form *better* has also been acquired:

(34) a.  and he is much *better* Chinese writer
     b.  the standard of living is much *better* than any other places
     c.  and she was *better* than me, you know, in English
     d.  this one *better* than the other one

Since the relexification hypothesis would seem to predict that the comparative would not be relexified as a suffix, Patty's acquisition of English affixal -*er* shows again that she has gone beyond relexification. There are many examples of affixal -*er* in the data, including the ones in (35).

(35) a.  you deserve a *nicer* person
     b.  their need are much *easier* to please than women
     c.  but my English is *lower*
     d.  but he feel # he feel *happier*
     e.  because Sri Lanka was *farer* away than Medan

With the sole exception of the doubly marked example *most unhappiest* in (30c) above (an error occasionally made by native speakers as well), Patty appears to have internalized the conditions determining the distribution of the suffixal vs. the full free forms for both the superlative and comparative constructions (including the "regularized" form in example (35e) above). There is no such morphosyntactic distinction for these lexical entries in her L1(s). If we look through the data at those contexts that include both entities under comparison using *than*, which is probably the closest we can come to establishing an obligatory context for the comparative, we find that Patty's suppliance of comparatives is completely consistent, regardless of whether the free or affixal form is required. Both the superlative and comparative suffixes are affixes she has completely acquired.

3.7 *Other affixes: derivational category-changing morphology*
One place where it appears that relexification can result in the acquisition of affixes (as opposed to major category free morphemes) is in derivational morphology, because derivational affixes are assumed to be listed in the lexicon with major categorial features. There are productive derivational affixes in Haitian Creole, which Lefebvre suggests are based on those of the substratum language Fongbe and have been relexified using French-based phonetic forms. As predicted by the relexification hypothesis, it is argued that the substratum language has contributed both the semantics of the Haitian affixes and the principles that govern their concatenation with their bases (p. 323). As for which affixes get relexified, Lefebvre writes: "Of course, they [the creators of the creole] would have identified only forms which corresponded to those of their native lexicons" (p. 324).

The first problem we encounter in assessing Patty's productive use of derivational morphology in English is establishing criteria for productivity. Lefebvre offers several criteria that work for an established creole—which is a *native language* for its speakers derived from, yet distinct from, its substrate and superstrate languages—but seem more problematic from the standpoint of SLA, where the L2 learner hopes to eventually achieve a grammatical representation that is as close as possible to that of the target language. For example, a form in Haitian is considered productive if: (i) it is found affixed to a base which is foreign to French (and thus could not have been learned as an unanalyzed whole from the superstrate language); (ii) it is used with a French base that in French does not take the equivalent affix; (iii) it appears in a different position from the parallel affix in French; (iv) the semantic and syntactic properties of a word it derives are different from those of the corresponding word in French; and (v) it takes part in a morphological process that has no counterpart in French (p. 304).

All of these criteria (except possibly (ii), which looks like a case of overgeneralization, common to all acquisition processes) would be at odds with what we would expect SLA data to look like. Take (i), for example. Since the only input a learner in Patty's situation is exposed to is from the target language (English), presumably none of the forms she hears will be "foreign to" that language, even if they were diachronically borrowed from some other language.

Looking at Patty's naturalistic production data, we can observe that she does occasionally make errors in derivational morphology, as the examples in (36) show:

(36)   a.   I tried to *analysis* what kind of person M. is
         b.   when my father went *bankruptcy*
         c.   it must be a huge *relieve*

    d.   her head circumference was not *growth* as normal
    e.   God ... try to give us his wisdom and *happy*
    f.   because he give us *sad*, you mean?
    g.   and her sister, who is a physical *therapy*
    h.   we are going to take her medical records ... to an expert *pediatric*

Nonetheless, she is aware of the syntactic categorial requirements for one form vs. another, as shown in the following examples:

(37)  a.   ... to do *gardening*
          or learn to be a great *gardener*
     b.   A. is ... so *generous* to my family and friends
          [he] has *generosity*
     c.   what are they *talking* about?
          if men can be a good listener and women become less *talkative*
     d.   she don't speak very *fluently*
          so after about a year I'm very *fluent* in Cantonese
     e.   but I know we have to be *patient*
          he has a lot of *patience*
          A. is more *impatient* than me
     f.   I have someone else *correct* my grammar
          he would look at my journal and give me *correction*
     g.   he is a *killer*
          he just want to *kill* them
     h.   look for *happiness* in everything
          no, I don't say that make # uh, God make us *happy*
          I say God doesn't want to give us ha # *unhappiness*
          I was very *unhappy*
     i.   I *believe* everything happen for a reason
          someone who will share your *belief*

In the following conversational excerpt, Patty recognizes and correctly nominalizes the verb *punish* from the immediately preceding turn of her native-speaker interlocutor:

(38)  Friend:   OK, because I did this, I'm being *punished.*
      Patty:    No ... there's no *punishment* from God.

There are many other similar examples in the data in which Patty uses more than one form of a word, adjusting her choice to the syntactic context. Note that in the examples above, Patty correctly uses seven different nominalized forms (not including words with the agentive *-er* affix, of which there are also many examples in the data): garden*ing*, generos*ity*, patien*ce*, correct*ion*, happi*ness*, belie*f*, punish*ment*. According to the list of derivational affixes provided in Li and Thompson (1981), there does not appear to be an equivalent for any one of these forms in her native Chinese, much less for all seven.

These examples certainly do not constitute proof that Patty has individual lexical entries for these particular word endings and affixes. It is possible (likely, from a lexeme- rather than morpheme-based morphological perspective) that she has learned that the entire word *punishment* is a nominalized resultative derivate of the verb *punish*, or that she has heard and learned the word *happiness* instead of productively (but incorrectly) producing something like *happiosity,* or *happy-un* instead of *unhappy*. The real learning problem here, and one that she sometimes struggles with, is retrieving the appropriate form of a word for the particular semantic and syntactic categorial context required, for example, *analyze* instead of *analysis* in example (36a) above. But she is also clearly not choosing relabeled L1 lexical entries.[5]

Control of derivational morphology has been associated with literacy in studies of native English-speaking schoolchildren. Whereas a few derivational affixes, such as agentive *-er*, are acquired very early in English L1 acquisition (Clark & Hecht 1982), other research has shown that productive knowledge of much category-changing derivational morphology may be acquired very late. Tyler and Nagy (1989) found that, by the 4th grade, children are able to recognize a familiar stem in a derivate; however, knowledge of the syntactic, and particularly the selectional, properties of particular derivational suffixes only very gradually increases through the 8th grade (the highest level they tested, at which there was still a substantial error rate in choosing correct suffixes for nonce words in particular syntactic contexts). One might hazard a guess, then, that whatever proficiency Patty does have in derivational morphology may have come about as a result of her very high level of attainment in her target language literacy—a factor that would almost certainly have been negligible in most situations of creole genesis.

## 4. *Conclusions*

To sum up, Patty's data suggest that, given unlimited access to the target language community, it does indeed appear possible to go well beyond

---

[5] A reviewer asks whether Chinese distinguishes between nouns and verbs. In general, it does so in the same way that all languages do—by virtue of the morphosyntactic company each category keeps. Thus, in Chinese, verbs are often accompanied by aspectual marking whereas nouns are accompanied by demonstratives and/or numerals plus classifiers. As for the type of category-changing derivational morphology that occurs widely in English, Li and Thompson (1981) point out that "there is very little morphological complexity in any of the Chinese languages" (p. 11). They list a derivational suffix *-huà* that derives verbs from nouns and adjectives, similar to English *-ize*, as in *yáng-huà* 'Western-ize' (p. 42), a suffix *-jiā* that derives an agentive or occupational noun from nouns or verbs similar to English *-ist*, as in *yùndùn-jiā* = athletics-ist 'athlete' or *zuò-jiā* = create-ist 'writer' (p. 41), along with a (very) few others. They do not list any derivational affixes for deriving nouns from verbs equivalent to the English examples mentioned above in the text.

relexification and acquire many of the semantic and syntactic properties of the target grammar in the L2 idiolect. This situation contrasts with that of creole genesis, but in the way that Lefebvre predicts, since creoles are generally created in contexts of severely restricted access.

Nonetheless, even with unlimited access, Patty's English idiolect is in other respects still far from target-like. This is especially obvious in the domain of inflectional morphology, as the very first set of examples provided earlier in (1) illustrates. We could conceivably argue that this is generally compatible with the relexification view, whereby relabeling proceeds on the basis of free morphemes in the superstrate language and thus the resulting new language tends to be an isolating language. What appears to be a universal tendency in creole genesis would presumably be intensified in Patty's particular case of L2 acquisition due to the fact that her native languages, Mandarin and Hokkien Chinese, are isolating, anyway. But as we have seen, when we take a closer look at her data, the relexification hypothesis often fails, and she appears in many respects to have far exceeded expectations based on its predictions.

Patty does produce morphological forms associated with the functional features of the target language, particularly in her writing, but in many cases these are highly inconsistent. Does this variability in production indicate that she has not acquired corresponding knowledge of the semantic and syntactic properties of the categories and features associated with these forms?

To further consider this question, let us turn to the possible role of maturational constraints in language acquisition by adults, for both SLA and creole genesis. Lefebvre writes that "by definition, relexification is a mental process that is available to speakers of a mature lexicon ... Hence according to the relexification hypothesis a creole is not created by children ... it is argued that creole languages must be created by adult speakers with a mature lexicon" (p. 10). In a series of tasks designed to directly address this claim, Hudson and Newport (1999) and Hudson-Kam and Newport (2005) used a miniature artificial-language-learning situation to investigate the extent to which both child and adult learners reproduced inconsistency in the input or categorically regularized it.

In their first experiment, adult native English speakers were randomly assigned to one of four input conditions in which they were presented with different rates of "determiners" co-occurring with nouns. The rates of co-occurrence between determiner and noun for the four input conditions were 45%, 60%, 75% and 100%, respectively. In a subsequent sentence production task, most of the adults approximately matched whatever rate of determiner omission they had been exposed to; that is, they produced determiners in their sentences roughly as often as they heard them in the input. Only those learners exposed to the 100% exposure condition produced them categorically. Results from an acceptability judgment task were similar: adults accepted sentences with missing determiners at approximately the same rate at which determiners were omitted in the exposure condition. Interestingly, adults in all exposure conditions judged sentences with missing determiners to be better than sentences with determiners in the wrong position. This finding is compatible with others from various L1 and L2 studies showing that, although inflection is often omitted, it is usually correct when it is supplied (see Lardiere 2000 for some discussion).

When Hudson-Kam and Newport (2005) (partially) replicated their experiment with children (ages 5 to 7), a very different picture emerged from that of adults. Most of the children systematically regularized their production, either categorically supplying or omitting determiners. Strikingly, they occasionally imposed regular patterns on their own output that did not even exist in the input, such as producing determiners according to whether the sentential verb was transitive or intransitive. Their acceptability judgments were also more categorical than those of adults and, like the adults, they also preferred sentences with missing determiners to those with incorrectly positioned ones.

On the basis of these experiments, the authors concluded that adults do not regularize perceived variability as they learn a language, whereas children "prefer regularity in language and sometimes perceive or produce such regularity even when it is not present in their input (Hudson-Kam & Newport 2005: 184). Regarding Lefebvre's claim that creole languages must be created by adult speakers with a mature lexicon, they hypothesize that, although adults may introduce the structure of the new language in creole genesis, children likely play a major role in regularizing it.

If these conclusions turn out to be correct, then they suggest that a preference for categorical consistency is a characteristic of children but not adults. Adults in fact seem quite "comfortable" with apparently random (i.e., unconditioned or unpredictable) variability. These findings may also be able to explain why creolization looks so different from adult SLA. In the case of creole genesis, adults with little access to the superstrate language relexify their own native language(s), as suggested by Lefebvre, not having enough exposure to go beyond the "initial" or "full transfer" stage of development. Subsequently, the "radicalness" of their new lingua franca is regularized and more categorically "set in stone" by their children, who are seeking maximum consistency. In adult SLA, on the other hand, greater access does lead to greater development that proceeds well beyond relexification, yet adult learners may nonetheless exhibit much more variable production than we find among native speakers of a creole.

We are still left with the question, however, of how to correlate regular vs. variable production with language knowledge in SLA: does inconsistent production necessarily reflect lack of knowledge of a particular functional category or feature? Hudson and Newport (1999) provide an interesting possible answer to our question, writing that "the source of the *structures* may not be the same as the source of the *consistency* and *obligatoriness*" (p. 266, their emphasis). In their view, the drive for categorical consistency is more likely to be part of non-language-specific processing or general learning mechanisms, which are likely to be distinct from the (possibly innate) language-specific features those mechanisms analyze (such as "verb transitivity"). Clearly, more research is needed as we continue trying to sort out how the UG-constrained representation of linguistic knowledge interacts with and informs language processing and learning mechanisms.

*References*
Baker, M. C. 2003. *Lexical Categories*. Cambridge: Cambridge University Press.
Bao, Z. 2005. The aspectual system of Singapore English and the systemic substratist explanation. *Journal of Linguistics* 41: 237–267.
Birdsong, D. 1999. Introduction: Whys and why nots of the Critical Period Hypothesis for second language acquisition. In *Second Language Acquisition and the Critical Period Hypothesis,* D. Birdsong (ed.), 1–22. Mahwah, NJ: Lawrence Erlbaum.
Bodman, N. C. 1987. *Spoken Amoy Hokkien*. Ithaca, NY: Spoken Language Services, Inc.
Chomsky, N. 1995. *The Minimalist Program*. Cambridge, MA: MIT Press.
Clark, E. V. and B. F. Hecht. 1982. Learning to coin agent and instrument nouns. *Cognition* 12: 1–24.
Freidin, R. 1999. Cyclicity and minimalism. In *Working Minimalism,* S. D. Epstein and N. Hornstein (eds.), 95–126. Cambridge, MA: MIT Press.
Ho, M.-L. and Platt, J. T. 1993. *Dynamics of a contact continuum: Singaporean English*. Oxford: Clarendon Press.
Hudson, C. L. and E. L. Newport. 1999. Creolization: Could adults really have done it all? In *Proceedings of BUCLD 23,* A. Greenhill, H. Littlefield and C. Tano (eds.), 265–276. Somerville, MA: Cascadilla Press.
Hudson-Kam, C. L. and E. L. Newport. 2005. Regularizing unpredictable variation: The roles of adult and child learners in language formation and change. *Language Learning and Development* 1: 151–195.
Hulk, A. 1986. Subject clitics and the pro-drop parameter. In *Formal Parameters of Generative Grammar,* P. Coopmans, I. Bordelois, and B. D. Smith (eds.), 107–121. Dordrecht: ICG Printing.
Jaeggli, O. A. 1984. Subject extraction and the null subject parameter. In *Proceedings of NELS 14,* C. Jones and P. Sells (eds.), 132–153. Amherst, MA: GLSA, University of Massachusetts at Amherst.
Kwan-Terry, A. 1989. The specification of stage by a child learning English and Cantonese simultaneously: A study of acquisition processes. In *Interlingual Processes,* H. W. Dechert and M. Raupach (eds.), 33–48. Tübingen: Gunter Narr Verlag.
Lardiere, D. 1998a. Case and tense in the "fossilized" steady state. *Second Language Research* 14: 1–26.
Lardiere, D. 1998b. Dissociating syntax from morphology in a divergent end-state grammar. *Second Language Research* 14: 359–375.

Lardiere, D. 2000. Mapping features to forms in second language acquisition. In J. Archibald (ed.), *Second language acquisition and linguistic theory*. Malden, MA: Blackwell.

Lardiere, D. 2003a. Second language knowledge of [±past] vs. [±finite]. In *Proceedings of the 6th Generative Approaches to Second Language Acquisition Conference (GASLA 2002)*, J. M. Liceras, H. Zobl and H. Goodluck (eds.), 176–189. Somerville, MA: Cascadilla Press.

Lardiere, D. 2003b. Revisiting the comparative fallacy: A reply to Lakshmanan and Selinker. *Second Language Research* 19: 129–143.

Lardiere, D. in press. Establishing ultimate attainment in a particular second language grammar. In *Studies in Fossilization,* Z. H. Han and T. Odlin (eds.). Clevedon: Multilingual Matters.

Lardiere, D. to appear. *Ultimate Attainment in Second Language Acquisition: A Case Study*. Mahwah, NJ: Erlbaum.

Lefebvre, C. 1998. *Creole Genesis and the Acquisition of Grammar*. Cambridge: Cambridge University Press.

Li, C. and S. Thompson. 1981. *Mandarin Chinese: A Functional Reference Grammar*. Berkeley, CA: University of California Press.

Ludlow, P. 1999. *Semantics, Tense and Time*. Cambridge, MA: MIT Press.

Muysken, P. C. 1981. Half-way between Quechua and Spanish: The case for "relexification". In *Historicity and Variation in Creole Studies,* A. R. Highfield and A. Valdman (eds.), 52–78. Ann Arbor, MI: Karoma.

Pienemann, M., Johnston, M., & Brindley, G. 1988. Constructing an acquisition-based procedure for second language assessment. *Studies in Second Language Acquisition* 10, 217-243.

Roberge, Y. 1990. *The Syntactic Recoverability of Null Arguments*. Kingston: McGill-Queen's University Press.

Schwartz, B. D. and R. A. Sprouse. 1994. Word order and nominative case in nonnative language acquisition: A longitudinal study of (L1 Turkish) German interlanguage. In *Language Acquisition Studies in Generative Grammar,* T. Hoekstra and B. D. Schwartz (eds.), 317–368. Amsterdam: John Benjamins.

Schwartz, B. D. and R. A. Sprouse. 1996. L2 cognitive states and the Full Transfer/Full Access model. *Second Language Research* 12: 40–72.

Tyler, A. and W. Nagy. 1989. The acquisition of English derivational morphology. *Journal of Memory and Language* 28: 649–667.

# INDEX OF LANGUAGES AND LANGUAGE FAMILIES

# INDEX OF SUBJECTS

In the series *Language Acquisition and Language Disorders* the following titles have been published thus far or are scheduled for publication: